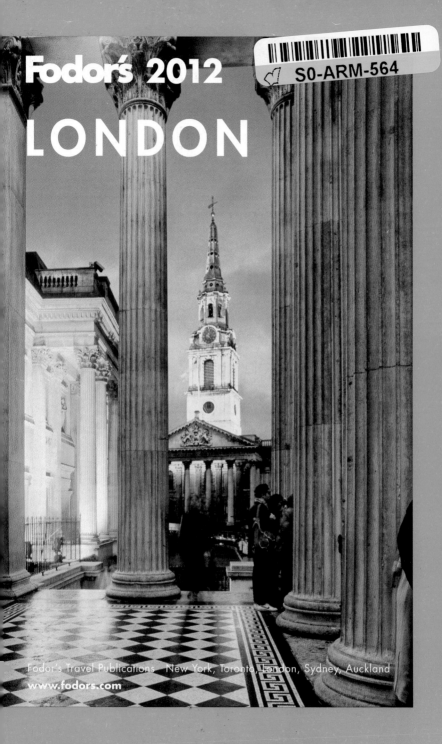

Fodor's 2012

LONDON

S0-ARM-564

Fodor's Travel Publications New York, Toronto, London, Sydney, Auckland
www.fodors.com

Eugene Fodor:
The Spy Who Loved Travel

As Fodor's celebrates our 75th anniversary, we are honoring the colorful and adventurous life of Eugene Fodor, who revolutionized guidebook publishing in 1936 with his first book, *On the Continent, The Entertaining Travel Annual.*

Eugene Fodor's life seemed to leap off the pages of a great spy novel. Born in Hungary, he spoke six languages and graduated from the Sorbonne and the London School of Economics. During World War II he joined the Office of Strategic Services, the budding spy agency for the United States. He commanded the team that went behind enemy lines to liberate Prague, and recommended to Generals Eisenhower, Bradley, and Patton that Allied troops move to the capital city. After the war, Fodor worked as a spy in Austria, posing as a U.S. diplomat.

In 1949 Eugene Fodor—with the help of the CIA—established Fodor's Modern Guides. He was passionate about travel and wanted to bring his insider's knowledge of Europe to a new generation of sophisticated Americans who wanted to explore and seek out experiences beyond their borders. Among his innovations were annual updates, consulting local experts, and including cultural and historical perspectives and an emphasis on people—not just sites. As Fodor described it, "The main interest and enjoyment of foreign travel lies not only in 'the sites,' . . . but in contact with people whose customs, habits, and general outlook are different from your own."

Eugene Fodor died in 1991, but his legacy, Fodor's Travel, continues. It is now one of the world's largest and most trusted brands in travel information, covering more than 600 destinations worldwide in guidebooks, on Fodors.com, and in ebooks and iPhone apps. Technology and the accessibility of travel may be changing, but Eugene Fodor's unique storytelling skills and reporting style are behind every word of today's Fodor's guides.

Our editors and writers continue to embrace Eugene Fodor's vision of building personal relationships through travel. We invite you to join the Fodor's community at fodors.com/community and share your experiences with like-minded travelers. Tell us when we're right. Tell us when we're wrong. And share fantastic travel secrets that aren't yet in Fodor's. Together, we will continue to deepen our understanding of our world.

Happy 75th Anniversary, Fodor's! Here's to many more.

Tim Jarrell, Publisher

FODOR'S LONDON 2012

Editors: Robert I. C. Fisher (lead editor), Carolyn Galgano (Restaurants and Hotels editor), Heidi Leigh Johansen

Editorial Contributors: Astrid DeRidder, Damian Harper, Julius Honnor, Erin Huebscher, Jack Jewers, Michelle Rosenberg, Ellin Stein, Alex Wijeratna

Production Editor: Carrie Parker
Maps & Illustrations: Mark Stroud, David Lindroth, *cartographers;* Bob Blake, Rebecca Baer, *map editors;* William Wu, *information graphics*
Design: Fabrizio La Rocca, *creative director;* Guido Caroti, Siobhan O'Hare, *art directors;* Tina Malaney, Nora Rosansky, Chie Ushio, *designers;* Melanie Marin, *senior picture editor*
Cover Photo: BildagenturHuber/Picture Finders/Fototeca 9x12
Production Manager: Angela L. McLean

ISBN 978–0–679–00928–3

ISSN 0149–631X

SPECIAL SALES

This book is available at special discounts for bulk purchases for sales promotions or premiums. Special editions, including personalized covers, excerpts of existing books, and corporate imprints, can be created in large quantities for special needs. For more information, write to Special Markets/Premium Sales, 1745 Broadway, MD 3-1, New York, NY 10019, or e-mail specialmarkets@randomhouse.com.

AN IMPORTANT TIP & AN INVITATION

Although all prices, opening times, and other details in this book are based on information supplied to us at press time, changes occur all the time in the travel world, and Fodor's cannot accept responsibility for facts that become outdated or for inadvertent errors or omissions. So **always confirm information when it matters**, especially if you're making a detour to visit a specific place. Your experiences—positive and negative—matter to us. If we have missed or misstated something, **please write to us**. Share your opinion instantly through our online feedback center at fodors.com/contact-us.

PRINTED IN COLOMBIA

10 9 8 7 6 5 4 3 2 1

CONTENTS

CONTENTS

ABOUT THIS BOOK

Our Ratings

At Fodor's, we spend considerable time choosing the best places in a destination so you don't have to. By default, anything we recommend in this book is worth visiting. But some sights, properties, and experiences are so great that we've recognized them with additional accolades. Orange **Fodor's Choice** stars indicate our top recommendations; black stars highlight places we deem **Highly Recommended**; and **Best Bets** call attention to top properties in various categories. Disagree with any of our choices? Care to nominate a new place? Visit our feedback center at www.fodors.com/feedback.

TripAdvisor ⦿⦿

Fodor's partnership with TripAdvisor helps to ensure that our hotel selections are timely and relevant, taking into account the latest customer feedback about each property. Our team of expert writers selects what we believe will be the top choices for lodging in a destination. Then, those choices are reinforced by TripAdvisor reviews, so only the best properties make the cut.

> For expanded hotel reviews, visit **Fodors.com**

Hotels

Hotels have private bath, phone, and TV, and do not offer meals unless we specify that in the review. We always list facilities but not whether you'll be charged an extra fee to use them.

Restaurants

Unless we state otherwise, restaurants are open for lunch and dinner daily. We mention dress only when there's a specific requirement and reservations only when they're essential or not accepted—it's always best to book ahead.

Credit Cards

We assume that restaurants and hotels accept credit cards. If not, we'll note it in the review.

Budget Well

Hotel and restaurant price categories from £ to £££££ are defined in the opening pages of the respective chapters. For attractions, we always give standard adult admission fees; reductions are usually available for children, students, and senior citizens.

Listings
★ Fodor's Choice
★ Highly recommended
⊠ Physical address
✛ Directions or Map coordinates
⌖ Mailing address
☎ Telephone
🖷 Fax
⊕ On the Web

✍ E-mail
🖾 Admission fee
⊘ Open/closed times
Ⓜ Metro stations
▭ No credit cards

Hotels & Restaurants
🖼 Hotel
⤹ Number of rooms
⌂ Facilities
⦙⦚ Meal plans
✕ Restaurant
⌕ Reservations
🏛 Dress code
⤢ Smoking

Outdoors
⚑ Golf
⟁ Camping

Other
🕭 Family-friendly
⇨ See also
⊠ Branch address
☞ Take note

Experience London

LONDON TODAY

If London contained only its landmarks—Buckingham Palace, Big Ben, the Tower of London—it would still rank as one of the world's top destinations. But England's capital is much more. It is a bevy of British bobbies, an ocean of black umbrellas, and an unconquered continuance of more than 2,000 years of history. A city that loves to be explored, London beckons with great museums, royal pageantry, and 1,001 historic delights. No matter that the weather stinks, no one smiles, and it takes far too long to get around—just what is it that makes London such a great place to be?

The World Comes to Town

Londoners are among the least xenophobic in Europe, and with one third of its residents born outside England, London is perhaps the most culturally diverse city on Earth. It's part indifference and part adaptability (heavily sprinkled with tolerance), but Londoners pay precious little attention to outsiders. This is undeniably part of London's charm: without the attentions of strangers, you can lose yourself here like in no other city. With more than 300 languages spoken on its streets—from the hybrid Multicultural London English to Pashto—the city is a terrific tangle of tongues. And as one of Europe's largest cities—whether it's cuisine, music, theater, poetry, or fashion—the outside world converges on London to leave its mark. London's global village can only become increasingly diverse—and unique—as the 2012 Olympics Games approach.

A City of Ideas

The capital of England's knowledge economy, London is foremost a city of ideas and creativity. From literati to glitterati, London is a vibrantly experimental capital and one of the destinations of choice for global culture hounds. Whether it's experimental drama, offbeat literature, street fashion, street performers, sparkling West End productions, cutting-edge art, urban music, or left-field public sculpture, the city is a refreshing haven for the inventive, innovative, and independent-minded. Scores of theaters in the West End make London a powerful magnet for drama enthusiasts, while the city's top-drawer museums embrace an almanac of human wisdom.

The Big Smoke?

London was once notorious for its pea-soup smog, and although a battery of measures has successfully cleaned up its

---

DID YOU KNOW?

With more than 7 million residents, London is the most populous city in the European Union, more than twice that of its nearest rival. It's among the most densely populated, too, after Copenhagen, Brussels, and Paris.

■ Up to around £2,000 (nearly $4,000) of taxpayers' money can be used to purchase a wig for a London judge, who often still wears the antiquated accessory. Barristers and solicitors (lawyers) must pay for their own wigs and often buy them used.

■ More than 120 species of fish, including smelt (which locals say has an odor resembling their beloved cucumber sandwiches), live in the Thames. It may look brown because of the sediment, but the Thames is actually Europe's cleanest metropolitan estuary.

skies the city still has some of the dirtiest air in Europe. Since 2008, the London Low Emission Zone has deterred heavily polluting large vehicles from entering the city area, while the Congestion Charge, charging vehicles £8 per day entering central London, has reduced both traffic and pollution. London's current mayor, tousle-haired Boris Johnson, is a great supporter of creating even more bicycle lanes, mandating public cycle hire initiatives, and prodding Londoners toward recycling. Johnson also keeps a close eye on London's fitness levels, supporting initiatives to combat obesity and promote exercise. Further good news is that only 15% of Londoners smoke cigarettes and in 2007 all enclosed public places (including pubs and restaurants) and places of work became smoke-free. The city's green lungs—its gorgeous and ample parkland—help keep the city oxygenated while Boris Johnson plans to spend £6 million on improving London's open spaces to make this the world's greenest city by 2012.

Have and Have-Nots

For the people who live here, money is what makes London's cogs go around. The credit crunch may have pierced its bubble of prosperity, but in 2009 the U.K. still replaced the U.S. as the world's leading financial center, with London leading the way. London's housing market enjoys its own economic micro-climate, with prices still rising as they fall elsewhere. Elegant areas such as Kensington and Knightsbridge are in a different world, with gravity-defying prices fed by waves of overseas investors and tycoons. The lead-up to the 2012 Olympics promises a further bonanza but gloom-mongering talk of double-dip recessions may upset the apple cart.

Today, The City contributes about 2.5% of the country's GDP, which highlights the pivotal role it plays in the country's economy. But while its Kazakh oligarchs, Saudi playboys, and cash-splashing freewheelers suggest a city endlessly flaunting its wealth, income disparities are colossal. London remains a reasonably safe city but it pays to keep your wits about you; gang culture and incidents of knife and gun crime conspire to make some neighborhoods a grittier and disadvantaged flip side to the city's flashier boroughs.

■ The Tube (the London Underground) is the world's oldest subway system, with the first line up and running in 1863. With 253 mi of track and 270 stations, it covers more ground than systems in New York, Paris, and Tokyo. More than a billion passenger journeys are made on the network every year.

■ London may have been credit-crunched, but the world's most expensive property—a central London flat—recently sold for more than £115 million.

■ The city is also the world's most expensive if you want to park your car. London's Congestion Charge Zone, where vehicles need to pay on weekdays to use the city center streets, is already the world's largest.

WHAT'S WHERE

The following numbers refer to chapters.

2 Westminster and Royal London. This is the place to embrace the "tourist" label. Snap pictures of the mounted Horse Guards, watch kids clambering onto the lions in Trafalgar Square, and visit stacks of art in the fantastic national galleries. Do brave the crowds to peruse historic Westminster Abbey and its ancient narrative in stone.

3 St. James's and Mayfair. You might not have the wallet for London's most prestigious district, but remember window-shopping in Mayfair is free. St. James's is the ultimate enclave of old money and gentleman's London. Here you'll find the noted private members' clubs of Pall Mall, and the starched shirts and cigars of Jermyn Street, where you can shop like the Duke of Windsor.

4 Soho and Covent Garden. More sophisticated than seedy these days, the heart of London puts Theaterland, strip joints, Chinatown, and the trendiest of film studios side by side. Nearby Charing Cross Road is a bibliophile's dream, but steer clear of the hectic hordes in Leicester Square, London's crowd-packed answer to Times Square.

5 Bloomsbury and Legal London. The literary and left-wing set that made Bloomsbury world famous has left its cerebral mark and this remains the heart of brainy London. The University of London and the Law Courts are worth a passing glance; save thorough exploration for the incomparable British Museum.

6 The City. London's Wall Street might be the oldest part of the capital, but thanks to futuristic skyscrapers and a sleek Millennium Bridge, it looks like the newest. Fans of history won't be short-changed, however: head for the dome of St. Paul's Cathedral, the storybook Tower Bridge, and grisly tales from the Tower of London.

7 The East End. Once famed for the 19th-century slums immortalized by Charles Dickens, today the area has become the razor-sharp cutting edge of London's contemporary art scene. For spit-and-sawdust sensations of market London on the weekend, dive headfirst into the wares at Spitalfields, Petticoat Lane, Brick Lane (popular for curry houses and bagel bakeries), and Columbia Road's much-loved flower market.

BLOOMSBURY

5

British
Museum

SPITALFIELDS

7

Liverpool
Street
Station

New Oxford St
High Holborn

Sir John Soane's
Museum

Barbican
Centre

BARBICAN
Museum of London

London Wall

BBC World
Service
Bush House

HOLBORN

Royal Courts
of Justice

THE
CITY

Guildhall

Old Bailey

Bank of
England

Helter
Skelter

Cheese
Grater

St. Paul's

Cheapside

Cornhill Leadenhall St.

Covent
Garden

Lombard St

Lloyd's of
London

National Portrait
Gallery

Somerset
House

The Temple

Cannon
Street
Station

Walkie Talkie

National
Gallery

Charing Cross
Station

Royal
National
Theatre

Shakespeare's
Globe Theatre

Tate Modern

Tower of
London

SOUTHWARK

Southwark
Cathedral

London
Bridge
Station

BERMONDSEY

London
Eye

Waterloo
Station

Shard

Westminster
Abbey

Houses of
Parliament

THE
BOROUGH

Lambeth Palace
Grounds

NEWINGTON

Tate
Britain

Lambeth
Palace

Hamsworth
Park

Elephant
And Castle

LAMBETH

KENNINGTON

VAUXHALL

The
Oval

Kennington
Park

Surrey
Gardens

Faraday
Gardens

Surrey
Sq. Park

WALWORTH

Burgess
Park

Bedmonsey
Spa

0   1/2 mi

0   1 km

WHAT'S WHERE

8 The South Bank. Die-hard culture vultures could spend a lifetime here. The Southbank Centre—including the Royal National Theatre and Royal Festival Hall, the National Film Theatre, Shakespeare's Globe, the Design Museum, and the Tate Modern—pretty much seals the artistic deal. Or put it all in sweeping perspective from high up on the London Eye.

9 Kensington, Chelsea, and Knightsbridge. Although the many boutiques of the King's Road have lost much of their heady 1960s swagger, the museums are as awe-inspiring as ever. The playful Science Museum and the magnificently overblown Natural History Museum are crucial must-sees for kids and toddlers. High St Ken (Kensington High Street) is slightly more affordable than the King's Road; otherwise, flash your cash at London's snazziest department stores, Harrods and Harvey Nichols ("Harvey Nicks" to insiders).

10 Notting Hill and Bayswater. For that effortlessly hip North London demeanor, hang out in its coolest residential post code. Around Portobello Road, Notting Hill Gate is a trendsetting square mile of multi-ethnicity, galleries, bijous shops, and see-and-be-seen-in restaurants. Bayswater mixes gaudy Arab fashions and fresh-food shops; some think it has an appealing edginess, others a nouveau-riche élan.

11 Regent's Park and Hampstead. For poetic inspiration, visit Keats House, where the poet penned his immortal "Ode to a Nightingale." Villagelike Hampstead is a must: cozy and wonderful streets, sidewalk cafés, delis, and outdoor swimming on the Heath in "the Lido."

12 Greenwich. Quaint Thames-side streets make for an excellent rummaging ground for trendy antiques. Throw in some brilliant sights, Christopher Wren architecture, and the Greenwich Meridian Line, and you have one of the best excursions beyond the cut-and-thrust of central London.

13 The Thames Upstream. As an idyllic retreat from the city, stroll around London's stately gardens and enjoy a beer close by once-powerful palaces at Chiswick, Kew, Richmond, and Putney. Better yet, take a river cruise along Old Father Thames for views of rolling greenery, and land up at the famous maze of Hampton Court Palace, England's version of Versailles.

LONDON PLANNER

When to Go

The heaviest tourist season runs mid-April through mid-October, with another peak around Christmas—though the tide never really ebbs. Spring is the time to see the countryside and the royal London parks and gardens at their freshest; fall to enjoy near-ideal exploring conditions. In late summer, be warned: air-conditioning is rarely found in places other than department stores, modern restaurants, hotels, and cinemas in London. Winter can be rather dismal, but all the theaters, concerts, and exhibitions go full speed ahead, and festive Christmas lights bring a glow. For a schedule of festivals, check ⊕ www.visitbritain.com.

When Not to Go

One good time to avoid is the October "half-term," when schools in the capital take a break for a week and nearly all attractions are flooded by children. Arriving at the start of August can be a very busy time, and the weather makes Tube travel a nightmare. And trying to shop in central London the week before Christmas is an insane idea best left only to desperate Londoners who have forgotten to buy presents.

Addresses

Central London and its surrounding districts are divided into 32 boroughs—33, counting the City of London. More useful for navigating, however, are the subdivisions of London into postal districts. Throughout the guide we've given the abbreviated postal code for most listings. The first one or two letters give the location: N means north, NW means northwest, and so on. Don't expect the numbering to be logical, however. (You won't, for example, find W2 next to W3.) The general rule is that the lower numbers, such as W1 or SW1, are closest to the city center.

Getting Around

London is, above all, a walker's city, and will repay every moment you spend exploring on foot. But if you're in a rush, here are other options.

By far the easiest and most practical way to get around is on the Underground, or "Tube."

Trains run daily from early morning to late at night. Buy an Oyster card for £3, which will allow you to use London's transport at a lower cost than using paper tickets. The plastic card can be topped up as often as you want, and your £3 will be reimbursed when you hand the card back. Alternatively, buy a Travelcard pass (from £5.10 per day), which offers unlimited use of the Tube, buses, and the commuter rail. Check ⊕ www.tfl.gov.uk for details on ongoing Tube renovations. The commuter rail system is an over-ground network that connects outlying districts and suburbs to the center. Prices are comparable to those of the Underground, and you can easily transfer between the Underground and other connecting rail lines at many Tube stations. Buses crisscross London and often have their own lanes, which only buses and taxis can use. They are a great way to see London, but routes are more complicated than the Tube's; scan the route posted at the bus stop and check the number and destination on the front of the bus. Service is frequent; most buses run from 5 am to midnight, others are night buses or operate 24 hours. For further details on transport around London, see the Travel Smart section at the end of this book.

London Hours

Most businesses are closed on Sunday and national ("bank") holidays. Banks are open weekdays 9:30–4:30; offices are generally open 9:30–5:30.

The major national museums and galleries are open daily, with shorter hours on weekends than weekdays. Often they are open late one night a week.

The usual shop hours are Monday–Saturday 9–5:30 and Sunday noon–5. Around Oxford Street, High Street Kensington, and Knightsbridge, hours are 9:30–6, with late-night hours (until 7:30 or 8) on Wednesday or Thursday.

Deal or No Deal?

There's no getting around it: Today's exchange rates really maul the pockets of American tourists. But it's much better to accept this fact in advance and factor it into your vacation planning, tailoring outings and trips that will reflect your interests—and your budget.

Often, booking in advance, harnessing low-season deals, and taking advantage of Internet specials for flights and hotel rooms can cut down on costs. London is also great at offering things for free, and the quality of the culture, entertainment, relaxation, and fun to be had in the city means that if you target your spending wisely, you'll go home penny-pinched but satisfied.

What It Costs

	IN LONDON	IN NEW YORK
Pair of theater tickets	£20–£70	$50–$200
Museum admission	Usually free; sometimes £4–£10	Usually $5–$20; sometimes free
Fast-food value meal	£4	$4
Tall latte	£2.15	$3.19
Pint of beer in a pub	£3 and up	$6 and up
1-mi taxi ride before tips	£5	$5
Subway ride within city center	£4 without Oyster or Travelcard	$2.25

How's the Weather?

It's a standard joke that Londoners—and English people in general—chat obsessively about meteorology. The London drizzle generates a fatalism that kicks off any conversation with a long-suffering nod to the weather. Winter is usually dreary and wet (with occasional snow), spring is colorful and fair, June to August can be anything from a total wash-out to a long, hot Indian summer and anything in-between, while autumn is cool and mild. Come prepared for anything: layers and an umbrella are your best friends. One thing is sure: it's virtually impossible to forecast London weather, but you can be fairly certain that it will *not* be what you expect.

The following are the average daily maximum and minimum temperatures for London.

AVERAGE LONDON TEMPERATURES

LONDON
TOP ATTRACTIONS

Westminster Abbey

(A) Steeped in history and tradition, the pillars of this great Christian edifice stand around the final resting place of the men and women who built Britain. The former monastery continues to play a role in the formation of the kingdom, with almost every sovereign being crowned at this site since 1066.

Buckingham Palace

(B) Not the prettiest royal residence, but a must-see for the glimpse it affords of the modern life of the monarchy. The opulence of the state rooms open to the public provides plenty of wow factor, and don't forget the collection of china and carriages at the Queen's Gallery and Royal Mews next door.

Tower of London

(C) The Tower is London at its majestic, idiosyncratic best. This is truly the heart of the kingdom—with foundations dating back nine centuries, every brick tells a story, and the ax-blows and fortunes that have risen and fallen within this turreted mini-city provide an inexhaustible supply of intrigue.

St. Paul's Cathedral

(D) No matter how many times you have been here before, the scale and elegance of Sir Christopher Wren's masterpiece never fail to take the breath away. Climb the enormous dome, one of the world's largest, to experience the freaky acoustics of the Whispering Gallery, and higher still to the Golden Gallery for far-reaching views across London.

British Museum

(E) If you want to journey through time and space without leaving the confines of Bloomsbury, a visit to the British Museum holds hours of eye-catching artifacts from the world's greatest civilizations, including the Elgin Marbles, the Rosetta Stone, and the Sutton Hoo treasure.

Shakespeare's Globe Theatre

(F) You can catch a Shakespeare play almost every night of the year in London. But standing in the Yard on a floor of leaves and sawdust in a scrupulously re-created version of the Tudor theater for which the Bard wrote is a genuine thrill.

Tate Modern

(G) More of an event than the average museum visit, Tate Modern, housed in the striking 1940s Bankside Power Station, is a hip and immensely successful feature of London's artistic landscape. Passing judgment on the latest controversial temporary exhibit inside the giant turbine hall has become almost a civic duty among art-loving Londoners.

London's Central Parks

(H) A whopping 25% of London is parkland, so it seems churlish to pick out just one in the middle of it all. The four central parks each have their own persona (but all are lovely): pick St. James's Park for fairy-tale views; Green Park for hillocks and wide boulevards; Regent's Park for its open-air theater and the London Zoo; and Hyde Park for rowing on the Serpentine Lido.

Hampton Court Palace

(I) This collection of buildings and gardens so captivated Henry VIII that it became his favorite royal residence. Its Tudor charm, augmented by Wren's touch, and a picturesque upstream Thames location make it a great day out—not even dour Oliver Cromwell, who moved here in 1653, could resist its charms.

National Gallery

(J) Whatever the collective noun is for a set of old masters—a palette? a canvas?—there are enough here to have the most casual art enthusiast cooing with admiration. When you've finished, enjoy pedestrianized Trafalgar Square on the doorstep of this collection.

LONDON'S ROYAL LEGACY

Don't know your House of York from your Houses of Parliament? Here's the low-down (or high-up) to the most famous kings and queens that have influenced London, and where you can still see their mark.

Queen Mary I

(A) "Bloody Mary" (r. 1553–58, House of Tudor), the Roman Catholic daughter of Henry VIII and his first wife, Catherine of Aragon, persecuted Protestants in an attempt to reverse the Reformation and return England to Catholicism. She imprisoned her half-sister, Elizabeth—daughter of Anne Boleyn—in the Tower, suspecting her of a plot against her, but there was no evidence and Elizabeth came to the throne after her death.

Edward the Confessor

(B) Edward (r. 1042–66) came to the throne in 1042 and ordered the construction of the original Westminster Abbey, which was consecrated in 1065, just a week before he died.

William the Conqueror

(C) The Battle of 1066 was won by William (r. 1066–87, House of Normandy) when he shot the then-king Harold through the eye with an arrow at the battle of Hastings. He is credited with starting the building of the White Tower in the Tower of London, though it wasn't completed until after his death.

Queen Elizabeth I

(D) The "Virgin Queen" (r. 1558–1603, House of Tudor) never married—perhaps because she thought that any man would try to wrest control from her (though she did move Robert Dudley, Earl of Leicester, into rooms close to her own at Hampton Court). She oversaw and supported a golden age of playwriting and poetry and famously inspired her troops as they prepared to battle the Spanish Armada.

1

Henry VIII
(E) A true Renaissance man, Henry (r. 1509–47, House of Tudor) was keen to bring new ideas to the Royal Court. All of Henry's six wives lived at Hampton Court Palace. Henry was desperate for a male heir—the main reason for having two of his wives executed: Anne Boleyn and Catherine Howard.

George III
(F) His frequent bouts of irrational behavior led to the nickname "The Mad One," but George (r. 1760–1820, House of Hanover) is now thought to have suffered from an inherited metabolic illness and often secluded himself at Kew Palace. With the Declaration of Independence in 1776, he lost the American colonies.

Duke & Duchess of Cambridge
(G) Now that you're in Merrie Olde England, just seeing the Queen Elizabeth II on a postage stamp doesn't seem to do the trick. It's far more exciting to catch the Windsors on a royal walkabout—so go to www.royal.gov.uk and search for the Diary of Events to catch Prince William and his new wife (as of April 29, 2011) at a public event.

Charles I
(H) "The Martyr" (r. 1625–49, House of Stuart) is famous for losing the English Civil War, and was beheaded at Banqueting House—a twist of fate as Charles had commissioned the palace to be decorated with paintings showing a monarch being received into heaven.

Queen Victoria
(I) Famous for the longest reign so far in British history, 63 years, Victoria (r. 1837–1901, House of Hanover) was born in, and spent her childhood at, Kensington Palace, where she learned she would become queen.

THE 2012 OLYMPIC GAMES

After Beijing's mind-boggling display at the 2008 Olympic Games, the baton was passed to London for the 2012 Olympic Games (⊕ *www.london2012.com*), to be held July 27 to August 12, 2012. London's handover performance at the Beijing Olympics curtain call—featuring a double-decker bus and umbrella-toting commuters—was a typically English affair: slapstick, tongue-in-cheek, and devoid of bombast. Overshadowed by the ambition of Beijing's mesmerizing show, some decried its lack of ambition. But it was a confident, offbeat, and fun display that was so very London. The unmistakable message was: come to London and enjoy yourself.

Hotels and Flights
London may have more than 100,000 hotel rooms but you will still need to book your room as far ahead as you can, especially if you want to be near the Olympic Park. Air tickets are also going to be snapped up close to the event.

Getting Around
More than £17 billion has been earmarked for transport development in the run-up to the 2012 Games in this city that sees 20 million trips daily on the transport system. Served by five airports, London has the world's second largest (and oldest) underground system, but pre-Olympics development saw the extension of the East London line (May 2010) and the Docklands Light Railway, the upgrading and modernization of all underground stations, investment on the Jubilee Line (serving Olympic facilities) to handle extra capacity, and a high-rail link between St Pancras International and Stratford International for the Olympic Park, shuttling spectators to the Games in seven minutes from central London.

New cycle and walking lanes are also planned to encourage healthier modes of transportation. London, however, remains one of the most congested cities in Europe, with an average vehicle speed of just under 12 mph.

Buying Tickets
Tickets for the London Olympics 2012 go on sale in 2011 and will generally be available until the start of each event unless sold out. Advance tickets start to go on sale beginning March 15 to April 26, 2011, through the Authorized Ticket Reseller, Cosport (⊕ *cosport.com*), or through the various offices of the National Olympic Committees of the International Olympic Committee (⊕ *www.olympic. org*). Tickets will include free public transport on the day of the event.

New London?
The 2008 Olympic Games in Beijing further marked the long-heralded shift eastward of the world economic axis. Back in London for the first time since 1948, the Olympic Games return to a nation increasingly at ease with its decreased global stature but just as eager to put on a show. Drawing on impressive reserves of cosmopolitan verve, creativity, and sheer élan, London aims to host the Olympic Games in striking fashion. While the Beijing Olympics purposefully declared the arrival of a new superpower, the 2012 Olympics will be about showing why London remains one of the world's most-loved and cosmopolitan cities.

The jigsaw-style logo for the London Olympics may have polarized opinion, but the Games have been applauded for their promise to revitalize areas of East London and swing the spotlight of global attention back to town. The Games are also an occasion to showcase some dramatic new architecture. And, Olympic visitors are expected to bring as much as £2.2 billion to the local economy in 2012, fueling the London feel-good factor.

London under Construction

London has focused its Olympic energies on transforming the deprived East London, where the Olympic Park is under construction, but the occasion has been seized on to overhaul public transport, to showcase some sparkling new architecture, and to convert some well-known landmarks into Olympic venues.

With the exceptions of Canary Wharf, the Swiss Re Headquarters (the "Gherkin"), the Lloyd's of London building, and the London Eye, London's skyline is typically low-key with little of the brash swagger of, say, Shanghai or Manhattan. But a spectacular crop of new architecture—the 945-foot (288-meter) "Helter-Skelter" Bishopsgate Tower, 740-foot (228-meter) Leadenhall Building "Cheese Grater," and 1,020 foot (310 meters) "Shard of Glass"—is set to inject fresh adrenaline into London's otherwise staid streetscapes and revitalize its skyline.

A curvilinear £303-million piece of eye candy due for completion in 2011, the gorgeous **Aquatics Centre** will be a centerpiece of London's Olympics display. Designed by Iraqi architect Zaha Hadid, the center's wavelike form has been scaled back from original designs, but it remains an impressive and inspirational building.

The **Olympic stadium's** design has divided opinion, with critics making unfavorable comparisons with Beijing's iconic Bird's Nest, but supporters have pointed to the 80,000-capacity stadium's ability to be dismantled as a major plus point.

Olympic Venues

Most big-ticket events will take place in the Olympic Park but some medals will be vied for in more unusual settings, many that are open to the public today.

Athletics events will all take place in the 80,000-capacity **Olympics Stadium.**

Gymnasts and basketball finalists will be limbering up in the **O2 Arena**, to be temporarily rechristened the **North Greenwich Arena 1**; badminton contestants and rhythmic gymnasts will aim for glory in the North Greenwich Arena 2.

The Beach Volleyball competition will be held in **Horse Guard's Parade** in Whitehall, a beach ball's toss from Downing Street and next to St. James's Park.

Road Cycling takes to **Regent's Park**. (For great views of the park and Central London head to nearby Primrose Hill.)

Football (soccer) matches will kick off in 90,000-seat **Wembley Stadium**, the home of the English National Football team.

Triathlon contestants and Marathon swimmers will make a splash in the Serpentine in **Hyde Park.**

Swimming and diving will be held in the astonishing form of the signature **Aquatics Centre.**

Lovely **Greenwich Park**—London's oldest Royal Park—is the venue for Equestrian events and Modern Pentathlon.

In Woolwich, shooting will be staged at the **Royal Artillery Barracks**, while **Lord's Cricket Ground** will host archery.

Tennis can really only be held at one venue—**Wimbledon**—with its famous grass courts, but rowers, canoeists, and kayakers will be heading off to Eton Dorney, near Windsor Castle.

GIVE THE SPORTS SCENE A GO

London will host the 2012 Olympic Games, but don't expect to see many city inhabitants practicing their javelin throws in Hyde Park or going for a synchronized swim across the Thames. Sport in the capital comes into its own when it's watched, rather than participated in. You'll most easily witness London's fervent sporting passions in front of a screen in a pub with a pint in hand. And those passions run deep.

If you're lucky enough to score a ticket for a big football match, you'll experience a seething, jeering mass of mockery and rude chants, especially if the opposition happens to be another London team. Amid all the aggression you might also catch a glimpse of why the excitement of English football makes it world sport's hottest media property right now.

And sport does mainly mean football (refer to it as "soccer" at your mortal peril). David Beckham is not alone in being overpaid for kicking a ball around—a generation of footballers lives the high life in London, their status somewhere between sporting rock stars and royalty. Cricket, rugby, and tennis briefly impinge on Londoners' sporting horizons at certain times of year, but you're unlikely to see grown men crying at the outcome of matches at Wimbledon, or beating each other up about the Ashes.

Football

The English may not be Brazil when it comes to football (returning home after an earlier-than-anticipated dismissal by arch-foe Germany at the 2010 World Cup in South Africa), but they invented the modern game and the sport is *the* national obsession. A self-deprecating expectation of failure accompanies the national team's performances, although current squad manager Fabio Capello has injected a new sense of purpose. London's top teams—Chelsea, Arsenal, Tottenham Hotspur, and West Ham—are world class (especially the first two), however, and regularly progress in the European Champions League, but rely heavily on foreign players.

It's unlikely you'll be able to get tickets for anything except the least popular Premier League games during the August–May season, despite absurdly high ticket prices (as much as £50 for a standard seat). Lower down football's hierarchical ladder, you'll have a much better chance of seeing a match. If you're engaging locals in sporting banter, it is imperative to know your way around the big teams.

Arsenal (aka the Gunners) is historically London's most successful club, and under the managerial reign of Arsene Wenger they have shed their boring image to become proponents of attractive, free-flowing football while hardly ever employing any English players, bar gifted winger Theo Walcott. ⊠ *Emirates Stadium, Dayton Park, London* ☎ *020/7704–4040* ⊕ *www.arsenal.com* Ⓤ *Arsenal.*

Chief rivals of Manchester United in the Premier League, Champions League finalists in 2008 and Premier League title and FA Cup winners in 2009, **Chelsea** (aka the Blues) is owned by one of Russia's richest men and has been forged in recent years into a formidable and ruthless footballing machine. ⊠ *Stamford Bridge, Fulham Rd., Fulham* ☎ *0871/984–1905* ⊕ *www.chelseafc.com* Ⓤ *Fulham Broadway.*

Tottenham Hotspur (aka Spurs)—bitter North London rivals of Arsenal—has underperformed for many years but there are strong hints of a revival with a bevy of England national team regulars from Peter Crouch to Jermaine Defoe and Aaron

Lennon. ✉ *White Hart La., 748 High Rd., London* ☎ *0844/499–5000* ⊕ *www.tottenhamhotspur.com* Ⓤ *National Rail: White Hart La.*

West Ham, despite the name, is the team of the East End. After a long period of failing to match their past success, the Hammers have created a more consistent team, but one unlikely to claim too many trophies. ✉ *Boleyn Ground, Green St., Upton Park* ☎ *0871/222–2700* ⊕ *www.whufc.com* Ⓤ *Upton Park.*

Cricket

At its best, cricket can be a slow-build of smoldering tension and excitement. At its worst, though, it can be unbearably tedious, as five-day games crawl toward a draw, or as the English weather interferes and rain stops play.

Lord's has been hallowed cricketing turf since 1811. Tickets are hard to come by: obtain an application form and enter the ballot (lottery) to purchase tickets. Forms are sent out in early December or you can apply online. Test Match tickets cost between £25 and £95. County matches (Middlesex plays here) can usually be seen by standing in line on match day. ✉ *St. John's Wood Rd., St. John's Wood* ☎ *020/7432–1000* ⊕ *www.lords.org* Ⓤ *St. John's Wood.*

Horse Racing

The Queen attends **Royal Ascot** (✉ *Grand Stand, Ascot, Berkshire* ☎ *0870/727–1234* ⊕ *www.ascot.co.uk*) in mid-June, driving from Windsor in an open carriage for a procession before the plebs. Grandstand tickets, which go on sale in November, cost £49–£69, although some tickets can usually be bought on the day of the race (generally on Tuesday or Wednesday) for £16. The real spectacle is the crowd itself, and those who arrive dressed inappropriately (jeans, shorts, sneakers) will be turned away from their grandstand seats.

Derby Day (✉ *The Grandstand, Epsom Downs, Surrey* ☎ *0844/579–3004* ⊕ *www.epsomderby.co.uk*), usually held on the first Saturday in June, is the second-biggest social event of the racing calendar. It's also one of the world's greatest horse races, first run in 1780. Tickets are between £20 and £100.

Tennis

The **Wimbledon Lawn Tennis Championships** are famous for the green grass of Centre Court and an old-fashioned insistence on players wearing white.

Rain, a perennial hazard even in the last-week-of-June–first-week-of-July timing, has been banished on Centre Court by the addition of a retractable roof.

Whether you can get grandstand tickets is literally down to the luck of the draw, because there's a ballot system (lottery) for advance purchase. For more information, see their Web site.

You can also buy entry to roam matches on the outside courts, where even the top-seeded players compete early.

Get to Southfields or Wimbledon Tube station as early as possible and get in line.

Five hundred show court tickets are also sold, but these usually go to those prepared to stand in line all night. ✉ *Ticket Office, All England Lawn Tennis & Croquet Club, Box 98, Church Rd., Wimbledon* ☎ *020/8944–1066* ⊕ *www.wimbledon.org.*

FREE (AND ALMOST FREE) THINGS TO DO

The exchange rate may vary, but there's one conversion that'll never change: £0 = $0. Here are our picks for the top free things to do in London.

Art

Many of London's biggest and best cultural attractions are free to enter, and the number of museums offering free entry is staggering. Donations are often more than welcome, and special exhibits usually cost extra.

Major Museums

British Museum
Imperial War Museum
Museum of London
National Gallery
National Maritime Museum, Queen's House, and Royal Observatory
National Portrait Gallery
Natural History Museum
Science Museum
Tate Britain
Tate Modern
Victoria & Albert Museum

Smaller Museums and Galleries

Courtauld Institute Gallery (Permanent Exhibition free on Monday only)
Geffrye Museum
Hogarth's House
Horniman Museum
Houses of Parliament
Institute of Contemporary Arts (ICA) Gallery
Museum of London Docklands
V&A Museum of Childhood
Saatchi Gallery
Serpentine Gallery
Sir John Soane's Museum
Wallace Collection

WHITECHAPEL ART GALLERY CONCERTS

St. Martin-in-the-Fields, St. Stephen Walbrook, and St. James's Church have regular lunchtime concerts, as does St. George Bloomsbury on Sunday, Hyde Park Chapel on Thursday, and St. Giles in the Fields on Friday. There are regular organ recitals at Westminster Abbey.

Of the music colleges, the Royal Academy of Music, the Royal College of Music, the Guildhall, the Trinity College of Music, and the Royal Opera House have regular free recitals.

For contemporary ears, the area outside the National Theatre on the South Bank (known as the Djanogly Concert Pitch) reverberates to an eclectic range of music weekdays at 5:45 pm, and on Saturday at 1 pm and 5:45 pm and Sunday at 1:45 pm. St. Olave's Church (Hart Street, EC3) has lunchtime recitals on Wednesday and Thursday at 1 pm.

Free jazz and classical evenings (sometimes there's a charge) are held on Thursday and Sunday at the excellent Dysart Arms (✆ 0208/940–8005 ⊕ www. thedysartarms.co.uk) in Richmond. Live Jazz also comes to the central and ancient Lamb and Flag (⊠ 33 Rose St., WC2 ✆ 0207/497–9504) on Sunday from 7 pm. For regular doses of free blues, down a drink at the Ain't Nothing But Blues Bar (⊠ 20 Kingly St. ✆ 020/7287–0514). The Notting Hill Arts Club (⊠ 21 Notting Hill Gate ✆ 0207/460–4459) has live bands on Saturday 4 to 8.

FILM, THEATER, AND OPERA

If all seats have been sold, the English National Opera sells standing tickets for the back of the Dress and Upper circles from £10 each. Check at the box office.

Standing-only tickets with obstructed views at the Royal Opera House are between £4 and £14.

"Groundling" standing-only tickets are a traditional way to experience the Globe Theatre from £5.

Sloane Square's Royal Court Theatre, one of the United Kingdom's best venues for new playwriting, has restricted-view, standing-room-only tickets at the downstairs Jerwood Theatre for 10 pence (yes, £0.10), available one hour before the performance.

Prince Charles Cinema in the West End shows weekday movie matinees for £4.

OFFBEAT EXPERIENCES

Take a walk down the Greenwich Foot Tunnel. Claustrophobics steer clear, but for those looking for a quirky journey, take the old lift or the spiral stairs down and stroll under the Thames from the Isle of Dogs to the *Cutty Sark* in Greenwich.

There are free spectacles throughout the year, but one of the most warmly enjoyed is Guy Fawkes' Night (November 5), when parks throughout the country hold spectacular fireworks displays.

On New Year's Eve thousands of revelers descend on Trafalgar Square and the South Bank to watch more free fireworks. The Underground usually runs for free well into the small hours.

Finally, set aside some time for random wandering. London is a great walking city because so many of its real treasures are untouted: tiny alleyways barely visible on the map, garden squares, churchyards, shop windows, sudden vistas of skyline or park. With comfortable, weatherproof shoes and an umbrella, walking might well become your favorite activity here.

However, **Barclays Cycle Hire** (☎ 0845/026–3630 ⊕ *www.tfl.gov.uk/barclayscyclehire*) has 330 docking stations housing 5,000 bicycles around Central London. The first 30 minutes is free, but then it's £1 for the first hour and then £4 for 90 minutes and you also need a £45 yearly membership to get a card (but casual use for non-U.K. residents is coming soon). Remember to cycle on the left!

SIGHTSEEING ON THE CHEAP

Join real Londoners on the top deck of a double-decker bus. Routes 9 and 15 also operate shortened Heritage routes on the traditional Routemaster buses. You can use your Oyster card or buy tickets from machines at the bus stops for the following routes:

Bus 11: King's Road, Sloane Square, Victoria Station, Westminster Abbey, Houses of Parliament and Big Ben, Whitehall, Trafalgar Square, the Strand, Fleet Street, and St. Paul's Cathedral.

Bus 12: Bayswater, Marble Arch, Oxford Street, Piccadilly Circus, Trafalgar Square, Horse Guards, Whitehall, Houses of Parliament and Big Ben, Westminster Bridge.

Bus 19: Sloane Square, Knightsbridge, Hyde Park Corner, Green Park, Piccadilly Circus, Shaftsbury Avenue, Oxford Street, Bloomsbury, Islington.

GREAT ITINERARIES

Crowning Glories

This regal runaround packs more into a day than most cities can offer in a week. Hit Westminster Abbey early to avoid the crowds, then cut through St. James's Park to catch the Changing the Guard at 11:30 am at Buckingham Palace. (If the palace doors are open, enjoy a peek at royal life.)

Take a quick detour to the Tudor delights of St. James's Palace, old haunt of Charles I, before a promenade down the Mall past the Regency glory of Carlton House Terrace and through Admiralty Arch to Trafalgar Square.

■ TIP→ Get an early start and a hearty breakfast, as this selection of treasures will likely keep you on your feet all day.

After lunch, choose from the canvases of the National Gallery, the Who's Who of the National Portrait Gallery, or a brass rubbing in the crypt of St. Martin-in-the-Fields if the children's interest is flagging.

This should leave time for a stately stroll down Whitehall—past Downing Street, Horse Guards Parade, and Banqueting House—to the Houses of Parliament, where you have the option of prebooking a tour or trying to get in to see a debate.

■ TIP→ Her Majesty's mounted guardsmen make a great photo op—you may even see Prince Harry, a member of the Regiment of the Blues and Royals, responsible for his grandmother's personal protection.

If you have any time or energy left, stroll through Green and Hyde parks to Kensington Palace, home to Queen Victoria in her childhood, and (for aspiring little princesses everywhere) the Royal Ceremonial Dress Collection.

Museum Magic

London has one of the finest collections of museums in the world, and certainly no other comparable city offers so much for free.

Many resemble state-of-the-art, hands-on playgrounds; others take a more classical approach.

One of the latter is the British Museum in Bloomsbury, an Aladdin's cave of artifacts from across the world that is ideal for either a half- or full-day browse.

If you want to bolt on additional visits, pop into the nearby museum of architect Sir John Soane, or transport yourself to the London Transport Museum.

■ TIP→ For a structured visit or if you're short of time, hop onto one of the British Museum's nine freebie 40-minute "eyeOpener" tours, join one of the three 90-minute "Highlights" tours, or grab an audio tour.

Alternatively, South Kensington's "Museum Mile" on Cromwell Road houses the triple whammy of the Victoria & Albert Museum, the Natural History Museum, and the Science Museum, any one of which would make for a substantial half-day's diversion.

Retail Therapy

Shopping 'til you drop in the West End is almost a national sport. New Bond Street—an awesome display of top names and sartorial finery—is the main stomping ground of the well-heeled and fastidiously dressed.

Nearby Oxford Street is more chaotic and department store–led, but finds itself at the very heart of London's commercial hubbub.

■TIP→ Men should not pass up a chance to browse the shirts and suits on show at nearby Savile Row (famed for its high-quality tailoring), and accessories on Jermyn Street.

Oxford Street encompasses four Tube stations and is unbeatable for mass-market shopping.

Run the gauntlet of high-street designers, cheap odds and ends, department stores, and ferocious pedestrians: it's seriously busy, but you're pretty much guaranteed a buy.

A more sedate but utterly fashionable experience can be found in Knightsbridge, wandering between Harvey Nichols and Harrods department stores.

Head south down Sloane Street to Sloane Square and head out along the King's Road, home to boutiques galore and once capital of London's swinging '60s.

■TIP→ To catch a glimpse of how to design your home to match your new couture clothes, visit the Conran Shop at 81 Fulham Road, parallel to the King's Road.

To dip into the ever-expanding world of urban chic, an afternoon in the Portobello street market should deposit remnants of bygone eras into your arms: glassware, furniture, art, and clothes, from boiler suits to Vietnamese silk dresses.

Portobello has wised up in recent years to tourist prices in recent years, so a trip out to Spitalfields (covered) market on a Sunday is worth considering instead, especially for a sample of the East End.

For the younger crowd, Camden market still has clubbing wear in spades.

Village People

The easiest village to reach is Hampstead, 20 minutes from the city center by Tube, but a world away in character.

It is home to a thriving arts scene, a history of left-wing poets and writers (including John Keats), some of the most gorgeous Georgian houses in London (hence the routine jibe of "Champagne Socialism"), and a great range of smart shops, bistros, and French delicatessens.

■TIP→ If you're in Hampstead, don't miss the chance to get out onto the Heath, moodier and wilder than many of London's other open spaces.

To the west, leave Richmond behind to get down to the riverside, or head for the vast expanse of the park next door, which breaks all remaining links with city life.

The fantastic views bestowed on Greenwich, southeast of the city center, ensure that you never forget how close the city is—and yet this village's nautical past creates an almost seaside feel.

The National Maritime Museum and its collection of fine buildings, as well as two very good markets, make it a worthwhile day trip.

Also in the southeast, leafy Dulwich Village possesses a delightful and genteel charm, with soaring horse chestnuts, the Dulwich Picture Gallery, and the green expanses of Dulwich Park.

Up the road in Forest Hill, the outstanding Horniman Museum is ensconced in exquisitely tended grounds. ■TIP→ To appreciate fully how tribal London's villagers can be, try asking which part of the city they come from or live in. The responses you'll get—"Haggerston," "Tufnell Park," "Turnham Green," "Camberwell," "Battersea"—indicate a dizzying array of identities, often consisting only of a few neighboring streets.

A LONDON HISTORIC PUB CRAWL

An excellent and beery way to see London and its back streets is on a "pub crawl"—this walk takes you through some of the city's most historically textured neighborhoods, crosses the Thames, and pops you in and out of a string of cheerful and ancient pubs. Remember to settle back several times with a pint and drink in all the history.

The South Bank

Like Chaucer's *Canterbury Tales* pilgrims, we start in Southwark. Head down Borough High Street to the **George Inn,** a long black-and-white affair with wonky galleries, warped beams, and smoothed stairs. Etched with age and first chronicled in 1542, the pub is mentioned in Dickens's *Little Dorrit.* Cross Borough High Street and take the Stoney Street entrance to **Borough Market**; at the arched entrance to Green Market, turn left and walk along Cathedral Street, with **Southwark Cathedral** on your right. At the fork head left to the **Golden Hind** and then walk along Pickfords Wharf to reach the **Anchor** when you hit Bankend. Although recently renovated, this historic pub proudly declares it was built in 1615; head up to the roof terrace for sterling views of the river and **St. Paul's.** It is here that it is thought that writer Samuel Pepys stood as he observed the 1666 fire of London.

Across the Thames

Cross Southwark Bridge to The City. On the corner of Bow Lane, **Ye Olde Watling** was originally built just before the Great Fire, and promptly torched. Rebuilt around 1668, again in 1901, and then again after the Blitz, it is named after Watling Street, the Roman Road it sits on.

Head west along Watling Street to magnificent St. Paul's Cathedral and take a left down Creed Lane from Ludgate Hill. Wind your way down to Queen Victoria Street and turn right to the **Black Friar** at No 174.

The spectacular Arts and Crafts interior is all marble and brass bas-reliefs of friars interspersed with aphorisms and quotes.

Head up New Bridge Street and turn left onto Fleet Street to dig out the **Ye Olde Cheshire Cheese** in a minute alley called Wine Office Court. Dictionary-scribe Dr. Johnson, who lived close nearby, used to have a tipple or two here, as did Dickens, Mark Twain, and Theodore Roosevelt.

Bloomsbury

Wander west along Fleet Street, then walk north along Fetter Lane to the **Ye Olde Mitre,** serving up brews since 1546 and rebuilt around 1772. Find the preserved trunk of a cherry tree that Elizabeth I supposedly once danced around.

Walk north up Gray's Inn Road, then left onto Theobalds Road before turning right onto Lamb's Conduit Street, to find the **Lamb.** Not far from the Dickens House Museum, the pub is notable for its wooden horseshoe bar with its etched-glass "snob screens" to shield the "pillars of society" when drinking with "women of dubious distinction." Head West along Great Ormond Street to the far side of Queen Square and the **Queen's Larder,** where Queen Charlotte reputedly rented out the cellar. Just north is the Russell Square tube station, or you can continue to the British Museum, opposite which is the Museum Tavern, where Karl Marx would loosen his neck-tie and take time off from researching *Das Kapital.*

Where to Start:	On the South Bank at the London Bridge Tube/rail station.
Length:	4 mi (about 1.5 hours without stopping). Just part of this walk will give you a taste of the oldest part of London.
Where to Stop:	Russell Square Tube station or Tottenham Court Road.
Best Time to Go:	Weekday mornings or afternoons (most pubs open late in the morning). Some of these pubs are shut on weekends.
Worst Time to Go:	Busy summer weekends may be too crowded.
Eating and Drinking:	All the pubs will serve food at lunchtime. Stop when you're hungry or pick up some tasty morsels in Borough Market and stop in either Gray's Inn Fields or Lincoln's Inn Fields for a picnic.
Diversions:	From the Anchor, consider continuing along the riverside to the Tate Modern, before crossing over the River Thames to ferret out Ye Olde Watling or the Black Friar.
Pub Highlights:	The Anchor, Black Friar, George Inn, the Lamb, Queen's Larder, Ye Old Watling, Ye Olde Mitre.

AFTERNOON TEA

Taking afternoon tea is the height of cool in London right now.

From Kate Moss to Cameron Diaz, everyone wants to sit up straight, stick their pinkie out, and sip hot tea in the company of friends and family—and preferably in the warm embrace of an established hotel tea salon.

So, what is Afternoon Tea, exactly? Well, it means real tea (Earl Grey, English Breakfast, Ceylon, Darjeeling or Assam Indian, or Chinese) brewed in a china pot, and served with china cups and saucers, milk, lemon, and silver spoons, between 3 and 5:30 pm.

In particularly grand places, there should be elegant finger foods on a three-tiered silver tea stand: crustless sandwiches on the bottom; fruit scones with Devonshire clotted cream and strawberry jam in the middle; and rich fruitcake, shortbread, patisseries, macaroons, and fancies on top.

Tea-goers dress up in posh hotels, and conversation (by tradition) avoids politics and religion.

Brown's Hotel. This classic Mayfair townhouse hotel sets the standard at the English Tea Room, where one of London's best-known Afternoon Teas is served (Afternoon Tea £35, Champagne Tea £45). ⊠ *33 Albermarle St., Mayfair* ☎ *020/7493-6020* ▭ *AE, DC, MC, V* ⊘ *Tea weekdays 3–6, weekends 1–6* Ⓤ *Green Park.*

Café at Sotheby's. What could be better than perusing the famous Mayfair auction house before afternoon tea? Breakfasts are from 9:30 am, then teas from 3 pm; teas are available from £6.50 (including tea cakes and scones) and up to £18.75 for Champagne Tea. ⊠ *Sotheby's, 34 New Bond St., Mayfair* ☎ *020/7293-5077*

⚠ *Reservations essential* ▭ *AE, DC, MC, V* ⊘ *Tea weekdays 3–4:45* Ⓤ *Green Park.*

The Dorchester. Amid a maze of marble and gold leaf, afternoon tea in the Promenade is best taken on comfy sofas and to the sound of the resident pianist. Teas are £35.50, £45.50 for Champagne Tea, and £49.50 for High Tea (with light bites like salmon and Cromer crab). Book well ahead. ⊠ *53 Park La.* ☎ *020/7629-8888* ⚠ *Reservations essential* ▭ *AE, DC, MC, V* ⊘ *Tea daily 2:30 and 4:45* Ⓤ *Hyde Park Corner.*

Fortnum & Mason. Upstairs at the revamped 300-year-old Queen's grocers, three set teas are ceremoniously served: Afternoon Tea (sandwiches, scones, and cakes: £344), old-fashioned High Tea (the traditional nursery meal, with scrambled eggs and salmon: £36), and Champagne Tea (price according to Champagne). Hours: teas, Monday–Saturday noon to 8, Sun. noon to 6. ⊠ *St. James's Restaurant, 4th fl., 181 Piccadilly, St. James's* ☎ *020/7734-8040* ▭ *AE, DC, MC, V* ⊘ *Tea Mon.–Sat. 2–7, Sun. noon–4:30* Ⓤ *Green Park.*

The Ritz. At the Ritz tea is served in the impressive Palm Court, with marble tables and Louis XIV chaises complete with musical accompaniment, giving the last morsel of Edwardian London. Afternoon Tea is £39 and Champagne Tea £50. Reserve two to three months ahead and remember to wear a jacket and tie. ⊠ *150 Piccadilly, St. James's* ☎ *020/7300-2309* ⚠ *Reservations essential* ▭ *AE, MC, V* ⊘ *Tea daily 11:30, 1:30, 3:30, 5:30, 7:30* Ⓤ *Green Park.*

LONDON LIKE A LOCAL

Unforgettable London moments are rarely captured in picture-postcard settings like Trafalgar Square or Piccadilly Circus, but tucked away off the main drag or in more prosaic and unexpected locales: with a pint at a hospitable pub, amid the tottering clutter of an antiques shop, on a park bench in a smart London garden, or in a welcoming centuries-old church beneath glass-and-steel towers in The City. Like a four-leaf clover, you'll come up them only unexpectedly.

Wander About A Market

London's markets are perfect for an aimless Sunday morning potter, along with locals who aren't quite sure what they're doing there either.

The most fun is Portobello, full of great clothes and jewelry from local designers, and plenty of cafés and pubs to drop into along the way.

Discover Pub Culture

Although fashionable coffee shops now dot every street, it's still the pub that Londoners are drawn to the minute the working day finishes.

Don't get sucked into the big chains, such as Pitcher and Piano or All Bar One—head instead for the ones with kooky names straight out of a Monty Python sketch. Scuffed carpets, dartboards, and old chaps propping up the bar are all essential.

Go to Any Football Match

Football fires up Londoners' blood and nowhere does it get more adoring, tribal, and high-pitched than at a 30,000-strong stadium on Match Day.

These are emotional pressure-cookers where fans come for moments of sporting epiphany or damnation. Tickets can be like gold dust, but lower-division teams (Barnet, Brentford, Charlton Athletic, Crystal Palace, Millwall, Leyton Orient, or Queens Park Rangers) will be less heavily booked up.

Eat at a Greasy Spoon

The fatty delights of a London greasy-spoon breakfast are well-known among London's party animals as a peerless hangover cure.

A classic "full English" breakfast—fried bacon, fried egg, baked beans, mushrooms, and tomatoes (and black pudding for the truly carefree)—all washed down with a mug of strong tea while reading the *Sun* or any other red-top rag is a sinful joy. Just don't tell your doctor.

Take a Night Bus Home

Like the street sweepers they overtake, these buses pick up the living leftovers of a thousand different nights out in the capital.

Sometimes there are so many stops that it seems it will be dawn before you get to where you want to go, but the endless procession of passengers (and the speed and humor of their banter) is what makes the trip interesting.

Party in Hoxton

This neighborhood is no longer the ultra-hip brother-in-charms to Manhattan's Lower East Side that it once was, but maybe it's for the better.

Nowadays, the mullet-headed fashionistas and art school dropouts accommodate angular City slickers in the most predictable destination for a guaranteed good night out.

Round off your night, or get it going, with a hearty curry on nearby Brick Lane, home to London's Bangladeshi community.

LONDON WITH KIDS

Education Without Yawns

London Dungeon. Gore galore (did you ever see a disembowelment?) plunges you into murky depths of history, with gruesome rides and special effects scary enough to frighten the coolest of cats.

London Zoo. City? What city? Disappear into the animal kingdom among the enclosures, complete with sessions for kids afraid of spiders (even bird-eating ones!), in this popular animal retreat set in Regent's Park.

Kew Gardens. If the sun penetrates the London clouds, Kew Gardens is great for kids, with family activities, the "climbers and creepers" playzone, zip wires, scramble slides, and children's trails; free for children.

Natural History Museum. It doesn't get much more awe-inspiring than bloodsucking bats, fake earthquakes, and a life-size blue whale. Just make sure you know your diplodocus from your dodo.

Science Museum. Special effects, virtual voyages, interactive galleries, puzzles, and mysteries from the world of science, with a fun-tastic play area for toddlers downstairs, featuring an excellent hands-on water activity game.

Tower of London. Perfect for playing princess in front of the crown jewels. Not so perfect for imagining what becomes of the fairy tale—watch your royal necks.

Performances

Applaud street performers. You can't beat the cacophony of jugglers, fire-eaters, unicyclists, and the human statues tantalizing crowds in Covent Garden.

Enjoy Regent's Park Open Air Theatre. Welcome to the land of fairy dust and magic. Don't miss an evening performance under the stars of *A Midsummer Night's Dream* in summer.

Sing along to musicals. Move over, Broadway: you can't beat a song and dance number from London's West End.

Activities

Ride the London Eye. Ferris wheel–loving kids will think they've hit the mother lode when they see Europe's biggest observation wheel.

Clamber on the lions. Challenge your child to pick a perch in Trafalgar Square, the capital's tourist hot spot, and climb one of the four tall stone lions at the foot of Nelson's column.

Ice-skating at the Natural History Museum. Send your kids whizzing, arms whirling, across ice from November to January at this fantastic ice rink right outside the museum.

Night at the Museum. Leave your children in the capable hands of the Natural History Museum and its toothy dinosaur collection for its monthly Dino Snores sleepover (minimum of five kids per group). Leave kids at 7 pm, pickup next morning at 9:50 am.

Paddle on the Serpentine. Pack a picnic and take a rowboat out into the middle of Hyde Park's famed lake; settle back and tuck in to lunch.

Lose your kids at Hampton Court. It might be more than 300 years old, but the quest to reach the middle of the world-famous hedge maze remains as challenging as ever.

Little Angel Theatre. Entertaining children since 1961, this Islington puppet theatre (⊠ *14 Dagmar Passage* ☎ *0207/226–1887* ⊕ *www.littleangeltheatre.com*) also has drama classes for young thespians.

Millennium Bridge and St. Paul's Cathedral.

THE BUILDING OF LONDON

The past is knit into the very fabric of the lives of Londoners: they live in Regency townhouses, worship in Baroque churches, and chill out in Edwardian-era parks. Unfolding like a gigantic historical pop-up book, London reveals—building by building—the pageant of a nation's history. To make sense of it all, here's a quick architectural tour through time.

Despite invading tribes, an epic fire, and 20th-century bombing, London has always survived, and a surprising amount of yesterday remains visible in its streets today. Starting with remnants of Londinium, the early Roman city contained by a defensive wall some 2,000 years ago, you can trace the city's beginnings. Only pieces of the wall remain, but the name of each entrance to the city has been preserved: Aldgate, Newgate, Bishopsgate, Cripplegate, Aldersgate, and Ludgate.

As commerce grew the city over the centuries, London expanded between two centers of power, Westminster in the west and the Tower in the east. Following both the Great Fire and World War II destruction, the need to rebuild outweighed the desire for sensible street layouts, and often any aesthetic considerations. In fact, London as a whole has rarely been planned, and the financial center is still roughly in the shape of that original Roman wall. London's haphazard streets and alleys are filled with diverse architectural styles side-by-side, each representing a piece of the city's history.

by Janice Fuscoe

TIMELINE

56, 64 BC Julius Caesar arrives on Britain's shores	43 AD–410 AD Roman rule	61 AD Boudicca attacks and destroys Londinium		600s Anglo-Saxon Lundenwic settlemen in Covent Garden are
	0	250	500	750

(top left) Statue of the Roman Emperor Trajan (r. AD 98-117) outside the largest remaining section of the Roman wall at Tower Hill. (right) Tower of London; (left) Carausius coin struck circa 288-290 AD at the Londinium mint.

Roman Londinium

Pre–410

As the Roman Empire expanded, Britain was conquered and the first city where London now stands began to develop along the Thames. Among many building projects, the Romans enclosed Londinium with a wall to protect against invading tribes after the Celtic warrior queen Boudicca razed the city. Today chunks of the ancient barrier remain in the City, and at the Guildhall art gallery you can see a partial Roman amphitheatre from this time.

■ Visit: Guildhall (Ch. 6), London Wall at Tower Hill Tube station (Ch. 6), Museum of London (Ch. 5)

Saxon and Medieval London

410–1485

Little is known of the 250 years after the Romans left London. Following these "Dark Ages," most medieval houses and bridges were built of timber or wattle and daub and the perishable materials didn't last in the changing city.

England's royalty began building heavily in the capital as a sign of strength and power, focusing on defensive structures. In 1042, the Saxon King Edward the Confessor moved his court and began a church on the site of the current Westminster Abbey, where almost all the monarchs of England have been crowned since. From

across the English Channel, William the Conqueror brought Norman architectural styles with him. William built the White Tower; later expanded, the solid castle became the heart of the Tower of London complex. His son and heir William II saw the construction of Westminster Hall, the oldest part of the Palace of Westminster (today's Houses of Parliament). St. Bartholomew's Hospital, founded in 1123, and the Guildhall, a center of commerce from the early 15th century, are among the few buildings that survived the later Great Fire.

■ Visit: Guildhall (Ch. 6), St. Bartholomew's Hospital (Ch. 6), Tower of London (Ch. 6)

1066 William the Conqueror becomes King of England	1240 Parliament sits at Westminster for the first time	1348 The Black Death	1605 Guy Fawkes's Gunpowder Plot uncovered 1534 Dissolution of the Monasteries	1642–51 Civil War 1666 Great Fire
1000	1250		1500	1750

1

IN FOCUS THE BUILDING OF LONDON

(top left) Painted ceiling of Banqueting House by Peter Paul Rubens; (top right) *The Great Fire of London, with Ludgate and old St Paul's;* (bottom right) St. Paul's Cathedral, built 1675–1708, designed by Christopher Wren

Tudor and Stuart London

1485–1700

As London grew, the Tudor royals influenced the architecture of London not only by creating, but also by destroying. Henry VII continued the expansion of Westminster Abbey and his successor, Henry VIII, resided at Hampton Court. The arts flourished under Elizabeth I, and the original Globe Theatre was built in 1599. Yet many fine medieval churches were torn down as England separated from the Roman Catholic Church.

Architects brought continental ideas to London, notably the influential Italian Palladian style introduced by Inigo Jones. You can see this classical style with it's mathematical proportions and balanced lines at the Queen's House in Greenwich and at Banqueting House, where Charles I was executed following the civil war. Eleven years later, Charles II was restored to the throne, returning from exile in France.

The Great Fire of 1666 destroyed five-sixths of London, but it also wiped out the plague that had ravaged the impoverished and overcrowded population the year before. Sir Christopher Wren was given the Herculean charge of rebuilding London. He wanted to map out a more organized grid for the city, but it was rebuilt on the old haphazard lines. It took Wren 35 years to build his baroque masterpiece, St. Paul's Cathedral. Wren also designed 50 other churches (only 23 still stand, including St. Bride's and St. Stephen Walbrook) and Monument to commemorate the fire. Nicholas Hawksmoor assisted Wren and designed his own highly original churches including the splendid Christ Church in Spitalfields.

■ Visit: Banqueting House (Ch. 2), Christ Church, Spitalfields (Ch. 7), Shakespeare's Globe Theatre (Ch. 8), Queen's House, Greenwich (Ch. 12), St. Bride's (Ch. 6), St. Paul's Cathedral (Ch. 6), St. Stephen Walbrook (Ch. 6), Hampton Court (Ch. 13)

(top left) Courtyard of Neo-classical Somerset House, built for George III. (right) The Rotunda of the Victoria and Albert (V&A) Museum with modern Chihuly sculpture; (bottom left) St Martin-in-the-Fields on Trafalgar Square.

Georgian Era

1700–1836

By the beginning of the 18th century, London was the biggest city in Europe and a center of world trade. This growth led to changes in politics, as power moved to a parliamentary system. Increased wealth led to an explosion of art and architecture.

Many different styles flourished—rococo, neo-classical, regency, and gothic revival. The predominant neo-classical, based on the styles of ancient Greece, can be seen in many stately homes. You can admire the elegant Regency terraces around John Nash's Regent's Park.

■ Visit: Regent's Park (Ch. 11), Somerset House (Ch. 4), St. Martin-in-the-Fields (Ch. 2)

Victorian Age

1837–1901

Queen Victoria ruled the British Empire for 63 years. London experienced the growth of wealth, industrialization, and philanthropy; this was also a period of desperate poverty, as depicted in Charles Dickens's novels. At the start of the 19th century the population of the city was over a million; by the end of Victoria's reign it was six million.

This rapid growth required many building programs, from worker housing to even bigger projects such as the bridges, government buildings, and the first subway system in the world. Businessmen, artists, and architects helped create many institutions that still exist today from the Tate Britain to the Ragged Schools and Foundling hospitals.

The clean, classical lines of the previous era gave way to more elaborate styles—which were considered more "English"—such as the Gothic Revival Houses of Parliament. Other Victorian projects included covered markets, canal locks, arcades, palaces, memorials, museums, theaters, and parks. So much building took place during this period that it's hard to miss the style: look for elaborate, highly decorated architecture.

■ Visit: Burlington Arcade (Ch. 3), Houses of Parliament (Ch. 2), Leadenhall Market in The City (Ch. 6), V&A and Natural History Museum (Ch. 9)

1851 Great Exhibition held in Hyde Park	1901 Death of Queen Victoria	1939–1945 WWII	1951 Festival of Britain
1863 Underground opens		1914–1918 WWI	
1870	1900	1930	1960

1

IN FOCUS THE BUILDING OF LONDON

(left) Theatregoers at The National Theatre on the South Bank of the Thames River; (right) Tower block at Barbican Centre, a 1980s complex of art venues and apartments.

20th-century building

1901–1979

The turn of the 20th century saw wealthy Westminster widening its streets to accommodate the arrival of motor cars and department stores. Even after the First World War, a "live for today" attitude continued among the upper classes, while the poorest Londoners suffered increasing prices and low wages. While modernism—a cultural movement embracing the future and rejecting anything associated with the past— was gathering pace in 1920s Europe, conservative British architecture continued to hark back to traditional influences of ancient Greece and the middle ages.

The WWII devastation of the Blitz bombings changed this and an enormous amount of post-war building was needed quickly. Émigrés such as Hungarian Ernö Goldfinger and Russian-born Berthold Lubetkin brought the modernist architectural movement to London with their high-rise buildings—a solution to the desperate housing shortage. One of the most exciting post-war projects was the 1951 Festival of Britain, celebrating the great inventions of the century. Out of a host of new architecture at the South Bank for this event, only the Royal Festival Hall remains.

Mass-produced concrete, steel, and glass ushered in the brutalist style in the '60s. This outgrowth of modernism can be seen in the Hayward Gallery and National Theatre. It was not a popular style, partly because the use of raw concrete—pioneered in the sunny south of France— looked gray, ugly, and even sinister against the backdrop of wet and windy London.

London's powers-that-be haven't always embraced modernist architecture, and many examples have been torn down. Today some iconic buildings are protected and the massive concrete Barbican Centre finally brought modernism right into the conservative City.

■ Visit: The Barbican Centre (Ch. 6), Hayward Gallery (Ch. 8), National Theatre (Ch. 8), Royal Festival Hall (Ch. 8) (left) Lloyd's of London by the Richard Rogers Pertnership, completed in 1986. (top right) Current design of the London Aquatics Centre by Zaha Hadid. (bottom right) The 2000 Great Court at the British Museum by Sir Norman Foster.

Modern and Millennium London

1980–Present

While the sun may have set on the British empire, London remains a global city, perhaps more now than ever before. The '80s saw changes in economic policy and ambitious building projects, including the Jubilee Line extension to the Underground system. Great business and banking centers reached higher into the sky as London's importance in financial markets increased. London's disused Docklands area got a revitalizing boost with the Canary Wharf development and the DLR (Docklands Light Railway).

Internationally-known architects began to make their mark on the city with creative projects. Known as Tower 42, the NatWest Tower opened in 1980 as the tallest skyscraper in the city—for a great view, head to its bar on the 42nd floor. The Richard Rogers Partnership designed the fabulous 1986 Lloyd's of London building. Sir Norman Foster and his associates have designed the Sackler Galleries at the Royal Academy of Arts, the British Museum's Great Court, City Hall, and the Swiss Re Headquarters (known as the Gherkin).

Building projects to celebrate the Millennium are now so beloved it's hard to imagine London without the pedestrian-only Millennium Bridge and the London Eye.

The "Helter Skelter" Bishopsgate Tower is to be completed in 2012, followed by the Richard Rogers Partnership's "Cheese Grater." Beijing's Olympic Games are a tough act to follow, but the eyes of the world will be on London as the 2012 host city. Everyone's waiting for the curvaceous Aquatics Center designed by world-renowned Zaha Hadid and the 1,016-foot "Shard of Glass" designed by Italian Renzo Piano—it will be the tallest building in the EU by 2012; but for future buildings...the sky's the limit.

■ Visit: Canary Wharf (Ch. 12), Lloyd's of London (Ch. 6), Swiss Re (Ch. 6)

Westminster and Royal London

WORD OF MOUTH

"I really, really recommend taking a verger's tour at Westminster Abbey—our guide really made history come alive. If you get to the Abbey when it opens, just sign up for the first tour of the day or you can sign up in advance the previous day."

—azzure

GETTING ORIENTED

TOP REASONS TO GO

Westminster Abbey: Steeped in history, this sublime Gothic church was not only the site of Prince William's 2011 marriage but also saw 38 hallowed coronations, starting with William the Conqueror in 1066.

Buckingham Palace: Keep pace with the marching soldiers and bands, resplendent in red and black, as they enact the time-honored ceremony of the "Changing of the Guard" in front of the residence of Her Majesty.

Leonardo da Vinci and Co.: Leonardo, Raphael, Van Eyck, Rembrandt, and Rubens…you get the picture. Enjoy one of the world's greatest collections of Old Master paintings in gorgously renovated rooms at the National Gallery.

Cabinet War Rooms: Listen to Churchill's wartime radio addresses to the British people from this cavernous underground wartime hideout.

Hearing Big Ben's Chimes: The 320-foot-high Clock Tower is as much a symbol of London as the Eiffel Tower is of Paris—hear its chimes from the Houses of Parliament to Trafalgar Square.

FEELING PECKISH?

Gordon's Wine Bar (⊠ *47 Villiers St.* ☎ *020/7930–1408* ⊕ *www.gordonswinebar.com*), the oldest in London, is hidden belowground among vaulted brick arches and bathed in candlelight. A range of bottles will suit any budget, and buffet food includes excellent beef.

There's great food and drink all year at **Inn the Park** (⊠ *St. James's Park* ☎ *020/7451–9999* ⊕ *www.innthepark.com*) and the outdoor pinewood deck makes for fantastic people-watching in summer.

At the **Vincent Rooms** (⊠ *Vincent Sq.* ☎ *020/7802–8391* ⊕ *www.thevincentrooms.com*) the kitchen of a top catering college offers offers haute cuisine at bargain prices.

GETTING THERE

Trafalgar Square—easy to access and smack-dab in the center of the action—is a good place to start. Take the Tube to Embankment (Northern, Bakerloo, District, and Circle lines) and walk north until you cross the Strand, or alight at the Charing Cross (Bakerloo and Northern lines) Northumberland Avenue exit. Buses are another great option, as almost all roads lead to Trafalgar Square, which also features on both Routemaster heritage routes London's classic double-deckers.

MAKING THE MOST OF YOUR TIME

A lifetime of exploring may still be insufficient to cover this historically rich part of London. More practically, two to three days can take in the highlights. For royal pageantry begin with Buckingham Palace, Westminster Abbey, the Queen's Gallery, and the Guards Museum. For more constitutional sightseeing, there's the Houses of Parliament and the Cabinet War Rooms. For art, the National Gallery and the Tate Britain head anyone's list.

NEAREST PUBLIC RESTROOMS

If you get caught short in Westminster Abbey, paid loos (50p) are across the street at the bottom of Victoria Street. Banqueting House and the Queen's Gallery have very elegant restrooms.

2

Sightseeing
★★★★★
Nightlife
★★
Dining
★★★
Lodging
★
Shopping
★★

This is postcard London at its best. Crammed with historic churches, grand state buildings, and major art collections, the area unites politics, high culture, and religion. (Oh, and the Queen lives here, too.) If you went no farther than these few acres, you would see many of the most famous sights, from the Houses of Parliament, Big Ben, Westminster Abbey, and Buckingham Palace to two of the world's greatest art collections, housed in the National and Tate galleries. Clearly, there is as much history in these few acres as in many entire cities, as the statues of kings, queens, soldiers, and statesmen that start guard at every corner attest—this is concentrated sightseeing, so pace yourself. If you have time to visit only one part of London, this is it.

Updated
by Damian
Harper

Royal London's basic layout can be divided into three distinct areas—Buckingham Palace, Whitehall, and Trafalgar Square—grouped at the corners of triangular St. James's Park.

Trafalgar Square is the official center of London. To its north are two major museums, the **National Gallery** and the **National Portrait Gallery.** From Trafalgar Square two boulevards lead to the seats of very different ideas of governance: **Whitehall** leads to the **Houses of Parliament,** whereas the **Mall,** a wide, pink avenue beyond the stone curtain of **Admiralty Arch,** heads toward the **Queen Victoria Memorial** and **Buckingham Palace,** the sovereign's official residence. Halfway down Whitehall, the Queen's Life Guards sit motionlessly on horses in front of Horse Guards Parade, adjacent to the glorious Banqueting House.

No. 10 Downing Street, diagonally opposite, is both the residence and the office of the prime minister. One of the most celebrated occupants, Winston Churchill, is commemorated in the **Cabinet War Rooms & Churchill**

A BRIEF HISTORY OF WESTMINSTER

The Romans may have gunned for The City, but England's royals went for Westminster. London's future home of democracy started out as Edward the Confessor's palace, when he moved his cramped court west in the 11th century. He founded Westminster Abbey in 1050, where every British monarch has been crowned since. Under the Normans, the palace of Westminster was an elaborate and French-speaking affair. The politicos finally got their hands on it in 1529 (when Henry VII and his court shifted up to the roomier Whitehall Palace), but nearly lost it forever with the Gunpowder Plot of 1605, when Catholic militants attempted to blow the prototypical Parliament to smithereens.

Inigo Jones's magnificent Banqueting House is the only surviving building of Whitehall Palace, and was the setting for the 1649 beheading of Charles I. The Westminster we see today took shape during the Georgian and Victorian periods, as Britain reached the zenith of its imperial power. Grand architecture sprang up, and Buckingham Palace became the principal royal residence in 1837, when Victoria acceded to the throne. Trafalgar Square and Nelson's Column were built in 1843, to commemorate Britain's most famous naval victory, and the Houses of Parliament were rebuilt in 1858 in the trendy neo-Gothic style of the time. The illustrious Clarence House, built in 1825 for the Duke of Clarence (later William IV), is now the home of Prince Charles and Camilla Parker Bowles, Duchess of Cornwall.

Museum, his underground wartime headquarters off Whitehall. Just down the road is the **Cenotaph,** which acts as a focal point for the annual remembrance of those lost in war, and at the end of Whitehall you'll find Parliament Square and the neo-Gothic **Houses of Parliament,** where members of both Houses (Commons and Lords) hold debates and vote on pending legislation.

On Parliament Square's west side is **Westminster Abbey,** a site of daily worship since the 10th century. Poets, political leaders, and 17 monarchs are buried in the 13th-century Gothic building. In its shadow is the 16th-century **St. Margaret's Church,** Parliament's "parish church." Heading west along **Birdcage Walk** will bring you to **Buckingham Palace.** The building is open to the public only in summer, but you can see much of the royal art collection in the Queen's Gallery and spectacular ceremonial coaches in the **Royal Mews,** both open all year. Finally, farther south toward Pimlico, **Tate Britain** focuses on prominent British artists from 1500 to today.

TOP ATTRACTIONS

Banqueting House. Built on the site of the original Tudor Palace of Whitehall, which was (according to one foreign visitor) "ill-built, and nothing but a heap of houses," James I commissioned Inigo Jones, one of England's great architects, to undertake a grand building. Influenced during a sojourn in Italy by Andrea Palladio's work, Jones brought Palladian sophistication and purity back to London with him. The resulting graceful and disciplined classical style of Banqueting House, completed in 1622, must have stunned its early occupants. In the quiet vaults beneath, James would escape the stresses of being a sovereign with a glass or two. His son Charles I enhanced the interior by employing the Flemish painter Peter Paul Rubens to glorify his father and the Stuart dynasty in vibrant painted

ceiling panels. As it turned out, these allegorical paintings, depicting a wise monarch being received into heaven, were the last thing Charles saw before he was beheaded by Cromwell's Parliamentarians in 1649. But his son, Charles II, was able to celebrate the restoration of the monarchy in this same place 20 years later. Banqueting House is also the setting for lunchtime classical concerts, held 1–2 pm. Call, or check the Web site for details. ✉ *Whitehall, Westminster* ☎ *020/3166–6154 or 020/3166–6155, 020/3166–6153 concert information* ⊕ *www.hrp.org.uk* 🖅 *£4.80, includes audio guide, concerts from £20* ⊙ *Mon.–Sat. 10–5, last admission 4:30. Closed Christmas wk. Liable to close at short notice for events so calling first is advisable* Ⓤ *Charing Cross, Embankment, Westminster.*

Fodor'sChoice
★
Buckingham Palace.
See the highlighted listing in this chapter.

☯
★
Cabinet War Rooms & Churchill Museum. It was from this small warren of underground rooms—beneath the vast government buildings of the Treasury—that Winston Churchill and his team directed troops in World War II. Designed to be bombproof, the whole complex has been preserved almost exactly as it was when the last light was turned off at the end of the war. Every clock shows almost 5 pm, and the furniture, fittings, and paraphernalia of a busy, round-the-clock war office are in situ, down to the colored map pins.

During air raids, the leading government ministers met here, and the Cabinet Room is still arranged as if a meeting were about to convene. In the Map Room, the Allied campaign is charted on wall-to-wall maps with a rash of pinholes showing the movements of convoys. In the hub of the room, a bank of different-color phones known as the "Beauty Chorus" linked the War Rooms to control rooms around the nation. The Prime Minister's Room holds the desk from which Churchill made his morale-boosting broadcasts; the Telephone Room (a converted broom cupboard) has his hotline to FDR. You can also see the restored suite of rooms that the PM used for dining, cooking, and sleeping. Telephonists and clerks who worked 16-hour shifts slept in lesser quarters in unenviable conditions; it would not have been unusual for a secretary in pajamas to scurry past a field marshal en route to a meeting.

An absorbing addition to the Cabinet War Rooms is the **Churchill Museum,** a tribute to the stirring politician and defiant wartime icon. Different zones explore his life and achievements—and failures, too—through objects and documents, many of which, such as his personal papers,

A classic photo op: cavalry from the Queen's Life Guard at Buckingham Palace.

had never previously been made public. Central to the exhibition is an interactive timeline, with layers of facts, figures, and tales. ✉ *Clive Steps, King Charles St., Westminster* ☎ *020/7930–6961* ⊕ *www.iwm. org.uk* 🎟 *£14.95, includes audio tour* ⊙ *Daily 9:30–6; last admission 5; disabled access* Ⓤ *Westminster.*

Clarence House. The London home of Queen Elizabeth the Queen Mother for nearly 50 years, Clarence House is now the Prince of Wales' and the Duchess of Cornwall's residence. The Regency mansion was built by John Nash for the Duke of Clarence, who found living in St. James's Palace quite unsuitable. Since then it has remained a royal home for princesses, dukes, and duchesses, including the present monarch, Queen Elizabeth, as a newlywed before her coronation. The rooms have been sensitively preserved to reflect the Queen Mother's taste, with the addition of many works of art from the Royal Collection, including works by Winterhalter, Augustus John, and Sickert. You'll find it less palace and more home (for the Prince and his sons William and Harry), with informal family pictures and comfortable sofas. The tour (by timed ticket entry only) is of the ground-floor rooms and includes the Lancaster Room, so called because of the marble chimneypiece presented by Lancaster County to the newly married Princess Elizabeth and the Duke of Edinburgh. Like Buckingham Palace, Clarence House is open only in August and September and tickets must be booked in advance. Visitors should note that there are no public restroom facilities at Clarence House. ✉ *Clarence House, St. James's Palace, St. James's* ☎ *020/7766–7303* ⊕ *www.royalcollection.org.uk* 🎟 *£8.50* ⊙ *Aug. and Sept.* Ⓤ *Green Park.*

BUCKINGHAM PALACE

✉ *Buckingham Palace Rd.,*
St. James ☎ *020/7766–7300*
⊕ *www.royalcollection.org.uk*
✆ *£17* ⊗ *Late July–late Sept.,*
daily 9:45–6 (last admission
3:45); times subject to change;
book ahead for disabled
access; check Web site before
visiting Ⓤ *Victoria, St. James's*
Park, Green Park.

TIPS

■ If bought directly from the
palace ticket office, tickets
are valid for a repeat visit
over the course of 12 months
from the first visit, so you can
return to Buckingham Palace
for another installment.

■ Admission is by timed ticket
with entry every 15 minutes
throughout the day. Allow up
to two hours.

■ A Royal Day Out ticket,
available only in August and
September, gives you the regal
triple whammy of the Royal
Mews, the Queen's Gallery, and
the State Rooms, and is valid
throughout the day. Tickets
cost £30.50. Allow four hours.

■ Get there by 10:30 to grab
a spot in the best viewing
section for the Changing the
Guard (www.changing-the-
guard.com), daily at 11:30 from
May until the end of July (varies according to troop deploy-
ment requirements) and on
alternate days for the rest of
the year, weather permitting.

It's rare to get a chance to see how the other half—well,
other minute fraction—lives and works. But when the
Queen heads off to Scotland on her annual summer
holiday (you can tell because the Union Jack flies above
the palace instead of the Royal Standard), the palace's
19 State Rooms open up to visitors (although the north
wing's private apartments remain behind closed doors).
With fabulous gilt moldings and walls adorned with
masterpieces by Rembrandt, Rubens, and other old
masters, the State Rooms are the grandest of the palace's 775 rooms.

HIGHLIGHTS

Inside the palace, the **Grand Hall,** followed by the
Grand Staircase and **Guard Room,** gives a taste of
what's to follow: marble, gold leaf galore, and massive,
twinkling chandeliers. Don't miss the theatrical **Throne
Room,** with the original 1953 coronation throne, or the
sword in **the Ballroom,** used by the Queen to bestow
knighthoods and other honors. Royal portraits line the
State Dining Room, and the **Blue Drawing Room** is
splendor in overdrive. The bow-shape **Music Room** features lapis lazuli columns between arched floor-to-ceiling windows, and the alabaster-and-gold plasterwork
of the **White Drawing Room** is a dramatic crescendo.
Spend some time ambling around the splendid gardens,
a gorgeous epilogue to the visit.

The **Changing the Guard,** also known as **Guard Mounting,** remains one of London's best free shows and culminates in front of the palace. Marching to live bands,
the old guard proceeds up the Mall from St. James's
Palace to Buckingham Palace. Shortly afterward, the
new guard approaches from Wellington Barracks. Then
within the forecourt, the captains of the old and new
guards symbolically transfer the keys to the palace.

BUCKINGHAM PALACE:GROUND FLOOR

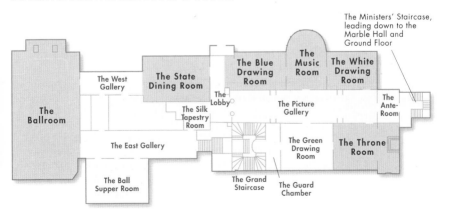

BUCKINGHAM PALACE:FIRST FLOOR

★ **Houses of Parliament.**
See the highlighted listing in this chapter.

⟳ **National Gallery.**
See the highlighted listing in this chapter.

Fodor's Choice
★

⟳ **National Portrait Gallery.** A suitably
Fodor's Choice idiosyncratic collection that pres-
★ ents a potted history of Britain through its people, past and present, this museum is an essential stop for all history and literature buffs, where you can choose to take in a little or a lot. The spacious, bright galleries are accessible via a state-of-the-art escalator. Pop into Portrait Explorer in the IT Gallery for computer-aided exploration. At the summit, the Portrait Restaurant (open an hour after gallery closing times on Thursday and Friday) will delight skyline aficionados. ■ TIP→ Here you'll see one of the best landscapes for real: a panoramic view of Nelson's Column and the backdrop along Whitehall to the Houses of Parliament.

Galleries are arranged chronologically from Tudor times on the second floor forward to contemporary Britain. In the Tudor Gallery—a modern update—on a Tudor long hall—is a Holbein cartoon of Henry VIII. Joshua Reynolds's self-portrait hangs in the refurbished 17th-century rooms; portraits of notables, including Shakespeare, the Brontë sisters, Jane Austen, and the Queen are always on display. Other faces are more obscure and will be just as unknown to you if you're English, because the portraits outlasted their sitters' fame—not so surprising when the portraitists are such greats as Reynolds, Gainsborough, Lawrence, Romney, and Hockney. Look for the four Andy Warhol *Queen Elizabeth II* silkscreens from 1985 and Maggi Hambling's surreal self-portrait. Contemporary portraits range from the iconic (*Julian with T-shirt*—an LCD screen on a continuous loop—by Julian Opie) to the creepy (Marc Quinn's *Self*, a realization of the artist's head in frozen blood) and the eccentric (Tim Noble's ghoulish *Head of Isabella Blow*). Temporary exhibitions can be explored in the Wolfson and Porter galleries. ⊠ *St. Martin's Pl., Covent Garden* ☎ *020/7312–2463, 020/730–0555 recorded switchboard information* ⊕ *www.npg.org.uk* ✉ *Free, charge for special exhibitions; £3 audiovisual guide* ☉ *Mon.–Wed. and weekends 10–6, Thurs. and Fri. 10–9, last admission 45 mins before closing* Ⓤ *Charing Cross, Leicester Sq.*

★ **The Queen's Gallery.** The former chapel at the south side of Buckingham Palace is now a temple of art and rare and exquisite objects, acquired by kings and queens over the centuries. Although Her Majesty herself is not the personal owner, she has the privilege of holding these works for the nation. Step through the splendid portico (designed by John Simpson) into elegantly restrained, spacious galleries whose walls are hung with some truly great works. An excellent audio guide takes you through the treasures.

A rough timeline of the major royal collectors starts with Charles I. An avid appreciator of painters, Charles established the basis of the Royal Collection, purchasing works by Mantegna, Raphael, Titian,

HOUSES OF PARLIAMENT

✉ *St. Stephen's Entrance, St. Margaret St., Westminster* ☎ *020/7219–4272 or 0844/847–1672* ⊕ *www.parliament.uk/visiting* 🎫 *Free; £14 Aug. and Sept. tours (weekdays) and Sat. through the year (must book ahead)* ⊙ *Call to confirm hrs* Ⓤ *Westminster.*

2

TIPS

■ The only guided tour nonresidents can go on is the paid-for (£14) tour offered on Saturday or during August and September (book through www.ticketmaster.co.uk).

■ However, nonresidents are able to watch debates when Parliament is in session if they wait in line for tickets. Embassies and High Commissions often have a quota of debate tickets available to their citizens, which can help you avoid long queues.

■ If you're pressed for time, queues for the House of Lords are often shorter than for the House of Commons. The easiest time to get into the Commons is during an evening session—Parliament is still sitting if the top of the Clock Tower is illuminated.

■ The most romantic view of the Houses is from the opposite (south) bank, across Lambeth Bridge. It is especially dramatic at night when floodlighted green and gold.

If you want to understand some of the centuries-old traditions and arcane idiosyncrasies that make up constitutionless British parliamentary democracy, the Palace of Westminster, as the complex is still properly called, is the place to come. The architecture in this 1,100-room labyrinth impresses, but the real excitement lies in stalking the corridors of power. A palace was first established on this site by Edward the Confessor in the 11th century. William II started building a new palace in 1087, and this gradually became the seat of English administrative power. However, the current building dates from the 19th century, when fire destroyed the rest of the complex in 1834.

HIGHLIGHTS

Visitors aren't allowed to snoop too much, but the **Visitors' Galleries** of the House of Commons do afford a view of democracy in process when the banks of green-leather benches are filled by opposing MPs (members of Parliament). When they speak, it's not directly to each other but through the Speaker, who also decides who will get time on the floor. Elaborate procedures notwithstanding, debate is often drowned out by raucous jeers. When MPs vote, they exit by the "Aye" or the "No" corridor, thus being counted by the party "tellers."

Westminster Hall, with its remarkable hammer-beam roof, was the work of William the Conqueror's son William Rufus. It's one of the largest remaining Norman halls in Europe, and its dramatic interior was the scene of the trial of Charles I.

After the 1834 fire, the **Clock Tower** was completed in 1858, and contains the 13-ton bell known as **Big Ben.** At the southwest end of the main Parliament building is the 323-foot-high Victoria Tower.

Caravaggio, and Dürer (it was under royal patronage that Rubens painted the Banqueting House ceiling). During the Civil War and in the aftermath of Charles's execution, many masterpieces were sold abroad and subsequently repatriated by Charles II. George III, who bought Buckingham House, scooped up a notable collection of Venetian (including Canaletto), Renaissance (Bellini and Raphael), and Dutch (Vermeer) art, and a large number of baroque drawings, in addition to patronizing English contemporary artists such as Gainsborough, Hoppner, and Beechey. He also took a liking to American artist Benjamin West. The Prince Regent, George IV, transformed his father's house into a palace, filling it with fine art from paintings to porcelain. In particular, he had a good eye for Rembrandt, contemporary equestrian works by Stubbs, and lavish portraits by Lawrence. Queen Victoria had a penchant for Landseer animals and landscapes, Frith's contemporary scenes, and portraits by Winterhalter. Finally, Edward VII indulged Queen Alexandra's love of Fabergé, and many royal tours around the empire produced gifts of gorgeous caliber, such as the Cullinan diamond from South Africa and an emerald-studded belt from India.

KEEP IN MIND

At the Queen's Gallery, look out for portraits of the Queen herself. She has the most reproduced image in history, with more than 180 billion incarnations on postage stamps alone.

The Queen's Gallery displays only a selection from the Royal Collection in themed exhibitions, while more than 3,000 objects reside in museums and galleries in the United Kingdom and abroad: check out the National Gallery, the Victoria & Albert Museum, the Museum of London, and the British Museum. ■ TIP→ The E-gallery provides an interactive electronic version of the collection, allowing the user to open lockets, remove a sword from its scabbard, or take apart the tulip vases. It's probably the closest you could get to eyeing practically every diamond in the sovereign's glittering diadem. ⊠ *Buckingham Palace, Buckingham Palace Rd., St. James's* ☎ *020/7766–7301* ⊕ *www.royal.gov.uk* ☑ *£8.50 with free audio guide, joint ticket with Royal Mews £15* ☉ *Daily 10–5:30; last admission 4:30* Ⓤ *Victoria, St. James's Park, Green Park.*

⟳ Fodor'sChoice ★ **St. James's Park.** With three palaces at its borders (the Palace of Westminster, the Tudor **St. James's Palace,** and Buckingham Palace), St. James's Park is acclaimed as the most royal of the royal parks. It's London's smallest, most ornamental park, as well as the oldest; once marshy water meadows, the land was acquired by Henry VIII in 1532 as a royal deer-hunting park (with dueling and sword fights forbidden); the public was always allowed access. James I improved the land and installed an aviary and zoo (complete with crocodiles). Charles II (after his exile in France, where he admired Louis XIV's formal Versailles Palace landscapes) had formal gardens laid out, with avenues, fruit orchards, and a canal. Lawns were grazed by goats, sheep, and deer, although in the 18th century it became a different kind of hunting ground, for wealthy lotharios looking to pick up nighttime escorts. In the early 19th century John Nash redesigned the landscape in a more naturalistic, romantic style, and if you gaze down the lake toward Buckingham Palace, you can believe you are on a country estate.

A large population of water fowl—including pelicans, geese, ducks, and swans (which belong to the Queen)—breed on and around Duck Island at the east end of the lake, while well-fed squirrels hop about on the grass. From April to September, the deck chairs (charge levied) come out for the longer days, crammed with office workers lunching while being serenaded by music from the bandstands. One of the best times to stroll the leafy walkways is after dark, with Westminster Abbey and the Houses of Parliament rising above the floodlighted lake. The popular Inn the Park restaurant is a wood-and-glass pavilion with a turf roof that blends in beautifully with the surrounding landscape; it's a good stopping place for a meal or a snack on a nice day. ⊠ *The Mall or Horse Guards approach, or Birdcage Walk, St. James's* ⊕ *www.royalparks.gov. uk* ☉ *Daily 5 am–midnight* Ⓤ *St. James's Park, Westminster.*

> ### GRANDMOTHER TIME
>
> In 1856, *The Times* noted "The singular structure that rises some three hundred feet high at the foot of Westminster Bridge, and looks the grandfather, or more properly the grandmother, of all kitchen clocks."

The Supreme Court. Officially opened by the Queen in 2009, the Supreme Court is the highest court of appeal in the UK. Housed in the carefully restored Middlesex Guildhall, visitors are welcome to pop in (for free) and look at the three courtrooms, including the impressive Court Room 1, on the second floor, with its magnificent carved wood ceiling. There is a café downstairs. ⊠ *Parliament Square, Westminster* ☎ *0207/960–1500* ⊕ *www.supremecourt.gov.uk* ☐ *Free* ☉ *9:30–4:30 weekdays.*

☾ **Tate Britain.** The stately neoclassical building may not be as ambitious
Fodor'sChoice as its sibling Tate Modern on the south bank, but Tate Britain's bright
★ galleries lure only a fraction of the Modern's crowds. A great place for exploring British art from 1500 to the present, the Tate Britain also hosts the annual Turner Prize exhibition, with its accompanying furor over the state of contemporary art, from about October to January each year. First opened in 1897, funded by the sugar magnate Sir Henry Tate, the museum includes the Linbury Galleries on the lower floors, which stage temporary exhibitions (which can get busy), whereas the upper floors show the permanent collection. Pictures are regularly re-hung so may be arranged chronologically or thematically. Whatever the presentation, you can find classic works by Constable, Gainsborough, Stubbs, David Wilkie, Francis Bacon, Duncan Grant, Barbara Hepworth, and Ben Nicholson and an outstanding display from J.M.W. Turner in the Clore Gallery, including many later vaporous and light-infused works such as *Sunrise with Sea Monsters*. Sumptuous Pre-Raphaelite pieces are a major drawcard while Contemporary British Art galleries bring you face to face with Damien Hirst's *Away from the Flock* and other recent conceptions.

Craving more art? Head down the river on the Tate-to-Tate shuttle boat to the Thames Modern, running between the two museums every 40 minutes. A River Roamer ticket permits additional stops

NATIONAL GALLERY

✉ *Trafalgar Sq.* ☎ *020/7747–2885* ⊕ *www.nationalgallery.org.uk* 🎫 *Free, charge for special exhibitions; audio guide £3* ⏱ *Sun.–Thurs. 10–6, Fri. 10–9* Ⓤ *Charing Cross, Embankment, Leicester Square.*

TIPS

■ Color coding throughout the galleries helps you keep track of the period you're immersed in.

■ Begin at an "Art Start" terminal in the Sainsbury Wing or East Wing Espresso Bar. The interactive screens give you access to information on all of the museum's holdings; you can choose your favorites, and print out a free personal tour map.

■ Want some stimulation? Try a free weekday lunchtime lecture, or Ten Minute Talk, which illuminates the story behind a key work of art.

■ One-hour free, guided tours start at the Sainsbury Wing daily at 11:30 and 2:30.

■ If you are eager for even more insight into the art, pick up a themed audio guide, which takes in about 20 paintings.

■ If you visit during school holidays, don't miss special programs for children. There are also free Family Sundays with special talks for children and their parents.

Standing proudly on the north side of Trafalgar Square is one of the world's supreme art collections, with more than 2,300 masterpieces on show. Picasso, van Gogh, Michelangelo, Leonardo, Monet, Turner, and more—all for free.

HIGHLIGHTS

This brief selection is your jumping-off point, but there are hundreds more, enough to fill a full day. In chronological order: (1) **Van Eyck** (circa 1395–1441), *The Arnolfini Portrait*—a solemn couple holds hands, the fish-eye mirror behind them mysteriously illuminating what can't be seen from the front view. (2) **Holbein** (1497–1543), *The Ambassadors*—two wealthy visitors from France stand surrounded by what were considered luxury goods at the time. Note the elongated skull at the bottom of the painting, which takes shape when viewed from an angle. (3) **Leonardo da Vinci** (1452–1519), *The Virgin and Child*—this exquisite black-chalk "Burlington Cartoon" has the master's most haunting Mary. (4) **Constable** (1776–1837), *The Hay Wain*—rendered overfamiliar by too many greeting cards, this is the definitive image of golden-age rural England. (5) **Turner** (1775–1851), *Rain, Steam and Speed: The Great Western Railway*, an astonishing whirl of rain, mist, steam, and locomotion (spot the hare). (6) **Caravaggio** (1573–1610), *The Supper at Emmaus*—a cinematically lightened, freshly resurrected Christ blesses bread in an astonishingly domestic vision from the master of chiaroscuro. (7) **Seurat** (1859–91), *Bathers at Asnières*—this static summer day's idyll is one of the pointillist extraordinaire's best-known works. (8) **Botticelli** (1445–1510), *Venus and Mars*—Mars sleeps, exhausted by the love goddess, oblivious to the lance wielded by mischievous cherubs.

at the London Eye and the Tower of London. ✉ *Millbank, Westminster* ☎ *020/7887–8888* ⊕ *www.tate.org.uk/britain* 🎫 *Free, exhibitions £5–£11* ⊘ *Daily 10–6, last entry at 5, 10–10 1st Friday of month* Ⓤ *Pimlico (signposted 5-min walk).*

NEED A BREAK?

Rather than search for a suitable place in Pimlico or Victoria, you can eat well right at the Tate. The Tate Britain Café has drinks, sandwiches, and cakes and is open daily from 10 am to 5:30 pm. The Rex Whistler Restaurant, also in the Tate Britain, is almost a destination in itself, with its celebrated Rex Whistler murals

BEARSKIN, NOT BUSBY

While on duty, guardsmen are required to remain utterly aloof—they may not speak (some people attempt to make them laugh), may not swat errant flies from their noses, and in theory may not keel over under the weight of their enormous, saunalike hats. Called bearskins (not busbies, as is sometimes incorrectly assumed) after the material from which they are made, the headdress was originally worn by the French Imperial Guard defeated in the Battle of Waterloo in 1815.

and a daily fixed-price three-course lunch menu (around £15) and à la carte choices. Ingredients celebrate British produce, such as Cornish crab, Welsh lamb, organic smoked salmon, and Stilton cheese. Children's portions are available. It's open for lunch Monday through Sunday noon to 3; afternoon tea and breakfast are also served on weekends.

Trafalgar Square. This is literally the center of London: a plaque on the corner of the Strand and Charing Cross Road marks the spot from which distances on U.K. signposts are measured. **Nelson's Column** stands at the heart of the square (which is named after the great admiral's most important victory), guarded by haughty lions designed by Sir Edwin Landseer and flanked by statues of two generals who helped establish the British Empire in India, **Charles Napier** and **Henry Havelock.** The fourth plinth is given over to rotating works by contemporary sculptors. Great events, such as New Year's Eve celebrations, political protests, and sporting triumphs always see the crowds gathering in the city's most famous square. Although Trafalgar Square is known to Chinese tourists as Pigeon Square, feeding the birds is now banned so the gray flocks have flown.

The commanding open space is built on the grand scale demanded by its central position. From the 13th century, the site housed the royal hawks and falcons until 1530, when these buildings were replaced by stabling for royal horses. This "Great Mews" was demolished in 1830 as part of John Nash's Charing Cross Improvement Scheme. Nash, who envisioned the square as a cultural space open to the public, exploited its natural north–south incline to create a succession of high points from which to look down imposing carriageways toward the Thames, the Houses of Parliament, and Buckingham Palace. Upon Nash's death, the design baton was passed to Sir Charles Barry and then to Sir Edwin Lutyens, and the square was finally completed in 1850.

The Tate Britain showcases British art from the last 500 years, including contemporary works.

At the southern point of the square, en route to Whitehall, is the **equestrian statue of Charles I.** After the Civil War and the king's execution, Oliver Cromwell, then the leader of the "Commonwealth," commissioned a scrap dealer, brazier John Rivett, to melt the statue. The story goes that Rivett buried it in his garden and made a fortune peddling knickknacks wrought, he claimed, from its metal, only to produce the statue miraculously unscathed after the restoration of the monarchy—and to make more cash reselling it to the authorities. In 1767 Charles II had it placed where it stands today, near the spot where his father was executed in 1649. Each year, on January 30, the day of the king's death, the Royal Stuart Society lays a wreath at the foot of the statue. ✉ *Trafalgar Sq., Westminster* Ⓤ *Charing Cross.*

Fodor's Choice **Westminster Abbey.**
★ *See the highlighted listing in this chapter.*

WORTH NOTING

Admiralty Arch. A stately and bombastic gateway to the Mall, this is one of the city's finest set pieces. On the southwest corner of Trafalgar Square, the arch, which was named after the adjacent Royal Navy headquarters, was designed in 1908–11 by Sir Aston Webb as a two-part memorial to Queen Victoria, along the ceremonial route to Buckingham Palace; the second part is the Victoria Memorial just outside the palace. Passing under one of its five arches—two for pedestrians, two for traffic, and a central arch, opened only for state occasions—one enters the Mall (rhymes with the American pronunciation of shall). A quirky feature of

ROYAL ATTRACTIONS

The Queen and the Royal Family attend hundreds of functions a year, and if you want to know what they are doing on any given date, turn to the *Court Circular*, printed in the major London dailiesthe *Times*, the *Telegraph*, and the *Scotsman*, or check out the Royal Family Web site, ⊕ *www.royal.gov.uk*, for the latest events on the *Royal Diary*. Trooping the Colour is usually held on the second Saturday in June, to celebrate the Queen's official birthday. This spectacular parade begins when she leaves Buckingham Palace in her carriage and rides down the Mall to arrive at Horse Guards Parade at 11 exactly. To watch, just line up along the Mall with your binoculars!

Another time you can catch the Queen in all her regalia is when she and the Duke of Edinburgh ride in state to Westminster to open the Houses of Parliament. The famous gilded black, gilt-trimmed Irish State Coach travels from Buckingham Palace, escorted by the brilliantly uniformed Household Cavalry—on a clear day, it's to be hoped, for this ceremony takes place in late October or early November, depending on the exigencies of Parliament. The Gold State Coach, an icon of fairy-tale glamour, is used for coronations and jubilees only.

But perhaps the most relaxed, least formal time to see the Queen is during Royal Ascot, held at the racetrack near Windsor Castle—a short train ride out of London—usually during the third week of June (Tuesday–Friday). The Queen and members of the Royal Family are driven down the track to the Royal Box in an open carriage, giving spectators a chance to see them. After several races, the Queen invariably walks down to the paddock, greeting race goers as she proceeds.

the arch is its curious "nose": about 7 feet up, on the inside wall of the most northerly arch is a noselike protrusion, said to be either based on Wellington's or Napoleon's nose. ⊠ *The Mall, Cockspur St., Trafalgar Sq., Westminster* Ⓤ *Charing Cross.*

Carlton House Terrace. Architect John Nash designed Carlton House, a glorious example of the Regency style. Between 1812 and 1830, under the patronage of George IV (Prince Regent until George III's death in 1820), Nash was the architect of the grand scheme for Regent Street, which started here and ended with the sweep of neoclassical houses encircling Regent's Park. The Prince Regent, who lived at Carlton House, had plans to build a country villa at Primrose Hill (to the north of the park), connected by a grand road—hence Regent Street. Even though it was considered a most extravagant building for its time, Carlton House was demolished after the prince's accession to the throne. Nash's Carlton House Terrace, no less imposing, with white-stucco facades and massive Corinthian columns, was built in its place. It was a smart address and one that prime ministers Gladstone (1856) and Palmerston (1857–75) enjoyed. Today Carlton House Terrace houses the Royal College of Pathologists (No. 2), the Royal Society (No. 6–9), whose members have included Isaac Newton and Charles Darwin, and the Turf Club (No. 5). ⊠ *The Mall, St. James's* Ⓤ *Charing Cross.*

Downing Street. Looking like an unassuming alley but for the iron gates at both its Whitehall and Horse Guards Road approaches, this is the location of the famous **No. 10,** London's modest version equivalent of the White House. The Georgian entrance is deceptive, though, since the old house now leads to a large mansion behind it, overlooking the Horse Guards Parade. Only three houses remain of the terrace built circa 1680 by Sir George Downing, who spent enough of his youth in America to graduate from Har-

vard—the second man ever to do so. **No. 11** is traditionally the residence of the chancellor of the exchequer (secretary of the treasury), and **No. 12** is the party whips' office. No. 10 has officially housed the prime minister since 1732. Just south of Downing Street, in the middle of Whitehall, you'll see the **Cenotaph,** a stark white monolith designed in 1920 by Edwin Lutyens to commemorate the 1918 armistice. On Remembrance Day (the Sunday nearest November 11, Armistice Day) it's strewn with red poppy wreaths to honor the dead of both world wars and all British and Commonwealth soldiers killed in action since; the first wreath is laid by the Queen or the senior member of the Royal Family present, and there's a march-past by war veterans, who salute their fallen comrades. ⊠ *Whitehall, Whitehall* Ⓤ *Westminster.*

Ⓒ **Household Cavalry Museum.** Horse lovers can see working horses belonging to the British Army's two senior regiments, the Life Guards and the Blues and Royals, being tended to in their stable block behind a glass wall. Located in the cavalry's original 17th-century stables, the museum has displays of uniforms and weapons going back to 1661 as well as interactive exhibits on the regiments' current operational roles. In the tack room you can handle saddles and bridles, and try on a trooper's uniform, including its distinctive brass helmet with horsehair plume. ⊠ *Horse Guards, Whitehall* ☎ *020/7930–3070* ⊕ *www. householdcavalrymuseum.org.uk* 🔖 *£6* ⊗ *Mar.–Sept., daily 10–6; Oct.–Feb., daily 10–5* Ⓤ *Charing Cross, Westminster.*

Ⓒ **Horse Guards Parade.** Once the tiltyard of Whitehall Palace, where jousting tournaments were held, the Horse Guards Parade is now notable mainly for the annual Trooping the Colour ceremony, in which the Queen takes the salute, her official birthday tribute, on the second Saturday in June. (Like Paddington Bear, the Queen has two birthdays; her real one is on April 21.) There is pageantry galore, with marching bands and throngs of onlookers. Covering the vast expanse of the square that faces Horse Guards Road, opposite St. James's Park at one end and Whitehall at the other, the ceremony is televised. At the Whitehall facade of Horse Guards, the changing of two mounted sentries known as the **Queen's Life Guard** provides what may be London's most popular photo opportunity. The ceremony last about half

an hour. The ceremony lasts about half an hour. ⊠ *Whitehall, Whitehall* ☏ *020/7930–4832* ⊙ *Changing of the Queen's Life Guard at 11 am Mon.–Sat. and 10 am Sun.; inspection of the Queen's Life Guard daily at 4 pm* Ⓤ *Westminster.*

The **Wesley Café** (⊠ *Storey's Gate, Westminster* ☏ *020/7222–8010*) is a popular budget haunt for office workers around Westminster, and a good stopping point if you don't want to go farther along Victoria Street in search of food. It's almost opposite Westminster Abbey, in the crypt of Methodist Central Hall.

Institute of Contemporary Arts (ICA). Behind its incongruous white-stucco facade on the Mall next to the Duke of York steps, the ICA has provided a stage for the avant-garde in performance, theater, dance, visual art, and music since it was established in 1947. There are two cinemas, a theater, three galleries, a cerebral bookshop, reading room, a café, a hip bar, and adventurous curators. ⊠ *The Mall, St. James's* ☏ *020/7930– 3647* ⊕ *www.ica.org.uk* 💷 *Free; £9 for cinema screenings* ⊙ *Galleries daily noon–7, Thurs. until 9* Ⓤ *Charing Cross, Piccadilly Circus.*

The **ICA Bar and Café** has a Modern British menu and windows overlooking the Mall—it's popular at lunchtime, so come early. Open daily from noon.

The Mall. This stately, 115-foot-wide processional route sweeping from Admiralty Arch to the Queen Victoria Memorial at Buckingham Palace is an updated 1904 version of the traditional rambling promenade that was used for centuries. The street was originally laid out around 1660 for the game of *paille-maille* (a type of croquet crossed with golf), which also gave the parallel road Pall Mall its name, and it quickly became the place to be seen. The **Duke of York Memorial** up the steps toward Carlton House Terrace is a towering column dedicated to George III's second son, further immortalized in the English nursery rhyme "The Grand old Duke of York." Sadly the internal spiral steps are inaccessible. ■TIP→ Be sure to stroll along the Mall on Sunday when the road is closed to traffic, or catch the bands and troops of the Household Division on their way from St. James's Palace to Buckingham Palace for the Changing the Guard. ⊠ *The Mall, St. James's* Ⓤ *Charing Cross, Green Park.*

Royal Mews. Fairy-tale gold-and-glass coaches and sleek Rolls-Royce state cars emanate from the Royal Mews, next door to the Queen's Gallery. The John Nash–designed Mews serves as the headquarters for Her Majesty's travel department (so beware of closures for state visits), complete with the Queen's own special breed of horses, ridden by wigged postilions decked in red-and-gold regalia. Between the stables and riding school arena are exhibits of polished saddlery and riding tack. The highlight of the Mews is the splendid Gold State Coach, not unlike an art gallery on wheels, with its sculpted tritons and sea gods. Mews were originally falcons' quarters (the name comes from their "mewing," or feather shedding), but the horses gradually eclipsed the birds. Royal Collection staff guide tours. ⊠ *Buckingham Palace Rd., St. James's* ☏ *020/7766–7302* ⊕ *www.royalcollection.org.uk* 💷 *£7.75, joint ticket with Queen's Gallery £15* ⊙ *Mar. 28–July 25 and Oct.,*

Sat.–Thurs. 11–4 (last admission 3:15); July–Sept., daily 10–5, no guided tours; last admission 4:15 Ⓤ *Victoria, St. James's Park.*

St. James's Palace. With its solitary sentry posted at the gate, this surprisingly small palace of Tudor brick was once a home for many British sovereigns, including the first Elizabeth and Charles I, who spent his last night here before his execution. Today it's the working office of another Charles—the Prince of Wales. The front door actually opens right onto the street,

but he always uses a back entrance to various departments of the Royal Household. Matters to ponder as you look (you can't go in): the palace was named after a hospital for women lepers that stood here during the 11th century; Henry VIII had it built; foreign ambassadors to Britain are still accredited to the Court of St. James's even though it has rarely been a primary royal residence; the present Queen made her first speech here; and after the death of a monarch, the accession of the new sovereign is announced by the Garter King of Arms from the Proclamation Gallery overlooking Friary Court. Friary Court out front is a splendid setting for Trooping the Colour, part of the Queen's official birthday celebrations. Everyone loves to take a snapshot of the scarlet-coated guardsman standing sentry outside the imposing Tudor gateway. Note that the Changing the Guard ceremony at St. James's Palace occurs only on days when the guard at Buckingham Palace is changed. See entry for Buckingham Palace for details. ⊠ *Friary Court, St. James's* ⊕ *www.royal.gov.uk* Ⓤ *Green Park.*

St. Margaret's Church. Dwarfed by its neighbor, Westminster Abbey, St. Margaret's was founded in the 11th century and rebuilt between 1488 and 1523. As the unofficial parish church of the House of Commons, St Margaret's is much sought after for weddings and memorial services. Samuel Pepys, Chaucer, and John Milton worshipped here, and Winston Churchill tied the knot here in 1908. Since 1681, a pew off the south aisle has been set aside for the Speaker of the House (look for the carved portcullis). The stained glass in the north windows is classically Victorian, facing abstract glass from John Piper in the south, replacing the originals, which were ruined in WWII. ⊠ *St. Margaret's St., Parliament Sq., Westminster* ☎ *020/7654–4847* ⊕ *www.westminster-abbey. org/st-margarets* ☉ *Weekdays 9:30–3:30, Sat. 9–1:30, Sun. 2–5 (entry via east door). Church may close on short notice for services, so call ahead* Ⓤ *Westminster.*

↻ **St. Martin-in-the-Fields.** One of London's best-loved and most welcoming of churches has been enhanced both inside and out by expensive and time-consuming refurbishment work; the building's array of functions continues unabated. It's a welcome sight for the homeless who have sought soup and shelter at this church—named after the saint who helped beggars—since 1914. For historical detailing, take the worthwhile audio tour. The church is also a haven for music lovers; the internationally known Academy of St. Martin-in-the-Fields was founded here, and a popular program of concerts continues today. (Although the interior is a wonderful setting, the wooden benches can make it hard to give your undivided attention to the music.) The crypt is a hive of activity, with a café and shop, plus the **London Brass-Rubbing Centre,** where you can make your own life-size souvenir knight, lady, or monarch from replica tomb brasses, with metallic waxes, paper, and instructions from about £4.50. St. Martin's is often called the royal parish church, partly because Charles II was christened here: the small medieval chapel that once stood here, probably used by the monks of Westminster Abbey, gave way to a grand rebuilding, completed in 1726, and James Gibbs's classical temple-with-spire design also became a familiar pattern for churches in early colonial America. Though it has to compete for attention with Trafalgar Square's many prominent structures, its spire is slightly taller than Nelson's Column. ⊠ *Trafalgar Sq., Covent Garden* ☎ *020/7766–1100, 020/7839–8362 brass rubbings; 020/7766–1122 evening-concert credit-card bookings* ⊕ *www.smitf.org* 🖼 *Concerts £6–£22; Church audio tour £3.50* ⊗ *Mon.–Sat. 8–6, Sun. 8–6 for worship; café Mon. and Tues. 8–8, Wed. 8–7, Thurs.–Sat. 8–9, Sun. 11–6* Ⓤ *Charing Cross, Leicester Sq.*

ST. MARTIN'S CONCERTS

Classical concerts (some candlelit) are held every Thursday to Saturday (and some Tuesdays) at 7.30 pm with evening jazz concerts in the crypt every Wednesday at 8 pm. Tickets are available from the box office in the crypt. Free (donation appreciated) lunch-time concerts take place Monday, Tuesday, and Friday, 1–2 pm.

QUICK BITES

The atmospheric St. Martin's Café in the Crypt, with its magnificent high-arched brick vault and gravestone floor, serves full English and Continental breakfasts, sandwiches, salads, snacks, afternoon tea, and wine. Lunch and dinner options include vegetarian meals and the setting, at the heart of London, is superb.

Wellington Barracks. These are the headquarters of the Guards Division, the Queen's five regiments of elite foot guards (Grenadier, Coldstream, Scots, Irish, and Welsh) who protect the sovereign and patrol her palaces dressed in tunics of gold-purled scarlet and tall bearskin caps. Guardsmen alternate these ceremonial postings with serving in current conflicts, for which they wear more practical uniforms. If you want to learn more about the guards, visit the **Guards Museum,** which has displays on all aspects of a guardsman's life in conflicts dating back to 1642; the entrance is next to the Guards Chapel. Next door is the **Guards Toy Soldier Centre,** a great place for a souvenir. ⊠ *Wellington Barracks, Birdcage Walk, Westminster* ☎ *020/7414–3428* ⊕ *www.theguardsmuseum.com* 🖼 *£4* ⊗ *Daily 10–4; last admission 3:30* Ⓤ *St. James's Park.*

Continued on page 70

WESTMINSTER ABBEY

A monument to the rich—and often bloody and scandalous—history of Great Britain, Westminster Abbey rises on the Thames skyline as one of the most iconic sites in London.

The mysterious gloom of the lofty medieval interior is home to more than 600 monuments and memorial statues. About 3,300 people, from kings to composers to wordsmiths, are buried in the abbey. It has been the scene of 14 royal weddings and no less than 38 coronations—the first in 1066, when William the Conqueror was made king here.

TOURING THE ABBEY

There's only one way around the abbey, and as there will almost certainly be a long stream of shuffling tourists at your heels, you'll need to be alert to catch the highlights. Enter by the north door.

When you enter the church, turn around and look up to see the ❶ painted-glass rose window, the largest of its kind.

The ❷ Coronation Chair, at the foot of the Henry VII Chapel, has been briefly graced by nearly every regal posterior since Edward I ordered it in 1301. Look for the graffiti on the back of the Coronation chair. It's the work of 18th- and 19th-century visitors and Westminster schoolboys who carved their names there.

The ❸ Henry VII's Lady Chapel contains the tombs of Henry VII and his queen, Elizabeth of York. Close by are monuments to the young daughters of James I, and an urn purported to hold the remains of the so-called Princes in the Tower—Edward V and Richard. Interestingly, arch enemies Elizabeth I and her half-sister Mary Tudor share a tomb here. Begun in 1503, the chapel is famed for its ceiling—a dazzling fan-vaulted roof with carved pendants—and the heraldic banners of living knights that hang above its oak stalls.

In front of the ❹ High Altar, which was used for the funerals of Princess Diana and the Queen Mother, is a black-and-white marble pavement laid in 1268. The intricate Italian Cosmati work contains three Latin inscriptions, one of which states that the world will last for 19,683 years.

The ❺ Shrine of St. Edward the Confessor contains the shrine to the pre-Norman king. Because of its great age, you must join a tour with the verger to be admitted to the chapel. (Details are available at the admission desk; there is a small extra charge.)

Geoffrey Chaucer was the first poet to be buried in ❻ Poets' Corner in 1400. Other memorials include: William Shakespeare, William Blake, John Milton, Jane Austen, Samuel Taylor Coleridge, William Wordsworth, and Charles Dickens.

A door from the south transept and south choir aisle leads to the calm of the ❼ Great Cloisters.

West Entrance

Choir

College Hall

Dean's Court

Deanery

Site of Refectory

North Entrance

1 North Transept

North Ambulatory

Sanctuary **5**

South Ambulatory

South Transept

6

8

9

10

2   **3**   **4**

and actual clothing of Charles II and Admiral Lord Nelson (complete with eye patch).

The **10** Little Cloister is a quiet haven, and just beyond, the **11** College Garden is a delightful diversion. Filled with medicinal herbs, it has been tended by monks for more than 900 years.

The **12** Dean's Yard is the best spot for a fine view of the massive flying buttresses above.

In the choir screen, north of the entrance to the choir, is a marble **13** monument to Sir Isaac Newton.

14 A plaque to Franklin D. Roosevelt is one of the Abbey's very few tributes to a foreigner.

The **15** Grave of the Unknown Warrior, in memory of the soldiers who lost their lives in both world wars, is near the exit of the abbey.

The medieval **8** Chapter House is adorned with 14th-century frescoes. The King's Council met here between 1257 and 1547. Be sure to look at the floor, one of the finest surviving tiled floors in the country.

The **9** Abbey Museum includes a collection of deliciously macabre effigies made from the death masks

QUIRKY LONDON

Near the Henry VII chapel, keep an eye open for St. Wilgefortis, who was so concerned to protect her chastity that she prayed to God for help and woke up one morning with a full growth of beard.

A BRIEF HISTORY

960 AD Benedictine monastery founded on the site by King Edward and King Dunstan.

1045–65 King Edward the Confessor enlarges the original monastery, erecting a stone church in honor of St. Paul the Apostle. Named "west minster" to distinguish from "east minster" (St. Paul's Cathedral).

1065 The church is consecrated on December 28. Edward doesn't live to see the ceremony.

1161 Following Edward's canonization, his body is moved by Henry III to a more elaborate resting place behind the High Altar. Other medieval kings are later buried around his tomb.

1245–54 Henry III pulls down the abbey and starts again with a new Gothic style influenced by his travels in France. Master mason Henry de Reyns ("of Rheims") constructs the transepts, north front, and rose windows, as well as part of the cloisters and Chapter House.

1269 The new abbey is consecrated and the choir is completed.

1350s Richard II resumes Henry III's plan to rebuild the monastery. Henry V and Henry VII continue as benefactors.

1503 The Lady Chapel is demolished and the foundation stone of Henry VII's Chapel is laid on the site.

1540 The abbey ceases to be used as a monastery.

1560 Elizabeth I refounds the abbey as a Collegiate Church. From this point on it is a "Royal Peculiar," exempt from the jurisdiction of bishops.

1745 The western towers, left unfinished from medieval times, are finally completed, based on a design by Sir Christopher Wren.

1995 Following a 25-year restoration program, saints and allegorical figures are added to the niches on the western towers and around the Great West Door.

PLANNING YOUR DAY

GETTING HERE: The closest Tube stop is Westminster. When you exit the station, walk west along Great George Street, away from the river. Turn left on St. Margaret Street.

CONTACT INFO: ✉ Broad Sanctuary, Westminster SW1 P3PA ☎ 020/7222–5152 ⊕ www.westminster-abbey.org.

ADMISSION: Adults: Abbey and museum £15. **Family ticket** (2 adults and 2 children): £30. **Children under 11:** free.

HOURS: The abbey is a house of worship. Services may cause changes to the visiting hours on any given day, so be sure to call ahead.
Abbey: Mon., Tues., Thurs., Fri. 9:30–4:30 (last admission 3:30); Wed. 9:30–7 (last general admission 6); Sat. 9:30–2:30; (last admission 1:30); Sun, worship only.
Museum: Mon.–Sat. 10:30–4.
Cloisters: Daily 8–6
College Garden: Tues.–Thurs. 10–6
Chapter House: Mon.–Sat. 10:30–4

WHAT'S NEARBY: To make the most of your day, arrive at the abbey early (doors open at 9:30), then make an afternoon visit to the Parliament buildings and finish with a sunset ride on the **London Eye**. Post-flight, take a walk along the fairy-lit South Bank and have dinner (or a drink in the bar) with a view, at the **Oxo Tower Restaurant** (☎ 020/7803–3888) or the Royal Festival Hall's **Skylon Restaurant** (☎ 020/7654–7800).

Please note that overseas visitors can no longer visit the **Houses of Parliament** during session. However, tours of the buildings are available in August and September. For more information and booking call ☎ 0870/906–3773. Also, it's advisable to prebook tickets for the London Eye. Do this online at www.londoneye.com, or call 0870/990–8883.

IN A HURRY?

If you're pressed for time, concentrate on the following four highlights: the Coronation Chair; Chapter House; Poets' Corner; and Grave of the Unknown Warrior.

THINGS TO KNOW

■ Photography and filming are not permitted anywhere in the abbey.

■ In winter the interior of the abbey can get quite cold; dress accordingly.

■ For an animated history of the museum, join one of the tours that depart from the information desk, tour times vary.

■ Touring the abbey can take half a day, especially in summer, when lines are long.

■ To avoid the crowds, make sure you arrive early. If you're first in line you can enjoy parts of the abbey in relative calm before the mad rush descends.

■ If you want to study up before you go, visit www.westminster-abbey.org, which includes an in-depth history and self-guided tour of the abbey. Otherwise pick up a free leaflet from the information desk.

■ On Sundays the abbey is not open to visitors. Join a service instead. Check the Web site for service times, as well as details of concerts, organ recitals, and special events.

Westminster Cathedral. Amid the concrete jungle of Victoria Street lies this remarkable neo-Byzantine find, seat of the Archbishop of Westminster, head of the Roman Catholic Church in Britain, and consequently of London's principal Roman Catholic church. Faced with the daunting proximity of Westminster Abbey, the architect, John Francis Bentley, flew in the face of fashion by rejecting neo-Gothic in favor of the Byzantine idiom, which still provides maximum contrast today. The asymmetrical redbrick Byzantine edifice, dating from 1903, is banded with stripes of Portland stone and abutted by a 273-foot-high bell tower containing Big Edward at the northwest corner, ascendable by elevator for sterling views. The interior remains incomplete and is unusual for the unfinished overhead brickwork of the ceiling, which lends the church a dark, brooding intensity. An optimistic watercolor from 1950 hangs from one of the internal pillars, revealing the church interior in an imagined state of resplendent completion. Several side chapels—such as the eastern-Roman styled Chapel of the Blessed Sacrament and the Holy Souls Chapel—are beautifully finished in glittering mosaics. The lovely Lady Chapel—dedicated to the Virgin Mary—is also sumptuously decorated. In front of the chapel, a small stone statue of Jesus' mother attracts particular veneration. Look out for the Stations of the Cross (stopping points for prayer or contemplation) by Eric Gill and the striking baldachin—the enormous stone canopy standing over the altar and giant cross suspended in front of it. Since his conversion to Catholicism, and a clearer calendar, ex–prime minister Tony Blair has been seen at the church on Sunday mornings. The nave is the widest in the country and is constructed in green marble, which also has a Byzantine connection—it was cut from the same place as the 6th-century St. Sophia's in Istanbul, and was almost confiscated by warring Turks as it traveled across the country. Just inside the main entrance is the tomb of Cardinal Basil Hume, head of the Catholic Church in the United Kingdom for more than 25 years. There's a café in the crypt. ⊠ *Ashley Pl., Westminster* ☎ *020/7798–9055* ⊕ *www.westminstercathedral. org.uk* ☎ *Tower £5, Bell Tower viewing gallery £5, Treasures of the Cathedral exhibition £5 (exhibition opening hrs weekdays 9:30–5 pm, weekends 9:30–6); joint ticket for both Bell Tower and exhibition £8* ⊙ *Weekdays 7–6, weekends 8–7* Ⓤ *Victoria.*

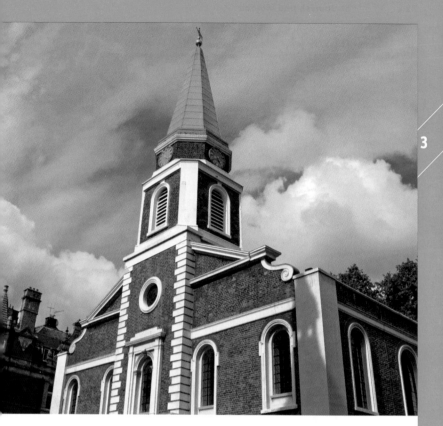

St. James's and Mayfair

WORD OF MOUTH

"We really liked being based in Mayfair, a very upscale area with many embassies and gorgeous town homes. The kids were impressed at the number of Bentleys, Aston Martins, and Ferraris. It's a short walk to Hyde Park or Green Park, and there are many restaurants and pubs to choose from."

—BelTib

GETTING ORIENTED

TOP REASONS TO GO

Claridge's Bar: Unwind with afternoon tea at this Art Deco gem after a shopping spree in Mayfair.

St. James's Church: Raise your spirits at this beautiful masterpiece by Sir Christopher Wren, the site of poet William Blake's baptism.

Fine Shopping: Balance your boutique stores (Stella McCartney and Burberry) with food emporium Fortnum & Mason and the designers on sale at gigantic Selfridges before relaxing at Waterstone's 5th View with a book and glass of wine at this mega–bookstore café.

Royal Academy of Arts: Visit the Summer Exhibition, usually between June and August, a breathtaking affair showcasing some of the best sculpture and painting in the art world.

St. George's Gardens: Escape from the congestion of central London in this hidden patch of green tucked behind chic Mount Street.

FEELING PECKISH?

Eating healthfully can be a challenge in London, but **Crussh** (⊠ *1 Curzon St., Mayfair* ☎ *020/7629–2554*) on Curzon Street serves excellent juices, smoothies, and soups as well as sandwiches, salads, and wraps to bring across to nearby Green Park.

Gordon Ramsay at Claridge's (⊠ *55 Brook St., Mayfair* ☎ *020/7499–0099*) takes fine dining to exquisite heights of elegance; it's the perfect marriage of Art Deco beauty and culinary genius from one of England's most celebrated chefs.

Since 1909, **Richoux** (⊠ *172 Piccadilly, Mayfair* ☎ *020/7493–2204*) is an affordable refuge from busy Piccadilly. Simple but well-executed French bistro food is served all day; save room for the excellent pastries.

GETTING THERE

There are three Tube stops on the Central Line that will leave you smack in the center of these neighborhoods: Marble Arch, Bond Street (also Jubilee Line), and Oxford Circus (also Victoria and Bakerloo lines).

You can also take the Piccadilly or Bakerloo line to the Piccadilly Circus Tube station, the Piccadilly to the Hyde Park Corner station, or the Piccadilly, Victoria, or Jubilee line to the Green Park station.

The best buses are the 8, which takes in Green Park, Berkeley Square, and New Bond Street, and the 9, one of the few routes that still use the traditional Routemaster model, which runs along Piccadilly.

MAKING THE MOST OF YOUR TIME

Reserve at least a day to see the sights in St. James's and Mayfair, but choose carefully, as this is one of London's most densely packed, and visited, districts.

The only areas to avoid are the Tube stations at rush hour, and Oxford Street if you don't like crowds.

At all costs, stay away from Oxford Circus around 5 pm, when the commuter rush can, at times, resemble an East African wildebeest migration.

3

Sightseeing
★★★★★

Nightlife
★★★

Dining
★★★★

Lodging
★★★★

Shopping
★★★★

St. James's and Mayfair form the very core of London's West End, the city's smartest central area. No textbook sights here; rather, these neighborhoods epitomize so much of the flavor that is peculiarly London's—the sense of being in a great, rich, (once) powerful city is almost palpable as you wander along its posh and polished streets.

Updated
by Damian
Harper

Smart and stylish Mayfair reflects the shiny affluence of London. This is where the city's financial set, British aristocrats, and the international rich live, as well as dine, play, and shop. Meanwhile, more sedate St. James's, with its old-money galleries, restaurants, and gentlemen's clubs, embodies the history and privilege of traditional London.

Despite being bounded by four of the busiest streets in London—bustling budget-shopping mecca Oxford Street to the north, traffic artery Park Lane with Hyde Park beyond to the west, and elegant boulevards Regent Street and Piccadilly to the east and south respectively—Mayfair itself is remarkably traffic-free and ideal for walking. Starting at **Selfridges** on Oxford Street, a southward stroll will take you through quiet residential streets lined with Georgian town houses (the area was largely developed in the 17th and 18th centuries).

Mayfair has three grand squares: **Grosvenor Square** and **Berkeley Square** lie to the quieter west side of **Bond Street,** the neighborhood's main luxury shopping street that bisects the area, and **Hanover Square,** with its splendid **St. George's Church** where Handel worshipped, is on the busier eastern side. South of Grosvenor Square is the quiet St. George's Gardens and beyond it the older part of Mayfair, a maze of atmospheric streets and mews.

Leading off Berkeley Square are two of London's most exclusive shopping destinations: **Mount Street** and **Bruton Street.** To the east of New Bond Street, Bruton Street turns into the equally fashionable **Conduit Street.** Between New Bond Street and Regent is **Savile Row,** famous as the source of the world's best made-to-measure suit. At the foot of Savile Row is the **Burlington Arcade** leading to Piccadilly, where you will find the **Royal Academy of Arts.** Architecture buffs will want to see

A BRIEF HISTORY

The name Mayfair derives from the 15-day May fair that was once held in the web of small streets known as Shepherd Market.

This, however, was brought to an end by the upper classes who lived there and felt it was drawing undesirables to their polished part of town.

The area was mostly fields and farms belonging to families whose names are commemorated in the surrounding streets—Grosvenor, Burlington, and Berkeley—until it was developed in the early 18th century.

The beautiful St. James's Park, meanwhile, stands as an idyllic emblem of this elite past.

It's the oldest royal park in London and all that remains of the royal hunting grounds that once traversed the city to Islington, Marylebone, and Hampstead.

Henry VIII acquired the land in 1532 for a deer park.

the Christopher Wren–designed **St. James's Church** just across the road. From this side of Piccadilly to Pall Mall, with Green Park to the west and Lower Regent Street to the east, is St. James's, Mayfair's more stealth-wealth neighbor.

A pedestrian passage alongside the church will take you to **Jermyn Street.** Continue south to **St. James's Square** and **Pall Mall,** with its private clubs tucked away in 18th- and 19th-century patrician buildings. On a more contemporary note, St James's is also home to the **White Cube Gallery,** a leading dealer in modern British art.

At the western end of Piccadilly at Hyde Park corner are two memorials to England's great hero the Duke of Wellington: **Wellington Arch** and the duke's restored London residence, **Apsley House.** From here a northbound bus will take you up Park Lane to **Speakers' Corner** and **Marble Arch.**

TOP ATTRACTIONS

Fodor's Choice
★

Apsley House (Wellington Museum). Once popularly known as No. 1, London, because it was the first and grandest house at the old tollgate from Knightsbridge village, this was long celebrated as the best address in town. Built by Robert Adam and later refaced and extended, it housed the Duke of Wellington from 1817 until his death in 1852, forming one of the many tributes gifted to the "Iron Duke" in thanks for his victory over Napoléon at the Battle of Waterloo in 1815. The years of war against the French made the duke—born in Ireland as Arthur Wellesley—the greatest soldier and statesman in the land, so much so that the house's location at Hyde Park Corner was soon nicknamed "hero's corner" (even in the subway, beneath the turmoil of traffic, the Duke of Wellington's heroic exploits are retold in murals). Before entering, note that the house is flanked by imposing statues: opposite is the 1828 Decimus Burton **Wellington Arch** with the four-horse chariot of peace at its pinnacle (open to the public as an exhibition area and viewing platform); just behind Apsley House, and cast from captured French

Old Bond Street is great for window-shopping—it has some of the most exclusive stores in London.

guns, the legendary **Achilles** statue (legendarily naked, to the titillation of countless Victorian matrons) points the way with thrusting shield to the ducal mansion from the edge of Hyde Park. Next to Apsley House is the elaborate gateway to the royal park, designed and built by Burton at the same time as the Wellington Arch.

As the Wellington Museum, the duke's former residence has been faithfully restored, down to Wellesley's uniforms, weapons, a fine collection of paintings (partially looted from his war campaigns), and his porcelain and plate collections acquired as a result of his military success, such as a Sévres dessert service commissioned by Napoléon for his empress, Josephine. His extensive art collection, much of it presented to him by admirers, includes works by Brueghel, Van Dyck, and Rubens, as well as the famous Veláquez portrait of Pope Innocent X and a portrait of Wellington himself on horseback by Goya. There are also numerous portraits of military comrades, allies, and even his main adversary, Napoléon Bonaparte. Unmissable, in every sense, is the gigantic Canova statue of a nude (but fig-leafed) Napoléon, which presides over the grand staircase that leads to the many elegant reception rooms in Apsley House. The sculptor chose to present his subject, at the time the most powerful man in Europe, as Mars the Peacemaker, depicting the short and stocky emperor as a classical god more than 11 feet tall with a perfect physique. Even so, Napoléon wasn't happy with either the nudity or the athleticism of Canova's approach and ordered the marble statue to be hidden behind a screen.

The free audio guide highlights the most significant works and the superb decor, notably the stunning Waterloo Gallery, where an annual banquet for officers who fought beside Wellington was held. With its heavily sculpted and gilded ceiling, its feast of old-master paintings on red damask walls, and commanding candelabra, it's a veritable orgy of opulence. Special events take place on the annual Waterloo weekend and occasionally on Waterloo Day (June 18) itself, in addition to other special events throughout the year. Call or check the Web site for details. ⊠ *149 Piccadilly, Hyde Park Corner, Mayfair* ☎ *020/7499–5676* ⊕ *www.english-heritage.org.uk* ⊗ *Mar.–Oct., Wed.–Sun. and bank holiday Mon. 11–5; Nov.–Feb., Wed.–Sun. 11–4* 🖃 *£6, joint ticket with Wellington Arch £7.40* Ⓤ *Hyde Park Corner.*

Bond Street. This world-class shopping haunt is divided into northern "New" (1710) and southern "Old" (1690) halves. You can spot the juncture by a bronzed bench on which Franklin D. Roosevelt sits companionably next to Winston Churchill. On New Bond Street you'll find **Sotheby's**, the world-famous auction house, at No. 35, as well as upscale retailers like Asprey's, Burberry, Louis Vuitton, Georg Jensen, and Church's. Among the fastidiously well-dressed pedestrians there are even more opportunities to flirt with financial ruin on Old Bond Street: flagship boutiques of top-end designers like Chanel, Gucci, and Yves St. Laurent; an array of fine jewelers including Tiffany's; and art dealers Colnaghi, Spink Leger, and Agnew's. **Cork Street,** which parallels the top half of Old Bond Street, is where London's top dealers in contemporary art have their galleries—you're welcome to browse. ⊠ *Bond St., Mayfair* Ⓤ *Bond St., Green Park.*

Burlington Arcade. Perhaps the finest of Mayfair's enchanting covered shopping alleys is the second oldest in London, built in 1819 for Lord Cavendish, to stop hoi polloi from jettisoning rubbish (oyster shells in particular) into his garden at Burlington House, behind the arcade. Top-hatted watchmen called Beadles—the world's smallest private police force—still patrol, preserving decorum by preventing you from singing, running, or carrying an open umbrella. The arcade is also the main link between the Royal Academy of Arts and its extended galleries at 6 Burlington Gardens. ⊠ *Piccadilly, Mayfair* Ⓤ *Green Park, Piccadilly Circus.*

Several of London's most storied and stylish hotels are in Mayfair. Even if you're not staying at one, sample the high life by popping into their glamorous bars for a cocktail or some afternoon tea. Claridge's Bar takes its cue from Art Deco, as do the Ritz's intimate Rivoli Bar and the eponymous Connaught Bar; the bar at Brown's Hotel is modernist.

Marble Arch. John Nash's 1827 arch, moved here from Buckingham Palace in 1851, stands amid the traffic whirlpool where Bayswater Road segues into Oxford Street, at the top of Park Lane. The arch actually contains three small chambers, which served as a police station until the mid-20th century. Search the sidewalk on the traffic island opposite the cinema for the stone plaque recalling the Tyburn Tree that stood here for 400 years, until 1783. The condemned would be conveyed to London's central gallows in their finest clothes from Newgate Prison, and were expected to affect a casual indifference, or face a merciless heckling from the crowds. Towering across the grass from the arch towards Tyburn Way is a vast patina-green statue of a horse's head called "Horse at Water" by sculptor Nic Fiddian, commissioned in 2010. Cross over (or under) to the northeastern corner of Hyde Park for Speakers' Corner. ⊠ *Park La., Mayfair* Ⓤ *Marble Arch.*

Piccadilly Circus. Although it may *seem* like a circus with its traffic and the camera-clickers clustered around the steps of **Eros,** the name refers to the five major roads that radiate from it. The origins of "Piccadilly" are from the humble tailor in the Strand named Robert Baker who sold picadils—a stiff ruffled collar all the rage in courtly circles—and built a house with the proceeds. Snobs dubbed his new-money mansion Piccadilly Hall, and the name stuck.

Eros, London's favorite statue and symbol of the *Evening Standard* newspaper, is not in fact the Greek god of erotic love at all. Neither is he the Angel of Christian Charity as is otherwise supposed, but rather he is Anteros, the Greek God of requited love. The work of young sculptor Alfred Gilbert in 1893 is a memorial to the selflessness of the philanthropic Earl of Shaftesbury (the god's bow and arrow are a sweet allusion to the earl's name). Gilbert cast the statue he called his "missile of kindness" in the novel medium of aluminum. Unfortunately, he spent most of his £8,000 fee ensuring the bronze fountain beneath was cast to his specifications. Already in debt, he eventually went bankrupt and fled the country. (Not to worry—he was knighted in the end.) Beneath the modern bank of neon advertisements are some of the most elegant Edwardian-era buildings in town. ⊠ *St. James's* Ⓤ *Piccadilly Circus.*

☯ **Ripley's Believe It Or Not!** London's latest tourist attraction contains five floors of curiosities: natural mutations (an albino alligator), cultural artifacts (Eucadorian shrunken heads), and historic memorabilia (a

Marble Arch was originally a gateway to Buckingham Palace before it was moved to the corner of Hyde Park.

piece of the Berlin Wall). ⊠ *1 Piccadilly Circus, Mayfair* ☎ *020/3238–0022* ⊕ *www.ripleyslondon.com* ⊟ *£23.25* ⊗ *Daily 10–midnight.*

Fodor's Choice ★ **Royal Academy of Arts.** Burlington House was originally built in 1664, with later Palladian additions for the 3rd Earl of Burlington in 1720. The piazza in front is a later conception from 1873, when the renaissance-style buildings around the courtyard were designed by Banks and Barry to house a gaggle of noble scientific societies, including the Royal Society of Chemistry, the Linnean Society of London and the Royal Astronomical Society. Burlington House itself houses the draw card tenant: the Royal Academy of Arts and, the statue of the academy's first president, Sir Joshua Reynolds, palette in hand, is prominent in the piazza of light stone with fountains by Sir Phillip King. Within the house and up the stairs are further statues of creative giants J.W.M. Turner and Thomas Gainsborough. The John Madejski Fine Rooms provide free art as well (but they are sometimes closed) and you can join free tours of part of the RA collection; there are also lectures on art and family programs. Further exhibition space exists at the Burlington Gardens end, reached via Burlington Arcade. The RA has an active program of temporary exhibitions, including the hugely successful "Byzantium" in 2008. Every June for the past 240 years, the RA has put on its Summer Exhibition, a huge and always surprising collection of art by living Royal Academicians and a plethora of other contemporary artists. ⊠ *Burlington House, Piccadilly, Mayfair* ☎ *020/7300–8000, 0207/300–5839 lectures, 0207/300–5995 family programs* ⊕ *www.royalacademy.org.uk* ⊟ *From £12; prices vary with exhibition* ⊗ *Sat.–Thurs. 10–6, Fri. 10–10; tours on Tues. 1, Wed.–Fri. 1 and 3, Sat. 11:30* Ⓤ *Piccadilly Circus, Green Park.*

Don't miss the globe-spanning Food Hall in the basement of Selfridges.

QUICK
BITES

The Royal Academy Restaurant (☎ 0207/300–5608) has hot dishes at lunchtime, good vegetarian options, and an extensive salad selection that is inexpensive for such a posh location. The walls are covered in Stanley Spencer murals. It's open weekdays 10–5:30, with a dinner menu on Friday from 6:15 to 10:30; live jazz takes place Friday nights, so book ahead. For something a little less substantial, have a snack at the Gallery Café, which offers a range of muffins, sandwiches, and pastries. Outdoor tables are available in the summer.

★ **Selfridges.** With its row of massive Ionic columns, this huge store was opened three years after Harry Gordon Selfridge came to London from Chicago in 1906. Now Selfridges is comparable to Harrods in size and scope, and, since investing in major face-lift operations, to Knightsbridge's Harvey Nichols in designer cachet. ✉ 400 Oxford St., Mayfair ☎ 020/7629–1234 ⊕ www.selfridges.com ⊙ Mon.–Sat. 9:30–9, Sun. noon–6 Ⓤ Marble Arch, Bond Street.

St. James's Church. Blitzed by the German Luftwaffe in 1940 and not restored under 1954, this was one of the last of Sir Christopher Wren's London churches—and his personal favorite. Completed in 1684, it envelops one of Grinling Gibbon's finest works, an ornate limewood reredos (the screen behind the altar). Brought here in 1691, the organ is a survivor of Whitehall Palace. A new restoration project is in the planning stages while the church remains a lively place, with all manner of lectures and (some free) concerts. The prayer screen behind the votive candles is pinned with written prayers, many quite poignant. A café enjoys a fine location right alongside the church, while a small, sedate garden is tucked away at the rear. The market out front is full of surprises, hosting antiques on Tuesday, and arts and crafts from Wednesday to Saturday. ✉ *197 Piccadilly, St. James's* ☎ *020/7734–4511, 020/7381–0441 concert program and tickets* ⊕ *www. st-james-piccadilly.org* Ⓤ *Piccadilly Circus, Green Park.*

Wellington Arch. Opposite the Duke of Wellington's mansion, Apsley House, this majestic stone arch surveys the busy traffic rushing around Hyde Park Corner. Designed by Decimus Burton and built in 1828, it was created as a grand entrance to the west side of London and echoes the design of that other landmark gate, Marble Arch. Both were triumphal arches commemorating Britain's victory against France in the Napoleonic Wars, and both were moved after their construction to ease the Victorian traffic situation. The Wellington Arch was constructed at the same time as the Hyde Park's Triumphal Screen (also Burton's design); you'll see the same highly ornamental green gates within the Wellington Arch. Atop the building, the Angel of Peace descends on the quadriga, or four-horse chariot of war. This replaced the Duke of Wellington on his horse, which was considered too large and hence moved to army barracks in Aldershot. A step inside the arch reveals the stories behind the building and statue, and explores other great arches around the world. Without doubt, the highlight is to walk around the top of the arch and enjoy the brilliant panoramas over the park, including glimpses into the private gardens of Buckingham Palace. ✉ *Hyde Park Corner, Mayfair* ☎ *020/7930–2726* ⊕ *www.english-heritage.org. uk* 🎫 *£3.50* ⊙ *Apr.–Oct., Wed.–Sun. 10–5; Nov.–Mar., Wed.–Sun. 10–4* Ⓤ *Hyde Park Corner.*

ROYALTY IN AISLE 9

Shoppers and historians alike will enjoy **Fortnum & Mason** at 181 Piccadilly. This old-fashioned fine-foods store feels lifted from another century, with ornate murals decorating the walls, glass cabinets, and brass fixtures casting a dazzling glow all around. Its restaurants, where you can find quintessentially British dishes like Welsh rarebit, and a fabulous ice-cream parlor, are beloved of country ladies who've come up for the day. Built in 1788, Fortnum & Mason sent hams to the Duke of Wellington's army and baskets of treats to Florence Nightingale in the Crimea. (It also happens to be the Queen's grocery store.)

WORTH NOTING

Grosvenor Square. Once a private square and damaged in WWII, leafy Grosvenor Square (pronounced *Grove*-na) was laid out in 1725–31. It is as desirable an address today as it was then. Americans certainly thought so—from John Adams, the second president, who as ambassador lived at No. 38, to Dwight D. Eisenhower, whose wartime headquarters was at No. 20. Now the massive 1960s block of the U.S. Embassy occupies the entire west side, and a British memorial to Franklin D. Roosevelt stands in the center. There is also a classically styled memorial to those who died in New York on September 11, 2001. The little brick chapel used by Eisenhower's men during World War II, the

1730 Grosvenor Chapel, stands a couple of blocks south of the square on South Audley Street, with the entrance to pretty **St. George's Gardens** to its left. Across the gardens is the headquarters of the English Jesuits as well as the society-wedding favorite, the mid-19th-century Church of the Immaculate Conception, known as Farm Street Church because of its location. A Barclays Cycle Hire docking station is immediately northeast of the square. ⊠ *Mayfair* Ⓤ *Bond St.*

★ **Handel House Museum.** The former home of the composer, where he lived for more than 30 years until his death in 1759, is a celebration of his genius. It's the first museum in London solely dedicated to one composer, and that is made much of with room settings in the contemporary fine Georgian style. You can linger over original manuscripts (there are more to be seen in the British Library) and gaze at portraits—accompanied by live music if the adjoining music rooms are being used by musicians in rehearsal. Some of the composer's most famous pieces were created here, including *Messiah* and *Music for the Royal Fireworks*. To hear a live concert here—there are Thursday evening performances, mostly of baroque music—is to imagine the atmosphere of rehearsals and "salon" music in its day. Handel House makes a perfect cultural pit stop after shopping on nearby Bond and Oxford streets, and if you come on Saturday, there is free admission for kids. The museum occupies both No. 25 and the adjoining house, where life in Georgian London is displayed, and where another musical star, Jimi Hendrix, lived for a brief time in the 1960s, as a blue plaque outside the house indicates—also look for the petite exhibition of photos. Tours of his flat, currently administrative offices and not usually open to the public, are offered twice a year. Phone or check the Web site for details. ⊠ *25 Brook St., entrance in Lancashire Court, Mayfair* ☎ *020/7495–1685* ⊕ *www.handelhouse.org* 🎫 *£5* ⏱ *Tues.–Sat. 10–6, Thurs. until 8, Sun. noon–6* Ⓤ *Bond St.*

★ **Spencer House.** Ancestral abode of the Spencers—Diana, Princess of Wales's family—this is perhaps the finest example of an elegant 18th-century town house extant in London. Reflecting his passion for the Grand Tour and classical antiquities, the first Earl Spencer commissioned architect John Vardy to adapt designs from ancient Rome for a magnificent private palace. Vardy was responsible for the external elevation, including the gorgeous west-facing Palladian facade, its pediment adorned with classical statues, and the ground-floor interiors, notably the lavish Palm Room, which boasts a spectacular screen of columns covered in gilded carvings that resemble gold palm trees. The purpose of the bling-tastic decor was not only to attest to Spencer's power and

Gentleman's shops in St. James's specialize in high-quality, handmade goods.

wealth but also to celebrate his marriage, a love match then rare in aristocratic circles (the palms are a symbol of marital fertility). Midway through construction—the house was built between 1756 and 1766— Spencer changed architects and hired James "Athenian" Stuart, whose designs were based on a classical Greek aesthetic, to decorate the gilded State Rooms on the first floor. These include the Painted Room, the first completely neoclassical room in Europe. In recent years the house was superlatively restored by Lord Rothschild (to impress close friend, Princess Diana, but in 2010 the Spencer family scandalously decided to sell off all the house's best furnishings and paintings at Christie's so that today's viewers now get to see a decidedly denuded house. The garden, of Henry Holland design, has also been replanted in the 18th- and 19th-century fashion. The house is open only on Sunday (closed January and August), and only to guided tours. The garden is open some Sundays in summer. Check the Web site for details. ⊠ *27 St. James's Pl., St. James's* ☎ *020/7499–8620* ⊕ *www.spencerhouse.co.uk* ⊠ *£9* ⊘ *Sept.–Dec. and Feb.–July, Sun. 10:30–5:45, last tour 4:45; tour leaves approx. every 25 mins; tickets on sale Sun. at 10:30* Ⓤ *Green Park*.

St. James's Square. One of London's oldest and leafiest squares was also the most snobbish address of all when it was laid out around 1670, with 14 resident dukes and earls installed by 1720. Since 1841, No. 14—one of the several 18th-century residences spared by World War II bombs—has housed the **London Library,** founded by Thomas Carlyle. With its million or so volumes, this is the world's largest independent lending library and is also considered the best private humanities library in the land. The workplace of literary luminaries from T.S. Eliot to Bruce Chatwin, Kingsley Amis, Winston Churchill, John Betjeman, and Charles Dickens, the library invited you to read famous authors' complaints in the comments book—but you'll need a £10 day or £30 week membership to peruse the collection (bring ID and proof of address). Other notable institutions around the square include the East India Club at No. 16, the Naval and Military Club (known as the "In and Out" after the signage on its gateposts) at No. 4, as well as Chatham House, a think-tank on international affairs. A small epitaph to WPC Yvonne Fletcher—shot by a Libyan gunman— can be found on the sidewalk around the square. ⊠ *St. James's* ⊕ *www. londonlibrary.co.uk* ⊗ *Mon.–Wed. 9:30–7:30, Thurs.–Sat. 9:30–5:30, closed Sun.* Ⓤ *Piccadilly Circus.*

Soho and
Covent Garden

WORD OF MOUTH

"From April through September, it stays light fairly late, and Covent Garden is very active until late: there are street entertainers, sidewalk cafes, shops in the main pavilion, and market staffs."
—Cathinjoetown

GETTING ORIENTED

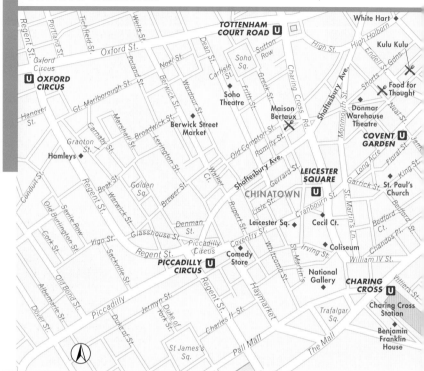

GETTING THERE	TOP REASONS TO GO
Almost all of the Tube lines cross the Covent Garden and Soho areas, so it's quite easy to hop off the Tube for a funky dinner or show in the hippest area of London. For Soho, take any train to Piccadilly Circus, or Leicester Square, Oxford Circus, or Tottenham Court Road. For Covent Garden, get off at the Covent Garden station on the Piccadilly Line, but be aware that this station can be severely crowded. It might be easier to exit the tube at Leicester Square or Holborn and take a short walk. Thirty buses connect to the Covent Garden area.	**Royal Opera House:** Make sure you visit (even if you're not going to the opera or ballet) for the beautiful architecture and sense of history. **Courtauld Gallery:** Admire your favorite Impressionist painting up close in the Courtauld Gallery, then discover Cranach the Elder's mischievous *Adam and Eve*. **Shaftesbury Avenue:** Take in a show on London's equivalent of Broadway, and snaffle half-price tickets at the Leicester Square kiosk. **Somerset House:** Watch the skaters and ice-wall climbers on a December evening. Otherwise, try the London Craft Fair, held each autumn in a specially designed pavilion. In summer, dine at the terrace restaurant overlooking the river. **London Transport Museum:** Explore the city's history with interactive installations about its public transport.

4

MAKING THE MOST OF YOUR TIME

You can comfortably tour all the sights in Covent Garden in a day. Visit the small but perfect Courtauld Gallery on Monday before 2 pm when it's free. That leaves plenty of time to visit the marketplace, watch the street entertainment, and do a bit of shopping, with energy left over for a night on the town (or "on the tiles," as the British say) in Soho.

GAY LONDON

Old Compton Street in Soho is the epicenter of London's affluent, stylish gay scene. There are some smart nightclubs in the area, with crowds forming in Soho Square, south of Oxford St.

Madame Jo Jo's (⌧ *8–10 Brewer St.* ☎ *020/7734–3040* ⊕ *www. madamejojos.com*) has been around for nearly 50 years, with a range of popular club nights. The club's *Kitsch Cabaret*, which can be booked online, is so popular (with straights as well as gays) that it's booked up weeks in advance.

FEELING PECKISH?

Although they may set out a few tables, the coffee shops and snack bars along the Covent Garden market buildings can be overpriced and of iffy quality. It's usually best to head for Soho when the munchies strike.

Food for Thought (⌧ *31 Neal St., Covent Garden* ☎ *020/7836–9072*) is always crowded, with hungry customers queuing outside for their delicious range of vegetarian dishes. Be prepared to share a table.

Kulu Kulu (⌧ *51–53 Shelton St., Covent Garden* ☎ *020/7240–5687*) offers fresh, good-value sushi. Dishes trundle around on a conveyor belt—ideal if you're pressed for time. There's another branch on Brewer Street in Soho.

Maison Bertaux (⌧ *28 Greek St., Soho* ☎ *020/7437–6007*) has been around since the end of the 19th century. Decor is spartan, but fab French cakes, tarts, and savory quiches more than make up for that. Nobody's mother ever baked this well.

Sightseeing
★★★
Nightlife
★★★★
Dining
★★★★
Lodging
★★
Shopping
★★★

Once a red-light district, today's Soho delivers more "grown-up" than "adult" entertainment, offering some of London's best nightclubs, live music venues, restaurants, and theaters. By day, this hotbed of media production reverts to the business side of its late-night scene. If Soho is all about showbiz, neighboring Covent Garden—once the stomping grounds of *My Fair Lady*'s Eliza Dolittle (before Henry Higgins's make-over) and landmark home to the Royal Opera House and Courtauld Institute Gallery—is devoted to culture. Both offer an abundance of narrow streets packed with one-of-a-kind shops and lots of character.

Updated
by Astrid
deRidder

The narrow, winding streets of Soho lie to the east of Regent Street and to the south of Oxford Street. To the west of Wardour Street there are lots of interesting boutiques around Foubert's Place and on Brewer and Lexington streets, which also boast some of London's best-value restaurants. To the east of Wardour Street is nightlife central. At its southern end is gay mecca Old Compton Street and beyond that Shaftesbury Avenue, London's equivalent of Broadway. Between here and **Leicester Square** is London's compact Chinatown. Charing Cross Road, to the east of the square, is famous for its secondhand bookshops, and tiny **Cecil Court** is a pedestrianized passage lined with small antiquarian book sellers.

To the east of Charing Cross Road lies Covent Garden. Just north of the **Piazza** and the adjoining **Royal Opera House**, busy Long Acre bisects the district on an east–west axis. On the north is a nexus of yet more narrow streets with lots of interesting shops and the **Donmar Warehouse**, one of London's best and most innovative theaters. Nearby Monmouth Street is the place to look for haute fashion. Wellington Street, south of Long Acre, has several reasonably priced restaurants for a quick pretheater bite.

DID YOU KNOW

Covent Garden was a convent garden for 300 years before it was Britain's first planned public square with a fruit and vegetable market. The 1840 market building and the courtyard still teem with shoppers.

aftershock

POLLOCK'S
TOY THEATRES

COVENT
GARDEN
MARKET

You can't miss the buskers performing in the streets of Soho and Covent Garden.

At the end of Wellington Street is the semicircular Aldwych, lined with grand buildings. Moving west down the Strand is the huge 18th-century piazza of **Somerset House,** which contains the **Courtauld Institute Gallery.** Just behind the Strand are small lanes that will make you feel you've stepped back into the 18th century. On the way to the verdant **Embankment Gardens** bordering the Thames, you may pass the **Adam Houses** and the **Benjamin Franklin House,** where the noted statesman lived in the years leading up to the American Revolution.

TOP ATTRACTIONS

Courtauld Institute Gallery. One of London's most beloved art collections, the Courtauld is to your left as you pass through the archway into the grounds of the beautifully restored, grand 18th-century classical **Somerset House.** Founded in 1931 by the textile magnate Samuel Courtauld to house his remarkable private collection, this is one of the world's finest Impressionist and post-Impressionist galleries, with artists ranging from Bonnard to van Gogh. A déjà-vu moment with Cézanne, Degas, Seurat, or Monet awaits on every wall (Manet's *Bar at the Folies-Bergère* is the star), with bonus post-Renaissance works thrown in. Botticelli, Brueghel, Tiepolo, and Rubens are also represented, thanks to the exquisite bequest of Count Antoine Seilern's Princes Gate collection. German Renaissance paintings, bequeathed in 1947, include the colorful and delightfully wicked *Adam and Eve* by Lucas Cranach the Elder. There are also some bold and bright Fauvist paintings. Don't miss the little café downstairs, which is a perfect place for a spot of tea. ⊠ *Somerset House, Strand, Covent Garden*

A BRIEF HISTORY

Almost as soon as a 17th-century housing development covered what had been a royal park and hunting ground, Soho earned a reputation for entertainment, bohemianism, and cosmopolitan tolerance. When the authorities introduced zero tolerance of soliciting in 1991 (the most recent of several attempts to end Soho's sex trade), they cracked down on an old neighborhood tradition that still resurfaces from time to time.

Successive waves of refugees, from French Huguenots in the 1680s followed by Germans, Russians, Poles, Greeks, Italians, and Chinese, settled and brought their ethnic cuisines with them. So when dining out became fashionable after World War I, Soho was the natural place for restaurants to flourish.

In the 1950s and '60s, Soho was London's main artists' quarter and the place to find the top jazz clubs and art galleries. Among the luminaries who have made their home here are landscape painter John Constable; Casanova; Canaletto, the great painter of Venice; William Blake; and Karl Marx.

Present-day Covent Garden took shape in the 1630s, when Inigo Jones turned what had been agricultural land into Britain's first planned public square. After the Great Fire of 1666, it became the site of England's largest fruit-and-vegetable market (the flower market arrived in the 19th century). This, along with the district's many theaters and taverns, gave the area a somewhat dubious reputation, and after the produce market relocated in 1973, the surviving buildings were scheduled for demolition. A local campaign saved them, and the restored market opened in 1980.

☎ *020/7848–2526* ⊕ *www.courtauld.ac.uk* 🖃 *£5, free Mon. 10–2, except bank holidays* ⊙ *Daily 10–6; last admission 5:30* Ⓤ *Covent Garden, Holborn, Temple.*

★ **Covent Garden Piazza.** Once home to London's main flower market, and former stomping ground of *My Fair Lady*'s Eliza Doolittle, the market building around which Covent Garden pivots is known as the Piazza. Inside, the shops are mostly higher-class clothing chains, plus several restaurants and cafés and knickknack stores that are good for gifts. One particular gem is Benjamin Pollock's Toyshop at No. 44 in the market. Established in the 1880s, it sells delightful toy theaters. There's the superior **Apple Market** for crafts on most days, too. On the south side of the Piazza, the indoor **Jubilee Market,** with its stalls of clothing, army-surplus gear, and more crafts and knickknacks, has a distinct flea-market feel. In summer it may seem that everyone you see around the Piazza (and the crowds are legion) is a fellow tourist, but there's still plenty of office life in the area. Londoners who shop here tend to head for Neal Street and the area to the north of Covent Garden tube station rather than the touristy market itself. In the Piazza, performers—from global musicians to jugglers and mimes—play to the crowds, as they have done since the first English Punch and Judy Show, staged here in the 17th century. ⊠ *Covent Garden* Ⓤ *Covent Garden.*

DID YOU KNOW?

Somerset House was lapped by the River Thames before the Victoria Embankment was built in the 19th century. The neoclassical building's grand courtyard is home to ice skating in winter and dancing fountains in summer.

London Transport Museum. Housed in the old flower market at the southeast corner of Covent Garden, this stimulating museum includes the interactive features that explain why London was the first world's city. As you watch the crowds gawk at the horse-drawn trams (and the piles of detritus that remained behind), the ever-fascinating steam locomotives, and trolley buses from the past, you're not sure who's enjoying it more, children or adults. This kid-friendly (under 16 admitted free) museum is filled with impressive poster, photograph, and vehicle collections. Best of all, the museum has a multilevel approach to education, including information for the youngest visitor to the most advanced transit aficionado. Food and drink are available at the aptly named Upper Deck café. ⊠ *Covent Garden Piazza* ☎ *020/7379–6344* ⊕ *www.ltmuseum.co.uk* ✉ *£10* ⊙ *Sat.–Thurs. 10–6 (last admission 5:15), Fri. 11–6 (last admission 5:15)* Ⓤ *Leicester Sq., Covent Garden.*

Royal Opera House. London's premier opera and ballet venue was *Fodor's Choice* designed in 1858 by E.M. Barry, son of Sir Charles, the House of Commons architect, and is the third theater on the site. The first theater opened in 1732 and burned down in 1808; the second opened a year later, only to succumb to fire in 1856. The entire building, which has been given a spectacular overhaul, retains the magic of the grand Victorian theater (but is now more accessible). The glass-and-steel Floral Hall is the most wonderful feature; you can wander around and drink in (literally, in the foyer café) the interior. The same is true of the Amphitheatre Bar and Piazza concourse, where you can have lunch while looking out at a splendid panorama across the city. There are free lunchtime chamber concerts and lectures, as well as tea dances and occasional free jazz concerts, which go a long way to making this venue a great space for the common people. ⊠ *Bow St., Covent Garden* ☎ *020/7240–1200* ⊕ *www.royalopera.org* Ⓤ *Covent Garden.*

Somerset House. An old royal palace once stood on the site, but it was eventually replaced by this 18th-century building, the work of Sir William Chambers (1726–96), during the reign of George III. It was built to house government offices, principally those of the Navy. For the first time in more than 100 years, these gracious rooms are on view, including the Seamen's Waiting Hall and the Nelson Stair. In addition, the Navy Commissioners' Barge has returned to dry dock at the Water Gate. The rooms are on the south side of the building, by the river. The **Courtauld Institute Gallery** occupies most of the north building, facing the busy

Strand. In between is the cobbled Italianate courtyard where Admiral Nelson used to walk, the scene of an ice rink in the winter holiday season as well as summer concerts and other cultural events. In the summer months, come early and bring a deck chair to catch a free, live telecast from the Royal Opera House. Tom's Kitchen, a new restaurant from top chef Tom Aikens, opened in the fall of 2010 and includes the latest in fresh British produce. A gallery devoted to contemporary art, design, fashion, architecture, and photography hosts three exhibitions a year. ⊠ *The Strand, Covent Garden* ☎ *020/7845–4600* ⊕ *www. somerset-house.org.uk* ✉ *Embankment Gallery £5, Courtauld Gallery £5, other areas free* ⊗ *Daily 10–6; last admission 5:30* Ⓤ *Charing Cross, Waterloo, Blackfriars.*

ICE-SKATING

It's hard to beat the skating experience at Somerset House, where from November through January a rink is set up in the grand courtyard of this central London palace. Check the Web site for current prices; its popularity is enormous, and if you can't get a ticket, other venues such as Hampton Court, the Tower of London, and the Natural History Museum are following Somerset House's lead in having temporary winter rinks. ☎ 0844/847–1520 ⊕ www.somerset-house.org.uk/ icerink.

WORTH NOTING

All that remains of what was once a regal riverfront row of houses on a 3-acre site, connected by arches and streets below grade, are a few of the structures, but such is their quality that they are worth a detour off the Strand to see. The work of 18th-century Scottish architects and interior designers (John, Robert, James, and William Adam, known collectively as the Adam brothers), the original development was damaged in the 19th century during the building of the embankment, and mostly demolished in 1936 to be replaced by an Art Deco tower. The original houses still standing are protected, and give a glimpse of their former grandeur. Nos. 1–4 Robert Street and Nos. 7 and 10 Adam Street are the best. At the **Royal Society of Arts** (⊠ *8 John Adam St.* ☎ *020/7930–5115* ⊕ *www.thersa.org* ✉ *Free* ⊗ *1st Sun. of month, 10–1*), you can see a suite of Adam rooms; no reservations are required. ⊠ *The Strand, Covent Garden* ⊗ *Closed weekends* Ⓤ *Charing Cross, Embankment.*

Benjamin Franklin House. Opened to the public for the first time in 2006, this architecturally significant 1730 house is the only surviving residence of American statesman, scientist, writer, and inventor Benjamin Franklin, who lived and worked here for 16 years preceding the American Revolution. The restored Georgian town house has been left unfurnished, the better to show off the original features—18th-century paneling, stoves, beams, bricks, and windows. Older children (under 16 admitted free) particularly enjoy the Student Science Centre, an interactive display of scientific experiments that contrasts historical with modern knowledge. There's also a glass harmonica (which Franklin

Leicester Square is home to many cinemas and a half-price theater ticket booth.

invented while living there) and a scholarship center with a complete collection of Franklin's papers. On Monday you can take a guided tour focusing on the architectural details of the building. ⊠ *36 Craven St., Covent Garden* ☎ *020/7839–2006, 020/7925–1405 booking line* ⊕ *www.benjaminfranklinhouse.org* 🎫 *£7* ⊗ *Wed.–Sun. noon–5.*

Leicester Square. Looking at the neon of the major movie houses, the fast-food outlets, and the disco entrances, you'd never guess that this square (pronounced *Lester*) was a model of formality and refinement when it was first laid out around 1630. By the 19th century it was already bustling and disreputable, and although today it's not a threatening place, you should still be on your guard, especially at night—any space so full of people is bound to attract pickpockets, and Leicester Square certainly does. Although it retains some residual glamour as the site of red-carpet film premieres, Londoners generally tend to avoid this windswept plaza, crowded as it is with suburban teenagers, wandering backpackers, and mimes. That said, the liveliness can be quite cheering. In the middle is a statue of a sulking Shakespeare, clearly wishing he were somewhere else and perhaps remembering the days when the cinemas were live theaters—burlesque houses, but live all the same. Here, too, are figures of Newton, Hogarth, Reynolds, and Charlie Chaplin. On the northeast corner, in Leicester Place, stands the church of **Notre Dame de France,** with a wonderful mural by Jean Cocteau in one of its side chapels. ⊠ *Covent Garden* Ⓤ *Leicester Sq.*

St. Paul's Church. If you want to commune with the spirits of Vivien Leigh, Noël Coward, Edith Evans, or Charlie Chaplin, this might be just the place. Memorials to them and many other theater greats are found in this 1633 work of the renowned Inigo Jones, who, as the King's Surveyor of Works, designed the whole of Covent Garden Piazza. St. Paul's Church has been known as "the actors' church" since the Restoration, thanks to the neighboring theater district and St. Paul's prominent parishioners. (Well-known actors often read the lessons at services, and the church still hosts concerts and small-scale productions.) Fittingly, the opening scene of Shaw's *Pygmalion* takes place under its Tuscan portico (you might know it better from the musical *My Fair Lady* starring Audrey Hepburn). The western end of the Piazza is a prime pitch for street entertainers, but if they're not to your liking, you can repair to the serenity of the garden entered from King or Bedford streets. ✉ *Bedford St., Covent Garden* Ⓤ *Covent Garden.*

CHEAP TICKETS

One landmark certainly worth visiting is the **Society of London Theatre ticket kiosk (TKTS)**, on the southwest corner of Leicester Square, which sells half-price tickets for many of that evening's performances. It's open Monday to Saturday from 10 to 7, and Sunday from noon to 3 pm. One window sells matinee tickets and the other sells tickets for evening performances, so make sure you join the correct line. Watch out for illegal ticket touts (scalpers), who target tourists around the square.

Theatre Royal, Drury Lane. This is London's best-known auditorium and almost its largest. Since World War II, its forte has been musicals (past ones have included *The King and I, My Fair Lady, South Pacific, Hello, Dolly!,* and *A Chorus Line*)—though David Garrick, who managed it from 1747 to 1776, made its name by reviving the works of the by-then-obscure William Shakespeare. It enjoys all the romantic accessories of a London theater—a history of fires (it burned down three times, once in a Wren-built incarnation), riots (in 1737, when a posse of footmen demanded free admission), attempted regicides (George II in 1716 and his grandson George III in 1800), and even sightings of the most famous phantom of theaterland, the Man in Grey (in the Circle during matinees). ✉ *Catherine St., Covent Garden* ☎ *020/7494–5000* ⊕ *www.theatre-royal.com* Ⓤ *Covent Garden.*

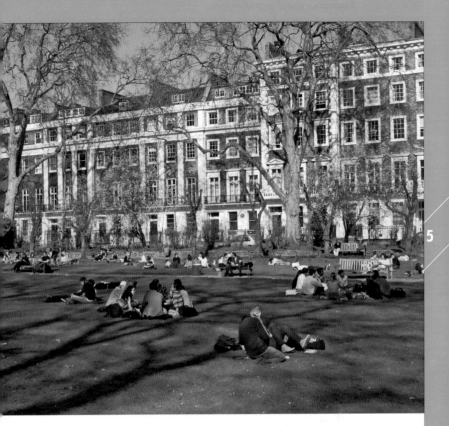

Bloomsbury and Legal London

WORD OF MOUTH

"We began to walk to the British Library in a leisurely manner. [Then] we spent over an hour oohing and aahing (quietly!). Austen, Shakespeare, Carroll, Bronte, Milton, Wordsworth, Beowulf, Gutenberg, Beatles, Handel. Beyond cool."

—texasbookworm

GETTING ORIENTED

TOP REASONS TO GO

British Museum: From the Rosetta Stone to the Elgin Marbles, this is the golden hoard of booty bought or "borrowed" by centuries of the British Empire.

The Inns of Court: When you hear the word "lawyer," the immediate tendency is to yawn, grimace, or check your wallet, but these gorgeous residences—the heart of Legal London—embody Enlightenment.

Sir John Soane's Museum: This fascinating ex-abode of one of Britain's best architects is full of antiquities, gargoyle heads, and a plethora of chunks of buildings, not to mention the Sarcophagus of Seti I.

British Library: Few traces remain of the personalities that brought Bloomsbury such intellectual fame—Virginia Woolf, Lytton Strachey, E. M. Forster—so head to this great repository to see the Magna Carta, a Gutenberg Bible, and Shakespeare's First Folio.

Charles Dickens Museum: Pay your respects to the beloved author of *Oliver Twist*.

FEELING PECKISH?

The Betjeman Arms (✉ *Unit 53, St. Pancras International Station* ☎ *020/7923–5440*), inside St. Pancras International's wonderfully Victorian station, is the perfect place to stop for a pint and grab some traditional pub fare. Perched above the tracks of the Eurostar Terminal, the view of the trains and travelers will keep you entertained for hours.

The Hare and Tortoise Dumpling & Noodle Bar (✉ *15–17 Brunswick Shopping Centre, opposite the Renoir Cinema, Brunswick Square, Bloomsbury* ☎ *020/7278–9799*) serves scrumptious Asian fast food. This bright café is a favorite with students, and it's easy to see why: Ingredients are all natural, the portions are huge, and the bill is always reasonable.

GETTING THERE

The Russell Square Tube stop on the Piccadilly Line leaves you right at the corner of Russell Square.

The best Tube stops for the Inns of Court are Holborn on the Central and Piccadilly lines or Chancery Lane on the Central Line.

Tottenham Court Road on the Northern and Central lines is best for the British Museum.

Once you're in Bloomsbury, you can easily get around on foot.

5

MAKING THE MOST OF YOUR TIME

Bloomsbury can be seen in a day, or in half a day, depending on your interests and your time constraints.

If you plan to visit the Inns of Court as well as the British Museum, and you'd also like to get a feel for the neighborhood, then you may wish to devote an entire day to this literary and legal enclave.

An alternative scenario is to come back on another day to visit the British Museum, which can be quite exhausting in itself.

Although there can be many students in the neighborhood, it's a pleasure to wander through the quiet, leafy squares, examining historic Blue Plaques or relaxing at a street-side café.

Sightseeing
★★★
Nightlife
★★
Dining
★★
Lodging
★★★★
Shopping
★★

The character of an area of London can change visibly from one street to the next. Nowhere is this so clear as in the contrast between fun-loving Soho and the hub of intellectual London, Bloomsbury, a mere 100 yards to the northeast, or between arty Covent Garden and, on the other side of Kingsway, sober Holborn. The first district is best known for the famous flowering of literary-arty bohemia, personified by the clique known as the Bloomsbury Group during the first three decades of the 20th century, and for the British Museum and University of London, which dominate it now. The second sounds as exciting as, say, a center for accountants, but don't be put off: filled with magnificently ancient buildings, it's more interesting and beautiful than you might suppose.

Updated
by Astrid
deRidder

Fundamental to the region's spirit of open expression and scholarly debate is the legacy of the Bloomsbury Group, an elite corps of artists and writers who lived in this neighborhood during the first part of the 20th century. **Gordon Square** was at one point home to Virginia Woolf, John Maynard Keynes (both at No. 46), and Lytton Strachey (at No. 51). Much like the Beat poets of San Francisco or the jazz artists of the Harlem Renaissance, they defined their neighborhood as well as an entire era. But perhaps the best-known square in Bloomsbury is the large, centrally located **Russell Square**, with gardens laid out by Humphry Repton, a prominent English landscape designer. Scattered around the **University of London** campus are Woburn Square, Torrington Square, Tavistock Square, and Gordon Square. The unforgettable **British Library** with its vast treasures is a few blocks north, across busy Euston Road.

The area from Somerset House on the Strand, all the way up Kingsway to the Euston Road, is known as London's **Museum Mile** for the myriad historic houses and museums that dot the area. **Charles Dickens Museum,** where the author wrote *Oliver Twist,* is one of the most-visited sites in the area. Artists' studios and design shops share space with tenants near the bright and modern **British Museum.** And guaranteed to raise a smile from the most blasé and footsore tourist is **Sir John Soane's Museum,** which hardly deserves the burden of its dry name.

Bloomsbury also happens to be where London's legal profession was born. In fact, the buildings associated with legal London were some of the few structures spared during the Great Fire of 1666, and so the serpentine alleys, cobbled courts, and historic halls frequented by the city's still-bewigged barristers ooze centuries of history. The massive Gothic-style **Royal Courts of Justice** ramble all the way to the Strand, and the **Inns of Court—Gray's Inn, Lincoln's Inn, Middle Temple,** and **Inner Temple—**are where most British trial lawyers have offices to this day. In the 14th century the inns were lodging houses where the barristers lived so that people would know how to easily find them (hence, the label "inn"). Also here are Temple Church, the 500-year-old Prince Henry's Room, and the Staple Inn, one of London's oldest surviving half-timber buildings.

TOP ATTRACTIONS

British Library. Formerly in the British Museum, the collection of around 18 million volumes now has a home in state-of-the-art surroundings. The library's greatest treasures are on view to the general public: Magna Carta, a Gutenberg Bible, Jane Austen's writings, Shakespeare's First Folio, and musical manuscripts by G.F. Handel as well as Sir Paul McCartney are on display in the Sir John Ritblat Gallery. Also in the gallery are headphones—you can listen to some of the most interesting pieces in a small showcase of the **National Sound Archive** (it's the world's largest collection), such as the voice of Florence Nightingale and an extract from the Beatles' last tour interview. On weekends and during school vacations there are hands-on demonstrations of how a book comes together. Feast your eyes also on the six-story glass tower that holds the 65,000-volume collection of George III, plus a permanent exhibition of rare stamps. If all this wordiness is just too much, you can relax in the library's piazza or restaurant, or take in one of the occasional free concerts in the amphitheater outside. ⊠ *96 Euston Rd., Bloomsbury* ☎ *0870/7412–7332* ⊕ *www.bl.uk* ⊠ *Free, donations appreciated, charge for special exhibitions* ⊗ *Mon. and Wed.–Fri. 9:30–6, Tues. 9:30–8, Sat. 9:30–5, Sun. and bank holiday Mon. 11–5* Ⓤ *Euston, Euston Sq., King's Cross.*

Fodor's Choice **British Museum.**
★ *See the highlighted listing in this chapter.*

Fodor's Choice **Sir John Soane's Museum.** Sir John (1753–1837), architect of the Bank of
★ England, bequeathed his house to the nation on condition that nothing be changed. He obviously had enormous fun with his home: in the Picture Room, for instance, two of Hogarth's *Rake's Progress* series are

Continued on page 110

THE BRITISH MUSEUM

Anybody writing about the British Museum had better have a large stack of superlatives close at hand: most, biggest, earliest, finest. This is the golden hoard of nearly three centuries of the Empire, the booty brought from Britain's far-flung colonies.

The first major pieces, among them the Rosetta Stone and the Parthenon Sculptures (Elgin Marbles), were "acquired" from the French, who "found" them in Egypt and Greece. The museum has since collected countless goodies of worldwide historical significance: the Black Obelisk, some of the Dead Sea Scrolls, the Lindow Man. And that only begins the list.

The British Museum is a vast space split into 94 galleries, generally divided by continent or period of history, with some areas spanning more than one level. There are marvels wherever you go, and—while we don't like to be pessimistic—it is, yes, impossible to fully appreciate everything in a day. So make the most of the tours, activity trails, and visitors guides that are available.

The following is a highly edited overview of the museum's greatest hits, organized by area. Pick one or two that

whet your appetite, then branch out from there, or spend two straight hours indulging in the company of a single favorite sculpture. There's no wrong way to experience the British Museum, just make sure you do!

✉ Great Russell St., Bloomsbury WC1

☎ 020/7323–8000

⊕ www.britishmuseum.org

🎟 Free; donations encouraged. Tickets for special exhibits vary in price.

🕙 Galleries, including special exhibits, Sat.–Wed. 10–5:30, Thurs. and Fri. 10–8:30. Great Court Sun.–Wed. 9–6, Thurs.–Sat. 9 am–11 pm.

Ⓤ Russell Square, Holborn, Tottenham Court Rd.

(left) The Great Court
(top) *Cradle to Grave* by Pharmacopoeia

MUSEUM HIGHLIGHTS

Ancient Civilizations

The Rosetta Stone. Found in 1799 and carved in 196 BC by decree of Ptolemy V in Egyptian hieroglyphics, demotic, and Greek, it was this multilingual inscription that provided French Egyptologist Jean-François Champollion with the key to deciphering hieroglyphics. *Room 4.*

Colossal statue of Ramesses II. A member of the 19th dynasty (ca. 1270 BC), Ramesses II commissioned innumerable statues of himself—more than any other preceding or succeeding king. This one, a 7-ton likeness of his perfectly posed upper half, comes from his mortuary temple, the Ramesseum, in western Thebes. *Room 4.*

(top) Portland vase
(bottom) Colossal statue of Ramesses II

The Parthenon Sculptures. Perhaps these marvelous treasures of Greece shouldn't be here—but while the debate rages on, you can steal your own moment with the Elgin Marbles. Carved in about 440 BC, these graceful decorations are displayed along with an in-depth, high-tech exhibit of the Acropolis; the **handless, footless Dionysus** who used to recline along its east pediment is especially well known. *Room 18.*

Mausoleum of Halikarnassos. All that remains of this, one of the Seven Wonders of the Ancient World, is a fragmented form of the original "mausoleum," the 4th-century tomb of Maussollos, King of Karia. The highlight of this gallery is the marble forepart of the **colossal chariot horse from the** *quadriga. Room 21.*

The Egyptian mummies. Another short flight of stairs takes you to the museum's most popular galleries, especially beloved by children: the Roxie Walker Galleries of Egyptian Funerary Archaeology have a fascinating collection of relics from the Egyptian realm of the dead. In addition to real corpses, wrapped mummies, and mummy cases, there's a menagerie of animal companions and curious items that were buried alongside them. *Rooms 62–63.*

Portland Vase. Made in Italy from cameo glass at the turn of the first century, it is named after the Dukes of Portland, who owned it from 1785 to 1945. It is considered a technical masterpiece—opaque white mythological figures cut by a gem-cutter are set on cobalt-blue background. *Room 70.*

The **Enlightenment Gallery** should be visited purely for the fact that its antiquarian cases hold the contents of the British Museum's first collections—Sir Hans Sloane's natural-history loot, as well as that of Sir Joseph Banks, who acquired specimens of everything from giant shells to fossils to rare plants to exotic beasts during his voyage to the Pacific aboard Captain Cook's *Endeavour*. *Room 1.*

IN FOCUS THE BRITISH MUSEUM

Asia Galleries

Egypt Galleries
60–66

Egyptian Mummies

67

TO
GALLERIES
90–94

North Korean
Socialist Realism Art

66

61 62 63 64 65

59 58 57 56 55 54 53

73

72

71

Greece & Rome
Galleries
69–73

70

Portland Vase

69a 69

68

36

40

41

42

37

Lindow Man

Prehistory
Galleries

Asia Galleries
91–94

94 93 92

91 90

TO
GALLERIES
36–67

UPPER FLOOR

52

51

50

Roman Britain
Gallery

49

Mildenhall
Treasure

Sutton Hoo
Treasure

43

44

Europe
Galleries
41–48

47 46 45

48

34

33a 33

33b

Americas
Galleries
26–27

Native
American
Skin Map

26 27

Cradle to Grave

World Cultures
Galleries

24

Mausoleum
of Halikarnassos

20

21

19

9 Rosetta
Stone

Greece
Galleries
11–23

22

18 17 23

8 Egypt
Galleries

16

10

Elgin
Marbles

15

7 4

14

Colossal Statue
of Ramesses II

GROUND FLOOR

13 6

12 11

35

Reading
Room

1

Enlightenment
Gallery

The
Great Court

3 2

Paul Hamlyn
Library

Great Russell St.
Entrance

Asia

The Korea Foundation Gallery. Delve into striking examples of **North Korean Socialist Realism art** from the 1950s to the present and a reconstruction of a **sarangbang**, a traditional scholar's study, complete with hanji paper walls and tea-making equipment. *Room 67.*

The Percival David Collection. More than 1400 pieces of Chinese ceramics (the most comprehensive collection outside China) are on display. *Room 95.*

World Cultures

The JP Morgan Chase North American Gallery. This is one of the largest collections of native culture outside North America, going back to the earliest hunters 10,000 years ago. Here a 1775 **native American skin map** serves as an example of the importance of such documents in the exploration and cartography of North America. Look for the beautifully displayed **native American costumes.** *Room 26.*

The Mexican Gallery. The most alluring pieces sit in this collection side by side: a 15th-century **turquoise mask of Xiuhtecuhtli**, the Mexican Fire God and Turquoise Lord, and a **double-headed serpent** from the same period. *Room 27.*

Britain and Europe

The Mildenhall Treasure. This glittering haul of 4th-century Roman silver tableware was found beneath the sod of a Suffolk field in 1942. *Room 49.*

The Sutton Hoo Treasure. Next door to the loot from Mildenhall—and equally splendid, including brooches, swords, and jewel-encrusted helmets—the treasure was buried at sea with (it is thought) Redwald, one of the first English kings, in the 7th century, and excavated from a Suffolk field in 1938–39. *Room 41.*

Lindow Man. "Pete Marsh"—so named by the archaeologists who unearthed the body from a Cheshire peat marsh—was ritually slain, probably as a human sacrifice, in the 1st century and lay perfectly pickled in his bog until 1984. *Room 50.*

Theme Galleries

Living & Dying. The "Cradle to Grave" installation pays homage to the British nation's wellbeing—or ill-being, as it were. More than 14,000 drugs (the number estimated to be prescribed to every person in the U.K. in his lifetime) are displayed in a colorful tapestry of pills and tablets. *Room 24.*

Colossal chariot horse from the *quadriga* of the Mausoleum at Halikarnassos

LOWER GALLERY

The three rooms that comprise the **Sainsbury African Galleries** are of the main interest here: together they present a staggering 200,000 objects, featuring intricate pieces of old ivory, gold, and wooden masks and carvings—highlighting such ancient kingdoms as the Benin and Asante. The displays include a collection of **55 throwing knives**; ceremonial garments including a dazzling pink and green **woman's coif** (*qufiya*) from Tunisia made of silk, metal, and cotton; and the *Oxford Man*, a 1992 woodcarving by Owen Ndou, depicting a man of ambiguous race clutching his Book of Knowledge.

THE NATION'S ATTIC: A HISTORY OF THE MUSEUM

The collection began when Sir Hans Sloane, physician to Queen Anne and George II, bequeathed his personal collection of curiosities and antiquities to the nation. The collection quickly grew, thanks to enthusiastic kleptomaniacs after the Napoleonic Wars—most notoriously the seventh Earl of Elgin, who obtained the marbles from the Parthenon and Erechtheion on the Acropolis in Athens during his term as British ambassador in Constantinople.

Soon thereafter, it seemed everyone had something to donate—George II gave the old Royal Library, Sir William Hamilton gave antique vases, Charles Townley gave sculptures, the Bank of England gave coins. When the first exhibition galleries opened to visitors in 1759, the trustees agreed to admit only small groups guided by curators. The British Museum quickly became one of the most fashionable places to be seen in the capital, and tickets, which had to be booked in advance, were treated like gold dust.

The museum's holdings quickly outgrew their original space in Montague House. After the addition of such major pieces as the Rosetta Stone and other Egyptian antiquities (spoils of the Napoleonic War) and the Parthenon sculptures, Robert Smirke was commissioned to build an appropriately large and monumental building on the same site. It's still a hot ticket: the British Museum now receives more than 5 million visitors every year.

THE GREAT COURT & THE READING ROOM

The museum's classical Greek-style facade features figures representing the progress of civilization, and the focal point is the awesome Great Court, a massive glass-roofed space. Here is the museum's inner courtyard (now the largest covered square in Europe) that, for more than 150 years, had been used for storage.

The 19th-century Reading Room, an impressive 106-foot-high blue-and-gold-domed library, forms the centerpiece of the Great Court. The 104,000 ancient tomes are at the British Library until 2012. H.G. Wells, Thomas Hardy, Lord Tennyson, Oscar Wilde, George Orwell, T.S. Elliot, and Beatrix Potter are just a few writers who have used this space as a literary and academic sanctuary over the past 150 years or so. Temporary exhibitions here now include China's Terracotta Army, Hadrian, and Shah 'Abbas.

(above) Reading Room

PLANNING YOUR VISIT

Tours

The **30–40 minute eyeOpener tour (free)** by museum guides does just what it says; ask for details at the information desk. After this tour, you can then dip back into the collections that most captured your imagination at your leisure.

An **audio version of the Highlights tour (£4.50)** is a less-animated but perhaps more relaxed way to navigate the galleries. Other audio tours focus on the Enlightenment and the Parthenon sculptures; another is designed for families.

Alternatively, the **Visitor's Guide (£5)** gives a brief but informative overview of the museum's history and is divided into self-guided themed tours.

Before you go, take a look at the online **COMPASS tour** using the museum's navigation tool (www.britishmuseum.org/compass), which allows users to browse past and present exhibits as well as search for specific objects. A children's version can also be found here. Computer stations in the Reading Room offer onsite access to COMPASS.

■ **TIP→** The closest underground station to the British Museum is Russell Square on the Piccadilly line. However, since you will be entering via the back entrance on Montague Place, you will not experience the full impact of the museum's grand facade. To do so, alight at Holborn on the Central and Piccadilly lines or Tottenham Court Road on the Central and Northern lines. The walk from these stations is about 10 minutes.

WITH KIDS

■ Take a look at the "Objects to see with Children" page online. All the items are also on the family audio tour.

■ The Paul Hamlyn Library has trails for kids ages 3 to 5 and 6 to 11. The Ford Centre for Young Visitors has free activity backpacks.

■ Art materials are available for free from information points, where you can also find out about workshops, performances, storytelling sessions, and other free events.

■ Around the museum, there are Hands On desks open daily 11–4, which let visitors handle objects from the collections.

WHERE TO REFUEL

The British Museum's self-service **Gallery Café** gets very crowded but serves an acceptable menu beneath a plaster cast of a part of the Parthenon frieze that Lord Elgin didn't remove. It's open daily, but isn't particularly family friendly.

The **café in the Great Court** keeps longer hours and is a great place to people-watch and admire the spectacular glass roof while you eat your salad and sandwich.

If the weather is nice, exit the museum via the back entrance on Montague Place and amble over to **Russell Square,** which has grassy lawns, water fountains, and a glass-fronted café for post-sandwich coffee and ice cream.

among the paintings on panels that swing away to reveal secret gallery pockets with even more paintings. Everywhere mirrors and colors play tricks with light and space, and split-level floors worthy of a fairground fun house disorient you. In a basement chamber sits the vast 1300 BC sarcophagus of Seti I, lit by a domed skylight two stories above. (When Sir John acquired this priceless object for £2,000, after it was rejected by the British Museum, he celebrated with a three-day party.) The elegant, tranquil courtyard gardens with statuary and plants are open to the public, and there's a below-street-level passage, which joins two of the courtyards to the museum. Because of the small size of the museum, limited numbers are allowed entry at any one time, so you may have a short wait outside. On the first Tuesday of the month, the museum opens for a special candle-light evening from 6 to 9 pm, but expect to wait in a queue for this unique experience. ⊠ *13 Lincoln's Inn Fields, Bloomsbury* ☎ *020/7405–2107* ⊕ *www.soane.org* ✆ *Free, Sat. tour £5* ☾ *Tues.–Sat. 10–5; also 6–9 on 1st Tues. of month* Ⓤ *Holborn.*

> **WORD OF MOUTH**
>
> "[For a nice stroll] head for Temple Tube station and walk east into inner/middle temple. Here you will find an oasis of calm, with just the sound of quill pens being wielded by all the barristers in their chambers. At lunchtime, the gardens of inner temple are open and make a nice spot for a picnic. Then cross over the strand, and wander around the Royal Courts of Justice—if you are interested, they hold the big libel trials and criminal appeals there—just ask at the enquiry desk at the entrance."
> —annhig

WORTH NOTING

★ **Charles Dickens Museum.** This is the only one of the many London houses Charles Dickens (1812–70) inhabited that is still standing, and it would have had a real claim to his fame in any case because he wrote *Oliver Twist* and *Nicholas Nickleby* and finished *Pickwick Papers* here between 1837 and 1839. The house looks exactly as it would have in Dickens's day, complete with first editions, letters, and a tall clerk's desk (where the master wrote standing up, often while chatting with visiting friends and relatives). Down in the basement is a replica of the Dingley Dell kitchen from *Pickwick Papers*. A program of changing special exhibitions gives insight into the Dickens family and the author's works, with sessions where, for instance, you can try your own hand with a quill pen. Visitors have reported a "presence" upstairs in the Mary Hogarth bedroom, where Dickens's sister-in-law died. Investigate yourself and decide whether you're spooked—or feel a sense of calm. Christmas is a memorable time to visit, as the rooms are decorated in traditional style: better than any televised costume drama, this is the real thing. ⊠ *48 Doughty St., Bloomsbury* ☎ *020/7405–2127* ⊕ *www.dickensmuseum.com* ✆ *£5* ☾ *Daily 10–5; last admission 4:30* Ⓤ *Chancery La., Russell Sq.*

Gray's Inn. Although the least architecturally interesting of the four Inns of Court and the one most damaged by German bombs in the 1940s, it still has its romantic associations. In 1594 Shakespeare's *Comedy of Errors* was performed for the first time in its hall—which was restored after World War II and has a fine Elizabethan screen of carved oak. You must make advance arrangements to view the hall, but the secluded and spacious gardens, first planted by Francis Bacon in 1606, are open to the public. ✉ *Gray's Inn Rd., Holborn* ☎ *020/7458–7800* ⊕ *www.graysinn. org.uk* ✉ *Free* ⊙ *Weekdays noon–2:30* Ⓤ *Holborn, Temple.*

★ **Lincoln's Inn.** There's plenty to see at one of the oldest, best preserved, and most attractive of the Inns of Court—from the Chancery Lane Tudor brick gatehouse to the wide-open, tree-lined, atmospheric Lincoln's Inn Fields and the 15th-century chapel remodeled by Inigo Jones in 1620. Visitors are welcome to attend Sunday services at the chapel; otherwise, to enter the buildings requires prior arrangement. ✉ *Chancery La., Bloomsbury* ☎ *020/7405–1393* ⊕ *www.lincolnsinn.org.uk* ✉ *Free* ⊙ *Gardens weekdays 7–7, chapel weekdays noon–2:30; public may also attend Sun. service in chapel at 11:30 during legal terms* Ⓤ *Chancery La.*

Royal Courts of Justice. Here is the vast Victorian Gothic pile of 35 million bricks containing the nation's principal law courts, with 1,000-odd rooms running off 3½ mi of corridor. And here are heard the most important civil law cases—that's everything from divorce to fraud, with libel in between. You can sit in the viewing gallery to watch any trial you like, for a live version of Court TV. The more dramatic criminal cases are heard at the Old Bailey. Other sights are the 238-foot-long main hall and the compact exhibition of judges' robes. ✉ *The Strand, Bloomsbury* ☎ *020/7947–6000* ⊕ *www.hmcourts-service.gov.uk* ✉ *Free* ⊙ *Weekdays 9–4:30; during Aug. there are no sittings and public areas close at 2:30* Ⓤ *Temple.*

Temple Church. Featuring "the Round"—a rare, circular nave—this church was built by the Knights Templar in the 12th century. The Red Knights (so called after the red crosses they wore—you can see them in effigy around the nave) held their secret initiation rites in the crypt here. Having started poor, holy, and dedicated to the protection of pilgrims, they grew rich from showers of royal gifts, until in the 14th century they were charged with heresy, blasphemy, and sodomy, thrown into the Tower, and stripped of their wealth. You might suppose the church to be thickly atmospheric, but Victorian and postwar restorers have tamed its air of antique mystery. It's a fine Gothic-Romanesque church, whose 1240 chancel ("the Oblong") has been accused of perfection. ✉ *King's Bench Walk, The Temple, Bloomsbury* ☎ *020/7353–8559* ⊕ *www.templechurch.com* ⊙ *Wed.–Sat. 11–4, Sun. 1–4; closures for special services* Ⓤ *Temple.*

KING'S CROSS STATION

Known for its 120-foot-tall clock tower, this yellow-brick, Italianate building with large, arched windows was constructed in 1851–52 as the London terminus for the Great Northern Railway. Harry Potter and fellow aspiring wizards took the *Hogwarts Express* to school from the imaginary platform 9¾ (platforms 4 and 5 were the actual shooting site) in the movies based on J. K. Rowling's popular novels. The station has put up a sign for platform 9¾ if you want to take a picture there—but please don't try to run through the wall.

5

University College London. The college was founded in 1826 and set in a classical edifice designed by the architect of the National Gallery, William Wilkins. In 1907 it became part of the University of London, providing higher education without religious exclusion. The college has within its portals the **Slade School of Fine Art,** which did for many of Britain's artists what the nearby Royal Academy of Dramatic Art (on Gower Street) did for actors. On view is a fine collection of sculpture by an alumnus, John Flaxman.

You can also see more Egyptian artifacts, if you didn't get enough at the neighboring British Museum, in the **Petrie Museum**(☎ *020/7679–2884* ⊕ *www.petrie.ucl.ac.uk* ✆ *Tues.–Sat. 1–5* ▱ *Free, donations appreciated*), accessed from the DMS Watson building. It houses an outstanding, huge collection of fascinating objects of Egyptian archaeology—jewelry, toys, papyri, and some of the world's oldest garments. The South Cloisters contain one of London's weirder treasures: the clothed skeleton of one of the university's founders, Jeremy Bentham, who bequeathed himself to the college. Stuffed with straw and topped with a wax head, it is probably the most famous item in the UCL collection. ⊠ *Malet Pl., Bloomsbury* Ⓤ *Euston Sq., Goodge St.*

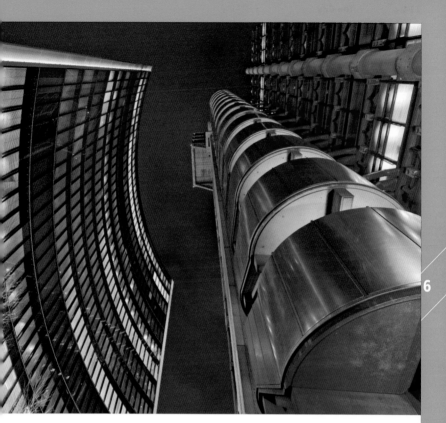

The City

WORD OF MOUTH

"Do you know about the Ceremony of the Keys at the Tower of London? Tickets are free, and attendees are limited to a small group. [Check out www.hrp.org.uk in advance.] It is a cool, and very authentic, ceremony they do every evening at sunset, to lock up the tower. They explain it as they go, and we thought it was neat to be there as the sun goes down."

—PeaceOut

GETTING ORIENTED

GETTING THERE

The City area is well served by a concentrated selection of Underground stops in London. St. Paul's and Bank are on the Central Line, and Mansion House, Cannon Street, and Monument are on the District and Circle lines. Liverpool Street and Aldgate border The City's eastern edge, whereas Chancery Lane and Farringdon lie to the west. Barbican and Moorgate provide easy access to the theaters and galleries of the Barbican, and Blackfriars, to the south, leads to Ludgate Circus and Fleet Street.

TOP REASONS TO GO

Tower of London: Nowhere else does London's history come to life so vividly as in this minicity of melodramatic towers stuffed to bursting with heraldry, quite a few pints of royal blood, and treasure, most notably, the stunning Crown Jewels (bring sunglasses).

St. Paul's Cathedral: The symbolic heart of London, St. Paul's rides high on the skyline although now nudged by ugly skyscrapers—once inside, however, you'll revel in Sir Christopher Wren's 17th-century masterpiece.

Museum of London: Oliver Cromwell's death mask, Queen Victoria's crinolined gowns, Selfridges' Art Déco elevators, and a Diorama of the Great Fire (sound effects! flickering flames!) all make this a gem of a museum.

The Millennium Bridge: Hurtle the centuries with this promenade between the Tate Modern and St. Paul's (with a great river view).

MAKING THE MOST OF YOUR TIME

The "Square Mile" is as compact as the nickname suggests, with little distance between points of interest, making it easy to dip into The City for an afternoon stroll. For full immersion in the Tower of London, however, set aside half a day, especially if seeing the Crown Jewels is a priority. Allow an hour minimum each for the Museum of London, St. Paul's Cathedral, and the Tower Bridge. On weekends, without the scurrying suits, The City is nearly deserted, making it hard to find lunch—and yet this is when the major attractions are at their busiest.

A GOOD WALK

Crossing the Millennium Bridge from the Tate Modern to St. Paul's is one of the finest walks in London for views of the river and the cathedral that towers over it. Dubbed the "blade of light," this shiny aluminum-and-steel construction was the result of a collaboration between architect Norman Foster and sculptor Anthony Caro.

FEELING PECKISH?

The friendly **Riverside Café Bar** (✉ *St. Katherine's Dock, St. Katherine's Way* ☎ *020/7481–1464*) is one of the few places you're sure to find a good cup of hot chocolate and hot and cold meals, with waterside views of the luxurious yachts and gin palaces moored at the docks.

Sweetings (✉ *39 Queen Victoria St.* ☎ *020/7248–3062*) has been here since 1889. It's not cheap, it's closed in the evenings, and takes no reservations, but it serves one of the best fish lunches in London. Refuel here on Dover sole and Black Velvet, the local brew, and observe the pinstripes at play in their natural habitat.

When you're finished exploring Fleet Street, head to the famed **Ye Olde Cheshire Cheese** (✉ *145 Fleet St.* ☎ *020/7353–6170*) for a pint of ale and a snack. Parts of the building date from 1667 and it's rightly admired for its roaring fires and dingy interior, barely changed since Dr. Johnson came here.

DID YOU KNOW?

In The City—the oldest part of London—streets still follow a medieval pattern. Here you can see financial institutions, and notable buildings, like the Bank of England and Lloyd's of London.

Sightseeing
★★★★★
Nightlife
★
Dining
★★★
Lodging
★
Shopping
★★★

The City, as opposed to the city, is the capital's fast-beating financial heart. Easy to walk around, the "Square Mile" also has currency as a religious and political center. St. Paul's Cathedral has looked after Londoners' souls since the 7th century, and the Tower of London—that moat-surrounded royal fortress, prison, and jewel house—has taken care of beheading them.

Updated
by Michelle
Rosenberg

There are many starting points to explore The City, but **Temple Bar Memorial,** at the top of the Strand, is the site of the only surviving entry point—the gate itself was moved closer to St. Paul's (brick by brick) in 1878 to widen the road. **Fleet Street,** the site of England's first printing press, was the undisputed seat of British journalism until the 1980s. The nearby church of **St. Bride's,** recognizable by its tiered wedding-cake steeple, is a Sir Christopher Wren mini-masterpiece and still the church for journalists.

Nestled behind Fleet Street is **Dr. Johnson's House,** former home of the man who claimed that to be bored of London was to be bored of life and author of *Dictionary of the English Language*. Eastward, London's most distinctive building, **St. Paul's Cathedral,** designed by Wren, has clear views of the **Millennium Bridge,** the pedestrian-only steel suspension bridge that links The City to the South Bank of the Thames. The **Central Criminal Court** (nicknamed **Old Bailey,** and home to London's most intriguing criminal trials) lies to the north, as does the 800-year-old **Smithfield Market,** whose Victorian halls are the site of a daily early-morning meat market and the ancient church of **St. Bartholomew the Great** and St. Bartholomew Hospital, both begun in 1123.

The **Museum of London,** where archaeological displays include a portion of the original **Roman Wall** that ringed The City, is a gateway to the modern **Barbican Centre,** a complex of arts venues and apartments. To the southeast lies the **Guildhall,** the site of the only Roman amphitheater in London. Nearby, the church of **St. Mary-le-Bow** and the narrow maze of streets just to its south, around **Bow Lane,** are great shopping haunts.

A BRIEF HISTORY

Rising from the mud of the Thames as the Roman settlement of Londinium, in AD 47, this area marks the beginnings of the capital. It gained immediate momentum as a trading center for materials and goods shipped in from all corners of the fledgling colony. Centuries later, William the Conqueror began building the palace that was to become the Tower of London. It went from being Henry III's defensive shelter in the 13th century to, by Tudor times, the world's most forbidding and grisly prison, where two of Henry VIII's six wives were executed. During the Middle Ages, powerful guilds that nurtured commerce took root, followed by the foundation of great trading companies, such as the Honourable East India Company, which started up in 1600.

The City's history has been punctuated by periods of chaos that have threatened to destroy it. The Great Fire of 1666 was the most serious, sparing only a few of the cramped, labyrinthine streets, where the Great Plague of the previous year had already wiped out a huge portion of the population. Yet the gutted wastelands enabled a new start, driving out the plague-carrying rodents that had menaced London since the Middle Ages and forcing an architectural renaissance, led by Sir Christopher Wren. Further punishment came during the Blitz of World War II, when German bombers destroyed many buildings. Today's eclectic skyline reflects every period of its history, some sublime, some hideous.

At the epicenter of The City is a powerful architectural triumvirate: the **Bank of England,** the **Royal Exchange,** and **Mansion House,** where the lord mayor of The City of London (not to be confused with the mayor of London, who works from City Hall on the South Bank) lives and entertains. The **Monument** was built to commemorate the Great Fire of London of 1666. Northeast of its 202-foot-high tower are excellent views of two unmissable members of The City skyline: the **Lloyd's of London Building,** and the **Swiss Re Tower,** popularly known as "the Gherkin." From here, the river leads to one of London's most absorbing and bloody attractions, the **Tower of London. Tower Bridge** is a suitably giddying finale.

TOP ATTRACTIONS

★ **Monument.** Commemorating the "dreadful visitation" of the Great Fire of 1666, this is the world's tallest isolated stone column. It is the work of Sir Christopher Wren and Dr. Robert Hooke, who were asked to erect it "on or as neere unto the place where the said Fire soe unhappily began as conveniently may be." And so here it is—at 202 feet, exactly as tall as the distance it stands from Farriner's baking house in Pudding Lane, where the fire started. If the thought of attempting the 311 steps is enough to put you off your lunch, cheat a little and watch the live views that are relayed from the top. ✉ *Monument St., The City* ☎ *020/7626–2717* ⊕ *www.themonument.info* ✉ *£3; combined ticket with Tower Bridge exhibition £8* ⊙ *Daily 9:30–5:30, last admission 5* Ⓤ *Monument.*

★ **Museum of London.** If there's one place to absorb the history of London, from 450,000 BC to the present day, it's here: Oliver Cromwell's death mask, Queen Victoria's crinoline gowns, Selfridges' Art Deco elevators, and the London's Burning exhibition are just some of the goodies. The museum appropriately shelters a section of the 2nd- to 4th-century London wall, which you can view from a window inside. Permanent displays include "London Before London," "Roman London," "Medieval London," and "Tudor London." The Galleries of

> **A VIEW TO REMEMBER**

At the top of the Monument's 311-step spiral staircase (a better workout than any StairMaster) is a gallery providing fantastic views from the heart of The City that is helpfully caged to prevent suicidal jumps, which were a trend for a while in the 19th century.

Modern London, which opened in 2010 following a £20 million modernization, are enthralling. Experience the "Expanding City," "People's City," and "World City" galleries, each one dealing with a section of London's history from 1666 until the 21st century. Innovative interactive displays include the fun "So You Want to be an Apprentice" quiz, with options including shoemaker, gunmaker, glassmaker, and watchmaker and around 7,000 objects to wonder at, from fans, guns, and jewelry to an original Newgate Prison Door and the incredible Blackett Dolls House, both dating from around the late 1700s. The archaeologists and curators at the museum regularly leap from AD to BC, as fresh building work in the city uncovers more treasures. ⊠ *London Wall, The City* ☎ *020/7001–9844* ⊕ *www.museumoflondon.org.uk* ⊠ *Free* ☽ *Mon.–Sun. 10–6; last admission 5:30* Ⓤ *Barbican, St. Paul's.*

Fodor's Choice
★   **St. Paul's Cathedral.**
See the highlighted listing in this chapter.

Ↄ   **Tower Bridge.** Despite its medieval, fairy-tale appearance, this is a Victorian youngster. Constructed of steel, then clothed in Portland stone, the Horace Jones masterpiece was deliberately styled in the Gothic persuasion to complement the Tower next door, and it's famous for its enormous bascules—the 1,200-ton "arms," which open to allow large ships through. This still happens occasionally, but when river traffic was dense, the bascules were raised about five times a day.

Fodor's Choice
★

The **Tower Bridge Exhibition** is a child-friendly tour where you can discover how one of the world's most famous bridges actually works and then head out onto the walkways for the wonderful city views. First, take in the romance of the panoramas from the east and west walkways between those grand turrets. On the east are the modern superstructures and ships of Docklands, and on the west is the best look at the steel-and-glass "futuristic mushroom" that is Greater London Assembly's City Hall, the Tower of London, St. Paul's, and the Monument. Then it's back down to explore the Victorian engine rooms and discover the inner workings, which you learn about through hands-on displays and films. ⊠ *Tower Bridge Rd., The City* ☎ *020/7403–3761* ⊕ *www.towerbridge. org.uk* ⊠ *£7* ☽ *Apr.–Sept., daily 10–6:30; Oct.–Mar., daily 9:30–6; last admission 30 min before closing* Ⓤ *Tower Hill.*

Fodor's Choice
★   **Tower of London.**
See the highlighted listing in this chapter.

Continued on page 126

ST. PAUL'S CATHEDRAL

Sir Christopher Wren's maxim "I build for eternity" proves no empty boast.

Sublime, awesome, majestic, and inspirational are just some of the words to describe Wren's masterpiece, St. Paul's Cathedral—even more so now that the restoration for the 300th anniversary is expected to finish in 2010.

This is the spiritual heart of the nation, where people and events are celebrated, mourned, and honored. As you approach the cathedral your eyes are inevitably drawn skyward to the great dome, one of the largest in the world and an amazing piece of engineering. Visit in the late afternoon for evensong, and let the choir's voices transport you to a world of absolute peace in a place of perfect beauty, as pristine as the day it was completed.

TOURING ST. PAUL'S

Enter the cathedral via the main west entrance, and walk straight down the length of the nave to the central Dome Altar. Nobody can resist making a beeline for the dome, so start your tour beneath it, standing dead center on the beautiful sunburst floor, Wren's focal mirror of the magnificent design above. A simple quotation marks the floor "Lector si momentum requiris, circumspice" (Reader if you seek his monument, look around). The dome crowns the center of the cathedral and rises to 364 feet—but save your strength for the "great climb" to get some fantastic views.

THE CATHEDRAL FLOOR

The North Transept is dominated by the Pre-Raphaelite painting **❶ The Light of the World** (1853) by William Holman Hunt. It is one of the best-known of English religious pictures of the nineteenth century.

North Transept ❶

North Aisle ❸

Nave ❷

South Aisle

Dome

❹

South Transept

❷ The Nave is formed of three aisles, and from here you can see right down to the High Altar at the far end of the Choir, more than 100 yards away. Take time to admire the mastery of space and light.

In the north aisle of the Nave is Flax-man's grandiose **❸ monument to the Duke of Wellington,** who sits astride his faithful charger, Copen-hagen, the horse that carried him through the Battle of Waterloo.

The South Transept displays a **❹ monument to Admiral Lord Nelson,** Britain's favorite naval hero, with an anchor. Other memorials commemorate the explorer Captain Robert Scott and the darling of British landscape painting J.M.W. Turner.

CELEBRITY STATUS

St. Paul's has witnessed many momentous processions along its checkered nave. The somber state funerals of heroes Admiral Lord Nelson and the Duke of Wellington, and of Sir Winston Churchill, drew huge crowds. It was here, also, that the fairy-tale wedding of Prince Charles and Lady Diana Spencer took place, and the jubilees of Queen Victoria, George V, and the present Queen were celebrated.

The North Choir Aisle features the beautiful ❺ **gilded gates** by Jean Tijou, perhaps the most accomplished artist in wrought iron of all time, as well as Henry Moore's sculpture ❻ *Mother and Child*, its simple lines complementing the ornate surroundings.

The Choir contains the ❽ **Bishop's Throne** or cathedra, hence the name cathedral. Look aloft to the fabulous mosaics. Don't miss the exquisite, delicate carvings by Grinling Gibbons, in particular on the case of the ❾ **grand organ,** one of the Cathedral's greatest artifacts. It was designed by Wren and played by such illustrious figures as Handel and Mendelssohn.

❿ **The High Altar,** with its glorious canopy, is a profusion of marble and carved and gilded oak.

North Choir Aisle

Apse

Choir (Quire)

South Choir Aisle

The Apse is home to the ⓫ **American Memorial Chapel,** which honors the more than 28,000 U.S. soldiers who died while stationed in the U.K. during World War II. The lime-wood paneling incorporates a rocket as a tribute to the United States' achievements in space.

The South Choir Aisle contains a ❼ **marble effigy of poet John Donne,** who was Dean of old St. Paul's for his final 10 years (he died in 1631). This is the only statue to have survived the Great Fire of London intact. You can see the scorch marks at the base of the statue.

MUSICAL FRICTION

The organ, with its cherubs and angels, was not installed without controversy. The mighty instrument proved a tight fit, and the maker, known as Father Schmidt, and Wren nearly came to blows. Wren was reputed to have said he would not adapt his cathedral for a mere "box of whistles."

IN FOCUS ST. PAUL'S CATHEDRAL

THE DOME

The dome is the crowning glory of the cathedral, a must for visitors.

At 99 feet, the **❶ Whispering Gallery** is reached by 259 spiral steps. This is the part of the cathedral with which you bribe children—they will be fascinated by the acoustic phenomenon: whisper something to the wall on one side, and a second later it transmits clearly to the other side, 107 feet away. The only problem is identifying your whisper from the cacophony of everyone else's. Look down onto the nave from here and up to the monochrome frescoes of St. Paul by Sir James Thornhill.

More stamina is required to reach the **❷ Stone Gallery,** at 173 feet and 378 steps from ground level. It is on the exterior of the cathedral and offers a vista of the city and the River Thames.

For the best views of all—at 280 feet and 530 steps from ground level—make the trek to the small **❸ Golden Gallery,** the highest point of the outer dome. A hole in the floor gives a vertiginous view down. You can see the lantern above through a circular opening called the oculus. If you have a head for heights you can walk outside for a spectacular panorama of London.

The top of the dome is crowned with a **❹ ball and cross.** At 23 feet high and weighing approximately 7 tons, it is the pinnacle of St. Paul's.

A BRIEF HISTORY

The cathedral is the masterpiece of Sir Christopher Wren (1632–1723), completed in 1710 after 35 years of building and much argument with the Royal Commission. Wren had originally been commissioned to restore Old St. Paul's, the Norman cathedral that had replaced, in its turn, three earlier versions, but the Great Fire left so little of it standing that a new cathedral was deemed necessary.

Wren's first plan, known as the New Model, did not make it past the drawing board; the second, known as the Great Model, got as far as the 20-foot oak rendering you can see here today before it, too, was rejected, whereupon Wren is said to have burst into tears. The third, however, known as the Warrant Design (because it received the royal warrant), was accepted, with the fortunate coda that the architect be allowed to make changes as he saw fit. Without that, there would be no dome, because the approved design had featured a steeple. Parliament felt that building was proceeding too slowly (in fact, 35 years is lightning speed, as cathedrals go) and withheld half of Wren's pay for the last 13 years of work. He was pushing 80 when Queen Anne finally coughed up the arrears.

■TIP→ **To see Wren's Great Model, you must join a Triforium Tour (Mon. and Tues. at 11:30 and 2, Fri. at 2).** These one-hour tours include a visit to the library and a glimpse of the famous Geometric staircase. The visit ends in the Trophy Room, where Wren's Great Model is on display. The tour costs £16 per person and includes entry to the cathedral and access to the crypt and galleries. It's best to book in advance by calling 020/7246–8357 or sending an e-mail to visits@stpaulscathedral.org.uk.

THE CRYPT

A visit to the vast crypt is a time for reflection and contemplation, with some 200 memorials to see. If it all becomes too somber, take solace in the café or shop near the crypt entrance.

Here lies ❶ **Admiral Nelson,** killed at the Battle of Trafalgar in 1805. His body was preserved in alcohol for the journey home, and his pickled remains were buried here beneath Cardinal Wolsey's unused 16th-century sarcophagus.

The ❷ **tomb of the Duke of Wellington** comprises a simple casket made from Cornish granite. He is remembered as a hero of battle, but his name lives on in the form of boots, cigars, beef Wellington, and the capital of New Zealand.

Surrounded by his family and close to a plethora of iconic artists, musicians, and scientists, the ❸ **tomb of Sir Christopher Wren** is a modest simple slab.

The beautiful ❹ **O.B.E. Chapel** (dedicated 1960) is a symbol of the Order of the British Empire, an order of chivalry established in 1917 by George V. The theme of sovereign and Commonwealth is represented in the glass panels.

The vast ❺ **treasury** houses the cathedral's plate, although a good deal has been lost or stolen over the centuries—in particular in a daring robbery of 1810—and much of the display comes from other London churches.

Entrance & Exit

The Refectory

Crypt Café

Cathedral Shop

Entrance

Entrance

5

7

1

2

4

3

PLANNING YOUR DAY

WHAT'S NEARBY: Stroll over the Millennium Bridge (look back for a great view of St. Paul's) and have lunch at Tate Modern. The restaurant at the top of the gallery has spectacular views of London. ■TIP➜ To avoid lines visit early in the morning. For a different experience return for Evensong at 5 pm.

CONTACT INFO: ✉ *St. Paul's Churchyard, Ludgate Hill EC4 8AD* ☎ *020/7236–4128* ⊕ *www.stpauls.co.uk* Ⓤ *St. Paul's*

ADMISSION: Adults: £14.50. **Family ticket** (2 adults, 2 children): £34.50. **Children 7–16:** £3.50.

TOURS: A guided tour of the cathedral, choir, Geometric staircase, and crypt lasts 1½–2 hours and costs £3. Tours start at 10:45, 11:15, 13:30, and 14:00. Multimedia rental guides are included in admission.

HOURS: The cathedral is a house of worship. Services may cause changes to the visiting hours on any given day, so be sure to call ahead.

Cathedral: Mon.–Sat. 8:30–4:30 (last admission at 4).
Shop: Mon.–Sat. 8:30–5, Sun. 10–4:30.
Crypt café: Mon.–Sat. 9–5, Sun. 12–4.

WORTH NOTING

SUMMER FESTIVAL

Every year, for three weeks in June and July, the City of London Festival (⊕ *www.colf.org*) has numerous walks, dances, street arts, and concerts taking place in buildings that are usually closed to the public.

Bank of England. Known for the past couple of centuries as "the Old Lady of Threadneedle Street," after the name appeared in a caption to a political cartoon (which can be seen in the museum), the country's top vault, which has been central to the British economy since 1694, manages the national debt and the foreign exchange reserves, issues banknotes, sets interest rates, looks after England's gold, and regulates the country's banking system. Sir John Soane designed the neoclassical hulk in 1788, wrapping it in windowless walls, which are all that survives of his original building. The bank's history is traced in the Bank of England Museum (entrance is around the corner on Bartholomew Lane). Here, the museum comes to life with the interactive exhibits that chart the bank's more recent history, including the chance to try your hand at controlling inflation, but most visitors still make a beeline for the solid-gold bar that can be stroked and held in the central trading hall (but before you get any ideas, there's security everywhere). ⊠ *Threadneedle St., The City* ☎ *020/7601–5545* ⊕ *www. bankofengland.co.uk* 🎫 *Free* ⊙ *Weekdays and Lord Mayor's Show day (2nd Sat. in Nov.)* 10–5 Ⓤ *Bank, Monument.*

★ **Barbican Centre.** With two theaters; the London Symphony Orchestra and its auditorium; the Guildhall School of Music and Drama; a major art gallery for touring and its own special exhibitions; two cinemas; a convention center; an upscale restaurant, cafés, terraces with fountains, and literary bookshops; and living space in some of the most desirable tower blocks in town, the Barbican is an enormous 1980s concrete maze that Londoners either love or hate. Navigation around the complex is via the yellow lines running, Wizard-of-Oz-like, along the floors, with signs on the walls, although it's still easy to get lost. Actors rate the theater acoustics especially highly, and the steep rake of the seating makes for a good stage view. The dance, music, and theater programs have been transformed into a yearlong fest named BITE, which stands for Barbican International Theatre Events, and encompasses dance, puppetry, and music. The emphasis is on presenting tomorrow's names today, although there are performances by established companies and artists, such as Merce Cunningham. ⊠ *Silk St., The City* ☎ *020/7638–8891 box office* ⊕ *www.barbican.org.uk* 🎫 *Barbican Centre free, art gallery £6–£8, films £8.50, concerts £6.50–£45, theater £7–£50* ⊙ *Barbican Centre Mon.–Sat. 9 am–11 pm, Sun. and holidays noon–11; gallery Thurs. 11–10, Mon., Fri.–Sun. 11–8, Tues.– Wed. 11–6* Ⓤ *Moorgate, Barbican.*

★ **Dr. Johnson's House.** This is where Samuel Johnson lived between 1748 and 1759, compiling his famous dictionary in the attic as his health deteriorated. Built in 1700, the elegant Georgian residence, with its paneled rooms and period furniture, is where the Great Bear (as he

Interior of the "Inside-Out" Lloyd's of London building, designed by Richard Rogers Partnership.

was known) compiled his *Dictionary of the English Language*—two early editions of which are among the mementos of Johnson and his friend, diarist, and later, his biographer, James Boswell. After soaking up the atmosphere, repair around the corner in Wine Office Court to the famed **Ye Olde Cheshire Cheese** pub, once Johnson and Boswell's favorite watering hole. ⊠ *17 Gough Sq., The City* ☎ *020/7353–3745* ⊕ *www.drjohnsonshouse.org* 🖼 *£4.50* 🕙 *May–Sept., Mon.–Sat. 11–5:30; Oct.–Apr., Mon.–Sat. 11–5; closed bank holidays* Ⓤ *Holborn, Chancery La.*

Guildhall. The Corporation of London, which oversees The City, has ceremonially elected and installed its lord mayor here for the last 800 years. The Guildhall was built in 1411, and though it failed to avoid either the 1666 or 1940 flames, its core survived. The Great Hall is a psychedelic patchwork of coats of arms and banners of the City Livery Companies, which inherited the mantle of the medieval trade guilds. Tradesmen couldn't even run a shop without kowtowing to these prototypical unions, and their grand banqueting halls, the plushest private dining venues in The City, are testimony to the wealth they amassed. Inside the hall, Gog and Magog, the pair of mythical giants who founded ancient Albion and the city of New Troy, upon which London was said to be built, glower down from their west-gallery grandstand in 9-foot-high painted lime wood. The hall was also the site of famous trials, including that of Lady Jane Grey in 1553, before her execution at the Tower of London. To the right of Guildhall Yard is the **Guildhall Art Gallery**, which includes portraits of the great and the good, cityscapes, famous battles, and a slightly cloying pre-Raphaelite section. The construction of the gallery led to the exciting discovery of London's only **Roman amphitheater,** which had lain underneath Guildhall Yard undisturbed for more than 1,800 years. It was excavated, and now visitors can walk among the remains, although most of the relics can be seen at the Museum of London, through which guided tours can be booked. ✉ *Aldermanbury, The City* ☎ *020/7606–3030, 020/7332–3700 gallery* ⊕ *www.cityoflondon.gov.uk* ▨ *Free; gallery and amphitheater £2.50* ⊙ *Mon.–Sat. 9:30–5; gallery Mon.–Sat. 10–5, Sun. noon–4, last admission 4:30 or 3:30* Ⓤ *St. Paul's, Moorgate, Bank, Mansion House.*

Old Bailey. If you're lucky, this is the place to watch the real-life drama of justice in action in one of the 16 courtrooms that are open to the public. Previous trials have included those of Crippen and Christie, two of England's most notorious wife murderers, as well as the controversial trial of Oscar Wilde and, less so, the notorious East End gangsters, the Kray twins. The day's hearings are posted on the sign outside, but your best bet is to consult the previous day's tabloid newspapers for an idea of the trials that are making waves. There are security restrictions, and children under 14 are not allowed in; call the information line first. The present-day **Central Criminal Court** is where Newgate Prison stood from the 12th century right until the beginning of the 20th century. Called by the novelist Henry Fielding the "prototype of hell," few survived for long in the version pulled down in 1770. The Central Criminal Court replaced Newgate in 1907, and the most famous feature of the solid Edwardian building is the 12-foot gilded statue of Justice perched on top; she was intended to mirror the dome of St. Paul's. ✉ *Newgate St., The City* ☎ *020/7248–3277 information* ⊕ *www.cityoflondon.gov. uk* ⊙ *Public Gallery weekdays 10–1 and 2–5 (approx.); line forms at Newgate St. entrance or in Warwick St. Passage; closed bank holidays and day after* Ⓤ *St. Paul's.*

St. Bartholomew the Great. Reached via a perfect half-timber gatehouse atop a 13th-century stone archway, this is one of London's oldest churches. Construction on the church and the hospital nearby was begun in 1123 by Henry I's favorite courtier, Rahere, who caught malaria and, surviving, vowed to dedicate his life to serving the saint who had visited him in his fevered dreams. With the Dissolution of the Monasteries, Henry VIII had most of it torn down; the Romanesque choir loft is all that survives from the 12th century. The ancient church has appeared in *The Other Boleyn Girl, Four Weddings and a Funeral,* and *Shakespeare in Love.* ✉ *Cloth Fair, West Smithfield, The City* ☎ *020/7606–5171* ⊕ *www.greatstbarts.com* ▨ *Church £4, museum free* ⊙ *Church weekdays 8:30–5 (Nov.–Feb. 8:30–4), Sat. 10:30–4, Sun 8:30–8. Museum Tues.–Fri. 10–4* Ⓤ *Barbican, Farringdon.*

St. Bride's. According to legend, the distinctively tiered steeple of this Christopher Wren–designed church gave rise to the shape of the traditional wedding cake. One early couple inspired to marry here were the parents of Virginia Dare, the first European child born in colonial America in 1587. As St. Paul's (in Covent Garden) is the actors' church, so St. Bride's belongs to journalists, many of whom have been buried or memorialized here. Samuel Richardson, one of the "Fathers of the English Novel," is buried here and by 1664 the crypts were so crowded that

Continued on page 136

THE TOWER OF LONDON

The Tower is a microcosm of the city itself—a sprawling, organic hodgepodge of buildings that inspires reverence and terror in equal measure. See the block on which Anne Boleyn was beheaded, marvel at the Crown Jewels, and pay homage to the ravens who keep the monarchy safe.

An architectural patchwork of time, the oldest building of the complex is the fairytale White Tower, conceived by William the Conqueror in 1078 as both a royal residence and a show of power to the troublesome Anglo-Saxons he had subdued at the Battle of Hastings. Today's Tower has seen everything, as a palace, barracks, a mint for producing coins, an armoury, and the Royal menagerie (home of the country's first elephant). The big draw is the stunning opulence of the Crown Jewels, kept on-site in the heavily fortified Jewel House. Most of all, though, the Tower is known for death: it's been a place of imprisonment, torture, and execution for the realm's most notorious traitors as well as its martyrs. These days, unless you count the killer admission fees, there are far less morbid activities taking place in the Tower, but it still breathes London's history and pageantry from its every brick and offers hours of exploration.

TOURING THE TOWER

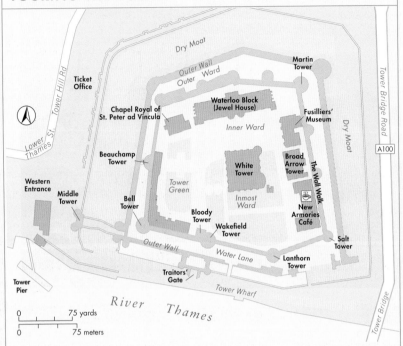

Entry to the Tower is via the **Western Entrance** and the **Middle Tower**, which feed into the outermost ring of the Tower's defenses.

Water Lane leads past the dread-inducing **Traitors' Gate**, the final point of entry for many Tower prisoners.

Toward the end of Water Lane, the **Lanthorn Tower** houses by night the ravens rumored to keep the kingdom safe, and by day a timely high-tech reconstruction of the Catholic Guy Fawkes's plot to blow up the Houses of Parliament in 1605.

The **Bloody Tower** earned its name as the apocryphal site

of the murder of two young princes, Edward and Richard, who disappeared from the Tower after being put there in 1483 by their uncle, Richard III. Two little skeletons (now in Westminster Abbey) were found buried close to the White Tower in 1674 and are thought to be theirs.

The **Beauchamp Tower** housed upper-class miscreants: Latin graffiti about Lady Jane Grey can be glimpsed today on its walls.

Like a prize gem set at the head of a royal crown, the **White Tower** is the centerpiece of the complex. Its four towers dominate the Inner

Ward, a fitting and forbidding reminder of Norman strength at the time of the conquest of England.

Once inside the White Tower, head upstairs for the **Armouries**, where the biggest attraction, quite literally,

ROYAL BLING

The Crown of Queen Elizabeth, the Queen Mother, from 1937, contains the exotic 105-carat Koh-i-Noor (mountain of light) diamond.

Jewel House, Waterloo Barracks

TIME KILLERS

Some prisoners managed to keep themselves plenty amused: Sir Walter Raleigh grew tobacco on Tower Green, and in 1561 suspected sorcerer Hugh Draper carved an intricate astronomical clock on the walls of his Salt Tower cell.

is the suit of armor worn by a well-endowed Henry VIII. There is a matching outfit for his horse.

Other fascinating exhibits include the set of Samurai armor presented to James I in 1613 by the emperor of Japan, and the tiny set of armor worn by Henry VIII's young son Edward.

The **Jewel House** in Waterloo Block is the Tower's biggest draw, perfect for playing pick-your-favorite-crown from the wrong side of bul-

letproof glass. Not only are these crowns, staffs, and orbs encrusted with heavy-duty gems, they are invested with the authority of monarchical power in England, dating back to the 1300s.

Outside, pause at **Tower Green,** permanent departure point for those of noble birth. The hoi polloi were dispatched at nearby Tower Hill. The Tower's most famous female victims—Anne Boleyn, Margaret Countess of Salisbury, Catherine Howard, and Lady Jane Grey—all went this "priviledged" way.

Behind a well-kept square of grass stands the **Chapel Royal of St. Peter ad Vincula,** a delightful Tudor church and final resting place of six beheaded Tudor bodies. ■TIP→ **Visitors are welcome for services and can also enter after 4:30 pm daily.**

The **Salt Tower,** reputedly the most haunted corner of the complex, marks the start of the **Wall Walk,** a bracing promenade along the stone spiral steps and battlements of the Tower that looks down on the trucks, taxis, and shimmering high-rises of modern London.

The Wall Walk ends at the **Martin Tower,** former home of the Crown Jewels and now host to the crowns and diamonds exhibition that explains the art of fashioning royal headwear and tells the story of some of the most famous stones.

On leaving the Tower, browse the gift shop, and wander the wharf that overlooks the Thames, leading to a picture-postcard view of Tower Bridge.

WHO ARE THE BEEFEATERS?

First of all, they're Yeoman Warders, but probably got the nickname "beefeater" from their position as Royal Bodyguards which entitled them to eat as much beef as they liked. Part of the "Yeoman of the Guard," started in the reign of Edmund IV, the warders have formed the Royal Bodyguard as far back as 1509 when Henry VIII left a dozen of the Yeoman of the Guard at the Tower to protect it.

Originally, the Yeoman Warders also served as jailers of the Tower, doubling as torturers when necessary. (So it would have been a Beefeater tightening the thumb screws, or ratchetting the rack another notch on some unfortunate prisoner. Smile nicely.) Today 36 Yeoman Warders (men and women since 2007), along with the Chief Yeoman Warder and the Yeoman Gaoler, live within the walls of the Tower with their families, in accommodations in the Outer Ward. They stand guard over the Tower, conduct tours, and lock up at 9:53 pm every night with the Ceremony of the Keys.

■ TIP➡ Free tickets to the Ceremony of the Keys are available by writing several months in advance; check the Tower Web site for details.

HARK THE RAVENS!

Legend has it that should the hulking black ravens ever leave, the White Tower will crumble and the kingdom fall. Charles II, no doubt jumpy after his father's execution and the monarchy's short-term fall from grace, made a royal decree in 1662 that there should be at least six of the carrion-eating nasties present at all times. There have been some close calls. During World War II, numbers dropped to one, echoing the precarious fate of the war-wracked country. In 2005, two (of eight) died over Christmas when Thor—the most intelligent but also the largest bully of the bunch—killed new recruit Gundolf, named after the Tower's 1070 designer. Pneumonia put an end to Bran, leaving lifelong partner Branwen without her mate.

■ DID YOU KNOW? In 1981 a raven named Grog, perhaps seduced by his alcoholic moniker, escaped after 21 years at the Tower. Others have been banished for "conduct unbecoming."

The six that remain, each one identified by a colored band around a claw, are much loved for their fidelity (they mate for life) and their cheek (capable of 440 noises, they are witty and scolding mimics). It's not only the diet

of blood-soaked biscuits, rabbit, and scraps from the mess kitchen that keeps them coming back. Their lifting feathers on one wing are trimmed, meaning they can manage the equivalent of a lop-sided air-bound hobble but not much more. For the first half of 2006 the ravens were moved indoors full-time as a preventive measure against avian flu but have since been allowed out and about again. In situ they are a territorial lot, sticking to Tower Green and the White Tower, and lodging nightly by Wakefield Tower. They've had free front-row seats at all the most grisly moments in Tower history—Anne Boleyn's execution included.

■ TIP➡ Don't get too close to the ravens: they are prone to pecking and not particularly fond of humans, unless you are the Tower's Raven Master.

And *WHAT* are they wearing?

A **pike** (or halberd), also known as a partisan, is the Yeoman Warder's weapon of choice. The Chief Warder carries a staff topped with a miniature silver model of the White Tower.

Anyone who refers to this as a costume will be lucky to leave the Tower with head still attached to body: this is the ceremonial uniform of the Yeoman Warders, and it comes at a cool £13,000 a throw.

The black Tudor **bonnet** is made of velvet; the blue undress consists of a felt top hat, with a single Tudor rose in the middle.

This **Tudor-style ruff** helps date the ceremonial uniform, which was first worn in 1552.

Insignia on a Yeoman Warder's upper right arm denote the rank he carried in the military.

The **medals** on a Yeoman Warder's chest are more than mere show: all of the men and women have served for at least 22 years in the armed forces.

This version of the **royal livery** bears the insignia of the current Queen ("E" for Elizabeth) but originally dates from Tudor times. The first letter changes according to the reigning monarch's Christian name; the second letter is always an "R" for *rex* (king) or *regina* (queen).

Slits in the **tunic** date from the times when Beefeaters were expected to ride a horse.

Red socks and **black patent shoes** are worn on special occasions. Visitors are more likely to see the regular blue undress, introduced in 1858 as the regular working dress of the Yeoman Warders.

The **red lines down the trousers** are a sign of the blood from the swords of the Yeoman Warders in their defense of the realm.

(IN)FAMOUS PRISONERS OF THE TOWER

Anne Boleyn　　　　　　Lady Jane Grey　　　　　　Sir Walter Raleigh

Sir Thomas More. A Catholic and Henry VIII's friend and chancellor, Sir Thomas refused to attend the coronation of Anne Boleyn (Henry VIII's second wife) or to recognize the multi-marrying king as head of the Church. Sent to the Tower for treason, in 1535 More was beheaded.

Anne Boleyn. The first of Henry VIII's wives to be beheaded, Anne, who failed to provide the king with a son, was accused of sleeping with five men, including her own brother. All six got the chop in 1536. Her severed head was held up to the crowd, and her lips were said to be mouthing prayer.

Margaret, Countess of Salisbury. Not the best-known prisoner in her lifetime, she has a reputation today for haunting the Tower. And no wonder: the elderly 70-year-old was condemned by Henry VIII in 1541 for a potentially treacherous bloodline (she was the last Plantagenet princess) and hacked to death by the executioner after she refused to put her head on the block like a common traitor and attempted to run away.

Queen Catherine Howard. Henry VIII's fifth wife was locked up for high treason and infidelity and beheaded in 1542 at age 20. Ever eager to please, she spent her final night practicing how to lay her head on the block.

Lady Jane Grey. The nine-days-queen lost her head in 1554 at age 16. Her death was the result of sibling rivalry gone seriously wrong, when Protestant Edward VI slighted his Catholic sister Mary in favor of Lady Jane as heir, and Mary decided to have none of it.

Guy Fawkes. The Roman Catholic soldier who tried to blow up the Houses of Parliament and kill the king in the 1605 Gunpowder plot was first incarcerated in the chambers of the Tower, where King James I requested he be tortured in ever-worsening ways. Perhaps unsurprisingly, he confessed. He met his seriously grisly end in the Old Palace Yard at Westminster, where he was hung, drawn, and quartered in 1607.

Sir Walter Raleigh. Once a favorite of Elizabeth I, he offended her by secretly marrying her Maid of Honor and was chucked in the Tower. Later, as a conspirator against James I, he paid with his life. A frequent visitor to the Tower (he spent 13 years there in three stints), he managed to get the Bloody Tower enlarged on account of his wife and growing family. He was finally executed in 1618 in Old Palace Yard, Westminster.

Josef Jakobs. The last man to be executed in the Tower was caught as a spy when parachuting in from Germany and executed by firing squad in 1941. The chair he sat in when he was shot is preserved in the Royal Armouries' artifacts store.

FOR FURTHER EVIDENCE . . .

A trio of buildings in the Inner Ward, the **Bloody Tower, Beauchamp Tower,** and **Queen's House,** all with excellent views of the execution scaffold in Tower Green, are the heart of the Tower's prison accommodations and home to a permanent exhibition about notable inmates.

TACKLING THE TOWER (without losing your head)

✉ H.M. Tower of London, Tower Hill
☎ 0844/482–7777, 0844/482–7799 tickets
⊕ www.hrp.org.uk 🎫 £19.80, children 16 and under £9.50, children under 5 free. Family tickets (2 adults, 3 children) £55 ⊙ Mar.–Oct., Tues.–Sat. 9–5:30, Sun. and Mon. 10–5:30; last admission at 5. Nov.–Feb., Tues.–Sat. 9–4:30, Sun. and Mon. 10–4:30; last admission at 4 Ⓤ Tower Hill

■ TIP → You can buy tickets from automatic kiosks on arrival, or up to seven days in advance at any Tube station. Avoid lines completely and save by booking discounted tickets online.

MAKING THE MOST OF YOUR TIME: Without doubt, the Tower is worth two to three hours. A full hour of that would be well spent by joining one of the Yeoman Warders' tours (included in admission). It's hard to better their insight, vitality, and humor—they are knights of the realm living their very own fairytale castle existence.

The Crown Jewels are worth the wait, the White Tower is essential, and the Medieval Palace and Bloody Tower should at least be breezed through.

■ TIP → It's best to visit on weekdays, when the crowds are smaller.

WITH KIDS: The Tower's centuries-old cobblestones are not exactly stroller-friendly, but strollers are permitted inside most of the buildings. If you do bring one, be prepared to leave it temporarily unsupervised (the stroller, that is—not your child) outside the White Tower, which has no access. There are baby-changing facilities in the Brick Tower restrooms behind the Jewel House. Look for regular free children's events such as the Knight's school where children can have a go at jousting, sword-fighting, and archery.

■ TIP → Tell your child to find one of the Yeoman Warders if he or she should get lost; they will in turn lead him or her to the Byward Tower, which is where you should meet.

IN A HURRY? If you have less than an hour, head down Wall Walk, through a succession of towers, which eventually spit you out at the Martin Tower. The view over modern London is quite a contrast.

TOURS: Tours given by a Yeoman Warder leave from the main entrance near Middle Tower every half-hour from 10–4, and last about an hour. Beefeaters give occasional 30-minute talks in the Lanthorn Tower about their daily lives. Both tours are free.

diarist Samuel Pepys, who was baptized here, had to bribe the grave-digger to "justle together" some bodies to make room for his deceased brother. Now the crypts house a museum of the church's rich history, and a bit of Roman sidewalk. ✉ *Fleet St., The City* ☎ *020/7427–0133* ⊕ *www.stbrides.com* 🎫 *Free* ☉ *Weekdays 8–6, Sat. 11–3, Sun. for services only 10–1 and 5–7:30* Ⓤ *St. Paul's, Blackfriars.*

St. Mary-le-Bow. This church is another classic City survivor; various versions have stood on the site since the 11th century. In 1284 a local goldsmith took refuge here after committing a murder, only to be killed inside the church by enraged relatives of his victim. The church was abandoned for a time afterward, but started up again, and was rebuilt in its current form after the Great Fire. Wren's 1673 incarnation has a tall steeple for a City church (only St. Bride's is taller) and one of the most famous sets of bells around—a Londoner must be born within the sound of the "Bow Bells" to be a true Cockney. The origin of that idea may have been the curfew rung on the bells during the 14th century, even though "Cockney" only came to mean "Londoner" centuries later, and then it was an insult. The Bow takes its name from the bow-shaped arches in the Norman crypt. The garden contains a statue of local boy Captain John Smith, who founded Virginia in 1606 and was later captured by Native Americans. ✉ *Cheapside, The City* ☎ *020/7248–5139* ⊕ *www.stmarylebow.co.uk* ☉ *Mon.–Wed. 7–6, Thurs. 7–6:30, Fri. 7–4; closed weekends* Ⓤ *Mansion House, St. Paul's.*

QUICK BITES

The Café Below (☎ *020/7329–0789* ⊕ *www.cafebelow.co.uk*), in St. Mary-le-Bow's Norman crypt, is packed with City workers weekdays from 7:30 am until 9 pm for a menu covering breakfasts, scrumptious light lunches, and delicious dinners.

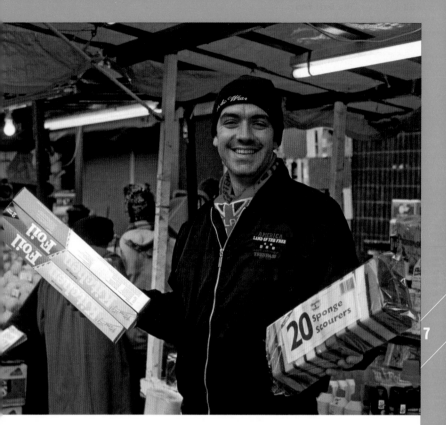

The East End

WORD OF MOUTH

"Spitalfields is busiest on Sundays; it has arty clothes, antiques, and bits and bobs. There are also more alternative craft and clothes stalls in a warehouse building on the corner of Hanbury Street and Brick Lane, which is also worth a visit. Petticoat Lane is a general market on Sundays only, mostly cheap clothes, accessories, and luggage."
—PatrickLondon

GETTING ORIENTED

TO
HOXTON

Dunston Rd.
Pownall Rd.
Regents Row
Bush Rd.
Northiam St.
Kingsland Rd.
Laburnum St.
Whiston Rd.
Hows St.
Appleby St.
Ormsby St.
Geffrye St.
Nuttall St.
Hoxton St.
Falkirk St.
Geffrye Museum
HAGGERSTON
Grand Union Canal
Haggerston Park
Dunloe St.
Hackney Rd.
Goldsmith's Row
Andrew's Rd.
Pritchards Rd.
Cambridge Heath Rd.
Bishop's Way
Cambridge Heath Station
Temple St.
Russia La.

SHOREDITCH
Columbia Road
Flower Market
Gosset St.
Warner Pl.
Barnet Grove
Old Bethnal Green Rd.
BETHNAL GREEN
V & A Museum of Childhood
U Bethnal Green
Victoria Pk. S.
White Cube
Old St.
Shoreditch High St.
Curtain Rd.
Swanfield St.
Brick La.
Turin St.
Arnold Circus
Vallance Rd.
Bethnal Green Rd.
Weavers Fields
Great Eastern St.
Redchurch St.
Bethnal Green Rd.
Cheshire St.
Dunbridge St.
Bethnal Green Station
Cottingwood St.
Cambridge Heath Rd.
Cleveland Way

Old Truman Brewery
U Bethnal Green
Quaker St.
Buxton St.
Spitalfields City Farm
Brady St.
Burial Ground
Commercial St.
Dennis Severs' House
Nude Espresso
SPITALFIELDS
Hanbury St.
Vallance Rd.
The Blind Beggar
Mile End Rd.
Lamb St.
Brick La.
Spitalfields Market
Brushfield St.
Christ Church, Spitalfields
Fashion St.
Hanbury St.
Greatorex St.
Old Montague St.
Whitechapel
U
Whitechapel Rd.
Raven Row
Stepney Way
Liverpool St. Station
Market Coffee House
White's Row
Royal London Hospital
Cavell St.
Sidney St.
U Liverpool Street
Bishopsgate
Houndsditch
Middlesex St.
Castle St.
Whitechapel Bell Foundry
Myrtle St.
New Rd.
Settles St.
Greenfield Rd.
Varden St.
Nelson St.
Stepney Way
Whitechapel Art Gallery
U Aldgate East
Adler St.
Ragged School Museum
Aldgate U
Whitechapel High St.
Braham St.
Alie St.
Gowers Wk.
Cannon St.
Commercial Rd.
Docklands
Bigland St.

0   1/4 mi
0   1/4 km

TOP REASONS TO GO

The Jack the Ripper Walk: Track the very footsteps of the world's most infamous serial killer through the Victorian slum streets he once called his own—unforgettable.

Geffrye Museum: This magical collection of period rooms—rich in antiques, brocades, and crystal—offers a peek into the lives of extraordinary Londoners through the years.

Fast Forward to the 1880s: Take a "candlelight" tour of a gorgeous Georgian town house, stage-set to replicate the life of a 19th-century grandee at Dennis Severs' House.

Skip the Light Fantastic: Have a hedonistic night out bar- and club-crawling in Hoxton and Shoreditch.

The Coolest, Hottest Art Scene: The East End isn't pictur-esque, but the art scene here is vibrant, colorful, and excit-ing—small galleries are interspersed with larger collections.

FEELING PECKISH?

Inside Spitalfields Market is **Canteen** (☎ 0845/686–1122), an open-floor-plan eatery with long communal tables that serves British dishes made with additive-free ingredients.

For some of the finest coffee in London (by way of New Zealand), go to **Nude Espresso** (✉ 26 Hanbury St. ☎ 0780/422–3590). The best beans, machines, and baristas are complemented by delicious sandwiches and cakes.

SAFETY

Around the central hubs of Hoxton, Shoreditch, Spitalfields, and Brick Lane, you're unlikely to experience any trouble during daylight hours; even after dark it's relatively safe. However, if you're venturing into Whitechapel or out toward Bethnal Green and Mile End, be on your guard at all times.

GETTING THERE

The best Tube stops to start from are Whitechapel or Aldgate East on the District–Hammersmith & City lines, and Aldgate on the Metropolitan and Circle lines.

MAKING THE MOST OF YOUR TIME

To experience the East End at its most lively, make sure you visit on the weekend—here it's possible to shop, eat, drink, and party your way through a whole 72 hours. Spitalfields Market bustles all weekend, whereas Brick Lane is at its best on a Sunday morning—also the time to visit Columbia Road for its glorious flower market.

If you're planning to explore the East End art scene, pick up a free art map at the Whitechapel Art Gallery to help you navigate around the many small galleries and art spaces.

As far as nightlife, there's no time limit here. Start after shop-ping—Hoxton's bars are your best bet—and finish as far into the following morning as your stamina will allow.

A GOOD WALK

There are some thrilling walks that illustrate the progress of Jack and other murderers around the East End: recom-mended is the **Blood and Tears Walk: London's Horrible Past** (☎ 020/7625–5155), led by researcher and actor Declan McHugh, which departs daily from Barbican Tube Station.

7

Made famous by Dickens and infamous by Jack the Ripper, the East End is one of London's most enduringly evocative neighborhoods. It may have fewer conventional tourist attractions but it's rich in folk history, architectural gems, and feisty burgeoning culture. Once home to French Huguenots, then Ashkenazi Jews, the area now has a large Bangladeshi community. Since the early 1990s the area has also attracted students and hipsters in the art and fashion fields, all lured by the grand old industrial spaces.

Updated
by Mish
Rosenberg

Nowadays the East End is London's most culturally diverse area. East of Whitechapel Road are the famous **Whitechapel Art Gallery;** the Whitechapel Bell Foundry; and **Brick Lane,** the heart of the Bangladeshi East End, filled with innumerable curry houses and glittering sari shops, and also home to the **Old Truman Brewery,** now converted to studios and gallery space. The Sunday morning junk market on Brick Lane adds further complements to the rewarding vintage-clothes shopping in this area.

Since the East End was heavily bombed in World War II, and subsequently rebuilt with public housing estates, it's not the best-looking part of the capital, although pockets of historic buildings do remain. Nicholas Hawksmoor's masterpiece, **Christ Church, Spitalfields** soars above Fournier Street, alongside some fine early Georgian houses. For a sensory experience of Georgian life, visit **Dennis Severs's House.** Kids enjoy **Spitalfields City Farm** and, to the east in Bethnal Green, the quirky **V&A Museum of Childhood.** Farther east still, toward Mile End, are the former Trinity Almshouses, with the statue of William Booth on the very spot where the first Salvation Army meetings were held, and the notorious **Blind Beggar** pub. The immense **Royal London Hospital** and its museum are just a few yards away.

Today Spitalfields and Shoreditch are London's most exciting bohemian neighborhoods, together with Hoxton, just north of here. There are stylish boutiques (especially on Cheshire Street) and cafés, artists' studios, and galleries in the plentiful old, derelict industrial spaces that were bought up cheaply and have been imaginatively remodeled. **Spitalfields Market,** with its arts and crafts and design booths, is open daily, but weekends are the liveliest. In Shoreditch, **Columbia Road** on Sunday (8–2) gets buried under forests of shrubs and blooms of all shapes and sizes during London's main plant and **flower market.** The **Geffrye Museum** occupies a row of early-18th-century almshouses, and that bastion of contemporary art, the East End branch of the **White Cube** gallery, lies to the west in the very hip Hoxton Square.

> **WORD OF MOUTH**
>
> "The Geffrye Museum is off the beaten tourist path. It's well worth checking out [the museum's] special events. I attended a ceramics fair there in the fall, which featured many wonderful contemporary artists. Around the holidays, various rooms are decorated in period style. My daughter and I have enjoyed that on a couple of occasions."
>
> —obxgirl

TOP ATTRACTIONS

Fodor'sChoice ★ **Geffrye Museum.** Here's where you can discover what life was really like for the general masses in London (and it's different from the grand, high-society town-house interiors of the rich royal boroughs). It's a small museum where you can walk through a series of room sets that re-create everyday domestic interiors from the Elizabethan period through postwar 1950s utility to the present day. Originally, the museum was a row of almshouses for the poor (built in 1716 by Sir Robert Geffrye, former lord mayor of London) that provided shelter for 50 pensioners over the course of 200 years. The houses were rescued from closure by keen petitioners (the inhabitants were relocated to a healthier part of town) and were transformed into the Geffrye Museum in 1914. The former almshouses were restored to their original condition, with most of the internal woodwork intact, including the staircase, upper floors, closets, and paneling. There are also displays on the almshouses' history and on the kinds of people who lived there. To discover more, you can also attend a regular "bring a room to life" talk. The museum's extension wing houses the 20th-century galleries, a lovely café overlooking the garden, and a bookshop. ⊠ *136 Kingsland Rd., East End* ☎ *020/7739–9893* ⊕ *www.geffrye-museum.org.uk* ✉ *Free* ☉ *Tues.–Sat. 10–5, Sun. and bank holidays noon–5* Ⓤ *Old St., then Bus 243; Liverpool St., then Bus 149 or 242.*

Fodor'sChoice ★ **Dennis Severs' House.** Enter this extraordinary time machine of a house with your imagination primed to take part in the plot. The Georgian terraced house belonged to the eponymous performer-designer-scholar from Escondido, California, who dedicated his life not only to restoring his house but also to raising the ghosts of a fictitious Jervis family that might have inhabited it over the course of two centuries. Dennis Severs (1944–99) created a replica of Georgian life, without electricity but with a butler in full 18th-century livery to light the candles and lay the fires—for the Jervises. The 10 rooms are shadowy set pieces

7

of rose-laden Victorian wallpapers, Jacobean paneling, Georgian wing chairs, baroque carved ornaments, "Protestant" colors (upstairs), and "Catholic" shades (downstairs). ■TIP→ The "Silent Night" candlelight tours, each Monday, are the most theatrical and memorable way to "feel" the house; a magical experience relished by both Londoners and out-of-towners. ⊠ *18 Folgate St., East End* ☎ *020/7247–4013* ⊕ *www. dennissevershouse.co.uk* ⊡ *£8 for Sun., £5 for Mon. open house; £12 for candlelight Mon. evening* ⊙ *1st and 3rd Sun. of month 2–5, 1st and 3rd Mon. noon–2. Call for hrs for "Silent Night" Mon., reservations essential* Ⓤ *Liverpool St.*

Spitalfields Market. There's been a market here since the mid-17th century, but the current version is overflowing with crafts and design shops, stalls, bars, and restaurants (with a global palette, from tapas to Thai), and different-purpose markets every day of the week. Look out for work by young designers, whose one-off accessories make original gifts, and join the office workers for some pie and mash. ■TIP→ The nearer the weekend, the busier it all gets, culminating in the arts-and-crafts and green market on Sunday—the best day to go. *For more on Spitalfields, see* ⇨ *Chapter 18, Shopping.* ⊠ *Commercial St. between Lamb and Brushfield Sts., East End* ☎ *020/7247–8556* ⊕ *www.visitspitalfields.com* ⊡ *Free* ⊙ *Daily 10–7; market stalls Thurs. and Fri, 10–4, Sun. 9–5* Ⓤ *Liverpool St.*

★ **V&A Museum of Childhood.** What more do you need to say? This is the world's biggest toy collection. Actually, the East End outpost of the Victoria & Albert Museum—in fact, this entire iron, glass, and brown-brick building was transported here from South Kensington in 1875—its contents have grown into a must-see for children of all ages. One highlight (among many) is the large Dolls' Houses collection—a bit like the Geffrye Museum zapped into miniature, with houses of every period. Each genre of plaything has its own enclosure, so if teddy bears are your weakness, you need waste no time with the train sets or board games. The museum's title is justified in the fascinating galleries on the social history of childhood from baby dolls to Beanie Babies. Don't miss the magnificent 18th-century puppet theater, thought to have been made in Venice to show *commedia dell'arte* (comedy of art) plays. ⊠ *Cambridge Heath Rd., East End* ☎ *020/8983–5200* ⊕ *www.vam.ac.uk/moc* ⊡ *Free* ⊙ *Daily 10–5:45, last admission 5:30* Ⓤ *Bethnal Green.*

★ **Whitechapel Art Gallery.** Founded in 1901, this gallery underwent an ambitious £13 million expansion program that doubled its exhibition space in 2009. The Whitechapel bought the library next door and has created fabulous new galleries alongside facilities for talks, events, film, music, and poetry. The Whitechapel has an international reputation for its shows, which are often on the cutting edge of contemporary art. The American painter Jackson Pollock exhibited here

DID YOU KNOW?

On Sunday, the Columbia Road Flower's Market opens at 8 am. Arrive early to see the photogenic market in full sway and at its best. Victorian shops nearby sell horticultural wares, accessories, and antiques.

EAST END STREET SMARTS

Brick Lane and the narrow streets running off it offer a paradigm of the East End's development. Its population has moved in waves: communities seeking refuge, others moving out in an upwardly mobile direction.

Brick Lane has seen the manufacture of bricks (during the 16th century), beer, and bagels, but nowadays it's becoming the hub of artistic bohemia, especially at the Old Truman Brewery with its calendar of diverse cultural activities. It's also the heart of Banglatown—Bangladeshis make up one-third of the population in this London borough, and you'll see that the surrounding streets have their names written in Bengali—where you find many kebab and curry houses along with shops selling videos, colorful saris, and stacks of sticky sweets. On Sunday morning the entire street becomes pedestrianized. Shops and cafés are open, and several stalls are set up making it a companion market to the nearby **Petticoat Lane.**

Flower and Dean streets, past the ugly 1970s housing project on **Thrawl Street** (and once the most disreputable street in London) was where Abe Saperstein, founder of the Harlem Globetrotters, was born in 1902.

Fournier Street contains fine examples of the neighborhood's characteristic Georgian terraced houses, many of them built by the richest of the early-18th-century Huguenot silk weavers (note the enlarged windows on the upper floors). Most of those along the north side of Fournier Street have been restored by conservationists; others still contain textile sweatshops—only now the workers are Bengali.

Wilkes Street, with more 1720s Huguenot houses, is north of the Christ Church, Spitalfields, and neighboring **Princelet Street** was once important to the East End's Jewish community. Where No. 6 stands now, the first of several thriving Yiddish theaters opened in 1886, playing to packed houses until the following year, when a false fire alarm, rung during a January performance, ended with 17 people being crushed to death and so demoralized the theater's actor-founder, Jacob Adler, that he moved his troupe to New York. Adler played a major role in founding that city's great Yiddish theater tradition—which, in turn, had a significant effect on Hollywood.

Elder Street, just off Folgate, is another gem of original 18th-century houses. On the south and east side of Spitalfields Market are yet more time-warp streets that are worth a wander, such as **Gun Street**, where artist Mark Gertler (1891–1939) lived at No. 32.

in the 1950s, as did pop artist Robert Rauschenberg in the 1960s; David Hockney had his first solo show here in the 1970s. Pick up a free East End art map to help you with the rest of your gallery hopping. ■TIP➜ Late-night music events take place on Friday in the café-bar from 8 pm to 11 pm. ✉ 77–82 *Whitechapel High St., East End* ☎ *020/7522–7888* ⊕ *www.whitechapelgallery.org* ✑ *Free* ☉ *Tues.– Sun. 11–6* Ⓤ *Aldgate East.*

CLOSE UP

Blimey, Gov'nor, It's Jack the Ripper!

Gigantic shadows, fires blazing on the corner, leering looks by the homeless, and the spirit of "Jack" himself: all may show up on one of London's most unforgettable experiences, the "Jack the Ripper Walk" that tracks the very footsteps of the world's most infamous serial killer. You'll see the deserted squares ("Did you know that you're standing on the very spot where his second victim was found?"), warehouse alleys, and the ground-floor flat—today occupied by an Indian restaurant—where he literally butchered poor Marie Kelly.

At No. 90 Whitechapel High Street once stood George Yard Buildings, where Jack the Ripper's first victim, Martha Turner, was discovered in August 1888. A second murder occurred some weeks later, and Hanbury Street, behind a seedy lodging house at No. 29, is where Jack the Ripper left his third mutilated victim, "Dark" Annie Chapman. A double murder followed, and then, after a month's lull, came the death on this street of Marie Kelly, the Ripper's last victim and his most revolting murder of all. He had been able to work indoors this time, and Kelly, a young widow, was found strewn all over the room, charred remains of her clothing in the fire grate. Jack the Ripper's identity never has been discovered, although theories abound, including, among others, the cover-up of a prominent member of the British aristocracy, the artist Walter Sickert, and Francis Tumblety, an American quack doctor.

Today, many outfitters offer walking tours of the Victorian slum streets that once Jack called his own: the most popular is run by Original London Walks (⊕ www.walks.com) and lead by Donald Rumbelow, "the leading authority on Jack the Ripper"; it leaves every night from Tower Hill at 7:30 pm (Don only shows up a few nights a week).

WORTH NOTING

The Blind Beggar. This is the dark and rather dingy Victorian den of iniquity where Salvation Army founder William Booth preached his first sermon. On the south side of the street stands a stone inscribed "Here William Booth commenced the work of the salvation army, July 1865," marking the position of the first Sally Army platform; back by the pub a statue of William Booth stands where the first meetings were held. Booth didn't supply the pub's main claim to fame, though. The Blind Beggar's real notoriety dates only from March 1966, when Ronnie Kray—one of the Kray twins, the former gangster kings of London's East End underworld—shot dead rival "godfather" George Cornell in the saloon bar. The original Albion Brewery, celebrated home to the first bottled brown ale, was next door. ⊠ 337 Whitechapel Rd., East End Ⓤ Whitechapel.

Christ Church, Spitalfields. This is the 1729 masterpiece of Sir Christopher Wren's associate Nicholas Hawksmoor. Hawksmoor built six London churches; this one was commissioned as part of Parliament's 1711 "Fifty New Churches Act." The idea was to score points for the Church of England against such nonconformists as the Protestant

On Sunday, additional clothing and crafts stalls surround Spitalfields covered market.

Huguenots. (It must have worked; in the churchyard, you can still see some of their gravestones, with epitaphs in French.) As the local silk industry declined, the church fell into disrepair, and by 1958 the structure was crumbling, with the looming prospect of demolition. But after 25 years—longer than it took to build—and a huge local effort to gather funds, the structure was completely restored and is a joy to behold, from the colonnaded portico and tall spire to its bold, strident baroque-style interior. As a concert venue it truly comes into its own. ■ TIP→ If you're lucky enough to be in town during the Spitalfields Festival held every summer and winter, don't miss the chance to attend a classical concert in this atmospheric ecclesiastical venue. ✉ *Commercial St., East End* ☎ *020/7377–2440* ☉ *Tues. 11–4, Sun. 1–4* Ⓤ *Aldgate East.*

OFF THE BEATEN PATH **Estorick Collection.** West of Hoxton, on the eastern end of the affluent, yuppie borough of Islington, is this small, restored Georgian mansion with an extraordinary collection of early-20th-century Italian art. The works were acquired by Eric Estorick, an American collector and sociologist, who was particularly keen on Italian Futurists; there are works by Balla, Boccioni, and Severini, among others. The downstairs Estorick Caffè is a good place to grab a bite, especially in summer when you can sit outdoors. ✉ *39A Canonbury Sq., off Canonbury Rd., Islington* ☎ *020/7704–9522* ⊕ *www.estorickcollection.com* 🎫 *£5* ☉ *Wed., Fri., and Sat. 11–6, Thurs. 11–8, Sun. noon–5* Ⓤ *Highbury & Islington.*

Old Truman Brewery. This is the only one of the former East End breweries still standing. It's a handsome example of Georgian and 19th-century industrial architecture; in 1873, it was the largest brewery in the world. The buildings, which straddle Brick Lane, are a conglomeration of art,

The East End Art Scene

It was only inevitable that the once arty Islington area (the N1 postal district, which rubs streets with the less elegant end of the Regent's Canal toward The City, EC1) would become too expensive and gentrified for the artists themselves. Hoxton, on a corner of Islington just off the City Road, with its cheap industrial units and more artisan Georgian–Victorian terraced streets, was the logical next stop.

The seal of boho approval came when Damien Hirst's agent and the most important modern art dealer in town, Jay Jopling, set up the White Cube gallery at 48 Hoxton Square. Impoverished artists, however, are not newcomers to the area—in the 1960s, Bridget Riley set up an outfit here to find affordable studio space for British artists—but the latest wave this side of the millennium has changed the face of this formerly down-at-the-heels neighborhood. It's now undeniably hip to be in Hoxton.

From the Barbican in The City to Whitechapel in the East End, as many as 25 art galleries have opened, showing the latest works of the YBAs (Young British Artists). A spread of trendy real estate has taken a firm grip across the City Road into E1, principally Shoreditch, Spitalfields, and "Banglatown"—the nickname for the neighborhood around Brick Lane where Bengali shops and homes have created a slice of south Asia. Where less-than-glam buildings for the poor (such as the Jewish Soup Kitchen off Commercial Street, Spitalfields) once stood are now loft-style luxury apartments. Boutiques, bars, clubs, and restaurants have followed in their wake, and the Eastside—as it has been coined—is unapologetically brimming with energy.

craft, and photo studios, and are now established as the capital of cool. The Atlantis Gallery, host of the sell-out *Body Worlds* exhibition in 2002, is a major focus—visitors were crammed inside to watch a live autopsy as part of the show. Less controversial events include fashion showcases for young, upcoming designers, and fringe events. The Vibe Bar is a hot spot to chill out behind a traditional Georgian facade—it also has a great outdoor space. ⊠ *91 Brick La., East End* ⊕ *www. trumanbrewery.com* Ⓤ *Aldgate East.*

Founded in 1740, the Royal London was once as nasty as its former neighborhood near the Tower of London. Waste was carried out in buckets and dumped in the street; bedbugs and alcoholic nurses were problems; according to hospital records patients didn't die— they were "relieved." In 1757 the hospital moved to its present site, and the original building forms the core of the one you see today. By then it had become one of the best hospitals in London, and it was enhanced further by the addition of a small medical school in 1785, and again, 70 years later, by an entire state-of-the-art medical college. Thomas John Barnardo, who went on to found the famous Dr. Barnardo's Homes for Orphans, came to train here in 1866. Ten years later the hospital grew to become the largest in the United Kingdom, and now, though mostly rebuilt since World War II, it remains one of London's most capacious. To get an idea of the huge medical leaps forward, walk through the main entrance and garden to the crypt of St. Augustine within St. Philip's Church (alternatively, go directly two blocks south to the entrance on Newark Street), to the **Royal London Hospital Museum** (☉ *Weekdays 10–4:30*), where displays of medical paraphernalia, objects, and documentation illustrate the more-than-250-year history of this East London institution. The museum often closes on short notice, so call before you go. ⊠ *Whitechapel Rd., East End* ☎ *020/7377–7608* ⊕ *www.medicalmuseums.org* ⊠ *Free* ☉ *Hospital and garden daily 9–6* Ⓤ *Whitechapel.*

☾　**Spitalfields City Farm.** This little community farm, squashed into an urban landscape, raises a selection of farm animals, including some rare breeds, to help educate city kids in country matters. A tiny farm shop sells freshly laid eggs and also organic seasonal produce. ⊠ *Buxton St., East End* ☎ *020/7247–8762* ⊕ *www.spitalfieldscityfarm.org* ⊠ *Free* ☉ *Tues.–Sun. 10–4:30* Ⓤ *Aldgate East, Whitechapel, Bethnal Green.*

White Cube. The original White Cube had cramped quarters in genteel St. James's—this outpost was set up to take advantage of the massive open spaces of the East End's former industrial units. Damien Hirst (arguably the leader of the Britart phenomenon who gained notoriety for preserving animals in formaldehyde as art, and whose recent auction of work netted a cool $198 million), Tracey Emin, Gilbert and George, Sam Taylor-Wood, and other trailblazers have shown here and gone on to become internationally renowned. The building looks, appropriately enough, like a white cube—it has a glassed-in upper level called "Inside the White Cube," where international guest curators are invited to show their projects. ⊠ *48 Hoxton Sq., Hoxton* ☎ *020/7930–5373* ⊕ *www. whitecube.com* ⊠ *Free* ☉ *Tues.–Sat. 10–6* Ⓤ *Old St.*

The South Bank

WORD OF MOUTH

"We did the Eye, buying tickets just before sunset on a clear day and felt it was worth the time and money. Line only took 5–10 minutes. Great experience, even those in our group who had issues with heights soon overcame that. . . . Agree it is so slow moving you won't have a 'ride' experience—it is for the VIEW."

—jeanOH

GETTING ORIENTED

GETTING THERE	TOP REASONS TO GO
For the South Bank use Westminster station on the Jubilee or Northern line, from where you can walk across Westminster Bridge; Embankment on District, Circle, Northern, and Bakerloo lines, where you can walk across Hungerford Bridge; or Waterloo on the Jubilee, Northern, and Bakerloo lines, where it's a 5-minute walk to the Royal Festival Hall. In the east, alternatively, use Tower Gateway on the Docklands Light Railway (DLR). London Bridge on the Northern and Jubilee lines is a 5-minute stroll from Borough Market and Southwark Cathedral.	**Shakespeare's Globe Theatre:** Catch a performance as a "groundling" (in the standing-room pit) while being caught up in a performance of one of the Bard's great plays in the recreated "Wooden O." **Tate Modern:** One of the world's great shrines of contemporary and modern art, this branch of the Tate is served up in a spectacularly renovated electric turbine hall. **The London Dungeon:** Did you ever imagine what a disembowelment looks like? Well, here's your chance to visit a real old-fashioned "chamber of horrors," which showcase tableaux depicting all forms of medieval torture. You'll be amazed how many children adore this place. **Borough Market:** Arrive hungry and gorge your way through stalls of organic produce at London's oldest food market. **Golden Jubilee Bridges:** Walk across the footbridge at dusk, then east along a fairy-light embankment toward the Oxo Tower.

MAKING THE MOST OF YOUR TIME

Don't attempt the South Bank all in one go. Not only will you exhaust yourself, but you will miss out on the varied delights that it has to offer.

The Tate Modern alone deserves a whole morning or afternoon, especially if you want to do justice to both the temporary exhibitions and the permanent collection.

The Globe requires about two hours for the exhibition theater tour and two to three hours for a performance. Finish with drinks or dinner at the Oxo Tower or a stroll west along the riverbank and then across the Golden Jubilee Bridges.

As for other ways of returning across the river to central London, keep in mind that you can use Southwark on the Jubilee Line from Tate Modern, although it's a good 15-minute walk from the station. It's perhaps more enjoyable to use St. Paul's on the Central Line, where you can cross the Millennium Bridge, or Embankment, which are longer walks, but pass through more alluring scenery.

8

FEELING PECKISH?

At Gabriel's Wharf have a sit-down meal at the **Gourmet Pizza Co.** (✉ *56 Upper Ground, Gabriel's Wharf* ☎ *020/7928–3188*) or grab a sandwich or coffee at one of the smaller establishments open during the day here.

For exquisite handmade pastries, along with daily specials such as chicken paella or vegetarian moussaka, stop at the bijou premises of **Konditor & Cook** (✉ *10 Stoney St.* ☎ *020/7407–5100*), one of the stars of the handful of eateries nearby Borough Market. Alternatively, just dive into the crowds of the market itself and grab something from its many and varied food stalls. It's all good.

SAFETY

At night, it's best to stick to where the action is at the Butler's Wharf and Gabriel's Wharf restaurants, the Oxo Tower, the National Theatre, the National Film Theatre, and the Royal Festival Hall. Stray farther south of the embankment and it quickly begins to feel deserted.

Sightseeing
★★★★★
Nightlife
★★★★
Dining
★★★
Lodging
★
Shopping
★★

That old, snide North London dig about needing a passport to cross the Thames has not been heard for the past five years. For decades, natives rarely ventured beyond the watery curtain that divides the city in half; tourists, too, rarely troubled the area unless they were departing from Waterloo Station. But lately, a host of new attractions are drawing even the most ardent Northerners across the great divide. The reconstructed Shakespeare's Globe Theatre—the most famous theater in the world—steals the show, but the Tate Modern is also a huge draw, a monolithic ex-power station turned museum. And dominating the skyline is the London Eye ferris wheel. In more ways that one, South Londoners are beginning to look down on their northern cousins.

Updated
by Mish
Rosenberg

Culture, history, sights: The South Bank has emerged as one of the capital's most creative hubs. Stretching from the Imperial War Museum in the southwest as far as the Design Museum in the east, high-caliber art, music, film, and theater venues at the **Globe Theatre** and **Tate Modern** are up alongside the likes of an aquarium, historic warships, and a foodie-favorite market. The **Southbank Centre** is home to the recently renovated **Royal Festival Hall**, the **Hayward Gallery**, the **BFI Southbank**, and the **National Theatre**. East near **Butlers Wharf**, the ultrachic Design Museum occupies what was once a dingy Dickensian shadowland.

Actually, it is fitting that so much of London's artistic life should once again be centered here on the South Bank—back in the days of Ye Olde London Towne, Southwark was the city's oldest borough and noted for being London's outlaw neighborhood. Just across London Bridge, it was conveniently outside the city walls and was therefore the ideal location for the theaters, taverns, and cock-fighting arenas—not to mention brothels—that served as after-hours entertainment in the Middle Ages. Today, however, the **Thames Path** is alive with legal activity, especially in summer, with skateboarders, secondhand-book stalls, and street entertainers. Several footbridges cross the Thames, including the curvaceous **Millennium Bridge,** connecting the Tate Modern to St. Paul's Cathedral, and the **Golden Jubilee Bridges,** with the best view of the Houses of Parliament on the embankment between Westminster and Lambeth bridges. In the shadow of the **Oxo Tower** sits **Gabriel's Wharf,** a small marketplace of shops and restaurants. Sir Francis Drake's ship, the *Golden Hinde,* nestles in Pickfords Wharf and the massive domed **City Hall** lies next to **Tower Bridge.** Just a short walk east, Bermondsey (or "Beormund's Eye" as it was known in Saxon times), with its artist studios and pretty streets, is being bought up by fashion-conscious homemakers in search of the new Hoxton. A millennium project that's a favorite with both Londoners and out-of-towners alike, the **London Eye** is next to the **London Aquarium.** The grisly delights of the **London Dungeon** is a favorite for kids. After all this sightseeing, grab a bite at the legendary **Borough Market** (the rowdier neighbor of **Southwark Cathedral**). "London's Larder" has become an essential foodie destination, where celebrity chefs go in search of farm-fresh produce.

TOP ATTRACTIONS

The Globe Theatre.

Fodor's Choice ★ *See the highlighted listing in this chapter.*

Golden Hinde. Sir Francis Drake circumnavigated the globe in this little galleon, or one just like it. This exact replica made a 23-year round-the-world voyage—much of it spent along U.S. coasts, both Pacific and Atlantic—and has settled here to continue its educational purpose. Call to confirm opening hours and for information on guided tours. ✉ *Units 1 & 2, Pickfords Wharf, Clink St., South Bank* ☎ *020/7403–0123* ⊕ *www.goldenhinde.com* 🎫 *£6* ⊗ *Daily 10–5:30* Ⓤ *London Bridge, Mansion House.*

QUICK BITES

Gabriel's Wharf. This cluster of specialty shops, cafés, and restaurants is part of the Coin Street Community neighborhood and bustles with activity during the daytime. You can rent bicycles here from the London Bicycle Tour Company (☎ *020/7928–6838*). ✉ *56 Upper Ground, South Bank* ☎ *020/7021–1686* ⊕ *www.coinstreet.org* 🎫 *Free* ⊗ *Shops and studios Tues.–Sun. 11–6* Ⓤ *Blackfriars, Waterloo.*

Hayward Gallery. The gray, windowless bunker tucked behind the Southbank Centre concert halls has had to bear the brunt of architectural criticism over the years, but that's changed with a foyer extension that gives more daylight, more space for exhibits, a café, and better access. The highlight of the project is an elliptical mirrored glass pavilion by New York–based artist Dan Graham. Exhibitions here encompass a range of art media, crossing history and cultures, bridging the experimental and established. It's consistently on the cutting edge of new developments in art and critical theory, finding new ways to present the well known, from

8

Picasso to Lichtenstein, and providing a prominent platform for up-and-coming artists. ■TIP→ A small part of the gallery is always reserved for free exhibitions. ⊠ *Southbank Centre, South Bank* ☎ *020/7921–0813* ⊕ *www. hayward.org.uk* ⊠ *Varies; usually around £10* ☉ *Sat.–Thurs. 10–6, Fri. 10–10* Ⓤ *Waterloo.*

☺ ★ **London Eye.** To mark the start of the new millennium, architects David Marks and Julia Barfield conceived an entirely new vision: a beautiful and celebratory structure that would allow people to see this great city from a completely new perspective—on a giant wheel. As well as representing the turning of the century, a wheel was seen as a symbol of regeneration and the passing of time. The London Eye is the largest observation wheel ever built and among the top 10 tallest structures in London. The 25-minute slow-motion ride inside one of the enclosed passenger capsules is so smooth you'd hardly know you were suspended over the Thames, moving slowly around. On a clear day you can take in a range of up to 25 mi, viewing London's most famous landmarks from a fascinating angle. If you're looking for a special place to celebrate, champagne and canapés can be arranged ahead of time. ■TIP→ Buy your ticket online, over the phone, or at the ticket office in advance to avoid the long lines and get a 10% discount. For an extra £10, you can save even more time with a Fast Track flight for which you check in 15 minutes before your "departure." There's also the option of buying a combination ticket for the Eye with other London attractions—check online for details. The London Eye sightseeing cruise also departs here for a 40-minute cruise of the Thames. ⊠ *Jubilee Gardens, South Bank* ☎ *0870/990–8883* ⊕ *www.londoneye.com* ⊠ *£17.95, cruise £12* ☉ *June and Sept., daily 10–9; July and Aug., daily 10–9:30; Oct.–Mar., daily 10–8* Ⓤ *Waterloo.*

Oxo Tower. Long a London landmark to the insider, the Art Deco–era Oxo building has graduated from its former incarnations as a power-generating station and warehouse into a vibrant community of artists' and designers' workshops, a pair of restaurants, and five floors of community homes. There's an observation deck for a super river vista (St. Paul's to the east and Somerset House to the west), and a performance area on the first floor, which comes alive all summer long—as does the entire surrounding neighborhood. All the artisans expect you to disturb them whenever they're open, whether buying, commissioning, or just browsing. The biggest draw remains the Oxo Tower Restaurant for a meal or a martini. ⊠ *Bargehouse St., South Bank* ☎ *020/7021–1686* ⊕ *www.oxotower.co.uk* ⊠ *Free*

THE ELEPHANT IN THE ROOM

Look at a map of south London, and just below the South Bank you'll see an area called Elephant and Castle. It's not one of London's nicer districts—don't bother visiting—but you might wonder how it got such a fairy-tale name. The most popular story concerns a Spanish princess, betrothed to a prince and sent to England while she was still a little girl. A castle was built for her just outside the city walls, where she was looked after until she was old enough to be married. The name is therefore thought to be a corruption of the Spanish *Infanta de Castile*.

Continued on page 160

"Within this wooden O..."

—William Shakespeare, Henry V

SHAKESPEARE AND THE GLOBE THEATRE

At Shakespeare's Globe Theatre, they say the Bard does not belong to the British; he belongs to the world. Not a day has gone by since the Restoration when one of his plays isn't being performed or reinterpreted somewhere. But here, at the site of the original Globe, in a painstaking reconstruction of Shakespeare's own open-air theater, is where seeing one of his plays can take on an ethereal quality.

If you are exceedingly well read and a lover of the Bard, then chances are a pilgrimage to his Globe Theatre is already on your list. But if Shakespeare's works leave you wondering why exactly the play is the thing, then a trip to the Globe—to learn more about his life or to see his words come alive—is a must.

The Globe Theatre in Shakespeare's Day

In the 16th and 17th centuries, a handful of theaters—the Rose, the Swan, the Globe, and others whose names are lost—rose above the higgledy-piggledy jumble of rooftops in London's rowdy Southwark neighborhood. They were round or octagonal open-air playhouses, with galleries for the "quality" members of society, and large, open pits for the raucous mobs. People from all social classes, from royalty down to the hoi polloi, shared the communal experience of drama in these places. Shakespeare's Globe was one.

A fire in 1613 destroyed the first Globe, which was quickly rebuilt; however, Oliver Cromwell and waves of other reformers put an end to all the Southwark playhouses in the 1640s. By the time American actor and director Sam Wanamaker visited in 1949, the only indication that the world's greatest dramatist created popular entertainment here was a plaque on a brewery wall. Wanamaker was shocked to find that all evidence of the playwright's legendary playhouse had vanished into air.

And thereby hangs a tale.

Wanamaker's Dream

Over the next several decades, Wanamaker devoted himself to the Bard. He was director of the New Shakespeare Theatre in Liverpool and, in 1959, joined the Shakespeare Memorial Theatre Company (now the Royal Shakespeare Company) at Stratford-upon-Avon. Finally, in the 1970s he began the project

8

SHAKESPEARE'S ALL-TIME TOP 10

1. *Romeo and Juliet.* Young love, teenage rebellion, and tragedy are the ingredients of the greatest tearjerker of all time.

2. *Hamlet* (*right*). The very model of a modern antihero and origin of the most quoted line of any play: "To be or not to be…"

3. *A Midsummer Night's Dream.* Spells and potions abound as the gods use humans for playthings; lovers' tiffs are followed by happy endings for all.

4. *Othello.* Jealousy poisons love and destroys a proud man.

5. *The Taming of the Shrew.* The eternal battle of the sexes.

6. *Macbeth.* Ambition, murder, and revenge. Evil gets its just reward.

7. *The Merry Wives of Windsor.* A two-timing rascal gets his comeuppance from a pack of hysterically funny gossips.

8. *Richard III.* One of literature's juiciest villains. The whole audience wants to hiss.

9. *The Tempest.* On a desert island, the concerns of men amaze and amuse the innocent Miranda: "Oh brave new world, that has such people in't."

10. *King Lear.* A tragedy of old age, filial love, and grasping, ungrateful children.

that would dominate the rest of his life: reconstructing Shakespeare's theater, as close to the original site as possible.

Today's Globe was re-created using authentic Elizabethan materials and craft techniques—green oak timbers joined only with wooden pegs and mortise-and-tenon joints; plaster made of lime, sand, and goat's hair; and the first thatched roof in London since the Great Fire of 1666. The complex, 200 yards from the site of the original Globe, includes an exhibition center, cafés, and restaurants. (The shell of a 17th-century-style theater, built adjacent to the Globe to a design by Inigo Jones, awaits further funds for completion.)

FUN FACT: Plays are presented in the open air (and sometimes the rain) to an audience of 1,000 on wooden benches in the bays, and 500 "groundlings," who stand on a carpet of hazelnut shells and cinder, just as they did nearly four centuries ago.

The eventual realization of Wanamaker's dream, a full-scale, accurate replica of the Globe, was the keystone that supported the revitalization of the entire district. The new Globe celebrates Shakespeare, his work, and his times, and as an educational trust it is dedicated to making the Bard continually fresh and accessible for new audiences. Sadly, Wanamaker died before construction was completed, in 1997. In Southwark Cathedral, a few hundred yards west of the Globe, a memorial to him stands beside the statue memorializing Shakespeare himself.

The season of plays is limited to the warmer months, from May to the first week in October, with the schedule announced in late January on the theater's Web site. Tickets go on sale in mid-February. The box office takes phone and mail orders as well as in-person sales, but the most convenient way to buy tickets is online. Book as early as possible.

FUN FACT: "Groundlings"—those with £5 standing-only tickets—are not allowed to sit during the performance. Reserve an actual seat, though, on any one of the theater's three levels, and you can join the "Elizabethan" crowd.

If you do have a seat, you can rent cushions for £1 (or bring your own) to soften the backless wooden benches. A limited number of backrests are also available for rent for £4. The show must go on, rain or shine, warm or chilly—so come prepared for whatever the weather throws at you. Umbrellas are banned, but you can bring a raincoat or buy a cheap Globe rain poncho, which doubles as a great souvenir.

MAKING THE MOST OF YOUR TIME
Give yourself plenty of time: there are several cafés and restaurants, as well as fascinating interactive exhibitions, and theater tours with occasional live demonstrations. Performances can last up to three hours.

SPECIAL EVENT

The Frost Fair, held annually the weekend before Christmas, commemorates several extraordinary winters in the 17th century when the Thames froze over and fairs took place on the ice. It includes street theater, Morris Dancing, sword fighting, and food and crafts stalls. Admission is free, and there is special reduced admission to the Theatre and Exhibition during the fair.

WITH CHILDREN
Childsplay, a program for 8- to 11-year-olds, is held every Saturday during the theatre season. While Mom and Dad enjoy the play, children—helped by actors, musicans, and teachers—learn the background and story and become accustomed to Shakespearean language. By the time they are admitted to the theater for the last 20 minutes of the play, the children have become Shakespeare enthusiasts for life. Workshops start at 1:30 pm and tickets are £12.50; book in advance.

IN FOCUS SHAKESPEARE AND THE GLOBE THEATRE

Year-Round at Shakespeare's Globe

Shakespeare's Globe Exhibition is a comprehensive display built under the theater (the entry is adjacent) that provides background material about the Elizabethan theater and about the surrounding neighborhood, Southwark. The exhibition describes the process of building the modern Globe and the serious research that went into it.

FUN FACT: In Shakespeare's day, this was a rough part of town. The Bear Gardens, around the corner from the Globe, was where bear baiting, a cruel animal sport, took place. Farther along, the Clink (now a museum) was the local *gaol* (jail).

Daily live demonstrations include Elizabethan dressing, stage fighting, and swordplay, performed by drama students and stage-fighting instructors from the Royal Academy of Dramatic Art (RADA) and the London Academy of Music and Dramatic Art (LAMDA).

FUN FACT: Many performances are done in Elizabethan dress. Costumes are handmade from period materials—wool, silk, cotton, animal skins, and natural dyes.

Admission also includes a tour of the theater. On matinee days, the tour visits the archaeological site of the nearby (and older) Rose Theatre.

FUN FACT: Shakespeare's casts were all male, with young men and boys playing the female roles. A live demonstration in the costume exhibit shows how this was done—and how convincing it can be.

Visiting the Globe

- ⊠ 21 New Globe Walk, Bankside, South Bank
- ☎ 020/7902–1400 box office, 7401–9919 New Shakespeare's Globe Exhibition
- ⊕ www.shakespeares-globe.org
- 🎫 Exhibition & tour £11.50, family ticket (2 adults, 3 children) £28; ticket prices for plays vary (£5–£37.50)
- ⊗ Exhibition daily 9–5; plays May—early Oct., call for performance schedule.
- Ⓤ Southwark, then walk to Blackfriars Bridge and descend the steps; Mansion House, then cross Southwark Bridge; Blackfriars, then walk across Blackfriars Bridge; St. Paul's, then cross Millennium Bridge.

⊘ *Studios and shops Tues.–Sun. 11–6* ⓤ *Blackfriars, Waterloo.*

Southwark Cathedral. Pronounced "Suth-uck," this is the second-oldest Gothic church in London, after Westminster Abbey, with parts dating back to the 12th century. Although it houses some remarkable memorials, not to mention a program of lunchtime concerts, it's seldom visited. It was promoted to cathedral status only in 1905; before that it was the priory church of St. Mary Overie (as in "over the water"—on the South Bank). Look for the gaudily renovated 1408 tomb of the poet John Gower, friend of Chaucer, and for the Harvard Chapel. Another notable buried here is Edmund Shakespeare, brother of William. ■TIP➔ The Refectory serves full English breakfasts, light lunches, and tea daily 10–6. ⊠ *London Bridge, South Bank* ☎ *020/7367–6700* ⊕ *www.southwark.anglican.org* 🎫 *Free, suggested donation £4* ⊘ *Daily 8–6* ⓤ *London Bridge.*

> **BEDLAM**
>
> The Imperial War Museum is in an elegant domed and colonnaded building, erected in the early 19th century to house the Bethlehem Hospital for the Insane, better known as the infamous Bedlam. By 1816, when the patients were moved here, they were no longer kept in cages to be taunted by tourists (see the final scene of Hogarth's *Rake's Progress* at Sir John Soane's Museum for a sense of how horrific it was), since reformers—and George III's madness—had effected more humane standards. Bedlam moved to Surrey in 1930.

Ⓒ **Tate Modern.**

Fodor'sChoice
★ *See the highlighted listing in this chapter.*

WORTH NOTING

Ⓒ **Dulwich Picture Gallery.** Famed for its regal Old Master painting collection, the Dulwich Picture Gallery (pronounced "Dull-ich") was
Fodor'sChoice
★ Europe's first purpose-built art museum when it opened in 1811. The permanent collection includes landmark works by Rembrandt, Van Dyck, Rubens, Poussin, and Gainsborough, and it also hosts three major international exhibitions each year. As one British art critic puts it, "we would all travel bravely for a day in Tuscany or Umbria in order to see much less." The gallery also has a lovely café serving meals and drinks. Most of the land around here belongs to Dulwich College, a local boys' school, which keeps strict control over development. Consequently, Dulwich Village feels a bit like a time capsule, with old-fashioned street signs and handsome 18th-century houses strung out along its main street. Take a short wander and you'll find a handful of cute clothing and crafts stores and the well-manicured Dulwich Park, with lakeside walks and a fine display of rhododendrons in late May. ⊠ *Gallery Rd., Dulwich Village, Southwark* ☎ *020/8693–5254* ⊕ *www.dulwichpicturegallery.org.uk* 🎫 *£5–£9. Free guided tours weekends at 3* ⊘ *Tues.–Sun. 10–5* ⓤ *National Rail: West Dulwich from Victoria or North Dulwich from London Bridge.*

TATE MODERN

✉ *Bankside, South Bank*
☎ *020/7887–8888*
⊕ *www.tate.org.uk/modern*
🎫 *Free, charge for special exhibitions* ⊙ *Sun.–Thurs. 10–6, Fri. and Sat. 10–10 (last admission to exhibitions 45 min before close)* Ⓤ *Blackfriars, Southwark.*

TIPS

■ Join one of the free, 45-minute guided tours. Each one covers a different gallery: Poetry and Dream at 11 am, Material Gestures at noon, States of Flux at 2, and Energy and Process at 3. No need to book; just show up in the appropriate room.

■ Level 4 is devoted to temporary exhibitions, for which there's usually a charge of around £15. Bypass it if you're just here to see the main collection, which is free.

■ Make it a two-for-one art day by taking advantage of the Tate Boat, which ships visitors back and forth between Tate Britain and Tate Modern every 40 minutes.

■ Private "Tate Tours for Two" can be booked online from £100 to £210 including a restaurant meal.

■ An ambitious—and controversial—extension to the front of the Tate Modern is scheduled to open in 2012. No closures had been announced at this writing, but check ahead.

Perhaps in keeping with Britain's most renowned contemporary artist, Damien Hirst (who often uses utensils, dead sharks, and other found objects), this spectacular art museum took something functional—a 1930s power station—and made it a place for creativity. Today, it is one of the greatest new museums devoted to modern and contemporary art. Besides a great permanent collection, ranging from Matisse to the most-talked-about British upstarts and not grouped by artist but are arranged thematically—Landscape, Still Life, and the Nude—the museum hosts its latest barnstorming exhibition, often a talking point at smart dinner parties across the art world. Autumn 2011 will see a vast retrospective of the great contemporary master Gerhard Richter.

8

HIGHLIGHTS

The vast **Turbine Hall** is a dramatic entrance point used to showcase big, audacious installations that tend to generate a lot of publicity. Past highlights include a massive glowing sun and, perhaps most bizarrely, a long crack in the floor.

The **Material Gestures** galleries on Level 3 feature an impressive offering of post–World War II painting and sculpture. Room 7 contains a breathtaking collection of Rothkos and Monets; there are also paintings by Matisse, Pollock, and Picasso, and newer works from the likes of the sculptor Anish Kapoor.

Head to the Restaurant on Level 7 or the Espresso Bar on Level 4 for stunning vistas of the Thames. The view of St. Paul's from the Espresso Bar's balcony is one of the best in London.

Florence Nightingale Museum. With the renovation bandages removed after a £1.4-million face lift to mark the centenary of Florence Nightingale's death, come here to learn all about the founder of the first school of nursing, that most famous of health-care reformers, "the Lady with the Lamp" known for tending soldiers during the Crimean War (1854–56). Compact, highly visual, and engaging, the museum is arranged around three areas, focusing on her Victorian childhood, the Crimean War, and health reform. The setup is creative and accessible, with photographic displays, displays of Florence's own books and bed, as well as interactive displays of instruments, medicinal herbs, and the famous lamp. ⊠ *2 Lambeth Palace Rd., South Bank* ☎ *020/7620–0374* ⊕ *www.florence-nightingale.co.uk* ☞ *£5.80* ⊙ *Weekdays 10–5, last admission 4, weekends 10–4:30, last admission 3:30* Ⓤ *Waterloo, Westminster, Lambeth North.*

★ **The Garden Museum.** A rather unassuming museum, it has a great story behind it and is supported by a dedicated team of volunteers. In the mid-1970s, two gardening enthusiasts were looking for the graves of the John Tradescants (the elder and younger), who were adventurous plant collectors, responsible for introducing many familiar blooms to these shores. Their search led them to a medieval church, right next to Lambeth Palace—which, they were horrified to discover, was about to be bulldozed. Inspired to action, they rescued the church and opened this museum, which has built one of the largest collections of historic garden tools, artifacts, and curiosities in the world. The museum also has its own beautiful walled gardens, which are maintained year-round with seasonal plants. One section contains a perfect replica of a 17th-century knot garden; another is devoted entirely to wildflowers. It's worth a visit to see the church itself, which also contains the tombs of William Bligh, captain of the *Bounty*, and several members of the Boleyn family. There's also a green-thumb gift shop and the **Garden Café** serving vegetarian lunches and home-baked cakes—the toffee-apple variety is a must! ⊠ *Lambeth Palace Rd., South Bank* ☎ *020/7401–8865* ⊕ *www.gardenmuseum.org.uk* ☞ *£6 (includes garden and all exhibitions)* ⊙ *Daily 10:30–5; closed 1st Mon. of month* Ⓤ *Vauxhall.*

☾ **HMS Belfast.** At 613 feet, this is one of the largest and most powerful cruisers the Royal Navy has ever had. It played an important role in the D-Day landings off Normandy, left for the Far East after the war, and has been moored in the relative calm of the Thames since 1971. On board there's a riveting interactive outpost of the **Imperial War Museum,** which tells the Royal Navy's story from 1914 to the present and shows you about life on a World War II battleship, from mess decks and bakery to punishment cells, and from operations room to engine room and armaments. ⊠ *Morgan's La., Tooley St., South Bank* ☎ *020/7940–6300* ⊕ *hmsbelfast.iwm.org.uk* ☞ *£12.95, children under 16 free* ⊙ *Mar.–Oct., daily 10–6; Nov.–Feb., daily 10–5; last admission 1 hr before closing* Ⓤ *London Bridge.*

★ **Imperial War Museum.** Despite its title, this museum of 20th-century warfare

---

COMBINATION TICKETS

If you're planning to visit the London Dungeon, Sea Life London Aquarium, and Madame Tussauds, save by booking a combination ticket on any of their Web sites.

does not glorify bloodshed but emphasizes understanding through evoking what life was like for citizens and soldiers alike through the two world wars and beyond. There's an impressive amount of hardware at the main entrance with accompanying interactive material, including a Battle of Britain Spitfire, a German V2 rocket, tanks, guns, and submarines—and from here you can peel off to the various sections of the museum. Sights, sounds, and smells are used to re-create the uncomfortable Trench Experience in the World War I gallery, which is just as effective as the "Blitz Experience" in the World War II gallery: a 10-minute taste of an air raid in a street of acrid smoke with sirens blaring and searchlights glaring. There are two galleries of war art on the second floor (by Henry Moore, John Singer Sargent, Stanley Spencer, and William Orpen, to name a few), poetry, photography, and documentary film footage. ⊠ *Lambeth Rd., South Bank* 🕾 *020/7416–5000* ⊕ *www.iwm.org.uk* 🖃 *Free (charge for special exhibits)* ⊙ *Daily 10–6* Ⓤ *Lambeth North.*

🏵 Fodor's Choice ★ **London Dungeon.** Here's the goriest, grisliest, most gruesome attraction in town, where realistic waxwork people are subjected in graphic detail to all the historical horrors the Tower of London merely tells you about. Perhaps the most shocking thing here is the mass of children lined up roaring to get in every day—kiddies absolutely adore this place, but some nervous types may find it too frightening (and that goes for the adults, too). Replete with campy mannequins, penny-dreadful stage-sets, and lurid colored spotlights, a series of tableaux depicts famous bloody moments—like Anne Boleyn's decapitation and the martyrdom of St. George—alongside the torture, murder, and ritual slaughter of lesser-known victims, all to a soundtrack of screaming, wailing, and agonized moaning. There are displays on the Great Plague, the Great Fire of London, and Jack the Ripper; to add to the fear and fun, costumed characters leap out of the gloom to bring the exhibits to life. And did you ever imagine what a disembowelment looks like? Well, here's your chance. Be sure to get the souvenir booklet to impress all your friends back home. ■ TIP➜ **Expect long lines on weekends and during school holidays. Booking online will save at least £5.** ⊠ *28–34 Tooley St., South Bank* 🕾 *0871/7403–7221* ⊕ *www. thedungeons.com* 🖃 *£23* ⊙ *Daily; opening times vary slightly, week by week, but generally Sept.–Mar. 10–5; Mar.–Sept. 9:30–6; Aug. 9:30–7; phone to confirm times* Ⓤ *London Bridge.*

🏵 **Sea Life London Aquarium.** The curved, colonnaded, neoclassic hulk of County Hall once housed London's local government administration (now at the Norman Foster–designed City Hall building farther downriver by Tower Bridge). Now it's where you can catch a dark and thrilling glimpse of the waters of the world, focused around a superb three-level aquarium full of sharks and stingrays, among other common and rarer breeds. There are also educational exhibits, feeding displays, and hands-on displays—including a tank full of nonvenomous rays that you can touch if they swim near enough—they seem to like having their backs tickled. It's not the biggest aquarium you've ever seen—especially if you've been to SeaWorld—but the exhibit is well arranged, with areas for different oceans, water environments, and climate zones, including a stunning coral reef and rain forest. There are regular feeding times and free talks throughout the day. Look out for new additions to the tanks from the conservation breeding program.

✉ *County Hall, Riverside Bldg., Westminster Bridge Rd., South Bank* ☎ *0871/663–1678* ⊕ *www.sealife.co.uk* 🎫 *£16* ⊗ *Mon.–Thurs. 10–6, last admission 5; Fri.–Sun. 10–7, last admission 6* Ⓤ *Westminster, Waterloo.*

Kensington, Chelsea, and Knightsbridge

WORD OF MOUTH

"The new V&A galleries are absolutely splendid. In a lesser city (i.e. anywhere else on earth) they'd be regarded as a major new museum in their own right."

—flanneruk

GETTING ORIENTED

GETTING THERE

There are several useful Tube stations for this area: Sloane Square and High Street Kensington on the District and Circle lines; Earl's Court, Kensington, Knightsbridge, and Hyde Park Corner on the Piccadilly Line; South Kensington and Gloucester Road on the District, Circle, and Piccadilly lines; and Victoria Station on the District, Circle, and Victoria lines.

SAFETY

This entire, posh region is quite safe but beware of pickpockets in shopping areas.

TOP REASONS TO GO

The V&A Museum: The greatest museum of decorative arts in the world—even Edwardians got "interactive" by sketching in the Sculpture Court (stools are still provided today).

Natural History Museum: Watch children catch on that the museum's animatronic T. rex has noticed *them*—and is licking its dinosaur chops. Then see some of those fearsome teeth for real in the dinosaur room.

Kensington Palace and Gardens: Address to everyone from Queen Victoria to Princess Diana, this holds an array of treasures, including the Royal Dress Collection.

Harrods' Food Hall: The granddaddy of all London department stores, even Harrods' decor glitters—note the shiny mosaic of fish in its famed food hall.

Linley Sambourne House: Stuffed with Edwardian antiques, 18 Stafford Terrace is almost like a theater set for *The Importance of Being Ernest*.

MAKING THE MOST OF YOUR TIME

You could fill three or four days in this borough: A shopping stroll along the length of the King's Road is easily half a day. Add lunch and some time weaving back and forth between the King's Road and the river and you can fill a day. Give yourself a half-day, at least, for the Victoria & Albert Museum and a half-day for either the Science or Natural History Museum.

FEELING PECKISH?

The Café at the V&A (✉ Victoria & Albert Museum, Cromwell Rd. ☎ 0207/942–2500) serves breakfast, light snacks, tea, and full meals throughout the day, all in a grand room at modest prices. You can eat in the courtyard if the weather's good, or have a buffet supper on late nights. Stop by just to see the original Arts and Crafts decor, one of William Morris's earliest commissions, with stained-glass panels by Edward Burne Jones.

NEAREST PUBLIC RESTROOMS

Most old-style public restrooms have been replaced by futuristic "autoloos"—podlike booths on street corners that usually cost £1 to use. If you're not brave enough to trust the push-button locks (and plenty of locals don't), try Peter Jones or Harvey Nicks department stores, which have several large, clean restrooms that are free to use. You could also try asking for the "loo" in any pub, but be prepared for short shrift if you're not a paying customer.

A GOOD RUN

The short circuit around the Thames between Chelsea Bridge and Albert Bridge is a pleasant 1½-mi run. From Chelsea Bridge run west along Chelsea Embankment. The wooded park on the other side is Battersea Park, with its Peace Pagoda in the middle. Turn left across the river on the Albert Bridge. Then turn left into Battersea Park and run along the cinder path beside the river. Now the view is of Chelsea. There are good public bathrooms and drinking fountains in the park. Emerge from the park and turn left across Chelsea Bridge back to the starting point.

9

Sightseeing
★★★★
Nightlife
★★
Dining
★★★★
Lodging
★★★★
Shopping
★★★★★

Even in these supposedly democratic days, you still some-times hear people say that the *only* place to live in London is in the Royal Borough of Kensington & Chelsea (or "K&C" as the locals call it). Head here to find London's ritziest pieces of real estate: Belgravia and Chelsea, the eastern and south-ern borders of K&C. Chelsea is where Henry James died, T. S. Eliot lived, and James McNeill Whistler painted his "noc-turnes." Today, the artists have moved out and the Gettys have moved in. Belgravia is another enclave of posh houses and splendid embassies. Past this streetscape, however, you'll find Museum Central—a cavalcade of great museums, including Victoria & Albert, the Natural History Museum, the Science Museum, and Kensington Palace. And in adjacent Knightsbridge, Britain's reputation as a nation of shopkeep-ers is well kept—this is *must*-go territory for shopaholics.

KENSINGTON AND CHELSEA

Updated by
Ellin Stein

Chelsea was settled before the Domesday Book and was already fash-ionable when two of Henry VIII's wives lived there. On the North side of the Thames, over from trendier but less well-heeled Battersea, are the impressive lawns of Wren's **Royal Hospital**. Walking along the Embank-ment, notice the **Albert Bridge**, a candy-color Victorian confection of a suspension bridge. The bridge, shimmering with thousands of lights, its reflection sparkling on the river, is one of London's great romantic views. **Cheyne Walk**, a lovely street dating back to the 18th century, has **Chelsea Physic Garden** and **Carlyle's House**, with all their arty and historic associations. The blue plaques commemorating important residents along here are amazing.

Nearby is a famous London shopping street, the **King's Road** (Charles II's private way from St. James's to Fulham). Leave time in your retail therapy schedule to stop at the relocated **Saatchi Gallery,** or explore the tiny Georgian lanes of pastel-color houses that veer off the King's Road to the north—especially **Jubilee Place** and **Burnsall Street,** leading to the hidden "village square" of **Chelsea Green.** On Saturday there's an excellent farmers' market up from the Saatchi Gallery selling artisanal cheese and chocolates, local oysters, and organic meats, plus stalls serving international food.

Kensington laid its first royal stake when King William III, fed up with the vapors of the Thames, bought a country place there in 1689 and converted it into **Kensington Palace.** Its **Orangery** is diagonally across the park, with the opulent **Kensington Palace Gardens** running behind it. Londoners call this street Billionaires' Row. Notice that there is no electric street lighting down here; it is still lighted exclusively by old Victorian gas lamps. Queen Victoria's consort, Prince Albert, added the jewel in the borough's crown when he turned the profits of the Great Exhibition of 1851 into South Kensington's metropolis of museums: **Victoria & Albert Museum (V&A),** the **Science Museum,** and the **Natural History Museum.** His namesakes in the area include **Royal Albert Hall,** with its bas-reliefs that make it resemble a giant, redbrick Wedgwood pot, and the lavish **Albert Memorial.**

Turn into Derry Street or Young Street and enter **Kensington Square,** one of the most complete 17th-century residential squares in London. Holland Park is about ¾ mi farther west; both **Leighton House** and **18 Stafford Terrace** are nearby as well.

EXPLORING

Albert Memorial. This gleaming, neo-Gothic shrine to Prince Albert created by George Gilbert Scott epitomizes the Victorian era. Albert's grieving widow, Queen Victoria, had this elaborate confection (including a 14-foot bronze statue of the prince) erected on the spot where his Great Exhibition had stood a decade before his early death, from typhoid, in 1861. ✉ *Kensington Gore, Hyde Park, Kensington.*

Fodor's Choice
★ **18 Stafford Terrace.** Filled with delightful Victorian and Edwardian antiques, fabrics, and paintings, the home of *Punch* cartoonist Edward Linley Sambourne in the 1870s is one of the most charming 19th-century London houses extant—small wonder that it was used in Merchant Ivory's *A Room with a View.* An Italianate house, it was the scene for society parties when Anne Messel was in residence in the 1940s. Being Kensington, there's a royal connection, too: her son, Antony Armstrong-Jones, married the late Princess Margaret, and their son has preserved the connection by taking the name Viscount Linley. Admission is by guided tours. Apart from the 11:15 tour on weekends and all Wednesday tours, these are given by costumed actors. ✉ *18 Stafford Terr., Kensington* ☎ *0207/602–3316* ⊕ *www.rbkc.gov.uk/subsites/museums. aspx* ✉ *£6* ⊙ *Guided tours Wed. 11:15, 2:15, weekends 11:15, 1, 2:15, 3:30. Closed mid-June–mid-Sept.* Ⓤ *High Street Kensington.*

Holland Park. The former grounds of the Jacobean Holland House opened to the public only in 1952. It was originally owned by Sir Walter Cope, the wealthy chancellor of James I, and many treats are to be found within its 60 acres. Holland House itself was nearly flattened by World War II bombs, but the east wing remains, now incorporated into a youth hostel and providing a fantastical stage for the April–September **Open Air Theatre** (☎ 0207/361–3570 box office ⊕ www.operahollandpark.com). The glass-wall Orangery also survived to host art exhibitions and other public events. Next door the former Summer Ballroom has

> **WORD OF MOUTH**
>
> "I have been lucky enough to visit the Chelsea Flower Show on two occasions... What you should do first of all is join the RHS. This allows you to book an entrance ticket for the two days immediately after the Royal Family has been. It's members only, which allows you to see the flowers at their best. You can lie on the lawn with an ice-cold Pimms and listen to the orchestra. Even treat yourself to a posh lunch with champagne. Now there's an idea!"
>
> —tod

become the upmarket Belvedere restaurant; nearby is a lovely café. From the Belvedere's terrace you see the formal Dutch Garden, planted by Lady Holland in the 1790s with the first English dahlias. North of that are woodland walks; lawns populated by peacocks, guinea fowl, and the odd, awkward emu; a fragrant rose garden; great banks of rhododendrons and azaleas, which bloom profusely in May; a well-supervised children's Adventure Playground; and a Japanese water garden, legacy of the London Festival of Japan. If that's not enough, you can watch cricket on the Cricket Lawn on the south side or tennis on the several courts. ☉ Daily dawn–dusk Ⓤ Holland Park, High Street Kensington.

★ **Kensington Palace.**
See the highlighted listing in this chapter.

Natural History Museum.
Fodor's Choice
★ See the highlighted listing in this chapter.

Royal Albert Hall. This domed, circular 5,223-seat auditorium (as well as the Albert Memorial, opposite) was made possible by the Victorian public, who donated funds for it. More money was raised by selling 1,300 future seats at £100 apiece—not for the first night but for every night for 999 years. Some descendants of purchasers still use them. ■TIP➔ The Royal Albert Hall is best known for its annual July–September BBC Promenade Concerts—the "Proms"—with bargain-price standing (or promenading, or sitting-on-the-floor) tickets sold on the night of the concert. On the last night only, the BBC hosts **Proms in the Park**, a series of free live concerts in Hyde Park and at other locations across the country, which culminate in a big-screen link-up with Royal Albert Hall for the grand finale. ✉ Kensington Gore, Kensington ☎ 0207/589–8212 ⊕ www.royalalberthall. com ☝ Prices vary with event Ⓤ South Kensington.

Royal Hospital, Chelsea. Charles II founded the hospice for elderly and infirm soldiers in 1682; his troops had hitherto enjoyed not so much as a meager pension, and they were growing restive after the civil wars

KENSINGTON PALACE

✉ *The Broad Walk, Kensington Gardens, Kensington*
☎ *0844/482–7799 advance booking, 0844/482–7777 information, 0203/166–6000 from outside U.K.* ⊕ *www.hrp.org.uk* 🎫 *£12.50* ⊘ *Mar.–Sept., daily 10–6; Oct.–Feb., daily 10–5; last admission 1 hr before closing* Ⓤ *Queensway, High Street Kensington.*

Not as splendid as Buckingham Palace, or as famous as Hampton Court, Kensington Palace is the most intimate of London's great royal residences. Bought in 1689 by Queen Mary and King William III, it was converted into a palace by Sir Christopher Wren and Nicholas Hawksmoor. Royals have been living here ever since, most famously Princess Diana, in the private part of the palace. The State Apartments, however, are open to the public and now house a temporary exhibition, "The Enchanted Palace," which evokes the seven princesses who have lived at KP through innovative installations that utilize gowns, artifacts, and soundscapes. Princess Diana, for example, is represented by one of her ball gowns in a glass vitrine surrounded by dozens of model butterflies.

From January 3, 2012 to March 25, 2012, the palace will be completely closed while the renovation is finished. The "new" palace will showcase four new exhibitions that unfold the palace saga: Queen Victoria (with the theme "love, duty and loss"); William and Mary and Queen Anne ("the private life of the Queen"); George II ("the curious world of the court"); and princesses Diana and Margaret ("it's not easy being a princess").

HIGHLIGHTS

In addition, KP is home to the **Royal Ceremonial Dress Collection,** including royal raiments ranging from the elaborate (an 18th-century mantua—a dazzling court dress with a 6-foot-wide skirt) to the downright odd (King George III's socks). Also look for the King's Staircase, with its panoramic trompe l'oeil painting, and the King's Gallery, with royal artworks in a jewelbox setting of rich red damask walls, intricate gilding, and a beautiful painted ceiling. Outside, the grounds are almost as lovely as the palace itself.

TIPS

■ If you also plan to visit the Tower of London, Hampton Court Palace, Banqueting House, or Kew Palace, become a member of Historic Royal Palaces. It costs £41 per person, or £80 for a family, and gives you free entry to all five sites for a year.

■ Picnicking is allowed on the benches in the palace grounds. (You can also picnic anywhere in the adjoining Kensington Gardens.)

■ There's a delightful café in the Orangery, near the Sunken Garden. Built for Queen Anne, it's a great place for formal afternoon tea, although you have to book ahead.

■ It's only recently that the palace has made much fuss over its most famous modern resident, the late Diana, Princess of Wales. One commemorative event was the Field of Flowers—an open-air art installation featuring thousands of dandelion heads arranged into giant flowers.

9

Ice-skaters outside the Natural History Museum in South Kensington.

of 1642–46 and 1648. Charles wisely appointed the great architect Sir Christopher Wren to design this small village of brick and Portland stone set in manicured gardens (which you can visit) surrounding the Figure Court—named after the 1682 bronze figure of Charles II dressed up as a Roman general—and the Great Hall (dining room) and chapel. The latter is enhanced by the choir stalls of Grinling Gibbons (who did the bronze of Charles, too), the former by a vast oil of Charles on horseback by Antonio Verrio, and both are open to the public at certain times during the day. There is a small museum here, detailing the history of the resident "Chelsea Pensioners," but it's the building and, of course, the pensioners themselves that are the real attraction. Recognizable by their traditional scarlet frock coats with gold buttons, medals, and tricorne hats, they are all actual veterans, who wear the uniform, and the history it conveys, with a great deal of pride. They celebrate Charles II's birthday—May 29, Founder's Day—by draping oak leaves on his statue and parading around it in memory of a hollow oak tree that expedited the king's miraculous escape from the 1651 Battle of Worcester. Also in May (usually the third week), the **Chelsea Flower Show**, the year's highlight for thousands of garden-obsessed Brits, is held here. Run by the Royal Horticultural Society (☎ *0844/338–7505 in U.K., 121/767–4063 from outside U.K.* ⊕ *www.rhs.org.uk*), this mammoth event takes up vast acreage, and the surrounding streets throng with visitors. ⊠ *Royal Hospital Rd., Chelsea* ☎ *0207/881–5298* ⊕ *www.chelsea-pensioners.org.uk* ⊡ *Free* ☉ *Museum open Apr.–Sept., Mon.–Sat. 10–noon and 2–4, Sun. 2–4. Closed Sun. Oct.–Mar., also closed holidays and for special events. Chapel, Courts, and Great Hall open daily, 10–noon and 2–4* Ⓤ *Sloane Sq.*

NATURAL HISTORY MUSEUM

✉ *Cromwell Rd., South Kensington* ☏ *0207/942–5000* ⊕ *www.nhm.ac.uk* 🚇 *Free (some fees for special exhibitions)* ⏱ *Daily 10–5:50, last admission at 5:30* Ⓤ *South Kensington.*

TIPS

■ "Nature Live" is a program of free, informal talks given by scientists, covering a wildly eclectic range of subjects, usually at 2:30 (and on some days at 12:30) in the David Attenborough Studio in the Darwin Centre.

■ The museum has an outdoor ice-skating rink from November to January, and a popular Christmas fair.

■ Free, daily behind-the-scenes Spirit collection tours of the museum can be booked on the day—although space is limited, so come early. Recommended for children over eight years old.

■ Got kids under seven with you? Check out the museum's "Explorer Backpacks." They contain a range of activity materials to keep the little ones amused, including a pair of binoculars and an explorer's hat. They're free, but you'll need to provide a £25 credit-card deposit.

The outrageously ornate terra-cotta facade of this enormous Victorian museum is strewn with relief panels, depicting living creatures to the left of the entrance and extinct ones to the right. It's an appropriate design, for within these walls lie more than 70 million different specimens.

Only a small percentage is on public display, but you could still spend a day here and not come close to seeing everything. The museum is full of cutting-edge exhibits, with all the wow-power and interactives necessary to secure interest from younger visitors.

HIGHLIGHTS

A giant diplodocus skeleton dominates the vaulted, cathedral-like entrance hall, affording you perhaps the most irresistible photo opportunity in the building. It's just a cast, but the **Dinosaur Gallery** (Gallery 21) contains plenty of real-life dino bones, fossils—and some extremely long teeth.

You'll also come face to face with a giant animatronic Tyrannosaurus rex—who is programmed to sense when human prey is near and "respond" in character. When he does, you can hear the shrieks of fear and delight all the way across the room.

A dizzyingly tall escalator takes you into a giant globe in the **Earth Galleries,** where there's a choice of levels—and Earth surfaces—to explore. Don't leave without checking out the earthquake simulation in Gallery 61.

The centerpiece of a major expansion is the **Darwin Centre,** which houses some of the (literally) millions of items they don't have room to display, including "Archie," a 28.3-foot giant squid.

9

CLOSE UP

Historic Plaque Hunt

As you wander around London, you'll see lots of small, blue, circular plaques on the sides and facades of buildings, describing which famous, infamous, or obscure but brilliant person once lived there. The first was placed outside Lord Byron's birthplace (now no more) by the Royal Society of Arts. There are around 700 blue plaques, erected by different bodies—you may even find some green ones that originated from Westminster City Council—but English Heritage now maintains the responsibility, and if you want to find out the latest, check the Web site ⊕ www.english-heritage.org.uk. Below are some of the highlights:

James Barrie (✉ 100 Bayswater Rd., Bayswater); Frederic Chopin (✉ 4 St. James's Place, St. James's); Sir Winston Churchill (✉ 28 Hyde Park Gate, Kensington Gore); Captain James Cook (✉ 88 Mile End Rd., Tower Hamlets); T.S. Eliot (✉ 3 Kensington Court Gardens, Kensington); Benjamin Franklin (✉ 36 Craven St., Westminster); Mahatma Gandhi (✉ 20 Baron's Court Rd., West Kensington); Jimi Hendrix (✉ 23 Brook St., Mayfair); Alfred Hitchcock (✉ 153 Cromwell Rd., Earl's Court); Wolfgang Amadeus Mozart (✉ 180 Ebury St., Pimlico); Horatio Nelson (✉ 103 New Bond St., Mayfair); Sir Isaac Newton (✉ 87 Jermyn St., St. James's); Florence Nightingale (✉ 10 South St., Mayfair); George Bernard Shaw (✉ 29 Fitzroy Sq., Fitzrovia); Percy Bysshe Shelley (✉ 15 Poland St., Soho); H. G. Wells (✉ 13 Hanover Terr., Regent's Park); Oscar Wilde (✉ 34 Tite St., Chelsea); William Butler Yeats (✉ 23 Fitzroy Rd., Primrose Hill).

Saatchi Gallery. Charles Saatchi, who made his fortune building an advertising empire that successfully "rebranded" Margaret Thatcher's Conservative Party, is an astute art collector whose avant-garde acquisitions regularly create headlines. The museum's home—its third in 10 years—is at the former Duke of York's HQ, just off the King's Road. Built in 1803, its suitably grand exterior belies an imaginative restoration, which transformed the interior into 14 gallery exhibition spaces of varying size and shape. Unlike the Tate Modern, there is no permanent collection; instead the galleries are given over to a single exhibition, which normally runs for about three months. Exhibitions have included a highly successful showcase for contemporary Chinese art. ✉ Duke of York's HQ Bldg., Kings Rd., Chelsea ☎ 0207/823-2332 ⊕ www.saatchigallery.com 🎫 Free ⊙ Daily 10–6 Ⓤ Sloane Sq.

★ **Science Museum.** This, one of the three great South Kensington museums, stands next to the Natural History Museum in a far plainer building. It has loads of hands-on exhibits, with entire schools of children apparently decanted inside to interact with them; but it is, after all, painlessly educational. Don't dismiss the Science Museum as just for kids, though. Highlights include the Launch Pad gallery, which demonstrates basic laws of physics; *Puffing Billy*, the oldest steam locomotive in the world; and the actual *Apollo 10* capsule. The six floors are devoted to subjects as diverse as the history of flight, space exploration, steam power, medicine, and a sublime exhibition on science in the 18th century. Overshadowed by a three-story blue-glass wall, the Wellcome Wing is an annex to the rear of the museum, devoted to contemporary science and technology. It contains a 450-seat IMAX cinema, and the ForceField ride—an advanced motion simulator that combines seat vibration with other technical gizmos to create such crowd-pleasing effects as flying past an explosion in space. ■TIP→ If you're a family of at least five, you might be able to get a place on one of the popular new Science Night sleepovers by booking well in advance. Aimed at kids 8–11 years old, these nighttime science workshops offer the chance to camp out in one of the galleries, and include a free IMAX show the next morning. Check the Web site for details. ⊠ *Exhibition Rd., South Kensington* ☎ *0870/870–4868* ⊕ *www.sciencemuseum.org.uk* ⊡ *Free, charge for cinema shows and special exhibitions* ⊙ *Daily 10–6* Ⓤ *South Kensington.*

ARTISTIC CHELSEA

Artists and writers flocked to the area in the 19th century, establishing a creative colony in Cheyne Walk; at one time Turner, Whistler, John Singer Sargent, Dante Gabriel Rossetti, and Oscar Wilde were residents. In the 1960s it was the turn of the Rolling Stones and the Beatles; in the 1970s Bob Marley wrote "I Shot the Sheriff" in a flat off Cheyne Walk. It's now one of London's most expensive streets, completely unaffordable for latter-day Bob Marleys.

Ⓒ **Victoria & Albert Museum.**

Fodor's Choice
★   *See the highlighted listing in this chapter.*

KNIGHTSBRIDGE

There's no getting away from it. This is shop-'til-you-drop territory of the highest order. With two world-famous department stores, **Harrods** and **Harvey Nichols**, a few hundred yards apart, and every bit of space between and around taken up with designer boutiques, chain stores, and jewelers, it's hard to imagine why anyone who doesn't like shopping would even think of coming here. If the department stores seem overwhelming, **Beauchamp Place** (pronounced "Beecham") is a good tonic. It's lined with equally chic and expensive boutiques, but they tend to be smaller, more personal, and less hectic. Nearby Sloane Street is lined with top-end designer boutiques such as Prada, Dior, and Tods.

Another place to find peace and quiet is a divinely peaceful stroll in fashionable Belgravia, one of the most gorgeous set-pieces of urban 19th-century planning. Street after street is lined with grand white terraces of aristocratic town houses, still part of the Grosvenor estate, and owned by the Dukes of Westminster. Many are leased to embassies, but a remarkable number around **Lowndes Square, Belgrave Square,** and **Eaton Square** remain homes of the discreet, private wealthy and outright superrich. Often, the only people on the streets are professional dog walkers and chauffeurs. Some people call the area near **Elizabeth Street** Belgravia, others Pimlico–Victoria. Either way, now that you've had a break, it's time to shop again, and this street is the place to be.

9

VICTORIA & ALBERT MUSEUM

✉ *Cromwell Rd., South Kensington* ☎ *0207/942–2000* ⊕ *www.vam.ac.uk* ▭ *Free* ⊙ *Sat.–Tues. 10–5:45, Fri. 10–10* Ⓤ *South Kensington.*

TIPS

■ The V&A is a tricky building to navigate so be sure to use the free map.

■ As a whirlwind introduction, you could take a free one-hour tour at 10:30, 11:30, 12:30, 1:30, 2:30, or 3:30. There are also tours devoted just to the British Galleries at 12:30 and 2:30.

■ Public lectures on Friday nights at 7 are delivered by visiting bigwigs from the art or fashion world (from £8). There are free lectures throughout the week given by museum staff.

■ Whatever time you visit, the spectacular sculpture hall will be filled with artists, both amateur and professional, sketching the myriad of artworks on display there. Don't be shy: Bring a pad and join in.

■ Although the permanent collection is free—and there's enough there to keep you busy for a week—the V&A also hosts high-profile special exhibitions that run for up to three months (from £5).

Always referred to as the V&A, this huge museum is devoted to the applied arts of all disciplines, all periods, and all nationalities. Full of innovation, it's a wonderful, generous place to get lost in. First opened as the South Kensington Museum in 1857, it was renamed in 1899, in honor of Queen Victoria's late husband and has since grown to become one of the country's best-loved cultural institutions.

Many collections at the V&A are presented not by period, but by category—textiles, sculpture, jewelry, and so on. Nowhere is the benefit of this more apparent than in the **Fashion Gallery** (Room 40), where formal 18th-century court dresses are displayed alongside the haute couture styles of contemporary designers, creating an arresting sense of visual continuity.

The **British Galleries** (rooms 52–58), devoted to British art and design from 1500 to 1900, are full of beautiful diversions—among them the Great Bed of Ware (immortalized in Shakespeare's *Twelfth Night*). Here, a series of actual rooms have been painstakingly reconstructed piece by piece after being rescued from historic buildings. These include an ornate music room, and the Henrietta St. Room, a breathtakingly serene parlor dating from 1722.

The **Asian Galleries** (rooms 44–47) are full of treasures, but among the most striking items on display is a remarkable collection of ornate samurai armor in the **Japanese Gallery** (Room 44). There are also galleries devoted to China, Korea, and the Islamic Middle East. Several new galleries opened in 2009: a Buddhist Sculpture gallery, a new Ceramics gallery, and a Medieval and Renaissance gallery, which has the largest collection of works from the period outside of Italy.

World-famous Harrods has been attracting shoppers since 1834.

EXPLORING

Belgrave Square. This is the heart of Belgravia, the epicenter of posh aristocratic London. The square, as well as the streets leading off it, is genuine grand territory and has been since it was built in the mid-1800s. The grand, porticoed mansions were created as town residences for courtiers, conveniently close to Buckingham Palace, just around the corner. These are some of the grandest houses in London, and although many of them are embassies, several are still private homes. Walk down Belgrave Place toward Eaton Place and you pass two of Belgravia's most beautiful mews: Eaton Mews North and Eccleston Mews, both fronted by grand rusticated entrances right out of a 19th-century engraving. ■ TIP→ Traffic really whips around Belgrave Square, so be careful.

Harrods. Just in case you don't notice it, this well-known shopping destination frames its domed terra-cotta Edwardian outline in thousands of white lights each night. The 4.5-acre store's sales weeks are top-notch, and inside it's as frenetic as a stock-market floor. Its motto, *Omnia, omnibus, ubique* (Everything, for everybody, everywhere) is not too far from the truth. Don't miss the extravagant Food Hall, with its stunning Art Nouveau tiling around the meat and poultry section and continuing to the fishmongers' territory, where its glory is rivaled by displays of the sea produce itself. *For more on Harrods, see ⇨ Shopping, Chapter 18.* ⊠ *87–135 Brompton Rd., Knightsbridge* ☎ *0207/730–1234* ⊕ *www.harrods.com* ☉ *Mon.–Sat. 10–8, Sun. 11:30–6* Ⓤ *Knightsbridge.*

9

Harvey Nichols. This is fashionista central and a must for anyone who has been watching *Absolutely Fabulous*, dahling—in which case you'll already know to call it Harvey Nicks. The Fifth Floor Restaurant, Café, and Bar offer outstanding views and stylish refreshments that attract an equally stylish clientele. *For more on Harvey Nichols, see* ⇨ *Shopping, Chapter 18.* ✉ *109–125 Knightsbridge, Knightsbridge* ☎ *0207/235–5000* ⊕ *www.harveynichols.com* ⊘ *Mon.–Sat. 10–8, Sun. 11:30–6* Ⓤ *Knightsbridge.*

Notting Hill and Bayswater

WORD OF MOUTH

"We stayed in Notting Hill for a week last summer and enjoyed the area. Where we stayed, farther west and therefore more in Notting Hill proper, it was a bit of a hike to the Tube, [so] we depended on buses. There are plenty of restaurants and pubs along Westbourne Grove and Queensway."

—Nikki

GETTING ORIENTED

GETTING THERE

For Portobello Market and environs, the best Tube stops are Ladbroke Grove and Westbourne Park (Hammersmith and City lines); ask for directions when you emerge. The Notting Hill stop on the District, Circle, and Central lines enables you to walk the length of Portobello Road on a downhill gradient.

A GOOD WALK

To gape at Notting Hill's grandest houses, stroll over to Lansdowne Road, Lansdowne Crescent, and Lansdowne Square—two blocks west of Kensington Park Row.

TOP REASONS TO GO

Portobello Road Market: Seek and ye shall find; go early-morning antique hunting at London's best and most famous market on Saturday for the top bargains, or come during the week for a leisurely browse.

Notting Hill shopping: In addition to Portobello Road Market, you can search for vintage designer pieces at the numerous secondhand and retro clothing stores.

Westbourne Grove: Watch these locals stroll the streets as if they were one big catwalk, then drop in for lunch at one of the Grove's colorful ethnic restaurants.

Electric Cinema: Catch a movie reclined on a two-seater leather sofa, beer and bar snacks in hand, at this restored early-20th-century theater–then splurge for dinner at its fantastic restaurant, the Electric Brasserie.

Café Society: There are few better places to people-watch and take in the passing fashion parade than from a sidewalk café seat here.

MAKING THE MOST OF YOUR TIME

Saturday is Notting Hill and Portobello Road's most fun and frenetic day. You could easily spend the whole day shopping, eating, and drinking here.

The market can get very crowded by noon in nice weather so come early if you are serious about shopping.

You may prefer to start at the end of Portobello Road and work backward, using the parks for relaxation after your shopping exertions. Do the same on Friday if you're a flea-market fan.

Sunday, the Hyde Park and Kensington Gardens railings all along Bayswater Road are hung with dubious art, which may slow your progress.

This is also the day when the well-heeled locals are out in force, filling the pubs at lunchtime or hitting the parks with their kids if it's sunny.

FEELING PECKISH?

There's cult appeal to the super-value **Churchill Thai Kitchen** (✉ *119 Kensington Church St., Notting Hill* ☎ *020/7792–1246*) attached to a traditional English pub swamped in Winston Churchill memorabilia. With large portions of all dishes priced around £7, it's a bargain for this part of town.

A haven for the health conscious, **Planet Organic** (✉ *42 Westbourne Grove* ☎ *020/7727–2227*) serves upscale vegetarian meals at nongourmet prices, with a wide selection of specials to take out.

SAFETY

At night, be wary of straying too far off the main streets, as it gets "edgier" toward Ladbroke Grove's high-rise estates and surrounding areas. Notting Hill Carnival attracts massive crowds and revelers should be wary of crime.

Sightseeing
★★
Nightlife
★★★
Dining
★★★
Lodging
★★★
Shopping
★★★★

Notting Hill is one of London's most famous trendsetting square miles of multi-ethnicity, music, and magnificent street markets. Throw in a goodly number of see-and-be-seen-in restaurants and a sprinkling of the younger and adventurous versions of the Cork Street modern-art galleries, and you see why it remains a favorite of the hip and happening set. That crowd of musician/novelist/filmbiz/drug-dealer/ fashion-victim local residents and hangers-out has been dubbed by the style-watching media the Notting Hillbillies. And the whole thing has mushroomed around one of the world's great antiques markets: the Portobello Road, a top spot to find treasures in the trash. There are few historic sites here, so just wander the streets to savor the flavor.

Updated by
Jack Jewers

The Notting Hill district is centered around the Portobello Road antiques market, bordered in the west by Landsdowne Road and Landsowne Crescent—address to the Hill's poshest 19th-century terraced row houses—and to the east by Chepstow Road, with Notting Hill Gate and Westbourne Grove Road marking the southern and northern boundaries. In between, Rastafarians rub elbows with wealthy young Brits (a.k.a. "Trustafarians") and such fashionable folk as reporter Christiane Amanpour and Lady Antonia Fraser have been spottted at the chic shops on Westbourne Grove and the lively cafés on Kensington Park Road.

Notting Hill as we know it was born in the 1840s, when the wealthy Ladbroke family laid out a small suburb to the west of London. Before then it had been known, informally, as "the Potteries and the Piggeries," in honor of its two industries: ceramics and pig farming. Notting Hill's transformation from poverty-stricken backwater to super-trendy enclave started in the 1980s and had reached its peak by the early 2000s—helped, in no small way, by the Julia Roberts' flick that bore its name. For the Notting Hill of the film sets (the Travel Bookshop on Blenheim Crescent is Hugh Grant's bookshop in the film *Notting Hill)*, head straight for **Westbourne Grove,** replete with chic boutiques and charity shops laden with the castoffs from wealthy residents. The whole area sprung up around **Portobello Road**, with the beautifully restored early-20th-century **Electric Cinema** at No. 191. The famous Saturday antiques market and shops are at the southern end; **Westway Portobello Green Market,** under the Westway overpass, is filled with bric-a-brac, secondhand threads, and clothes and accessories by young, up-and-coming designers. Nearby on Acklam Road are the **Westbourne Studios,** an office complex with a gallery, restaurant, and bar open to the public, and the capital's best skateboarding park, **Bay Sixty6.**

In Bayswater—found north of the royal parks and a welcome hub of tourist restaurants and midprice hotels—the main thoroughfare of **Queensway** is a rather peculiar, cosmopolitan street of ethnic confusion, late-night cafés and restaurants, a skating rink, and the **Whiteleys** shopping-and-movie mall. Nearby **Paddington Station** is the namesake for the marmalade-loving Paddington Bear.

EXPLORING

- ↻ **Hyde Park and Kensington Gardens.**
- ★ *See the highlighted listing in this chapter.*
- ↻ **Museum of Brands, Packaging and Advertising.** This extraordinary little museum does exactly what it says on the box. Its massive collection of toys, fashion, food wrappers, advertising, and the assorted detritus of everyday life is from all corners of the globe. It's a fascinating and eccentric chronicle of how consumer culture has developed since the Victorian age. ✉ *2 Colville Mews, Lonsdale Rd., Notting Hill* ☎ *020/7908–0880* ⊕ *www.museumofbrands.com* 🖃 *£5.80* ⊙ *Tues.– Sat. 10–6, Sun. 11–5; last entry 45 min before closing. Closed during Notting Hill Carnival* Ⓤ *Notting Hill.*
- ★ **Portobello Road.** Tempted by tassels, looking for a 19th-century snuff spoon or dashingly Deco frock (just don't believe the dealer when he says the Vionnet label just fell off), or hunting for a gracefully Georgian silhouette of the Earl of Chesterfield? Head to Portobello Road, world famous for its Saturday antiques market (arrive at about 9 am to find the real treasures-in-the-trash; after ten, the crowds pack in wall to wall. Actually, the Portobello Market is three markets: Antiques, "fruit and veg," and a flea market. The street begins at Notting Hill Gate, though the antique stalls start a couple of blocks north, around Chepstow Villas. Lining the sloping street are also dozens of antiques shops and indoor markets, open most days—in fact, serious collectors will want to do Portobello on a weekday, when they can explore the 90-some antique and art stores in relative peace. Where the road levels off, around Elgin Crescent, youth culture and a vibrant neighborhood life kicks in, with all manner of interesting small stores and restaurants interspersed with the fruit and vegetable market. This

Continued on page 190

10

HYDE PARK AND KENSINGTON GARDENS

Every year millions of visitors descend on the royal parks of Hyde Park and Kensington Gardens, which sit side by side and roll out over 625 acres of grassy expanses that provide much-craved-for respite from London's frenetic pace. The two parks incorporate formal gardens, fountains, sports fields, great picnic spots, shady clusters of ancient trees, and even an outdoor swimming pool.

Although it's probably been centuries since any major royal had a casual stroll here—you're more likely to bump into Chris Martin and Gwyneth Paltrow than Her Royal Highness these days—the parks remain the property of the Crown, which saved them from being devoured by the city's late-18th-century growth spurt.

Today the luxury of such wide open spaces continues to be appreciated by the Londoners who steal into the parks before work for a session of tai chi, say, or on weekends when the sun is shining. Simply sitting back in a hired deck chair or strolling through the varied terrain is one of the most enjoyable ways to spend time here.

KENSINGTON GARDENS

At the end of the 17th century, William III moved his court to the impeccably kept green space that is now **Kensington Gardens**. He was attracted to the location for its clean air and tranquillity and subsequently commissioned Sir Christopher Wren to overhaul the original redbrick building, resulting in the splendid **Kensington Palace**.

To the north of the palace complex is the early-20th-century **Sunken Garden**, complete with a living tunnel of lime trees (i.e., linden trees) and golden laburnum.

On western side of the **Long Water** is George Frampton's 1912 *Peter Pan*, a bronze of the boy who lived on an island in the Serpentine and never grew up and whose creator, J.M. Barrie, lived at 100 Bayswater Road, not 500 yards from here.

Back toward Kensington Palace, at the intersection of several paths, is George Frederick Watts's 1904 bronze of a muscle-bound horse and rider, entitled **Physical Energy**. The **Round Pond** is a magnet for model-boat enthusiasts and duck feeders.

Near the Broad Walk, toward Black Lion Gate, is the **Diana Princess of Wales**

Diana Memorial Walk

LANCASTER GATE U

QUEENSWAY U
NOTTING HILL GATE
Diana Princess of Wales Memorial Playground
BLACK LION GATE
Bayswater Rd.
LANCASTER GATE
Italian Gardens
The Fountains
Peter Pan

Kensington Gardens

Elfin Oak

(RESTRICTED AREA)
Kensington Palace Gardens

Orangery

Sunken Garden

Kensington Palace

The Round Pond

Physical Energy

Broad Walk

Lancaster Walk

The Long Water

Serpentine Gallery

The Ring

Flower Walk

Kensington Rd.
QUEEN'S GATE
Albert Memorial
Kensingto
ALEXANDR GATE

Afternoon tea taken at the Orangery, a short walk from the Sunken Garden on the palace grounds, is a quintessentially English experience.

Memorial Playground, an enclosed space with specially designed structures and areas on the theme of Barrie's Neverland. Hook's ship, crocodiles, "jungles" of foliage, and islands of sand provide a fantasy land for kids—more than 70,000 visit every year. Just outside its bounds is Ivor Innes's *Elfin Oak*, the remains of a tree carved with scores of tiny woodland creatures.

One of the park's most striking monuments is the **Albert Memorial**. This Victorian high-Gothic celebration of Prince Albert is

adorned with marble statues representing his interests and amusements.

Diminutive as it may be, the **Serpentine Gallery** has not been afraid of courting controversy with its temporary exhibitions of challenging contemporary works.

Hyde Park was once the hunting ground of King Henry VIII. This stout, bawdy royal more or less stole Hyde Park, along with the smaller St. James's and Green parks, from the monks of Westminster in 1536. The public wasn't to be granted access

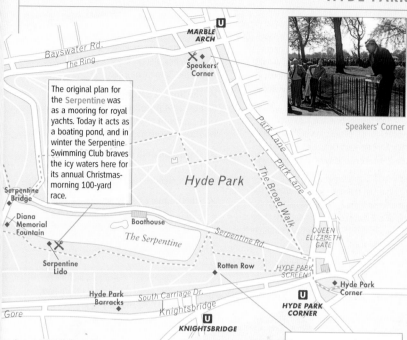

HYDE PARK

The original plan for the Serpentine was as a mooring for royal yachts. Today it acts as a boating pond, and in winter the Serpentine Swimming Club braves the icy waters here for its annual Christmas-morning 100-yard race.

Speakers' Corner

MARBLE ARCH

Speakers' Corner

Bayswater Rd.

The Ring

Park Lane

Park Lane

The Broad Walk

Hyde Park

Serpentine Bridge

Diana Memorial Fountain

Boathouse

The Serpentine

Serpentine Rd.

QUEEN ELIZABETH GATE

Serpentine Lido

Rotten Row

HYDE PARK SCREEN

Hyde Park Corner

Hyde Park Barracks

South Carriage Dr.

Knightsbridge

HYDE PARK CORNER

Gore

KNIGHTSBRIDGE

IN FOCUS HYDE PARK AND KENSINGTON GARDENS

10

to Hyde Park's delights until James I came to the throne and opened up limited parts to "respectably dressed" plebeians.

It was Charles I, in the 1700s, however, who was to shape the Hyde Park that visitors see today. Once he had created the Ring (North Carriage Drive), which forms a curve north of the Serpentine and boathouses, Charles allowed the general public to roam free. During the Great Plague of 1665, East Enders and City dwellers fled to the park, seeking refuge from the black bilious disease.

The Serpentine Bridge, built

in 1826 by George Rennie, marks the boundary between Hyde Park and Kensington Gardens. Rotten Row, a corruption of the French *route de roi* (king's road), runs along the southeastern edge of Hyde Park and is still used by the Household Cavalry, who live at the Hyde Park Barracks—a high-rise and a long, low, red block—to the left. This is where the brigade that mounts the guard at Buckingham Palace resides; you can see them at about 10:30 am, as they leave to perform their duty in full regalia, or await the return of the guard about noon.

Rotten Row was the first artificially lit highway in Britain. In the late 17th century, William III was concerned that his walk to from Kensington Palace to St. James's Park was too dangerous, so he ordered 300 lamps to be placed along the route.

On the south side of the 1930s Serpentine Lido (open to swimmers from June to September) is the £3.6 million oval Diana Memorial Fountain.

Ever since the 1827 legislation of public assembly, Speakers' Corner near Marble Arch has provided an outlet for political debate: on Sundays, it's a spectacle of vehement, sometimes comical, and always entertaining orators.

ENJOYING THE PARKS

Ride. **Hyde Park Riding Stables** keeps horses for hacking the sand tracks. Group lessons (usually just a few people) are £59 per person per hour. Private lessons are £89 Tuesday–Friday, £99 on weekends. ⊠ 63 Bathurst Mews, Bayswater W2 ☎ 020/7723–2813 ⊕ www.hyde-parkstables.com Ⓤ Lancaster Gate.

Row. **The Serpentine** has paddleboats and rowboats for £9 per person per hour, kids £2.50, April through October from 10 am to dusk, later in good weather in summer. ☎ 020/7262–1330.

Run. You can run a **4-mi route** around the perimeter of Hyde Park and Kensington Gardens or a **2½-mi route** in Hyde Park alone if you start at Hyde Park Corner or Marble Arch and encircle the Serpentine.

Skate. On Friday, skaters of intermediate ability and upward meet at 8 pm at the Duke of Wellington Arch, Hyde Park Corner, for the **Friday Night Skate**, an enthusiastic two-hour mass skating session, complete with music and whistles. If you're a bit unsure on your wheels, arrive at 6:30 pm for the free lesson on how to stop. The **Sunday Rollerstroll**, a more laid-back version of the same thing, runs on Sunday afternoons; meet at 2 pm on the east side of Serpentine Road ⊕ www.thefns.com Ⓤ Hyde Park Corner.

Swim. **Serpentine Lido** is technically a beach on a lake, but a hot day in Hyde Park is surreally reminiscent of the seaside. There are changing facilities, and the swimming section is chlorinated. There is also a paddling pool, sandpit, and kids' entertainer in the afternoons. It's open daily from June through September, 10–5:30; admission £4, ☎ 020/7706–3422 ⊕ www.royalparks.co.uk Ⓤ Knightsbridge.

WHERE TO REFUEL

✗ The **Lido Café**, near the Diana Memorial Fountain, has plenty of seating with views across the Serpentine Lake.

✗ The **Honest Sausage** at Speakers' Corner is the place to grab a free-range sausage sandwich or organic bacon roll before enjoying the circus of debate.

✗ The **Broadwalk Café & Playcafe** next to the Diana Memorial Playground has a children's menu.

✗ The **Orangery** beside Kensington Palace is a distinctly more grown-up affair for tea and cakes.

SPEAKERS' CORNER

Once the site of public executions and the Tyburn hanging trees, the corner of Hyde Park at Cumberland Gate and Park Lane now harbors one of London's most public spectacles: Speakers' Corner. This has been a place of assembly and vitriolic outpourings and debates since the mid-19th century. The pageant of free speech takes place every Sunday afternoon.

Anyone is welcome to mount a soapbox and declaim upon any topic, which makes for an irresistible showcase of eccentricity—one such being the (now-deceased) Protein Man. Wearing his publicity board, the Protein Man proclaimed that the eating of meat, cheese, and peanuts led to uncontrollable acts of passion that would destroy Western civilization. The pamphlets he sold for four decades are now collector's items. Other more strait-laced campaigns have been launched here by the Chartists, the Reform League, the May Day demonstrators, and the Suffragettes.

PRACTICAL INFO

ADMISSION: Free for both parks

HOURS: Kensington Gardens 6 am–dusk; Hyde Park 5 am–midnight

CONTACT INFO: ☎ 020/7298–2141, ⊕ www.royalparks.org.uk

GETTING HERE: Ⓤ Kensington Gardens: Kensington High Street, Queensway, Lancaster Gate, South Kensington. **Hyde Park:** Hyde Park Corner, Knightsbridge, Lancaster Gate, Marble Arch

EVENTS: Major events, such as rock concerts and festivals, road races, and talks, are regular features of the parks' calendar; check online for what's on during your visit.

Each summer, a different modern architect designs an outdoor pavilion for the contemporary Serpentine Gallery, the venue for outdoor film screenings, readings, and other such cultural soirees.

From June to August, Hyde Park hosts the Royal Parks Summer Festival, with live jazz evenings, opera, and plays all over the park grounds.

(left) Horseback riding, Hyde Park

(top) The Fountains, Kensington Gardens

(bottom) Both parks are lovely year-round, but spring blooms are spectacular.

TOURS: There are **themed guided walks** about once a month, usually on Thursday or Friday afternoons. They are free but must be booked in advance. Check online or call the park offices for dates and details.

A 45-minute tour (£4.50) of the **Albert Memorial** is available. It's held at 2 and 3 pm on the first Sunday of the month from March to December. There's no need to book in advance unless you are part of a big group, in which case call ☎ 020/7495–0916.

Kensington Palace is open for the "Enchanted Palace" show until Jan. 3, 2012. After closing for several months, the entire palace and its Royal Dress Collection will reopen for guided tours on March 25, 2010. Hours are March to September, daily, from 10 to 6 and October to February, daily, from 10 to 5. For tickets £12.50 and information call ☎ 0844/482–7777 or visit ⊕ www.hrp.org.uk.

continues to the Westway overpass ("flyover" in British), where London's best flea market (high-class, vintage, antique, and second-hand clothing; jewelry; and junk) happens Fridays and Saturdays, then on up to Goldbourne Road. There's a strong West Indian flavor to Notting Hill, with a Trinidad-style Carnival centered along Portobello Road on the August bank-holiday weekend. *For more on Portobello Road, see* ⇨ *Shopping, Chapter 18.* Ⓤ *Notting Hill Gate, Ladbroke Grove.*

NOTTING HILL CARNIVAL

Loud, colorful, and very, very crowded, the annual Carnival (⊕ *www.nottinghillcarnival.biz*) is a massive event that was started by Afro-Caribbean immigrants in 1965. Held the last weekend in August, it attracts hundreds of thousands of visitors, mostly young and often raucous. Be aware that crime is rife and has grown in recent years—be careful.

Queens Ice and Bowl. This is London's most central year-round ice-skating rink. The per-session cost, including skate rental, is £10 plus £2 skate rental for both adults and children. ⊠ *17 Queensway, Bayswater* ☎ *020/7229–0172* ⊕ *www. queensiceandbowl.co.uk* ⊙ *Sun.–Fri. 10–6:45, 8–10:45, Sat. 10–6:45, 7:30–10:45* Ⓤ *Queensway.*

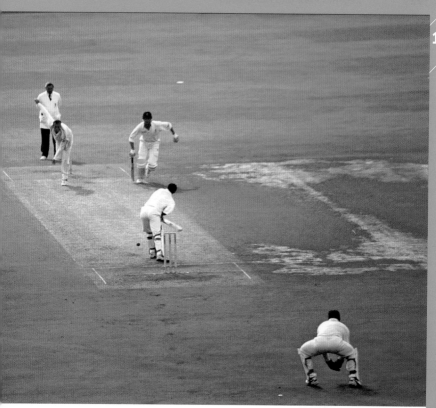

Regent's Park and Hampstead

WORD OF MOUTH

"Kenwood House on the Heath is a rather beautiful building with a good art collection. There's also the Freud Museum and Keats House in the area. If you're a '60s fan, then you can see Abbey Road studios and the zebra crossing from the cover of the Abbey Road album."

—djkbooks

GETTING ORIENTED

TOP REASONS TO GO

Strawberry Beatles Forever: No. 3 Abbey Road is the beloved Beatles building, Abbey Road Studios, in front of which is the most famous zebra-crossing in the world.

Elegant Regency-era Architecture: Which is grander—John Nash's Grecian-templelike Cumberland Terrace, found on Chester Road, or his Chester Place extravaganza?

Keats House: Stroll through the very garden that inspired the great Romantic to write "Ode to a Nightingale."

Wallace Collection: This 18th-century mansion's impressive art collection includes Fragonard's best 18th-century frolic, *The Swing*.

Marylebone High Street: Although it's just north of frenetic Oxford Street, you'll feel a whole world away as you wander by the chic restaurants and boutiques.

FEELING PECKISH?

Family-friendly and thoroughly modern, **Ginger and White** (✉ *9 South End Rd., Hampstead* ☎ *020/7431–9098* ⊕ *www.gingerandwhite.com*) is a delightful fusion of continental-style coffee shop and traditional British eatery—all bound up with a sophisticated Hampstead vibe.

Marine Ices (✉ *8 Haverstock Hill, Camden Town* ☎ *020/7482–9003* ⊕ *www.marineices.co.uk*) has some of London's best ice cream, while the indoor restaurant here lures diners near the Camden Lock market.

SAFETY

It's best to stay out of Hampstead Heath and Regent's Park proper late at night unless there's an event (such as a play or concert) taking place. Camden High Street and the Canal towpath should be avoided after dark.

GETTING THERE

Reaching Hampstead by Tube is as easy as it looks: Simply take the Edgware branch of the Northern Line to the Hampstead station, or the overground North London line to Hampstead Heath. The south side of Hampstead Heath can also be reached by the Gospel Oak station on the North London line. To get to Regent's Park, take the Bakerloo Line to Regent's Park Tube station or, for Primrose Hill, the Chalk Farm stop on the Northern Line.

MAKING THE MOST OF YOUR TIME

Depending on your pace and inclination, Marylebone, Regent's Park, and Hampstead can realistically be covered in a day. It might be best to spend the morning in Hampstead, then head south toward Regent's Park and Marylebone in the afternoon so that you're closer to central London come nightfall, if that is where your hotel is located.

A GOOD WALK

There really are no bad walks to be had in Hampstead. Once there, the village is best explored on foot, and Hampstead Heath will lead you by way of marked footpaths on a healthy jaunt through its sprawling green spaces. The neighborhoods around Regent's Park—as well as the park itself—are also best explored on foot.

Sightseeing
★★★★

Nightlife
★★★

Dining
★★

Lodging
★★

Shopping
★★★

London becomes noticeably calmer and greener as you head north from Oxford Street. From the civilized shopping streets of Marylebone, through the well-tended parks of Regent's Park and Primrose Hill up to the open spaces of Hampstead Heath and the handsome Georgian streets of Hampstead itself, this area will provide a taste of how laid-back (moneyed) Londoners can be.

Updated by
Jack Jewers

The Regent's Park area is the showcase for some of the most aristocratic architecture in the world, thanks to the "terraces" and town houses of John Nash, 19th-century design whiz. They provide the setting for some splendid sights, which range from Keats House to—Strawberry Beatles Forever!—Abbey Road, the favorite studio of the Fab Four. Northwards lies Hampstead, which continues its historic tradition of providing a haven for literati and some of the most stunning town-house architecture in England (think any Merchant Ivory film) while Primrose Hill is home to models and movie stars. Excellent bookshops, contemporary boutiques, and cozy cafés line tree-shaded blocks abuzz with locals: you won't find any souvenir stands here.

The residential areas hereabouts are usually considered "leafy" and therefore highly desirable by the garden-loving British. **Hampstead Heath** is a huge swath of countryside in the city, offering spectacular views. At the northern end is **Kenwood House,** a Georgian villa with a remarkable art collection that includes Vermeer's unforgettable *Guitar Player.* To the west of the Heath are the charming streets of Hampstead itself. Here you will find **Fenton House,** a Georgian town house with a period walled garden, and the **Freud Museum,** the last home of the founder of psychiatry.

A walk down Haverstock Hill will bring you to **Primrose Hill,** a manicured green park boasting yet another city panorama. The adjoining "village" of the same name has several fashionable boutiques and restaurants popular with actors, musicians, and celebs (Madonna bought her first London house here). To the east of Primrose Hill is lively

A BRIEF HISTORY

11

Much like New York City's Greenwich Village, the cliché about the enclaves north of Regent's Park (Primrose Hill, Belsize Park, and Hampstead) is that several of the residents claim to be artists—and yet the cost of a coffee at a café along Regent's Park Road will run you as much as, if not more than, one in central London. In the last decade, real estate prices have skyrocketed, and the elephants of the London Zoo now call some of the best-dressed folks in town neighbors.

In the early 18th century, the commercial development of the mineral springs in Hampstead led to its success as a spa; people traveled from miles around to drink the pure waters from Hampstead Wells, and small cottages were hastily built to accommodate the influx. Though the spa phenomenon was short-lived, Hampstead remained a favorite place for many artistic figures whose legacies still permeate the landscape.

Camden Market, a magnet for dedicated followers of fashion. The **Jewish Museum** traces the history of the Jewish community in Britain.

At the bottom of Primrose Hill is the **London Zoo,** at the northern end of **Regent's Park.** From here a westward detour will take you to **Lord's Cricket Ground & Museum,** and continuing south toward Queen Mary's Garden will take you past the **Open-Air Theatre.** Leaving the park on the southern end is to return to the busy urban center. The southeastern exit is near two of London's traditional tourist destinations, the **Sherlock Holmes Museum** and **Madame Tussauds.** The park's southwestern exit takes you onto handsome Portland Place. To the west of this street lies stylish **Marylebone High Street** and, just north of Oxford Street, the magnificent **Wallace Collection,** London's prime repository of 18th-century French art and artifacts.

TOP ATTRACTIONS

Fodor'sChoice
★

Hampstead Heath. For an escape from the ordered prettiness of Hampstead, head to the Heath—unique remnant of London's original countryside with habitats ranging from wide grasslands to ancient woodlands—spread over some 791 acres to the north. Parliament Hill, one of the highest points in London, offers a stunning panorama over the city. There are signposted paths, but these can be confusing. Maps are available from Kenwood House, or the Education Centre near the Lido off Gordon House Road, where you can also get details about the history of the Heath and the flora and fauna growing there. An excellent café near the Athletics Field offers light refreshment under the trees. ⊠ *Hampstead* ☎ *020/7482–7073 Heath Education Centre* ⊕ *www.cityoflondon. gov.uk/hampstead* Ⓤ *Gospel Oak or Hampstead Heath North London Overground Line from Highbury & Islington underground for south of Heath; Hampstead underground, then walk through Flask Walk, Well Walk for east of Heath; Golders Green underground, then Bus 210, 268 to Whitestone Pond for north and west of Heath.*

★ **Highgate Cemetery.** Highgate is not the oldest cemetery in London, but it is probably the best known. When the cemetery was consecrated in 1839, Victorians came from miles around to appreciate the ornate headstones, the impressive tombs, and the view. Such was its popularity that 19 acres on the other side of the road were acquired in 1850, and this additional East Cemetery contains what may be the most visited grave, of Karl Marx, as well as that of George Eliot, among other famous names. Much of the west side's 17 acres were once grounds

WORD OF MOUTH

"The heath is particularly beautiful in the morning, and at dusk. I recommend you pick a nice, relatively clear day and take the northern (black) Tube line and head up to Hampstead Heath—on a clear day, you can spot the London Eye from up there. Wear comfy shoes that you don't mind getting muddied. This was as close as I got to actually hiking—it was just lovely."
—Magellan_5

belonging to Sir William Ashurst, lord mayor of London in 1693. At the summit is the Circle of Lebanon, a ring of vaults built around an ancient cypress tree—a legacy of Ashurst's garden. Leading from it is the Egyptian Avenue, a subterranean stone tunnel lined with catacombs, itself approached by a dramatic colonnade that screens the main cemetery from the road. Both sides are impressive, with a grand (locked) iron gate leading to a sweeping courtyard for horses and carriages. By the 1970s the cemetery had become unkempt and neglected until a group of volunteers, the Friends of Highgate Cemetery, undertook the huge upkeep. Tours are arranged by the Friends, and among the wide variety of interesting statuary—memorials once hidden by overgrowth—they will show you the most notable graves and significant buildings. The west side is accessible only by tour. ■ TIP→ Children under eight are not admitted; nor are dogs, tripods, or video cameras. ⊠ *Swains La., Highgate* 🕾 *020/8340–1834* ⊕ *www.highgate-cemetery.org* 🖾 *East Cemetery £3, tours £7; Western Cemetery tours £7* ☉ *Daily; call for opening times, as hrs vary according to whether a funeral service is scheduled. East Cemetery tours, 2:30 pm, Sat. 11 am, noon, 1, 2, 3; also 4 pm Apr.–Oct.* Ⓤ *Archway, then Bus 210, 271, or 143 to Highgate Village.*

Keats House. Here you can see the plum tree under which the young Romantic poet composed "Ode to a Nightingale," many of his original manuscripts, his library, and other possessions he managed to acquire in his short life. It was in February 1820 that Keats coughed blood up into his handkerchief and exclaimed, "I know the color of that blood; it is arterial blood. I cannot be deceived in that color. That drop of blood is my death warrant. I must die." He left this house in September, moved to Rome, and died of consumption there, in early 1821, at age 25. There are frequent guided tours and special events, such as poetry readings. A major refurbishment in 2009 saw the house decorated to match its original Regency Style; new exhibition spaces; and a redesign of the gardens, inspired by elements of Keats' poetry, such as "autumn" and "nightingale." ■ TIP→ Picnics can be taken into the grounds during the summer. ⊠ *Wentworth Pl., Keats Grove, Hampstead* 🕾 *020/7332–3868* ⊕ *www.keatshouse.cityoflondon. gov.uk* 🖾 *£5* ☉ *Apr.–Oct., Tues.–Sun. 1–5; Nov.–Mar., Fri.–Sun. 1–5;*

closed Good Friday and Christmas wk Ⓤ *Hampstead; North London Line overground: Hampstead Heath from Highbury & Islington.*

Ⓒ ★ **Kenwood House.** This gracious Georgian villa was first built in 1616 and remodeled by Robert Adam between 1764 and 1779. Adam refaced most of the exterior and added the splendid library, which, with its curved painted ceiling, rather garish coloring, and gilded detailing, is the highlight of the house for decorative arts and interior design buffs. What is not to be missed here is the **Iveagh Bequest,** a collection of paintings that the Earl of Iveagh gave the nation in 1927, including a wonderful self-portrait by Rembrandt and works by Reynolds, Van Dyck, Hals, Gainsborough, and Turner. Top billing goes to Vermeer's *Guitar Player,* considered by some to be one of the most beautiful paintings in the world. In front of the house, a graceful lawn slopes down to a little lake crossed by a trompe-l'oeil bridge—all in perfect 18th-century upper-class taste. The rest of the grounds are skirted by Hampstead Heath. ■TIP➡ In summer the grounds host a series of popular and classical concerts, culminating in fireworks on the last night. A popular café, the Brew House, is part of the old coach house, and has outdoor tables in the courtyard and terraced garden. ✉ *Hampstead La., Hampstead* ☎ *020/8348–1286* ⊕ *www.english-heritage.org.uk* 🎫 *Free* ☉ *House daily except Dec. 24–26 and Jan. 1, 11:30–4. Gardens daily dawn–dusk* Ⓤ *Golders Green, then Bus 210.*

Ⓒ Fodor'sChoice ★ **London Zoo.** The zoo, owned by the Zoological Society of London (a charity), opened in 1828 and peaked in popularity during the 1950s, when more than 3 million people passed through its turnstiles every year. A recent modernization program has seen several big attractions open up, with a definite focus on wildlife conservation, education, and the breeding of endangered species. A great example of this is the huge BUGS pavilion (Biodiversity Underpinning Global Survival), a self-sustaining, contained ecosystem with 140 species of exotic plants, animals, and creepy-crawlies. At Gorilla Kingdom you can watch the four resident gorillas—Effie, Mjukuu, Bobby, and Zaire—at close range. Also popular is the Clore Rainforest Lookout, home to tiny primates such as marmosets and golden lion tamarins and a large collection of other rainforest-dwelling creatures. The Blackburn Pavilion contains hundreds of tropical bird species, including the largest collection of hummingbirds in the United Kingdom. Other zoo highlights (unchanged over the years, because of English Heritage conservation listing) include the graceful Snowdon Aviary, spacious enough to allow its tenants free flight; the Butterfly Paradise, which includes a pupae room in which its possible to see the creatures emerging from their chrysalises; and Berthold Lubetkin's 1936 Art Deco Penguin Pool, currently used for special exhibitions. Don't miss the penguins' new home, though, where feeding time tends to send small children into raptures. ■TIP➡ For animal encounter sessions with keepers, and feeding times, check the information board at admission. ✉ *Regent's Park* ☎ *020/7722–3333* ⊕ *www.zsl.org* 🎫 *£16.20–£19.80 depending on season* ☉ *Nov.–Feb., daily 10–4; Mar.–1st wk in Sept., daily 10–6; mid-Sept.–Oct. 10–5:30; 1st wk in Nov. 10–4:30; last admission 1 hr before closing* Ⓤ *Camden Town, then Bus 274.*

Something is always in bloom at Queen Mary's Gardens, within the Inner Circle of Regent's Park.

★ **Marylebone High Street.** A favorite of style sections everywhere, this street forms the heart of Marylebone (pronounced "Marr-le-bone") Village, a vibrant, upscale residential neighborhood that encompasses the squares and streets around the High Street and nearby Marylebone Lane. It's hard to believe that you're just a few blocks north of Oxford Street as you wander in and out of Marylebone's shops and boutiques. Some noteworthy stops along the way are La Fromagerie (2–4 Moxon Street), an excellent cheese shop; Daunt Books (Nos. 83–84), a travel bookshop; the Saturday afternoon "Cabbages and Frocks" market on the grounds of the St. Marylebone Parish Church, which purveys specialty foods and vintage clothing; and on Sunday 10–2, a large farmers' market in a parking lot on Cramer Street, just behind the High Street. It becomes less intimate when you get to busy Marylebone Road, but Marylebone Town Hall is worth a look if you're heading that way—perhaps for a stroll in the park or to take the kids to Madame Tussauds. ■ TIP➜ Marylebone Lane has an unusual, curved shape because it was built along the banks of the River Tyburn—which is now completely underground. ⊠ *Marylebone* Ⓤ *Bond St.*

↻ **Regent's Park.**
★ *See the highlighted listing in this chapter.*

↻ **Wallace Collection.** Assembled by four generations of marquesses of
★ Hertford and given to the nation by the widow of Sir Richard Wallace, illegitimate son of the fourth, this collection of art and artifacts is important, exciting, undervisited—and free. As at the Frick Collection in New York, Hertford House itself is part of the show: the fine late-18th-century mansion, built for the Duke of Manchester, contains

a basement floor with educational activities, several galleries, and a courtyard covered by a glass roof, with the upscale Wallace Restaurant.

The first marquess was a patron of Sir Joshua Reynolds, the second bought Hertford House, the third—a flamboyant socialite—favored Sèvres porcelain and 17th-century Dutch painting; but it was the eccentric fourth marquess who, from his self-imposed exile in Paris, really built the collection, snapping up Bouchers, Fragonards, Watteaus, and Lancrets for a song (the French Revolution having rendered them dangerously unfashionable), augmenting these with furniture and sculpture. Richard Wallace continued acquiring treasures after his father's death, scouring Italy for majolica and Renaissance gold, then moving most of it to London. Look for Rembrandt's portrait of his son, the Rubens landscape, Gainsborough and Romney portraits, the Van Dycks and Canalettos, the French rooms, and of course the porcelain. The highlight is Fragonard's *The Swing*, which conjures up the 18th century's let-them-eat-cake frivolity better than any other painting around. Don't forget to smile back at Frans Hals's *Laughing Cavalier* in the Great Gallery or pay your respects to Thomas Sully's enchanting *Queen Victoria*, which resides in a rouge-pink salon (just to the right of the main entrance). ✉ *Hertford House, Manchester Sq., Marylebone* ☎ *020/7563–9500* ⊕ *www.wallacecollection.org* 🎫 *Free* ⊗ *Daily 10–5* Ⓤ *Bond St.*

QUICK BITES — The **Wallace Restaurant** brings the outside in, in the elegant setting of the glass-roofed courtyard of the Wallace Collection. It's open for breakfast, lunch, and afternoon tea, and for dinner on weekends. The brasserie menu highlights French food from pâtés and cheeses to oysters, lobster, and succulent steaks. If you don't want to indulge your budget too much, you can just linger over coffee or afternoon tea in the gorgeous surroundings. It's open Sunday–Thursday 10–5, Friday and Saturday 10 am–11 pm.

WORTH NOTING

☺ **Camden Market.** What started as a small group of clothing stalls in the 1970s has since grown into one of London's biggest (and most crowded) tourist attractions. Centered on the Grand Union Canal, this isn't actually a single market, but a vast honeycomb of them that sell just about everything, but mostly crafts, clothing (vintage, ethnic, and young designer), and antiques. Here, especially on weekends, the crowds are dense, young, and relentless. **Camden Lock Market** specializes in crafts; **Camden Stables Market** is popular with Goth kids and aspiring rock stars; and the **Electric Ballroom** (✉ *184 Camden High St.* ☎ *020/7485–9006*) is a nightclub that doubles as a retro/designer fashion and music market on weekends. Just around the corner, the **Hawley Arms Pub** (✉ *2 Castlehaven Rd.* ☎ *020/7428–5979*) gained fame as a hangout for celebrities such as Amy Winehouse and Kate Moss, and has now been completely renovated after a devastating fire in 2008. It's a good spot for an inexpensive pub lunch. ■TIP➔ Print out the (appropriately psychedelic) map of Camden Market from the Web site before coming; it's super helpful for first-time visitors. *For more on Camden Lock, see ⇨ Shopping, Chapter 18.* ✉ *Camden High St., Camden Town* ⊕ *www.camdenmarkets.org* ⊗ *Daily 10–6* Ⓤ *Camden Town, Chalk Farm.*

REGENT'S PARK

✉ *Marylebone Rd., Regent's Park* ☎ *020/7486–7905*
⊕ *www.royalparks.gov.uk*
🎫 *Free* ⊙ *5 am–dusk*
Ⓤ *Baker St., Regent's Park, Great Portland St.*

Cultivated and formal—compared with the relative wildness of Hampstead Heath—Regent's Park was laid out in 1812 by John Nash, in honor of the Prince Regent (hence the name), who was later crowned George IV. The idea was to re-create the feel of a grand country residence close to the center of town, with all those magnificent white-stucco terraces facing in on the park. Most of Nash's plans were carried out successfully, although the focus of it all—a palace for the prince—was never built. Now it's a destination for sporty types and dog owners—not for nothing did Dodie Smith set her novel *A Hundred and One Dalmatians* in an Outer Circle house. (Nearby along East Heath Road is the Gothic manse that inspired Cruella DeVil's Hell Hall.)

HIGHLIGHTS
The most famous and impressive of Nash's terraces, **Cumberland Terrace** has a central block of Ionic columns surmounted by a triangular Wedgwood-blue pediment that looks like a giant cameo. The noted architectural historian Sir John Summerson described it as "easily the most breathtaking architectural panorama in London." You can spend a vigorous afternoon rowing about **Regent's Park Boating Lake** (☎ 020/7724–4069), where rowboats hold up to five adults and cost £6.50 per hour per person. Times vary with seasons and weather. The **Broad Walk** is a good vantage point from which to glimpse the minaret and the golden dome of the **London Central Mosque** on the far west side of the park. As in all London parks, planting here is planned with the aim of having something in bloom in all seasons, but if you hit the park in summer, head first to the Inner Circle. Your nostrils should lead you to **Queen Mary's Gardens,** a fragrant 17-acre circle that riots with 400 different varieties of roses in summer.

TIPS

■ Soccer, rugby, tennis, hockey, and softball are all played on the park's many sports grounds. Head up to the area around the Hub (020/7935–2458)—a state-of-the-art sports pavilion—to watch some action. You'll have to book in advance if you want to join in, but you're just as likely to find an informal soccer match in progress anywhere in the park, especially on a warm Sunday afternoon.

■ At the Garden Café (Inner Circle, Regent's Park; 020/7935–5729), enjoy breakfast, lunch, or supper on a patio next to the rose gardens, or take away some smoked-salmon bagels and champagne (or cappuccinos) for an elegant picnic.

■ Check the Regent's Park Open-Air Theatre schedule—they have been mounting summer Shakespeare productions here since 1932 (0844/826–4242; www.open-airtheatre.org).

■ Don't leave without exploring London Zoo—it's at the very edge of the park on the northeastern side.

A TRIP TO ABBEY ROAD

For countless Beatlemaniacs and baby boomers, No. 3 Abbey Road is one of the most beloved spots in London. Here, outside the legendary Abbey Road Studios, is the most famous zebra crossing in the world, immortalized on the Beatles' 1969 *Abbey Road* album. This footpath became a mod monument when, on August 8 of that year, John, Paul, George, and Ringo posed—walking symbolically *away* from the recording facility—for photographer Iain Macmillan for the famous cover shot. In fact, the recording facility's Studio 2 is where the Beatles recorded their entire output, from "Love Me Do" onward, including *Sgt. Pepper's Lonely Hearts Club Band* (early 1967).

Meanwhile, there's never any shortage of tourists recreating "the photo" outside. ■TIP→ Be very careful if you're going to attempt this. Abbey Road is a dangerous intersection. One of the best—and safer—ways Beatle lovers can enjoy the history of the group is to take one of the smashing walking tours offered by the **Original London Walks** (☎ *020/7624–3978* ⊕ *www. walks.com*), including **The Beatles In-My-Life Walk** (11:20 am outside Marylebone Underground on Saturday and Tuesday) and **The Beatles Magical Mystery Tour** (Wednesday at 2 pm, Thursday at 11 am, and Sunday at 11 am at Underground Exit 3, Tottenham Court Road), which cover nostalgic landmark Beatles spots in the city.

Abbey Road is in the elegant neighborhood of St. John's Wood, a 10-minute ride on the Tube from central London. Take the Jubilee Line to the St. John's Wood Tube stop, head southwest three blocks down Grove End Road, and be prepared for a heart-stopping vista right out of Memory Lane.

QUICK BITES

You will not go hungry in Camden Town, with its countless cafés, bars, and pubs, plus appealing restaurants at all price points on Parkway. Within the market at Camden Lock there are various stalls selling the usual hot dogs and burgers, but you can also find good value at the stalls selling ethnic food if you don't mind standing as you eat outdoors, or perching on a canalside bench.

Fenton House. This is Hampstead's oldest surviving house. Now a National Trust property, it has fine collections of porcelain and Georgian furniture, along with a superb walled garden, complete with an apple orchard that dates back to the 17th century. Baroque music enthusiasts can join a tour of the important collection of keyboard instruments, and there's a summer series of concerts on these very same instruments on Thursday evenings. Check the Web site for details. ⊠ *Hampstead Grove, Hampstead* ☎ *020/7435–3471* ⊕ *www.nationaltrust.org.uk* 🖃 *£5.40, garden only £1* ☉ *Late Mar.–Oct., Wed.–Fri. 2–5; weekends 11–5 (hrs vary; call to confirm). Last admission 30 min before closing* Ⓤ *Hampstead*.

Freud Museum. The father of psychoanalysis lived here for a year, between his escape from Nazi persecution in his native Vienna in 1938 and his death in 1939. Many of his possessions emigrated with him and were

The fabled cover of the Beatles Abbey Road album, with Hampstead's most famous traffic crossing.

set up by his daughter, Anna (herself a pioneer of child psychoanalysis), as a shrine to her father's life and work. Four years after Anna's death in 1982 the house was opened as a museum. It replicates Freud's famous consulting rooms, particularly through the presence of *the* couch. You'll find Freud-related books, lectures, and study groups here, too. ⊠ *20 Maresfield Gardens, Hampstead* ☎ *020/7435–2002* ⊕ *www.freud.org. uk* 🖭 *£6* ☉ *Wed.–Sun. noon–5* Ⓤ *Swiss Cottage, Finchley Rd.*

Jewish Museum. Reopened in 2010 after a £10-million refurbishment, this museum traces the history of the Jewish people in Britain from medieval times to the present day, although most of the exhibits date from the 17th century—when Cromwell repealed the laws against Jewish settlement—and later. The collection is spread over four galleries. "History: A British Story" provides a general overview of British Jewish people over the centuries, through a mix of rare artifacts and interactive displays, including a re-creation of a Victorian street from what was then the Jewish Quarter of East London. The Holocaust Gallery focuses on the incredible story of Leon Greenman (1910–2008), a British Jew who survived six concentration camps—including Auschwitz—and later became a prominent anti-racism campaigner. There are also galleries on modern Judaism, a changing exhibition space, and a free overview of the collection on the ground floor, including a medieval *mikveh* (ritual bath), excavated in 2001. ⊠ *Raymond Burton House, 129–131 Albert St., Camden Town* ☎ *020/7284–7384* ⊕ *www. jewishmuseum.org.uk* 🖭 *£7* ☉ *Sun.–Wed. 10–5, Thurs. 10–9, Fri. 10–2. Last admission 30 min before closing. Closed Sat. and on major Jewish festivals* Ⓤ *Camden Town.*

PUBS WITH A PAST

Hampstead has some of the most storied pubs in London—although a few have distinctly shady pasts.

The quaintest pub in Hampstead, complete with fireplace and timber frame, is the **Holly Bush** (⊠ *22 Holly Mount, Hampstead* ☎ *020/7435–2892*), which dates back to 1807. Tucked away on a side street, with cozy wooden booths inside, it's open until 11 each night and serves traditional English lunches and dinners.

The legendary highwayman Dick Turpin is said to have been born at the **Spaniard's Inn** (⊠ *Spaniards Rd.* ☎ *020/8731–8406*), which was once frequented by the likes of Dickens, Shelley, and Stoker. The owners will happily tell you how the latter borrowed one of their many resident

ghost stories to furnish the plot of *Dracula*. After a few hours in this atmospheric spot, you might even believe it.

A plaque outside the **Wells** (⊠ *30 Well Walk* ☎ *020/7794–3785*) delicately informs visitors that this (now terribly upscale) pub was originally built to provide "facilities for the celebration of unpremeditated and clandestine marriages."

Meanwhile, a much sadder tale is associated with the **Magdala** (⊠ *2A South Hill Park* ☎ *020/7435–2503*), the site of a notorious murder in 1955 for which Ruth Ellis was the last woman in Britain to be hanged. It's a sedate place these days, but the famous bullet holes near the door have been left untouched.

OFF THE BEATEN PATH

London Canal Museum. Near the St. Pancras International train station, in a former ice-storage house, you can learn about the rise and fall of London's once extensive canal network. Children enjoy the activity zone and learning about Henrietta, the museum's horse. Outside, on the Battlebridge Basin, float the painted narrow boats of modern canal dwellers— a few steps and a world away from King's Cross, which was once one of London's least salubrious neighborhoods. The quirky little museum is a half-hour walk along the towpath from Camden Lock—you can download a free audio tour to accompany the route, or join one of their several guided walking tours (£6 per person). ⊠ *12–13 New Wharf Rd., King's Cross* ☎ *020/7713–0836* ⊕ *www.canalmuseum.org.uk* ⊠ *£3* ☉ *Tues.– Sun. and holiday Mon. 10–4:30; last admission 30 min before closing. First Thurs. open until 7:30. Closed Dec. 24–Jan. 1* Ⓤ *King's Cross.*

🅒 **Lord's Cricket Ground & Museum.** If you can't manage to lay your hands on tickets for a cricket match, the next best thing is to take a tour of the spiritual home of this most English of games. Founded by Thomas Lord, the headquarters of the MCC (Marylebone Cricket Club) opens its "behind the scenes" areas to visitors. You can see the Long Room with cricketing art on display; the players' dressing rooms; and the world's oldest sporting museum, where the progress from gentlemanly village-green game to world-class sport over 400 years is charted. Don't miss the prize exhibit: the urn containing the Ashes (reputedly the remains of a cricket ball presented to the English captain in 1883, a jokey allusion to a newspaper's premature obituary for the death of English cricket published after the home team's defeat by Australia), and even smaller,

221B Baker Street and "Holmes" himself.

the poor sparrow that met its death by a bowled ball. More up-to-date is the eye-catching Media Centre building, which achieved high scores in the architectural league. The tour is not available during major matches (it's offered during smaller "county" matches), but the museum remains open to match ticket holders. ⊠ *St. John's Wood Rd., St. John's Wood* ☎ *020/7616–8595* ⊕ *www.lords.org* ✉ *£14. Museum only, £3 match days* ⊙ *Museum Apr.–Sept., daily 9:30–5, except during major matches; Oct.–Mar., daily 11–5 (closes at 4 Fri.). Tours Apr.–Oct., daily 10, noon, and 2; Nov.–Mar, weekdays noon and 2; weekends 10* Ⓤ *St. John's Wood.*

☃ **Madame Tussauds.** One of London's busiest sights, this is nothing more and nothing less than the world's premier exhibition of lifelike waxwork models of celebrities. Madame T. learned her craft while making death masks of French Revolution victims, and in 1835 set up her first show of the famous ones near this spot. Top billing still goes to the murderers in the Chamber of Horrors, who stare glassy-eyed at visitors—one from an electric chair, one sitting next to the tin bath where he dissolved several wives in quicklime. What, aside from ghoulish prurience, makes people stand in line to invest in one of London's most expensive museum tickets? It must be the thrill of photo opportunities with royalty, Hollywood stars, and world leaders—all in a single day. ■ **TIP**➡ Beat the crowds by calling in advance for timed entry tickets, or booking online. ⊠ *Marylebone Rd., Regent's Park* ☎ *0870/400–3000 for timed entry tickets* ⊕ *www. madame-tussauds.com* ✉ *£14–£28 according to time; call or check Web site. Combination ticket with London Eye, London Dungeons, and London Aquarium from £57.50* ⊙ *Weekdays 9–5:30 (last admission); weekends 9:30–6 (last admission)* Ⓤ *Baker St.*

Regent's Park Open-Air Theatre. The theater has mounted productions of Shakespeare productions every summer since 1932; everyone from Vivien Leigh to Jeremy Irons has performed here. Today it also hosts musicals, concerts, and comedy shows. However, *A Midsummer Night's Dream* is the one to catch— never is that enchanted Greek wood more lifelike than it is here,

enhanced by genuine birdsong and a rising moon. You can buy light suppers or choose from a (somewhat limited) barbecue selection in the evening, or prebook a picnic lunch for matinees. The park can get chilly, so bring a blanket; only very heavy rain stops the plays, in which case you can exchange your ticket (umbrellas aren't allowed during performances). ✉ *Open-Air Theatre, Inner Circle Regent's Park* ☎ *0844/826–4242* ⊕ *www.openairtheatre.org* 💷 *£15–£42.50* 🕙 *June–mid-Sept., evening performances at 8, matinees at 2:30* Ⓤ *Baker St., Regent's Park.*

Sherlock Holmes Museum. Outside Baker Street station, by the Marylebone Road exit, is a 9-foot-high bronze statue of the celebrated detective. Nearby is number 221B Baker Street—the address of Arthur Conan Doyle's fictional detective. Inside, Mrs. Hudson, "Holmes's housekeeper," conducts you into a series of Victorian rooms full of Sherlock-abilia. There's more than enough photo ops, and it's all so realistic, you may actually begin to believe that the fictional "great detective" really lived there. ✉ *221B Baker St., Regent's Park* ☎ *020/7224–3688* ⊕ *www.sherlock-holmes.co.uk* 💷 *£6* 🕙 *Daily 9:30–6* Ⓤ *Baker St.*

Greenwich

WORD OF MOUTH

"The elevated automated metro, the Docklands Railway (DLR), was created to ferry folks from the city to the new world financial hub in and around the Canary Wharf DLR. To me riding the DLR thru the Docklands and onto Greenwich is one of my very favorite things to do in London."

— Palenque

GETTING ORIENTED

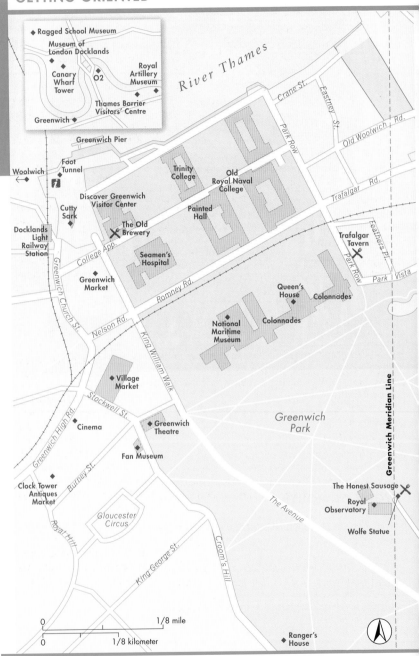

Ragged School Museum
Museum of London Docklands
Canary Wharf Tower
O2
Royal Artillery Museum
Thames Barrier Visitors' Centre
Greenwich

River Thames

Crane St.
Eastney St.
Old Woolwich Rd.
Park Row
Trafalgar Rd.
Feathers Pl.

Greenwich Pier

Woolwich

Foot Tunnel

Discover Greenwich Visitor Center

Cutty Sark

Docklands Light Railway Station

Greenwich Church St.

College App.

Trinity College

Old Royal Naval College

Painted Hall

The Old Brewery

Seamen's Hospital

Greenwich Market

Romney Rd.

Nelson Rd.

King William Walk

Trafalgar Tavern

Park Row

Park Vista

Queen's House
Colonnades

National Maritime Museum
Colonnades

Village Market

Stockwell St.

Cinema

Greenwich Theatre

Fan Museum

Burney St.

Clock Tower Antiques Market

Greenwich High Rd.

Gloucester Circus

Royal Hill

King George St.

Croom's Hill

Greenwich Park

The Avenue

The Honest Sausage

Royal Observatory

Wolfe Statue

Greenwich Meridian Line

0   1/8 mile
0   1/8 kilometer

Ranger's House

TOP REASONS TO GO

Greenwich Meridian Line: Stand astride time at the Royal Observatory—where the world's time is set—and be in the Eastern and Western hemispheres simultaneously.

Sir Inigo Jones's Queen's House: In the 17th century, this "avant-garde" building was the first to use the lessons of the Italian Renaissance in England—pay a call and see what all the fuss was about.

Cutty Sark: Discover Britain's seafaring past at this last extant 19th-century tea clipper, then head a few blocks away to visit the National Maritime Museum.

Greenwich (Village): Like its namesake in New York City, the village of Greenwich is also filled with quaint streets and fun outdoor markets.

Walk under the Thames to Docklands: Emerge from a Victorian tunnel to see London's "Manhattan"—Canary Wharf's financial skyscapers—rising up from a former warehouse district.

FEELING PECKISH?

With excellent vista of the Thames, there is no more handsomely situated pub in Greenwich than the **Trafalgar Tavern** (⌧ *Park Row* ☎ *020/8858–2909* ⊕ *www.trafalgartavern. co.uk*). Featured in Charles Dickens's *Our Mutual Friend,* it's still as grand a place to have a pint and some (upscale) pub grub as it ever was.

Right next to Discover Greenwich, the **Old Brewery** (⌧ *Pepys Bldg., Royal Naval College, Greenwich* ☎ *020/3327–1280* ⊕ www.oldbrewerygreenwich.com) is a relaxed café by day and a sophisticated restaurant at night. The artful, high-ceiling dining room is worth the trip alone but the modern British cuisine is also among the best in this part of London—and reasonably priced, too. The suave bar serves 200 different ales.

GETTING THERE

Sitting at the front of a Docklands Light Railway (DLR) train can be disconcerting, as you watch the controls in the fully automated driver's cab move about, as if a ghost were at the helm. It remains a zippy way to get to Cutty Sark station, from Canary Wharf and Bank Tube stations in The City. Or take the DLR to Island Gardens and walk the old Victorian Foot Tunnel under the river. The best way to arrive, however—time and weather permitting—is like a sea admiral of old: by water (though this way takes an hour from central London ⇨ *For more on cruising the Thames, see Chapter 13*).

MAKING THE MOST OF YOUR TIME

Set apart from the rest of London, Greenwich is worth a day to itself, to make the most of walks in the rolling parklands and to immerse yourself in its richness of maritime art and entertainment. The boat trip takes about an hour from Westminster Pier (next to Big Ben), or 25 minutes from the Tower of London, so factor in enough time for the round-trip.

NEAREST PUBLIC RESTROOMS

Duck into the tourist information center (near the Old Royal Naval College), where loos are free.

Sightseeing
★★★★
Nightlife
★
Dining
★★
Lodging
★
Shopping
★★★

The smart borough of Greenwich is on the Greenwich Meridian Line at 0° longitude, the official starting point for every new day, month, and year. The island nation of Britain—and the district—boasts an incredible maritime history. Even though star attraction *Cutty Sark*—the world's last remaining tea clipper—was tragically damaged by fire in 2007, Greenwich still preserves its unique charm, from its earthy markets to its distinctive Palladian architecture.

Updated by
Jack Jewers

A visit to Greenwich feels like a trip to a seaside town—but one with more than its fair share of historic sites and visitor attractions, all fairly close to one another—that's designated a UNESCO World Heritage Site. The grandiose Christopher Wren–designed **Old Royal Naval Hospital** was originally erected as Greenwich Hospital, a home for veteran sailors. It closed in 1869 and was reincarnated for training young officers; today it's the setting of many a blockbuster period film.

Greenwich was originally home to one of England's finest Tudor palaces, and the birthplace of Henry VIII, Elizabeth I, and Mary I. The masterful Inigo Jones built what is considered the first "classical" building in England in 1616—the **Queen's House,** now housing a collection of fine art. Right next door, one of the world's largest maritime museums, the **National Maritime Museum,** details stories of Britain's seafaring past and also houses Nelson's bullet-pierced coat from his last battle.

Verdant **Greenwich Park** is London's oldest royal park; here Henry VIII introduced deer so that he could hunt. The **Ranger's House** now houses a private art collection, next door to a beautifully tended rose garden. Atop the park's hill is the **Royal Observatory,** where you can bestride two hemispheres by standing over the **Greenwich Meridian Line** and see a planetarium show.

In town, opposite the Greenwich Theatre, the **Fan Museum** is home to 4,000 fans dating as far back as the 11th century. The **Clock Tower Antiques Market** and the lively **Greenwich Market** keep browsers busy on weekends.

Toward north Greenwich, the hopelessly ambitious Millennium Dome has been successfully reborn as the O2 and has hosted a string of the world's biggest bands and stand-up comedians in memorable, if wallet-busting, gigs. Now the most popular concert venue in London, it's slated to host the gymnastics and basketball events of the 2012 Olympic Games. In the opposite direction, downstream in Woolwich, lies the **Thames Flood Barrier.**

FUN FACT

Prance around the lightning-cracked Elizabeth Oak in Greenwich Park and you'll be in good historic company—it's so called because Elizabeth I is supposed to have played in its branches as a girl.

12

TOP ATTRACTIONS

Clock Tower Antiques Market. The weekend Clock Tower Antiques Market on Greenwich High Road has more vintage shopping, and browsing among the "small collectibles" makes for a good half-hour diversion.

Discover Greenwich. Intended as a kind of anchor point for Greenwich's big three attractions—the Old Royal Naval College, *Cutty Sark,* and National Maritime Museum—this excellent new visitor center includes large, interactive exhibitions on the history of Greenwich, plus an assortment of local treasures and artifacts. Most intriguing among them is a 17th-century "witch bottle," once used to ward off evil spirits, modern x-rays have revealed it to contain a mixture of human hair, fingernails, and urine. ⊠ *Pepys Bldg., King William Walk, Greenwich* ☎ *020/8269–4799* ⊕ *www.oldroyalnavalcollege.org* ✉ *Free* ☉ *Daily 10–5* Ⓤ *DLR: Greenwich.*

Greenwich Market. Established as a fruit-and-vegetable market in 1700, and granted a royal charter in 1849, the covered market now offers mixed stalls of homewares on Wednesday, antiques, and collectibles on Thursday and Friday, and arts and crafts on Saturday and Sunday. You can get food-to-go on each market day, although it's usually best on weekends. Shopping for handicrafts is a pleasure, as in most cases you're buying directly from the artist. ⊠ *College Approach, Greenwich* ☎ *020/8269–5096* ⊕ *www.greenwichmarket.net* ☉ *Wed.–Sun. 10–5:30* Ⓤ *DLR: Cutty Sark.*

National Maritime Museum. Following a millennial face-lift, one of Greenwich's star attractions has been completely updated to make it one of London's most enjoyable museums. Its glass-covered courtyard of beautifully grand stone, dominated by a huge revolving propeller from a powerful frigate, is reminiscent of the British Museum. The collection spans seascape paintings to scientific instruments, interspersed with the heroes of the waves. A permanent Nelson gallery contains the uniform he wore, complete with bloodstain, when he met his end in 1805. ■TIP➜ The museum has a good café with views over Greenwich Park. The **Queen's House** is home to the largest collection of maritime art in the world, including works by William Hogarth, Canaletto, and Joshua Reynolds. Construction was granted by Queen Anne only on condition that the river vista from the house be

ROYAL OBSERVATORY

✉ *Romney Rd., Greenwich*
☎ *020/8858–4422*
⊕ *www.rog.nmm.ac.uk*
🎫 *Free, planetarium shows*
£6 ⊙ *Daily 10–5 (May–Aug.,*
Meridian courtyard until 6);
last entry 30 min before clos-
ing; last planetarium show 4
Ⓤ *DLR: Greenwich.*

TIPS

■ A brass line laid among the cobblestones here marks the meridian, one side being the Eastern, one the Western hemisphere. As darkness falls, a funky green laser shoots out across London for several miles, following exactly the path of the meridian line.

■ The Time Ball atop Flamsteed House is one of the world's earliest time signals. Each day at 12:55, it rises halfway up its mast. At 12:58 it rises all the way to the top, and at 1 exactly, the ball falls.

■ The steep hill home to the observatory gives fantastic views across London, topped off with £1-a-slot telescopes to scour the skyline. Time a walk to catch the golden glow of late-afternoon sun on Canary Wharf Tower and head back into Greenwich via the rose garden behind Ranger's House.

■ Youngsters under five are not usually allowed into the auditorium. Tickets can be purchased ahead online.

Since 1884, the ultimate standard for time around the world has been set here: Greenwich is on the prime meridian at 0° longitude. Why was Greenwich adopted as the international standard? The reason was due to Britain's preeminence as a naval power. A redesign in 2007 split the observatory into two sites—one devoted to the study of the stars, the other to the study of time—and added new exhibition spaces.

HIGHLIGHTS
The recently opened south site, not previously accessible to the public, is the location of the enchanting **Peter Harrison Planetarium,** now London's only planetarium, its bronze-clad turret poking out of the ground like a crashed UFO. Shows on black holes and how to interpret the night sky entrance visitors. If you come with children, don't miss the high-technology rooms of the **Astronomy Galleries,** where cutting-edge touch screens and interactive programs give young explorers the chance to run their own space missions to Ganymede, one of Jupiter's moons.

Across the way is **Flamsteed House,** designed by Christopher Wren in 1675 for John Flamsteed, the first Royal Astronomer. A climb to the top of the house reveals the **28-inch telescope,** built in 1893 and now housed inside an onion-shaped fiberglass dome. It doesn't compare with the range of modern telescopes, but it is the largest in the United Kingdom, and regular viewing evenings still reveal startling, detailed views of the lunar surface. In the **Time Galleries,** linger over the superb workmanship of John Harrison (1693–1776), whose famous **Maritime Clocks** won him the Longitude Prize for solving the problem of accurate timekeeping at sea and greatly improved navigation.

DID YOU KNOW?

Once sailors could determine their distance from the Greenwich meridian (Longitude), maritime navigation was greatly improved. Look for the brass line marking the two hemispheres throughout the cobblestone streets.

preserved, and there are few more majestic views in London than Inigo Jones's awe-inspiring symmetry. Completed around 1638, the Tulip Stair, named for the fleur-de-lis–style pattern on the balustrade, is especially fine, spiraling up without a central support to the Great Hall. The Great Hall itself is a perfect cube, exactly 40 feet in all three dimensions, decorated with paintings of the Muses and the Virtues. ⊠ *Romney Rd., Greenwich* ☎ *020/8858–4422* ⊕ *www.nmm. ac.uk* 🎟 *Free* ⊙ *Daily 10–5; last admission 30 min before closing* Ⓤ *DLR: Greenwich.*

Old Royal Naval College. Begun by Christopher Wren in 1694 as a rest home for ancient mariners, it became instead a school for young

GREENWICH FOOT TUNNEL

In a brilliant piece of foresight, Greenwich Hospital bought Island Gardens, on the other side of the Thames, in 1849 to prevent anticipated industrial expansion and preserve the view back toward Greenwich. Take the stone spiral steps down into Greenwich Foot Tunnel and head under the Thames (enjoy the echo during the foreboding walk) to Island Gardens, at the southern tip of the Isle of Dogs, for a magnificent view back over the river, of the Old Royal Naval College and Queen's House, framed by the park.

ones in 1873. Today the University of Greenwich and Trinity College of Music have classes here. Architecturally, you'll notice how the structures part to reveal the **Queen's House** across the central lawns. Behind the college are two more buildings you can visit: the **Painted Hall,** the college's dining hall, derives its name from the baroque murals of William and Mary (reigned 1689–95; William alone 1695–1702) and assorted allegorical figures. James Thornhill's frescoes, depicting scenes of naval grandeur with a suitably pro-British note of propaganda, were painstakingly done over installments in 1708–12 and 1718–26, and were good enough to earn him a knighthood. In the opposite building stands the **College Chapel,** which was rebuilt after a fire in 1779 in an altogether more restrained, neo-Grecian style. ■ TIP→ Trinity College of Music holds free classical music concerts in the chapel every Tuesday lunchtime during the school year. ⊠ *Old Royal Naval College, King William Walk, Greenwich* ☎ *020/8269–4747* ⊕ *www.oldroyalnavalcollege.org* 🎟 *Free, guided tours £5* ⊙ *Painted Hall and chapel daily 10–5 (Sun. chapel from 12:30); grounds 8–6* Ⓤ *DLR: Greenwich.*

Royal Observatory.
See the highlighted listing in this chapter.

WORTH NOTING

Cutty Sark. At this writing, the famous tea clipper itself remains closed until winter 2011. In addition to repairing the damage from the 2007 fire, the ship is being raised and other work is taking place to make it more accessible to visitors. This sleek, romantic clipper was built in 1869, one among fleets and fleets of similar tall-masted wooden ships that plied oceanic highways of the 19th century, trading in exotic commodities—tea, in this case. The *Cutty Sark* was also the fastest,

Without a central support, the Tulip Stair spirals up to the Great Hall of Queen's House.

sailing the China–London route in 1871 in only 107 days. ⊠ *King William Walk, Greenwich* ☎ *020/8858–2698* ⊕ *www.cuttysark.org. uk* Ⓤ *DLR: Cutty Sark.*

Fan Museum. The 2,000 fans here, housed in two restored 1820s buildings opposite the Greenwich Theatre, date from the 17th century onward and make up the world's only such collection. The history and purpose of these objects, often exquisitely crafted from ivory, mother-of-pearl, and tortoiseshell, are explained in satisfying detail. It was the personal vision—and fan collection—of Helene Alexander that brought it into being, and the workshop and conservation–study center that she has also set up ensure that this anachronistic art has a future. If your interest is really piqued, you can attend fan-making workshops (on the first Saturday of every month only—£20 for the afternoon; call ahead or visit the Web site for booking details). ■TIP➜ Afternoon tea is served in the café on Tuesday and Sunday at 3 pm. ⊠ *12 Croom's Hill, Greenwich* ☎ *020/8305–1441* ⊕ *www.fan-museum.org* ▱ *£4* ⊙ *Tues.–Sat. 11–5, Sun. noon–5* Ⓤ *DLR: Greenwich.*

Ranger's House. This handsome, early-18th-century villa, which was the Greenwich Park ranger's official residence during the 19th century, is hung with Stuart and Jacobean portraits. But the most interesting diversion is the Wernher Collection, more than 700 works of art with a northern European flavor, amassed by diamond millionaire Julius Wernher at the turn of the 20th century. After making his money in diamond mining, he amassed an eclectic art collection, from jewelry (one of the largest in the country), porcelain, and enamels, to some particularly bizarre curios. Wernher's American wife, Birdie, was a strong influence

DID YOU KNOW?

The Docklands Light Rail (DLR) connects former warehouses that have been converted to museums and malls, such as Hay's and Butler's wharves, and the gleaming office buildings of Canary Wharf shown here.

THE DOCKLANDS RESISTANCE

12

If it hadn't been for the Thames, Roman Londinium, with its sea link to the rest of the world, would not have grown into a world power. For centuries, life was played out by the riverside, and palaces redolent of Venice—such as Westminster and Whitehall—were built.

Dock warehouses sprang up during the 18th century from the trade with the Indies for tea and coffee, spices, and silks. Trade took a gradual downturn after World War II, leading to the docks' degeneration when larger vessels pushed trade farther downriver to Tilbury.

It took a driverless railway and Britain's tallest building—Canary Wharf Tower—to start a renaissance. Now, what was once a desolate quarter near Greenwich is known as the Docklands, a peninsula of waterways with cutting-edge architecture, offices, water-based leisure and cultural activities, restaurants, and bars. Some of the warehouses have been converted into museums and malls, such as Hay's and Butler's wharves.

The best way to explore is on the **Docklands Light Railway (DLR)**, whose elevated track appears to skim over the water past the swanky glass buildings where the railway is reflected in the windows. On foot, however, the Thames Path has helpful plaques along the way, with nuggets of historical information.

The **Museum of London Docklands**, on a quaint cobbled quayside, beside the tower of Canary Wharf, is worth a visit for its warehouse building alone. With uneven wood floors, beams, and pillars, the museum used to be a storehouse for coffee, tea, sugar, and rum from the West Indies—hence the name West India Quay.

The fascinating story of the old port and the river is told using films, together with interactive displays and reconstructions. The museum runs a highlights tour (free) on Wednesday and Sunday at 3 pm. There are also a handful of special themed tours per season; call or see the Web site for details. ✉ *No. 1 Warehouse, West India Quay, Hertsmere Rd., East End* ☎ *020/7001–9844* ⊕ *www.museumindocklands. org.uk* 🎟 *Free* ◷ *Daily 10–6; last admission 5:30* Ⓤ *Canary Wharf; DLR: West India Quay.*

☉ In its time, the **Ragged School Museum** was the largest school in London and a place where impoverished children could get free education and a good meal. The museum re-creates a classroom dating from the 1880s. It's an eye-opener for adults, and fun for kids, who get the chance to work just like Victorian children did in one of the many organized workshops.

If you really want to get into the spirit, visitors of all ages can attend a Victorian-style lesson (complete with fully costumed schoolmistress) from 2:15 to 3:30 on the first Sunday of every month. ✉ *46–50 Copperfield Rd., East End* ☎ *020/8980–6405* ⊕ *www.raggedschoolmuseum.org.uk* 🎟 *Free; £2 donation requested for Victorian lessons* ◷ *Wed. and Thurs. 10–5, 1st Sun. of month 2–5* Ⓤ *Mile End; DLR: Limehouse.*

and personality during the belle époque, which is easy to imagine from her striking portrait by Sargent. ⊠ *Chesterfield Walk, Greenwich Park, Greenwich* ☎ *020/8853–0035* ⊕ *www.english-heritage.org.uk* 🎟 *£6* ⊗ *Apr.–Sept., Mon.–Wed. guided tours only, 11:30 and 2:30, Sun. 11–5; call ahead to confirm* Ⓤ *DLR: Greenwich; no direct bus access, only to Vanbrugh Hill (from east) and Blackheath Hill (from west).*

OFF THE BEATEN PATH

Thames Barrier Visitors' Centre. Learn what comes between London and its famous river—a futuristic-looking metal barrier that has been described as the eighth wonder of the world. Multimedia presentations, a film on the Thames's history, working models, and views of the barrier itself put the importance of the relationship between London and its river in perspective. ⊠ *Unity Way, Eastmoor St., Woolwich* ☎ *020/8305–4188* ⊕ *www.environment-agency.gov.uk* 🎟 *£3.50* ⊗ *Apr.–Sept., daily 10:30–4:30; Oct.–Mar., daily 11–3:30; last entry 30 min before closing* Ⓤ *National Rail: Charlton (from London Bridge), then Bus 177 or 180; North Greenwich (Jubilee Line), then Bus 161 or 472.*

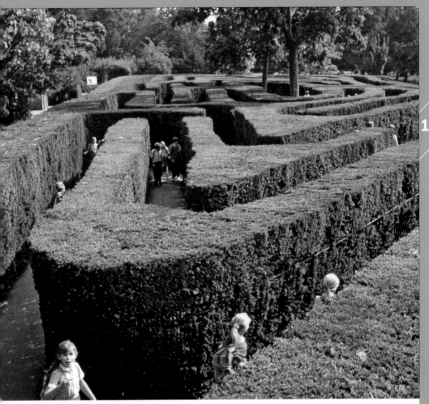

The Thames Upstream

WORD OF MOUTH

"We have in past visits . . . made a day of it by either taking a leisurely cruise from Westminster Pier up to the landing at Hampton Court and catching the train back or vice-versa. Between the two choices, I would say the train in the morning is better, allowing one to stroll through the garden paths up to the palace tearoom for breakfast."

—tod

GETTING ORIENTED

A GOOD WALK

From Chiswick House, follow Burlington Lane and take a left onto Hogarth Lane—which is anything but a lane—to reach Hogarth's House. Chiswick's Church Street is the nearest thing to a sleepy country village street in all of London. Follow it down to the Thames and turn left at the bottom to reach the 18th-century riverfront houses of Chiswick Mall, referred to by locals as "Millionaire's Row" (with runaway inflation, some realtors call it "Billionaire's Row"). There are several pretty riverside pubs near Hammersmith Bridge.

MAKING THE MOST OF YOUR TIME

Hampton Court Palace requires at least half a day to experience its magic fully, although you could make do with an afternoon at Richmond Park, or a couple of hours for any of the other attractions. Because of the distance between the sights, too much traveling eats into your day. The best option is to concentrate on one of the principal sights, adding in a brisk park visit, one stately home, and a riverside promenade before rounding off with an evening pint.

FEELING PECKISH?

The Original Maids of Honour (✉ 288 Kew Rd., Kew ☎ 020/8940–2752 ⊕ www.theoriginalmaidsofhonour.co.uk), the most traditional of Old English tearooms, is named for the famous tarts invented here and still baked by hand on the premises. Tea is served daily 2:30–6. They also serve lunch daily, in two sittings at 12:30 and 1:30. Or opt for take-out to picnic at Kew Gardens or on Kew Green.

13

GETTING THERE

The District Line is the best of the Tube options, stopping at Turnham Green (in the heart of Chiswick but a fair walk from the houses), Gunnersbury (for Syon Park), Kew Gardens, and Richmond. For Hampton Court, overland train is your quickest option: South West trains run from Waterloo twice an hour, with most requiring a change at Surbiton. There are also regular, direct trains from Waterloo to Chiswick station (best for Chiswick House), Kew Bridge, Richmond (for Ham House), and St. Margaret's (best for Marble Hill House). London Overground trains also stop at Gunnersbury, Kew Gardens, and Richmond. A pleasant, if slow, way to go is by river. Boats depart upriver from Westminster Pier, by Big Ben, for Kew (1½ hours), Richmond (2 hours), and Hampton Court (3 hours) several times a day in summer, less frequently from October through March. The boat trip is worth taking only if you make it an integral part of your day out, and be aware that it can get very breezy on the water.

TOP REASONS TO GO

Hampton Court Palace: Get lost in the leafy walls of the palace's maze as dusk falls.

Strawberry Hill: The 19th-century birthplace of connoisseur Horace Walpole's "Gothick" style, this mock castle just reopened its doors to the public in 2010.

Richmond: Browse the antiques shops and travel back in time of this lovely "village."

Kew Gardens: See the earth from above, by visiting Kew's treetop walkway, at the Royal Botanic Gardens.

Thames-side Views: Enjoy a pint from the creaking balcony of a centuries-old riverside pub as you watch the boats row home.

NEAREST PUBLIC RESTROOMS

Richmond Park, Kew Gardens, and all the stately homes have public restrooms available.

Sightseeing
★★★★
Nightlife
★★
Dining
★★★
Lodging
★★
Shopping
★★

The upper stretch of the Thames unites a string of lustrous riverside pearls—Chiswick, Kew, Richmond, Putney, and Strawberry Hill—taking in friendly streets, horticultural delights, regal magnificence, and Henry VIII's fiendish outdoor labyrinth at Hampton Court Palace. The neighborhoods dotted along the way are as proud of their village-y feel as of their stately history, with many a pleasing pub nestled at the water's edge. After the busyness of the West End, it's easy to forget you're in a capital city.

CHISWICK AND KEW

Updated by
Jack Jewers

Chiswick is the nearest Thames-side destination to central London. It's a low-key district, content with its good run of restaurants, stylish shops, and film-star residents, but it is also proud of the seething moral authority of its most famous son: William Hogarth, one of Britain's best-loved painters, lived here, and tore the fabric of the 18th-century nation to pieces in his slew of satirical engravings. Incongruously stranded among Chiswick's terraced homes are a number of fine 18th-century houses, and a charming little village survives, populated by London's affluent middle-class families. A mile or so beyond Chiswick is Kew, and the village atmosphere here makes this one of the most desirable areas of outer London. The biggest draw for visitors, though, is the Royal Botanic Gardens.

EXPLORING

★ **Chiswick House.** Completed in 1729 by the 3rd Earl of Burlington (of Burlington House—home of the Royal Academy—and Burlington Arcade fame), this extraordinary Palladian mansion was envisaged as a kind of temple to the arts. Burlington was fascinated by the architecture he saw in Italy while on the Grand Tour as a young man. When his country home was destroyed by fire in 1725, he seized the chance to rebuild it in homage to those classical and Renaissance styles. The building is loosely modeled on the Villa Capra near Vicenza, while the colonnaded frontage is a partial replica of the Pantheon in Rome (which also inspired the domed roof).

The sumptuous interiors were the work of William Kent (1685–1748), his most extraordinary achievement being the Blue Velvet Room, with its gilded decoration and intricate painted ceiling. The design of Chiswick House sparked a great deal of interest—such ideas were radical in England at the time—and you'll see its influence reflected in numerous later buildings. The rambling gardens are one of the hidden gems of West London. Italianate in style (of course), they are filled with classical temples, statues, and obelisks. A £12 million restoration of the grounds was completed in 2010, adding a new café and a children's play area. ⊠ *Burlington La., Chiswick* ☎ *020/8995–0508* ⊕ *www.chgt.org.uk* ☑ *£5* ⊙ *Grounds daily 7–dusk; house daily 10–4, Mar.–Oct.* Ⓤ *Turnham Green, Chiswick*.

Hogarth's House. Besieged by a roaring highway that somewhat spoils the atmosphere, the home of the satirist and painter William Hogarth (1697–1764) is still worth a visit by art lovers, especially for fans of his amusing, moralistic engravings (such as "The Rake's Progress" and "Marriage à la Mode"). At this writing, Hogarth House is preparing to reopen after a long period of restoration because of fire damage in 2008. This will include an expanded museum, with new exhibits and educational programs. Hogarth's tomb can be found in the cemetery of St. Nicholas's church on Chiswick Mall. ⊠ *Hogarth La., Great West Rd., Chiswick* ☎ *020/8994–6757* ⊕ *www.hounslow.info/ arts/hogarthshouse* ☑ *Free* ⊙ *Tentative at this writing, but probably Apr.–Sept., Tues.–Fri. 1–5, weekends 1–6; Oct.–Mar., Tues.–Fri. 1–4, weekends 1–5* Ⓤ *Turnham Green.*

HOGARTH HEAVEN

A great place to buy Hogarth prints is at **Fosters Bookshop** (⊠ *183 Chiswick High Rd.* ☎ *020/8995-2768* ⊕ *www. fostersbookshop.co.uk*), the oldest shop in Chiswick. The shop has its original Georgian frontage, creaking floorboards, and a glorious number of original Victorian novels and essays. It also offers handwritten gift vouchers from £10 to £50,000.

13

QUICK BITES

Pubs are the name of the game here at Chiswick's portion of the Thames. Many pubs sit on the bank of the river, offering watery vistas to accompany stout pints of brew. The **Blue Anchor** (⊠ *13 Lower Mall, Hammersmith* ☎ *020/8748-5774* ⊕ *www.blueanchorlondon.com*) is a cozy 18th-century watering hole, with rowing memorabilia lining the walls. The **City Barge** (⊠ *27 Strand-on-the-Green, Chiswick* ☎ *020/8994–2148*) on the north bank of the Thames has a lovely riverside terrace and honest pub grub. The **Dove Inn** (⊠ *19 Upper Mall, Hammersmith* ☎ *020/8748-9474*) retains the charm of its 300-plus-year heritage. If you can find a spot on the tiny terrace, it's a tranquil place to watch the energetic oarsmen. The food is good here, too (especially Sunday lunch).

♨ **Kew Gardens.**

★ *See the highlighted listing in this chapter.*

Kew Palace and Queen Charlotte's Cottage. To this day quietly domestic Kew Palace remains the smallest royal palace in the land. The house and gardens offer a glimpse into the 17th century. Originally known as the Dutch House, it was bought by King George II to provide more room in addition to the White House (another royal residence that used to exist on the grounds) for the extended Royal Family. In spring there's a romantic haze of bluebells. ⊠ *Kew Gardens, Kew* ⊕ *www.hrp.org.uk* ✉ *£5, in addition to ticket for Kew Gardens* ⊘ *Apr.–Sept., Tues.–Sun. 10–5, Mon. 11–5* Ⓤ *Kew Gardens.*

RICHMOND

Named after the palace Henry VII built here in 1500, Richmond is still a welcoming and extremely pretty riverside "village," with many handsome (and expensive) houses, antiques shops, a Victorian theater, London's grandest stately home, and, best of all, the largest of London's royal parks.

EXPLORING

★ **Ham House.** To the west of Richmond Park, overlooking the Thames and nearly opposite the oddly named Eel Pie Island, the house was built in 1610 by Sir Thomas Vavasour, knight marshal to James I, then refurbished later in the century by the Duke and Duchess of Lauderdale, who managed to produce one of the finest houses in Britain at the time. It's one of the most complete examples in Europe of a lavish Restoration period house, with a restored formal garden, which has become an influential source for other European palaces and grand villas. The original decorations in the Great Hall, Round Gallery, and Great Staircase have been replicated, and all the furniture and fittings are on permanent loan from the Victoria & Albert Museum. A tranquil and scenic way to reach the house is on foot, which takes about 30 minutes, along the eastern riverbank south from Richmond Bridge. ⊠ *Ham St., Richmond* ☎ *020/8940–1950* ⊕ *www.nationaltrust.org.uk* ✉ *House, gardens, and outbuildings £10; gardens only £3.50* ⊘ *House mid-Mar. to Oct., Sat.–Wed. noon–4; late Feb. and early Mar., weekends noon–4 (limited guided tours only). Gardens mid-Feb.–Oct., Sat.–Wed. 11–5; early Nov.–mid-Dec., weekends 11–5; Jan.–early Feb., weekends 11–4.* Ⓤ *Richmond, then Bus 65 or 371.*

Fodor's Choice **Hampton Court Palace.**

★ *See the highlighted listing in this chapter.*

Marble Hill House. On the northern bank of the Thames, almost opposite Ham House, stands another mansion, this one a near-perfect example of a Palladian villa. Set in 66 acres of parkland, Marble Hill House was built in the 1720s by George II for his mistress, the "exceedingly respectable and respected" Henrietta Howard. Later the house was occupied by Mrs. Fitzherbert, who was secretly married to the Prince Regent (later George IV) in 1785. Marble Hill House was restored in 1901 and opened to the public two years later, looking very much

KEW GARDENS

✉ *Royal Botanic Gardens, Kew, Richmond, Surrey (main entrance is between Richmond Circus and traffic circle at Mortlake Rd.)*
☎ *020/8332–5655*
🌐 *www.kew.org* 🎟 *£13.50*
🕐 *Feb., daily 9:30–5:30; Mar.–Aug., weekdays 9:30–6:30, weekends 9:30–7:30; Sept. and Oct., 9:30–6; Nov.–Feb. 9:30–4:15* Ⓤ *Kew Gardens.*

13

TIPS

■ Guided tours with nature-loving volunteers leave daily from the Guides' desk inside Victoria Plaza at 11 and 2.

■ Can't tell your False acacia from your Corsican pine? The 90-minute Tree Identification Tour leaves from Museum No. 1 (opposite the Palm House) on Saturday at 11:30, £5. Book ahead (020/8332–5604).

■ Fresh air and natural beauty made you peckish? Treat your taste buds to a light tea at the Victoria Terrace Café, dine outside at White Peaks, or go elegant at the Orangery.

■ Hire a Kew Ranger—an interactive handheld GPS that will lead you to highlights, give hints and snippets of history, and even give kids "hunting clues" to keep them occupied. Pick one up from Victoria Gate for £4.95.

Enter Kew Gardens and you are enveloped by blazes of color, extraordinary blooms, hidden trails, magnificent buildings, and centuries of endeavor aimed at getting to grips with the mysteries of plants that entrance, medicate, and excite. Even today academics are hard at work on more than 300 scientific projects across as many acres, researching everything from the cacti of eastern Brazil to the yams of Madagascar. First opened to the public in 1840, Kew has been supported by royalty and nurtured by landscapers, botanists, and architects since the 1720s, and with more than 30,000 species of plants, there is interest and beauty in spades.

Although the plant houses make Kew worth visiting even in the depths of winter (there's also a seasonal garden), the flower beds come into their own in spring and summer.

HIGHLIGHTS

Two great 19th-century greenhouses—the **Palm House** and the **Temperate House**—are filled with exotic blooms, and many of the plants have been there since the final glass panel was fixed into place. The Temperate House, once the biggest greenhouse in the world, today contains the largest greenhouse plant in the world, a Chilean wine palm rooted in 1846. You can climb the spiral staircase to the roof and look down on it and the dense tropical profusion from the walkway. Architect Sir William Chambers built a series of temples and follies, of which the crazy 50-story **Pagoda,** visible for miles around, is the star turn. The Princess of Wales conservatory houses 10 climate zones, and the Rhizotron & Xstrata treetop walkway takes you 59 feet up into the air.

like it did in Georgian times, with extravagant gilded rooms in which Ms. Howard entertained famous poets and wits of the age, including Pope, Gay, and Swift. A ferry service operates during the summer from Ham House across the river; access on foot is a half-hour walk south along the west bank from Richmond Bridge. Guided tours by volunteers from the local history group, the Marble Hill Society, are at noon on Saturday, 11 and 2:30 Sunday. They cost £5, which includes the entrance fee to the house. ⊠ *Richmond Rd., Twickenham, Richmond* ☎ *020/8892–5115* ⊕ *www.english-heritage.org.uk* 🖾 *£5* ⊙ *Apr.–Oct., Sat. 10–2, Sun. and bank holidays 10–5; Nov.–Mar., prebooked tours only* Ⓤ *Richmond.*

WORD OF MOUTH

"We found the boat trip from Richmond to Hampton Court Palace one of the highlights of our most recent visit to Britain. And everybody else on the boat was pretty happy also. Nice being carried gently along past pubs and houses with boats tied up in front and greening parks and trees. You do want good weather for this; May is the perfect time of year."

—Mimar

Richmond Park. Charles I enclosed this one in 1637 for hunting purposes, like practically all the other parks. Unlike the others, however, Richmond Park still has wild red and fallow deer roaming its 2,360 acres (that's three times the size of New York's Central Park!) of grassland and heath and the oldest oaks you're likely to see—vestiges of the forests that encroached on London from all sides in medieval times. The Isabella Plantation (near the Ham Gate entrance) is an enchanting and colorful woodland garden, first laid out in 1831. ■TIP→ There's a splendid, protected view of St. Paul's Cathedral from King Henry VIII's Mound. Established in 1710, it measures 10 mi and is the bane of overenthusiastic town planners. Find it and you have a piece of magic in your sights. The park is also home to White Lodge, a 1727 hunting lodge that now houses the Royal Ballet School. Though the school isn't open to the public, it does contain the small **White Lodge Museum** (☎ *020/8392–8440* ⊕ *www.royal-ballet-school.org.uk*) dedicated to the history of the school and ballet in general. Entry is on Tuesday and Thursday afternoons during the school year only and prebooking is essential. *Richmond* ☎ *020/8948–3209* ⊕ *www.royalparks.org.uk* ⊙ *Mar.–late Dec., daily 7–dusk; late Dec.–Feb., daily 7:30–dusk* Ⓤ *Richmond, then Bus 371 or 65.*

QUICK BITES

The White Cross (⊠ *Water La., Richmond* ☎ *020/8940–6844*), on the site of a monastery, serves traditional pub grub.

Syon House and Park. The residence of the Duke and Duchess of Northumberland, this is one of England's most sumptuous stately homes, and certainly the only one that's near a Tube station. Set in a 55-acre park landscaped by Capability Brown, the core of the house is Tudor—Henry VIII's fifth wife, Catherine Howard, and the extremely short-lived monarch, Lady Jane Grey ("Queen for thirteen days"), made pit stops here before they were sent to the Tower—but it was remodeled in the Georgian style in 1761 by famed decorator Robert

Fodor's Choice
★

HAMPTON COURT PALACE

⌧ *Hampton Court Palace, East Molesley, Surrey* ☎ *0844/482–7799 tickets, 0844/482-7777 information* ⊕ *www.hrp.org.uk/hamptoncourtpalace* 🎫 *£14* ⊘ *Late Mar.–Oct., daily 10–6 (last ticket sold at 5; last entry to maze at 5:15); Nov.– late Mar., daily 10–4:30 (last ticket sold at 3:30; last entry to maze at 3:45); check Web site before visiting* ⓤ *Richmond, then Bus R68; National Rail, South West: Hampton Court Station, 35 min from Waterloo (most trains require change at Surbiton).*

13

TIPS

■ Avoid the queue and save by buying your tickets online.

■ In a group? Save nearly £10 on admission with a £38 family ticket (two adults, three children).

■ Choose which parts of the palace to explore based on a number of self-guided audio walking tours.

■ Come Christmastime, there's ice-skating on a rink before the West Front of the palace—an unmissable mixture of pleasantry and pageantry.

■ Special programs, such as cooking demonstrations in the cavernous Tudor kitchens, also make history fun for young royal-watchers.

Today the royal palace that sits beside the slow-moving Thames gives you two palaces for the price of one: The magnificent Tudor redbrick mansion that was begun in 1514 by Cardinal Wolsey to impress the young Henry, and the larger 17th-century baroque offering, for which the graceful south wing was designed by Christopher Wren of St. Paul's fame. The first buildings of Hampton Court belonged to a religious order founded in the 11th century and were expanded over the years by its many subsequent residents, none more important than Henry VIII and his six wives. Henry spent a king's ransom (today's equivalent of £18 million or $27.5 million) expanding and refurbishing the palace.

HIGHLIGHTS

If Tudor takes your fancy, wander through the **State Apartments,** hung with priceless paintings, and on to the wood-beamed magnificence of **Henry's Great Hall,** lined with tapestries and the mustiness of old, before taking in the strikingly azure ceiling of the **Chapel Royal.** Topping it all is the Great House of Easement, a lavatory that could sit 28 people at a time.

Feel a chill in the air? Watch out for the ghost of Henry VIII's doomed fifth wife, Catherine Howard, who literally lost her head yet apparently still screams her way along the **Haunted Gallery.** The latter-day baroque transformers of the palace, William and Mary, maintained beautiful **King's and Queen's Apartments, Georgian Rooms,** and fine collections of porcelain.

Don't miss the world's most famous maze, its ½ mi of pathways among clipped hedgerows still fiendish to negotiate. There's a trick, but we won't give it away here: it's much more fun to go and lose yourself.

In summer months, consider arriving in style by riverboat (see "A Tour of the Thames" special section) at Hampton Court.

Adam. He had just returned from studying the sights of classical antiquity in Italy and created two rooms here worthy of any Caesar: the entryway is an amazing study in black and white, pairing neoclassical marbles with antique bronzes, and the Ante-Room contains 12 enormous verd-antique columns surmounted by statues of gold—this, no less, was meant to be a waiting room for the duke's servants and retainers. The Red Drawing Room is covered with crimson Spitalfields silk, and the Long Gallery is one of Adam's noblest creations. In the grounds of Syon Park, the **Tropical Zoo** (☎ *020/8847–4730* ⊕ *www. tropicalzoo.org*) is a rescue sanctuary for abused, abandoned, and illegally kept exotic pets, from snakes and tarantulas to marmosets and crocodiles. Kids even get to handle (some of) the creatures themselves at 11, 2, and 4 on weekends, and sometimes during the week if you call ahead. ■TIP→ On certain bank holidays and Sundays in the summer you can take a miniature steam-train ride in the grounds. ⊠ *Syon Park, Brentford* ☎ *020/8560–0882* ⊕ *www.syonpark.co.uk* ☜ *£9 for house, gardens, conservatory, and rose garden; £4.50 for gardens and conservatory; £6.50 for Tropical Zoo* ☉ *House mid-Mar.–Oct., Wed., Thurs., Sun., and bank holidays 11–5; gardens daily mid-Mar.–Oct. 10:30–5; Nov.–mid-Mar. 10:30–4; Tropical Zoo daily 10–5:30. Last admission 1 hr before closing* Ⓤ *Gunnersbury, then Bus 237 or 267 to Brentlea stop.*

★ **Strawberry Hill.** From the outside, this Rococo mish-mash of towers, crenulations, and dazzling white stucco is almost fairytale-ish in its faux-medieval splendor. Its architect, Sir Horace Walpole (1717–1797), knew a thing or two about imaginative flights of fancy—the flamboyant son of the first British prime minister, he all but single-handedly invented the Gothic Revival style with his novel *The Castle of Otranto* (1764). Once inside, the forbidding exterior gives way to a veritable explosion of color and light for Walpole boldly decided to take elements from the exteriors of Gothic cathedrals and move them inside for interior accents. Constructed from 1748 onwards, the detail is extraordinary, from the cavernous entrance hall with its vast Gothic trompe l'oeil, to the Great Parlour with its Renaissance stained glass, to the Gallery, whose extraordinary fan vaulting was an amazing replica of the vaults found in Henry VIII's chapel at Westminster Abbey. Neglected for years, Strawberry Hill re-opened in April 2011 after a £9 million restoration (which also used brilliant white stucco to cover up a time-burnished, centuries-old exterior). ⊠ *268 Waldegrave Rd., Twickenham* ☎ *020/8744–3124* ⊕ *www.strawberryhillhouse.org.uk* ☜ *£8* ☉ *Apr.–early Nov., Sat.–Sun. noon–4:20, Mon.–Wed. 2–4:20* Ⓤ *Richmond, then bus 33; National Rail: Strawberry Hill Station.*

Tower Bridge

A TOUR OF THE THAMES

"I have seen the Mississippi. That is muddy water.
I have seen the St. Lawrence. That is crystal water.
But the Thames is liquid history."
—*John Burns*

The twists and turns of the Thames River through the heart of the capital make it London's best thoroughfare and most compelling viewing point. Once famous for sludge, silt, and sewage, the Thames is now the cleanest city river in the world. Whether you take a river cruise or a leisurely stroll along its banks and bridges, traveling on or alongside the river is an unforgettable way to soak up views of the city.

HAMPTON COURT PALACE TO PUTNEY

The Great Conservatory at Syon Park

Waterlily House at Kew Gardens

Hampton Court Palace is a suitably lavish start or end to any trip on the Thames. The river skirts the grounds, giving magnificent views over the Tudor palace that Henry VIII and his daughter Elizabeth I made home, and continues north to **Kingston Bridge**, starting point for the river voyage of Jerome K. Jerome's *Three Men in a Boat* and home to hectic summer regattas. At **Teddington**, where the poet Alexander Pope and writer Horace Walpole entertained their female admirers in the 18th century, the river turns tidal but remains quiet and unspoiled all the way to **Kew**, passing herons and fine stately homes standing proud on the banks. From **Twickenham Bridge** you round the old deer park (to the south) and **Syon Park** (north), which has belonged to the Duke of Nor-

thumberland's family for centuries. Beyond that is an even greater treat—the UNESCO World Heritage Site of **Kew Botanical Gardens**. All manner of rowboats set up for one, two, four, or eight people pull hard under **Chiswick Bridge** and **Barnes (railway) Bridge**, past the expensive riverside frontage of Chiswick Mall and under **Hammersmith Bridge**, to **Putney** and **Fulham**— smart urban villages facing each other across the banks.

Syon Park

Kew Botanical Gardens

Twickenham Br.

Richmond Landing Stage

Richmond Br.

Marble Hill Park

Eel Pie Island

Teddington

Kingston Br.

Bushy Park

Hampton Ct. Br.

Hampton Court Palace

Hampton Court Pier

0   1 mi

0   1 km

The stretch between Kew and Hammersmith is real rowing and riverside-pub territory, with a picturesque parade past Strand-on-the-Green by Kew Bridge.

ROWERS' ROW Every spring Britain's oldest universities, Oxford and Cambridge, compete not with their brains but with their brawn, in the **Boat Race**, which began in 1829. The race is 4¼ miles upstream from Putney Bridge to Chiswick Bridge: expect clashing oars, clenched teeth, and the occasional sinking (there have been six). The best views are from Hammersmith at the Surrey bend, which is also where most of the pubs are clustered. ⊕ www.theboatrace.org

A BRIEF HISTORY

An engraving by Claes Van Visscher showing Old London Bridge in 1616, with Southwark Cathedral in the foreground

The Thames has come a long way—and not just from its 344-km (214-mi) journey from a remote Gloucestershire

meadow to the sea. In the mid-19th century, the river was dying, poisoned by sewers that flushed into the river. The "Big Stink" was so awful that cholera and typhoid killed more than 10,000 in 1853, and Parliament abandoned sitting in 1858. "The odour is hardly that of frankincense," said one contemporary of the 1884 drought that forced down water levels, leaving elegant Victorian nostrils exposed to slimy ooze on the banks.

Joseph Bazalgette, star civil engineer of his time, was commissioned to design a new sewage system, and by the 1900s nearly all was forgiven. (His efforts did not go unappreciated: Bazalgette was later knighted.) Today 7.2 million people get their drinking water from the Thames River.

WANDSWORTH TO BLACKFRIARS

Parliament

Blackfriars Bridge at night.

Battersea Br.

Albert Br.

Chelsea Harbour Pier

Chelsea Br.

Grosvenor Br.

South Park

Battersea Park

Wandsworth Br.

Battersea Power Station

0   1/2 mi

0   1/2 km

WALKING THE THAMES

Even if you lack sea legs, you can still enjoy the river: not much beats a wander beside London's waterway. The Thames Path (www.nationaltrail.co.uk) follows the river 184 miles, from its source to the flood barriers in Greenwich. Some of the best riverside strolls:

- Hammersmith Bridge to Chiswick Mall
- Golden Jubilee Bridges to the South Bank's Queen's Walk
- Cleopatra's Needle to Parliament along Victoria Embankment
- Tate Modern to St. Paul's over Millennium Bridge

Beyond **Wandsworth Bridge**, the early part of this stretch by Battersea Bridge, rebuilt in 1890, was London's real industrial heartland, the southern side chock full of cottage housing for laborers, artisans at work, and factories.

View from London Eye (left); House's of Parliament (right)

The real treat of this stretch is the view of the **Houses of Parliament** and, beyond that, **Westminster Abbey**. **Victoria Embankment**, stretching all the way from Westminster to Blackfriars, was once all grim mudflats. In 1878 it became the country's first electrically illuminated street, and today its fine architecture, trees, and gardens are perfect strolling territory.

You can't miss the **London Eye**, whose parts were brought down the Thames one by one before being assembled on-location. Look out too for the London Aquarium and the Dalí museum, housed in the baroque-style County Hall.

Cleopatra's Needle, overlooking the Thames by Embankment, dates back to Heliopolis in 1450 BC. Look for World War I shrapnel holes and gouges at the base.

After **Albert Bridge**—glorious at night, with lights like luminescent pearls sweeping down on strings—the Thames is a metropolitan glory of a river, charging through fashionable **Chelsea** and past the now derelict **Battersea Power Station**, under Chelsea, Vauxhall and Lambeth Bridges, with **Lambeth Palace** to the south.

The **Golden Jubilee Bridges** by **Embankment**, two beautifully lit steel-cabled pedestrian walkways, are perfect for reaching the **South Bank**.

Look out for the golden eagle, a monument to World War I RAF fighters, and **Cleopatra's Needle**. For the ultimate double-decker bus-viewing moment, look at **Waterloo Bridge**, once known as Ladies Bridge because it was built by female labor during World War II. The bridge has great views of the South Bank.

Further on is the **Oxo Tower**, whose red-glass letters were designed in 1928 to spell out the brand name while circumventing tight laws on exterior advertising.

By **Blackfriars Bridge**, named after the monks who wore black robes and lived on the north bank during the Middle Ages, the river used to run red by the riverside tanneries and slaughterhouses.

Blackfriars Bridge

MILLENNIUM BRIDGE TO THAMES FLOOD BARRIER

Tower Bridge

The **Millennium Bridge** is the newest span across the river: **St. Paul's Cathedral** and **Tate Modern** eye each other magnificently from either side of the once worryingly wobbly strip of a bridge. Farther east, the reconstructed **Shakespeare's Globe Theatre** is resplendent in whitewash and brown timber on the South Bank.

Between Southwark and London bridges, look for the southside *Golden Hinde*, an exact scale reconstruction of Sir Francis Drake's galleon that sailed around the world.

Moored outside the Victorian shopping mall **Hay's Galleria** is **HMS** *Belfast*, Europe's last existing armored warship that saw action in World War II, now a floating naval museum on nine decks.

London Bridge is admittedly not the river's finest, but it is the birthplace of the city. Some say the river ceases to be picturesque after St. Paul's, but we disagree: look for the flaming crown of the **Monument**, Sir Christopher Wren's tribute to those who died in the 1666 Great Fire of London.

The splendid **Tower of London** sits proudly opposite the shining egg of **City Hall** (also referred to by the former London mayor Ken Livingstone as a giant "glass testicle"—a fine match for its phallic friend across the river, the **Swiss Re Building**, aka the Gherkin, both designed by a mischievous Norman Foster). They frame the 1894 **Tower Bridge**, a magnificent feat of engineering and style, which leads past the elegant confines of **St. Katharine's Docks**, the trendy restaurants of **Butler's Wharf**, and the **Design Museum**.

LONDON BRIDGE

Viking invaders destroyed London Bridge in 1014, hence the nursery rhyme "London Bridge is falling down." By 1962, London Bridge really was falling down again, its 1831 incarnation unable to take the strain of traffic. It was saved by American tycoon Robert McCulloch, who—possibly confusing the bridge with its much more splendid neighbor, Tower Bridge—bought it in 1968 for $2.46 million and had it shipped, stone by stone, to Lake Havasu in Arizona.

Thames Flood Barrier

For the pièce de résistance of London's redevelopment, stay on the river until you reach the bright lights and tall reflective sides of **Canary Wharf**, the city's new business district, robotic in its modernity.

Step back in time at **Greenwich**, with the glorious **Royal Naval College** and the **National Maritime Museum**. Round the bend and you're back to the future, with the alien spaceship **O2** (formerly the Millennium Dome) and the **Thames Flood Barrier** looming.

Walking bridge at Canary Wharf

Limehouse Basin

Canary Wharf

Canary Wharf Pier

Hilton Docklands Nelson Dock Pier

West India Millwall Docks

Design Museum

O2

Greenland Docks

Greenland Pier

Millwall Outer Docks

Thames Flood Barrier

Masthouse Terrace Pier

Royal Naval College

Greenwich Pier

National Maritime Museum

Greenwich

Greenwich Park

0   1/4 mi
0   1/4 km

PLANNING A THAMES BOAT TOUR

"On the smallest pretext of holiday or fine weather the mighty population takes to the boats," wrote Henry James in 1877. You can follow in the footsteps of James, who took a boat trip from Westminster to Greenwich, or make up your own itinerary.

■ Frequent daily tourist-boat services are at their height between April and October.

■ In most cases you can turn up at a pier, and the next departure won't be far away. However, it never hurts to book ahead if you can.

■ Westminster and Tower piers are the busiest starting points, usually with boats heading east.

■ TIP→ For a rundown of all the options, along with prices and timetables, contact **London River Services** (☎ 0843/ 222–1234 ⊕ www.tfl.gov.uk/river), which gives details of all the operators sailing various sections of the river.

■ The trip between Westminster Pier and the Tower of London takes about 30 minutes, as does the trip between the Tower and Greenwich.

■ A full round-trip can take several hours. Ask about flexible fares and hop on/off options at the various piers.

THE BEST WAYS TO EXPERIENCE THE THAMES WHILE...

GOING OFF THE BEATEN PATH (LITERALLY)	020/7928–3132	www.londonducktours.co.uk	£20
	London Ducktours offers sightseeing with a twist—amphibious patrol vehicles used in World War II have been painted like rubber duckies and traverse land and sea.		Departs from the London Eye (on land): Summer, daily approx. every 30 mins 9:30–6; times vary in winter.
SAVING TIME AND MONEY	020/7887–8888	www.tate.org.uk/tatetotate	£5 one-way
	The playfully polka-dotted *Tate Boat* ferries passengers across the river from the Tate Britain to the Tate Modern.		Departs from the pier at either museum: Daily every 40 mins. Approximately 18 mins. one-way.
IMPRESSING A DATE OR CLIENT	020/7695–1800	www.bateauxlondon.com	£27.50–£39.50 (lunch), £75–£120 (dinner)
	For ultimate glamour (and expense), look into lunch and dinner cruises with **Bateaux London**, often formal affairs with surprisingly good two- to five-course meals. Variations include jazz brunch cruises on Sundays.		Departs from Embankment Pier for lunch: Apr.–Dec., Wed.–Sat. (also Tues. in Jul. and Aug.), 12; Jan.–Mar., Thur.–Sat., 12; for dinner: Apr.–Dec., daily 7:30; Jan.–Mar., Tue.–Sat., 7:30.
ENJOYING ON-BOARD ENTERTAINMENT	020/7740–0400	www.citycruises.com	£75
	The *London Showboat* lives up to its name, with four-course meals, snazzy cabaret acts from West End musicals, and after-dinner dancing.		Departs from Westminster Pier: Apr.–Oct., Wed.–Sun. 7:30 pm; Nov., Dec., Mar., Thurs.–Sat. 7:30 pm; Jan.–Feb., Fri.–Sat. 7:30 pm (boarding starts 15 mins. prior to departure). Approximately 3½ hours. Book 48 hours in advance.

Where to Eat

WORD OF MOUTH

"I can recommend Le Gavroche. Not sure it could be described as 'hot', but excellent it certainly is—expensive, old-school French with old fashioned décor (jacket required for gentlemen)."

—Odin

THE SCENE

Updated
by Alex
Wijeratna

London rivals Tokyo, New York, and Paris as one of the best places to eat in the world right now. The sheer diversity of restaurants here is unparalleled. Among the city's 6,700 restaurants are see-and-be-seen hot spots, casual ethnic eateries, innovative gastropubs, and hotel-based temples to haute cuisine.

To measure London's spectacular culinary rise, note that it was once a common dictum that the British ate to live, whereas the French lived to eat. The best of British food—local, seasonal, wild, and regional—is now all the rage and appears on more menus by the day. Waste not, want not "nose-to-tail" eating—where every scrap of meat is deemed fair game for the plate—has made a spectacular comeback at St. John in Clerkenwell, and fits perfectly with the age of austerity. Meanwhile, the haute cuisine scene powers serenely on. Clare Smyth sets the highest bar as head chef at Restaurant Gordon Ramsay; Marcus Wareing wows at the Berkeley; Brett Graham is cooking on gas at the Ledbury; and Hélène Darroze does it for the girls at the Connaught.

For cheap eats, don't miss the city's unofficial dish, the ubiquitous Indian curry. The quality of other international cuisines also has grown in recent years, with London becoming known for its Thai, Malaysian, Spanish, Turkish, and North African restaurants. With all of the choices, traditional British food, when you track it down, appears as just one more exotic cuisine in the pantheon.

Whatever eating experience you seek, London can likely deliver. From dirt-cheap street food to posh multicourse meals, the city has become a destination for gustatory adventurers. In this chapter, we've uncovered the best of the best. Dig in, and enjoy!

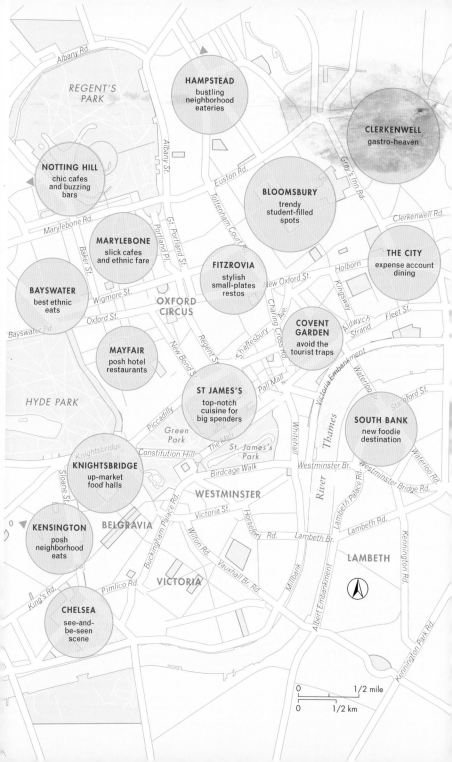

REGENT'S PARK

HAMPSTEAD
bustling neighborhood eateries

CLERKENWELL
gastro-heaven

NOTTING HILL
chic cafes and buzzing bars

BLOOMSBURY
trendy student-filled spots

MARYLEBONE
slick cafes and ethnic fare

THE CITY
expense account dining

FITZROVIA
stylish small-plates restos

BAYSWATER
best ethnic eats

OXFORD CIRCUS

COVENT GARDEN
avoid the tourist traps

MAYFAIR
posh hotel restaurants

HYDE PARK

ST JAMES'S
top-notch cuisine for big spenders

SOUTH BANK
new foodie destination

KNIGHTSBRIDGE
up-market food halls

Green Park

St. James's Park

WESTMINSTER

KENSINGTON
posh neighborhood eats

BELGRAVIA

LAMBETH

VICTORIA

CHELSEA
see-and-be-seen scene

Albany Rd.
Albany St.
Euston Rd.
Gt. Portland St.
Portland Pl.
Tottenham Court Rd.
Gray's Inn Rd.
Clerkenwell Rd.
Marylebone Rd.
Baker St.
Wigmore St.
New Oxford St.
Holborn
Kingsway
Aldwych
Fleet St.
Strand
Oxford St.
Bayswater Rd.
New Bond St.
Charing Cross Ave.
Shaftesbury
Regent St.
Pall Mall
Victoria Embankment
Waterloo Br.
Stamford St.
Waterloo Rd.
Piccadilly
The Mall
Whitehall
Thames
Westminster Br.
Westminster Bridge Rd.
Knightsbridge
Constitution Hill
Birdcage Walk
Sloane St.
Victoria St.
Buckingham Palace Rd.
Wilton Rd.
Horseferry Rd.
Lambeth Palace Rd.
Lambeth Br.
Lambeth Rd.
River
Millbank
Albert Embankment
Kennington Rd.
Kennington Park Rd.
King's Rd.
Pimlico Rd.
Vauxhall Br. Rd.

0   1/2 mile
0   1/2 km

WHERE TO EAT PLANNER

Eating Out Strategy

Where should you eat? With thousands of London eateries competing for your attention, it may seem like a daunting question. But fret not—our expert writers and editors have done most of the legwork. The selections here represent the best this city has to offer—from hot pudding to haute cuisine. Search "Best Bets" for top recommendations by price, cuisine, and experience. Sample local flavor in the neighborhood features. Or find a review quickly in the neighborhood listings. Whichever way you look at it, you're sure to get a taste of London!

Reservations

Plan ahead if you're determined to snag a sought-after reservation. Some renowned restaurants are booked weeks or months in advance. In the reviews, we mention reservations only when they're essential or not accepted, though it's always a good idea to book as far ahead as you can and reconfirm when you arrive in London. Note that some top restaurants also now take credit-card details and charge a penalty fee if you're a no-show.

What to Wear

When in England's style capital, do as the natives do: Dress up to eat out. Whatever your style, dial it up a notch. Have some fun while you're at it. Pull out the clothes you've been saving for a "special" occasion and get a little glamorous. As unfair as it seems, the way you look can influence how you're treated—and where you're seated. Generally speaking, jeans and a button-down shirt will suffice at most table-service restaurants in the £ to ££ range. Moving up from there, many pricier restaurants require jackets, and some insist on ties. Shorts, sweatpants, and sports jerseys are rarely appropriate. Note that in reviews we mention dress only when men are required to wear a jacket, or a jacket and tie.

Tipping and Taxes

Do not tip bar staff in pubs and bars—though you can always offer to buy them a drink. In restaurants, tip 10% to 12.5% of the check for full meals if service is not already included; tip a small token if you're just having coffee or tea. If paying by credit card, double-check that a tip has not already been included in the bill.

Children

Unless your children behave impeccably, it's best to avoid the high-class establishments; you're unlikely to find a children's menu there, anyway. London's many Italian restaurants and pizzerias are popular with kids. Other family-friendly establishments include chains like Byron, Pizza Express, Wagamama, and Carluccio's.

Hours

In London you can find breakfast all day, but it's generally served between 7 am and 11 am. Workmen's cafés and sandwich bars for office workers are sometimes open from 7 am, more upscale cafés from 7 am to 11:30 am. Lunch is between noon and 3 pm. Tea, often a meal in itself, is taken between 3:30 pm and 6 pm, and dinner or supper is typically eaten between 7 pm and 11 pm, though it can be taken earlier. Many ethnic restaurants, especially Indian, serve food until midnight. Sunday is proper lunch day, and some restaurants are open for lunch only. Other restaurants are closed entirely on Sunday and on public holidays. Over the Christmas period, London virtually shuts down and it seems only hotels are prepared to feed travelers. Unless otherwise noted, the restaurants listed in this guide are open daily for lunch and dinner.

Prices

The democratization of restaurants in London has not translated into smaller checks, and London is an extortionate city by global standards. A modest meal for two can easily cost £40, and the £120-a-head meal is not unknown. Damage-control strategies include making lunch your main meal—the top places have bargain midday menus—going for early evening deals, bringing your own wine to an ethnic eatery with a BYOB license, or sharing an à la carte entrée and ordering a second appetizer instead. (Note that an appetizer, usually known as a "starter" or "first course," is sometimes called an "entrée," as it is in France, and that entrées in England are dubbed "main courses" or simply "mains.") Seek out fixed-price menus, and watch for hidden extras on the check, that is, bread or vegetables charged separately.

WHAT IT COSTS

	£	££	£££	££££	£££££
At Dinner	under £10	£10–£16	£17–£23	£24–£32	over £32

Price per person for an average main course or equivalent combination of smaller dishes at dinner. Note: If a restaurant offers only prix-fixe (set-price) meals, it has been given the price category that reflects the full prix-fixe price.

In This Chapter

14

Using the Maps

Throughout the chapter, you'll see mapping symbols and coordinates (✛ 3:F2) after property names or reviews. To locate the property on a map, turn to the London Dining and Lodging Atlas at the end of this chapter. The first number after the ✛ symbol indicates the map number. Following that is the property's coordinates on the map grid.

BEST BETS FOR LONDON DINING

With thousands of restaurants to choose from, how will you decide where to eat? Fodor's writers and editors have selected their favorite restaurants by price, cuisine, and experience in the Best Bets lists below. In the first column, Fodor's Choice properties represent the "best of the best" in every price category. You can also search by neighborhood for excellent eats—just peruse the following pages. Or find specific details about a restaurant in the full reviews, listed later in the chapter by neighborhood.

Fodor's Choice ★

Busaba Eathai, p. 262
Dean Street Townhouse, p. 263
Dinner by Heston Blumenthal, p. 274
Giaconda Dining Room, p. 263
Goodman, p. 258
Great Queen Street, p. 265
Harwood Arms, p. 271
Hix, p. 263
Hunan, p. 272
Marcus Wareing at the Berkeley, p. 275
The Ledbury, p. 277
The Orange, p. 272
Scott's, p. 259
St. John, p. 269
Viajante, p, 269

Best by Price

£

Baozi Inn, p. 261
Busaba Eathai, p. 262
Côte, p. 263
Golden Hind, p. 260
Koya, p. 264

££

Giaconda Dining Room, p. 263
Harwood Arms, p. 271
The Pig's Ear, p. 272
The Orange, p. 272
St. John Bread & Wine, p. 268

£££

Dean Street Townhouse, p. 263
Great Queen Street, p. 265
Hix, p. 263
St. John, p. 269

Viajante, p. 269

££££

L'Atelier de Joël Robuchon, p. 265
The Ledbury, p. 277
Scott's, p. 259
Tom Aikens, p. 271

£££££

Dinner by Heston Blumenthal, p. 274
Hélène Darroze at the Connaught, p. 258
Hunan, p. 272
Marcus Wareing at the Berkeley, p. 275
Restaurant Gordon Ramsay, p. 272

Best by Cuisine

BRITISH

Great Queen Street, p. 265

Harwood Arms, p. 271
Hereford Road, p. 277
Hix, p. 263
The Orange, p. 272
St. John, p. 269

CHINESE

Baozi Inn, p. 261
Hunan, p. 272
Royal China, p. 279
Yauatcha, p. 264

FRENCH

Hélène Darroze at the Connaught, p. 258
Koffmann's, p. 274
La Petite Maison, p. 258
Restaurant Gordon Ramsay, p. 272
Seven Park Place, p. 256
The Ledbury, p. 277

ITALIAN

Bocca di Lupo, p. 262
Cecconi's, p. 257
L'Anima, p. 267
River Café, p. 280

JAPANESE

Aqua Kyoto, p. 260
Koya, p. 264
Zuma, p. 275

SEAFOOD

Golden Hind, p. 260
J Sheekey, p. 265
North Sea Fish Restaurant, p. 266
Scott's, p. 259
Sweetings, p. 268

Best by Experience

BRASSERIE

Cecconi's, p. 257
Côte, p. 263
Electric Brasserie, p. 276
Racine, p. 272
The Wolseley, p. 256

BRUNCH

Cecconi's, p. 257
Côte, p. 263
Dean Street Townhouse, p. 263
PJ's Bar & Grill, p. 270

BUSINESS DINING

Bistrot Bruno Loubet, p. 269
Corrigan's Mayfair, p. 257
L'Anima, p. 267
The Greenhouse, p. 258
Savoy Grill, p. 266
The Square, p. 259

CELEB SPOTTING

Dean Street Townhouse, p. 263
J Sheekey, p. 265
Le Caprice, p. 256
Nobu Berkeley Street, p. 259
The Ivy, p. 265
Scott's, p. 259
The Wolseley, p. 256

GASTROPUBS

Anchor & Hope, p. 269
Great Queen Street, p. 265
Harwood Arms, p. 271
The Pig's Ear, p. 272
The Orange, p. 272

GOOD FOR GROUPS

Boundary, p. 267
Goodman, p. 258
Lemonia, p. 279
The Orange, p. 272
Zuma, p. 275

GREAT VIEWS

Paramount, p. 264
River Café, p. 280

HISTORIC

Maison Bertaux, p. 264
Rules, p. 266
Simpson's Tavern, p. 268
Sweetings, p. 268
Wiltons, p. 256

HOTEL DINING

Bar Boulud at the Marndarin Oriental, p. 274
Bistro Bruno Loubet at The Zetter, p. 269
Dinner by Heston Blumenthal at the Mandarin Oriental, p. 274
Hélène Darroze at the Connaught, p. 258
Koffmann's at the Berkeley, p. 274

Marcus Wareing at the Berkeley, p. 275

HOT SPOTS

Dean Street Townhouse, p. 263
Hix, p. 263
The Ledbury, p. 277
Scott's, p. 259
Viajante, p. 269

LATE-NIGHT DINING

Dean Street Townhouse, p. 263
J Sheekey, p. 265
The Wolseley, p. 256

LOCAL FAVORITES

Alounak, p. 277
Chez Bruce, p. 270
Hunan, p. 272
La Trompette, p. 279
Lemonia, p. 279
Tom Ilić, p. 270

LUNCH PRIX-FIXE

Andrew Edmunds, p. 260
Arbutus, p. 261
Galvin Bistrot de Luxe, p. 260
Le Gavroche, p. 259
The Ledbury, p. 277
Wild Honey, p. 259

PRETHEATER

Arbutus, p. 261
Dean Street Townhouse, p. 263
L'Atelier de Joël Robuchon, p. 265
Savoy Grill, p. 266

Wild Honey, p. 259

ROMANTIC

Andrew Edmunds, p. 260
J Sheekey, p. 265
Hélène Darroze at the Connaught, p. 258
Restaurant Gordon Ramsay, p. 272
Scott's, p. 259

QUIET MEAL

Hibiscus, p. 258
L'Oranger, p. 256
The Greenhouse, p. 258
The Square, p. 259

SPECIAL OCCASION

Dinner by Heston Blumental, p. 274
Marcus Wareing at the Berkeley, p. 275
Restaurant Gordon Ramsay, p. 272
Hélène Darroze at the Connaught, p. 258
The Ledbury, p. 277

WINE LISTS

The Greenhouse, p. 258
The Ledbury, p. 277
Marcus Wareing at the Berkeley, p. 275
Restaurant Gordon Ramsay, p. 272
The Square, p. 259

14

ST. JAMES'S, MAYFAIR, AND MARYLEBONE

Mayfair and St. James's—home to Buckingham Palace and Clarence House, where Prince Charles and Camilla live—have a decidedly old-world, royal feel. Appropriately, most of the restaurants here are fit for a king or queen.

This is where you'll find London's top restaurants, including Scott's, Corrigan's Mayfair, Le Gavroche, La Petite Maison, and L'Oranger—dining experiences that are geared toward a well-heeled, deep-pocketed clientele. Mere mortals should make reservations well in advance to dine at any of these restaurants for dinner. But last-minute tables often crop up, and lunching here can be a great money-saving strategy.

If you're looking for something more low-key and wallet-friendly, head north to Marylebone where the scenery changes dramatically. Old-world elegance is replaced by funky little cafés and restaurants with a more indie spirit. Everything from Moroccan and Turkish to Thai is available here, as well as numerous local favorites. Just follow your nose.

HOTEL DINING

Some of London's finest restaurants can be found inside its top-end hotels. **Koffmann's** (⊠ *The Berkeley, Wilton Pl., Knightsbridge* ☎ *20/7235–6000*) at the Berkeley serves signature pig's trotters and calf's liver Lyonnaise. Admirable Frenchwoman Hélène Darroze shows off virtuoso skills at her self-named wood-paneled dining room at the **Connaught** (⊠ *16 Carlos Pl., Mayfair* ☎ *020/3147–7200*), and star chef Daniel Boulud pulls in a crowd for his posh French charcuterie and Yankee hamburgers and fries at **Bar Boulud** at the Mandarin Oriental in Knightsbridge (⊠ *Mandarin Oriental Hyde Park, 66 Knightsbridge, Knightsbridge*).

LONDON'S HOTTEST TABLES

These restaurants are more than just see-and-be-seen hot spots—excellent food adds to the buzz. If you're looking to save, visit at lunch, when the set menu is usually half of what it would cost to eat there at night.

✕ **Dean Street Townhouse:** Spot a celeb at this ravishing Soho dining salon and media meeting point on Dean Street. Expect no-nonsense British classics, like wild rabbit and black pudding or Lincolnshire onion tart. ✉ *69–71 Dean St., Soho* ⊕ *www.deanstreettownhouse.com* ☎ *020/7434–1775* ✛ *3:D5.*

✕ **Dinner by Heston Blumenthal:** Book three months ahead for super-chef Heston Blumenthal's old English gastronomy. Sample historic dishes, from cod cheeks-and-beetroot 'Savoury Porridge' (c.1660) to hay smoked mackerel (c.1730). ✉ *66 Knightsbridge., Knightsbridge* ⊕ *www.dinnerbyheston. com* ☎ *020/7201–3833* ✛ *4:F1.*

✕ **Giaconda Dining Room:** Enjoy inventive dishes like sautéed duck breast, celeriac purée, and cherry sauce at absurdly low prices at this 35-seat Australian-run beacon on London's Tin Pan Alley. ✉ *9 Denmark St., Soho* ⊕ *www.giacondadining. com* ☎ *020/7240–3344* ✛ *3:D4.*

✕ **Hix:** Long forgotten British dishes like *brawn* (head cheese) with *piccalilli* (pickled vegetable relish) are served at this slick Soho award-winner. ✉ *66–70 Brewer St., Soho* ☎ *020/7292–3518* ✛ *3:C5.*

✕ **The Ledbury:** Chef Brett Graham burnishes his world-class status with complex modern French cuisine in this handsome Notting Hill restaurant. ✉ *127 Ledbury Rd., Notting Hill* ☎ *020/7792–9090* ✛ *1:A4.*

✕ **Marcus Wareing at the Berkeley:** Marcus Wareing and his 100-strong kitchen brigade turn out arguably the most remarkable French haute cuisine in town at this showpiece at the Berkeley. ✉ *The Berkeley, Wilton Pl., Knightsbridge S* ☎ *020/7235–1200* ✛ *4:G1.*

TEA TIME

Fashionistas splurge on flourless caramel spongecake for a chic champagne tea at the wonderfully elegant **Connaught** (✉ *Carlos Place, Mayfair* ⊕ *www. the-connaught.co.uk* ☎ *020/3147–7100*). Loyalists come for the open fires, Laurent-Perrier bubbles, smoked salmon and wasabi sandwiches, and loose-leaf Ceylon tea. A less fancy, more bohemian crowd slip into **Mô Café** attached to **Momo** restaurant (✉ *23–25 Heddon St., Mayfair* ⊕ *www.momoresto. com* ☎ *020/7434–4040*), off Regent Street, and pay £9.50 to £32 for North African-inspired mint, green date, or cardamom-scented afternoon tea, with pastries and Moroccan chicken wraps. Finally, treat your mum to a Mother's Day posh afternoon tea at **Claridge's** (✉ *Brook St., Mayfair* ⊕ *www.claridges. co.uk* ☎ *020/7629–8860*), where she can enjoy the Hungarian string quartet, elegant service, and scones, finger sandwiches, fancy cakes, and refreshing loose-leaf tea.

14

SOHO AND COVENT GARDEN

Soho and Covent Garden are the city's playground, an all-day, all-night jostling wonderland of glitz, glamour, grit, and greasepaint.

This area is London's cultural heart, with old and new media companies, late-night bars, popular musicals, and highbrow theater and opera productions. In the last decade, high rents have forced out many of Soho's seedy businesses and ushered in top-notch restaurants, including **Yauatcha** and high-quality Spanish tapas bar **Barrafina,** a haven for creative modern Iberian food. Because of its popularity with visitors, Soho prices can be absurdly steep: £13 cocktails and £32 main courses are not unheard of. For a quick bite without breaking the bank, head to Chinatown's cobbled streets. The roast duck is world-class and made to a secret recipe at the **Four Seasons,** or try Indian street food like a lamb *tikka* roomali roll and spiced chai tea at nearby **Dishoom,** a cute take on a Bombay Persian-run Irani café.

BARS AND PUBS

Café Boheme (✉ *13 Old Compton St., Soho* ☎ *020/7734–0623* ✛ *3:D5*) has an atmospheric zinc bar, curbside tables, and is popular with models, photographers, and the fashion crowd. It's open until 3 am Monday–Saturday. The snazzy basement hangout **Mark's Bar** (✉ *66–70 Brewer St., Soho* ☎ *020/7292–3518* ⊕ *www.hixsoho.co.uk* ✛ *3:C5*) below Hix restaurant has old-fashioned bar billiards and English heritage cocktails. One of the best places for a romantic date is the elegant champagne bar at **Brasserie Max** inside the Covent Garden Hotel (✉ *10 Monmouth St., Covent Garden* ☎ *020/7806–1000* ✛ *3:E4*).

MEAL DEALS AND STEALS

PRE- AND POST-THEATER DINING

For a £19.50 romantic French meal in a covered indoor court-yard, head to **Clos Maggiore** (✉ *33 King St., Covent Garden* ☎ *020/7379–9696* ⊕ *www.closmaggiore.com* ⊹ *3:F5*), off the Covent Garden piazza. Meander through French artisan charcuterie and biodynamic or unfiltered natural terroirs-based wines at **Terroirs** (✉ *5 William IV St., Covent Garden* ☎ *020/7036–0660* ⊕ *www.terroirswinebar.com* ⊹ *3:E6*). Or try inventive modern European dishes (squid burger, anyone?) at **Arbutus** (✉ *63–64 Frith St., Soho* ☎ *020/7734–4545* ⊕ *www. arbutusrestaurant.co.uk* ⊹ *3:D4*), where three courses before 7 pm cost £18.95. **Dehesa** (✉ *25 Ganton St., Soho* ☎ *020/7494–4170* ⊕ *www.dehesa.co.uk* ⊹ *3:B5*) near Carnaby Street mixes Italian and Spanish tapas to dazzling effect. The A-list and opening–night theater and film stars file into **J Sheekey** (✉ *28–32 St. Martin's Ct., Covent Garden* ☎ *020/7240–2565* ⊕ *www.j-sheekey.co.uk* ⊹ *3:E6*) for seafood dishes in a low-lighted chic salon and raised-counter oyster bar.

BUDGET EATS

European: Regular tweets from the restaurant about their exceptional European stews, soups, and cheese and cured meat baguettes pull in the punters at **Fernandez & Wells** (✉ *43 Lexington St., Soho* ☎ *020/7734–1546* ⊕ *www. fernandezandwells.com* ⊹ *3:B5*). And there is always a crush at the no-bookings vegetarian **Mildred's** (✉ *45 Lexington St., Soho* ☎ *020/7494–1634* ⊕ *www.mildreds.co.uk* ⊹ *3:B5*) can-teen, where all mains are less than £9.50.

Pan-Asian: There's rated Japanese udon noodles with mack-erel and green leaves for £9.50 at no-reservations **Koya** (✉ *49 Frith St., Soho* ☎ *020/7434–4463* ⊕ *www.koya.co.uk* ⊹ *3:D5*), or those who prefer authentic Thai, there's always **Busaba Eathai** (✉ *106–110 Wardour St., Soho* ☎ *020/7255–8686* ⊕ *www.busaba.com* ⊹ *3:C4*), a wildly popular Thai canteen with wooden bench seats and shared tables.

STREET EATS

Head to **Mooli's** (✉ *50 Frith St., Soho* ☎ *020/7494–9075* ⊕ *www.moolis.com* ⊹ *3:D4*), where you can get Indian street food that's sweeping Soho. Try the unleavened flatbread roti wraps crammed with Punjabi goat and cumin potato. Other good-to-go rotis, which all cost under £5, are stuffed with Goan pork and pomegran-ate seeds, Keralan beef with coconut, or cubes of white paneer cheese with grated carrot and tomato chutney. Just around the corner, there's a friendly welcome, comfy booths, and a longer street-based Thai menu at **Rosa's** (✉ *48 Dean St., Soho* ☎ *020/7494–1638* ⊕ *www.rosaslondon.com* ⊹ *3:D5*), where it would be a crime to miss the deep-fried Thai calamari, soft shell crab with mint and chili, or the prawn green curry, with *auber-gine* (eggplant), bamboo shoots, and sweet basil.

14

BLOOMSBURY, FITZROVIA, REGENT'S PARK, AND HAMPSTEAD

From the bluestocking and intellectual haunts of Bloomsbury and the chic dining scene of Fitzrovia to the leafy tranquillity of Hampstead, this area offers diverse dining experiences.

Bloomsbury is known as London's literary and academic center with the British Museum, the University of London, Royal Academy of Dramatic Arts, leading hospitals, and numerous bookstores. Although Bloomsbury is known more as a residential area, there are many hotels in Russell Square, which is a convenient central location for visitors. To the west of Bloomsbury, Fitzrovia has striking town houses as well as a wealth of stylish shops, hip bars, and trendy restaurants.

Hampstead village lies in the north of London, and is best described as a leafy, quiet hilltop suburb. This neighborhood is a popular excursion destination for Londoners who want to escape the city with a stroll through peaceful Hampstead Heath to appreciate its meadows and woodland. The area is steeped in artistic and literary history. Now it has the highest concentration of millionaires in Britain, but nonetheless Hampstead has a number of cozy cafés, restaurants, and bustling pubs.

SUNDAY ROAST

Experience classic English flavor at one of Hampstead's homey Georgian gastro-pubs: the **Wells** (⌧ *30 Well Walk* ☎ *020/7794–3785* ⊕ *www. thewellshampstead. co.uk* ✛ *1:E1*) serves a traditional Sunday roast with roast beef, Yorkshire pudding, and roasted vegetables for about £16. For the "olde English" pub experience, soak up the ambience farther up at the **Holly Bush** (⌧ *22 Holly Mount* ☎ *020/7435–2892* ✛ *1:E1*), housed in a 200-year-old building. The upscale pub fare emphasizes organic and local products, with homemade pies (try beef and Harvey's ale) and a Sunday roast.

DINING TWO WAYS

	SAVE	SPLURGE
French	Le Relais de Venise L'Entrecôte (✉ 120 Marylebone La., Fitzrovia ☎ 020/7486-0878 ✛ 1:H3) is a beloved no-choice, no-bookings steak, frites, and walnut salad Parisian-style brasserie.	Galvin Bistrot de Luxe (✉ 66 Baker St., Fitzrovia ☎ 020/7935-4007 ✛ 1:G3) offers exemplary upmarket French bistro food in a handsome and grown up brasserie on Baker Street.
Modern European	The Engineer (✉ 65 Gloucester Ave., Regent's Park ☎ 020/7722-0950 ✛ 1:H1) doles out pot-roast partridge and game chips for £18 in a rustic gastro-pub and beer-garden setting.	Roux at the Landau (✉ 1c Portland Pl., Bloomsbury ☎ 020/7965-0165 ✛ 2:A5) at the Langham wows with a classic seven-course blowout for £135 with paired wines.
Japanese	Sushi of Shiori (✉ 44 Drummond St. Heath St., Regent's Park ☎ 020/7388-9962 ✛ 2:B3) offers mind-blowing sushi canapés or omakase chef's selection sushi and sashimi at this tiny nine-seater in Euston.	Roka's (✉ 37 Charlotte St., Fitzrovia ☎ 020/7580-6464 ✛ 3:C2) robata grill attracts a glamour crowd for its noted black cod, king crab, scallops, and skewered chicken dishes.

CUPCAKE CENTRAL

London's turning into cupcake central, and Bea's of Bloomsbury (✉ *44 Theobald's St., Bloomsbury* ☎ *020/7242-8330* ⊕ *www.beasofbloomsbury. com* ✛ *3:H1*) is one of the best teashops and cupcake joints in town. With its on-site bakery, Bea's churns out freshly baked sugary delights like the raspberry cupcake with vanilla sponge, butter cream, and a fresh raspberry on top, and the heavenly chocolate fudge cupcake with fudge ganache icing. Don't miss the brightly colored gingerbread, praline, or carrot cake cupcakes, and try not to drool over the cornucopia of impeccable three-layered chocolate truffle cakes, New York cheese cakes, lemon drizzle Bundts, fruit cakes, and pecan pies. Afternoon tea (2:30–5:30 pm weekdays, and noon–5:30 pm on weekends) with cupcakes, scones, mini-meringues, and Valrhona brownies is £9.90.

GLOBAL TAPAS

The small-plates trend is gathering steam in London, especially in Bloomsbury and Fitzrovia. Here's where to go: **Barrica** (✉ *62 Goode St., Fitzrovia* ☎ *020/7436-9448* ✛ *3:B2*) serves notable Spanish tapas in an authentic and Madrid taverna-style long tapa room. Plough through multiple dishes, or try the various meats and cheeses. At **Salt Yard** (✉ *54 Goode St., Fitzrovia* ☎ *020/7637-0657* ✛ *3:B2*) the small plates have a seamless Spanish–Italian twist. And **Siam Central** (✉ *14 Charlotte St., Fitzrovia* ☎ *020/7436-7460* ✛ *3:C2*) is a popular spot that offers 30 Thai tapas, such as tamarind duck and "drunken" noodles with scallops.

14

THE CITY, CLERKENWELL, AND SOUTH BANK

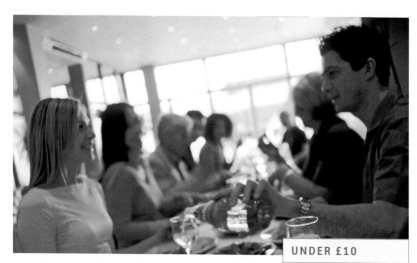

Historic and just-beyond-the-City-limits, Clerkenwell is one of the most cutting-edge, radical, and trendy quarters for London gastro-dining, which sets it in marked contrast to the adjacent City, which is conservative-minded and caters overwhelmingly to business-focused dining.

Across the River Thames, the South Bank has always been outside the historically stifling bounds of The City and has freer rein to experiment, and now anchors itself firmly around the foodie mecca that is Borough food market. Unrepentant City bankers troop over to **Hawksmoor** (⌧ 157 Commercial St., The City ☎ 020/7247–7392 ⊕ www.thehawksmoor.com ✛ 2:G1) for dictionary-thick 35-day-aged char-grilled British Longhorn steaks. Farther north, there's a more trendy, relaxed vibe, where you'll find Aussie/Kiwi–inspired fare at **Caravan** (⌧ 11–13 Exmouth Market, Islington ☎ 020/7833–8115 ⊕ www. caravanonexmouth.co.uk ✛ 2:E3). **Morito** (⌧ 32 Exmouth Market, Islington ☎ 020/7608–1550 ✛ 2:E3) does cheap and consistently high-quality Spanish tapas at fair prices.

UNDER £10

You can get smoked mackerel superfood salad and a banana split at "fresh fast food" restaurant **Leon** (⌧ 12 Ludgate Circus, Blackfriars ☎ 020/7489–1580 ⊕ www.leonrestaurants. co.uk ✛ 2:F5) for less than £10. Brightly colored **Applebee's Café** (⌧ 5 Stoney St., Borough ☎ 020/7407–5777 ⊕ www. applebeesfish.com ✛ 5:H1) conjures up a hearty Italian fish soup and garlic saffron brushetta for £9.50. For olde English fare, treat yourself to half a dozen Dorset rock oysters for £10.50 at **Wright Brothers Oyster & Porter House** (⌧ 11 Stoney St., Borough ☎ 020/7403–9554 ⊕ www. wrightbros.eu.com ✛ 5:H1).

OFF THE TOURIST TRACK

CHEF-CENTRIC CLERKENWELL

The area where the starchiness of The City fades into the relaxed artiness of Islington is a fertile ground for chefs and restaurants. Within walking distance of Farringdon Tube, **Bistrot Bruno Loubet** (⊠ *86–88 Clerkenwell Rd., Clerkenwell* ☎ *020/7324–4455* ⊕ *www.bistrotbrunoloubet. com* ✛ *2:F3*) serves highly expressive southwestern French cuisine. At the tucked-away **Clerkenwell Kitchen** (⊠ *27–31 Clerkenwell Close, Clerkenwell* ☎ *020/7101–9959* ⊕ *www. theclerkenwellkitchen.co.uk* ✛ *2:F3*) the focus is on organic, seasonal, and sustainable dishes.

On St. John's Square, New Zealander Anna Hansen's the **Modern Pantry** (⊠ *47–48 St. John's Sq., Clerkenwell* ☎ *020/7553–9210* ⊕ *www.themodernpantry.co.uk* ✛ *2:F3*) is doing something special with modern fusion food at this all-day pantry and deli. At **St. John** (⊠ *26 St. John St., Smithfield* ☎ *020/7251–0848* ⊕ *www.stjohnrestaurant. com* ✛ *2:F4*) Fergus Henderson prepares British nose-to-tail carnivorous cuisine, famed for its no-nonsense approach to offal and all bits in between.

BUSTLING BOROUGH MARKET

First mentioned in 1276 and believed to have existed in Roman times, Borough Market is a favorite with tourists, London's top chefs and foodies alike. From Thursday to Saturday, the unassuming location under Victorian wrought-iron railway arches at London Bridge is packed with foodies eager to pick up the finest and freshest food in the capital. There are more than 130 stalls, plus specialist shops like **Neal's Yard Dairy** (⊠ *6 Park St., Borough* ☎ *020/7367–0799* ⊕ *www. nealsyarddairy.co.uk* ✛ *5:H1*), where great truckles of Stilton cheese are stacked floor to ceiling. Foodies keen on sampling British roast beef with all the trimmings should head to **Roast** (⊠ *Floral Hall, Stoney St., Borough Market, Borough* ☎ *020/7940–1300* ⊕ *www.roast-restaurant.com* ✛ *5:H1*).

MONDO VINO

It's all about the wine at **28°–50°** (⊠ *140 Fetter La., The City* ☎ *020/7242–8877* ⊕ *www.2850.co.uk* ✛ *2:E5*), French restaurant and occasional wine tasting venue, where co-owner and sommelier Xavier Rousset has assembled a striking wine list of 40-odd wines available in tasting portions, by the glass, carafe, and bottle. An awesome collectors' wine list has some rare vintages seldom seen in London restaurants (and sold at bargain prices), such as Château Léoville Las Cases 1989 from St. Julien in Bordeaux for £275, or a highly prized Château Rieussec 1983 Sauternes sweet dessert wine for a knock-down £119. There are authentic French breads, charcuterie, duck rillettes, and cheese selections to provide a tasty foil for the outstanding oenological offerings.

14

KENSINGTON, CHELSEA, AND KNIGHTSBRIDGE

If you're famous, fabulous, wealthy, or all three, chances are you'll be living—and dining—in one of these neighborhoods among its world-class museums, parks, shops, hotels, and architecture.

Kensington, Chelsea, and Knightsbridge have some of the city's best restaurants and fashion stores. (Do super chef Heston Blumenthal and Harvey Nichols ring a bell?) Chelsea, made famous in the swinging 1960s, is where today's yummy mummies bomb around in Range Rovers, which locals have nicknamed Chelsea tractors. Known for its shopping, Chelsea's restaurants range from glamorous boîtes to little places ideal for a girly gossip and a bite on the go.

In upscale Knightsbridge, you'll find Harrods department store and the high-end fashion boutiques of Sloane Street, and the hotel-based restaurants are just as polished as the residents. Come here for an amazing dining experience, but don't expect bargains. Nearby, Kensington is a residential neighborhood with a wider range of restaurants, from little French bistros to funky Vietnamese hideaways.

CULTURAL EATS

The food's almost as good as the art and artifacts at London's best cultural spaces. Marvel at portraits of pop star Lily Allen or of Mary, Queen of Scots, before getting a seat with a view at the roof-top **Portrait Restaurant** (✉ *National Portrait Gallery, St. Martin's Pl., St. James's* ☎ *020/7312-2490* ⊕ *www.npg.org.uk* ✛ *3:E6*), which has fine British fare. At the world-famous auction house, the **Cafe at Sotheby's** (✉ *34–35 New Bond St., Mayfair* ☎ *020/7293-5077* ⊕ *www.sothebys.com/ cafe* ✛ *5:A1*) attracts a classy well-to-do crowd for their bargain afternoon tea services for only £6.50 to £11.

PIT STOPS FOR SHOPPERS

Whether you're looking for a quick bite or a more relaxing meal, there are plenty of options for every shopper.

Londoners love **Wagamama** (✉ *Lower ground floor, Harvey Nichols, 109–125 Knightsbridge* ☎ *020/7201-8000* ⊕ *www.wagamama.com* ✛ *4:F1*) for its healthful, cheap, and cheerful noodles, ramen and rice dishes. This branch is inside Harvey Nichols department store.

Slip in for a seasonal salad or lemon sole at the **Botanist** (✉ *7 Sloane Sq., Chelsea* ☎ *020/7730-0077* ⊕ *www.thebotanistonsloanesquare.com* ✛ *4:G2*), the ultimate posh hangout on Sloane Square.

Down a cheeseburger topped with Monterey Jack and deep-fried and thinly sliced zucchini fries at **Byron** (✉ *300 King's Road, Chelsea SW3* ☎ *020/7352-6040* ⊕ *www.byronhamburgers.com* ✛ *4:D4*). It's bright and perfect for the family, with two courses designed for kids for £6.

Another casual option is the **Pig's Ear** (✉ *35 Old Church St., Chelsea* ☎ *020/7352-2908* ⊕ *www.thepigsear.info* ✛ *4:E4*), where you can start with beers in the saloon bar before enjoying a meal in the dining room. Note that the deep-fried pigs' ears aren't to everyone's liking.

RISING STAR: NUNO MENDES

El Bulli–trained **Nuno Mendes** is the most exciting culinary talent in London. Armed with tweezers, micro-herbs, and urban foraged vegetation, Mendes takes diners on the most amazing avant-garde culinary journey with his set meals at **Viajante** (✉ *Patriot Sq., entrance on Cambridge Heath Rd., East End* ☎ *020/7584-2003* ⊕ *www.viajante.co.uk* ✛ *2:H1*). From homemade bread and a roast celeriac and tapioca starter, to an unusually flavored lemon sole and yeast main dish, Portuguese-born Mendes creates utterly unique tastes and flavors, always pushing the boundaries.

MUSICAL FOOD

It's hard to hear yourself speak, and the food is a bit pricey, but everyone enjoys the 1950s bohemian scene, live music, and poetry readings at the **Troubadour** (✉ *263–267 Old Brompton Rd., Chelsea* ☎ *020/7370-1434* ⊕ *www.troubadour.co.uk* ✛ *4:B3*), a restaurant, coffee shop, and music venue. The site of Bob Dylan's first London gig and previously host to Led Zepplin and Jimmy Hendrix, this place is where latter-day bohemians lounge around and dine on breakfasts, burgers, pastas, omelets, and strong coffee. Nearby off King's Road, there's more live music at the **606 Club** (✉ *90 Lots Rd., Chelsea* ☎ *020/7352-5953* ⊕ *www.606club.co.uk* ✛ *4:C6*), where you can dine on grilled sea bass with fennel, or Welsh lamb and gravy while enjoying up-close-and-personal live jazz sessions in an intimate basement setting.

14

NOTTING HILL AND BAYSWATER

World renowed Notting Hill's trendy atmosphere, designer shops, and oh-so-hip residents, and nearby Bayswater's ethnic eateries, entice Londoners and travelers in droves.

Notting Hill has a reputation as one of London's more fashionable neighborhoods, with numerous boutiques, chic cafés, pâtisseries and restaurants, buzzing bars, and the famous Portobello Road Market's collection of antiques shops, vintage-clothing stands, and delicious food stalls. The gentrification of Notting Hill has led to hordes of bankers and high flyers moving to the area, and hence prices are stratospheric. If you are in London at the end of August, be sure to check out the revelry and fanfare of the multiethnic Notting Hill Carnival street parade—a celebration of West Indian culture.

Bayswater is seedier, more transient, and known for its diversity. This neighborhood's main artery, Queensway, boasts some of the best cheap ethnic restaurants in London. Here, the Greek, Indian, Chinese, and Persian restaurants are all cheek by jowl. Affordable accommodation and shops are plentiful here, making this a popular destination for visitors.

SNACKING SPOT

Portobello Road Market is one of London's most popular outdoor street markets. Get there early on Saturday morning (the market is open 8 am–6 pm) to beat the crowds. Peruse the antiques and vintage clothes, and when you've built up an appetite, head to the north end of the market for snacks. You'll find fresh fruit and vegetable stands, bakeries, olive and cheese purveyors, and numerous hot food stalls peddling sweet and savory crepes, hamburgers, wraps, bagels, paella, fried prawns, noodles, and kebabs.

How to get there: Take the Tube to Ladbroke Grove or Notting Hill Gate station and follow the signs (and crowds).

GASTROPUB TOUR

These upscale pubs specialize in high-quality, innovative fare in a low-key bar setting. The **Cow** (✉ *89 Westbourne Park Rd., Notting Hill* ☎ *020/7221–0021* ⊕ *www.thecowlondon.co.uk* ✛ *1:B3*) is one of the best-known gastropubs in London. Eat oysters or prawns and down a Guinness at the stylish bar or head upstairs to the slightly more formal dining room. Over the road, the **Westbourne** (✉ *101 Westbourne Park Villas, Notting Hill* ☎ *020/7221–1332* ⊕ *www.thewestbourne.com* ✛ *1:A3*) attracts a boho-chic good-looking set and serves hearty regional food and rustic dishes, with specials like cuttlefish with capers, and roast pheasant with bacon. Lauded Italian eatery **Assaggi** (✉ *1st fl., 39 Chepstow Rd., Notting Hill* ☎ *020/792–5501* ✛ *1:B4*) sits above the Chepstow pub and fine regional dishes like stuffed squid and grilled sea bass. The quintessential **Ladbroke Arms** (✉ *54 Ladbroke Rd., Notting Hill* ☎ *020/7727–6648* ✛ *1:A5*) is an upmarket Sloaney neighborhood gastropub with a delightful beer terrace out front. The menu changes frequently, but chocolate fondant is a specialty.

CHEAP EATS

If you're looking for a filling meal that's not too pricey, head to Bayswater and Queensway. **Alounak** (✉ *44 Westbourne Grove, Bayswater* ☎ *020/7229–4158* ✛ *1:B4*) is a local favorite featuring reliable Persian cuisine served in a cramped dining room. Lobster noodles, king oysters, and fried baby squid are three legendary dishes at the **Mandarin Kitchen** (✉ *14–16 Queensway, Queensway* ☎ *020/7727–9012* ✛ *1:C5*). **Hereford Road** (✉ *3 Hereford Rd., Bayswater* ☎ *020/7727–1144* ⊕ *www.herefordroad.org; see review* ✛ *1:B4*) serves British seasonal fare like cod roe on toast, and rice pudding. There's always a big fat Greek party going on at **Aphrodite Taverna** (✉ *15 Hereford Rd., Queensway* ☎ *020/7221–1415* ⊕ *www.aphroditerestaurant.co.uk* ✛ *1:B4*), festooned with Greek drachmas, bouzouki mandolins, and a giant bottle of Metaxa brandy.

AROUND THE PARK

A Sunday afternoon stroll around Holland Park can lead you in many culinary directions. After a glimpse of its resident peacocks, you may be inclined to stop for a scoop or two of luscious Italian ice cream at **Gelato Mio** (✉ *138 Holland Park Ave., Notting Hill* ☎ *020/7727–4117* ⊕ *www.gelatomio.co.uk* ✛ *1:A5*), an ice-cream parlor on nearby Holland Park Avenue. Try hazelnut and chocolate, *biscotto* (cookies and cream), or black cherry. If you're not in the mood for ice cream, head down Portland Road and sit outside at pavement tables at **Julie's Restaurant & Bar** (✉ *135 Portland Rd., Notting Hill* ☎ *020/7229–8331* ⊕ *www.juliesrestaurant. com* ✛ *1:A5*) at quaint Clarendon Cross, and enjoy a Kir Royale or dry Martini, along with a bowl of vegetable tempura with French beans and sage leaves.

14

RESTAURANT REVIEWS

Listed alphabetically within neighborhoods.

ST. JAMES'S AND MAYFAIR

ST. JAMES'S

££££
MODERN BRITISH
✕ **Le Caprice.** Old-timer Le Caprice commands the deepest loyalty of any restaurant in London. Why? Because it gets practically everything right. It's the celebrity history—think Liz Taylor and Lady Di—the David Bailey black-and-white prints, perfect service, and appealing menu that sits somewhere between Euro peasant and trendy fashion plate. Sit at the raised counter and enjoy calves' liver with crispy bacon, red-legged partridge, and signature Scandinavian iced berries with white chocolate sauce—all served with an ample dollop of celebrity spotting. ⊠ *Arlington House, Arlington St., St. James's* ☎ *020/7629–2239* ⊕ *www. caprice-holdings.co.uk* ⚑ *Reservations essential* ▤ *AE, DC, MC, V* Ⓤ *Green Park* ✛ *5:A1.*

££££
FRENCH
✕ **L'Oranger.** French haute cuisine reaches gobsmacking heights at this old-school aristocratic spot in St. James's, whether it's scallop carpaccio, sea bass with pomegranate, beef *en croûte* (beef wrapped in pastry and baked), or fig tart with Muscovado ice cream. The charming dining room is intimate and attractive—polished silver, oak panels, cut flowers, and French windows—and service is formal. Royal courtiers from nearby Clarence House and business barons wallow in the plush surroundings. ⊠ *5 St. James's St., St. James's* ☎ *020/7839–3774* ⊕ *www. loranger.co.uk* ⚑ *Reservations essential* ▤ *AE, DC, MC, V* ☯ *Closed Sun. No lunch Sat.* Ⓤ *Green Park* ✛ *5:A1.*

££££
FRENCH
✕ **Seven Park Place.** The incredible clarity of chef William Drabble's neo-French haute cuisine is turning heads at the St. James's Club and Hotel. Serious foodies squeeze into a Diana Vreeland–esq opulent wonderland of patterned wallpaper and striking portraits for Drabble's three- to six-course set meals, which might include sublime poached lobster tails with caramelized cauliflower or unbeatable Lune valley lamb with garlic purée. Immaculate desserts like the coconut parfait with dark chocolate are miniature works of art. ⊠ *7–8 Park Pl., St. James's* ☎ *020/7316–1600* ⚑ *Reservations essential* ▤ *AE, MC, V* Ⓤ *Green Park* ✛ *5:A1.*

££££
BRITISH
✕ **Wiltons.** Blue-bloods, aristocrats, and the well-to-do blow the bank at this 1742 bastion of fine dining. Gentlemen are required to wear a jacket for lunch and dinner at this clubby time capsule and ode to all things English. Posh patrons take half-a-dozen finest Colchester oysters, followed by grilled Dover sole on the bone, or fabulous game in season, like woodcock, grouse, and teal. Old-fashioned savories like anchovies on toast are also enjoyed. Service is formal and discreet. ⊠ *55 Jermyn St., St. James's* ☎ *020/7629–9955* ⊕ *www.wiltons.co.uk* ⚑ *Reservations essential* �🏛 *Jacket required* ▤ *AE, DC, MC, V* ☯ *Closed weekends* Ⓤ *Green Park* ✛ *5:A1.*

£££
AUSTRIAN
✕ **The Wolseley.** The whole of London seems to love the spectacle and grand elegance at this Viennese-style café on Piccadilly. The brasserie begins its long days with breakfast at 7 am and stays serving until midnight. Linger for Hungarian goulash, Viennese boiled beef *Tafelspitz*

A juicy burger and fries served at meat-specialist, Goodman.

(with apple sauce and sour cream), cod-like whiting, chopped liver, flaked haddock kedgeree rice, Matjes herrings, or Wiener schnitzel. For dessert, go for apple strudel or *kaiserschmarren*—a pancake with stewed fruit and raisins. ⊠ *160 Piccadilly, St. James's* ☎ *020/7499–6996* ⊕ *www.thewolseley.com* ⊟ *AE, DC, MC, V* Ⓤ *Green Park* ✛ *5:A1.*

MAYFAIR

£££ ✕ **Cecconi's.** Wedged strategically between Savile Row, Cork Street, and
ITALIAN Old Bond Street, and across from the Royal Academy on Burlington Gardens, this fashionable Italian brasserie is where the jet set come for breakfast, brunch, and *cicchetti* (Italian tapas) and return later for something more substantial. Ilse Crawford's green-and-brown interior is a stylish backdrop for classics like veal Milanese, Venetian calves' liver, crab ravioli, and tiramisu. Note: This is a good place for a pit stop during a West End shopping spree. ⊠ *5A Burlington Gardens, Mayfair* ☎ *020/7434–1500* ⊕ *www.cecconis.co.uk* ⊟ *AE, DC, MC, V* Ⓤ *Green Park, Piccadilly Circus* ✛ *3:A6.*

££££ ✕ **Corrigan's Mayfair.** The nearby Mayfair streets may be quiet but there's
MODERN BRITISH a lively scene and a warm welcome at burly Irish chef Richard Corrigan's flagship haute cuisine venture off Park Lane. Self-assured and on top of its game, the battle-ship dark blue banquettes and crisp Irish linen provide a handsome setting for a high-powered clientele who love the game-bird salad with walnuts, wild duck, and sour cherries, and heartier dishes like grouse pie or braised haunch of venison. ⊠ *28 Upper Grosvenor St., Mayfair* ☎ *020/7499–9943* ⊕ *www.corrigansmayfair. com* ⌲ *Reservations essential* ⊟ *AE, MC, V* Ⓤ *Marble Arch* ✛ *1:G5.*

£££   ✕**Goodman.** This Russian-owned, Manhattan-themed, Mayfair-based
STEAK   restaurant, named after Chicago jazz legend Benny Goodman, has
Fodor'sChoice   everyone in agreement—here you'll find the best steaks in town. U.S.
★   Angus T-bones, sirloin, rib eye, and porterhouses compete for taste and
tenderness with prime cuts from Ireland, Canada, Britain, and Australia.
There's token Russian sweet herring and lobster bisque, but everyone's
here for one thing: the juicy charcoal grilled steaks, which come with
fries, creamed spinach and luscious béarnaise or Stilton sauce. ⊠ *26
Maddox St., Mayfair* ☎ *020/7499–3776* ⊕ *www.goodmanrestaurants.
com* ♧ *Reservations essential* ▤ *AE, DC, MC, V* ☉ *Closed Sun.* ⓤ *Oxford Circus* ✚ *1:H4.*

££££   ✕**The Greenhouse.** Tucked away amid imposing Mayfair mansions and
FRENCH   approached via a spotlighted deck garden, this elegant ground-floor
salon is for aficionados of top-class French haute cuisine at any price.
Sit by a garden window and feast on John Dory, Scottish lobster with
champagne sauce, or Anjou pigeon. The mainly business clientele appre-
ciate the smooth service and the highly acclaimed 90-page wine list,
which has 3,000 bottles and 36 wines served by the glass. ⊠ *27A Hay's
Mews, Mayfair* ☎ *020/7499–3331* ⊕ *www.greenhouserestaurant.co.uk*
♧ *Reservations essential* ▤ *AE, DC, MC, V* ☉ *Closed Sun. No lunch
Sat.* ⓤ *Green Park* ✚ *1:H5.*

£££££   ✕**Hélène Darroze at the Connaught.** The crème de la crème flock to Hélène
FRENCH   Darroze at the Connaught for dazzling regional French haute cuisine,
served in an Edwardian wood-paneled hotel dining room. Taking inspiration from Les Landes in southwest France, Darroze sallies forth with
a procession of magical dishes. Caviar d'Acquitaine wows with oyster
tartare in a stylish martini glass, topped with black caviar jelly and white
haricot bean velouté. Spit-roasted and flambéed grouse is served delightfully pink, with duck foie gras, and mini–Brussels sprouts. To finish,
enjoy Madagascar chocolate ganache with *galangal* (Asian root) crème
brûlée. Note that the prices are high: £35 for lunch, and £75 or £85 for
the set dinners. ⊠ *The Connaught, Carlos Pl., Mayfair* ☎ *020/3147–7200*
⊕ *www.the-connaught.co.uk* ♧ *Reservations essential* �🍽 *Jacket required*
☉ *Closed Sun. and Mon.* ▤ *AE, MC, V* ⓤ *Green Park* ✚ *1:H5.*

££££   ✕**Hibiscus.** French chef Claude Bosi excels at one of London's finest
MODERN FRENCH   modern French restaurants, tucked away on Maddox Street in Mayfair. Bosi's effortless cuisine is sure to impress with frogs' leg fricassée,
Cornish pollock with clams, Glenham salmon with eucalyptus, or Lyonnaise tripe with cuttlefish and pig's ear. Rice soufflé and pineapple sorbet
will send you home happy. ⊠ *29 Maddox St., Mayfair* ☎ *020/7629–
2999* ⊕ *www.hibiscusrestaurant.co.uk* ▤ *AE, MC, V* ☉ *No lunch Sat.
Closed Sun. and Mon.* ⓤ *Oxford Circus, Piccadilly* ✚ *3:A5.*

£££   ✕**La Petite Maison.** American in London star Gwyneth Paltrow blogs that
FRENCH   La Petite Maison is her all-time favorite London restaurant, and no wonder—there's nothing on the impeccably well-sourced French Mediterranean and Provençale menu that fails to delight. Try a crab and lobster
salad, a soft Burrata cheese, Datterini tomato and basil spread, or an
aromatic baked turbot with artichokes, chorizo, and white wine sauce.
Based on the style of the original La Petite Maison in Nice in France,
dishes come to the table when they're ready, and the friendly staff make

for a convivial vibe. ⊠ *53–54 Brook's Mews, Mayfair* ☎ *020/7495–4774* ⊕ *www.lpmlondon.co.uk* ▭ *AE, MC, V* Ⓤ *Bond St.* ✛ *1:H4.*

£££££
FRENCH
✕ **Le Gavroche.** Master chef judge Michel Roux Jr. thrives at this 44-year-old clubby basement haven in Mayfair, which some rate as the best formal dining in London. With silver domes and unpriced ladies' menus, Roux's mastery of classic French cuisine dazzles with signatures like foie gras with cinnamon-scented crispy duck pancake, langoustine with snails and Hollandaise sauce, or Pyrennean lamb with *flageolets* (French kidney-shaped beans). Desserts like the chocolate omelet soufflé are equally accomplished. The weekday set lunch is a relatively affordable treat at £48.90—with a half bottle of wine, water, coffee, and petits fours. ⊠ *43 Upper Brook St., Mayfair* ☎ *020/7408–0881* ⊕ *www.le-gavroche.co.uk* ⌂ *Reservations essential* 🏛 *Jacket required* ▭ *AE, DC, MC, V* ⊘ *Closed Sun. and 10 days at Christmas* Ⓤ *Marble Arch* ✛ *1:G5.*

££££
JAPANESE
✕ **Nobu Berkeley Street.** Supermodels, soccer stars, and the global fashion crowd pay silly money for new-style sashimi with Peruvian flair at this so-hip-it-hurts Nobu spin-off near Piccadilly. More trendy than nearby flagship Nobu on Park Lane, this version seems to triple up successfully with a combined restaurant, cocktail bar, and nightclub feel. Once seated, the beautiful people go bonkers for miso black cod, California sushi rolls, tuna teriyaki, yellowtail sashimi, Bento boxes, and grilled Wagyu beef. Prices are downtown-Tokyo extreme, but the hot people-watching is just *so* good. ⊠ *15 Berkeley St., Mayfair* ☎ *020/7290–9222* ⊕ *www.noburestaurants.com* ▭ *AE, MC, V* Ⓤ *Green Park* ✛ *1:H5.*

££££
SEAFOOD
Fodor's Choice
★
✕ **Scott's.** This is where the A-list come to dine. Founded in 1851, and reborn as a glamorous seafood haven and oyster bar, Scott's draws movers-and-shakers and the beautiful people who pick at Cumbrae oysters, Dublin Bay prawns, and Stargazy pie (Cornish pie with fish heads gazing out of a pastry crust). Standouts like cod with chorizo, ray wings, and brown butter or padron peppers are to die for. Prices are super high, but not to worry: this really is *the* hottest joint in town. ⊠ *20 Mount St., Mayfair* ☎ *020/7495–7309* ⊕ *www.scotts-restaurant. com* ⌂ *Reservations essential* ▭ *AE, DC, MC, V* Ⓤ *Bond St.* ✛ *1:G5.*

££££
FRENCH
✕ **The Square.** The Square in Mayfair is a favorite among corporate folk due to the impeccable food, the impressive wine selection, and unparalleled service. Philip Howard's sophisticated French haute cuisine, which may include langoustine tails, red mullet, Lincolnshire hare, and Brillat-Savarin cheesecake has the mainly business clientele coming back for more. ⊠ *6–10 Bruton St., Mayfair* ☎ *020/7495–7100* ⊕ *www. squarerestaurant.com* ⌂ *Reservations essential* ▭ *AE, MC, V* ⊘ *No lunch weekends* Ⓤ *Green Park* ✛ *1:H5.*

£££
MODERN
EUROPEAN
✕ **Wild Honey.** Wild Honey's notable set lunch or pre- and posttheater evening deals (£19.95–£22.95) are wildly popular. Book ahead at this wood-paneled clublike salon, with bright modern pictures and comfy booths, in swanky Mayfair. Try the tasty Exmouth crab and white peach, Marseille bouillabaisse, Dorset plaice with Swiss chard, panna cotta, or signature wild honey ice cream with crushed honeycomb. The food is unpretentious, and all 50-odd wines come in handy third-of-a-bottle carafes. ⊠ *12 St. George St., Mayfair* ☎ *020/7758–9160* ⊕ *www. wildhoneyrestaurant.co.uk* ▭ *AE, MC, V* Ⓤ *Oxford Circus* ✛ *3:A5.*

14

MARYLEBONE

£££   ✕ **Galvin Bistrot de Luxe.** The hard-working Galvin brothers blaze a trail
BISTRO   for the deluxe bistro concept on a no-man's-land stretch of Baker Street
in Marylebone. Feted chefs Chris and Jeff forsake Michelin stars and cut
loose under the brasserie banner. Loyal fans and a more mature crowd
enjoy impeccable service in a handsome slate floor and mahogany-
paneled salon. There's no finer crab lasagna around, and mains punch
above their weight: gilthead bream, calves liver with Morteaux sausage,
stuffed pig's trotter, and the veal kidneys with girolles mushrooms are all
a triumph. The £17.50 set lunch or £19.50 early evening dinners (6–7
pm) are unbeatable and there's monthly live Sunday evening jazz performed by the students from the nearby Royal Academy of Music. ⊠ 66
Baker St., Marylebone ☎ *020/7935–4007* ⊕ *www.galvinrestaurants.
com* ⊟ *AE, MC, V* Ⓤ *Baker St.* ✛ *1:G3.*

£   ✕ **Golden Hind.** You'll find some of the best fish-and-chips in London
SEAFOOD   at the Golden Hind, a British chippy (a shop serving traditional fish
and chips) in a retro 1914 Art Deco café, off Marylebone High Street.
Locals and tourists alike love the fresh calamari, skate wings, and fish
cakes, but it's the perfect—nongreasy—deep-fried or steamed battered
cod, plaice, and haddock from Grimsby, the classic hand-cut chips,
and mushy peas that are the big draw. It's corkage-free BYO and it's
open noon–3 pm weekdays and 6–10 pm Monday through Saturday.
⊠ *73 Marylebone La., Marylebone* ☎ *020/7486–3644* ⊟ *AE, MC, V*
Ⓟ *BYOB* ☺ *No lunch Sat. Closed Sun.* Ⓤ *Bond St.* ✛ *1:H3.*

SOHO AND COVENT GARDEN

SOHO

££   ✕ **Andrew Edmunds.** Rustic food at realistic prices defines this perpetu-
MEDITERRANEAN   ally jammed, Dickensian, softly lighted romantic Soho restaurant—
though it could be larger and the wooden bench seats more forgiving.
Tucked away behind Carnaby Street, it's a favorite with the Soho media
crowd that come for daily changing, fixed-price lunch menus. Starters
and main courses draw on the taste of Ireland, the Mediterranean, and
Middle East. Pigeon breast, Roquefort soufflé, and swordfish with
basil mayonnaise are all hale and hearty. ⊠ *46 Lexington St., Soho*
☎ *020/7437–5708* ⊴ *Reservations essential* ⊟ *MC, V* Ⓤ *Oxford Circus,
Piccadilly Circus* ✛ *3:C5.*

££   ✕ **Aqua Kyoto.** Japanese spectacular Aqua Kyoto off Regent Street is
JAPANESE   a high-concept import from Hong Kong that looks like a set from a
moody James Bond film, with a sunken central sushi counter that's
straight out of the Starship *Enterprise.* Set on the fifth floor of the
former Dickens & Jones building, there's enough culinary theatre and
beautiful bento boxes, sushi, sashimi, and tempura to keep the rich kids
and smart executives here coming back. Sample expert beef teriyaki
with chili ponzu sauce, flying fish roe sashimi and ubiquitious black
cod, but be warned: It's not cheap. ⊠ *5th fl., 240 Regents St. (entrance
on Argyll St.), Soho* ☎ *020/7478–0540* ⊕ *www.aqua-london.com*
⊴ *Reservations essential* ⊟ *AE, MC, V* Ⓤ *Piccadilly Circus, Oxford
Circus* ✛ *3:A4.*

AFTERNOON TEA

Afternoon tea is the height of fashion, and here are some of the best around. Tea at the **Ritz** (✉ *The Ritz, 150 Piccadilly, St. James's* ☎ *020/7493–8181* ⊕ *www. theritzlondon.com*) is still the ultimate afternoon tea experience, where you'll enjoy live music and cucumber sandwiches on silver cake stands at the gilded Palm Court (£39–£59). Super model Kate Moss enjoys old-school elegance at **Claridge's** tearoom (✉ *Claridge's, Carlos Pl., Mayfair* ☎ *020/7499–7070* ⊕ *www.the-connaught.co.uk*), where strawberry choux and champagne tea are on offer for £45. Posh mums and daughters scoff scones and clotted cream at **Fortnum & Mason** (✉ *St. James's Restaurant, Fortnum & Mason, 181 Piccadilly, St. James's* ☎ *0845/602–5694* ⊕ *www. fortnumandmason.com*) in the fifth-floor St. James's restaurant (£20). Fashionistas quaff designer pâtisserie among low seats and chandeliers at **Palour at Sketch** (✉ *9 Conduit St., Mayfair* ☎ *0870/777–4488* ⊕ *www.sketch.uk.com*) for £9.50. Finally, the **Wolseley** on Piccadilly (✉ *160 Piccadilly, St. James's* ☎ *020/7499–6996* ⊕ *www. thewolseley.com*) does gooey pastries and fine Ceylon tea for £21.

14

££
MODERN BRITISH
✗ **Arbutus.** Serious cuisine at midrange prices has established Arbutus in the winners' circle of favorite Soho eateries. The £16.95 three-course lunch or £18.95 pretheater special are bargains of the year. Chef Anthony Demetre might surprise with squid-and-mackerel burger, rabbit cottage pie, or Icelandic cod and sea purslane, and finishes off with English trifle or French *clafoutis* with William pears. All wines are offered in third-of-a-bottle carafes—a great way to sample new delights. ✉ *63–64 Frith St., Soho* ☎ *020/7734–4545* ⊕ *www.arbutusrestaurant. co.uk* ⊟ *AE, MC, V* Ⓤ *Tottenham Court Rd.* ✛ *3:D4.*

£
CHINESE
✗ **Baozi Inn.** Vintage Chairman Mao posters and paraphernalia decorate the interior of this hole-in-the-wall Sichuan café on a busy side street in Chinatown. Baozi steamed buns—pork and onion, or shrimp and radish—are house specials, and there's dragon wonton broth or Chengdu pork dumplings with chili oil (£5.50). Try ginger juice spinach (£4.90), or peace and happiness noodle soup, topped with duck, garlic, and Chinese toon tree shoots (£6.50). Tables are cramped, turnover is fast, and service is speedy. ✉ *25 Newport Ct., Soho* ☎ *020/7287–6877* ☙ *Reservations not accepted* ⊟ *AE, MC, V* Ⓤ *Leicester Sq.* ✛ *3:E5.*

£
CAFÉ
✗ **Bar Italia.** This football-mad Frith Street 1949 landmark Italian coffee bar is a 24-hour Soho institution. Grab a frothy cappuccino or sobering macchiato and wolf down a slice of pizza, panettone, or rich chocolate cake at the mirrored counter. The walls are plastered with old pictures of Italian singers, sports stars, and movie legends, and it's the *primo numero uno* spot in London to watch Italy play in—or get knocked out of—the soccer World Cup. ✉ *22 Frith St., Soho* ☎ *020/7437–4520* ⊕ *www.baritaliasoho.co.uk* ⊟ *AE, MC, V* Ⓤ *Leicester Sq.* ✛ *3:D5.*

££
SPANISH
✗ **Barrafina.** Soho's favorite tapas bar on Frith Street is modeled on Cal Pep the famed tapas bar in Barcelona, and similarly has only a few (23 in total) raised counter seats. It's a no-reservations spot and there will likely be a wait, but the authentic tapas are worth it. Nosh on shrimp,

Busaba Eathai's tasty fried calamari.

chorizo, quail, sardines, and octopus, or classics like cured Jabugo ham and Spanish tortillas. You can check out the scene—or who's waiting in line—at the Barrafina webcam. ✉ *54 Frith St., Soho* ☎ *020/7440–1463* ⊕ *www.barrafina.co.uk* ⟡ *Reservations not accepted* ▭ *AE, MC, V* Ⓤ *Tottenham Court Rd.* ✛ *3:D4.*

£££
ITALIAN
✕ **Bocca di Lupo.** The place is always packed, tables are jammed too close together, and the acoustics are particularly lousy, but everyone comes for the brilliant regional Italian cuisine. Set in an unlikely street off Soho's red-light district, here you'll find succession of small plates and dishes from Bologna to Veneto. Try fried anchovies, grilled red prawns, lamb *prosciutto*, cannellini beans, or rustic pork and foie gras sausages. You may not be able to hear yourselves speak, but at least the amazing milk-free espresso ice cream makes up for the loss. ✉ *12 Archer St., Soho* ☎ *020/7734–2223* ⊕ *www.boccadilupo.com* ⟡ *Reservations essential* ▭ *AE, MC, V* ☽ *Closed Sun.* Ⓤ *Piccadilly Circus* ✛ *3:C5.*

£
THAI
Fodor'sChoice
★
✕ **Busaba Eathai.** It's top Thai nosh for little money at this no-reservations eatery in the heart of Soho. Fitted with wooden bench seats and hardwood tables, this flagship restaurant has communal dining, rapid service, and a fast-moving queue. The menu includes noodles, curries, soups, and stir-fries. Pour yourself a lemongrass tea, then try the chicken with shiitake, cuttlefish curry, or vermicelli with prawns, squid, and scallops. It's always handy as a shopping pit stop. ✉ *106–110 Wardour St., Soho* ☎ *020/7255–8686* ⊕ *www.busaba.com* ⟡ *Reservations not accepted* ▭ *AE, MC, V* Ⓤ *Tottenham Court Rd.* ✛ *3:C4.*

£
CHINESE
✕ **Cha Cha Moon.** Alan Yau's slump-proof Chinese noodle canteen off Carnaby Street charges under £10 for all mains and sides, so it's no wonder the communal tables are usually crammed like a Hong Kong

rush hour subway train. Pick wisely from the long menu and you can score a tasty meal for £17. Stick to the hand-pulled *lao mian* noodles, rice-based curries, or the prawn dumplings. ✉ *15–21 Ganton St., Soho* ☎ *020/7297–9800* ⊕ *www.chachamoon.com* ✍ *Reservations not accepted* ▬ *AE, MC, V* Ⓤ *Oxford Circus* ✛ *3:B5.*

£ ✕**Côte.** Where else can you get a surprisingly good three-course French
FRENCH meal for £11.95? The Côte French brasserie—softly lighted and smoothly decked out with grey and white striped awning, banquettes, and Parisian-style round tables—does just the trick, and offers these deals weekdays from 3 pm until 7 pm, and weekends noon to 6 pm. With four choices per course, you'll find all your favorites: Bayonne ham, beef Bourguignon, Les Landes chicken, *moules marinières* (steamed mussels with white wine), tuna Niçoise, minced beef steak haché patties, and crème caramel. ✉ *124–126 Wardour St., Soho* ☎ *020/7287–9280* ⊕ *www.cote-restaurants.co.uk* ▬ *AE, MC, V* Ⓤ *Tottenham Court Rd., Piccadilly Circus* ✛ *3:C4.*

£££ ✕**Dean Street Townhouse.** It's impossible not to feel glamorous at this
BRITISH packed and buzzing restaurant, attached to the stylish hotel of the same
Fodor'sChoice name. Soft lighting, dark-wood floors, red banquettes, raised bar seats
★ and walls crammed with monochromes by Brit artists Tracy Emin and Mat Collishaw create a hip atmosphere for London's good-looking media elite. No-frills, no-fuss retro-British favorites include smoked haddock soufflé, fish fingers, or toad-in-the-hole, plus sherry trifle, treacle tart, and bread-and-butter pudding. You'll find buttered crumpets for afternoon tea, as well as a high tea service, and weekend brunch, plus a few celebrities dotted around the place, too. ✉ *69–71 Dean St., Soho* ☎ *020/7434–1775* ⊕ *www.deanstreettownhouse.com* ✍ *Reservations essential* ▬ *AE, MC, V* Ⓤ *Tottenham Court Rd.* ✛ *3:D5.*

££ ✕**Giaconda Dining Room.** A gastro-landmark with an indie spirit on Den-
MODERN mark Street's Tin Pan Alley (think Bowie, Marley, and the Clash), the
EUROPEAN friendly Australian-run two-room dining room may only seat 35, but
Fodor'sChoice the eclectic menu is inspired. Chef Paul Merrony sends out mighty start-
★ ers—creamed shallots with horseradish, crab linguine, or lamb with cocoa beans—and a full range of luscious main entrées at extremely low prices. Try the fish cakes, pig's trotters, salmon and fennel, or hearty dishes like veal kidneys, Italian pork sausage stew, or ham-hock hash with a fried egg on top. ✉ *9 Denmark St., Soho* ☎ *020/7240–3334* ⊕ *www.giacondadining.com* ▬ *AE, MC, V* ☉ *No lunch Sat. Closed Sun. and Mon.* Ⓤ *Tottenham Court Rd.* ✛ *3:D4.*

£££ ✕**Hix.** Hix, a spiffy Soho establishment on Brewer Street that oozes
BRITISH class, style, and panache, serves brilliant but simple British fare: think
Fodor'sChoice flat-iron steak with a huge chunk of bone marrow, Aryshire veal with
★ Mendip snails, or *gurnard* (a white fish) with cockles and sea *purslane* (green leaves). You can also find epic feasts for the whole table, such as goose, chop, and oysters, or suckling pig, plus riffs on classics, like rabbit and crayfish Stargazy pie. Check out Brit artists Sarah Lucas and Damian Hirst mobiles, plus old-fashioned bar billiards, kilim rugs, and famed mixologist Nick Strangeway's cocktails in the winning basement bar. ✉ *66–70 Brewer St., Soho* ☎ *020/7292–3518* ⊕ *www.hixsoho.co.uk* ✍ *Reservations essential* ▬ *AE, MC, V* Ⓤ *Piccadilly Circus* ✛ *3:C5.*

14

£ ✕**Koya.** Is it the hours of foot kneading (albeit under plastic canvas, to
JAPANESE allay hygene concerns) that makes the udon wheat-flour noodles here
so springy, spongy, and ultimately addictive? Lines of Japanese diners
and trendy Soho-ites are a testament to the allure of the dishes served
at this no-reservations, tiny, Zen-like cult *udon-ya* (noodle house). Once
inside, start with cold udon on a bamboo basket with pungent miso
and pickled pork, and then—if you're up for it—slurp hot udon with
mixed seaweed. There are also pickled plums and pork belly dishes,
but it's the humble udon noodle that prevails. ✉ *49 Frith St., Soho*
☎ *020/7434–4463* ⊕ *www.koya.co.uk* ✍ *Reservations not accepted*
⊟ *MC, V* ☻ *Closed Sun.* Ⓤ *Tottenham Court Rd.* ✛ *3:D5.*

£ ✕**Maison Bertaux.** Romantics cherish this tiny, two-story 1871 French
CAFÉ pâtisserie, where nothing seems to have changed in the past few decades.
Framed with a vintage blue-and-white awning, the *choux* pastry and
gooey cakes at this time-warp Soho institution are renowned and baked
on-site. The chocolate éclairs, Black Forest gâteaux, and almond crois-
sants always delight. Run by Soho legend Michelle Wade, Maison Bertaux also hosts a cheery tea service, which comes with tasty savories,
like broccoli quiche or Dijon slice (cheese, peppers, and Dijon mustard).
✉ *28 Greek St., Soho* ☎ *020/7437–6007* ⊕ *www.maisonbertaux.com*
⊟ *No credit cards* Ⓤ *Leicester Sq.* ✛ *3:D5.*

£££ ✕**Paramount.** Unrivaled panoramic views of London are the big draw at
BRITISH this 32nd-floor restaurant at Centre Point near Tottenham Court Road.
Ask to dine by the window at dusk and look east as the lights come on
at the London Eye, Tower Bridge, the Gherkin, along the Thames, and
at the cluster of towers at Canary Wharf. Despite hosting possibly the
best views in London, the pricey food is only fairly decent, and no match
for the majesty on offer. Our advice? Chin up, have a cocktail, admire
London from above, and stick to the less fiddly dishes on the menu,
such as roast Cobb chicken with Somerset truffles or Denham Castle
lamb with wild garlic. ✉ *101–103 New Oxford St., Soho* ☎ *020/7420–*
2900 ⊕ *www.paramount.uk.net* ✍ *Reservations essential* ⊟ *AE, MC,*
V ☻ *Closed Sun.* Ⓤ *Tottenham Court Rd.* ✛ *3:D3.*

££ ✕**Yauatcha.** It's all-day dim sum at this superbly lighted slinky Soho
CHINESE classic. Well designed by Christian Liaigre—with black granite floors,
aquarium, candles, and a starry ceiling—the food is a match for the
seductive setting. There's wicked dim sum (try prawns or scallops), crispy
duck rolls, silver cod, fancy cocktails, tea and colorful cakes in the first-
floor tearoom. Note the quick table turns, and ask to dine in the more
romantic basement at night. ✉ *15 Broadwick St., Soho* ☎ *020/7494–*
8888 ⊕ *www.yauatcha.com* ✍ *Reservations essential* ⊟ *AE, MC, V*
Ⓤ *Oxford Circus* ✛ *3:C4.*

COVENT GARDEN

£ ✕**Canela.** Hidden behind Neal Street in Covent Garden, this laid-back
PORTUGUESE Portuguese–Brazilian café serves unusual savories, pastries, and strong
coffee. Portuguese snacks including chicken-stuffed *coxinha* dumplings
are £2.50, and mains like *feijoada* (black bean stew and smoked pork),
meatballs in tomato sauce, or bacalhau salt cod with fried potatoes are
less than £10. There's a collection of wheat- and gluten-free coconut,
chocolate, orange and carrot cakes. ✉ *33 Earlham St., Covent Garden*

☎ *020/7240–6926* ⊕ *www.canelacafe.com* ▭ *MC, V* Ⓤ *Covent Garden, Holborn* ✛ *3:E4.*

£
VEGETARIAN

✕ **Food for Thought.** This 1970s-style subterranean vegetarian café without a liquor license (BYO without a corkage fee) on Neal Street, has got a cult following, so be prepared to wait. You'll find wooden communal tables and a daily menu of soups, salads, stews, quiches, stir-fries, bakes, and casseroles. Wheat-free, gluten-free, genetically modified–free, and vegan options are available. Note that it's open noon until 8:30 pm Monday–Saturday, and to 5 pm Sunday. ✉ *31 Neal St., Covent Garden* ☎ *020/7836–9072* ⌂ *Reservations not accepted* ▭ *No credit cards* ⌘ *BYOB* Ⓤ *Covent Garden* ✛ *3:F4.*

£££
MODERN BRITISH
Fodor's Choice
★

✕ **Great Queen Street.** Expect crowds at Covent Garden's leading gastropub that showcases classic British dishes in a burgundy and bare oak-floor-and-table setting. Old-fashioned offerings like pressed tongue, mackerel and gooseberry, Old Spot pork, and mussels and brown crab on toast may be revived from a bygone era, but Londoners absolutely adore them. Venison pie and dishes for the whole table—like seven-hour shoulder of lamb—are highly convivial. There's little for nonmeat eaters, and no dinner Sunday. ✉ *32 Great Queen St., Covent Garden* ☎ *020/7242–0622* ⌂ *Reservations essential* ▭ *MC, V* ☾ *No dinner Sun.* Ⓤ *Covent Garden, Holborn* ✛ *3:G4.*

£££
BRITISH

✕ **The Ivy.** The A-list tend to spurn the Ivy for other hot spots like Scott's, J Sheekey, and Hix, but it's still hard to get a table here. A mix of TV stars and out-of-towners dine on Moroccan spiced lamb and smoked *aubergine* (eggplant), salmon fish cakes, eggs Benedict, and English classics like shepherd's pie and *kedgeree* (curried rice with flaked haddock, parsley, and boiled egg) in a handsome stained-glass and wood-paneled dining salon. For midrange West End star-spotting this is a prime spot. If you can't score a reservation, try walking in for a table at the last moment—it's been known to work. ✉ *1–5 West St., Covent Garden* ☎ *020/7836–4751* ⊕ *www.the-ivy.co.uk* ⌂ *Reservations essential* ▭ *AE, DC, MC, V* Ⓤ *Covent Garden* ✛ *3:E5.*

£££
SEAFOOD

✕ **J Sheekey.** West End theater and movie stars slip into this famous seafood haunt as an alternative to Scott's or Hix. Linked with nearby Theaterland and Shaftesbury Avenue, J Sheekey is one of Londoners' all-time favorite West End haunts. It charms with warm wood paneling, showbiz monochromes, a warren of alcove tables, and lava-rock bar tops. Opt for Arctic herring, Dover sole, Cornish sardines, monkfish, or famous Sheekey fish pie. Have champagne and West Mersea oysters at the original mirrored oyster bar for the ultimate in true romance, or enjoy the £25.50 weekend set lunch. ✉ *28–32 St. Martin's Ct., Covent Garden* ☎ *020/7240–2565* ⊕ *www.j-sheekey.co.uk* ▭ *AE, DC, MC, V* Ⓤ *Leicester Sq.* ✛ *3:E6.*

££££
FRENCH

✕ **L'Atelier de Joël Robuchon.** Foodies and glitterati sit at the counter and graze tapas-style at Joël Robuchon's super-seductive West End outpost. Counter seating frames the ground-floor open kitchen creating a spectacle that is pure culinary theater. Indulge yourself in exquisite French tapas—from frogs' legs and egg cocotte to scallops, pig's trotters, and quail with truffle mash. The £125 eight-course tasting menu is a decadent way to blow a pay check, but the set £23 and £27

14

deals are the sensible way to go. There's also a bar and a more formal restaurant, La Cuisine, on the first floor. ⊠ *13–15 West St., Covent Garden* ☎ *020/7010–8600* ⊕ *www.joel-robuchon.com* ⊟ *AE, MC, V* Ⓤ *Leicester Sq.* ✛ *3:E5.*

££££   ✕ **Rules.** Come here to escape the 21st century. Opened by Thomas Rule
BRITISH   in 1798, London's oldest restaurant has hosted everyone from novelist Charles Dickens to actor Laurence Olivier and the current Prince of Wales. This most traditional of English dining salons has plush red banquettes and lacquered yellow walls crammed with old oil paintings, antique clocks, prints, engravings, and Victorian cartoons. Try pricey and historic British dishes—steak-and-kidney pie, perhaps, or roast beef and Yorkshire pudding—for a taste of the 18th century. In season, daily specials include game from the restaurant's High Pennines estate, including teal, snipe, woodcock, and grouse. ⊠ *35 Maiden La., Covent Garden* ☎ *020/7836–5314* ⊕ *www.rules.co.uk* ⊟ *AE, MC, V* Ⓤ *Covent Garden* ✛ *3:F6.*

£££££   ✕ **Savoy Grill.** You can feel the history at this 1889 art deco power din-
GRILL   ing salon at the Savoy, which has hosted everyone from Oscar Wilde and Winston Churchill, to Marilyn Monroe and Audrey Hepburn. Nowadays, business blue-bloods and top-end tourists enjoy the Grill's famous table-side daily trolley, which might have roast rack of pork, or traditional roast beef Wellington. T-bone, rib-eye, and porterhouse steaks sizzle straight off the flame grill. Puddings like mandarin baked Alaska are from a bye-gone age. ⊠ *The Savoy, 100 Strand, Covent Garden* ☎ *020/7592–1600* ⊕ *www.gordonramsay.com/thesavoygrill* ⌕ *Reservations essential* ⊟ *AE, DC, MC, V* Ⓤ *Charing Cross, Covent Garden.* ✛ *3:G5.*

£   ✕ **Wahaca.** Expect a wait for the fab-value Mexican street food at this
MEXICAN   brightly colored Covent Garden favorite. Mud walls and bench seats make for buzzy basement surroundings, but it's the cheap £3.85–£8.95 tacos, enchiladas, quesadillas, and burritos that pull in the student crowds. A £19.95 spread for two will produce a feast of broad bean quesadillas, pork tacos, slaw, green rice, black beans, and guacamole, but note that reservations aren't taken and that it's often full by 6:30 pm. ⊠ *66 Chandos Pl., Covent Garden* ☎ *020/7240–1883* ⊕ *www. wahaca.co.uk* ⌕ *Reservations not accepted* ⊟ *AE, MC, V* Ⓤ *Charing Cross* ✛ *3:F6.*

BLOOMSBURY AND LEGAL LONDON

£   ✕ **North Sea Fish Restaurant.** Come here for the British national dish of
SEAFOOD   fish-and-chips—battered cod, thick fries with salt and malt vinegar, and a dollop of homemade tartar sauce. Note that the restaurant is tricky to find: Head three blocks south of St. Pancras station and the British Library, then down Judd Street. It has net curtains, velvet seats, and worn carpet, and it's filled with students, pensioners, and academics from the Library's Reading Room. There's freshly caught cod, plaice, haddock, sea bass, and salmon, with mushy peas, as well as dishes like breaded scampi or chicken salad. ⊠ *7–8 Leigh St., Bloomsbury* ☎ *020/7387–5892* ⊟ *MC, V* ☾ *Closed Sun.* Ⓤ *Russell Sq.* ✛ *2:C3.*

THE CITY

£££ ✕ **Boundary.** Design guru and restaurateur Sir Terence Conran scores
FRENCH a bull's-eye at Boundary in über-fashionable Hoxton–Shoreditch. A
theatrical glass-fronted open kitchen and sparkling lighting, acoustics,
and Technicolor seats, make this plush 100-plus seat basement French
brasserie the *glamorati's* east-end destination of choice. The menu's a
wish list of crowd-pleasers designed to impress: shellfish bisque, escar-
gots à la Bourguignonne, *cassoulet Toulousain* (haricot bean stew with
pork, lamb, duck, and garlic sausage), *lapin à la moutarde* (rabbit with
mustard), and roast Les Landes chicken. Desserts like the *tarte au citron*
(a classic lemon tart) are tasty and reasonably priced. ⊠ *2–4 Boundary
St., entrance at 9 Redchurch St., The City* ☎ *020/7729–1051* ⊕ *www.
theboundary.co.uk* ⌲ *Reservations essential* ⊟ *AE, MC, V* ⊗ *No lunch
Mon.* Ⓜ *Liverpool St.* ✛ *2:G1.*

£ ✕ **E Pellicci.** It's Cockney chitchat and all-day English breakfast at this 1900
CAFÉ family-run listed landmark café near Brick Lane and Columbia Road
markets. With stained glass, Art Deco marquetry, and pics autographed
by *East Enders* TV soap stars, it's the hole-in-the-wall for the fry-ups that
Londoners love: eggs, bacon, beans, toast, tomato, black pudding, and
bubble 'n' squeak (cabbage and mash potatoes). Your arteries may clog
up, but at least the wallet survives: Everything's less than £8, but remember it's cash-only. ⊠ *332 Bethnal Green Rd., The City* ☎ *020/7739–4873*
⊟ *No credit cards* ⊗ *Closed Sun.* Ⓤ *Bethnal Green* ✛ *2:H1.*

£££ ✕ **L'Anima.** Brilliant Southern Italian cuisine in a love-it-or-loathe-it
ITALIAN modern glass-fronted box of a restaurant characterizes the scene at
L'Anima. Chef Francesco Mazzei draws inspiration from Sicily, Sar-
dinia, and Calabria, and works the floor, bar, and clear-fronted kitchen
like the proud owner he is. Simple, modern dishes like wild mushroom
and black truffle *tagliolini* are near perfection, as is the wood-roasted
turbot with clams—as succulent as you could wish. Dessert puddings,
like cappuchino tiramisu, are *belissimo*; the wines are mainly Italian.
⊠ *1 Snowden St., The City* ☎ *020/7422–7000* ⊕ *www.lanima.co.uk*
⊟ *AE, DC, MC, V* ⊗ *Closed Sun.* Ⓤ *Liverpool St.* ✛ *2:G1.*

£ ✕ **Lahore Kebab House.** Best budget curries in London is the mantra at
PAKISTANI the Lahore Kebab House in Whitechapel. It may be no-frills and free
BYO, but the Pakistani home-style cooking is cheap and brilliant—
popular with locals. Tandoor-grilled mutton *tikka*, grilled lamb chops,
creamy *tarka daal* lentils, *masala* fish curry, and *karahi* chicken are all
super-spiced and fiery. A £15-a-head spread knocks spots off anything
on offer in nearby Brick Lane's so-called curry mile. ⊠ *2 Umberston St.,
The City* ☎ *020/7481–9737* ⊕ *www.lahore-kebabhouse.com* ⊟ *MC, V*
⌖ *BYOB* Ⓤ *Aldgate or Whitechapel* ✛ *2:H2.*

£££ ✕ **Moro.** Up from the City, near Clerkenwell and Sadler's Wells con-
MEDITERRANEAN temporary dance theater, is Exmouth Market, a cluster of cute shops, a
few delis, an Italian church, and fine restaurants like Moro. The menu
includes a mélange of Spanish and North African flavors. Spiced meats,
Serrano ham, salt cod, and wood-fired and char-grilled offerings are the
secret to Moro's success. Wood-roasted sea bass with capers and fennel
sauce stands out. Sidle up to the zinc bar, or squeeze into a tiny table
and lean in—it's noisy here. But then again, that's part of the charm.

14

✉ *34–36 Exmouth Market, The City* ☎ *020/7833–8336* ⊕ *www.moro. co.uk* ✍ *Reservations essential* ▭ *AE, DC, MC, V* ☾ *Closed Sun.* Ⓤ *Farringdon* ✛ *2:E3.*

£   ✗ **Simpson's Tavern.** This Dickensian back-alley City chophouse was
BRITISH   founded in 1757 and is as raucous as the day it opened. It draws pinstriped City folk, who love the boardinghouse scene and old-school grub: oxtail stew, steak-and-kidney pie, potted shrimp (brown shrimp preserved in a pot of butter), and "stewed cheese" house special (cheese on toast with Béchamel sauce). The grumpy service and shared oak bench stalls are all part of the charm. Note that it's open weekdays only from noon until 3. ✉ *38½ Cornhill, at Ball Ct., The City* ☎ *020/7626–9985* ⊕ *www.simpsonstavern.co.uk* ▭ *AE, DC, MC, V* ☾ *Closed weekends. No dinner* Ⓤ *Bank* ✛ *2:G2.*

£   ✗ **Sông Quê Café.** An urban trawl through Hoxton's trendy boutiques,
VIETNAMESE record shops, and art galleries is topped off at this great-value Vietnamese canteen. Block out the scruffy Kingsland Road location and the gaudy green decor and instead sample a slew of the 180 dishes—including green papaya salad, tamarind prawns, Vietnamese pancakes, pork vermicelli, stir-fried tofu, and oodles of *pho* (beef broth with steak and rice noodles). ✉ *134 Kingsland Rd., The City* ☎ *020/7613–3222* ▭ *MC, V* Ⓤ *Old St.* ✛ *2:G1.*

££   ✗ **St. John Bread & Wine.** The younger sibling of nose-to-tail specialists
MODERN BRITISH St. John in Clerkenwell is a winner no matter what meal of the day: try porridge, prunes, and *pikelets* (small pancakes) and jam for breakfast; beetroot and pickled walnuts for lunch, and smoked sprats (a herringlike fish) for dinner. It's similar to St. John in that you'll find ox heart, pigskin, blood cake, and duck eggs on the menu. You can feast on a whole roast suckling pig that feeds 14. Note that it's a handy spot before or after visits to nearby Brick Lane or Old Spitalfields markets. ✉ *94–96 Commercial St., The City* ☎ *020/7251–0848* ⊕ *www.stjohnrestaurant. com* ▭ *AE, MC, V* Ⓤ *Aldgate East, Liverpool St.* ✛ *2:G2.*

£££   ✗ **Sweetings.** Established in 1889, Sweetings is a remnant from the old
SEAFOOD   imperial City of London heyday. There are some things Sweetings *doesn't* do: reservations, dinner, coffee, weekends. It does, however, do seafood. Not far from St. Paul's Cathedral, it's patronized by self-assured City gents who drink tankards of Black Velvet (Guinness and champagne) and eat soused herrings, roe on toast, and skate wings with black butter at linen-covered raised counters. The oysters are fresh and desserts like spotted dick and syrup pudding are classic favorites. ✉ *39 Queen Victoria St., The City* ☎ *020/7248–3062* ✍ *Reservations not accepted* ▭ *AE, MC, V* ☾ *Closed weekends. No dinner* Ⓤ *Mansion House* ✛ *2:H6.*

£   ✗ **Tayyabs.** Blythe City bankers and medics from the Royal London
PAKISTANI Hospital swamp this no-reservations high-turnover Pakistani curry canteen in Whitechapel. Expect a wait after dark, and bear in mind that it's corkage-free BYO, jam-packed, noisy, and maddeningly chaotic. Nonetheless, prices are cheap and you can gorge handsomely for £17 on minced meat seekh kebabs, karahi prawns, or marinated and char-grilled lamb chops. ✉ *83 Fieldgate St., The City* ☎ *020/7247–9543* ⊕ *www.tayyabs.co.uk* ✍ *Reservations not accepted* ▭ *AE, MC, V* 🍷 *BYOB* Ⓤ *Aldgate East* ✛ *2:H2.*

CLERKENWELL

£££ ✕ **Bistrot Bruno Loubet.** Beloved French chef Bruno Loubet creates so many
FRENCH distinctive dishes, it's hard to decide which ones to choose. Deliciously
pink quail comes with pistachio and soft egg-yolk ravioli, and guinea
fowl *boudin blanc* sausage sits perfectly with leek fondue and chervil
sauce. You'll find stewed beef daube Provençale, crêpe Suzette in a
shiny copper pan, and Pernod floating island, all served in a ground-
floor dining room with retro lamps and artifacts overlooking St. John's
Square. Watch out for the £30 three-course foragers' menu, which may
include hedge sorrel, dill pollen, dandelion, and *marsh samphire* (an
edible green plant that grows by the sea). ⌧ *The Zetter, 86–88 Clerkenwell Rd, Clerkenwell* ☎ *020/7324–4455* ⊕ *www.bistrotbrunoloubet.
com* ⌕ *Reservations essential* ▭ *AE, MC, V* Ⓜ *Farringdon St.* ✛ *2:F3.*

£££ ✕ **St. John.** Foodies travel the world for chef Fergus Henderson's ultra-
BRITISH British nose-to-tail cooking at this no-frills stark-white converted
Fodor's Choice smokehouse in Clerkenwell. His chutzpah is laudable: One appetizer
★ is pigskin, and others, like ox heart or pig spleen and bacon, are margin-
ally less extreme. Signature dishes like bone marrow and parsley salad,
or chitterlings with dandelion appear stark on the plate but arrive with
aplomb. Expect an all-French wine list and finish with quince jelly and
Jersey cream or half a dozen golden Madeleines. ⌧ *26 St. John St.,
Clerkenwell* ☎ *020/7251–0848* ⊕ *www.stjohnrestaurant.com* ▭ *AE,
DC, MC, V* ☺ *No dinner Sun.* Ⓤ *Farringdon* ✛ *2:F4.*

THE EAST END

£££ ✕ **Viajante.** It's a massive schlep from the West End to Viajante in Beth-
MODERN nal Green, but chef Nuno Mendes's ultra-contemporary, avant-garde
EUROPEAN cuisine is the hottest, most exciting in London—bar none. Armed with
Fodor's Choice tweezers in a fascinating open-kitchen, Mendes creates 3- to 12-course
★ extravaganzas (£24–£150) in the serene converted former Bethnal
Green Town Hall. Unlikely tastes, textures, and flavors abound—like
iced green tea and Japanese purple shiso herb leaves, or Thai basil
panna cotta—but everything excels, and looks like high art. Expect
rare micro-herbs and local urban-foraged goodies, such as wood sorrel, sweet violets, and honeysuckle. Our advice is simple: Go! ⌧ *Town
Hall Hotel, Patriot Sq., East End* ☎ *020/7871–0461* ⊕ *www.viajante.
co.uk* ⌕ *Reservations essential* ▭ *AE, MC, V* Ⓤ *Bethnal Green tube/
rail, Cambridge Heath rail* ✛ *3:H2.*

THE SOUTH BANK

££ ✕ **Anchor & Hope.** Great meaty dishes at friendly prices are prepared in the
MODERN BRITISH open kitchen at this permanently packed, no-reservations, leading gastropub on the Cut in Waterloo: pot-roast duck, Herefordshire beef, and
skate wings stand out. It's a few doors down from the fabulous Young Vic
contemporary theater and bear in mind that it's noisy, cramped, and informal. That said, it's highly original, and there are great dishes for groups,
like slow-roasted leg of lamb. Expect to share one of the wooden tables
with other diners, too. ⌧ *36 The Cut, South Bank* ☎ *020/7928–9898*
⌕ *Reservations not accepted* ▭ *MC, V* Ⓤ *Waterloo, Southwark* ✛ *5:F2.*

14

£££ ✕ **Chez Bruce.** Gutsy French cuisine, perfect service, a winning wine list
MODERN FRENCH and a local neighborhood vibe make for one of London's all-time favorite celebration restaurants. Take the overland train south of the river to this cozy haunt overlooking Wandsworth Common and expect wonders ranging from delicious offal to lighter, simply grilled fish dishes. Rump of lamb with aubergine purée, or roast cod with *gremolata* (chopped parsley, garlic, and lemon zest) are immaculately prepared. The wines are great, the sommelier is superb, and all in all it's hard to beat. ⊠ 2 *Bellevue Rd., Wandsworth* ☎ *020/8672–0114* ⊕ *www.chezbruce.co.uk* ⌂ *Reservations essential* ▭ *AE, DC, MC, V* ✛ *4:E6.*

££ ✕ **Magdalen.** South of the river between London and Tower bridges, and
MODERN BRITISH a hop and a skip from the London Assembly headquarters, Magdalen is a self-assured beacon of class in an up-and-coming part of town. It specialized in inventive modern British cuisine at keen prices; fried calves brain (£7.50), braised Welsh lamb (£15.50), wild turbot and cockles (£18), and cow's curd and honey for £6 will hardly break the bank. With dark-wood and aubergine-color surroundings, sit back with a clever 70-bottle wine list that carries 19 by the carafe. ⊠ *152 Tooley St., South Bank* ☎ *020/7403–1342* ⊕ *www.magdalenrestaurant.co.uk* ▭ *AE, MC, V* ☉ *No lunch Sat. Closed Sun.* Ⓤ *London Bridge* ✛ *5:H2.*

££ ✕ **Tom Ilić.** The eponymous Serbian-born chef cooks with technical bril-
MODERN liance but charges only neighborhood prices at this haven in Battersea.
EUROPEAN Big on meat, especially pork, gob-smacked locals lap up dishes like pig's cheek with chorizo, pork, or a trio of lamb with spiced aubergine. Desserts like banana tart tatin are highly rated, and set lunches offer outstanding value at £14.50, or £16.95 on Sunday. It's south of the Thames, and best approached by taxi or overland train. ⊠ *123 Queenstown Rd., South Bank* ☎ *020/7622–0555* ⊕ *www.tomilic.com* ▭ *AE, MC, V* Ⓤ *National Rail: Queenstown Rd. or Battersea Park* ✛ *4:H6.*

KENSINGTON, CHELSEA, AND KNIGHTSBRIDGE

KENSINGTON

£££ ✕ **Bibendum.** Vibrant Art Deco prints and awesome stained-glass win-
MODERN BRITISH dows of cycling Michelin men set the tone at this former tire showroom and smooth-running London showpiece. Chef Matthew Harris cooks with Euro-Brit flair. Try langoustine salad, escargot, risotto, grilled rabbit, monkfish linguine, ox cheeks, or tripe (just as it ought to be cooked). The £29.50 fixed-price lunch menu is money well spent. ⊠ *Michelin House, 81 Fulham Rd., Kensington* ☎ *020/7581–5817* ⊕ *www.bibendum.co.uk* ▭ *AE, DC, MC, V* Ⓤ *South Kensington* ✛ *4:E3.*

££ ✕ **PJ's Bar & Grill.** Enter PJ's and assume the Polo Joe lifestyle: wooden
AMERICAN floors and stained glass, a slowly revolving propeller from a 1919 Vickers Vimy flying bomber, and vintage polo gear galore. The place is packed, relaxed, and efficient, and the menu, which includes all-American staples like organic Scottish steaks, salads, and brownies, pleases all except vegetarians. Weekend brunch is a must with the wealthy Chelsea jet set. ⊠ *52 Fulham Rd., Kensington* ☎ *020/7581–0025* ⊕ *www.pjsbarandgrill.co.uk* ▭ *AE, MC, V* Ⓤ *South Kensington* ✛ *4:E3.*

Harwood Arms' modern take on the classic British dish, scotch eggs.

££££ ✗**Tom Aikens.** Wonder chef Tom Aikens trained under French stars
FRENCH Pierre Koffmann and Joël Robuchon and excels at his eponymous place
in upmarket Chelsea. The dining room is decorated with sleek grey
walls and black leather seats but some say it's a little subdued. Aikens
is prone to flights of fancy in the kitchen, but his food is technically
superb. You'll swoon over his foie gras with Sauternes jelly, sea bass
with pickled fennel, partridge with truffle mash, and his honeycomb
and poppy seed ice cream. There's an expert sommelier to help navigate
the wine list, and the £49 set lunch offer is a good treat. ⊠ *43 Elystan
St., Kensington* ☎ *020/7584–2003* ⊕ *www.tomaikens.co.uk* ⌕ *Reservations essential* ▭ *AE, MC, V* Ⓤ *South Kensington* ✛ *4:E3.*

CHELSEA

££ ✗**Aubaine.** Loads of pretty women hang out at Aubaine at Brompton
FRENCH Cross in the summer. They love the distressed gray wooden furniture,
cut flowers, in-house pâtisserie, terrace tables, and people-watching.
Not to mention the figure-friendly menu choices, like prawn and Niçoise
salads, risottos, grilled lemon sole, eggplant cassoulet, and chicken tar-
tines. Sit by Brompton Road and enjoy the best free catwalk in town.
⊠ *260–262 Brompton Rd., Chelsea* ☎ *020/7052–0100* ⊕ *www.aubaine.
co.uk* ▭ *AE, MC, V* Ⓤ *South Kensington* ✛ *4:E2.*

££ ✗**Harwood Arms.** Modern British game doesn't get any better—or
MODERN BRITISH more inventive—than at this unassuming gastro pub. The co-owner
Fodor's Choice Mike Robinson shoots all the venison on the menu in season, and
★ you'll find a catalogue of awesome dishes like Berkshire roe deer with
Douglas fir sausages or whole North Yorkshire grouse with water-
cress. Tuck into stout-soaked beef cheeks with Herefordshire snails, or

wood pigeon with pickled apricots. Some dishes are served on a slab of wood, and there are popular carve-your-own whole-roast joints for the entire table. ✉ *27 Walham Grove, Chelsea* ☎ *020/7386–1847* ⊕ *www. harwoodarms.com* ⌂ *Reservations essential* ⊟ *AE, MC, V* ⊙ *No lunch Mon.* Ⓤ *Fulham Broadway* ✛ *4:A5.*

£££££
CHINESE
Fodor's Choice
★

✕ **Hunan.** There's no menu at this quirky, top-rated family-run Chinese restaurant in Pimlico. Instead diners state their preferences to owner-chef Peng, or his son Michael, and sit back, relax, and plough through a succession of highly tasty items to share. A seasoned crowd might enjoy 14 to 18 unfailingly delicious dishes like Hunan water-fried dumplings, sliced duck, pork broth, crispy frogs' legs, pig's ears and tongues, and crab noodle soup. There's no real logic to what you might receive, but portion sizes are generous, and the not knowing is all part of the fun. ✉ *51 Pimlico Rd., Chelsea* ☎ *020/7730–5712* ⊕ *www.hunanlondon.com* ⌂ *Reservations essential* ⊟ *AE, MC, V* ⊙ *Closed Sun.* Ⓤ *Sloane Sq.* ✛ *4:G3.*

££
MODERN BRITISH
Fodor's Choice
★

✕ **The Orange.** The handsome Orange gastropub in Pimlico gets everything right, which seems appropriate because most nights and weekends the place is full. It's light and airy, with stripped wood, an ochra color–scheme, and mini-potted orange trees; service is noticeably smiley and well-mannered. Try the chicken liver parfait and wood-fired pizzas, or enjoy a leisurely Sunday roast like Castle of Mey beef, Kilravock pork, or chicken with sage and bacon, all served with duck-fat roast potatoes, Yorkshire pudding, and braised red cabbage. ✉ *37–39 Pimlico Rd., Chelsea* ☎ *020/7881–9844* ⊕ *www.theorange.co.uk* ⌂ *Reservations essential* ⊟ *AE, MC, V* Ⓤ *Sloane Sq.* ✛ *4:G3.*

££
MODERN BRITISH

✕ **The Pig's Ear.** Heir to the throne Prince William once came with friends and split the bill in the first-floor dining room at this classic Sloaney boho-chic gastropub off the King's Road. Elbow in for space at the crowded ground-floor pub area, or choose a more formal vibe in the dark wood-paneled salon upstairs. You'll find creative dishes on a short menu, like pig's ear, Cornish crab, wild mallard, lamb neck, veal and bone marrow and braised pork belly, which are all typical, and executed . . . royally. ✉ *35 Old Church St., Chelsea* ☎ *020/7352–2908* ⊕ *www.thepigsear.info* ⊟ *AE, MC, V* Ⓤ *Sloane Sq.* ✛ *4:D4.*

£££
BRASSERIE

✕ **Racine.** There's an upscale buzz at this star of the Brompton Road dining scene, not far from the V&A museum, Harrods department store, and Holy Trinity Brompton church. This smooth-running chic French brasserie excels in doing simple things well—and not overcharging. Chef Henry Harris's classics like melted Raclette cheese, roast partridge, paté-like Middlewhite pork rillette, and rack of lamb all hit the high notes. Many of the patrons are wealthy local regulars, and the £15–£17.50 set lunch or early evening dinners (6–7:30 pm) are deservedly popular. ✉ *239 Brompton Rd., Chelsea* ☎ *020/7584–4477* ⊕ *www. racine-restaurant.com* ⊟ *AE, MC, V* Ⓤ *South Kensington* ✛ *4:E2.*

£££££
FRENCH

✕ **Restaurant Gordon Ramsay.** Gordon Ramsay protégée and head chef Clare Smyth wins the highest accolades in London at this special occasion showpiece near Chelsea Embankment. It's mighty hard to book a table, but if you do, you can splurge on the £120 seven-course tasting menu, where you'll experience divine dishes like lobster ravioli with tomato chutney, Bresse pigeon with baby beetroot and date

LONDON'S BEST CURRIES

Curry has become England's surrogate national dish and in London you'll find some of the best.

✕ **Dishoom** is modeled on the Persian-run all-day Irani cafés of Victorian Bombay and it skillfully churns out marvelous street food, from naan bread and roti wraps, to masala Bombay sausages, sweet yogurt-and-milk-based *lassi* drinks. Average price of dinner for two: £24. ✉ *12 Upper St. Martin's La., Covent Garden* ☎ *020/7420–9320* ⊕ *www.dishoom. com* Ⓤ *Leicester Sq.* ✛ *3:E5.*

✕ **Hot Stuff** in Vauxhall offers some of the best-loved and best-priced curries in London. Run by the Dawood family, it's a BYO café with two tables. Home-cooked specials include rice and king prawn *biryani*, thick chicken bhuna curry, and chili paneer cubed white cheese. There's wonderful rice, onion bhagi snacks, naan bread, and earthy *daal* (spiced lentils). Average price of dinner for two: £24. ✉ *19 Wilcox Rd., South Bank* ☎ *020/7720–1480* ⊕ *www. eathotstuff.com* ⓨ *BYOB* Ⓤ *Vauxhall* ✛ *5:C6.*

✕ **Indian Zing**'s chef-owner Manoj Vasaikar woos the west London curry mafia with updated eclectic Indian cuisine. Start with Rasam mussels and tamarind broth and try Khyber Pass shoulder of lamb or duck with Chettinad spices. Average price of dinner for two: £65. ✉ *236 King St.,* *Hammersmith* ☎ *020/8748–5959* ⊕ *www.indianzing.co.uk* Ⓤ *Hammersmith* ✛ *1:A2.*

✕ **Rasoi**'s chef-owner Vineet Bhatia prepares modern Indian cuisine at this special occasion Chelsea town house, where fans swoon over skewered scallops, tandoori salmon, confit duck samosas, South Indian crab cakes, and Keralean lamb lasagne. Average price of dinner for two: £160. ✉ *10 Lincoln St., Knightsbridge* ☎ *020/72251–1881* ⊕ *www. rasoirestaurant.co.uk* Ⓤ *Sloane Sq.* ✛ *4:F3*

✕ **Tayyabs** attracts queues for its Pakistani curries, grilled meats, and spicy seekh kebabs at this throbbing Whitechapel mecca and all-round curry madhouse. Average price of dinner for two: £30. ✉ *83 Fieldgate St., The City* ☎ *020/7247–9543* ⊕ *www.tayyabs.co.uk* ⓨ *BYOB* Ⓤ *Aldgate East* ✛ *2:H4.*

✕ **Trishna**'s £34.50, five-course tasting menus are the way to enjoy this Mumbai-inspired seafood specialist in Marylebone. Shrimp with carom seed, minted bream, tiger prawns, fish curry, and spiced king crab come with basmati rice, naan bread, and a choice of Indian puddings. Average price for dinner for two: £95. ✉ *15–17 Blandford St., Marylebone* ☎ *020/79351–5624* ⊕ *www.trishnalondon.com* Ⓤ *Bond St.* ✛ *1:G3.*

14

sauce, turbot with *cep velouté foam*, and a dessert of bitter chocolate and hazelnut cylinder with black current and ginger mousse. Service is neat and flawless, and the wine list goes on forever. ✉ *68 Royal Hospital Rd., Chelsea* ☎ *020/7352–4441* ⊕ *www.gordonramsay. com/royalhospitalroad* ⚓ *Reservations essential* ▬ *AE, DC, MC, V* ☽ *Closed weekends* Ⓤ *Sloane Sq.* ✛ *4:F4.*

Prosciutto-topped wood-fired pizza served at The Orange.

KNIGHTSBRIDGE

£££
FRENCH

✕ **Bar Boulud.** Star chef Daniel Boulud successfully mixes the best of French high-end brasserie fare with a dash of gourmet burgers and fries, at this popular ground-level haunt in the Mandarin Oriental. Small-board platters of the most delicate Gilles Verot charcuterie, or chunky Beaujolaise sausages with Lyonnaise mashed potatoes are followed by fist-sized New York hamburgers in a sesame seed bun with *pommes frites* on the side. The appealing grazing menu and informal wait staff make for a friendly and convivial vibe in a handy spot opposite the Harvey Nichols department store. ✉ *Mandarin Oriental Hyde Park, 66 Knightsbridge, Knightsbridge* ☎ *020/7201–3899* ⊕ *www.barboulud. com/barbouludlondon.html* ⚲ *Reservations essential* ▬ *AE, MC, V* Ⓤ *Knightsbridge* ✣ *4:F1.*

£££££
BRITISH
Fodor'sChoice
★

✕ **Dinner by Heston Blumenthal.** Medieval and historically-inspired English dishes executed with modern precision is the draw at Heston Blumenthal's London outpost. The "Meat Fruit" starter (c.1500) is shaped like a mandarin, and encases creamy chicken liver parfait. Beef Royale (c.1720) of Angus rib is cooked sous-vide in a water bath for 72 hours at 56°C to create a layered depth of flavor. Other historic treats include, "Rice and Flesh" (c.1390), featuring calf's tail and red wine, and a dish called "Salamagundy" (c.1720), with chicken oysters, bone marrow, and horseradish cream. ✉ *Mandarin Oriental Hyde Park, 66 Knights-bridge, Knightsbridge* ☎ *020/7201–3833* ⊕ *www.dinnerbyheston.com* ⚲ *Reservations essential* ▬ *AE, DC, MC, V* Ⓤ *Knightsbridge* ✣ *4:F1.*

£££
FRENCH

✕ **Koffmann's.** Perfectly seared scallops with black squid ink and gelati-nous pig's trotters stuffed with sweetbreads and morel mushrooms are two all-time French classics at Pierre Koffmann's eponymous last-hurrah at the Berkeley. Coaxed out of retirement and in his early sixties, and the antithesis of a celebrity chef, Koffmann showcases 35 years of experience and the best of regional Gascony cuisine in a well-appointed basement setting. Try his snail with mushrooms and mash, roast wild duck à l'orange, and his feather-light pistachio soufflé with pistachio ice cream. ⊠ *The Berkeley, Wilton Place, Knightsbridge* ☎ *020/7235–1010* ☆ *Reservations essential* ▭ *AE, MC, V* Ⓤ *Knightsbridge 4:G1.*

£££££ ✕ **Marcus Wareing at the Berkeley.** Relentless master chef Marcus Ware-
MODERN ing vies to be the best in London at his eponymous restaurant at the
EUROPEAN Berkeley. Opulently designed by David Collins—all clarets, carpet, and
Fodor'sChoice burgundy leather seats—Wareing pulls out all the haute cuisine stops
★ with a succession of world-class dishes. Standouts include Orkney scallops with blueberries, a fine chunk of Scottish halibut with charred leeks or Anjou pigeon with Amaretti. An oozing hot chocolate *moëlleux* pudding with salted caramel, or lemon crème with spiced brioche are absolutely flawless, and the wine list includes page after page of famous names. ⊠ *The Berkeley, Wilton Pl., Knightsbridge* ☎ *020/7235–1200* ⊕ *www.the-berkeley.co.uk* ☆ *Reservations essential* ▭ *AE, DC, MC, V* ☉ *Closed Sun. No lunch Sat.* Ⓤ *Knightsbridge* ✛ *4:G1.*

£££££ ✕ **Rasoi.** Chef-proprietor Vineet Bhatia showcases the finest new Indian
INDIAN cuisine at this tony Victorian town-house restaurant off the King's Road. Ring the door bell before entering at this super-seductive venue, which is decked with colorful Indian silks, prints, masks, bells, and ornaments. Bhatia pushes the boundaries with signatures like wild mushroom rice with tomato ice cream, lamb lasagna with coconut chutney, or grilled lobster dusted with cocoa and sour spices. Prices are extreme, but don't leave without sampling chai panna cotta or the famous warm chocolate samosas. ⊠ *10 Lincoln St., Knightsbridge* ☎ *020/7225–1881* ⊕ *www. rasoirestaurant.co.uk* ▭ *AE, DC, MC, V* Ⓤ *Sloane Sq.* ✛ *4:F3.*

£££ ✕ **Zuma.** Hurrah for this buzzing, ever fashionable, Tokyo-style sushi
JAPANESE restaurant near Harrods. Well lighted and designed, with polished granite, blond wood, exposed pipes, and open timberwork, it includes a sake bar, robata grill, and sushi counter. Try California maki rolls, sea bass sashimi, eel sushi, black cod, or robata-grilled Wagyu beef on a hoba leaf. Make sure that you grab the sake sommelier to help navigate the 40 varieties of rice wine and Japanese spirits. ⊠ *5 Raphael St., Knights-bridge* ☎ *020/7584–1010* ⊕ *www.zumarestaurant.com* ☆ *Reservations essential* ▭ *AE, DC, MC, V* Ⓤ *Knightsbridge* ✛ *4:F1.*

NOTTING HILL AND BAYSWATER

NOTTING HILL

£££ ✕ **The Cow.** A popular boho-chic gastropub, the Cow comprises a faux-
MODERN BRITISH Dublin 1950s backroom saloon that serves Fines de Claires oysters, *whelks and winkles* (sea snails and gastropods), and whole Dorset crab. Upstairs the chef whips up Brit specialties like deviled lamb with artichokes, Stilton cheese and hazelnut salad, black bream, and sea trout with shrimp. Notting Hill locals love the house special in the packed bar: draft cold Guinness with a pint of prawns and mayonnaise (£5.25). ⊠ *89 Westbourne Park Rd., Notting Hill* ☎ *020/7221–0021* ⊕ *www. thecowlondon.co.uk* ▭ *MC, V* Ⓤ *Westbourne Park* ✛ *1:B3.*

British Food Decoder

In London, local could mean any global flavor, but for pure Britishness, roast beef and Yorkshire pudding top the list. If you want the best-value traditional Sunday lunch, go to a pub. Gastropubs, where Sunday roasts are generally made on-site with top-quality ingredients, are an excellent bet, too. The meat is usually served with duck-fat crisp roast potatoes and carrots, and with Yorkshire pudding, a savory batter baked in the oven until crisp. A rich, dark, meaty gravy is poured on top.

Other tummy liners include shepherd's pie, made with stewed minced lamb and a mashed-potato topping and baked until lightly browned on top; cottage pie is a similar dish, but made with minced beef instead of lamb. Steak-and-kidney pie is a delight when done properly: with chunks of lean beef and ox kidneys, braised with onions and mushrooms in a thick meaty gravy, and topped with a light puff-pastry crust.

Fish-and-chips, usually battered deep-fried cod, haddock or plaice, comes with thick chips, or french fries, as we call them in the States. A plough-man's lunch in a pub is crusty bread, a strong-flavored English cheese with bite (cheddar, blue Stilton, crumbly white Cheshire, or smooth red Leicester), and tangy pickles with a side-salad garnish. For a hot, comforting dessert, seek out a sweet bread-and-butter pudding, made from layers of bread and dried currants baked in cream until crisp. And one can't forgo English cream tea, which consists of scones served with jam and clotted cream, and sandwiches made with wafer-thin slices of cucumber—served as an accompaniment to properly brewed tea.

✕E&O. _ASIAN_ The global jet set and fashionistas hang out here, one of London's most successful hip bar scene and restaurant, off Portobello Road street market. E&O means "Eastern and Oriental," and the mix of Chinese, Japanese, Vietnamese, and Thai dishes includes a slew of figure-friendly, low-carb vegetarian options. Don't skip the lychee martinis, miso black cod, chili tofu, Thai rare beef, papaya salad or green fried rice; the sea bass sashimi is fresh. There are pavement tables and curbside bench seats to watch the world go by on Portobello. ⊠ _14 Blenheim Crescent, Notting Hill_ ☎ _020/7229–5454_ ⊕ _www.rickerrestaurants. com/eando_ ☰ _AE, DC, MC, V_ Ⓤ _Ladbroke Grove_ ✛ _1:B1._

✕Electric Brasserie. _BRASSERIE_ There's no better people-watching than at the Electric, a popular Portobello Road market hangout from morning 'til night. Expect oysters, steaks, roasts, hearty sandwiches, and seafood platters. The zinc bar's a neat place to meet up with friends—or strike up with new ones. Check out the cocktail list, with a broad selection of martinis and champagne cocktails. ⊠ _191 Portobello Rd., Notting Hill_ ☎ _020/7908–9696_ ⊕ _www.the-electric.co.uk_ ☰ _AE, MC, V_ Ⓤ _Notting Hill Gate_ ✛ _1:B1._

✕Julie's. _BRITISH_ The warren of peekaboo alcoves and opulent dining rooms at this cute 1969 throwback ooze Victorian sensuality and _allegedly_ have witnessed all manner of naughtiness over the years (noted is the draped-off downstairs dining room known as the "G-Spot"). Royalty and rockers—from Mick Jagger to Lady Di—have famously cavorted here. The food is pricey and unremarkable, but the old memories abound. Poached lobster with Russian salad, swordfish carpaccio, pork and Calvados, quail with Swiss *rösti* (grated potatoes), and crab spaghetti are all popular favorites. ⊠ *135 Portland Rd., Notting Hill* ☎ *020/7727–7985* ⊕ *www.juliesrestaurant.com* ⊟ *AE, MC, V* Ⓤ *Holland Park* ✢ *1:B1.*

££££ ✕ **The Ledbury.** Australian-born chef Brett Graham's fantastic fine-dining
MODERN FRENCH housed in a handsome high-ceiling dining room, full of drapes, mirrors,
Fodor'sChoice and leather seats continues to impress. The £40 weekend set lunch is
★ a tour de force that weaves from monkfish and truffle purée to ceviche of scallops and seaweed, to Pyrennean lamb with Chinese artichokes. Graham is known for his desserts, so finish with unusual olive oil panna cotta and fig leaf ice cream. Excellent service and a confident sommelier round out this winning proposition. ⊠ *127 Ledbury Rd., Notting Hill* ☎ *0207/7792–9090* ⊕ *www.theledbury.com* ⊟ *AE, MC, V* Ⓤ *Westbourne Park* ✢ *1:A4.*

£££ ✕ **Notting Hill Brasserie.** There's something quietly seductive about the
MODERN Notting Hill Brasserie, with its side entrance, twinkle of live jazz piano
EUROPEAN in the bar, muted conversation, African artifacts, mini-armchairs, and friendly service. Definitely a restaurant and less of a brasserie, it's in a converted Victorian town houses; the food is imaginative with strong and confident flavors. Feeling like fish? Try sole with brown shrimp, halibut with white beans, or cod and Spanish chorizo. Meat lovers might like the rabbit with pea purée and the Brillat-Savarin cheesecake will surely send you home happy. ⊠ *92 Kensington Park Rd., Notting Hill* ☎ *020/7229–4481* ⊕ *www.nottinghillbrasserie.com* ⊟ *AE, MC, V* Ⓤ *Notting Hill Gate* ✢ *1:A4.*

BAYSWATER

££ ✕ **Alounak.** The food at this lively Persian canteen on Westbourne Grove
MIDDLE EASTERN may be tried and tested, but lines still form for the hot bread and grilled kebabs that emerge from the clay oven. Try chicken kebab or the *zereshk polo* (chicken with Iranian berries). Take Persian black tea and sweets, but know that the sour yogurt drinks are not to everyone's taste. ⊠ *44 Westbourne Grove, Bayswater* ☎ *020/7229–4158* ⊟ *DC, MC, V* Ⓤ *Queensway* ✢ *1:B4.*

£££ ✕ **Angelus.** Owner, sommelier, and former pro-rugby player Thierry
FRENCH Tomasin scores a converted try at this distinctive French brasserie in Lancaster Gate. Styled with Art Deco mirrors and button-back banquettes in a 200-year-old converted former pub, Angelus has a reputation for unrivaled Paris-style brasserie cuisine. The foie gras crème brûlée, egg cocotte, duck with polenta, quail with bacon or chocolate soufflé are as good as they get. Light bites, such as beef baguette or banana bread, are served at the bar and Tomasin is sure to select a classy bottle from the wine list focused mainly on France. ⊠ *4 Bathurst St., Bayswater* ☎ *020/402–0083* ⊕ *www.angelusrestaurant.co.uk* ⊟ *AE, MC, V* Ⓤ *Lancaster Gate* ✢ *1:D4.*

£££ ✕ **Hereford Road.** Chef and co-owner Tom Pemberton mans the front-of-
MODERN BRITISH house grill at this must-visit Bayswater favorite, which specializes in pared-down British fare. With an accent on well-sourced regional and seasonal ingredients, many dishes are as unfussy as you'll find. Work your way

LOCAL CHAINS WORTH A TASTE

When you're on the go or don't have time for a leisurely meal, you might want to try a local chain restaurant or sandwich bar. The ones listed below are well priced and are the best in their category.

✗ **Busaba Eathai:** It's always jam-packed at these five Thai canteen supremos where you'll find Thai noodles, rice dishes, and spicy all-in-one meals in a bowl in sultry dark-wood surrounds. ⊕ www.busaba.com.

✗ **Byron:** Bright and child-friendly, this 10-strong line of superior hamburger joints storms the market with its delicious Aberdeen Angus Scotch hamburgers, onion rings and fries. ⊕ www.byronhamburgers.com.

✗ **Café Rouge:** A classic 30-strong French bistro chain that's been around for ages and does great prix-fixe deals—so uncool that it's now almost fashionable. ⊕ www.caferouge.co.uk.

✗ **Carluccio's Caffè:** The Carluccio's chain of 22 all-day Italian café/bar/food shops are freshly sourced, family-friendly, and make for brilliant pasta and salad stops on a shopping spree. ⊕ www.carluccios.com.

✗ **Ed's Easy Diner:** Overdose on milk shakes, ice-cream floats, chili dogs, and made-to-order hamburgers at this chain of shiny, retro 1950s-theme American diners. ⊕ www.edseasydiner.com.

✗ **Le Pain Quotidien:** Try tartine open sandwiches, and salads at the communal wooden tables. There are 16 branches, including at the stunning St. Pancras station and Eurostar terminus. ⊕ www.lepainquotidien.co.uk.

✗ **Pizza Express:** Serving classic thin-crust pizzas, old-favorite Pizza Express is everywhere (there are nearly 100 in London). The Soho branch has a famed live jazz program. ⊕ www.pizzaexpress.com.

✗ **Pret A Manger:** London's high-street take-out supremo isn't just for store-made sandwiches: there are wraps, toasties, noodles, sushi, salads, fruit, and tea cakes, too. ⊕ www.pret.com.

✗ **Ranoush Juice:** Shawarma lamb kebabs are the draw at these mirrored late-night kebab and juice bars (open 8 am to 3 am daily). They also serve falafel, meze, and tabbouleh. ⊕ www.maroush.com.

✗ **Strada:** Stop at this 28-strong chain for authentic hand-stretched pizzas baked over a wood fire, plus classic pastas, steaks, and risottos. It's cheap, stylish, and packed. ⊕ www.strada.co.uk.

✗ **Wagamama:** Londoners drain bowls of noodle soup at this child-friendly chain. ⊕ www.wagamama.com

though razor clams and lovage, smoked eels with horseradish, and buttermilk pudding. ⊠ *3 Hereford Rd., Bayswater* ☎ *020/7727–1144* ⊕ *www.herefordroad.org* ▭ *AE, MC, V* Ⓤ *Bayswater, Queensway* ✛ *1:B4.*

£
ASIAN ✗ **Mandalay.** Bargain hunters love this 28-seat Burmese café on windswept Edgware Road run by the friendly Ally brothers. All dishes are less than £8 and reservations are recommended. Don't go for atmosphere, romance, or to impress a hot date, but instead, focus on the delicious papaya-and-cucumber salad, shrimp fritters, fish curry, bottle

gourd soup, and chili king prawns. Completely stuffed, you'll leave with change from £15. ⊠ *444 Edgware Rd., Bayswater* ☎ *020/7258–3696* ⊕ *www.mandalayway.com* ⌲ *Reservations essential* ▭ *AE, MC, V* Ⓤ *Edgware Rd.* ✛ *1:E2.*

£ ✕ **Royal China.** The black-and-gold 1970s Biba-style decor is half the
CHINESE fun at this flagship dim sum palace on Queensway. Expect fast-moving
Ⓒ queues and mirrored ceilings at this longtime favorite that churns out stacks of dim sum at a furious pace. Start with dumplings stuffed with pork, squid, duck, prawns, scallops, or crab, and follow up with pork spareribs and Chinese greens, and pots of Chinese tea. ⊠ *13 Queensway, Bayswater* ☎ *020/7221–2535* ⊕ *www.royalchinagroup.co.uk* ⌲ *Reservations not accepted* ▭ *AE, MC, V* Ⓤ *Queensway, Bayswater* ✛ *1:B5.*

14

REGENT'S PARK AND HAMPSTEAD

REGENT'S PARK

££ ✕ **Lemonia.** Primrose Hill's favorite Greek Cypriot restaurant, vine-
GREEK decked and taverna-style Lemonia is large and light, and always packed with hungry North London customers. Besides an endless supply of small-dish *mezédes* dips and starters, there are rustic mains like baked lamb in lemon, and beef stewed in red wine. Expect Greek hospitality, hordes of locals, loads of noise, and the boho chic Primrose Hill set. Top-value weekday three-course lunch is £10.50. ⊠ *89 Regent's Park Rd., Regent's Park* ☎ *020/7586–7454* ▭ *MC, V* ☾ *No lunch Sat. No dinner Sun.* Ⓤ *Chalk Farm* ✛ *1:F1.*

ISLINGTON

££ ✕ **Ottolenghi.** Fabulously colorful foodie window displays and a funky
CAFÉ modern all-white interior characterize this flagship Mediterranean and
Ⓒ North African deli–bakery–café in Islington's main drag that serves fresh salads, savories, soups, pastries, and cakes. Sit at shared tables and tuck into butternut squash with sage fritters, Tunisian chili *harissa* chicken with pink grapefruit, or opt for arugula-and-herb salad with pomegranate and Greek feta cheese. Go home with a takeaway chocolate meringue, or roasted plum and quince with yoghurt cream and caramelized pistachios. ⊠ *287 Upper St., Islington* ☎ *020/7288–1454* ⊕ *www.ottolenghi.co.uk* ▭ *AE, MC, V* Ⓤ *Angel* ✛ *2:F1.*

THE THAMES UPSTREAM

£££ ✕ **La Trompette.** Top-notch neighborhood dining doesn't get much better
FRENCH than this. In outlying Chiswick, La Trompette has a serious west London following that goes gaga for the elegant food, spiffy service, and chic surroundings. An unpretentious £23.50 weekday lunch might impress with *goujons* (thin breaded strips) of plaice, rump of lamb with coucous, or cod with samphire. The desserts match the mains and the sommelier is charm personified. ⊠ *5–7 Devonshire Rd., Chiswick* ☎ *020/8747–1836* ⊕ *www.latrompette.co.uk* ▭ *AE, MC, V* Ⓤ *Turnham Green* ✛ *4:A3.*

££ ✕ **Princess Victoria.** This renovated 1829 former gin palace—high ceil-
BRITISH ings, gilded mirrors, etched glass, and carved wood bars—makes for a magnificent gastropub setting on a bleak stretch of Uxbridge Road in

Shepherd's Bush. With main courses under £16, top dishes range from steak and triple-cooked chips to green pea risotto and sea trout and mash. The 350-strong wine list is overseen by sommelier and co-owner Matt Wilkin, with a particular focus on boutique growers from the Rhône in France. ⊠ *217 Uxbridge Rd., Shepherd's Bush* ☎ *020/8749–5886* ⊕ *www.princessvictoria.co.uk* ⊟ *MC, V* Ⓤ *Shepherd's Bush, Uxbridge Rd.* ✚ *1:A1.*

££££

ITALIAN

✕ **River Café.** The open-kitchen Italian restaurant sets the standard with its simple roasts, fresh salads, pastas, and char-grilled meats. The chefs source ultrafresh, impeccable seasonal ingredients, so expect Tuscan bread soup, handmade nettle-and-ricotta pasta, veal shin with lemon and sage, and signature chocolate nemesis cake—plus one of London's highest bills. This is in distant Hammersmith in west London, so if you get a table, remember that you'll need to book a cab ahead or walk about 15 minutes to the closest Tube. Note that tables are cleared by 11 pm on Monday–Thursday, and 11:20 pm Friday and Saturday. ⊠ *Thames Wharf, Rainville Rd., Hammersmith* ☎ *020/7386–4200* ⊕ *www.rivercafe.co.uk* ⌂ *Reservations essential* ⊟ *AE, DC, MC, V* Ⓤ *Hammersmith* ✚ *4:A4.*

London Dining and Lodging Atlas

ISLINGTON

KILBURN

KENSAL RISE

WEST KILBURN

ST JOHN'S WOOD

Regent's Park

KENSAL TOWN

MAIDA VALE

NORTH KENSINGTON

CAMDEN TOWN

KING'S CROSS

HOXTON

HAGGERSTON

SHOREDITCH

SPITALFIELDS

BLOOMSBURY

2

COVENT GARDEN

3

SOHO

THE CITY

BAYSWATER

1

NOTTING HILL

Kensington Gardens

Hyde Park

MAYFAIR

SOUTHWARK

BERMONDSEY

ST. JAMES'S

KENSINGTON

BROMPTON

WESTMINSTER

SOUTH BANK

NEWINGTON

WEST KENSINGTON

SOUTH KENSINGTON

BELGRAVIA

CHELSEA

VICTORIA

LAMBETH

5

KENNINGTON

EARLS COURT

4

WEST BROMPTON

VAUXHALL

WALWORTH

River Thames

Battersea Park

FULHAM

SANDS END

SOUTH LAMBETH

CAMBERWELL

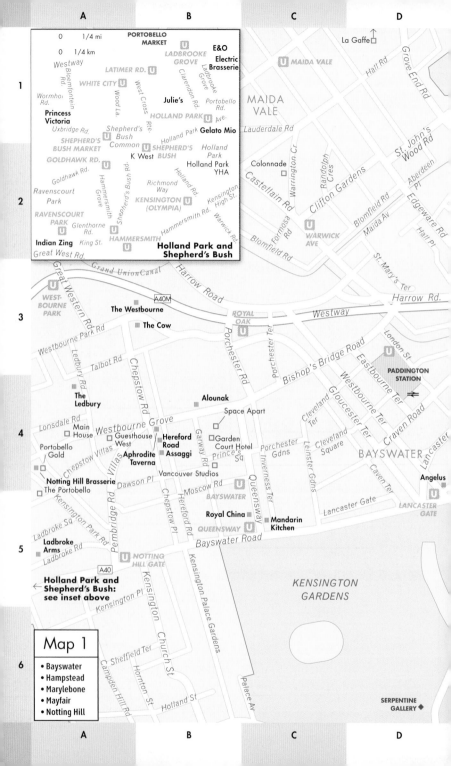

Map 1

- Bayswater
- Hampstead
- Marylebone
- Mayfair
- Notting Hill

Holland Park and Shepherd's Bush: see inset above

Holland Park and Shepherd's Bush

PORTOBELLO MARKET

LADBROOKE GROVE

E&O
Electric Brasserie

Westway

LATIMER RD.

WHITE CITY

Julie's

Princess Victoria

HOLLAND PARK

Gelato Mio

SHEPHERD'S BUSH MARKET

GOLDHAWK RD.

Shepherd's Bush Common

SHEPHERD'S BUSH

K West

Holland Park

Holland Park YHA

Ravenscourt Park

RAVENSCOURT PARK

Richmond Way

KENSINGTON (OLYMPIA)

Kensington High St.

Glenthorne Rd.

HAMMERSMITH

Indian Zing

King St.

Great West Rd.

MAIDA VALE

La Gaffe

MAIDA VALE

Lauderdale Rd

Colonnade

Castellain Rd

WARWICK AVE

St. John's Wood Rd

Clifton Gardens

PADDINGTON STATION

Grand Union Canal

Harrow Road

WESTBOURNE PARK

A40M

ROYAL OAK

Westway

Harrow Rd.

The Westbourne

The Cow

Bishop's Bridge Road

The Ledbury

Alounak

Space Apart

BAYSWATER

Main House

Westbourne Grove

Guesthouse West

Hereford Road

Assaggi

Garden Court Hotel

Portobello Gold

Aphrodite Taverna

Vancouver Studios

Prince's Sq.

Notting Hill Brasserie

The Portobello

Moscow Rd.

Angelus

BAYSWATER

Royal China

QUEENSWAY

Mandarin Kitchen

LANCASTER GATE

Ladbroke Arms

NOTTING HILL GATE

Bayswater Road

A40

KENSINGTON GARDENS

Holland St.

SERPENTINE GALLERY

0 1/4 mi
0 1/4 km

Lord's Cricket Ground

The Wells
The Holly Bush
Lemonia
The Engineer

E F G H

1

REGENT'S PARK

Outer Circle

Lodge Rd

Paveley St

Park Road

Inner Circle

Queen Mary's Gardens

Chester Rd

Outer Circle

Orchardson St

Lisson Grove

Church St

Rossmore Rd

Batcombe St

SHERLOCK HOLMES MUSEUM

Allsop Pl

York Br

Park Sq W

Park Sq E

REGENT'S PARK

Park Crescent

2

Ashmill St

Penfold St

Lisson St

Bell St

MARYLEBONE

Melcombe Pl

Dorset Square Hotel

The Landmark

Marylebone Road

MADAME TUSSAUD'S

Marylebone Rd

BAKER STREET

Park Plaza Sherlock Holmes

Marylebone High St

Devonshire St

Portland Pl

Mandalay

A5

EDGEWARE ROAD

Chapel St

Old Road

York St

Crawford St

22 York St.

Paddington St

New Cavendish St

Weymouth St

Baker Street

Harley St

3

Praed St.

Star St

Radnor

Norfolk

Edgware Rd

Seymour Pl

Montagu Sq

Gloucester Pl

George St

Galvin Bistrot de Luxe

Trishna's

Durrants

Le Relais de Venise L'Entrecote

Golden Hind

Wimpole St

Cavendish Pl

Stylotel

Sussex Gardens

Sussex Pl

Hyde Park St

Connaught St

A5

Montcalm

Cumberland Pl

Upper Berkeley St

Wigmore St

James St

SELFRIDGE'S

Henrietta Pl

Café at Sotheby's

4

Europa House Hotel

Stanhope Ter

Bayswater Road

Cumberland

MARBLE ARCH

Marble Arch

Park St

N. Audley St

Oxford St

Duke St

Davies St

A40

New Bond St

Claridge's

La Petite Maison

5

HYDE PARK

Park Ln

Park Ln

SPEAKER'S CORNER

Marriott Park Lane

Corrigan's Mayfair

Le Gavroche

Upper Brook St

Upper Grosvenor St

S. Audley St

Grosvenor Square

Hélène Darroze at the Connaught

Connaught

Scott's

Mount St

MAYFAIR

Brown's

The Square

Berkeley Sq.

Berkeley St

Nobu Berkeley Street

The Greenhouse

Charles St

Chesterfield Mayfair

Curzon St

The Dorchester

Le Meriden Piccadilly

6

The Serpentine

0   500 yards
0   500 m

Athenaeum Hotel and Apartments

Piccadilly

InterContinental London Park Lane

Green Park

E F G H

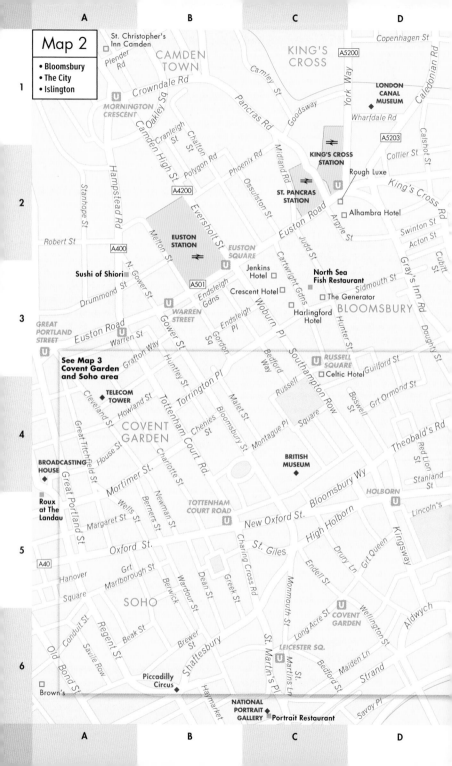

Map 2

- Bloomsbury
- The City
- Islington

A

St. Christopher's Inn Camden
CAMDEN TOWN
Plender Rd
Crowndale Rd
MORNINGTON CRESCENT
Oakley Sq
Camden High St
Cranleigh St
Chalton St
Polygon Rd
Hampstead Rd
Stanhope St
Robert St
A400
Melton St
EUSTON STATION
Eversholt St
N Gower St
Sushi of Shiori
Drummond St
Gower St
A501
Endsleigh Gdns
WARREN STREET
GREAT PORTLAND STREET
Euston Road
Warren St
Gower St

B

Camley St
Pancras Rd
Phoenix Rd
Ossulston St
A4200
EUSTON SQUARE
Jenkins Hotel
Endsleigh Pl
Crescent Hotel
Woburn Pl
Endsleigh Gdns
See Map 3
Covent Garden and Soho area
TELECOM TOWER
Cleveland St
Howland St
Torrington Pl
Huntley St
Grafton Way
COVENT GARDEN
Great Titchfield St
House St
Chenies St
Charlotte St
Tottenham Court Rd.
Bloomsbury St
Malet St
BROADCASTING HOUSE
Mortimer St
Wells St
Newman St
Berners St
TOTTENHAM COURT ROAD
Roux at The Landau
Margaret St
Oxford St.
Grt Marlborough St
Wardour St
Dean St
Greek St
Charing Cross Rd
A40
Hanover Square
Conduit St
Savile Row
Regent St
Beak St
Berwick St
Brewer St
SOHO
Shaftesbury
Brown's
Old Bond St
Piccadilly Circus
Haymarket

C

KING'S CROSS
Goodsway
Midland Rd
KING'S CROSS STATION
ST. PANCRAS STATION
Euston Road
Judd St
Cartwright Gdns
North Sea Fish Restaurant
The Generator
Harlingford Hotel
Hunter St
BLOOMSBURY
Bedford Way
Southampton Row
RUSSELL SQUARE
Celtic Hotel
Russell Square
Montague Pl
BRITISH MUSEUM
Bloomsbury Wy
New Oxford St.
High Holborn
St. Giles
St. Giles
Monmouth St
Endell St
Long Acre
COVENT GARDEN
Wellington St
LEICESTER SQ.
St. Martin's Pl
St. Martins Ln
Maiden Ln
Bedford St
NATIONAL PORTRAIT GALLERY
Portrait Restaurant

D

Copenhagen St
A5200
York Way
Caledonian Rd
LONDON CANAL MUSEUM
Wharfdale Rd
A5203
Collier St
Calshot St
Rough Luxe
Alhambra Hotel
King's Cross Rd
Swinton St
Acton St
Cubitt St
Gray's Inn Rd
Sidmouth St
Doughty St
Guilford St
Boswell St
Grt Ormond St
Theobald's Rd
Red Lion St
Stanland St
HOLBORN
Lincoln's
Kingsway
Aldwych
Strand
Savoy Pl

1
2
3
4
5
6

E **F** **G** **H**

Ottolenghi
A104
A1

Essex Rd

Liverpool Rd

Upper St

Barnsbury St

Wynford St

Rodney St

Donegal St

ANGEL

Pentonville Road

Grt Percy

Myddelton

Square

Wharton St

Amwell St

Margery St

Lloyd Baker St

Roseberry Avenue

Skinner St

Spencer St

St. John St

City Road

Goswell Road

Colebrook Row

Noel Rd

Hilton London
Islington

Caravan Moro
Morito

The Clerkenwell
Kitchen

The Modern
Pantry
Bistrot Bruno
Loubet
The Zetter

Farringdon Road

Bowling
Green Ln

Aylesbury St

Percival St

Seward St

Goswell Road

Central St

Lever St

OLD
STREET

Old Street

Whitecross St

Golden Ln

Bunhill Row

Dufferin St

Featherstone

City Road

Bath St

Shorditch,
Whitechapel and
Bethnall Green:
see inset above →

Phoenix Pl

Gough St

Clerkenwell Road

Leather Ln

Halton St

The Rookery

Malmaison

FARRINGDON

Cowcross St

St. Johns St

St. John

Charterhouse St

Fann St

BARBICAN

Beech St

Aldersgate

Silk St

Moore St

Moorfields

Moorgate

Chiswell St

BARBICAN
CENTRE ◆

Jockey's
Fields

Gray's Inn Rd

Greville St

Long Ln

Little
Britain

W Smithfield

London Wall

Wood St

MOORGATE

High Holborn
A40

Holborn Viaduct

Giltspur St

Angel
St

Gresham St

GUILDHALL ◆

Cheapside

BANK OF
ENGLAND ◆

Chancery
Ln

Carey St

Fetter Ln

St-Bride St

Shoe Ln

Old Bailey

Warwick

Leon

Ludgate Hill

ST.
PAUL'S ◆

Watling St

King
William St

BANK

HOLBORN

28°
50°

Fleet St

New Bridge St

THE CITY

London St. Paul's YHA
Carter Ln

Cannon St

Sweetings

Inn Fields

THE
TEMPLE ◆

Mtre Ct

Tudor St

Crowne Plaza
London

Queen Victoria St

Upper Thames St

CANNON ST.
STATION

TEMPLE

Temple Pl

Victoria Embankment

Blackfriars Br

BLACKFRIARS

Southwark Br

CANNON
STREET
STATION

RIVER THAMES

0 ——— 500 yards
0 ——— 500 m

E **F** **G** **H**

Sông Qué HOXTON CAMBRIDGE
HEATH

Haggerston
Park

Old St.

Kingsland Rd

Hackney Rd

Columbia
Rd

Gosset St

Hackney
Green Rd

Old Bethnall
Green Rd

Viajante

Victoria
Park
Gardens

1/4 mi
1/4 km

The
Hoxton

Boundary

Shoreditch
High St

Great
Eastern St

Bethnal
Green

Weavers
Fields

E Pellici

BETHNAL
GREEN

Valance Rd

Cambridge Heath Rd

1

SHOREDITCH
HIGH ST.

Buxton St.

L'Anima

Hawksmoor

Sun St
Passage

Bishopsgate

Commercial
St

WHITECHAPEL

St. John
Bread & Wine

Whitechapel Rd

Sidney St

Andaz

London
Wall

Threadneedle
St.

Thread-
needles

Simpson's
Tavern

Grange
City

LIVERPOOL ST.

ALDGATE

Bevis
Marks

Aldgate
High St

Leman
St

Mansell
St

Tayyabs

Lahore
Kebab
House

Cannon St. Rd

Commercial Rd

Commercial St

Ramada
Docklands

2

MONUMENT

Minories

Fenchurch St

TOWER HILL

Dock
St

**Shorditch,
Whitechapel and
Bethnall Green**

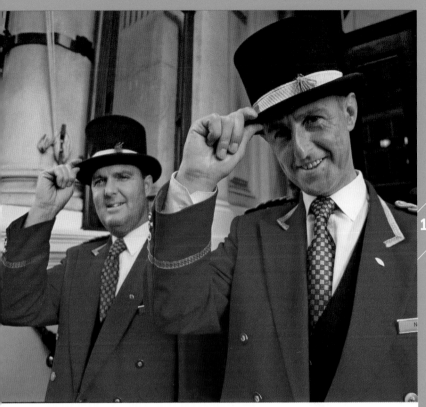

Where to Stay

WORD OF MOUTH

"My daughter and I stayed at the Morgan and liked it. The room was small, as was the bathroom (shower only), but the location is great. It's just off Oxford Street, right next door to the British Museum, walking distance to Covent Garden theaters, and the owners are just super."

—Carolyn

THE SCENE

Updated by
Jack Jewers

You'll find many things in London hotels: luxury, extraordinary service, and incredible views. But one thing you'll look long and hard for is a bargain. Rooms have traditionally been expensive, and the wild swings of the exchange rate make it hard to predict just how much you'll end up paying.

Meanwhile, the London hotel market is focusing on luxury, luxury, luxury. Five-star hotels close, renovate, and reopen with increased prices at a dizzying pace. If it's any consolation, London does luxury better than just about any city, so you'll get your money's worth.

However, it's not all bad news for those on more realistic budgets. The city's midrange hotel scene is at long last getting its act together, and there is now a small but solid range of reasonably priced, high-quality hotels that regularly offer good deals and bargain rates. Leaders in this field are places like the Hoxton—which even makes a handful of rooms available for £1 per night, if you're lucky enough to snatch one. The swanky Dean Street Townhouse also offers one of its rooms at a permanently low £95-a-night rate. There's also a clutch of new budget boutique hotels that are a real step forward for the city—places like Stylotel and the Church Street Hotel, which have both been making heads turn for their small-is-beautiful approach, eye for stylish detail, and down-at-home comforts. The downside is that these places tend to be a little out of the way, but that's often a price worth paying.

A newly attractive alternative are hotels in the Premier and Millennium chains, which offer sleek, modern rooms, lots of modern conveniences, and sales that frequently bring room prices well below £100 a night.

At the budget level, small bed-and-breakfasts still dominate, although most are quite battered and basic. An alternative to that is the easyHotel chain, with its tiny, bright orange "pod" rooms. There's also the more sophisticated (and more expensive) base2stay, which falls somewhere between budget and moderate.

WHERE SHOULD I STAY?

	NEIGHBORHOOD VIBE	PROS	CONS
Westminster and Royal London	This historic section, aka "Royal London," is home to major tourist attractions like Buckingham Palace.	Central area near tourist sites; easy Tube access; considered a safe area to stay.	Mostly expensive lodging options; few restaurants and entertainment venues nearby.
St. James and Mayfair	Traditional, old money; a mixture of the business and fiancial set with fashionable shops.	In the heart of the action; some of London's best hotels are found here.	Pricey part of town; the city-that-never-sleeps buzz makes peace and quiet hard to come by.
Soho and Covent Garden	A tourist hub with endless entertainment on the streets and in theaters and clubs—it's party central for young adults.	Buzzing area with plenty to see and do; late-night entertainment abounds; wonderful shopping district.	The area tends to be noisy at night; few budget hotels; keep your wits about you at night, and watch out for pickpockets.
Bloomsbury, Holborn, Hampstead, and Islington	Diverse area that is part bustling business center and part tranquil respite with tree-lined streets and meadows.	Easy access to Tube, and 15 minutes to city center; major sights, like British Museum are here; buzzing nightlife in Islington.	Busy streets filled with honking trucks and roving students; the area around King's Cross can be sketchy—avoid it at night.
The City and South Bank	London's financial district, where most of the city's banks and businesses are headquartered.	Central location with easy transportation access; great hotel deals in South Bank; many major sights nearby.	It can be as quiet as a tomb after 8 pm; many nearby restaurants and shops close over the weekend.
East End	Increasingly trendy area east of the town center, with a great arts scene.	Great for art lovers, shoppers, and business execs with meetings in Canary Wharf.	Still a transitional area, parts of Hoxton can be a bit dodgy at night; 20-minute Tube ride from central London.
Kensington, Chelsea, and Knightsbridge	This is one of London's most upscale neighborhoods and a center of London's tourist universe. A glittering galaxy of posh department stores, boutiques, and fabulous hotels.	Diverse hotel selection; great area for meandering walks; superb shopping district. London's capital of high-end shopping with Harrods; easy Tube access; gorgeous architecture.	Depending on where you are, the nearest Tube might be a hike; residential area might be too quiet for some. Few budget hotel or restaurant options; beware of pickpockets.
Notting Hill and Bayswater	Plenty of hotel options in an upscale, trendy area favored by locals and tourists.	Hotel deals abound in Bayswater; gorgeous greenery in Hyde Park; great shopping districts.	Few budget lodging options; residential areas may be too quiet at night for some.
Regent's Park and Hampstead	A mix of arty, fashionable districts with a village-like feel in other places.	Good access to central London; easy to fall in love with this part of town.	Surprisingly easy to stray into "edgier" neighborhoods.

15

WHERE TO STAY PLANNER

Lodging Strategy

Where should you stay? With hundreds of London hotels, it may seem like a daunting question. But it doesn't have to be. The 100-plus selections here represent the best this city has to offer—from the most-for-your-money budget motels to the sleekest designer hotels. Scan "Best Bets" on the following pages for top recommendations by price and experience. Or look through the reviews. To find one quickly, search by neighborhood, then alphabetically. Happy hunting!

Need a Reservation?

Yes. Hotel reservations are an absolute necessity when planning your trip to London, so book your room as far in advance as possible. The further in advance you can book, the better the deal you're likely to get. On the other hand, it is possible to find some pretty amazing last-minute deals at mid- to high-range places, but this is a real gamble as you could just as easily end up paying full rate. Fierce competition means properties undergo frequent improvements. When booking inquire about any ongoing renovations.

Checking In

Typical check-in and checkout times are 2 pm and noon, respectively. Many flights from North America arrive early in the morning, but having to wait six hours for a room after arriving jet-lagged at 8 am isn't the ideal way to start a vacation. Alert the hotel of your early arrival; large hotels can often make special early check-in arrangements, but be prepared to drop off your bags and strike out to amuse yourself for a few hours. On the plus side, this can effectively give you a whole extra day for sightseeing.

Hotel Quality

Note that rooms can vary considerably in a single hotel. If you don't like the room you're given, ask to see another. Be prepared for the fact that, while smoking is now banned in public, this doesn't apply to hotel rooms—so be firm and ask to change if you're given a smoking room and didn't request one. Hotels often renovate room by room—you might find yourself allocated a dark, unrenovated room, whereas a bright, newly decorated room awaits just down the hall.

Breakfast

Most hotels include breakfast in the price of the room. In England, though, breakfast is almost always exactly the same—one fried egg, two sausage links, two slices of bacon, grilled tomato slice, sautéed mushrooms, and toast. This is known as the "full English," and it's a great way to fuel you up for a day's sightseeing—until about Day 3 when you may be prepared to gnaw off your own hand for a bit of variety. In most budget hotels and B&Bs, this is the only hot breakfast available. Pancakes, French toast, waffles, and omelets are not common here, and usually just the most expensive hotels (or the most imaginative small ones) will offer anything along those lines. Luckily, virtually all accommodations also offer packaged cereals, muffins, yogurt, and fresh fruit, so when the sausage-and-bacon brigade begins to get you down, go Continental.

Facilities

The lodgings listed are the cream of the crop in each price category. All available facilities are mentioned, but some do cost extra. When pricing accommodations, always ask what's included. Modern hotels usually have air-conditioning, but B&Bs and hotels in older buildings often do not, and it is generally not the norm in London. You should specify if you wish to have a double bed. All hotels listed have private baths unless otherwise noted. Whatever the price, *don't* expect a room that's large by American standards. As in most of Europe, space is at a premium here.

Prices

Many central London hotels—particularly those in The City, Bloomsbury, and Holborn—are popular with business travelers and offer significant discounts for weekend stays. Almost all major properties have steeply discounted rates in the off-season. If you're planning to visit in the fall, winter, or early spring, start monitoring online prices a few months before your trip and book whenever you see a good rate. Chains such as Hilton, Premier, and Millennium are known for their low-season sales in which prices can be as little as half the normal rate.

The farther you go out of the city center, the better the deal. New hotels in far east and west London are cheaper than those in the center of town, but you'll spend a bit more time on the Tube every day.

Lastly, be aware that as this book was being written, Britain was in the process of raising V.A.T., or sales tax, which applies to hotel rooms. Wherever possible we've taken this into account, but occasionally you may you find prices to be around 3%–5% higher. ■TIP→ **The Visit London Accommodation Booking Service (☎020/7932–2020 ⊕www.visitlondon.com) offers a best-price guarantee.**

WHAT IT COSTS IN POUNDS

	£	££	£££	££££	£££££
For Two People	under £80	£80–£140	£141–£200	£201–£300	over £300

Prices are for two people in a standard double room in high season, V.A.T. included.

In This Chapter

15

Using the Maps

Throughout the chapter, you'll see mapping symbols and coordinates (✛ *3:F2*) after property names or reviews. To locate the property on a map, turn to the London Dining and Lodging Atlas at the end of the Where to Eat chapter. The first number after the ✛ symbol indicates the map number. Following that is the property's coordinate on the map grid.

HOTELS REVIEWS

Listed alphabetically by neighborhood. Use the coordinate (✛ 1:B2) at the end of each listing to locate a site on the corresponding map. For expanded hotel reviews, visit Fodors.com.

WESTMINSTER AND ROYAL LONDON

WESTMINSTER

£££–££££
Mint Hotel Westminster. In a rather stark, steel-and-glass building steps from the Tate Britain, this member of a small U.K. chain has some rooms with spectacular views of Big Ben and the London Eye; extras like floor-to-ceiling windows and flat-screen TVs complement the contemporary, monochrome guest rooms. **Pros:** amazing views; lots of high-tech toys, including iMac computers. **Cons:** with more than 400 rooms, you're just a number. **TripAdvisor:** "standard of food was really good," "modern and clean hotel," "sound proofing very good." ⊠ *30 John Islip St., Westminster* ☎ *020/7630–1000* ⊕ *www.minthotel.com* ⤳ *444 rooms, 16 suites* ⏥ *In-room: a/c, safe, DVD, Wi-Fi. In-hotel: restaurant, room service, bar, gym, laundry service, parking (paid)* ⊟ *AE, MC, V* Ⓤ *Pimlico* ✛ *5:C4.*

£–££
Vandon House Hotel. Popular with students, backpackers, and families on a budget, this simply decorated hotel is close to Westminster Abbey and Buckingham Palace; the accommodations on offer are the very definition of cheap and cheerful. **Pros:** handy location; comfortable beds. **Cons:** simple decor; few extras; some rooms share bathrooms. **TripAdvisor:** "cozy place," "great value and location," "bring your ear plugs." ⊠ *1 Vandon St., Westminster* ☎ *020/7799–6780* ⊕ *www.vandonhouse.com* ⤳ *32 rooms* ⏥ *In-room: no a/c, Wi-Fi. In-hotel: bar, laundry service* ⊟ *MC, V* �‖ *Breakfast* Ⓤ *St. James's Park* ✛ *5:B3.*

VICTORIA

£££££
41. This luxurious abode's designer credentials are everywhere, from the unusual tiled floors to the extraordinary furnishings drawn from every corner of the globe. **Pros:** unique place opposite Buckingham Palace; great service. **Cons:** the unusual design is not for everyone. **TripAdvisor:** "whole experience was first class," "very expensive but worth it," "very English." ⊠ *41 Buckingham Palace Rd., Victoria* ☎ *020/7300–0041* ⊕ *www.41hotel.com* ⤳ *26 rooms, 4 suites, 2 apartments* ⏥ *In-room: a/c, safe, Internet. In-hotel: room service, bar, Wi-Fi, laundry service, parking (paid)* ⊟ *AE, DC, MC, V* �‖ *Breakfast* Ⓤ *Victoria* ✛ *5:A3.*

££
B&B Belgravia. This modern guesthouse a short walk from Victoria Station has cool all-white decor—white chairs and walls, white pillars and desks, white linens and towels; it all looks a bit ethereal, which is what they're aiming for. **Pros:** nice extras like free use of a laptop in the hotel lounge; coffee and tea always available. **Cons:** bathrooms and rooms are small; no hotel restaurant or bar. **TripAdvisor:** "clean and comfortable," "almost a brilliant place to stay," "good value." **TripAdvisor:** "location is perfect," "inconsistent cleaning and room service," "best cheap accommodation in London." ⊠ *64–66 Ebury St., Victoria* ☎ *020/7259–8570* ⊕ *www.bb-belgravia.com* ⤳ *17 rooms* ⏥ *In-room: no a/c. In-hotel: Wi-Fi* ⊟ *AE, DC, MC, V* �‖ *Breakfast* Ⓤ *Knightsbridge* ✛ *4:H2.*

BEST BETS FOR LONDON LODGING

Fodor's offers a selective listing of high-quality lodging experiences at every price range, from the city's best budget motel to its most sophisticated luxury hotel. Here, we've compiled our top recommendations by price and experience. The very best properties—in other words, those that provide a particularly remarkable experience in their price range—are designated in the listings with the Fodor's Choice logo.

15

£££££ ⬚ **The Goring.** Buckingham Palace is just around the corner, and visiting VIPs use the Goring as a convenient, suitably dignified base for royal occasions. **Pros:** comfortable beds; spacious rooms. **Cons:** price is too high for what you get; decor is a bit fussy. **TripAdvisor:** "friendly and attentive management," "excellent breakfasts," "great location."✉ *15 Beeston Pl., Grosvenor Gardens, Victoria* ☎ *020/7396–9000* ⊕ *www. thegoring.com* ✆ *68 rooms, 6 suites* ♿ *In-room: a/c, safe, Internet. In-hotel: restaurant, room service, bar, gym, laundry service, parking (paid)* ▭ *AE, DC, MC, V* ⓤ *Victoria* ✛ *5:A3.*

££–£££ ⬚ **Lime Tree Hotel.** On a street filled with budget hotels, the homey Lime Tree stands out for its gracious proprietors, the Davies family, who also act as concierges. **Pros:** friendly and cheap; great location. **Cons:** some rooms are up several flights of stairs, and there's no elevator; family rooms don't allow kids under five. **TripAdvisor:** "staff were exceptionally friendly," "bathroom was spotless," "beautiful neighborhood."✉ *135–137 Ebury St., Victoria* ☎ *020/7730–8191* ⊕ *www.limetreehotel.co.uk* ✆ *25 rooms* ♿ *In-room: no a/c, safe, Wi-Fi. In-hotel: no kids under 5* ▭ *MC, V* ⦿*Breakfast* ⓤ *Victoria* ✛ *4:H2.*

££ ⬚ **Studios @ 82.** These self-catering apartments represent fantastic value for money; after checking in at the main B&B, you're left entirely to your own devices in the newly converted apartments. **Pros:** great price; lovely location; all the independence of self-catering. **Cons:** lots of stairs and no elevator. ✉ *64–66 Ebury St., Victoria* ☎ *020/7259–8570* ⊕ *www.bb-belgravia.com* ✆ *9 apartments* ♿ *In-room: no a/c, Wi-Fi* ▭ *AE, DC, MC, V* ⦿*Breakfast* ⓤ *Knightsbridge* ✛ *4:H2.*

££ ⬚ **Windermere Hotel.** This sweet little hotel, which is draped with charmingly sunny floral fabrics that look appropriate on the antique beds, will not let you forget that it stands on the site of London's first B&B, which opened here in 1881. **Pros:** attractive rooms; good location. **Cons:** price is a bit high for what you get; rooms and bathrooms are tiny; no elevator. **TripAdvisor:** "staff are friendly and helpful," "very clean and comfortable," "room was quite small."✉ *142–144 Warwick Way, Victoria* ☎ *020/7834–5163* ⊕ *www.windermere-hotel.co.uk* ✆ *22 rooms* ♿ *In-room: a/c, Internet. In-hotel: room service, bar, Wi-Fi hotspot* ▭ *MC, V* ⓤ *Victoria* ✛ *4:H3.*

ST. JAMES'S AND MAYFAIR

ST. JAMES'S

£££ ⬚ **Best Western Shaftesbury.** This Best Western chain in the midst of his-
☺ toric London does an admirable job of fitting in, while using as much chrome and frosted glass as anybody could ask. **Pros:** free Internet in all rooms; great location for theaters, shopping, and museums. **Cons:** rooms are tiny; the price is clearly based on its location, rather than its amenities. **TripAdvisor:** "staff were friendly and helpful," "very clean with plenty of space," "great location for the theatre."✉ *65–73 Shaftesbury Ave., Piccadilly* ☎ *020/7871–6000, 866/891–7710 in U.S.* ⊕ *www. shaftesburyhotel.co.uk* ✆ *69 rooms* ♿ *In-room: a/c, DVD, Internet (free). In-hotel: restaurant, bar, Wi-Fi, laundry service* ▭ *AE, MC, V* ⓤ *Piccadilly Circus* ✛ *3:C5.*

£££££–£££££   🏨 **Claridge's.** Stay here, and you're staying at a hotel legend with one
🛏   of the world's classiest guest lists around. The friendly staff are not in
Fodor's Choice   the least condescending, and the rooms are never less than luxurious.
★   **Pros:** serious luxury everywhere—this is an old-money hotel; kids won't
be bored, with comics, books, and DVDs to help keep them amused.
Cons: it's a bit pretentious—the guests in the hotel bar can be almost
cartoonishly snobbish. **TripAdvisor:** "old world charm with impeccable
service," "well equipped and clean," "lovely art deco."✉ *Brook St., St.
James's* ☎ *020/7629–8860, 866/599–6991 in U.S.* ⊕ *www.claridges.
co.uk* 🛏 *203 rooms* ⚒ *In-room: a/c, safe, DVD, Wi-Fi. In-hotel: restaurant, bar, gym, spa, laundry service, parking (paid)* ═ *AE, DC, MC,
V* Ⓤ *Bond St.* ✛ *1:H4.*

£££££   🏨 **Dukes Hotel.** This small, exclusive hotel in a discreet cul-de-sac recently
underwent a renovation that changed it from Edwardian to contem-
porary in one fell swoop. **Pros:** low-key ambience; peaceful setting.
Cons: can be a bit quiet for some; price is still rather high for what's
available. **TripAdvisor:** "room service was prompt and good," "service
in the bar was excellent," "great location."✉ *35 St. James's Pl., St.
James's* ☎ *020/7491–4840, 800/381–4702 in U.S.* ⊕ *www.dukeshotel.
com* 🛏 *78 rooms, 12 suites* ⚒ *In-room: a/c, safe, refrigerator, DVD
(some), Wi-Fi. In-hotel: restaurant, bar, gym, spa, laundry service, parking (paid)* ═ *AE, DC, MC, V* Ⓤ *Green Park* ✛ *5:A1.*

£££££–£££££   🏨 **The Stafford London by Kempinski.** This is a rare find: a posh hotel that
Fodor's Choice   is equal parts elegance and friendliness; it's hard to check in without
★   meeting the gregarious manager, and his unshakable cheeriness must
be infectious, for the staff are also upbeat and helpful. **Pros:** great staff;
big, luxurious rooms; quiet location. **Cons:** traditional decor is not to
all tastes; men must wear jackets in the bar. **TripAdvisor:** "a hidden
gem," "loads of character and charm," "service is constant but never
officious."✉ *St. James's Pl., St. James's* ☎ *020/7493–0111* ⊕ *www.
kempinski.com/london* 🛏 *81 rooms* ⚒ *In-room: a/c, Wi-Fi. In-hotel:
restaurant, bar* ═ *AE, DC, MC, V* Ⓤ *Green Park* ✛ *5:A1.*

MAYFAIR

£££££–£££££   🏨 **Athenaeum Hotel and Apartments.** This grand hotel overlooking Green
Park offers plenty for the money; rooms are both comfortable and lavishly decorated, with deeply comfortable Hypnos beds, plasma-screen
TVs, luxurious fabrics, and original contemporary artworks. **Pros:**
peaceful park views; handy for Buckingham Palace and Piccadilly; great
value for elegant setting. **Cons:** some rooms could use a decor update;
bathrooms are almost all small. **TripAdvisor:** "super friendly and helpful staff," "amazingly comfortable," "great location and value."✉ *116
Piccadilly, Mayfair* ☎ *020/7499–3464* ⊕ *www.athenaeumhotel.com*
🛏 *111 rooms, 46 suites and apartments* ⚒ *In-room: a/c, safe, kitchen
(some), DVD, Wi-Fi. In-hotel: restaurant, room service, bar, gym, spa*
═ *AE, MC, V* 🍽 *Breakfast* Ⓤ *Green Park* ✛ *1:H6.*

£££££   🏨 **Brown's Hotel.** Founded in 1837 by James Brown, Lord Byron's "gentleman's gentleman," this hotel, made up of 11 Georgian town houses,
holds a treasured place in London society. **Pros:** elegant space; attentive
service. **Cons:** everything costs here. **TripAdvisor:** "rooms are classic
and modern," "unbelievably clean," "fabulous luxury and attentive

15

service."✉ *34 Albemarle St., Mayfair* ☎ *020/7493–6020* ⊕ *www. brownshotel.com* ⇗ *88 rooms, 29 suites* ⌂ *In-room: a/c, safe, refrigerator, DVD, Internet. In-hotel: 2 restaurants, room service, bar, gym, spa* ⊟ *AE, DC, MC, V* Ⓤ *Green Park* ✛ *1:H5.*

££££–£££££ 🛏 **Chesterfield Mayfair Hotel.** Set deep in the heart of Mayfair, this four-star hotel is the former town house of the Earl of Chesterfield; the welcoming wood-and-leather public rooms match the dark-wood furnishings in the tiny bedrooms, which are done in burgundy, browns, and forest green. **Pros:** friendly service, laid-backatmosphere. **Cons:** prices are a bit high for what you get and have gone up recently; some rooms are very small. **TripAdvisor:** "hotel is distinctly English," "friendly, attentive service," "perfect in every aspect."✉ *35 Charles St., Mayfair* ☎ *020/7491–2622, 877/955–1515 in U.S.* ⊕ *www.chesterfieldmayfair. com* ⇗ *94 rooms, 13 suites* ⌂ *In-room: a/c, safe (some), Internet, Wi-Fi. In-hotel: 2 restaurants, room service, bar, gym, laundry service* ⊟ *AE, DC, MC, V* Ⓤ *Green Park* ✛ *1:H5.*

£££££ 🛏 **The Connaught.** Many of the classic Connaught touches (the grand oak
Fodor's Choice staircase, for example, and the small, elegant bars) remain, but the hotel
★ has a modern look since a thorough 2007 renovation. **Pros:** legendary hotel; great for star-spotting. **Cons:** history comes at a price; bathrooms are tiny. **TripAdvisor:** "world class service," "elegant hotel with elegant guests," "rooms are hit or miss."✉ *Carlos Pl., Mayfair* ☎ *020/7499– 7070* ⊕ *www.the-connaught.co.uk* ⇗ *92 rooms* ⌂ *In-room: a/c, safe, refrigerator, DVD, Wi-Fi. In-hotel: 2 restaurants, room service, bars, gym, spa, laundry service, Internet terminal, parking (paid)* ⊟ *AE, DC, MC, V* Ⓤ *Bond St.* ✛ *1:H5.*

£££££ 🛏 **The Dorchester.** The glamour level is off the scale here with 1,500 square
Fodor's Choice yards of gold leaf and 1,100 square yards of marble; bedrooms (some not
★ as spacious as you might expect) have Irish linen sheets on canopied beds, brocades, velvets, and Italian marble and etched-glass bathrooms with exclusive toiletries created by Floris. **Pros:** historic luxury; lovely views of Hyde Park; top-notch star-spotting. **Cons:** traditional look is not to all tastes; prices are high. **TripAdvisor:** "lovely furnishings and gorgeous food," "bathrooms are huge," "elegant but welcoming."✉ *Park Lane, Mayfair* ☎ *020/7629–8888* ⊕ *www.thedorchester.com* ⇗ *195 rooms, 55 suites* ⌂ *In-room: a/c, safe, DVD, Internet. In-hotel: 3 restaurants, bar, gym, spa, Wi-Fi, laundry service, parking (paid)* ⊟ *AE, DC, MC, V* Ⓤ *Marble Arch, Hyde Park Corner* ✛ *1:H5.*

£££ 🛏 **Durrants Hotel.** A stone's throw from Oxford Street and the smaller, posher shops of Marylebone High Street, Durrants sits on a quiet corner not far from the Wallace Collection. **Pros:** comfortable; relaxed base for exploring. **Cons:** not all rooms are air-conditioned; some rooms are quite small. **TripAdvisor:** "very quiet during the night," "quintessentially English hotel," "enjoyable stay and great location."✉ *26–32 George St., Mayfair* ☎ *020/7935–8131* ⊕ *www.durrantshotel.co.uk* ⇗ *87 rooms, 5 suites* ⌂ *In-room: no a/c (some), Internet. In-hotel: restaurant, room service, bar, laundry service* ⊟ *AE, MC, V* Ⓤ *Bond St.* ✛ *1:G3.*

££££–£££££ 🛏 **InterContinental London Park Lane.** The InterContinental London Park Lane, overlooking busy Hyde Park Corner and the Queen's back garden, offers luxurious rooms that appeal to the high-end business traveler. **Pros:** central location; business facilities; full-service spa. **Cons:** muzak in lobby; no outward views from standard rooms; charging £15 a day for internet access is a bit rich given the room rates. **TripAdvisor:** "great sleep provided every night," "overall feel is crammed," "staff is very friendly and proactive." ✉ *One Hamilton Pl., Park Lane, Mayfair* ☎ *020/7409–3131 or 871/423–4901* ⊕ *www.intercontinental.com* ⤵ *447 rooms* ♿ *In-room: a/c, safe, DVD, Internet. In-hotel: 2 restaurants, room service, bar, gym, spa, laundry service, Internet terminal, parking (paid)* ☰ *AE, DC, MC, V* Ⓤ *Hyde Park Corner* ✛ *1:H6.*

££££–£££££ 🏨 **LondonMarriott Park Lane.** The ornate facade and beautiful interior of this swanky Marriott date to 1919; today its useful location at the Oxford Street end of Park Lane gives access to great shopping on Bond Street and lovely strolls through Hyde Park. **Pros:** great location; big bedrooms. **Cons:** a bit nondescript; very busy streets outside. **TripAdvisor:** "breakfasts are very good," "perfect for a weekend," "great location." ✉ *140 Park La., Mayfair* ☎ *020/7493–7000* ⊕ *www.marriott.co.uk* ⤵ *148 rooms, 9 suites* ♿ *In-room: a/c, safe, refrigerator, Internet, Wi-Fi. In-hotel: restaurant, room service, pool, gym, spa, laundry service, parking (paid)* ☰ *AE, DC, MC, V* Ⓤ *Marble Arch* ✛ *1:G4.*

££££–£££££ 🏨 **The Montcalm.** A traditional grand hotel at the edge of Park Lane, the Montcalm gears itself to both business and leisure travelers in search of luxury. **Pros:** great location off Park Lane; dedication to luxury and comfort. **Cons:** old-fashioned approach might seem stuffy to some. **TripAdvisor:** "staff were friendly and professional," "décor is modern and stylish," "better choices in the area." ✉ *34–40 Great Cumberland Pl., Mayfair* ☎ *0207/402–4288* ⊕ *www.montcalm.co.uk* ⤵ *170 rooms* ♿ *In-room: a/c, safe, refrigerator (some), DVD, Wi-Fi. In-hotel: restaurant, room service, bar, pool, gym, spa, laundry service* ☰ *AE, MC, V* ⏹ *Breakfast* Ⓜ *Marble Arch* ✛ *1:G4.*

££££–£££££ 🏨 **No. 5 Maddox Street.** It doesn't get more boutique than this. With 12 luxury suites, each filled with everything you could ever need, this hotel is a great option for those who tire quickly of traditional travel. **Pros:** handy kitchens get you out of restaurants; everything can be delivered to your door. **Cons:** you can feel isolated, as there's no communal lobby. **TripAdvisor:** "London's hidden gem," "best location in London," "great for self catering." ✉ *5 Maddox St., Mayfair* ☎ *020/7647–0200* ⊕ *www.living-rooms.co.uk* ⤵ *12 suites* ♿ *In-room: a/c, safe, kitchen, refrigerator, DVD, Wi-Fi. In-hotel: room service, laundry service, parking (paid)* ☰ *AE, DC, MC, V* Ⓤ *Oxford Circus* ✛ *3:A5.*

MARYLEBONE

££ 🏨 **22 York Street.** This Georgian town house has a cozy, family feel with polished pine floors and plenty of quilts and antiques. **Pros:** handy guesthouse in a great location for shoppers. **Cons:** price is a bit steep for what is, in the end, a glorified B&B. **TripAdvisor:** "feels like home," "nice ambiance," "rooms ooze with charm." ✉ *22 York St., Mayfair* ☎ *020/7224–2990* ⊕ *www.22yorkstreet.co.uk* ⤵ *10 rooms* ♿ *In-room: no a/c. In-hotel: bar* ☰ *AE, MC, V* ⏹ *Breakfast* Ⓤ *Baker St.* ✛ *1:G3.*

£££££ 🏨 **The Landmark London Hotel.** One of the true grande dame London hotels, the Landmark has an historic pedigree. Built by a wealthy industrialist to serve the planned Channel Tunnel rail link in 1899, it was the

Claridge's

The Connaught

The Dorchester

The Stafford London by Kempinski

victim of atrocious timing twice in its life—first at the tail end of the Victorian era when the original Tunnel was canceled, and then 40 later when World War II saw it requisitioned by the army; decades of ruin followed until it was lavishly reborn in the late 1990s, and has been going full steam ahead ever since. **Pros:** amazing levels of luxury; spacious rooms; one of the few really posh London hotels that doesn't make you dress up. **Cons:** busy neighborhood outside; traditional decor. **TripAdvisor:** "rooms were spacious and comfortable," "lobby and atrium are wonderful," "would definitely stay here again." ✉ *222 Marylebone Rd., Marylebone* ☎ *020/7631–8000* ⊕ *www.landmarklondon.co.uk* ⟿ *299 rooms, 47 suites* ⚲ *In-room: a/c, safe, refrigerator, Internet. In-hotel: 2 restaurants, bars, pool, gym, spa, laundry service* ▭ *AE, DC, MC, V* Ⓤ *Marylebone* ✛ *1:F3.*

£££–££££   🛇 **Park Plaza Sherlock Holmes Hotel.** This was once a rather ordinary Hilton, until somebody had the idea of exploiting the Sherlock Holmes connection (the fictional detective had his home on Baker Street); making it a boutique hotel; adding a beautiful bar for a bit of local buzz, and—presto!—the place took off like a rocket. **Pros:** nicely decorated; good location for fans of shopping and Holmes. **Cons:** have to walk through the bar to get to reception; not well soundproofed from the noisy street. **TripAdvisor:** "staff were friendly and very helpful," "quiet and spotlessly clean room," "great location for getting around." ✉ *108 Baker St., Marylebone* ☎ *020/7486–6161* ⊕ *www.sherlockholmeshotel.com* ⟿ *119 rooms* ⚲ *In-room: a/c, safe, refrigerator, Wi-Fi. In-hotel: restaurant, room service, bar, gym, spa* ▭ *AE, DC, MC, V* Ⓤ *Baker St.* ✛ *1:G3.*

SOHO AND COVENT GARDEN

SOHO

£££–££££   🛇 **Dean Street Townhouse.** An adjunct to the private member's club, Soho House, and much beloved of the glitterati, this chic boutique hotel offers a discreet, unpretentious, but oh-so-stylish place to stay in the heart of Soho. **Pros:** über-cool; an amazing bargain if you can get the one cheap room. **Cons:** at full rate you're paying more for the address than what you get; rooms at the front can be noisy, especially on weekends. **TripAdvisor:** "very quiet," "wonderfully comfortable," "great location." ✉ *69–71 Dean St., Soho* ☎ *020/7434–1775* ⊕ *www.deanstreettownhouse.com* ⚲ *In-room: a/c, DVD, Wi-Fi. In-hotel: restaurant, bar* ▭ *AE, MC, V* Ⓤ *Leicester Sq., Tottenham Court Rd.* ✛ *3:D5.*

££££–£££££   🛇 **Hazlitt's.** Three connected early-18th-century houses, one of which was the last home of essayist William Hazlitt (1778–1830), make up this charming Soho hotel. **Pros:** great for art and antiques lovers; historic atmosphere; truly beautiful and relaxed. **Cons:** no in-house restaurant; breakfast is extra; no elevators. **TripAdvisor:** "staff were very friendly," "beautifully decorated," "modern facilities." ✉ *6 Frith St., Soho* ☎ *020/7434–1771* ⊕ *www.hazlittshotel.com* ⟿ *20 rooms, 3 suites* ⚲ *In-room: a/c, Wi-Fi. In-hotel: room service, laundry service, parking (paid), some pets allowed* ▭ *AE, DC, MC, V* Ⓤ *Tottenham Court Rd.* ✛ *3:D4.*

£££££   🛇 **TheSoho Hotel.** This redbrick, loftlike boutique hotel's public rooms are boldly designed with bright colors and big artworks, but the large bedrooms are calmer, most with neutral, beige-and-cream tones, or subtle,

BED-AND-BREAKFASTS

You can stay in small, homey B&Bs for an up-close-and-personal brush with city life (Arosfa Hotel), or find yourself in what is really a modern guesthouse, where you never meet the owners (B&B Belgravia). The main benefit of staying in a B&B is that the price is usually cheaper than a hotel room of comparable quality, and you receive more personal service. The limitations may be few in number, but can be off-putting for some: although you can sometimes arrange for daily maid service, there is no restaurant or bar, and no concierge should you have a question. If you book a room in a privately owned house through an agency, prices start as low as £70 a night, and go up for more central neighborhoods and larger and more luxurious homes. It's a nice option, both for seasoned travelers and for those trying to travel well without busting their budgets. Search the Web and call around to find the place that's right for you.

Contacts **Host & Guest Service** can find you a room in London as well as the rest of the United Kingdom. It's a great way to find bargains, knowing that all have been vetted by the agency, but the Web site functionality is a bit creaky. ✉ *103 Dawes Rd., Fulham* ☎ *020/7385–9922* ⊕ *www.host-guest.co.uk* ▭ *MC, V* ☞ *Full payment in advance.*

The long-established family-run agency **London B&B** has some truly spectacular—and some more modest—homes in central London. Most cost $130–$150 per night. You can check many of them online, but you still have to call to find out prices. ✉ *437 J St., Suite 210, San Diego, CA* ☎ *800/872-2632* ⊕ *www.londonbandb.com* ☞ *30% deposit required.*

sophisticated pinstripes, all offset by modern furniture. **Pros:** small and sophisticated; comfortable beds, in-house restaurant hot spot. **Cons:** bar can be crowded and noisy on weeknights. **TripAdvisor:** "quiet setting," "had everything necessary," "rooms feel welcoming." ✉ *4 Richmond Mews, off Dean St., Soho* ☎ *020/7559–3000* ⊕ *www.sohohotel.com* ☞ *85 rooms, 6 apartments* ☼ *In-room: a/c, DVD, Internet. In-hotel: room service, gym* ▭ *AE, MC, V* Ⓤ *Tottenham Court Rd.* ✛ *3:C4.*

COVENT GARDEN

££££–£££££   ⚏ **Covent Garden Hotel.** In the midst of boisterous Covent Garden, this hotel is now the London home-away-from-home for a mélange of off-duty celebrities, actors, and style mavens. **Pros:** great for star-spotting, and movie buffs. **Cons:** you can feel you don't matter if you're not a film star. **TripAdvisor:** "staff was mostly friendly and helpful," "room service never gets the order right.," "quite refreshing for London."✉ *10 Monmouth St., Covent Garden* ☎ *020/7806–1000, 800/553–6674 in U.S.* ⊕ *www.firmdale.com* ☞ *55 rooms, 3 suites* ☼ *In-room: a/c, safe, DVD, Wi-Fi. In-hotel: restaurant, room service, gym, spa, laundry service* ▭ *AE, MC, V* Ⓤ *Covent Garden* ✛ *3:E4.*

£££££   ⚏ **One Aldwych.** Flawlessly designed inside an Edwardian building,
Fodor's Choice   One Aldwych is coolly eclectic, with an artsy lobby, feather duvets,
★   Italian linen sheets, and ample elegance; it's an understated blend of

contemporary and classic, resulting in pure, modern luxury. **Pros:** understated (and underwater) luxury; ultra-cool atmosphere. **Cons:** all this luxury doesn't come cheap; fashionable ambience not always relaxing; design sometimes verges on form over function. **TripAdvisor:** "special mention to the housekeeping," "great location and fabulous service," "pleasant and efficient staff."⊠ *1 Aldwych, Covent Garden* ☎ *020/7300–1000* ⊕ *www.onealdwych.co.uk* ⤴ *93 rooms, 12 suites* ⛄ *In-room: a/c, safe, kitchen (some), refrigerator, Wi-Fi. In-hotel: 2 restaurants, room service, bars, pool, gym, spa, laundry service, parking (paid)* ⊟ *AE, MC, V* Ⓤ *Charing Cross, Covent Garden* ✛ *3:G5.*

£££££
Fodor's Choice
★

⊡ **The Savoy.** Reopened in late 2010 after a £220 million renovation, the Savoy is one of London's most famous hotels—and undoubtedly one of its best, too. As face-lifts go, this is surgical enhancement par excellence—the edges have been smoothed out, the creases ironed away, and the old girl is looking like a star again. **Pros:** historic hotel; gorgeous location; luxurious surroundings; less snooty than many others of its pedigree. **Cons:** everything comes with a price tag (even Wi-Fi); bedrooms can be surprisingly noisy; particularly on lower floors. **TripAdvisor:** "a haven of calm," "lots of energy but still elegant," "surprisingly large."⊠ *Strand, Covent Garden* ☎ *020/7836–4343, 800/257–7544 in U.S.* ⊕ *www.the-savoy.com* ⛄ *In-room: a/c, safe, Wi-Fi. In-hotel: 3 restaurants, 2 bars, room service, gym, pool, laundry service, parking* ⊟ *AE, DC, MC, V* Ⓤ *Covent Garden, Charing Cross* ✛ *3:G5.*

££££–£££££
⊡ **The Trafalgar London.** This fresh, contemporary hotel defies the Hilton norm; rooms here, in either sky-blue or beige color schemes, keep many of the 19th-century office building's original features, and some have floor-to-ceiling windows with extraordinary views of Trafalgar Square and the city. **Pros:** amazing location and views; spacious rooms; weekend rates have come down recently. **Cons:** decor is somewhat austere; service is patchy. **TripAdvisor:** "we were treated like family," "rooms are spacious," "great location for seeing the sights."⊠ *2 Spring Gardens, Covent Garden* ☎ *020/7870–2900* ⊕ *www.hilton.co.uk* ⤴ *127 rooms, 2 suites* ⛄ *In-room: a/c, safe, DVD, Internet. In-hotel: restaurant, room service, bar, laundry service, parking (paid)* ⊟ *AE, DC, MC, V* Ⓤ *Charing Cross* ✛ *5:C1.*

££££–£££££
⊡ **Waldorf Hilton.** After a massive overhaul, the Waldorf now has frosted glass, white marble, and understated bedrooms. **Pros:** tradition meets modern life comfortably here. **Cons:** prices are quite high for a Hilton; few discounts or deals. **TripAdvisor:** "pure luxury without the stuffiness," "rooms were disappointingly small," "clean and well located."⊠ *Aldwych, Covent Garden* ☎ *020/7836–2400* ⊕ *www. hilton.co.uk* ⤴ *303 rooms* ⛄ *In-room: a/c, safe, refrigerator, Internet. In-hotel: restaurant, room service, bar, pool, gym, spa, laundry service, parking (paid)* ⊟ *AE, DC, MC, V* Ⓤ *Charing Cross* ✛ *3:H5.*

HOLBORN

££££–£££££
Fodor's Choice
★

⊡ **Renaissance Chancery Court.** This landmark structure, built by the Pearl Assurance Company in 1914, houses a beautiful Marriott hotel; so striking is the architecture that the building was featured in the film *Howards End.* **Pros:** gorgeous space; great spa; your every need catered to. **Cons:** area is deserted at night and on weekends. **TripAdvisor:**

15

"bathroom was large and spotlessly clean," "rooms were spacious and relatively quiet," "great base for tourists visiting London." ✉ *252 High Holborn, Holborn* ☎ *020/7829–9888* ⊕ *www.marriott.com* ↪ *342 rooms, 14 suites* ♿ *In-room: a/c, safe, refrigerator, Internet. In-hotel: restaurant, room service, bar, gym, spa, laundry service* 🖃 *AE, MC, V* Ⓤ *Holborn* ✛ *3:G3.*

£££–££££ 🏛 **SACO Serviced Apartments, Holborn.** Down a quiet backstreet, a 10-minute walk from the British Museum, these fully serviced apartments are ideal for those who fancy living more like locals during their stay—not that many Londoners could afford to live in a place like this. **Pros:** more independence than hotels; freedom from having to eat in restaurants all the time. **Cons:** not everyone wants to buy groceries on vacation. **TripAdvisor:** "bathroom is quite narrow," "modern and roomy," "spacious living area." ✉ *82 Lamb's Conduit St., Holborn* ☎ *0207/269–9930* ⊕ *www.sacoapartments.co.uk* ↪ *30 apartments (mixture of studios, 1, 2, and 3 bed)* ♿ *In-room: no a/c, kitchen, Internet, TV, DVD. In-hotel: laundry service, parking* 🖃 *MC, V* Ⓤ *Russell Sq.* ✛ *3:G1.*

BLOOMSBURY AND LEGAL LONDON

£ 🏛 **Alhambra Hotel.** One of the best bargains in Bloomsbury, this family-run hotel has singles as low as £50 and doubles as low as £60; the place is not fancy, but it certainly is cheap. **Pros:** low price; friendly service; great location. **Cons:** very much a no-frills option; some rooms have shared bathrooms. **TripAdvisor:** "very clean and comfortable," "rooms small by American standards," "good value." ✉ *17–19 Argyle St., Bloomsbury* ☎ *020/7837–9575* ⊕ *www.alhambrahotel.com* ↪ *52 rooms* ♿ *In-room: no a/c, no phone, Wi-Fi. In-hotel: parking (paid)* 🖃 *AE, MC, V* ⦿| *Breakfast* Ⓤ *King's Cross* ✛ *2:C2.*

££ 🏛 **Arosfa Hotel.** The friendly owners and interesting historical background (the property once was the home of pre-Raphaelite painter Sir John Everett Millais) sets this B&B apart from the Gower Street hotel pack. **Pros:** friendly staff; check-in from 7 am; good location for museums and theaters. **Cons:** some rooms are very small; few services. **TripAdvisor:** "very good value," "a real mixed experience," "cleaner than a hospital." ✉ *83 Gower St., Bloomsbury* ☎ *020/7636–2115* ⊕ *www. arosfalondon.com* ↪ *15 rooms* ♿ *In-room: no a/c, Wi-Fi. In-hotel: bar* 🖃 *MC, V* ⦿| *Breakfast* Ⓤ *Goodge St.* ✛ *3:D1.*

£ 🏛 **Celtic Hotel.** Here you'll find a clean and comfortable budget accommodation with basic amenities; at this writing, a two-year renovation of the bedrooms was coming to an end, providing a few much-needed improvements like new TVs and Wi-Fi in all the rooms. **Pros:** good prices; friendly service; handy location at the edge of Bloomsbury. **Cons:** no-frills approach means few extras; cheaper rooms don't have private bathrooms. **TripAdvisor:** "building was very secure," "staff was friendly and helpful," "service was excellent." ✉ *61–63 Guilford St., Bloomsbury* ☎ *0207/837–6737* ↪ *35 rooms* ♿ *In-room: no a/c, no phone. In-hotel: Wi-Fi hotspot* 🖃 *MC, V* ⦿| *Breakfast* Ⓜ *Russell Sq.* ✛ *2:C3.*

££££–£££££ 🏛 **Charlotte Street Hotel.** On a busy street in the media hub around Soho, this hotel fuses the modern and traditional with real style. **Pros:** elegant, luxurious; great attention to detail. **Cons:** the popular bar can be noisy;

reservations are necessary for the restaurant. **TripAdvisor:** "perfect London hideaway," "rooms are nice but no view," "cozy and elegant." ✉ *15 Charlotte St., Bloomsbury* ☎ *020/7806–2000, 800/553–6674 in U.S.* ⊕ *www.charlottestreethotel.com* ⇆ *46 rooms, 6 suites* ♿ *In-room: safe, refrigerator, DVD, Wi-Fi. In-hotel: restaurant, room service, bar, gym, laundry service* ⊟ *AE, DC, MC, V* Ⓤ *Goodge St.* ✚ *3:C2.*

££ ⌂ **Crescent Hotel London.** On one of Bloomsbury's grand old squares, the Crescent is a friendly, attractive B&B. **Pros:** lovely, convenient location; friendly staff. **Cons:** basic decor; no elevator. **TripAdvisor:** "strictly for travelers," "comfortable with modern amenities," "clean and well located." ✉ *49–50 Cartright Gardens, Bloomsbury* ☎ *020/7387–1515* ⊕ *www.crescenthoteloflondon.com* ⇆ *27 rooms, 10 with bath* ♿ *In-room: no a/c, Internet. In-hotel: tennis court* ⊟ *MC, V* ◉ *Breakfast* Ⓤ *Russell Sq.* ✚ *2:C3.*

£ ⌂ **The Generator, London.** This is where the young, enthusiastic traveler

Fodor's Choice
★

comes to find fellow partyers. Set in a former police barracks, the decor makes the most of the bunk beds and dim lighting. **Pros:** funky, youthful attitude; great location. **Cons:** bar is crowded and noisy; party atmosphere is not for everyone. **TripAdvisor:** "fun if you are under 20," "awesome for meeting people," "good security in rooms." ✉ *MacNaghten House, Compton Pl. off 37 Tavistock Pl., Bloomsbury* ☎ *020/7388–7666* ⊕ *www.generatorhostels.com/london* ⇆ *214 beds* ♿ *In-room: no a/c, no phone, no TV. In-hotel: restaurant, bars, Internet terminal, parking (paid)* ⊟ *MC, V* ◉ *Breakfast* Ⓤ *Russell Sq.* ✚ *2:C3.*

££–£££ ⌂ **Grange Blooms Hotel.** Part of the reliable Grange hotels chain, this white Georgian town-house hotel offers a pleasant home away from home in a building just around the corner from the British Museum. **Pros:** great location; good prices if you book early. **Cons:** bathrooms could use an upgrade; outdated decor. **TripAdvisor:** "staff were friendly and helpful," "bathrooms nice and clean," "very clean yet very small." ✉ *7 Montague St., Bloomsbury* ☎ *020/7323–1717* ⊕ *www. grangehotels.com* ⇆ *26 rooms, 1 suite* ♿ *In-room: no a/c, Internet. room service, bar, some pets allowed* ⊟ *AE, DC, MC, V* Ⓤ *Russell Sq.* ✚ *3:F2.*

££ ⌂ **Harlingford Hotel.** The Harlingford is by far the sleekest and most contemporary of the Cartwright Gardens hotels; bold color schemes and beautifully tiled bathrooms enliven the family-run place. **Pros:** good location; friendly staff; wider breakfast choice than many small London hotels. **Cons:** rooms are quite small; no elevator. **TripAdvisor:** "staff are friendly and helpful," "clean and warm," "rooms are larger than most hotels." ✉ *61–63 Cartwright Gardens, Bloomsbury* ☎ *020/7387–1551* ⊕ *www.harlingfordhotel.com* ⇆ *43 rooms* ♿ *In-room: no a/c, Internet. In-hotel: bar, tennis court* ⊟ *AE, DC, MC, V* ◉ *Full breakfast* Ⓤ *Russell Sq.* ✚ *2:C2.*

£–££ ⌂ **Jenkins Hotel.** This small, moderately priced hotel has a classic Georgian exterior that belies its simply designed interior. **Pros:** good location for theaters and restaurants. **Cons:** thin mattresses; very small bathrooms; cheaper rooms have shared bathroom; lots of stairs but no elevator. **TripAdvisor:** "quiet yet handy," "great base for exploring London," "quite charming and clean." ✉ *45 Cartwright Gardens, Bloomsbury*

15

☎ 020/7387–2067 ⊕ *www.jenkinshotel.demon.co.uk* ⟲ *14 rooms* ♨ *In-room: no a/c, safe, refrigerator, Internet* ▭ *MC, V* |◯| *Breakfast* Ⓤ *Russell Sq., King's Cross, Euston* ✛ *2:C3.*

££ 🍴 **Morgan Hotel.** This family-run Georgian row-house hotel is a handy option for those traveling on a budget—but don't expect many bells or whistles; rooms are basic but attractive—some, though not all, are even quite spacious—but the best are the little apartments (£170–£240), which give you a bit more space to move around in and have a tiny kitchen. **Pros:** friendly staff; double and triple rooms are large by London standards; right by the museum and near West End theaters. **Cons:** mattresses are quite thin, as are walls; no elevator. **TripAdvisor:** "small by US standards," "great value," "comfortable and in a great location." ✉ *24 Bloomsbury St., Bloomsbury* ☎ *020/7636–3735* ⊕ *www.morganhotel.co.uk* ⟲ *15 rooms, 5 apartments* ♨ *In-room: a/c (some), refrigerator (some), Internet* ▭ *MC, V* |◯| *Breakfast* Ⓤ *Tottenham Court Rd., Russell Sq.* ✛ *3:E2.*

££–£££ 🍴 **The Portland Hotel.** Just around the corner from leafy Russell Square, the Portland is one of several hotels on the same street that are owned by the same Grange Hotels chain. This occasionally means that you can book into one hotel and actually end up staying in another, and while the quality is comparable, not all amenities are the same—so be quite clear of your requirements when you book. **Pros:** great location; large rooms; kitchenettes free you from restaurants. **Cons:** restaurant located in neighboring hotel means walk down the street to breakfast. **TripAdvisor:** "great position for sightseeing," "rooms were quite large," "only stay in cool weather." ✉ *31–32 Bedford Pl., Bloomsbury* ☎ *020/7580–7088* ⊕ *www.grangehotels.com* ⟲ *18 rooms* ♨ *In-room: no a/c, kitchen, DVD, Internet. In-hotel: restaurant* ▭ *MC, V* Ⓤ *Holborn Rd.* ✛ *3:F2*

£ 🍴 **The Ridgemount Hotel.** Mere blocks away from the British Museum and
☾ London's West End theaters is this handsomely fronted guesthouse that has clean and neat rooms at a bargain. **Pros:** good location for theaters and museum; family rooms accommodate up to five. **Cons:** decor is basic; no customer services; cheapest rooms have shared bathrooms. **TripAdvisor:** "rooms are small," "amazing price for central London," "great location to tube and buses." ✉ *65 Gower St., Bloomsbury* ☎ *020/7636–1141* ⊕ *www.ridgemounthotel.co.uk* ⟲ *32 rooms, 15 with bath* ♨ *In-room: no a/c, no phone* ▭ *MC, V* |◯| *Breakfast* Ⓤ *Goodge St.* ✛ *3:D1.*

£££–££££ 🍴 **Rough Luxe.** Bloomsbury's quirkiest hotel is, as its name implies, a strange combination of shabby chic and swanky luxury; in a 19th-century building near King's Cross train station in a neighborhood locals would describe as "dodgy," its rooms have been renovated to keep bits of their old battered walls and flooring in place so that the elegant new beds, designer lighting, and original artwork are cast in stark relief. **Pros:** art and design lovers will be dazzled; it's all very avant-garde. **Cons:** not everybody likes avant-garde; no restaurant or bar; neighborhood is a bit scary; some rooms share baths. **TripAdvisor:** "outstanding atmosphere," "unique style," "hidden gem of eclecticness." ✉ *1 Birkenhead St., Bloomsbury* ☎ *0207/837–5338* ⊕ *www. roughluxe.co.uk* ⟲ *10 rooms* ♨ *In-room: no a/c, no TV (some), Wi-Fi. In-hotel: Wi-Fi hotspot* ▭ *MC, V* Ⓜ *Kings Cross* ✛ *2:C2.*

££££–£££££ 🍴 **Sanderson Hotel.** This surreal "urban spa" is housed in a converted 1950s textile factory with a lobby that looks like a design museum: billowy

Renaissance Chancery Court

One Aldwych

The Generator, London

LONDON CHAIN HOTEL PRIMER

England has a number of hotel chains—worth considering—some are moderately priced, others are luxurious. Here's a quick run-down of our favorites:

easyhotel: One of the first chains to bring so-called "pod hotels" to London, the easyhotel chain specializes in very cheap (less than £50 a night for a double) rooms that are clean, secure and offer all the basics, but are teeny-tiny, and have no extras at all. ⊕ www.easyhotel.com.

Grange Hotels: This chain includes a good mix of large and small hotels, with reliable (if somewhat dull) neutral decor, good service, and plenty of gadgets for business travelers. Prices vary, although most are moderately priced.
⊕ www.grangehotels.com.

Malmaison: With lavish, elegant small hotels around the country, this upscale chain offers luxurious

designer style, good restaurants, and trendy bars. ⊕ www.malmaison.com.

Millennium: Similar in style to Premier Inns, Millennium (and its other brand, Copthorne) hotels are targeted at both business and leisure travelers. They offer well-designed rooms with plenty of gadgets and have frequent sales.
⊕ www.millenniumhotels.co.uk.

myhotel: A small chain of pricey boutique hotels, with a designer decor, trendy bars, and a modern approach, myhotels offer reliable comfort and service, if you don't mind the price tag.
⊕ www.myhotels.com.

Premier Inns: This widespread chain features medium-size, moderately priced hotels. They're known for their attractive if bland look, and for frequent sales, which keep prices cheap. ⊕ www.premierinn.com.

fabrics serve as bathroom doors, and bedrooms have sleigh beds. **Pros:** popular with design mavens; your every whim gratified. **Cons:** "designer cool" can be self-consciously hip; bar and restaurant are so exclusive it's hard to get in. **TripAdvisor:** "made us feel like VIPs," "room service prices are excessively high," "great location and comfortable rooms." ⊠ *50 Berners St., Bloomsbury* ☎ *020/7300–1400* ⊕ *www.sandersonlondon.com* ⤶ *150 rooms* ⌂ *In-room: a/c, safe, DVD, Wi-Fi. In-hotel: restaurant, room service, bars, gym, spa, laundry service, parking (paid)* ▭ *AE, DC, MC, V* Ⓤ *Oxford Circus, Tottenham Court Rd.* ✛ *3:B3.*

££ 🖫 **Thistle Bloomsbury Park Hotel.** A block away from leafy Russell Square and a short stroll from the British Museum, the location of the Thistle Bloomsbury Park Hotel is outstanding, though once you get past the handsome frontage and gleaming lobby, everything seems decidedly more average—though not necessarily in a bad way. **Pros:** affordable option in a great location; good deals and discounts; family rooms cost only slightly more than doubles. **Cons:** small rooms; tired decor; cheap furnishings. **TripAdvisor:** "spotlessly clean," "fairly spacious and cozy," "bathroom was well equipped." ⊠ *126 Southampton Row, Bloomsbury* ☎ *0871/376–9007* ⊕ *www.thistle.com* ⤶ *95 rooms* ⌂ *In-room: no a/c, Wi-Fi (hotspot). In-hotel: restaurant, bar* ▭ *MC, V* ❘⊙❘ *Breakfast* Ⓤ *Russell Sq.* ✛ *3:F1.*

THE CITY

££££ ⊞ **Crowne Plaza London—The City.** The shell of an old stationery warehouse, on the former site of Henry VIII's Bridewell Palace, is now in its "nth" reincarnation as a polished hotel. **Pros:** good prices available with advance booking; lots of amenities in rooms. **Cons:** neighborhood is busy during the day and quiet at night. **TripAdvisor:** "exceptionally clean and tidy," "lovely hotel for sightseeing," "breakfast was very good." ✉ *19 New Bridge St., The City* ☎ *0871/423–4901* ⊕ *www. crowneplaza.com* ⤵ *203 rooms, 14 suites* ⌂ *In-room: a/c, safe, refrigerator, DVD (some), Internet, Wi-Fi. In-hotel: restaurant, room service, bar, gym, laundry service, parking (paid)* Ⓤ *Blackfriars* ✛ *2:F6.*

££££ ⊞ **Grange City Hotel.** With an eye on business, this sleek hotel in London's City has everything the workaholic needs to feel right at home—chic bedrooms subtly decorated in creams and chocolates, modern furnishings, plenty of space (by London standards), Internet and direct-dial phones, and more. **Pros:** good-size rooms; women-only wing makes it extra safe for female travelers. **Cons:** location is a bit off the tourist track; online discounts tend to not allow changes or cancellation. **TripAdvisor:** "bright and clean," "fantastic view," "very good service." ✉ *8–14 Cooper's Row, The City* ☎ *020/7863–3700* ⊕ *www.grangehotels.com* ⤵ *307 rooms* ⌂ *In-room: a/c, safe, refrigerator, Internet. In-hotel: 2 restaurants, room service, bar, pool, gym, spa, laundry service* ▭ *AE, MC, V* Ⓤ *Tower Hill, Aldgate, Monument* ✛ *2:G2.*

£££££ ⊞ **The London Mal.** Part of a small chain of well-regarded U.K. boutique hotels, this Clerkenwell-based property is filled with elegant furnishings, clean lines, and all the electronic extras. **Pros:** luxurious rooms; excellent service. **Cons:** neighborhood is off the tourist track; area can be quiet at night. **TripAdvisor:** "very comfortable and elegantly furnished," "check in was fast," "particularly good value." ✉ *18–21 Charterhouse Sq., The City* ☎ *020/7012–3700* ⊕ *www.malmaison.com* ⤵ *95 rooms, 2 suites* ⌂ *In-room: a/c, safe, refrigerator, Internet. In-hotel: restaurant, room service, bar, gym, laundry service* ▭ *AE, MC, V* ⧙❍⧘ *Breakfast* Ⓤ *Barbican, Farringdon* ✛ *2:F4.*

£ ⊞ **London St. Pauls YHA.** On the doorstep of this hostel are St. Paul's Cathedral and the Millennium Bridge that leads to the Tate Modern. **Pros:** outstanding location; friendly and safe. **Cons:** lively atmosphere can keep you up nights; piped music in some public areas; geared to the young. **TripAdvisor:** "fantastic location," "good if you're not fussy," "cheapest for a reason." ✉ *36 Carter La., The City* ☎ *0845/371–9012* ⊕ *www.yha.org.uk* ⤵ *210 beds* ⌂ *In-room: no a/c, no phone, TV (some). In-hotel: restaurant, bar, laundry facilities, Internet terminal* ▭ *AE, MC, V* ⧙❍⧘ *Breakfast* Ⓤ *St. Paul's* ✛ *2:F5.*

££££–£££££ ⊞ **The Rookery.** This beautiful 1725 town house, surrounded by office
Fodor's Choice buildings, is tucked away down a discreet alleyway in the heart of
★ London's business district. Bedrooms are huge, wood-paneled affairs, with heavy raw silk drapes and antique furniture. Some also have four-poster beds and little sitting rooms off to the side—perfect for relaxing with one of the antiquarian books that have been artfully scattered around here and there. **Pros:** absolutely unique and beautiful; helpful staff; good deals to be had in the off-season. **Cons:** breakfast costs

15

extra. **TripAdvisor:** "try the room service for breakfast," "the antiques make a good touch," "very clean and quiet." ⊠ *12 Peter's La., at Cowcross St., The City* ☎ *020/7336–0931* ⊕ *www.rookeryhotel.com* ↝ *30 rooms, 3 suites* ⚒ *In-room: a/c, safe, refrigerator, Internet. In-hotel: room service, bar, laundry service, parking (paid)* ⊟ *AE, DC, MC, V* Ⓤ *Farringdon* ✛ *2:F4.*

£££££   📷 **Threadneedles Hotel.** The elaborate building housing this grand hotel is a former bank, and the vast old banking hall has been beautifully adapted along with its luxurious marble and mahogany panels; given its location in the financial district, it's no surprise that this place looks as if it were custom-designed to please business travelers—the hotel even provides personalized business cards to all guests as a basic amenity. **Pros:** lap of luxury; excellent service. **Cons:** a bit stuffy for some tastes; The City is quiet at night. **TripAdvisor:** "friendly and helpful staff," "very high standard," "excellent value." ⊠ *5 Threadneedle St., The City* ☎ *020/7657–8080* ⊕ *www.theetoncollection.com* ↝ *63 rooms, 6 suites* ⚒ *In-room: a/c, safe, refrigerator, DVD, Wi-Fi. In-hotel: restaurant, room service, bar, laundry service* ⊟ *AE, DC, MC, V* Ⓤ *Bank* ✛ *2:G2.*

££££   📷 **The Zetter.** By day, nothing but business suits buzz through the area
Fodor's Choice between Holborn and Clerkenwell, and by night, the ties are loosened
★ and it's all oh-so-trendy. **Pros:** big rooms; lots of gadgets; free Wi-Fi; gorgeous "Rainforest" showers. **Cons:** rooms with good views cost more. **TripAdvisor:** "comfortable and well equipped," "staff were very friendly," "room was bigger than I expected." ⊠ *86–88 Clerkenwell Rd., Holborn* ☎ *020/7324–4444* ⊕ *www.thezetter.com* ↝ *59 rooms* ⚒ *In-room: a/c, safe, refrigerator, DVD, Internet. In-hotel: restaurant, room service, bar, laundry service* ⊟ *AE, MC, V* Ⓤ *Farringdon* ✛ *2:F3.*

THE EAST END

£££–££££   📷 **Andaz.** This swanky, upscale hotel owned by the Hyatt group opened in 2007 and immediately made headlines for its modern, masculine design and unconventional approach; instead of checking in at a desk, guests sit in a lounge while a staff member with a handheld computer takes their information. **Pros:** nice attention to detail; guests can borrow an iPod from the front desk; no standing in line to check in. **Cons:** sparse decor is not for all. **TripAdvisor:** "rooms were spacious and immaculate," "very good mattress," "great location." ⊠ *40 Liverpool St., East End* ☎ *020/7961–1234* ⊕ *london.liverpoolstreet.andaz.hyatt.com* ↝ *267 rooms* ⚒ *In-room: a/c, safe, Wi-Fi. In-hotel: restaurant, room service, bar, gym, laundry service, parking (paid)* ⊟ *MC, V* Ⓤ *Liverpool St.* ✛ *2:G2.*

££–£££   📷 **The Hoxton Hotel.** This trendy, East London hotel sits in the epony-
Fodor's Choice mous neighborhood and is designed to reflect the funky galleries and
★ small boutiques for which the area is known. **Pros:** cool-looking place; price includes one hour of free international calls; every night five rooms in this hotel are priced at £1, but you'll need to join the mailing list. **Cons:** restaurant and bar can be crowded in the evening; area is a bit off the beaten tourist track. **TripAdvisor:** "stylish fittings," "bathrooms are immaculate," "hip and happening hotel." ⊠ *81 Great Eastern St., East End* ☎ *020/7550–1000* ⊕ *www.hoxtonhotels.com* ↝ *205 rooms*

In-room: a/c, safe, Internet, Wi-Fi. In-hotel: restaurant, room service, bar = AE, MC, V ⦿ Breakfast Ⓤ Old St. ⊹ 2:G1.

££ 🏨 **Ramada Hotel and Suites Docklands.** Built in a dramatic waterfront location, this modern hotel is in the rejuvenated Docklands area of East London. **Pros:** waterfront views. **Cons:** hotel lacks character; area is quiet on weekends; about a 20-minute Tube ride to central London. **TripAdvisor:** "excellent value," "incredibly quiet," "very handy location." ⊠ ExCel, 2 Festoon Way, Royal Victoria Dock, East End ☎ 020/7540–4820 ⊕ www.ramadadocklands.co.uk ⥂ 224 rooms In-room: a/c, safe, Internet. In-hotel: restaurant, room service, bar, gym = AE, MC, V ⦿ Breakfast Ⓤ Old St. ⊹ 2:H2.

£££–££££ 🏨 **Town Hall Hotel.** This building used to be one of London's living ghosts—an Art Deco Town Hall that was abandoned by the city in the early 1980s and literally untouched until it was turned into a chic hotel in 2010. Fortunately the new owners have done a good job in keeping the building's more elegant original features, while creating a stylish and modern new place to stay in a neglected corner of the East End. **Pros:** beautifully designed; lovely staff; close to a tube station; big discounts for weekend stays. **Cons:** not a great part of town; far from tourist sights. **TripAdvisor:** "staff were helpful and friendly," "relatively expensive," "beautiful building." ⊠ Patriot Square, Bethnal Green, East End ☎ 020/7657–8080 ⊕ www.townhallhotel.com In-room: a/c, DVD, Wi-Fi. In-hotel: restaurant, room service, bar, pool, spa, gym = AE, DC, MC, V Ⓤ Bethnal Green ⊹ 2:H2.

THE SOUTH BANK

££ 🏨 **Church Street Hotel.** Above a popular tapas restaurant, this immensely
Fodor's Choice welcoming boutique hotel is like a ray of sunshine in gritty South Lon-
★ don; each room is individually decorated in rich, bold tones and authentic Central American touches, from elaborately painted crucifixes to tiles that were handmade in Guadalajara. **Pros:** unique and funky; great breakfasts; lovely staff; closer to central London than it might appear. **Cons:** not a great part of town; would suit adventurous young things more than families; far from a tube station; some rooms have shared bathroom. **TripAdvisor:** "staff was extraordinarily friendly," "fresh and colorful," "very clean." ⊠ 29–33 Camberwell Church St., South East ☎ 020/7961–1234 ⊕ www.churchstreethotel.com ⥂ 267 rooms In-room: a/c, safe, Wi-Fi. In-hotel: restaurant, bar = AE, MC, V Ⓤ Oval St. ⊹ 5:H6.

£££–££££ 🏨 **London Bridge Hotel.** Just steps away from the London Bridge rail and Tube station, this thoroughly modern, stylish hotel is popular with business travelers, but leisure travelers find it just as handy. **Pros:** good location to visit South Bank attractions; good deals available on its Web site in the off-season. **Cons:** small rooms; bathrooms underwhelming for the price. **TripAdvisor:** "small but well stocked," "we felt like royalty," "a glimpse of "real" London." ⊠ 8–18 London Bridge St., South Bank ☎ 020/7855–2200 ⊕ www.london-bridge-hotel.co.uk ⥂ 138 rooms, 3 apartments In-room: a/c, safe, kitchen (some), refrigerator, Wi-Fi (free). In-hotel: restaurant, room service, bar, gym, laundry service, parking (paid) = AE, DC, MC, V Ⓤ London Bridge ⊹ 5:H1.

15

£££–££££   🏠 **London Marriott Hotel County Hall.** Housed in part of what was, until the 1980s, the seat of London's government, this grand hotel on the Thames has perhaps the most iconic view of any in London: right next door is the London Eye, and directly across the River Thames are Big Ben and the Houses of Parliament. **Pros:** handy location for South Bank arts scene, London Eye and Westminster; great gym; good weekend discounts. **Cons:** decor is overdone; breakfasts are pricey; rooms facing Parliament inevitably cost extra. **TripAdvisor:** "unbeatable location," "first class service," "surprisingly child-friendly." ⊠ *County Hall, Westminster Bridge Rd., South Bank* 🕿 *020/7928–5200* ⊕ *www.marriott.com* ↘ *200 rooms* ♿ *In-room: a/c, safe, refrigerator, Wi-Fi. In-hotel: 2 restaurants, room service, bars, pool, gym, spa, laundry service, parking (paid)* ⊟ *AE, DC, MC, V* Ⓤ *Westminster* ✛ *5:D2.*

££   🏠 **Premier Travel Inn County Hall.** Although part of the same former
Ⓒ   County Hall complex as the London Marriott Hotel County Hall, it shares none of its spectacular riverside views; that said, it is every bit as convenient a location, and decidedly cheaper, too. **Pros:** good location for the South Bank; bargains to be had if you book in advance. **Cons:** denied great views by other buildings nearby; limited services. **TripAdvisor:** "staff are extremely courteous," "excellent value and great location," "bedroom was clean and comfortable." ⊠ *Belvedere Rd., South Bank* 🕿 *0871/527–8648* ⊕ *www.premiertravelinn.com* ↘ *313 rooms* ♿ *In-room: no a/c, Internet. In-hotel: 2 restaurants, bar, parking (paid)* ⊟ *AE, DC, MC, V* Ⓤ *Westminster* ✛ *5:D2.*

££   🏠 **Premier Travel Inn Southwark.** This excellent branch of the Premier Travel Inn chain is a bit out of the way on the South Bank, but it sits on a quiet cobbled lane, and is ideally located for visiting the Tate Modern or the Globe Theatre. **Pros:** great location for the South Bank; quiet street. **Cons:** small rooms; limited customer services. **TripAdvisor:** "beautifully decorated rooms," "excellent value," "location was superb." ⊠ *34 Park St., South Bank* 🕿 *0871/527–8676* ⊕ *www.premiertravelinn.com* ↘ *56 rooms* ♿ *In-room: a/c, Internet. In-hotel: parking (paid)* ⊟ *AE, DC, MC, V* Ⓤ *London Bridge* ✛ *5:H1.*

KENSINGTON, CHELSEA, AND KNIGHTSBRIDGE

KENSINGTON

££–£££   🏠 **Astons Apartments.** Three redbrick Victorian town houses on a quiet residential street hold Astons's comfortable studios and apartments; all are simple and small but well designed with tiny kitchenettes, and the apartments (£££) have marble bathrooms and other extra touches as well. **Pros:** kitchenettes free you from restaurant tyranny; good way to save money on long stays. **Cons:** furnishings advertised as "designer" but look a bit cheap; few customer services; weekly discounts are hardly generous. **TripAdvisor:** "very helpful staff," "well looked after," "great location." ⊠ *31 Rosary Gardens, South Kensington* 🕿 *020/7590–6000, 800/525–2810 in U.S.* ⊕ *www.astons-apartments.com* ↘ *43 rooms, 12 suites* ♿ *In-room: no a/c, safe, kitchen, refrigerator, Internet. In-hotel: parking (paid), some pets allowed* ⊟ *AE, MC, V* Ⓤ *Gloucester Rd.* ✛ *4:D3.*

££–£££ 🖼 **base2stay Kensington.** In a creamy white Georgian town house in chic Kensington, this hotel is a near-budget option with comfortable double rooms; some even have bunk beds for traveling friends or children. **Pros:** attractive rooms; handy mini-kitchens; guests can hire electric car for £4 an hour. **Cons:** prices are a bit high for what you get; bathrooms are tiny. **TripAdvisor:** "room was compact but very clean," "has every amenity one needs," "great location, honest staff." ✉ *25 Courtfield Gardens, South Kensington* ☎ *020/7244–2255, 800/511–9821 in U.S.* ⊕ *www.base2stay.com* 🛏 *67 rooms* ♿ *In-room: a/c, kitchen, Internet. In-hotel: Wi-Fi* ⊟ *MC, V* Ⓤ *Earls Court Station* ✚ *4:B3.*

£££–££££ 🖼 **The Bentley London.** This opulent hotel is an elegant escape in Kensington; housed in a creamy-white Victorian building, its lobby is a gorgeous explosion of marble, with high ceilings and chandeliers, and bedrooms are almost palatial in size (by London standards), with silk wallpaper, golden furnishings, and fine marble bathrooms with whirlpool baths—some even have steam rooms. **Pros:** luxurious rooms; gorgeous spa; great location. **Cons:** can be a bit stuffy; old-fashioned style won't please everyone. **TripAdvisor:** "nice neighborhoods," "comfortable smallish hotel," "no complaints." ✉ *27–33 Harrington Gardens, South Kensington* ☎ *020/7244–5555* ⊕ *www.thebentley-hotel.com* 🛏 *52 rooms, 12 suites* ♿ *In-room: a/c, safe, refrigerator, DVD, Internet. In-hotel: restaurant, room service, bar, gym, spa, laundry service, parking (paid), some pets allowed* ⊟ *AE, D, MC, V* Ⓤ *Gloucester Rd.* ✚ *4:C3.*

£££ 🖼 **Best Western Premier Shaftesbury Kensington.** Just steps from Earl's Court Tube station at the edge of Kensington, this hotel complex offers a lot for your money. **Pros:** good neighborhood; two-minute walk from the Tube; free Wi-Fi; frequent online sales. **Cons:** small rooms; temperamental booking system, so make sure you bring your confirmation details; at the far edge of Kensington, farther than you might expect. **TripAdvisor:** "staff were friendly and obliging," "clean and modern," "good value and very quiet." ✉ *33–37 Hogarth Rd., Kensington* ☎ *020/7370–6831* ⊕ *www.bw-shaftesburykensingtonhotel.co.uk* 🛏 *133 rooms* ♿ *In-room: a/c, safe, refrigerator, Wi-Fi. In-hotel: restaurant, room service* ⊟ *AE, MC, V* 🍽 *Breakfast* Ⓤ *Earl's Court* ✚ *4:B3.*

£££–££££ 🖼 **Collingham Suites.** In an attractive Georgian building in Kensington, the Collingham is filled with suites and small apartments; all rooms are tastefully decorated in contemporary style, with neutral carpets and a creamy pallet. **Pros:** more space than you usually get with a serviced apartment; no minimum length of stay. **Cons:** still a bit pricey for what you get; no in-house restaurant or bar. **TripAdvisor:** "staff are wonderfully friendly," "pleasant alternative to a hotel stay," "great location and easy tube access." ✉ *26–27 Collingham Gardens, Kensington* ☎ *0207/244–8677* ⊕ *www.collinghamapartments.com* 🛏 *26 rooms* ♿ *In-room: a/c, kitchen, refrigerator, Wi-Fi* ⊟ *MC, V* Ⓜ *Gloucester Rd.* ✚ *4:C3.*

£££ 🖼 **The Cranley Hotel.** Old-fashioned British propriety is the overall feeling here at this small, Victorian town-house hotel; high ceilings, huge windows, and a pale, creamy color scheme make the bedrooms light and bright. **Pros:** good-size rooms; friendly staff; free evening nibbles are a nice touch. **Cons:** steep stairs into lobby; no restaurant. **TripAdvisor:** "all staff were friendly," "immaculately clean," "charming and great

Fodor's Choice ★

Mandarin Oriental Hyde Park

Church Street Hotel

The Hoxton

Number Sixteen

The Zetter

The Rookery

location." ✉ *10–12 Bina Gardens, South Kensington* ☎ *020/7373–0123* ⊕ *www.thecranley.com* ⊷ *29 rooms, 5 suites, 4 apartments* ⌕ *In-room: a/c, safe, Internet. In-hotel: Wi-Fi (free), parking (paid)* ▭ *AE, DC, MC, V* Ⓤ *Gloucester Rd.* ✛ *4:C3.*

£ 🏨**easyHotel South Kensington.** This budget hotel, which opened in 2005 as London's first "pod hotel," has 34 tiny rooms, all with a double bed, private bathroom, and little else. **Pros:** amazing price; safe and pleasant space. **Cons:** not for the claustrophobic; six floors, no elevator; no services; everything costs extra, from a TV in your room (£5 per day), to Wi-Fi (£3 per hour) and even fresh towels (£1 each). **TripAdvisor:** "friendly and helpful staff," "do not expect any frills," "very modern and clean." ✉ *14 Lexham Gardens, Kensington* ☎ *020/7216–1717* ⊕ *www.easyhotel.com* ⊷ *34 rooms* ⌕ *In-room: no a/c, no phone* ▭ *MC, V* Ⓤ *Gloucester Rd.* ✛ *4:B2.*

£££–££££ 🏨**The Gore Hotel.** Just down the road from the Albert Hall, this gorgeous, friendly hotel has a luxurious mixture of the comfortable and the extraordinary; the lobby evokes a wealthy estate from centuries past, and upstairs most rooms are spacious and decorated in calming neutral tones with rich fabrics. **Pros:** small scale means the staff can lavish attention on you; spacious rooms. **Cons:** prices still rather high; bar can be noisy. **TripAdvisor:** "staff are friendly and helpful," "real gem of a find," "pleasant surrounding and a great location." ✉ *189 Queen's Gate, Kensington* ☎ *020/7584–6601, 888/757–5587 in U.S* ⊕ *www. gorehotel.com* ⊷ *50 rooms* ⌕ *In-room: no a/c, safe, refrigerator, Wi-Fi. In-hotel: restaurant, room service, bar, laundry service* ▭ *AE, DC, MC, V* Ⓤ *Gloucester Rd.* ✛ *4:D1.*

£ 🏨**Holland Park YHA.** Ah, the 1970s. In what other decade would the London authorities have agreed to let someone convert a historic Jacobean mansion, in one of the city's most exclusive residential districts, into a gigantic youth hostel? Happily for the modern-day traveler, the result is perhaps the most celebrated (and certainly the most pastoral) of London's super-cheap places to stay. **Pros:** friendly and bright; beautiful setting. **Cons:** youthful atmosphere can be quite boisterous. **TripAdvisor:** "comfortable and well-kept," "nice place but not for sleeping," "security was paramount." ✉ *Holland Walk, Kensington* ☎ *0845/371–9122* ⊕ *www.yha.org.uk* ⊷ *200 beds* ⌕ *In-room: no a/c, no phone, no TV. In-hotel: bar, tennis courts, laundry facilities, Internet terminal* ▭ *AE, MC, V* ❙◯❙ *Breakfast* Ⓤ *High Street Kensington* ✛ *1:A5.*

££–£££ 🏨**Kensington House Hotel.** This refurbished 19th-century town house off High Street Kensington has streamlined rooms with a creamy, contemporary look. **Pros:** attractive design; relaxing setting; free Wi-Fi. **Cons:** rooms are small; bathrooms are minuscule; the elevator is Lilliputian. **TripAdvisor:** "room was smaller than expected," "polite and efficient staff," "no traffic noise at all." ✉ *15–16 Prince of Wales Terr., Kensington* ☎ *020/7937–2345* ⊕ *www.kenhouse.com* ⊷ *41 rooms* ⌕ *In-room: no a/c, safe, Wi-Fi. In-hotel: room service, bar, laundry service, parking (paid)* ▭ *AE, DC, MC, V* ❙◯❙ *Breakfast* Ⓤ *High Street Kensington* ✛ *4:C1.*

££££–£££££ 🏨**Milestone Hotel & Apartments.** This pair of intricately decorated Victorian town houses overlooking Kensington Palace and Gardens is an intimate, luxurious alternative to the city's more famous high-end hotels.

15

Pros: beautiful space; big rooms. **Cons:** service can be a bit stuffy (it seems you're not expected to do anything for yourself). **TripAdvisor:** "service is world class," "definition of refined elegance," "great location to all the shops." ⊠ *1 Kensington Ct., Kensington* ☎ *020/7917–1000* ⊕ *www.milestonehotel.com* ↩ *44 rooms, 12 suites, 6 apartments* ⚒ *In-room: a/c, safe, kitchen (some), refrigerator, DVD, Wi-Fi. In-hotel: 2 restaurants, room service, bar, gym, laundry service, some pets allowed* ▭ *AE, DC, MC, V* Ⓤ *High Street Kensington* ✛ *4:C1.*

££–£££ 🖼 **Millennium Gloucester.** Refurbished in 2007, the hotel has a sleek lobby with polished wood columns, a warming fireplace, and glittering chandeliers; guest rooms are done in neutral creams and earth tones, and blondwood desks and leather chairs have a blandly masculine look. **Pros:** good deals available if you book in advance. **Cons:** lighting in some bedrooms is a bit too subtle; public areas and restaurant can get crowded. **TripAdvisor:** "staff were friendly and helpful," "would definitely stay again," "very good location." ⊠ *4–18 Harrington Gardens, Kensington* ☎ *020/7373–6030* ⊕ *www.millenniumhotels.co.uk/millenniumgloucester* ↩ *143 rooms* ⚒ *In-room: a/c, safe, refrigerator, Wi-Fi. In-hotel: restaurant, room service* ▭ *AE, DC, MC, V* ⏐◯⏐ *Breakfast* Ⓤ *Gloucester Rd.* ✛ *4:C2.*

£££–££££ 🖼 **Number Sixteen.** A more boutique-style offering from the same peo-
Fodor's Choice   ple behind the elegant Charlotte Street Hotel, Number Sixteen is a
★   lovely luxury guesthouse just around the corner from the Victoria & Albert Museum. **Pros:** just the right level of helpful service; decor is gorgeous. **Cons:** there's no restaurant; small elevator. **TripAdvisor:** "room was clean but small," "breakfast was a little funky," "very good service." ⊠ *16 Sumner Pl., South Kensington* ☎ *020/7589–5232, 800/553–6674 in U.S.* ⊕ *www.firmdale.com* ↩ *42 rooms* ⚒ *In-room: no a/c (some), safe, refrigerator, Wi-Fi. In-hotel: room service, bar, laundry service* ▭ *AE, MC, V* ⏐◯⏐ *Breakfast* Ⓤ *South Kensington* ✛ *4:D3.*

££££ 🖼 **The Pelham Hotel.** Museum lovers flock to this sweet hotel across the street from the South Kensington Tube station. The Natural History, Science, and V&A museums are all a short stroll away, as is the King's Road. **Pros:** great location for museum-hopping; gorgeous bathrooms; good package deals for online booking. **Cons:** taller guests will find themselves cursing the top-floor rooms. **TripAdvisor:** "very charming hotel," "everything was perfect," "location is also very good." ⊠ *15 Cromwell Pl., South Kensington* ☎ *020/7589–8288, 888/757–5587 in U.S.* ⊕ *www.pelhamhotel.co.uk* ↩ *48 rooms, 4 suites* ⚒ *In-room: a/c, safe (some), refrigerator, Wi-Fi. In-hotel: restaurant, room service, bar, gym, parking (paid)* ▭ *AE, MC, V* Ⓤ *South Kensington* ✛ *4:D2.*

£££–££££ 🖼 **The Sumner.** This elegant Georgian town house on a quiet residential street is the kind of place where you can feel yourself relaxing the minute you enter. **Pros:** small enough that the staff know your name. **Cons:** services are limited but prices high. **TripAdvisor:** "tidy bathroom and a massive shower," "quiet location with excellent staff," "rooms are comfortable." ⊠ *5 Sumner Pl., South Kensington* ☎ *020/7723–2244* ⊕ *www.thesumner.com* ↩ *20 rooms* ⚒ *In-room: a/c, refrigerator, Internet. In-hotel: room service, parking (paid)* ▭ *AE, MC, V* ⏐◯⏐ *Breakfast* Ⓤ *South Kensington* ✛ *4:D3.*

££–£££ ☶ **Think Earl's Court.** Accommodations in this part of town more commonly pretend they're in Kensington rather than neighboring Earl's Court, but don't be fooled by the name—these brand new serviced apartments are a stone's throw from Kensington High Street. **Pros:** brand new building; self-catering offers greater independence. **Cons:** payment is made when you book; biggest apartments are two-bedroom, so not really geared to families. **TripAdvisor:** "clean and spacious," "felt like home from home," "wonderful alternative to a hotel." ✉ *26A Adam and Eve Mews, Kensington* ☎ *0845/602–9437 or 020/7795–6880* ⊕ *www.think-apartments.com* ☞ *133 rooms* ♨ *In-room: a/c, kitchen, Wi-Fi* ⊟ *AE, MC, V* Ⓤ *High Street Kensington* ✛ *4:B1.*

CHELSEA

££££–£££££ ☶ **The Cadogan Hotel.** This is one of London's most historically naughty hotels; it was once the home of Lillie Langtry, a scandalous actress and King Edward's mistress in the 1890s. **Pros:** luxurious but not stuffy; friendly staff; great location for shopping. **Cons:** rooms are quite small, as are the bar and restaurant. **TripAdvisor:** "so friendly and helpful," "interesting history," "great location for shopping." ✉ *75 Sloane St., Chelsea* ☎ *020/7235–7141* ⊕ *www.cadogan.com* ☞ *65 rooms* ♨ *In-room: a/c, refrigerator, Wi-Fi. In-hotel: restaurant, room service, bar, tennis courts, laundry service* ⊟ *AE, MC, V* Ⓤ *Sloane Sq.* ✛ *4:F2.*

15

££££ ☶ **myhotel chelsea.** This small, chic hotel tucked away down a Chelsea side street is a charmer; rooms are bijou small but sophisticated, with mauve satin throws atop crisp white down comforters. **Pros:** stylish rooms made for relaxation; upscale neighborhood. **Cons:** tiny rooms; no restaurant. **TripAdvisor:** "friendly reception staff," "bar was cold and uninviting," "staff was very friendly." ✉ *35 Ixworth Pl., Chelsea* ☎ *020/7225–7500* ⊕ *www.myhotels.com* ☞ *45 rooms, 9 suites* ♨ *In-room: a/c, safe, refrigerator, DVD, Wi-Fi. In-hotel: room service, bar, gym, spa, laundry service, some pets allowed* ⊟ *AE, D, MC, V* Ⓤ *South Kensington* ✛ *4:E3.*

KNIGHTSBRIDGE

££££–£££££ ☶ **The Beaufort.** At this elegant, modern-style boutique guesthouse, you get many amenities for your money like a front-door key, access to the honor bar in the drawing room, and an in-room music system with CDs and radio. **Pros:** gorgeous decor; friendly staff. **Cons:** standard doubles are much smaller than the price might indicate. **TripAdvisor:** "staff are extremely friendly," "rooms are small," "great location." ✉ *33 Beaufort Gardens, Knightsbridge* ☎ *020/7584–5252, 866/866–7599 in U.S.* ⊕ *www.thebeaufort.co.uk* ☞ *20 rooms, 7 suites* ♨ *In-room: a/c, safe, Wi-Fi. In-hotel: room service, bar, laundry service* ⊟ *AE, DC, MC, V* ⋈ *Breakfast* Ⓤ *Knightsbridge* ✛ *4:F1.*

£££££ ☶ **The Berkeley.** The elegant Berkeley is increasingly known for its luxurious, modern approach, which culminates in its splendid penthouse swimming pool. **Pros:** lavish luxury; attentive service; handy location for shopping. **Cons:** stratospheric prices; you'll need designer clothes to fit in here. **TripAdvisor:** "room was spacious and stylish," "service is hit or miss," "luxurious yet homey." ✉ *Wilton Pl., Knightsbridge* ☎ *020/7235–6000, 800/637–2869 in U.S.* ⊕ *www. the-berkeley.co.uk* ☞ *103 rooms, 55 suites* ♨ *In-room: a/c, safe,*

APARTMENT RENTALS & HOME EXCHANGES

APARTMENT RENTALS

For a home base that's roomy enough for a family and that comes with cooking facilities, consider renting furnished "flats" (the British word for apartments). These can save you money, especially if you're traveling as a family or with a group. You also have the freedom to cook for yourselves if you want—surprisingly liberating after several days of restaurant food. If you're interested in home exchange, but don't feel like sharing, some home-exchange directories list rentals as well. If you want to deal directly with local agents, get a personal recommendation from someone who has used the company; there's no accredited rating system for apartment-rental standards like the one for hotels.

International Agents Hideaways International (✉ *767 Islington St., Portsmouth, NH* ☎ *603/430–4433 or 800/843–4433* ⊕ *www.hideaways. com*) offers boutique hotels, tours, and cruises. Its offerings in London are extremely exclusive. Annual membership is $195.

Interhome (✉ *c/o ResortQuest, 2860 State Rd. 84, Suite 116–PMB 214, Fort Lauderdale, FL* ☎ *800/882–6864* ⊕ *www.interhome.us*) has dozens of rather pricey, but luxurious, flats all over London starting at about £400 per week, rising to more than 10 times that for those with money to burn.

Villanet (✉ *1251 N.W. 116th St., Seattle, WA* ☎ *206/417–3444 or 877/250–4366* ⊕ *www.rentavilla. com*) has hundreds of flats in residential neighborhoods all over London, with prices starting at about £1,000 per week.

The Villas International (✉ *17 Fox La., San Anselmo, CA* ☎ *415/499–9490 or 800/221–2260* ⊕ *www. villasintl.com*) agency has exclusively priced flats all over London that start around £1,800 per week—some sleep up to 10 people.

Local Agents Acorn Apartments (✉ *Ground Fl., 19 Bedford Pl.* ☎ *020/7636–8325* ⊕ *www.acorn-apartments.co.uk*) offers attractive small central apartments starting at around £100, however the Web site is not very good and it may be easier to call for information.

The Apartment Service (✉ *5 Francis Grove, Wimbledon* ☎ *020/8944–1444* ⊕ *www.apartmentservice. com*) specializes in executive apartments for business travelers in and around The City, so prices are high, but so is the level of quality. Aside from a few super-cheap places in parts of town you wouldn't want to stay in, prices start at £74 per night for a one-bedroom near the Olympic Village, rising to £585 per night for a four-bedroom near Buckingham Palace.

The Bed and Breakfast Club (✉ *Suite 192, 405 Kings Rd., Chelsea* ☎ *0870/803–4414* ⊕ *www. thebedandbreakfastclub.co.uk* ⊟ *AE, MC, V* ☞ *There's a 2.5% fee for using a credit card; debit cards incur no fees; the full price of room must be paid in advance. Check cancellation policies carefully*) offers delightful little London flats in Knightsbridge, Kensington, and Chelsea. Most properties are available for £60–£125 per night with full English breakfasts.

Stay in the properties of Londoners who are temporarily away with **Coach House London Vacation Rentals** (✉ *2 Tunley Rd., Balham* ☎ *020/8133–8332* ⊕ *www.rentals.chslondon.com* ▭ *AE, MC, V* ☞ *Payment by credit card only; 10% deposit required*). Attractive apartments and houses are primarily in Notting Hill, Kensington, and Chelsea, and most cost around £125 per night. The minimum booking of five to seven nights is a bit limiting, though, and you must make a substantial security deposit (usually between £200 and £1,000), which is returned after your stay.

Landmark Trust (☎ *01628/825–925* ⊕ *www.landmarktrust.org.uk*) has London apartments in unusual and historic buildings; prices start at around £100 a night, but many buildings require a minimum stay of seven days.

Uptown Reservations (☎ *020/7937–2001* ⊕ *www.uptownres.co.uk* ▭ *AE, MC, V*) accepts only upscale addresses, and specializes in hosted homes or apartments for Americans, often business executives. Nearly all the homes on its register are in Knightsbridge, Belgravia, Kensington, and Chelsea. Prices start at £105 per person, per night. There's limited information on their Web site; bookings must be made over the phone. A nonrefundable deposit is required.

Additionally, travelers at Fodors.com recommend these rental services:

"I've used **London Guest Suites** (⊕ *www.londonguestsuites.com*) many times and like them. They have rentals of all lengths. I also just booked a flat at **A Place Like Home**

(⊕ *www.aplacelikehome.co.uk*)."
—carrybean

"We stayed in 1 Sloane Ave. and were extremely happy and pleased with the apartment and the company **The Apartments** (⊕ *www.theapartments.co.uk*)." —jrecm

"Try the biggest rental site in Europe: **Holiday-Rentals from Home Away** (⊕ *www.holiday-rentals.co.uk*)."
—travel_tomato

"Check out **VRBO** (⊕ *www.vrbo.com*), lots of London listings, and **Farnum-Christ** (⊕ *www.farnum-christ.com*), which is a high-ish end agency with some wonderful flats." —janisj

"I've used **London Connections** (⊕ *www.londonconnections.com*) several times and I've been very pleased." —Tinathread

HOME EXCHANGES
If you would like to exchange your home for someone else's, join a home-exchange organization, which will send you its updated listings of available exchanges for a year and will include your own listing in at least one of them. It's up to you to make specific arrangements.

Exchange Clubs HomeLink International (✉ *2937 NW 9th Terr., Fort Lauderdale, FL* ☎ *954/566–2687 or 800/638–3841* ⊕ *www.homelink.org*); $119 yearly for a listing and online access.

Intervac U.S (✉ *Box 590504, San Franciso, CA 94159* ☎ *800/756–4663* ⊕ *www.intervacus.com*); $99 yearly for a listing and online access.

15

refrigerator, DVD, Internet. In-hotel: restaurant, room service, bar, pool, gym, spa, laundry service, parking (paid) ⊟ *AE, DC, MC, V* Ⓤ *Knightsbridge* ✛ *4:G1.*

££££££ 🏨 **The Capital Hotel.** This is a true boutique hotel, with subtle, elegant decor, spacious rooms, and understated service. **Pros:** beautiful space; handy for shopping at Harrods. **Cons:** you'll pay dearly for this luxury. **TripAdvisor:** "luxury hotel of an exceptional standard," "the location can't be beat," "gorgeous rooms and wonderful bar." ⊠ *22–24 Basil St., Knightsbridge* ☏ *020/7589–5171, 800/628–8929 in U.S.* ⊕ *www.capitalhotel.co.uk* ⇆ *42 rooms, 8 suites* ⚹ *In-room: a/c, safe, refrigerator, Internet. In-hotel: Wi-Fi, restaurant, room service, bar, laundry service, parking (paid), some pets allowed* ⊟ *AE, DC, MC, V* Ⓤ *Knightsbridge* ✛ *4:F1.*

££££–£££££ 🏨 **Egerton House.** This utterly peaceful, small hotel specializes in a traditional concept of luxury; walking around the public spaced can feel like a private tour of an art gallery with works on display that include originals by Matisse, Picasso, and Toulouse-Lautrec. **Pros:** staff is helpful; location is great for Knightsbridge shopping. **Cons:** Toulouse-Lautrec may have approved, but some may find the decor a little too Moulin Rouge for their taste. **TripAdvisor:** "exceedingly attentive front desk," "atmosphere is delightful," "rooms perfectly presented." ⊠ *17–19 Egerton Terr., Knightsbridge* ☏ *020/7589–2412, 877/955–1515 in U.S.* ⊕ *www. egertonhousehotel.co.uk* ⇆ *22 rooms, 6 suites* ⚹ *In-room: a/c, refrigerator, Internet. In-hotel: room service, bar, laundry service, parking (paid)* ⊟ *AE, DC, MC, V* Ⓤ *Knightsbridge, South Kensington* ✛ *4:F2.*

£££££ 🏨 **The Lanesborough.** Everything exudes richness here at this grand hotel that is now part of the St. Regis group—from the magnificent 19th century antiques in the luxurious guestrooms, to the personal butler service that caters to your every whim. **Pros:** lap of luxury; your wish is their command. **Cons:** prices are extraordinary; not everybody likes constantly hovering service. **TripAdvisor:** "service was impeccable," "beautifully furnished and equipped," "state of the art." ⊠ *Hyde Park Corner, Belgravia* ☏ *020/7259–5599, 800/999–1828 in U.S.* ⊕ *www. lanesborough.com* ⇆ *52 rooms, 43 suites* ⚹ *In-room: a/c, safe, refrigerator, Wi-Fi. In-hotel: restaurant, room service, bar, spa, gym, laundry service, parking (paid)* ⊟ *AE, DC, MC, V* Ⓤ *Hyde Park Corner* ✛ *4:G1.*

££££–£££££ 🏨 **The Levin Hotel.** This posh boutique hotel created by the people behind the Capital Hotel is owned by luxury-loving oenophiles; expect smooth, duck-egg-blue walls, hyper-modern furnishings, and a champagne bar in every room. **Pros:** your own champagne bar; sauntering to Harrods. **Cons:** no elevator; few bargains to be had. **TripAdvisor:** "beautifully decorated," "friendly and helpful personnel," "not inexpensive." ⊠ *28 Basil St., Knightsbridge* ☏ *020/7589–6286* ⊕ *www.thelevinhotel.co.uk* ⇆ *12 rooms, 1 suite* ⚹ *In-room: a/c, DVD, Internet. In-hotel: restaurant, bar, parking (paid)* ⊟ *AE, DC, MC, V* ⦿ *Breakfast* Ⓤ *Knightsbridge* ✛ *4:F1.*

£££££

Fodor's Choice

★

🏨 **Mandarin Oriental Hyde Park.** Stay here, and the three greats of Knightsbridge—Hyde Park, Harrods, and Harvey Nichols—are at your doorstep. Built in 1880, the Mandarin Oriental is one of London's most elegant hotels. **Pros:** amazing views of Hyde Park; excellent service.

HOSTELS AND UNIVERSITIES

Bargains are undeniably hard to find in London, but if you don't mind sharing bathrooms, TVs, and sofas with a few hundred of your newest friends, you can save a lot of cash.

HOSTELS

No matter what your age, you can save on lodging costs by staying at hostels. In some 4,500 locations in more than 70 countries around the world, Hostelling International (HI), the umbrella group for a number of national youth-hostel associations, has single-sex, dorm-style beds and, at many hostels, rooms for couples and family accommodations. Membership in any HI national hostel association, open to travelers of all ages, allows you to stay in HI-affiliated hostels at member rates; one-year membership is about $28 for adults; hostels charge about $15–$40 per night. Members have priority if the hostel is full; they're also eligible for other discounts.

Contacts Hostelling International—Canada (✉ 205 Catherine St., Suite 400, Ottawa, Ontario ☎ 613/237–7884 or 800/663–5777 ⊕ www.hihostels.ca). Hostelling International—USA (✉ 8401 Colesville Rd., Suite 600, Silver Spring, MD ☎ 301/495–1240 ⊕ www.hiusa.org). YHA England and Wales (✉ Trevelyan House, Dimple Rd., Matlock, Derbyshire, UK ☎ 0162/959–2700 or 080/0019–1700 ⊕ www.yha.org.uk).

UNIVERSITY RESIDENCE HALLS

University student dorms (Halls of Residence) can be ideal for single travelers as well as those on a tight budget who want to come to London in summer when deals on other lodgings are scarce. Walter Sickert Hall has year-round lodging in its "executive rooms" (six single and three twin), and breakfast is even delivered to your room. Beds are usually available for a week around Easter, and from mid-June to mid-September in all the university accommodations around town. As you might expect, showers and toilets are shared.

Contacts City University Hall of Residence: Walter Sickert Hall (✉ Graham St. ☎ 020/7040–8037 ⊕ www.city.ac.uk/ems) has rooms starting at £21 per person, per night. London School of Economics Vacations (☎ 020/7955–7575 ⊕ www.lsevacations.co.uk) costs around £50 for a double without a toilet to £72 for a double with a toilet. You can choose from a variety of rooms in their many halls of residence around London. The LSE also rent out self-catering apartments starting at around £90 per night. University College London (✉ Residence Manager, Campbell House, 5–10 Taviton St. ☎ 020/7679–2000 ⊕ www.ucl.ac.uk/residences) is open from mid-June to mid-September.

15

Cons: nothing here comes cheap; you must dress for dinner (and lunch and breakfast). **TripAdvisor:** "made to feel very welcome," "very good but understandably expensive," "staff were super friendly and helpful." ✉ 66 Knightsbridge, Knightsbridge ☎ 020/7235–2000 ⊕ www.mandarinoriental.com/london ➵ 177 rooms, 23 suites ⌂ In-room: a/c, safe, refrigerator, DVD (some), Wi-Fi. In-hotel: 2 restaurants, room service, bar, gym, spa, laundry service, parking (paid) ▭ AE, DC, MC, V Ⓤ Knightsbridge ✛ 4:F1.

NOTTING HILL AND BAYSWATER

NOTTING HILL

££ ⊤ **TheMain House.** A brass lion door knocker marks Main House's Victorian front door, typical of Notting Hill. With just four rooms, this hotel offers nothing but a good night's sleep in a Victorian home. **Pros:** unusual option; great location. **Cons:** few rooms mean it books up far in advance; two-night minimum stay; no room service. **TripAdvisor:** "felt very homey," "very spacious and bright," "charm and chic in buckets."⊠ *6 Colvile Rd., Notting Hill* ☎ *020/7221–9691* ⊕ *www.themainhouse.com* ↵ *4 rooms* △ *In-room: a/c (some), Wi-Fi (some). In-hotel: bicycles, laundry service, parking (paid)* ⊟ *MC, V* ¦○¦ *Breakfast* Ⓤ *Notting Hill Gate* ✛ *1:A4.*

££££–£££££ ⊤ **The Portobello Hotel.** One of London's most famous hotels, the little Portobello (formed from two adjoining Victorian houses) is seriously hip and attracts scores of celebrities. **Pros:** stylish; great for celebrity-spotting; good location. **Cons:** most rooms are quite small; may be too eccentric for some. **TripAdvisor:** "colonial decadence," "really quirky," "on the shabby side of chic."⊠ *22 Stanley Gardens, Notting Hill* ☎ *020/7727–2777* ⊕ *www.portobello-hotel.co.uk* ↵ *24 rooms* △ *In-room: no a/c (some), safe, refrigerator, Internet. In-hotel: restaurant, room service, bar* ⊟ *AE, MC, V* ⊙ *Closed 10 days at Christmas* ¦○¦ *Breakfast* Ⓤ *Notting Hill Gate* ✛ *1:A5.*

£–££ ⊤ **Portobello Gold.** This no-frills B&B in the heart of the Portobello Road antiques area is on the floor above the pub and restaurant of the same name; flat-screen TVs are mounted on the wall, and the beds take up almost the entire tiny room in the doubles. **Pros:** great location; laid-back atmosphere; good advance deals. **Cons:** rooms are tiny; can be noisy; no elevator. **TripAdvisor:** "atmosphere was great," "ideal for solo traveler," "small but cozy."⊠ *95–97 Portobello Rd., Notting Hill* ☎ *020/7460–4910* ⊕ *www.portobellogold.com* ↵ *6 rooms, 1 apartment* △ *In-room: a/c, Wi-Fi. In-hotel: restaurant, room service, bar* ⊟ *MC, V* ¦○¦ *Breakfast* Ⓤ *Notting Hill Gate* ✛ *1:A4.*

BAYSWATER

££££ ⊤ **Colonnade.** Near a canal filled with colorful narrow boats, this lovely town house rests in a quiet, residential area known as "Little Venice." **Pros:** beautifully decorated; Frette sheets; frequent online sales that can cut the price by £100. **Cons:** a bit far from popular sights; rooms are small. **TripAdvisor:** "always feel spoiled when I go," "very comfortable and elegantly furnished," "all in all a lovely room."⊠ *2 Warrington Crescent, Bayswater* ☎ *020/7286–1052* ⊕ *www.theetoncollection.com* ↵ *15 rooms, 28 suites* △ *In-room: a/c, safe, Internet. In-hotel: restaurant, room service, bars, laundry service, parking (paid), some pets allowed* ⊟ *AE, DC, MC, V* Ⓤ *Warwick Ave.* ✛ *1:C2.*

£ ⊤ **Europa House Hotel.** This modest family-run B&B near Hyde Park is a decent, unfussy alternative to overpriced, impersonal chain hotels. **Pros:** bargain price; close to two Tube stations. **Cons:** dated decor; few amenities; no elevator. **TripAdvisor:** "very small space," "shower had very limited space," "would definitely stay again."⊠ *151 Sussex Gardens, Bayswater* ☎ *020/7723–7343* ⊕ *www.europahousehotel.org.uk* △ *In-room: no a/c* ⊟ *AE, DC, MC, V* Ⓤ *Paddington, Lancaster Gate* ✛ *1:E2.*

£–££ 🛏 **Garden Court Hotel.** This small hotel is formed from two 19th-century town houses in a quiet garden square; rooms with toilet and shower cost an extra £30, and a hot breakfast also ups the bill. **Pros:** lovely garden; lots of charm; new elevator makes the upper floors more pleasant. **Cons:** not all rooms have private baths; some rooms need updating. **TripAdvisor:** "staff is friendly and helpful," "excellent, good value," "very quiet." ⊠ *30–31 Kensington Gardens Sq., Bayswater* ☎ *020/7229–2553* ⊕ *www.gardencourthotel.co.uk* ⇆ *12 rooms, 10 with bath* ♿ *In-room: no a/c. In-hotel: bar, Wi-Fi hotspot, some pets allowed* ⊟ *MC, V* 🍴 *Breakfast* Ⓤ *Bayswater, Queensway* ✛ *1:B4.*

££ 🛏 **Space Apart Hotel.** This Georgian hotel near Hyde Park is a great find with 30 studio apartments that have all been recently renovated in stellar style. **Pros:** the price is right; the larger suites have space for four people. **Cons:** no in-house restaurant or bar; minimum two-night stay required. **TripAdvisor:** "spotlessly clean," "very warm and inviting," "rooms ultra modern and stylish." ⊠ *32–37 Kensington Gardens Sq., Bayswater* ☎ *0207/908–1340* ⊕ *www.aparthotel-london.co.uk* ⇆ *30 rooms* ♿ *In-room: a/c, no phone, kitchen, refrigerator, Wi-Fi, DVD* ⊟ *MC, V* Ⓜ *Bayswater* ✛ *1:B4.*

£ 🛏 **Stylotel.** Just around the corner from Paddington station, this is a wry, funky-looking little place that conceals a smoothly run operation underneath its rather camp exterior. **Pros:** bargain price; helpful staff; unique style. **Cons:** style will be too unique for some; small bedrooms and bathrooms; serves breakfast only—you have to eat out every night; Web site is frequently down, which makes booking online a challenge. **TripAdvisor:** "perfect location for shopping," "rooms are extremely cool and modern," "comfortable and very clean." ⊠ *160–162 Sussex Gardens Sq., Bayswater* ☎ *0207/223–1026* ⊕ *www.stylotel.com* ♿ *In-room: no a/c, Wi-Fi (paid). In-hotel: parking (paid)* ⊟ *AE, MC, V* Ⓜ *Paddington, Edgware Rd* ✛ *1:E4.*

££ 🛏 **Vancouver Studios.** This little hotel in a heritage-listed Victorian town house is perfect for those wanting a home away from home. **Pros:** more space than a hotel room; unique little apartments. **Cons:** a bit out of the way; a bargain only if several people share the space. **TripAdvisor:** "room was spotless," "internet is slow in the evening," "shower is tiny." ⊠ *30 Prince's Sq., Bayswater* ☎ *020/7243–1270* ⊕ *www.vancouverstudios.co.uk* ⇆ *45 studios* ♿ *In-room: no a/c, kitchen, refrigerator, DVD, Wi-Fi. In-hotel: room service, bar, laundry facilities, laundry service, parking (paid)* ⊟ *AE, DC, MC, V* Ⓤ *Bayswater, Queensway* ✛ *1:B4.*

REGENT'S PARK AND HAMPSTEAD

££ 🛏 **La Gaffe.** Italian Bernardo Stella has welcomed people back to these early-18th-century row houses, a short walk up one of Hampstead's magnificent hills, for more than 20 years. **Pros:** pretty area of town; friendly staff. **Cons:** bathrooms have showers only; few services; no elevator. **TripAdvisor:** "very clean," "great location," "beds were firm." ⊠ *107–111 Heath St., Hampstead* ☎ *020/7435–8965* ⊕ *www.lagaffe.co.uk* ⇆ *18 rooms, 3 suites* ♿ *In-room: no a/c. In-hotel: restau-*

15

rant, bar, laundry facilities, parking (free) ⊟ *AE, MC, V* ⦿ *Breakfast* Ⓤ *Hampstead* ✛ *1:D1.*

£££–££££ Ⓣ **Hilton London Islington.** Next door to the Islington Business Design Centre, this hotel is sleek and modern, standing out starkly in historic Islington. **Pros:** lots of amenities for business travelers; handy restaurant and bar. **Cons:** not many amenities for leisure travelers. **TripAdvisor:** "staff were all friendly and helpful," "very good value," "very nice and ultra modern."⊠ *53 Upper St., Islington* ☎ *020/7354–7700* ⊕ *www.hilton.co.uk/islington* ⇱ *183 rooms, 6 suites* ⚹ *In-room: a/c, safe, Internet. In-hotel: 3 restaurants, room service, bar, gym, spa* ⊟ *AE, DC, MC, V* ⦿ *Breakfast* Ⓤ *Angel* ✛ *2:F1.*

CAMDEN TOWN

££ Ⓣ **66 Camden Square.** This beautiful B&B is run by an architect and his wife, so it comes as no surprise to find that the space within is tastefully done; the owners, Sue and Roger Davis, are gracious and personable hosts, with an encyclopedic knowledge of what the area has to offer in terms of pubs, restaurants, and nightlife. **Pros:** lovely owners; unique place; inexpensive. **Cons:** few extras; bathrooms not en suite (but not shared either); maximum stay of one week; no Web site. ⊠ *66 Camden Sq., Camden Town* ☎ *020/7485–4622* ⇱ *35 rooms, 3 suites* ⚹ *In-room: no a/c, Wi-Fi. In-hotel: parking (paid)* Ⓤ *Camden Rd.* ✛ *2:B1.*

£ Ⓣ **St. Christopher's Inn Camden.** In bustling, hippie Camden Town just north of the center of London, this branch of the local hostel and backpacker hotel chain is perfectly situated for wandering around Camden Lock and Camden Market. **Pros:** clean, safe, and friendly places in London really don't come cheaper than this; funky neighborhood. **Cons:** a bit noisy and boisterous. **TripAdvisor:** "not the best but not bad," "great for meeting people," "good food and friendly staff."⊠ *48–50 Camden High St., Camden Town* ☎ *020/7388–1012* ⊕ *www.st-christophers.co.uk* ⇱ *52 beds, some without bath* ⚹ *In-room: Wi-Fi, no a/c, no phone, no TV. In-hotel: restaurant, bar, laundry facilities, Internet terminal* ⊟ *MC, V* ⦿ *Breakfast* Ⓤ *Camden Town, Mornington Crescent* ✛ *2:A1.*

THE THAMES UPSTREAM

££–£££ Ⓣ **K West Hotel.** The proudly edgy K West is hidden away inside a featureless glass-and-steel building near the Shepherd's Bush Tube stop, just outside Notting Hill. This is definitely a grown-up place, more popular with business types and young couples, rather than families with young kids. **Pros:** sleek, modern decor; funky attitude. **Cons:** not a great neighborhood; bar is loud on weekends; hotel service can be patchy. **TripAdvisor:** "well decorated and comfortable," "modern and trendy," "excellent value."⊠ *Richmond Way, Shepherd's Bush* ☎ *020/8008–6600* ⊕ *www.k-west.co.uk* ⇱ *216 rooms, 6 suites* ⚹ *In-room: a/c, safe, DVD, Wi-Fi. In-hotel: restaurant, room service, bar, gym, spa, laundry service, Internet terminal, parking (paid)* ⊟ *AE, DC, MC, V* ⦿ *Breakfast* Ⓤ *Shepherd's Bush* ✛ *1:B2.*

Pubs and Nightlife

WORD OF MOUTH

"London has two types of pubs. One is the local where neighbors visit. The second is an open type hosting casual visitors. Inquire at your hotel about a local. Be prepared to buy a round. At the casual bar, ask for a recommendation of a beer or ale. Ask at your hotel for a nearby pub with the best pub grub."

—GSteed

PUBS AND NIGHTLIFE PLANNER

Getting Around

If you're out past 12:30 am, the best way to get home is by taxi (the Tube stops running around 12:30 am Monday–Saturday and midnight on Sunday). The best place to hail a taxi is at the front door of one of the major hotels; you can also have the staff at your last stop of the evening call one for you. Avoid unlicensed taxis that tout for business around closing time.

Liquor Laws, Smoking Laws

In 2005, England relaxed its licensing laws and as many as 5,200 drinking establishments in London extended their opening hours beyond their traditional 11 pm closing. And although it's controversial, the new development translates into only a modest increase in overall licensing hours; most still close at 11, and others at midnight or a few short hours later. A bigger change to many has been the 2007 law that bans smoking inside any public building. Many in the nightlife industry opposed the changes, worried that it would have a negative effect on their businesses. On the other hand, London's venues have become much more family-friendly and healthier as a result.

Can I Take My Kids to the Pub?

As pubs increasingly emphasize what's coming out of the kitchen rather than what's flowing from the tap, whether to bring the kids has become a frequent question. The law dictates that patrons must be 18 years of age or older to drink alcohol in a pub.

Children 14 to 17 may enter a pub but are not permitted to purchase or drink alcohol, and children under 14 are not permitted in the bar area of a pub unless the pub has a "Children's Certificate" and they are accompanied by an adult. In general, however, some pubs have a section set aside for families, especially during the day.

What to Wear

As a general rule, you can dress as you would for an evening in New York City; however, you see fewer people in the upscale London nightspots wearing jeans and sneakers. British women are also prone to baring a bit more skin, so that sparkly, backless top you were saving for a Caribbean soirée might be just as suitable for a night out in London. In general, people are more likely to dress down than up for a trip to a gig or to the pub.

Find Out What's Playing Where

Because today's cool spot is often tomorrow's forgotten or closed venue, you'll want to be sure to check out the weekly listings in one of several publications. There are several Web sites, in addition to the print publications the *Evening Standard, Time Out London, Where London,* and *In London,* that will tell you who's playing where and when, from theater presentations to jazz clubs to hot danceterias. To find your comfort level, read between the lines in the listings. *Tatler,* the monthly, super-stylish magazine about England's blue-blood set, is the insider's bible for the hottest places to go. Although many clubs are for underthirties, many others make for a popular night out for all ages and types. Check out ⊕ www.londontown.com, ⊕ www.allinlondon.co.uk, or ⊕ www.viewlondon.co.uk.

Updated by
Julius Honnor

There isn't a London nightlife scene—there are lots of them. As long as there are crowds for obscure teenage rock bands, Dickensian-style pubs, comedy cabarets, and "bodysonic" dance nights, someone will create clubs and venues for them in London. The result? London has become a veritable utopia for excitement junkies, culture fiends, and those who—simply put—like to party. Nearly everyone who visits London these days will be mesmerized by the city's energy, which reveals itself in layers. Whether you prefer rhythm and blues with fine French food, the gritty guitar riffs of East London, a pint and gourmet pizza at a local gastro-pub, or swanky cocktails and sushi at London's sexiest lair, the U.K. capital is sure to feed your fancy.

16

PUBS

The English take their drink very seriously, and pubs are where Londoners go to hang out, to see and be seen, act out the drama of life, and, for some, occasionally drink themselves into varying degrees of oblivion. Even today, competing with a thoroughly modern entertainment industry, the traditional pub is still a vital part of British life. It also should be a part of the visitor's experience, as there are few better places to meet Londoners in their local habitat. There are thousands of pubs in London—ever fewer of which still have original Victorian etched glass, Edwardian panels, and Art Nouveau carvings. The list below offers a few pubs selected for central location, historical interest, a pleasant garden, music, or good food, but you might just as happily adopt your own temporary "local."

REGENT'S PARK

Albany Rd.

HAMPSTEAD
villagey pubs
for long Sunday
lunches

CLERKENWELL
urban
cutting edge

Albany St.

Euston Rd.

Clerkenwell Rd.

Gt. Portland St.

Portland Pl.

Tottenham Court Rd.

Gray's Inn Rd.

BLOOMSBURY
heritage,
learning,
bowling

NOTTING HILL
arty but smart
and rich-hip
drinking holes

Marylebone Rd.

Baker St.

HOXTON
arty and
on the pulse

Holborn

New Oxford St.

Wigmore St.

Kingsway

Fleet St.

FITZROVIA
secret chic

**OXFORD
CIRCUS**

Oxford St.

Charing Cross Rd.

Aldwych

Strand

Bayswater Rd.

COVENT GARDEN
a drink before
the show

Regent St.

SOHO
lowlife and
highlife,
music and dance

Victoria Embankment

MAYFAIR
wine and
spirits

New Bond St.

Pall Mall

Stamford St.

Waterloo Br.

HYDE PARK

ST JAMES'S
jacket
required

SOUTH BANK
real ale,
real food

Piccadilly

Green
Park

River

Thames

Waterloo Rd.

Knightsbridge

St. James's
Park

Whitehall

KNIGHTSBRIDGE
hotel bar
martinis

Constitution Hill

The Mall

Westminster Bridge Rd.

Birdcage Walk

Westminster Br.

Sloane St.

HAMMERSMITH
relaxed and
upmarket,
evenings
by the river

WESTMINSTER

Lambeth Palace Rd.

Lambeth Rd.

Kennington Rd.

BELGRAVIA
hidden mews
gems

Victoria St.

Horseferry Rd.

Lambeth Br.

LAMBETH

Buckingham Palace Rd.

Wilton Rd.

Vauxhall Br. Rd.

Millbank

Albert Embankment

King's Rd.

Pimlico Rd.

VICTORIA

CHELSEA
sophisticated
and moneyed

Kennington Park Rd.

0   1/2 mile

0   1/2 km

Pubs in the capital are changing: 90-year-old licensing laws have finally been modernized, gastropub fever has swept through London, and smoking in all pubs has been illegal since 2007. At many places, char-grills are installed in the kitchen out back and nouveau pub grub, such as Moroccan chicken, is on the menu. Regardless of what you eat, however, you'll definitely want to order a pint.

Once you decide where to drink, the big decision is *what* to drink. The beer of choice among Britons is **"bitter,"** a lightly fermented beer with an amber color that gets its bitterness from hops. It is usually served at cellar temperature (that is, cooler than room temperature but not actually chilled). Real **ale,** served from wooded kegs and made without chilling, filtering, or pasteurization, is flatter than regular bitters. **Stouts,** like Guinness, are a meal in themselves and something of an acquired taste—they have a burnt flavor and look like thickened flat Coke with a frothy top. **Lagers,** most familiar to American drinkers, are light-color and carbonated. ■TIP➔ Remember that what Americans call beer, the British call lager, often beers from continental Europe. At the same time, designer and American **beers** have been making their way to bars across the country. Note that many English pubs are affiliated with particular breweries and are beholden to sell only beers produced by that brewery. Some of the larger chains, identified on the pub's sign, include Bass, Chef and Brewer, Courage, Samuel Smith, and Whitbread. In contrast, independently owned pubs, called "free houses," can serve whatever they wish and tend to offer a more extensive selection. Other potations now available also include **ciders,** ranging from sweet to dry, which are made from apples (Irish cider, served over ice, is now ubiquitously fashionable) and **shandies,** a mix of lager and lemonade. Friendly pubs will usually be happy to give you a taste of the brew of your choice before you order. After discussing your choice of drink with the barman, turn to your neighbor, raise the glass, and utter that most pleasant of toasts, "Cheers."

16

BLOOMSBURY AND LEGAL LONDON

BLOOMSBURY

★ **The Lamb.** Charles Dickens and his contemporaries drank here, but today's enthusiastic clientele make sure this intimate and eternally popular pub avoids the pitfalls of feeling too old-fashioned. For private chats at the bar, you can close the delicate etched-glass "snob screen" to the bar staff, opening it only when you fancy another pint. ⊠ *94 Lamb's Conduit St., Bloomsbury* ☎ *020/7405–0713* Ⓤ *Russell Sq.*

★ **Museum Tavern.** Across the street from the British Museum, this friendly and classy Victorian pub makes an ideal resting place after the rigors of the culture trail. Karl Marx unwound here after a hard day in the

Market Porter pub is directly across from foodie favorite Borough Market.

Library. He could have spent his *Kapital* on any of seven well-kept beers available on tap. ⊠ *49 Great Russell St., Bloomsbury* ☎ *020/7242–8987* Ⓤ *Tottenham Court Rd.*

The Queen's Larder. The royal name of this tiny pub comes from Queen Charlotte, who is said to have stored food here for her "mad" husband, George III, when he was being treated nearby. The interior preserves its antique feel, with dark wood and old posters, but it gets very "today" when jammed with tourists and office workers. In good weather, you might prefer to grab one of the seats outdoors. ⊠ *1 Queen's Sq., Bloomsbury* ☎ *020/7837–5627* ⊕ *www.queenslarder.co.uk* Ⓤ *Russel Sq.*

HOLBORN

Princess Louise. This fine, popular pub has over-the-top Victorian interior-glazed tiles and intricately engraved glass screens that divide the bar area into cozy little annexes. It's not all show, either: There's a good selection of excellent-value Yorkshire real ales. ⊠ *208 High Holborn, Holborn* ☎ *020/7405–8816* Ⓤ *Holborn.*

THE CITY AND CLERKENWELL

THE CITY

Fodor's Choice ★ **Black Friar.** A step from Blackfriars Tube stop, this spectacular pub has an Arts-and-Crafts interior that is entertainingly, satirically ecclesiastical, with inlaid mother-of-pearl, wood carvings, stained glass, and marble pillars all over the place. In spite of the finely lettered temperance tracts on view just below the reliefs of monks, fairies, and friars, there is a nice group of ales on tap from independent brewers. ⊠ *174 Queen Victoria St., The City* ☎ *020/7236–5474* Ⓤ *Blackfriars.*

Viaduct Tavern. Queen Victoria opened the nearby Holborn Viaduct in 1869, and this eponymous pub honored the waterway by serving its first pint the same year. Much of the Victorian decoration is still extant, with gilded mirrors, carved wood, and engraved glass. The Viaduct Tavern's haunted reputation stems from its proximity to the former Newgate Gaol, which once stood on the site (in fact, ex-prison cells in the basement can be seen with a free tour before or after the lunchtime rush and before 5 pm). There are usually three or four ales on tap; lunch is also served. ⊠ *126 Newgate St., The City* ☎ *020/600–1863* ◎ *Closed weekends* Ⓤ *St. Paul's.*

Ye Olde Cheshire Cheese. Yes, it's full of tourists, but it's also an extremely historic pub (it dates from 1667, the year after the Great Fire of London), and it deserves a visit for its sawdust-covered floors, low wood-beam ceilings, and the 14th-century crypt of Whitefriars' monastery under the cellar bar. This was the most regular of Dr. Johnson's and Dickens's *many* locals. ⊠ *145 Fleet St., The City* ☎ *020/7353–6170* Ⓤ *Blackfriars.*

Ye Olde Mitre. Hidden off the side of 8 Hatton Gardens, this cozy pub's roots go back to 1547, though it was rebuilt around 1772. Originally built for the staff of the Bishop of Ely, whose London residence was next door, it remained officially part of Cambridgeshire until the 20th century. It's a friendly little place, with a fireplace, well-kept ales, wooden beams, and traditional bar snacks. ⊠ *1 Ely Ct., The City* ☎ *020/7405–4751* ◎ *Closed weekends* Ⓤ *Chancery La.*

Ye Olde Watling. This busy corner pub has been rebuilt at least three times since 1666. One of its incarnations was supposedly as a hostel for Christopher Wren's workmen while nearby St. Paul's was being built. The ground floor is a laid-back pub, while upstairs houses an atmospheric restaurant, complete with wooden beams and trestle tables, with a basic English pub menu. ⊠ *29 Watling St., The City* ☎ *020/248–8935* Ⓤ *Mansion House.*

CLERKENWELL

Fodor'sChoice **Jerusalem Tavern.** Owned by the well-respected St. Peter's Brewery from
★ Suffolk, the Jerusalem Tavern is one-of-a-kind, small and endearingly eccentric. Ancient Delft-style tiles meld with wood and concrete in a converted watchmaker and jeweler's shop dating back to the 18th century. The beer, both bottled and on tap, is some of the best available anywhere in London. It's often busy, especially after work. ⊠ *55 Britton St., Clerkenwell* ☎ *020/7490–4281* Ⓤ *Farringdon.*

THE EAST END

Prospect of Whitby. Named after a ship, this is London's oldest riverside pub, dating from around 1520. Once upon a time it was called the Devil's Tavern because of the lowlife criminals—thieves and smugglers—who congregated here. Ornamented with pewter ware and nautical objects, this much-loved "boozer" is often pointed out from boat trips up the Thames. ⊠ *57 Wapping Wall, East End* ☎ *020/7481–1095* Ⓤ *Wapping.*

CHELSEA AND KNIGHTSBRIDGE

CHELSEA

Admiral Codrington. Named after a hero of the Napoleonic Wars, this smart pub was once the most popular meeting place for the upwardly mobile of Sloane Square (Lady Diana Spencer is said to have been a regular in her teaching days). The "Admiral Cod," as it's known, now houses a modern restaurant where excellent English fare is served at lunch and dinnertime (treat yourself to a delicious raspberry soufflé to finish). Activity at the island bar centers on the wine list; well-off Chelsea residents pack the bare wood interior on weekend evenings. ⊠ *17 Mossop St., Chelsea* ☎ *020/7581–0005* ⊕ *www.theadmiralcodrington. co.uk* Ⓤ *South Kensington.*

KNIGHTSBRIDGE

★ **The Nag's Head.** It's best not to upset the landlord in this classic little mews pub in Belgravia—he runs a tight ship, and no cell phones are allowed. If that sounds like misery, the lovingly collected Victorian artifacts (including antique penny arcade games), high-quality beer, and old-fashioned pub grub should make up for it. ⊠ *53 Kinnerton St., Belgravia* ☎ *020/7235–1135* Ⓤ *Hyde Park Corner.*

MAYFAIR

The Running Horse. Wood paneling gives this smart Mayfair pub an authentic feel, although the bright Art Deco lights may seem a bit out of place. Pub grub is served, and it's a pleasant stopover during your jaunt around the elegant neighborhood. ⊠ *50 Davies St., Mayfair* ☎ *020/7493–1275* ⊕ *www.therunninghorselondon.co.uk* Ⓤ *Bond St.*

NOTTING HILL

Fodor'sChoice
★ **The Cow.** Back in 1999 Tom Conran, a scion of the design-mad Conrans, opened this as the first shot in the gastro-pub revolution—a tiny, chic mix of fun, haute food and friendly, quaint decor. Notting Hillbillies and other stylish folk flocked to this place, just off Portobello Road, and couldn't get enough of the special: a half-dozen Irish rock oysters with a pint of Guinness. Today, crowds still head here for Guinness and oysters, either enjoying them in the unpretentious downstairs bar or the upstairs more formal restaurant. The food is still excellent, if pricey for pub grub, with lots of seafood and steaks (and sometimes a mix, as in the smoked eel with mash and bacon). The atmosphere? Always warm, welcoming, and buzzing. ⊠ *89 Westbourne Park Rd., Notting Hill* ☎ *020/7221–0021* ⊕ *www.thecowlondon.co.uk* Ⓤ *Royal Oak, Westbourne Park.*

REGENT'S PARK AND HAMPSTEAD

REGENT'S PARK

Camden Arms. On the site of the last fatal duel in Britain, this funky-yet-chill place has plenty of interesting features. Check out the ornate spiral staircase after a good pint of beer. House tunes spun by DJs pervade this pub–lounge every Friday night, and often on Saturday. Modern cocktails are served alongside Thai cuisine. ⊠ *1 Randolph St., Camden* ☎ *020/7267–9829* ⊕ *www.thecamdenarms.com* Ⓤ *Camden.*

HAMPSTEAD

Spaniards Inn. Ideal as a refueling point when you're on a Hampstead Heath hike, this historic oak-beam pub has a gorgeous garden, scene of the tea party in Dickens's *Pickwick Papers.* Dick Turpin, the highwayman, frequented the inn. Before Dickens's time, Shelley, Keats, and Byron hung out here as well. It's extremely popular, especially on Sunday, when Londoners roll in. It's also very dog friendly—there's even a dog wash in the garden. ⊠ *Spaniards Rd., Hampstead* ☎ *020/8731–8406* ⊕ *www.thespaniardshampstead.co.uk* Ⓤ *Hampstead.*

PRIMROSE HILL

Engineer. A gastropub before anyone knew what the term meant, the children-friendly Engineer has an upscale restaurant area (serving breakfast, lunch, and dinner), a stylish carved wooden bar with some good beers on tap, and a garden as well. Expect fresh-cut flowers, a modern British menu on the chalkboard, and lots of young, beautiful people. ⊠ *65 Gloucester Ave., Primrose Hill* ☎ *020/7722–0950* ⊕ *www. the-engineer.com* Ⓤ *Chalk Farm.*

16

SOUTHBANK

Fodor's Choice
★

Anchor & Hope. One of London's most popular gastropubs, the Anchor & Hope doesn't take reservations (except for Sunday lunch), meaning queuing would-be diners snake around the red-walled, wooden-floored pub, kept happy by some good real ales and a fine wine list as they wait for hours for a table. The food is old-fashioned English (think salt cod, tripe, and chips) with a few modern twists. ⊠ *36 The Cut, South Bank* ☎ *020/7928–9898* Ⓤ *Southwark.*

The George Inn. This Southwark pub has quite a history: Shakespeare drank here, Dickens featured it in his writing, and it's the last galleried inn in London. Now owned by the National Trust, it has a cobblestoned courtyard, which can be a great place for a drink when the weather's good and there aren't too many passing tour parties. Inside, several small, low-ceilinged rooms lead through to a middling restaurant, but some say the best way to soak up all the atmosphere is with some pints at the bar. ⊠ *77 Borough High St., South Bank* ☎ *020/7407–2056* Ⓤ *London Bridge.*

Mayflower. An atmospheric 17th-century riverside inn (rebuilt in the following century) with exposed beams and a terrace, this is practically the very place from which the Pilgrims set sail for Plymouth Rock in 1620. The pub has a jetty where customers can sit or opt to enjoy the quaint wood-beamed interiors, although its rooms can get quite packed with sightseers. ⊠ *117 Rotherhithe St., South Bank* ☎ *020/7237–4088* Ⓤ *Rotherhithe.*

COVENT GARDEN AND SOHO

COVENT GARDEN

Harp. This is the sort of friendly little local you might find on some out-of-the-way backstreet, except that it's right in the middle of town, between Trafalgar Square and Covent Garden. As a result, the Harp can get crowded, but the squeeze is worth it for the excellent real ales (there are usually eight traditional ales available, often featuring rare) and a no-frills menu of high-quality British sausages, cooked behind the bar. ⊠ *47 Chandos Pl., Covent Garden* ☎ *020/7836–0291* Ⓤ *Charing Cross.*

Lamb & Flag. This refreshingly un-gentrified 17th-century pub was once known as the Bucket of Blood because the upstairs room was used as a ring for bare-knuckle boxing. Now it's a friendly—and bloodless— pub, serving food (lunch only) and real ale. It's on the edge of Covent Garden, off Garrick Street. ⊠ *33 Rose St., Covent Garden* ☎ *020/7497– 9504* Ⓤ *Covent Garden.*

★ **White Hart.** This elegant, family-owned pub on Drury Lane is one of the best places to mix with cast and crew of the stage. A female-friendly environment, a cheery skylight above the lounge area, a late license, and above-average pub fare make the White Hart a particularly sociable spot for a drink. ⊠ *191 Drury La., Covent Garden* ☎ *020/7242–2317* ⊕ *www.whitehartdrurylane.co.uk* Ⓤ *Holborn, Covent Garden, Tottenham Court Rd.*

SOHO

French House. In the pub where the French Resistance convened during World War II, Soho hipsters and eccentrics rub shoulders now with theater people and the literati—more than shoulders, actually, because this tiny, tricolor-waving, photograph-lined pub is almost always packed. Note that in French style, beer is served here in half-pints only. ⊠ *49 Dean St., Soho* ☎ *020/7437–2799* ⊕ *www.frenchhousesoho.com* Ⓤ *Tottenham Court Rd.*

THE THAMES UPSTREAM

HAMMERSMITH

Blue Anchor. This unaltered Georgian pub has been seen in the movie *Sliding Doors* and was the site where *The Planets* composer Gustav Holst wrote his *Hammersmith Suite.* Sit out by the river, or shelter inside with a good ale. ⊠ *13 Lower Mall, Hammersmith* ☎ *020/8748– 5774* ⊕ *www.blueanchorlondon.com* Ⓤ *Hammersmith.*

Dove Inn. Read the list of famous ex-regulars, from Charles II and Nell Gwyn to Ernest Hemingway, as you wait for a beer at this smart, comely, and popular 16th-century riverside pub by Hammersmith Bridge. After a few pints you can practice your singing skills to the English patriotic song that was composed here, "Rule, Britannia!" If (as is often the case) the Dove is too full, stroll upstream along the bank to the Old Ship or the Blue Anchor. ⊠ *19 Upper Mall, Hammersmith* ☎ *020/8748–9474* Ⓤ *Hammersmith.*

Order a pint at the 17th-century Lamb & Flag pub in Covent Garden.

RICHMOND

Roebuck. Perched on top of Richmond Hill, the Roebuck has perhaps the best view of any pub in London. The most sought-after seats are the benches found directly across the road, which look out over the Thames as it winds its way into the countryside below. Friendly and surprisingly unpretentious, given its lofty surrounds, it is well worth the long climb up the hill from the center of Richmond. ⊠ *130 Richmond Hill, Richmond* ☎ *020/8948–2329* Ⓤ *Richmond.*

NIGHTLIFE

As is true of nearly all cosmopolitan centers, the pace with which bars and clubs go in and out of fashion in London is mind-boggling. The dreaded velvet rope has been usurped by the doorbell-ringing mystique of members-only drinking clubs and the understated glamour of North London's Primrose Hill, which makes movie stars feel so at ease, might be considered dull by the über-trendy club goers of London's East End. In addition, the price of a pint in Chelsea would be dubbed blasphemous by the musicians and poets of racially diverse Brixton. Meanwhile, some of the city's most talked-about nightlife spots are turning out to be those attached to some of its best restaurants and hotels—no wonder, when you consider the increased popularity of London cuisine in international circles. Moreover, the gay scene in London continues to flourish.

Whatever your pleasure, however your whim turns come evening, chances are you'll find what you're looking for in London's ever-changing arena of activity and invention.

BARS

Today the London bar scene is known for its bizarre blends, its pioneering panache, and its highly stylish regulars. Time was, bars in London were just a stopover in an evening full of fun—perhaps the pub first, then a bar, and then it's off to boogie the night away at the nearest dance club. These days, however, bars have become less pit stops and more all-night and all-day destinations in themselves. With the addition of dinner menus, DJs, dance floors, and the still-new later opening hours, people now stay into the wee small hours of the morning at many of London's most fashionable bars. From exotic spaces designed to look like African villages to classic Art Deco creations to cavernous structures housed in old railway stations, London's bar culture is as diverse as it is delicious.

COMEDY AND CABARET

From renowned comedians such as Eddie Izzard to amateurs who try their luck on stage, there are plenty of comedy and cabaret acts to keep you entertained all night long.

DANCE CLUBS

The city that practically invented raves is always on the verge of creating something new, and on any given night there's a club playing the latest in dance music. Because London is so ethnically diverse, the tunes that emanate from the DJ box are equally varied—an amalgamation of sounds infusing drum 'n' bass, hip-hop, deep house, Latin house, breakbeat, indie, and R&B.

The club scene here ranges from mammoth-size playgrounds like Fabric and Cargo to more intimate venues where you can actually hear your friends talk. Check the daily listings in *Time Out* for "club nights," which are theme nights that take place the same night every week, sometimes at the same clubs but often shifting locations. Another good way to learn about club nights is by picking up flyers in your favorite bar.

ECLECTIC MUSIC

The eclectic music scene in London is constantly becoming more mishmashed—the electro scene has evolved into the "nu rave" scene, and the constant arrival of new bands adds to the capital's already diverse music scene.

JAZZ AND BLUES

Jazz in London is highly eclectic. You can expect anything from danceable, smooth tunes played at a supper club to groovy New Orleans–style blues to exotic world-beat rhythms, which can be heard at some of the less central venues throughout the capital. London hosts the **London Jazz Festival** (⊕ *www.londonjazzfestival.org.uk*) in November, which showcases top and emerging artists in experimental jazz. The **Ealing Jazz Festival** (⊕ *www.ealing.gov.uk*), at the end of July, claims to be the biggest free jazz event in Europe.

ROCK

Ever since the Beatles hit the world stage in the early 1960s, London has been at the epicenter of rock and roll. The city is a given stop on any burgeoning or established band's international tour. These days, since rock clubs have been granted later licenses, many shows now go past 11 pm. Fans here are both loyal and enthusiastic. It is, therefore, a good idea to buy show tickets ahead of time. The "Gigs and Tickets" section on ⊕ *www.nme.com* is a comprehensive search engine where you can easily book tickets online; *Time Out* is another good source for upcoming shows.

BLOOMSBURY, FITZROVIA

BLOOMSBURY

BARS

All Star Lanes. One of London's most chic bars is an unlikely combination—it's in a sleek, underground, retro bowling alley in the heart of literary Bloomsbury. Here, surrounded by 1950s Americana, you can sit on the red leather seats and choose from the largest selection of bourbons in London. DJs play on Friday and Saturday nights and there are also locations in Bayswater and Brick Lane. ⊠ *Victoria House, Bloomsbury Pl., Bloomsbury* ☎ *020/7025–2676* ⊕ *www.allstarlanes. co.uk* ⊗ *Mon.–Wed. 5 pm–11:30 pm, Thurs. 5–midnight, Fri. and Sat. noon–2 am, Sun. noon–11* Ⓤ *Holborn.*

ROCK

Water Rats. This high-spirited pub hosted Bob Dylan on his 1963 tour, as well as the first Oasis gig. Alt-country, hip-hop, and indie guitar bands thrash it out most nights of the week. ⊠ *328 Gray's Inn Rd., Bloomsbury* ☎ *020/7837–7269* ⊕ *www.themonto.com* ☎ *£6 and up* ⊗ *Mon.–Sat. noon–11:30* Ⓤ *King's Cross.*

SOHO

ECLECTIC MUSIC

12 Bar Club. This rough-and-ready acoustic club hosts notable singer-songwriters. Four different acts of new folk, contemporary country, blues, and even ska and punk perform each night in the intimate venue. There's a good selection of bottled beer and gastropub food here. ⊠ *22–23 Denmark Pl., Soho* ☎ *020/7240–2622* ⊕ *www.12barclub. com* ☎ *£3–£10* ⊗ *Fri. and Sat. 7 pm–3 am, Sun. 6 pm–12:30 am. Café serves food 9–9* Ⓤ *Tottenham Court Rd.*

FITZROVIA

Fodor'sChoice
★

Crazy Bear. This sexy basement bar with cowhide stools and croc-skin tables feels like Casablanca in Fitzrovia. As you enter Crazy Bear, a spiral staircase leads to a mirrored parlor over which presides a 1947 Murano chandelier. But don't let the opulence fool you: Waitstaff here are warm and welcoming to an all-ages international crowd abuzz with chatter. The menu advertises high quality Thai, Chinese, and Japanese food alongside the drinks. ⊠ *26–28 Whitfield St., Fitzrovia* ☎ *020/7631–0088* ⊕ *www.crazybeargroup.co.uk* ⊗ *Sun.–Wed. noon–midnight, Thurs.–Sat. noon–1 am* Ⓤ *Goodge St.*

16

THE GAY SCENE

The U.K. capital's gay and lesbian culture is as thriving as it is in New York or Los Angeles, with Soho serving as the hub of gay London.

Clubs in London cater to almost every desire, whether that be the suited-up Tommy Hilfiger–look-alike scene, cruisers taking on dingy dives, flamboyant drag shows, lesbian tea dances, or themed fetish nights.

There's also a cornucopia of queer theater and performance art that runs throughout the year. Whatever your tastes, you'll be able to satisfy them with a night on the town in London.

Choices are admittedly much better for males than females here; although many of the gay clubs are female-friendly, those catering strictly to lesbians are in the minority.

The British Film Institute puts on the BFI London Lesbian and Gay Film Festival in late March and early April (⊕ www.bfi.org.uk./llgff/) every year.

Pride London in June (an annual event encompassing a parade, sports, art, comedy, theater, music, cabaret, and dance) welcomes anyone and everyone, and claimed a million participants in 2010.

This extravagant pageant spirals its way through London's streets, with major events taking place in Trafalgar Square and Leicester Square, then culminates in Victoria Embankment with ticketed parties continuing on afterward (⊕ www.pridelondon.org for details).

For up-to-date listings, consult *Time Out* (⊕ www.timeout.com/london/gay), *Boyz* (⊕ www.boyz.co.uk),

Gay Times (⊕ www.gaytimes.co.uk), *Attitude* (⊕ www.attitude.co.uk), or the lesbian monthly *Diva* (⊕ www.divamag.co.uk).

Online resources include Rainbow Network (⊕ www.rainbownetwork.com).

Trade. This London institution among the hedonistic muscle boys is now more than a decade old, and begins when many clubs are closing. The Trade brand has events all over the country—check online for dates. Most of the London events take place at the Ministry of Sound. ■TIP➔ Its schedule is irregular, so check the Web site for dates. ☎ 020/7609–8364 ⊕ www.tradeuk.net ⌂ £15 in advance (book at www.ticketweb.co.uk), £18 at door ⊗ Days vary, 6 am–4 pm.

BARS, CAFÉS, AND PUBS
Most bars in London are gay-friendly, though there are a number of cafés and pubs that are known as gay hangouts after-hours. The latest serve drinks until 3 am (11 pm on Sunday).

CLUBS
Many of London's best gay dance clubs are in mixed clubs like Fabric on theme nights designated for gays.

Almost all dance clubs in London are gay-friendly, but if you want to cruise or mingle only with other gays, it's best to call ahead or check Web-site listings.

Long Bar at Sanderson Hotel. The 80-foot-long shimmering white onyx island bar in the Philippe Starck–designed Sanderson Hotel attracts a cliquish and trendy crowd. The large but welcoming outdoor area exudes a Zen-like feel, with soothing running water mixed with dim lighting and decorative vegetation providing a truly relaxing experience. For a more intimate and romantic setting, the hotel's **Purple Bar** serves excellent chocolate martinis. ⊠ *50 Berners St., Fitzrovia* ☎ *020/7300–1444* ⊕ *www.sandersonlondon.com* ⊘ *Mon. 11 am–1 am, Tues. and Wed. 11 am–1:30 am, Thurs.–Sat. 11 am–3 am, Sun. noon–10:30 pm* Ⓤ *Oxford Circus.*

THE EAST END

HOXTON

DANCE CLUBS

Fabric. This sprawling subterranean club is now a firm fixture on the London scene. "Fabric Live" hosts drum 'n' bass, dubstep, and hip-hop crews and live acts on Friday; international big-name DJs play slow, sexy bass lines and cutting-edge music on Saturday. The devastating sound system and "bodysonic" dance floor ensure that bass riffs vibrate through your entire body. ■ TIP➔ Get there early to avoid a lengthy queue, and don't wear a suit. ⊠ *77A Charterhouse St., East End* ☎ *020/7336–8898* ⊕ *www.fabriclondon.com* ⊡ *£13–£16* ⊘ *Fri. 10 pm–6 am, Sat. 11 pm–8 am, Sun. 11 pm–6 am* Ⓤ *Farringdon.*

SHOREDITCH

BARS

Book Club. Light and friendly, the Book Club is a fine example of Shoreditch's fashionable industrial chic with an extra dose of culture on top. White tiles, bricks, and big black and white photos set the tone and there's a separate room for table-tennis. Breakfast is served morning weekdays, a full lunch menu is offered through the week, and a modern menu of cocktails accompanies music, book launches, and workshops in the evenings. ⊠ *100 Leonard St., Shoreditch* ☎ *020/7684–8618* ⊕ *www.wearetbc.com* ⊘ *Mon.–Wed. 8 am–midnight, Thurs.–Sat. 8 am–2 am, Sun. 10 am–midnight.*

DANCE CLUBS

Cargo. Housed under a series of old railway arches, this vast brick-wall bar, restaurant, dance floor, and live-music venue pulls a young, international crowd with its hip vibe and diverse selection of music. Long tables bring people together, as does the food, which draws on global influences and is served tapas-style. ⊠ *83 Rivington St., Shoreditch* ☎ *020/7739–3440* ⊕ *www.cargo-london.com* ⊡ *Free–£20* ⊘ *Mon.–Thurs. noon–1 am, Fri. noon–3 am, Sat. 6 pm–3 am, Sun. 1 pm–midnight* Ⓤ *Old St.*

333. The last word in dance music for the trendy Shoreditch crowd. Fashionable bright young things dance to drum 'n' bass, twisted disco, and underground dance genres. There are three floors, each with its own theme. You can chill on leather sofas at the relaxed Mother Bar upstairs, open from 8 pm daily, which always has DJs. ⊠ *333 Old St., Shoreditch* ☎ *020/7739–5949* ⊕ *www.333mother.com* ⊡ *Free–£10* ⊘ *Fri. and Sat. 10 pm–3 am, bar Mon.–Sun., 8 pm–3 am* Ⓤ *Old St.*

16

KENSINGTON, CHELSEA, AND KNIGHTSBRIDGE

CHELSEA

JAZZ AND BLUES

606 Club. Expect a civilized Chelsea club that showcases mainstream and contemporary jazz by well-known British-based musicians. ■TIP→ You must eat a meal in order to consume alcohol, so allow for an extra £20. Reservations are advisable. Sunday lunchtime jazz takes place once or twice a month; call ahead. ⊠ *90 Lots Rd., Chelsea* ☎ *020/7352–5953* ⊕ *www.606club.co.uk* 🔊 *£8–£12 music charge added to bill* ☉ *Mon. 7:30 pm–12:30 am, Tues.–Thurs. 7 pm–12:30 am, Fri. and Sat. 8 pm–1:30 am, Sun. 7 pm–midnight* Ⓤ *Earl's Court, Fulham Broadway.*

KNIGHTSBRIDGE

BARS

Fodor's Choice   **The Blue Bar at the Berkeley Hotel.** With low-slung gray-blue walls this
★   hotel bar is ever so slightly sexy. Immaculate service, an excellent cocktail list—try the Sex in the City—and a trendy David Collins design, make this an ideal spot for a secretive tête-à-tête, complete with jazzy music in the background. ⊠ *Wilton Pl., Knightsbridge* ☎ *020/291–1680* ⊕ *the-berkeley.co.uk* ☉ *Mon. 4 pm–1 am, Tues.–Sat. 9 am–1 am, Sun. 4–11 pm* Ⓤ *Knightsbridge.*

NOTTING HILL

NOTTING HILL

BARS

Beach Blanket Babylon. In a Georgian house in Notting Hill, close to Portobello Market, this always-packed bar is distinguishable by its eclectic indoor-outdoor spaces with Gaudí-esque curves and snuggly corners—like a fairy-tale grotto or a medieval dungeon. A sister restaurant-bar-gallery offers a slightly more modern take on similar themes in an ex-warehouse in Shoreditch (at 19 Bethnal Green Road). ⊠ *45 Ledbury Rd., Notting Hill* ☎ *020/7229–2907* ⊕ *www. beachblanket.co.uk* ☉ *Mon.–Sat. noon–midnight, Sun. noon–11:30 pm* Ⓤ *Notting Hill Gate.*

DANCE CLUBS

★   **Notting Hill Arts Club.** Rock stars like Liam Gallagher and Courtney Love have been seen at this small basement club-bar. An alternative crowd swills beer to eclectic music that spans Asian underground, hip-hop, Latin-inspired funk, deep house, and jazzy grooves. What it lacks in looks it makes up for in mood. ⊠ *21 Notting Hill Gate, Notting Hill* ☎ *020/7460–4459* ⊕ *www.nottinghillartsclub.com* 🔊 *Free–£8* ☉ *Weekdays 7 pm–2 am, Sat. 4 pm–2 am, Sun. 4 pm–1 am* Ⓤ *Notting Hill Gate.*

Cargo dance club is a huge venue for live music of all types.

ST. JAMES'S AND MAYFAIR

MAYFAIR

BARS

Claridge's Bar. This elegant Mayfair meeting place remains unpretentious even when it brims with beautiful people. The bar has an Art Deco heritage made hip by the sophisticated touch of designer David Collins. A library of rare champagnes and brandies as well as a delicious choice of traditional and exotic cocktails—try the Flapper or the Black Pearl—will occupy your taste buds. Request a glass of vintage Cristal in the Macanudo Fumoir. ⊠ *55 Brook St., Mayfair* ☎ *020/7629–8860* ⊕ *www.claridges.co.uk* ⊗ *Mon.–Sat. noon–1 am, Sun. noon–midnight* Ⓤ *Bond St.*

DANCE CLUBS

Vendome Mayfair. This classy club draws a trendy crowd for house music, colorful furnishings, and futuristic designs with '70s retro disco decor. The revolving DJ booth at the center of the club, the Renaissance-like entrance, the individually themed booths, and the faux snakeskin banisters shout out pure decadence. ⊠ *85 Piccadilly, Mayfair* ☎ *020/495–2595* ⊕ *www.vendomemayfair.com* ⊠ *£20* ⊗ *Mon., Tues., and Thurs. 10 pm–3 am, Fri. and Sat. 10 pm–4 am.*

JAZZ AND BLUES

Dover Street Restaurant & Jazz Bar. Put on your blue-suede shoes and prepare to dance the night away—that is, after you've feasted from the French Mediterranean menu. Fun for dates as well as groups, Dover Street Restaurant has three bars, a DJ, and a stage with the latest live bands performing everything from jazz to soul to R&B, all this

The Thameside Bulls Head has live jazz every night.

encircling linen-covered tables with a friendly staff catering to your every whim. ✉ *8–10 Dover St., Mayfair* ☎ *020/7491–7509* ⊕ *www. doverst.co.uk* 💷 *Free–£15* 🕐 *Mon.–Thurs. noon–3 pm and 5:30 pm–3 am, Fri. noon–3 pm and 7 pm–3 am, Sat. 7 pm–3 am* Ⓤ *Green Park.*

ST. JAMES'S
BARS

★ **American Bar.** Festooned with a chin-dropping array of club ties, signed celebrity photographs, sporting mementos, and baseball caps, this sensational hotel cocktail bar has superb martinis. ■ TIP→ Jacket required. ✉ *Stafford Hotel, 16–18 St. James's Pl., St. James's* ☎ *020/518–1253* ⊕ *www.thestaffordhotel.co.uk* 🕐 *Weekdays 11:30–11, weekends noon–11* Ⓤ *Green Park.*

THE SOUTH

BRIXTON
BARS

★ **Dogstar.** This popular South London hangout is frequented by local hipsters and counterculture types. It was the first DJ bar in the world and has since enjoyed a fabulous reputation. The vibe at this "surrealist boudoir" is unpretentious, with top-name DJs playing cutting-edge sounds every night (free Tuesday–Thursday). ✉ *389 Coldharbour La., Brixton* ☎ *020/7733–7515* ⊕ *www.antic-ltd.com/dogstar* 💷 *Free–£8* 🕐 *Tues.–Thurs. 4 pm–2 am, Fri. 4 pm–4 am, Sat. noon–4 am, Sun. noon–2 am* Ⓤ *Brixton.*

DANCE CLUBS

Mass. In what was previously St. Matthew's Church (whose crypt holds the Babalou bar), Mass is an atmospheric club with Gothic overtones. Winding stone steps lead to the main room where an extended balcony hangs over the dance floor. An unpretentious and friendly crowd dances, on rotating club nights, to reggae, drum 'n' bass, and R&B. ☒ *Brixton Hill, St. Matthew's Church, Brixton* ☎ *020/7738–7875* ⊕ *www.mass-club.com* 🎫 *£5–£20* ⊙ *Wed. and Thurs. 10 pm–2 am, Fri. and Sat. 9 pm–6 am* Ⓤ *Brixton.*

ECLECTIC MUSIC

Fodor'sChoice **O2 Academy Brixton.** This legendary Brixton venue has seen it all—mods
★ and rockers, hippies and punks. Despite a capacity for almost 5,000 people, this refurbished Victorian hall with original Art Deco fixtures retains a clublike charm; it has plenty of bars and upstairs seating. ☒ *211 Stockwell Rd., Brixton* ☎ *020/7771–3000* ⊕ *www.brixton-academy.co.uk* 🎫 *£10–£50* ⊙ *Opening hrs vary* Ⓤ *Brixton.*

SOUTH BANK

DANCE CLUBS

Ministry of Sound. It's more of an industry than a club, with its own record label, online radio station, and international DJs. The stripped-down warehouse-style club has a super sound system and pulls in the world's most legendary names in dance. There are chill-out rooms, two bars, and three dance floors. ☒ *103 Gaunt St., South Bank* ☎ *020/740–8600* ⊕ *www.ministryofsound.com* 🎫 *£15–£23* ⊙ *Fri. 10:30 pm–6 am, Sat. 11 pm–7 am* Ⓤ *Elephant & Castle.*

16

SOHO AND COVENT GARDEN

LEICESTER SQUARE

BARS

Le Beaujolais. Around 60 lovingly selected French wines are available here, where you can snack on olives, charcuterie, and homemade *croque monsieur* (grilled ham and cheese) sandwiches while snug and warm under the bottle-laden ceiling as a funky blues sound track plays. It's a romantic little spot and can get crowded just before theater performances, but it has room again once the shows begin. ☒ *25 Litchfield St., Leicester Square* ☎ *020/7836–2955* ⊙ *Weekdays noon–11, Sat. 5–11* Ⓤ *Leicester Sq.*

★ **Le Salon Bar.** Renowned chef Joël Robuchon's intimate, relaxed, and elegant bar with red undertones is in the same premises as his L'Atelier and La Cuisine restaurants. New cocktails await you, as the drink menu changes every six months, with new flavors and textures sure to entice your taste buds. If you're feeling generous, treat yourself to an unforgettable dinner at the restaurant pre- or post-drinks—try the Fois Gras Chaud. ☒ *13–15 West St., Leicester Square* ☎ *020/7010–8600* ⊕ *www.joel-robuchon.com* ⊙ *Mon.–Sat. 2:30 pm–2 am, Sun. 2:30 pm–10:30 pm* Ⓜ *Leicester Sq.*

COVENT GARDEN

BARS

Cafe des Amis. This relaxed basement wine bar near the Royal Opera House is the perfect pre- or post-theater spot, popular among musicians and performers alike—and a friendly enough place to go on your own. More than 30 wines are served by the glass, along with a good selection of cheeses and plates of charcuterie as well as more substantial dishes for those with more of an appetite (there's also a French restaurant with a Mediterranean twist on the ground floor serving everything from moules marinieres to risotto). ⊠ *11–14 Hanover Pl., Covent Garden* ☎ *020/7379–3444* ⊕ *www.cafedesamis.co.uk* ⊗ *Mon.–Sat. 11:30 am–1 am* Ⓤ *Covent Garden.*

THE GAY SCENE

Fodor'sChoice
★
Heaven. With by far the best light show on any London dance floor, Heaven is unpretentious, loud, and huge, with a labyrinth of rooms, bars, and live-music parlors. Friday and Saturday nights there's a gay comedy night (£10 in advance, 7–10 pm). If you go to just one gay club, Heaven should be it. ⊠ *The Arches, Villiers St., Covent Garden* ☎ *020/7930–2020* ⊕ *www.heaven-london.com* 🖃 *£4–£12* ⊗ *Mon. 11 pm–6 am, Tues.–Thurs. 11 pm–5 am, Wed. 10:30 pm–4 am, Fri. 11 pm–5 am, Sat. 10:30 pm–5 am* Ⓤ *Charing Cross, Embankment.*

SOHO

BARS

★
Nordic. With shooters called "Husky Poo" and "Danish Bacon Surprise" and crayfish tails and meatballs on the smorgasbord menu, Nordic takes its Scandinavian feel the whole way. This secluded, shabby-chic bar serves many couples cozied up among travel brochures promoting the Viking lands. If you can't decide what to drink, the cocktail roulette wheel on the wall may help. ⊠ *25 Newman St., Soho* ☎ *020/7631–3174* ⊕ *www.nordicbar.com* ⊗ *Mon.–Thurs. noon–11 pm, Fri. noon–midnight, Sat. 6 pm–midnight* Ⓤ *Tottenham Court Rd.*

Sketch. At this esoteric living room bar one seat never looks like the next. A patisserie during the day, the exclusive Parlour Bar exudes plenty of rarefied charm while the intimate East Bar at the back is reminiscent of a sci-fi film set. ⊠ *9 Conduit St., Soho* ☎ *020/7659–4500* ⊕ *www.sketch.uk.com* ⊗ *Parlour Bar Mon.–Thurs. 6:30–10 pm, Fri. and Sat. 6:30–9 pm, members only after 9 pm; East Bar Mon.–Thurs. 6 pm–1 am, Fri. and Sat. 6 pm–2 am* Ⓤ *Oxford Circus.*

COMEDY AND CABARET

Amused Moose. This Soho basement/retro nightclub is widely considered the best place to see breaking talent as well as household names doing "secret" shows. Ricky Gervais, Eddie Izzard, and Russell Brand are among those who have graced this stage, and every summer a handful of the Edinburgh Fringe comedians preview here. The bar is open late (and serves food), and there's a DJ and dancing until 5 am after the show. Tickets are often discounted with a printout from their Web site, and shows are mainly on Saturday. ⊠ *Moonlighting, 17 Greek St., Soho* ☎ *020/7287–3727* ⊕ *www.amusedmoose.com* 🖃 *£9 and up* ⊗ *Doors open at 7:30 pm* Ⓤ *Tottenham Court Rd.*

★ **Comedy Store.** Known as the birthplace of alternative comedy, this is where the United Kingdom's funniest stand-ups have cut their teeth before being launched onto prime-time TV. Comedy Store Players, a team with six comedians doing improvisation with audience suggestions, entertain audiences on Wednesday and Sunday; the Cutting Edge team steps in every Tuesday; and on the last Monday of every month the King Gong show (£5) hits the stage, where amateur comedians try their luck. Thursday, Friday, and Saturday have the best stand-up acts. There's also a bar with food. ■ TIP➜ Tickets can be booked through Ticketmaster or over the phone. Note that children under 18 are not admitted to this venue. ⊠ *1A Oxendon St., Soho* ☎ *0844/847–1728* ⊕ *www.thecomedystore.co.uk* ⊠ *£13–£18* ⊘ *Shows daily 8 pm, with extra shows Fri. and Sat. at midnight* Ⓤ *Piccadilly Circus, Leicester Sq.*

100 Club. Since it opened in 1942, all the greats have played here, from Glenn Miller and Louis Armstrong on down to the best traditional jazz artists, British and American blues, R&B, and punk. This cool, inexpensive club now reverberates to rock, indie, and R&B—as well as jazz, of course. You can still take jitterbug and jive lessons from the London Swing Dance Society. ⊠ *100 Oxford St., Soho* ☎ *020/7636–0933* ⊕ *www.the100club.co.uk* ⊠ *£7–£15* ⊘ *Mon. 7:30–midnight, Tues.–Thurs. 7:30–11, Fri. 7:30 pm–12:30 am, Sat. 7:30 pm–2 am, Sun. 7:30–11* Ⓤ *Oxford Circus, Tottenham Court Rd.*

JAZZ AND BLUES

Ain't Nothin' but . . . The Blues Bar. The name sums up this bar that whips up a sweaty environment. Local musicians, as well as some notable names, squeeze onto the tiny stage. There's good bar food of the chili-and-gumbo variety. Most weekday nights there's no cover. ⊠ *20 Kingly St., Soho* ☎ *020/7287–0514* ⊕ *www.aintnothinbut.co.uk* ⊠ *Free–£5* ⊘ *Mon.–Thurs. 6 pm–1 am, Fri. 5 pm–3 am, Sat. 3 pm–3 am, Sun. 3 pm–midnight* Ⓤ *Oxford Circus.*

Fodor'sChoice **Pizza Express Jazz Club Soho.** One of the capital's most ubiquitous pizza ★ chains also runs a great Soho jazz venue. The dimly lighted restaurant hosts top-quality international jazz acts every night. The Italian-style thin-crust pizzas are good, too, though on the small side. ⊠ *10 Dean St., Soho* ☎ *0845/602–7017* ⊕ *www.pizzaexpresslive.com* ⊠ *£10–£25* ⊘ *Daily from 11:30 am for food; music 7:30 pm–11 pm* Ⓤ *Tottenham Court Rd.*

Ronnie Scott's. Since the 1960s, this legendary jazz club has attracted big names. It's usually crowded and hot, the food isn't great, and service is slow—but the mood can't be beat, even since the sad departure of its eponymous founder and saxophonist. Reservations are recommended. ⊠ *47 Frith St., Soho* ☎ *020/7439–0747* ⊕ *www.ronniescotts.co.uk* ⊠ *£20–£36 nonmembers, 20% off for members, annual membership £175* ⊘ *Mon.–Sat. 6 pm–3 am, Sun. 6:30 pm–11 pm* Ⓤ *Leicester Sq.*

THE GAY SCENE

Box. True to its name, this modern, industrial-chic café–bar is small and square. It's a staple on the preclub circuit and gets packed to the hilt with muscular men. For peckish punters, food is served until 9 pm (except on Saturday until 5 pm) daily. ⊠ *32–34 Monmouth St.,*

16

Soho ☎ *020/7240–5828* ⊕ *www.boxbar.com* ⊘ *Weekdays noon–11, weekends noon–10:30* Ⓤ *Leicester Sq.*

Candy Bar. The United Kingdom's first girls' bar is intimate, chilled, and cruisey, with DJs mixing the latest sounds. Pole dancing and striptease are now also features on some nights. Men are welcome only as guests. ✉ *4 Carlisle St., Soho* ☎ *020/7287–5041* ⊕ *www.candybarsoho.com* 🖃 *Obligatory £5 membership fee* ⊘ *Mon.–Wed. 4 pm–1 am, Thurs. 4 pm–3 am, Fri. and Sat. 3 pm–3 am, Sun. 4 pm–12:30 am* Ⓤ *Tottenham Court Rd.*

Fodor's Choice
★ **Friendly Society.** This haute moderne hot spot hops with activity almost any night of the week; the basement feels a bit like something out of *Star Trek* with its white-leather pod seats. The place is known for being gay yet female-friendly. ✉ *79 Wardour St., Soho* ☎ *020/7434–3805* ⊘ *Weekdays 4–11, Sat. 2–11, Sun. 2–10:30* Ⓤ *Leicester Sq.*

Rupert Street. For smart boyz, this gay chic island among the sleaze has a lounge feel with brown-leather sofas and floor-to-ceiling windows. It's crowded and cruisey at night with preclubbers, civilized and café-like by day: a good spot for brunch. Traditional British food is served until 10 pm. ✉ *50 Rupert St., Soho* ☎ *020/7494–3059* ⊘ *Mon.–Wed. noon–11, Thurs.–Sat. noon–11:30, Sun. noon–10:30* Ⓤ *Leicester Sq., Piccadilly Circus.*

★ **The Shadow Lounge.** This fabulous little lounge and dance club glitters with faux jewels and twinkling fiber-optic lights over its sunken dance floor, which comes complete with pole for those inclined to do their thing around it. It has a serious A-list celebrity factor, with the glamorous London glitterati camping out in the VIP booth. Members are given entrance priority when the place gets full, especially on weekends, so show up early or prepare to queue. Free entry on Monday. ✉ *5 Brewer St., Soho* ☎ *020/7287–7988* ⊕ *www.theshadowlounge.co.uk* 🖃 *£5–£10* ⊘ *Mon.–Sat. 10 pm–3 am* Ⓤ *Leicester Sq.*

REGENT'S PARK AND HAMPSTEAD

CAMDEN

DANCE CLUBS

★ **KOKO.** This Victorian theater, formerly known as Camden Palace, has seen acts from Charlie Chaplin to Madonna, and genres from punk to rave. Updated with lush reds not unlike a cockney Moulin Rouge, this is still one of London's most stunning venues. Sounds of live indie rock, cabaret, funky house, and club classics keep the big dance floor moving, even when it's not heaving. ✉ *1A Camden High St., Camden Town* ☎ *0870/432–5527* ⊕ *www.koko.uk.com* 🖃 *£3–£20* ⊘ *Opening hrs vary, depending on shows* Ⓤ *Mornington Crescent.*

JAZZ AND BLUES

★ **Jazz Café.** A palace of high-tech cool in bohemian Camden—it remains an essential hangout for fans of both the mainstream end of the repertoire and hip-hop, funk, rap, and Latin fusion. Book ahead if you want a prime table overlooking the stage, in the balcony restaurant. ✉ *5 Pkwy., Camden Town* ☎ *020/7688–8899 restaurant reservations,*

0870/060–3777 standing tickets ⊕ www.jazzcafe.co.uk ⊟£10–£25 ⊙ Daily 7 pm–2 am ⓤ Camden Town.

ROCK

★ **Barfly Club.** At one of the finest small clubs in the capital, punk, indie guitar bands, and new metal rock attract a nonmainstream crowd. Weekend club nights upstairs host DJs (and live bands) who rock the decks. The Baryfly's sister club, **The Fly,** is at 36/38 New Oxford Street. ⊠ *49 Chalk Farm Rd., Camden Town* ☎ *020/7688–8994* ⊕ *www.barflyclub. com* ⊟ *£5–£8* ⊙ *Mon. and Tues. 7–midnight, Wed. and Thurs. 7 pm–2 am, Fri. and Sat. 7 pm–3 am* ⓤ *Camden Town, Chalk Farm.*

ISLINGTON

ECLECTIC

★ **Union Chapel.** This beautiful old chapel has excellent acoustics and sublime architecture. The beauty of the space and its impressive multicultural programming have made it one of London's best musical venues, especially for acoustic shows. Performers have included Björk, Beck, and Goldfrapp, though now you're more likely to hear lower-key alternative country, world music, and jazz. ⊠ *Compton Terr., Islington* ☎ *020/7226–1686* ⊕ *www.unionchapel.org.uk* ⊟ *Free–£25* ⊙ *Opening hrs vary* ⓤ *Highbury & Islington.*

KENTISH TOWN

ROCK

The HMV Forum. The best medium-to-big-name rock performers consistently play at the 2,000-capacity club. It's a converted 1920 Art Deco cinema, with a balcony overlooking the dance floor. Consult the Web site for current listings. ⊠ *9–17 Highgate Rd., Kentish Town* ☎ *020/7428–4099* ⊕ *www.kentishtownforum.com* ⊟ *£12–£25* ⊙ *Opening hrs vary, depending on concert schedule* ⓤ *Kentish Town.*

LITTLE VENICE

COMEDY AND CABARET

Canal Café Theatre. Famous comics and cabaret stars perform every night of the week in this intimate, canal-side venue. The long-running News-Revue is a topical song-and-sketch show every night, Thursday–Sunday. ⊠ *Bridge House, Delamere Terr., Little Venice* ☎ *020/7289–6054* ⊕ *www.canalcafetheatre.com* ⊟ *£5–£11* ⊙ *Mon.–Sat. 7:30–11, Sun. 7–10:30* ⓤ *Warwick Ave., Royal Oak, Paddington.*

WESTMINSTER

CHARING CROSS

BARS

Bedford and Strand. The wine bar enjoyed something of a renaissance in the first decade of the 21st century in London, and this is one of the best of a new generation. It's sunk atmospherically down below the streets of Covent Garden, with dark wood and hanging shades; the wine list is short but well chosen, the service is faultless, and the bistro food is created with plenty of care. ⊠ *1A Bedford St., Charing Cross* ☎ *020/7836–3033* ⊕ *www.bedford-strand.com* ⊙ *Mon.–Sat. noon–midnight* ⓤ *Charing Cross.*

16

HAYMARKET

BARS

The Mint Leaf Bar. Renowned for its long bar, this restaurant's bar–lounge has more than 500 spirits and serves more than 1,000 well-prepared cocktails. Nibbles and light snacks with an Indian twist are available, and if you're up for some more substantial spicy food, treat yourself to a meal at the sophisticated restaurant. There is also a sister bar and restaurant located in Angel Court in The City. ✉ *Suffolk Pl., Haymarket* ☎ *020/7930–9020* ⊕ *www.mintleafrestaurant.com* ☽ *Mon.–Wed. noon–midnight, Thurs. and Fri. noon–1 am, Sat. 5 pm–1 am, Sun. 5 pm–midnight* Ⓤ *Piccadilly Circus.*

VICTORIA

DANCE CLUBS

Pacha. London's version of the Ibizan superclub is in a restored 1920s dance hall next to Victoria Coach Station. The hedonistic surroundings include a (smoking) roof terrace for alfresco clubbing and a state-of-the-art VIP room. The crowd is slightly older than average and stylish, but not necessarily as moneyed as you might expect. ✉ *Terminus Pl., Victoria* ☎ *0845/371–4489* ⊕ *www.pachalondon.com* 🎟 *£5–£20* ☽ *Fri. and Sat. 10 pm–5 am* Ⓤ *Victoria.*

WESTMINSTER

BARS

Cinnamon Club. In the basement of what was once Old Westminster Library, the Club Bar of this contemporary Indian restaurant (treat yourself to a superb curry) has Bollywood scenes playing on a large screen, Asian-theme cocktails (mango mojitos, Delhi mules), delicious bar snacks, and a clientele that includes fashionable young politicos. Upstairs, the Library Bar also serves cocktails through the day. ✉ *The Old Westminster Library, Great Smith St., Westminster* ☎ *020/7222–2555* ⊕ *www.cinnamonclub.com* ☽ *Mon.–Sat. 6–11:45 pm* Ⓤ *Westminster.*

Arts and Entertainment

WORD OF MOUTH

"We bought standing-room tickets to the Proms which go on sale a couple of hours before the concert. You don't really stand but sit on the floor in the top gallery. It's like a big picnic. It was fun!"

—Marija

ARTS AND ENTERTAINMENT PLANNER

Find Out What's Playing Where

To find out what's showing now, the weekly magazine *Time Out* (£2.99, issued every Tuesday) is invaluable.

The newly free *Evening Standard* carries listings, many of which are available online at ⊕ *www.thisislondon.co.uk*. *Metro*, London's other widely available free newspaper, is also worth checking out, as are many Sunday papers, and the Saturday *Independent*, *Guardian*, and *Times*.

You can pick up the free fortnightly *London Theatre Guide* from hotels and tourist-information centers.

There are hundreds of small private galleries all over London with interesting work by famous and not-yet-famous artists.

The bimonthly free pamphlet "new exhibitions of contemporary art" (⊕ *www.newexhibitions. com*), available at most galleries, lists and maps nearly 200 art spaces in London.

Expect to pay around £10 for entry into touring exhibitions, but most permanent displays and commercial galleries are free.

Top Five for the Arts

Stand with the "plebs" in Shakespeare's Globe Theatre. There are seats, but to really experience theater Shakespearean-style you should stand in the yard, with the stage at eye level (plus it's a bargain at £5).

Visit the latest grand art installation in the Turbine Hall at the Tate Modern. The enormity of the Tate's central space either intimidates or inspires artists challenged to fill it.

Catch a world-class performance at the Proms. There's a surprisingly down-to-earth atmosphere among the elated company at these great concerts.

Enjoy a night at the National Film Theatre. Mingle with the real aficionados at screenings of foreign, classic, or experimental films.

Watch a Hollywood star in a West End production. Film stars often come to London to boost their artistic credibility in small-scale theaters.

Top Theater Tips

Behind the pillars. Many theaters and concert halls sell discounted seats with restricted views.

Matinees. Afternoon performances are almost always a better value than evening ones.

Previews. Tickets to shows are usually less expensive in the first few weeks of their run, before the critics have had their say.

Monday. Most cinemas, and some theaters, including the Royal Court, have a reduced-price ticketing policy on Monday.

Standing. The Globe Theatre and the Proms are the two most prominent occasions where remaining upright saves you money.

Updated by
Julius Honnor

"All the world's a stage," said Shakespeare, immortal words heard for the first time right here in London. And whether you prefer your art classical or modern, or as a contemporary twist on a time-honored classic, you'll find that London's vibrant cultural scene holds its own on the world stage.

17

Divas sing original-language librettos at the Royal Opera House, Shakespeare's plays are brought to life at the reconstructed Globe Theatre, and challenging new writing is produced at the Royal Court. Whether you feel like the lighthearted extravagance of a West End musical or the next shark-in-formaldehyde at the White Cube, the choice is yours.

Shakespearean theater and contemporary musicals, enormous art installations and tiny Renaissance portraits, magnificent operas and cutting-edge physical theater—if you're into going out, London will suit your fancy. There are international theater festivals, innovative music festivals, and critically acclaimed seasons of postmodern dance. Short trip or long, you'll find the cultural scene in London is ever-changing, ever-expanding, and ever-exciting.

This chapter is organized, after starting out with a section devoted to the two main performing arts centers in London—the Barbican Centre and the Southbank Centre—by neighborhood, listed alphabetically. Within each neighborhood is a list of the main art or performing arts venue of that city region. In addition, "What's Happening Now" boxes highlight the current state of the arts in each of the main art groups, such as Dance, Theater, Opera, and Film. No matter where you head, you'll find that London's art and performing arts scenes have been setting global trends for decades—and when you include Shakespearian theater and Handel oratorios, for centuries. Fringe theater, classical ballet, participatory chorales, you name it, London probably did it first and often does it best.

Random Dance Company performs at Sadler's Wells.

THE TWO MAIN PERFORMING ARTS CENTERS

Barbican Centre. Opened in 1982, the Brutalist-style Barbican is the largest performing arts center in Europe. Two galleries, three cinemas, and an array of spaces host a wide range of arts while the main concrete theater is most famous as the home of the London Symphony Orchestra. As well as the LSO (⊕ *www.lso.co.uk*), the Barbican is frequent host of the English Chamber Orchestra and the BBC Symphony Orchestra, and has an excellent concert season of big-name virtuosos. Performances by British and international theater companies make up part of its year-round **B.I.T.E.** (Barbican International Theatre Events), which also features groundbreaking performance, dance, drama, and musical theater. Innovative exhibitions of 20th-century and current art and design are shown in the Barbican Gallery and the Curve (✉ *Usually free*). In addition to Hollywood films, obscure classics and film festivals with Screen Talks are programmed in the three cinemas here. Saturday Family Film Club has adventure and animation to please all ages. Just last season at the Barbican, you could catch "The Directorspective" on the films of Michelangelo Antonioni, see "Future Beauty: Thirty Years of Japanese Fashion," check out a "Reggae Britannia" concert, and tune into an array of musical events, all in one evening. ✉ *Silk St., The City* ☎ *020/7382–7000 information, 020/7638–8891 box office* ⊕ *www.barbican.org.uk* ☉ *Mon., Fri. and weekends 11–8, Tues., Wed. 11–6, Thurs. 11–10* Ⓤ *Barbican*.

THE ARTS FOR FREE

CLASSICAL MUSIC AND JAZZ

The Barbican, the Royal National Theatre, and the Royal Opera House often have free music in their foyers or in dedicated spaces, usually of high standard. On the South Bank, free festivals and special performances often take place alongside the river.

Many of London's world-class music colleges give free concerts several times a week. The Royal Academy of Music and the Royal College of Music often have free recitals. St. Martin-in-the-Fields has free lunchtime concerts, as does Christchurch Spitalfields. Other churches, including Westminster Abbey, St. James's Piccadilly, and St. Paul's in Covent Garden, also have frequent free music. For the Proms, which run from July to September at the Royal Albert Hall, good seats are expensive, but hundreds of standing tickets are available at £5: not quite free, but a good value.

CONTEMPORARY MUSIC

Brixton's Dogstar pub has a great selection of DJs playing for free on weekday evenings. Ain't Nothing But the Blues Bar in Soho has live music most nights, often without a cover charge, and pubs such as the Monarch and the Hawley Arms near Camden Market offer the chance to see tomorrow's indie stars today. The largest of the music superstores, such as HMV Oxford Street, have occasional live performances of pop and rock bands, often to accompany album or single launches.

DRAMA AND PERFORMANCE ARTS

Look out for occasional festivals where innovative performances take place on the South Bank. Check the newspapers and *Time Out* for upcoming performances.

MUSEUMS AND GALLERIES

Few if any other cities in the world equal the number of free art venues offered in London. Most of the city's museums and galleries do not charge entrance fees. The monthly *Galleries* magazine, available from galleries themselves or online at ⊕ *www.artefact.co.uk*, has listings for all private galleries in the capital.

PARK LIFE

London's parks come to life in summer with a wide-ranging program of music, dance, and visual arts (⊕ *www.royalparks.gov.uk* for details or ☎ *020/7298–2000*). There are several summer festivals in London parks, some with lots of big-name pop stars, like the Wireless festival in Hyde Park and the somewhat more indie Lovebox in Victoria Park. Notable contemporary art fairs are October's Frieze in Regent's Park (⊕ *www.friezeartfair.com*) and the Affordable Art Fair in Battersea Park (⊕ *www.affordableartfair.com*).

RADIO AND TELEVISION

With so much broadcast material made in London, much of it recorded in front of live audiences, there are often opportunities to watch a free quiz show, current-affairs debate, comedy, or even drama. Check the BBC Web site for forthcoming recordings (⊕ *www.bbc.co.uk/tickets*). **Hat Trick Productions** (☎ *020/184–7777* ⊕ *www.hattrick.co.uk*) makes a number of good comedy programs, including the satirical current-affairs program *Have I Got News for You.*

17

The Proms at Royal Albert Hall have standing tickets for £5 on the night of the concerts.

★ **Southbank Centre.** After a £90 million refurbishment, the Royal Festival Hall reopened in 2007 with large-scale choral and orchestral works in newly improved acoustic surroundings. Both the Philharmonia and the London Philharmonic orchestras are based here. Another £20 million has been spent on the rest of the Southbank Centre, where other venues host smaller-scale music performances as well as art and dance along with the celebrated theatrical performance mounted by the National Theatre—everything from Zoe Wanamaker in *The Cherry Orchard* to a new mounting of *Frankenstein* to the celebrated worldwide sensation, *War Horse*. The Queen Elizabeth Hall has chamber orchestras and top-tier soloists, and in the intimate Purcell Room you can listen to chamber music and solo recitals. A diverse and exciting season of international and British-based contemporary dance companies is also presented in these spaces. Also part of the complex is the **Hayward Gallery** (Sat.–Wed. 10–6, Thurs. and Fri. 10–8 during exhibitions), a landmark Brutalist-style 1960s building and still one of London's major venues for contemporary art exhibitions. ✉ *Belvedere Rd., South Bank* ☎ *020/7960 4200* ⊕ *www.southbankcentre.co.uk* Ⓤ *Waterloo.*

BLOOMSBURY, ISLINGTON, KILBURN, AND KING'S CROSS

BLOOMSBURY

DANCE

Peacock Theatre. Sadler's Wells's West End annex, this modernist theater near the London School of Economics focuses on younger companies and shows in popular dance genres like flamenco, tango, and hip-hop. ⊠ *Portugal St., Holborn* ☎ *0844/412–4322* ⊕ *www.peacocktheatre.com/* Ⓤ *Holborn.*

The Place. The Robin Howard Dance Theatre is London's only theater dedicated to contemporary dance, and with tickets between £6 and £17 it's good value, too. "Resolution!" is the United Kingdom's biggest platform event for new choreographers. ⊠ *17 Duke's Rd., Bloomsbury* ☎ *020/7121–1100* ⊕ *www.theplace.org.uk* Ⓤ *Euston.*

ISLINGTON

ART GALLERY

Victoria Miro Gallery. This important commercial gallery has exhibited some of the biggest names on the British contemporary art scene—Chris Ofili, the Chapman brothers, and Peter Doig, to name a few. It also brings in exciting new talent from abroad. ⊠ *16 Wharf Rd., Islington* ☎ *020/7336–8109* ⊕ *www.victoria-miro.com* ⊠ *Free* ☼ *Tues.–Sat. 10–6* Ⓤ *Old St., Angel.*

DANCE

Fodor's Choice **Sadler's Wells.** This gleaming building opened in 1998, the seventh on
★ the site in its 300-year history, and is devoted to presenting leading classical and contemporary dance companies. The Random Dance Company is in residence. The little Lilian Baylis Theatre here has more left-field pieces. ⊠ *Rosebery Ave., Islington* ☎ *0844/412–4300* ⊕ *www. sadlerswells.com* Ⓤ *Angel.*

THEATRE

★ **Almeida Theatre.** This Off–West End venue premieres excellent new plays and exciting twists on the classics, often featuring high profile actors. The Almeida Opera Festival in July has an adventurous program of new opera and musical theater. ⊠ *Almeida St., Islington* ☎ *020/7359–4404* ⊕ *www.almeida.co.uk* Ⓤ *Angel, Highbury & Islington.*

KILBURN

FILM AND THEATER

Tricycle Theatre. The Tricycle is committed to the best in Irish, African-Caribbean, Asian, and political drama, and the promotion of new plays. There is also a gallery and cinema: expect the best of new British, European, and World Cinema, as well as films from the United States. There are occasional Irish, black, and Asian film festivals, as well as a year-round program of film-related activities for children. Discounted cinema tickets are available on Monday. ⊠ *269 Kilburn High Rd., Kilburn*

17

DANCE: WHAT'S HAPPENING NOW

Dance fans in London can enjoy the classicism of the world-renowned Royal Ballet, as well as innovative works by several contemporary dance companies—including Rambert Dance Company, Matthew Bourne's New Adventures, and the Wheeldon Company—and scores of independent choreographers. The English National Ballet and visiting international companies perform at the Coliseum and at Sadler's Wells, which also hosts various other ballet companies and dance troupes. Encompassing the newly refurbished Royal Festival Hall, the Southbank Centre has a seriously good contemporary dance program that hosts top international companies and important U.K. choreographers, as well as multicultural offerings ranging from Japanese Butoh and Indian Kathak to hip-hop. The Place and the Lilian Bayliss Theatre at Sadler's Wells are where you'll find the most daring, cutting-edge performances.

The following theaters are the key dance venues. Also check ⊕ www.londondance.com for current performances and fringe venues.

The biggest annual event is **Dance Umbrella** (☎ *0208/741–4040* ⊕ *www.danceumbrella.co.uk*), a four-week season in October that hosts international and British-based artists at various venues across the city.

☎ *020/7328–1900 information, 020/7328–1000 box office* ⊕ *www.tricycle.co.uk* Ⓤ *Kilburn.*

KING'S CROSS

CLASSICAL MUSIC

Kings Place. This airy new concert venue, opened in October 2008—the first in London for 25 years—by the Eurostar terminal in King's Cross, is the permanent home of the London Sinfonietta and the Orchestra of the Age of Enlightenment. It offers weeklong programs by musicians in a range of genres, and the London Chamber Music Society performs Sunday concerts. The past season saw a staggering array of fascinating options, ranging from a mini-festival celebrating the Liszt Bicentenary, "Tasmin Little & Friends: Violin Journeys," a series of Mozart Unwrapped concerts, and the "Off With Their Heads" Comedy Festival 2011. ✉ *90 York Way, King's Cross* ☎ *0207/520–1490* ⊕ *www.kingsplace.co.uk* Ⓤ *King's Cross.*

THE CITY AND SOUTH BANK

THE CITY

See the Barbican Centre in the Two Main Performing Arts Centers, at the top of this chapter.

SOUTH BANK

Also see the Southbank Centre in the Two Main Performing Arts Centers, at the top of this chapter.

ART GALLERY

Fodor's Choice ★ **Tate Modern.** This converted power station is one of the largest modern-art galleries in the world, so give yourself ample time to take it all in. The permanent collection includes work by all the major 20th-century artists, though only a fraction is shown at any one time. There are also blockbuster touring shows and solo exhibitions of international artists. ■ TIP➔ The bar on the top floor has gorgeous views overlooking the Thames and St. Paul's Cathedral. ⊠ *Bankside, South Bank* ☎ *020/7887–8888* ⊕ *www.tate.org.uk* 🎟 *Free–£12.50* ☉ *Sun.–Thurs. 10–6, Fri. and Sat. 10–10* Ⓤ *Southwark, St. Paul's, London Bridge.*

FILM

BFI London IMAX Cinema. The British Film Institute's glazed drum-shaped IMAX theater has the largest screen in the United Kingdom (approximately 75 feet wide and the height of five double-decker buses) playing state-of-the-art 2-D and 3-D films. ⊠ *1 Charlie Chaplin Walk, South Bank* ☎ *0870/787–2525* ⊕ *www.bfi.org.uk/imax* Ⓤ *Waterloo.*

☼ ★ **BFI Southbank.** With easily the best repertory programming in London, the three cinemas and studio at what was previously known as the National Film Theatre are effectively a national film center run by the British Film Institute. They show more than 1,000 titles each year, favoring art-house, foreign, silent, overlooked, classic, noir, and short films over Hollywood blockbusters. After a recent rejuvenation and expansion, the center also has a gallery, bookshop, and "mediatheque," where visitors can watch film and television from the National Archive. This is one of the venues for the Times BFI London Film Festival; throughout the year there are minifestivals, seminars, and guest speakers. ■ TIP➔ Members (£40) get priority bookings (useful for special events) and £1.40 off each screening. ⊠ *Belvedere Rd., South Bank* ☎ *020/7928–3535 information, 020/7928–3232 box office* ⊕ *www.bfi.org.uk* Ⓤ *Waterloo.*

THEATER

★ **BAC.** Battersea Arts Centre has a reputation for producing innovative new work. Check out Scratch, a spring festival of low-tech cabaret theater by emerging artists where the audience provides feedback on works-in-progress. Tuesday shows usually have pay-what-you-can entry. ⊠ *176 Lavender Hill, Battersea* ☎ *020/7223–2223* ⊕ *www.bac.org.uk* Ⓤ *British Rail: Clapham Junction.*

★ **National Theatre.** When this theater opened in 1976, Londoners generally felt the same way about the low-slung, multilayered "Brutalist" block the color of heavy storm clouds (designed by Sir Denys Lasdun) as they would feel a decade later about the Barbican Centre. Prince Charles described the building as "a clever way of building a nuclear power station in the middle of London without anyone objecting." But whatever its merits or demerits as a feature on the landscape, the Royal National Theatre's interior spaces are definitely worth a tour. Interspersed with the three theaters, the 1,120-seat Olivier, the 890-seat Lyttelton, and the 300-seat Cottesloe, is a multilayered foyer with

17

CLASSICAL MUSIC: LONDON TODAY

Whether it's a concert by cellist Yo-Yo Ma or a Mozart requiem by candlelight, it's possible to hear first-rate musicians in world-class venues almost every day of the year. The London Symphony Orchestra is in residence at the Barbican Centre, although other top orchestras—including the Philharmonia and the Royal Philharmonic—also perform here. The Barbican also hosts chamber-music concerts, with celebrated orchestras such as the City of London Sinfonia. Wigmore Hall, a lovely venue for chamber music, is renowned for its song recitals by up-and-coming young singers. The Southbank Centre has an impressive international music season, held in the Queen Elizabeth Hall and the small Purcell Room as well as in the Royal Festival Hall, now completely refurbished. Full houses are rare, so even at the biggest concert halls you should be able to get a ticket for £12. If you can't book in advance, arrive at the hall an hour before the performance for a chance at returns.

■TIP➔ Lunchtime concerts take place all over the city in smaller concert halls, the big arts-center foyers, and churches; they usually cost less than £5 or are free, and feature string quartets, singers, jazz ensembles, or gospel choirs. St. John's, Smith Square, and St. Martin-in-the-Fields are popular locations. Performances usually begin about 1 pm and last one hour.

Classical-music festivals range from the stimulating avant-garde Meltdown (⊕ www.meltdown. southbankcentre.co.uk), curated each year by a prominent musician—recently Patti Smith or David Bowie—at the Southbank Centre in June, to church hall recitals including the Spitalfields Festival (⊕ www. spitalfieldsfestival.org.uk), a program of recitals held in beautiful, historic East End churches in June, December, and January, and the monthlong City of London Festival (⊕ www. colf.org) in the Square Mile during the summer. A great British tradition since 1895, the Henry Wood Promenade Concerts (more commonly known as the "Proms" ⊕ www.bbc. co.uk/proms) run eight weeks, from July to September, at the Royal Albert Hall. Despite an extraordinary quantity of high-quality concerts, it's renowned for its (atypical) last night: a madly jingoistic display of singing "Land of Hope and Glory," Union Jack–waving, and general madness. For regular Proms, tickets run £5–£90, with hundreds of standing tickets for £5 available at the hall on the night of the concert.

■TIP➔ The last night is broadcast in Hyde Park on a jumbo screen, but even here a seat on the grass requires a paid ticket that can set you back around £25.

exhibitions, bars, and restaurants, and free entertainment. Musicals, classics, and new plays are performed by a top-flight company. Some shows offer £10 ticket deals. ⊠ *Southbank Centre, Belvedere Rd., South Bank* ☎ *020/7452–3000 box office, 0207/452–3400 information* ⊕ *www.nationaltheatre.org.uk* ☜ *Tour £5.90* ☉ *Foyer Mon.–Sat. 9:30 am–11 pm; 75-min tour backstage up to 6 times daily weekdays, twice on Sat., often on Sun.* Ⓤ *Waterloo.*

The Old Vic. Who would have thought it? This grand old theater, former haunting grounds of such stage legends as John Gielgud, Vivien Leigh, Peter O'Toole, Richard Burton, and Judi Dench is now masterminded by noted American actor Kevin Spacey. Even though Laurence Olivier called this grand 1818 Victorian theater his favorite, the theater had suffered decades of financial duress. Before being shut down, however, the Old Vic was brought under the ownership of a dedicated trust headed by Spacey. His production record so far has been spotty but there are high hopes, at this writing, for his interpretation of Shakespeare's *Richard III.* ⊠ *The Cut, Southwark* ☎ *0844/871–7628* ⊕ *www. oldvictheatre.com* Ⓤ *Waterloo.*

Fodor's Choice ★ **Shakespeare's Globe Theatre.** Making world headlines when the Globe "reopened" in 1996 to wide acclaim, this faithful reconstruction of the open-air playhouse where Shakespeare worked and wrote many of his greatest plays marvelously re-creates the 16th-century theatergoing experience. Standing room in the "pit" right in front of the stage costs £5. The season runs April through October. ⇨ *For more on the Globe Theatre, see our special photo-feature, "Shakespeare and the Globe Theater" in Chapter 8.* ⊠ *21 New Globe Walk, Bankside, South Bank* ☎ *020/7401–9919* ⊕ *www.shakespeares-globe.org* Ⓤ *Southwark, then walk to Blackfriars Bridge and descend steps; Mansion House, then cross Southwark Bridge; Blackfriars, then walk across Blackfriars Bridge; St. Paul's, then cross Millenium Bridge.*

Young Vic. Ensconced in a new home near Waterloo, big names perform here alongside young talent, often in daring, innovative productions of classic plays. ⊠ *66 The Cut, Waterloo, South Bank* ☎ *020/922–2922* ⊕ *www.youngvic.org* Ⓤ *Waterloo.*

THE EAST END

HACKNEY

THEATER

★ **Hackney Empire.** The history of this treasure of a theater is drama in its own right. Charlie Chaplin is said to have appeared here during its days as a thriving variety theater and music hall in the early 1900s. After a major refurbishment in the last decade, it now hosts traditional family entertainment and variety shows, opera, musical theater, dance, and drama, often with a multicultural slant. ⊠ *291 Mare St., Hackney* ☎ *020/8985–2424* ⊕ *www.hackneyempire.co.uk* Ⓤ *National Rail: Hackney Central.*

HOXTON

ART GALLERY

★ **White Cube.** The English role in the exploding contemporary art scene has been a major one, thanks in good portion to Jay Joplin's influential gallery. Housed in a 1920s light-industrial building on Hoxton Square, it is home-base for an array of artists who have won the Turner Prize—Hirst, Emin, Hume, et al.—with many of these superstars now residing

FILM: WHAT'S HAPPENING NOW

There are many wonderful movie theaters in London and several that are committed to nonmainstream and repertory cinema, in particular the National Film Theatre. Now over 50 years old, the **Times BFI London Film Festival** (⊕ *www.lff.org.uk*) brings hundreds of films made by masters of world cinema to London for 16 days each October into November, accompanied by often-sold-out events. The smaller, avant-garde **Raindance Film Festival** (⊕ *www.raindance.co.uk*) highlights independent filmmaking, September into October.

West End movie theaters continue to do good business. Most of the major houses, such as the Odeon Leicester Square and the Empire, are in the Leicester Square–Piccadilly Circus area, where tickets average £15. Monday and matinees are often cheaper, at around £6–£10, and there are also fewer crowds.

Check out *Time Out*, one of the London papers, or ⊕ *www.viewlondon.co.uk* for listings.

in the East End (which supposedly has the highest concentration of artists in Europe). Farther west, White Cube now has a second gallery in a striking building in Mason's Yard, St. James's, reflecting its central status in London's art world. ⊠ *48 Hoxton Sq., Hoxton* ☎ *020/7930–5373* ⊕ *www.whitecube.com* ▢ *Free* ☉ *Tues.–Sat. 10–6* Ⓤ *Old St.*

SHOREDITCH

ART GALLERY

★ **Whitechapel Art Gallery.** Established in 1897 and newly expanded, this large, independent East End gallery is one of London's most innovative and consistently interesting. Jeff Wall, Bill Viola, Gary Hume, and Janet Cardiff have exhibited here and there is an interesting program of events as well as an excellent restaurant. Closed Monday. ⊠ *80–82 Whitechapel High St., Shoreditch* ☎ *020/7522–7888* ⊕ *www.whitechapel.org* ▢ *Free* ☉ *Tues., Wed., Fri.–Sun. 11 am–6 pm, Thurs. 11 am–9 pm* Ⓤ *Aldgate East.*

KENSINGTON, CHELSEA, AND KNIGHTSBRIDGE

CHELSEA

ART GALLERY

Saatchi Gallery. If there was one man who lit the fuse to the contemporary art explosion as of late, it is probably Charles Saatchi and his cutting-edge art collection. After migrating to several museums and being shown around the world, it found a permanent home in 2008 in this ultramodern gallery, which now sprawls through the 70,000 square feet of the Duke of York's HQ building in Chelsea, complete with a bookshop and café-bar. ⊠ *Duke of York's HQ, Sloane Sq., Chelsea* ☎ *020/7823–2332* ⊕ *www.saatchi-gallery.co.uk* ▢ *Free* ☉ *Daily 10 am–6 pm* Ⓤ *Sloane Sq.*

OPERA: WHAT'S HAPPENING NOW

The two key players in London's opera scene are the Royal Opera House (which ranks with the Metropolitan Opera House in New York) and the more innovative English National Opera (ENO), which presents English-language productions at the London Coliseum. Only the Theatre Royal, Drury Lane, has a longer theatrical history than the Royal Opera House—the third theater to be built on the site since 1858.

Despite occasional performances by the likes of Björk, the Royal Opera House struggles to shrug off its reputation for elitism and ticket prices that can rise to £200. It is, however, more accessible than it used to be— the cheapest tickets are under £10.

Conditions of purchase vary; call for information. Prices for the ENO are generally lower, ranging from around £17 to £85. You can get same-day balcony seats for as little as £5.

Almeida Opera is a festival that showcases new and often cutting-edge opera. In summer, the increasingly adventurous Opera Holland Park presents the usual chestnuts alongside some obscure works under a newly enlarged canopy in leafy Holland Park.

International touring companies often perform at Sadler's Wells, the Barbican, the Southbank Centre, and Wigmore Hall, so check the weekly listings for details.

17

THEATER

★ **Royal Court Theatre.** Britain's undisputed epicenter of new writing, the RCT is now 50 years old and continues to produce gritty British and international drama. ■TIP→ Don't miss the best deal in town—10-pence standing tickets go on sale one hour before each performance, and there are £10 tickets on Monday. ⊠ *Sloane Sq., Chelsea* ☎ *020/7565–5000* ⊕ *www.royalcourttheatre.com* Ⓤ *Sloane Sq.*

KENSINGTON

ART GALLERY

Serpentine Gallery. Built in 1934 as a tea pavilion in Kensington Gardens, the Serpentine has an international reputation for exhibitions of modern and contemporary art. Man Ray, Henry Moore, Andy Warhol, Bridget Riley, Damien Hirst, and Rachel Whiteread are a few of the artists who have had exhibits here. The annual Summer Pavilion, a striking temporary structure designed by a different leading architect every year, is always worth catching. ⊠ *Kensington Gardens, South Kensington* ☎ *020/7402–6075* ⊕ *www.serpentinegallery.org* ⊠ *Free* ⊗ *Daily 10–6* Ⓤ *South Kensington, Lancaster Gate.*

CLASSICAL MUSIC

Cadogan Hall. Formerly a church, Cadogan Hall has been turned into a spacious concert venue, home to the Royal Philharmonic Orchestra, and where the English Chamber Orchestra performs regularly. ⊠ *5 Sloane Terr., Kensington* ☎ *020/7730–4500* ⊕ *www.cadoganhall.com* Ⓤ *Sloane Sq.*

★ **Royal Albert Hall.** Built in 1871, this splendid iron-and-glass–dome auditorium hosts music programs in a wide range of genres, including top-flight

London's Royal Opera House is also home to the Royal Ballet and an in-house orchestra.

pop artists, as well as being the home of Europe's most democratic music festival, the Proms. The hall is also open daily for daytime guided tours (£8) and occasional backstage tours (£12). ⊠ *Kensington Gore, Kensington* ☏ *020/7589–8212* ⊕ *www.royalalberthall.com* Ⓤ *South Kensington.*

OPERA

Opera Holland Park. In summer, well-loved operas and imaginative productions of relatively unknown works are presented under a spectacular new canopy against the remains of Holland House, one of the first great houses built in Kensington. Ticket prices range from £10 to £57, with 1,200 tickets offered free to young people ages 9–18 every season. Tickets go on sale in April. ⊠ *Holland Park, Kensington High St., Kensington* ☏ *0845/230–9769* ⊕ *www.operahollandpark.com* Ⓤ *High Street Kensington, Holland Park.*

GREATER LONDON

OPERA

★ **Glyndebourne.** Fifty-four miles south of London, Glyndebourne is one of the most famous opera houses in the world. During its glamorous summer festival, six operas are presented from mid-May to late August. The best route by car is the M23 to Brighton, then the A27 toward Lewes. There are regular trains from London (Victoria) to Lewes with coach connections to and from Glyndebourne. Call the information office for recommended trains for each performance. ⊠ *Lewes* ☏ *01273/815–000* ⊕ *www.glyndebourne.com.*

NOTTING HILL

FILM

The Electric Cinema. This refurbished Portobello Road art house screens mainstream and international movies. The emphasis is on comfort, with leather sofas, armchairs, footstools, and mini–coffee tables for your tapas-style food and wine. Saturday matinees for kids are popular. The Electric now has an equally sumptuous sister cinema in east London—the Aubin, on Redchurch Street. ⊠ *191 Portobello Rd., Notting Hill* ☎ *020/7908–9696* ⊕ *www.electriccinema.co.uk* Ⓤ *Ladbroke Grove, Notting Hill Gate.*

REGENT'S PARK

THEATER

Fodor's Choice ★ Open Air Theatre. On a warm summer evening, classical theater in the pastoral and royal Regent's Park is hard to beat for magical adventure. Enjoy a supper before the performance, a bite during the intermission on the picnic lawn, or drinks in the spacious bar. ⊠ *Inner Circle, Regent's Park* ☎ *0844/826–4242* ⊕ *www.openairtheatre.org* Ⓤ *Baker St., Regent's Park.*

ST. JAMES'S, MAYFAIR, AND MARYLEBONE

MARYLEBONE

ART GALLERY

Lisson. Owner Nicholas Logsdail represents about 40 blue-chip artists, including minimalist Sol Lewitt and Dan Graham, at arguably the most respected gallery in London. The gallery is most associated with New Object sculptors like Anish Kapoor and Richard Deacon, many of whom have won the Turner Prize. A branch down the road at 29 Bell Street features work by younger, up-and-coming artists. ⊠ *52–54 Bell St., Marylebone* ☎ *020/7724–2739* ⊕ *www.lissongallery.com* 🎟 *Free* ☉ *Weekdays 10–6, Sat. 11–5* Ⓤ *Edgware Rd., Marylebone.*

CLASSICAL MUSIC

Fodor's Choice ★ Wigmore Hall. Hear chamber music and song recitals in this charming hall with near-perfect acoustics. Don't miss the midmorning Sunday concerts (11:30 am). ⊠ *36 Wigmore St., Marylebone* ☎ *020/7935–2141* ⊕ *www.wigmore-hall.org.uk* Ⓤ *Bond St.*

MAYFAIR

ART GALLERY

Royal Academy of Arts. Housed in an aristocratic mansion and home to Britain's first art school (founded in 1768), the academy is best known for its blockbuster special exhibitions—like the record-breaking Monet, and the controversial Sensation show drawn from the Saatchi collection. The annual Summer Exhibition has been a popular London tradition since 1769. ⊠ *Burlington House, Mayfair* ☎ *020/7300–8000* ⊕ *www. royalacademy.org.uk* 🎟 *From £10, prices vary with exhibition* ☉ *Daily 10–6, except Fri. 10–10* Ⓤ *Piccadilly Circus.*

17

ST. JAMES'S

ART GALLERY

Institute of Contemporary Arts. Housed in an elegant John Nash–designed Regency terrace, the ICA's two galleries have changing exhibitions of contemporary visual art. The ICA also programs performance, underground and vintage movies, new media, literary talks, and photography. There's also an arts bookstore, cafeteria, and bar. ⊠ *Nash House, The Mall, St. James's* ☎ *020/7930–3647* ⊕ *www.ica.org.uk* ✉ *Free* ☾ *Mon.–Wed. noon–11* Ⓤ *Charing Cross.*

> ### WORD OF MOUTH
>
> "For me one thing stands out above all the others: London Theatre, where the houses are generally small, you can nearly always get a seat to almost any show at half price, and nobody races out before the curtain calls."
>
> —NeoPatrick

CLASSICAL MUSIC

St. James's Church. The organ was brought here in 1691 after fire destroyed its former home, the Palace of Whitehall. St. James's holds regular classical-music concerts and free lunchtime recitals Monday, Wednesday, and Friday at 1:10 pm (free but donations suggested). ⊠ *197 Piccadilly, St. James's* ☎ *020/7381–0441 concert program and tickets* ⊕ *www.st-james-piccadilly.org* Ⓤ *Piccadilly Circus, Green Park.*

SOHO AND COVENT GARDEN

COVENT GARDEN

CLASSICAL MUSIC

★ **St. Martin-in-the-Fields.** Popular lunchtime concerts (free but £3.50 donation suggested) are held in this lovely 1726 church, as are regular evening concerts. ■ TIP→ Stop for a snack at the Café in the Crypt. ⊠ *Trafalgar Sq., Covent Garden* ☎ *020/7766–1100* ⊕ *www.stmartin-in-the-fields.org* Ⓤ *Charing Cross.*

DANCE

The London Coliseum. Ballet troupes are often booked into the spectacular Coliseum—a true Edwardian extravaganza of architecture—during the summer and also during the Christmas season, and generally any time when the resident English National Opera is not holding down the fort here. The restored Edwardian baroque theater (1904) is known for its magnificent auditorium and a rooftop glass dome The top dance company to perform here is the English National Ballet (⊕ *www.ballet.org. uk*). ⊠ *St. Martin's La., Covent Garden* ☎ *020/7632–8300* ⊕ *www.eno. org* Ⓤ *Leicester Sq.*

Fodor'sChoice ★ **Royal Opera House.** The renowned Royal Ballet performs classical and contemporary repertoire in this spectacular theater, where the decor may be Victorian but the stagecraft behind the red velvet curtain is state-of-the-art. ⊠ *Bow St., Covent Garden* ☎ *020/7304–4000* ⊕ *www. roh.org.uk* Ⓤ *Covent Garden.*

THEATER: WHAT'S HAPPENING NOW

In London the play really *is* the thing, ranging from a long-running popular musical like *Mamma Mia!*, a groundbreaking reworking of Pinter, imaginative physical theater from an experimental company like *Complicite*, a lavish Disney spectacle, or a small fringe production above a pub. West End glitz and glamour continue to pull in the audiences, and so do the more innovative productions. Only in London will a Tuesday matinee of the Royal Shakespeare Company's *Henry IV* sell out a 1,200-seat theater.

In London the words radical and quality, or classical and experimental are not mutually exclusive. The Royal Shakespeare Company (⊕ *www.rsc.org.uk*) and the National Theatre (⊕ *www.nationaltheatre.org.uk*) often stage contemporary versions of the classics. The Almeida, Battersea Arts Centre (BAC), Donmar Warehouse, Royal Court Theatre, Soho Theatre, and Old Vic attract famous actors and have excellent reputations for new writing and innovative theatrical approaches. These are the venues where you'll see an original production before it becomes a hit in the West End or on Broadway (and for a fraction of the cost).

The London theater scene remains vibrant throughout the summer months. Open-air productions of Shakespeare are particularly well served, whether in the faithful reconstruction of the Elizabethan Globe Theatre or under the stars in Regent's Park's Open Air Theatre. Theater festivals such as LIFT (⊕ *www.liftfest.org.uk*), the London International Festival of Theatre, and B.I.T.E. (Barbican International Theater Events ⊕ *www.barbican.org.uk*) provide the chance to see international and cutting-edge companies throughout the year.

Theatergoing isn't cheap. Tickets less than £10 are a rarity, although designated productions at the National Theatre have seats at this price. At the commercial theaters you should expect to pay from £15 for a seat in the upper balcony to at least £25 for a good one in the stalls (orchestra) or dress circle (mezzanine). However, last-minute returns available on the night may provide some good deals. Tickets may be booked through ticket agents, at individual theater box offices, or over the phone by credit card. Be sure to inquire about any extra fees—prices can vary enormously, but agents are legally obliged to reveal the face value of the ticket if you ask. All the larger hotels offer theater bookings, but they tack on a hefty service charge. ■TIP→Be very wary of ticket touts (scalpers) and unscrupulous ticket agents outside theaters and working the line at "tkts" (a half-price ticket booth, www.tkts.co.uk).

Ticketmaster (☎ 0844/277–4321 ⊕ *www.ticketmaster.co.uk*) sells tickets to a number of different theaters, although they charge a booking fee. For discount tickets, **Society of London Theatre** (☎ 020/7557–6700 ⊕ *www.tkts.co.uk*) operates "tkts," a half-price ticket booth on the southwest corner of Leicester Square, and sells the best available seats to performances at about 25 theaters. It's open Monday–Saturday 10–7, Sunday noon–3; there's a £3 service charge (included in the price). Major credit cards are accepted.

17

THEATER

Fodor's Choice
★

Donmar Warehouse. Hollywood stars often perform here in diverse and daring new works, bold interpretations of the classics, and small-scale musicals. Under current Artistic Director Michael Grandage, who succeeded Sam Mendes, Nicole Kidman, Gwyneth Paltrow, and Ewan McGregor have all been featured. ⊠ *41 Earlham St., Covent Garden* ☎ *0844/871–7624* ⊕ *www.donmarwarehouse.com* Ⓤ *Covent Garden.*

Novello Theatre. Dating back to 1905 and refurbished a century later, the Novello specializes in popular contemporary musicals and serves as the Royal Shakespeare Company's London base. ⊠ *Aldwych, Covent Garden* ☎ *0844/482–5170* ⊕ *www.delfontmackintosh.co.uk* Ⓤ *Covent Garden, Temple.*

OPERA

The London Coliseum. Opera is the mainstay of London's biggest theater, along with ballet in the summer and Christmas season. A vertiable architectural extravaganza of Edwardian exoticism, the restored baroque-style theater (1904) has a magnificent auditorium and a rooftop glass dome with a bar and great views. As one of the city's largest and most venerable theaters, the Coliseum functions mainly as the home of the English National Opera. Despite financial problems, ENO continues to produce innovative opera for lower prices than the Royal Opera House. During opera's off-season, the house hosts a number of dance troupes, including the English National Ballet (⊕ *www.ballet. org.uk*). ⊠ *St. Martin's La., Covent Garden* ☎ *020/7632–8300* ⊕ *www. eno.org* Ⓤ *Leicester Sq.*

Fodor's Choice
★

Royal Opera House. Along with Milan's La Scala, New York's Metropolitan, and Paris's Palais Garnier, this is one of the world's greatest opera houses. The resident troupe has mounted famously spectacular productions in the past. As for the present, it should be noted that the current vogue for dramatic, "director-driven" concepts has led this company to economize on spectacle and mount quite a number of stark, minimalist, and modern-dress opera productions instead (even with its sky-high prices). At least the extravagant theater itself—also home to the famed Royal Ballet—delivers a full dose of opulence. Tickets range in price from £4 to £210. ■ TIP➔ It may be worth showing up on the morning of a performance to purchase a same-day seat, of which 67 are offered. The box office opens at 10 am, but queues for popular productions can start as early as 7 am and unsold tickets are offered at half price four hours before a performance. There are free lunchtime recitals most Mondays in the Linbury Studio Theatre or the Crush Room (arrive early to get a ticket—between 11 am and noon), and three summer concerts are broadcast live to a large screen in Covent Garden Piazza. ⊠ *Bow St., Covent Garden* ☎ *020/7304–4000* ⊕ *www. royalopera.org* Ⓤ *Covent Garden.*

Dominique Gonzalez-Foerster's installation, TH.2058, in the Turbine Hall of the Tate Modern.

SOHO

ART GALLERY

★ **Photographer's Gallery.** Britain's first photography gallery brought world-famous photographers like André Kertesz, Jacques-Henri Lartigue, and Irving Penn to the United Kingdom, and continues to program cutting-edge and provocative photography. The prestigious annual Deutsche Börse Photography Prize is exhibited and awarded here annually. There is a print sales room, a bookstore, and a café. ⊠ *16–18 Ramillies St., off Oxford St.* ☎ *020/7831–1772* ⊕ *www.photonet.org.uk* ✉ *Free* ☉ *Tues., Wed., and Sat. 11 am–6 pm, Thurs. and Fri. 11 am–8 pm, Sun. noon–6 pm* Ⓤ *Oxford Circus.*

Riflemaker. In London's oldest public building and a former Georgian riflemaker's workshop, this gallery exhibits ambitious works by emerging artists, having housed debuts by Francesca Lowe, Chosil Kil, Jaime Gili, and Jamie Shovin. ⊠ *79 Beak St., Soho* ☎ *020/7439–0000* ⊕ *www.riflemaker.org* ☉ *Weekdays 10 am–6 pm, Sat. noon–6 pm* Ⓤ *Piccadilly Circus, Oxford Circus.*

FILM

★ **Curzon Soho.** This comfortable cinema runs an artsy program of mixed repertoire and mainstream films. There are also branches in Mayfair, Bloomsbury, Chelsea, and Richmond. Members (£50) get discounts. ⊠ *99 Shaftesbury Ave., Soho* ☎ *0871/703–3988* Ⓤ *Piccadilly Circus, Leicester Sq.* ⊠ *38 Curzon St., Mayfair* ☎ *0871/703–3989* ⊕ *www.curzoncinemas.com* Ⓤ *Green Park.*

CONTEMPORARY ART: LONDON TODAY

In the 21st century, the focus of the city's art scene has shifted from the past to the future. Helped by the prominence of the Tate Modern, London's contemporary art scene has never been so high profile. In publicly funded exhibition spaces like the Barbican Gallery, the Hayward Gallery, the Institute of Contemporary Arts, and the Serpentine Gallery, London now has a modern-art environment on a par with Bilbao and New York. Young British Artists (YBAs, though no longer as young as they once were) Damien Hirst, Tracey Emin, and others are firmly planted in the public imagination. The celebrity status of British artists is in part thanks to the annual Turner Prize, which always stirs up controversy in the media during a monthlong display of the work, usually at Tate Britain.

Depending on whom you talk to, the Saatchi Gallery is considered to be either the savior of contemporary art or the wardrobe of the emperor's new clothes. It recently reopened in the former Duke of York's barracks off Chelsea's Kings Road.

The South Bank's Tate Modern may house the giants of modern art, but East London is where the innovative action is. There are dozens of galleries in the fashionable spaces around Old Street, and the truly hip have already moved even farther east, to areas such as Bethnal Green. The Whitechapel Art Gallery and Jay Jopling's influential White Cube in Hoxton Square remain at the epicenter of the new art establishment and continue to show exciting work by emerging British artists.

On the first Thursday of every month, more than 100 museums and galleries of East London stay open 'til late (more information at ⊕ www.firstthursdays.co.uk). For information about upcoming events and new young British artists visit ⊕ www.murmurart.com.

☾ **Prince Charles Cinema.** This repertory cinema right off Leicester Square offers a chance to catch up with independent features, documentaries, and even blockbusters you may have missed, and tickets are only £5 and under. A new second screen upstairs shows newer movies at more usual West End prices. This is where the "sing-along" screening originated—you can come in character and warble along to *The Sound of Music* and *The Rocky Horror Picture Show*. ⊠ *7 Leicester Pl., Soho* ☏ *0207/494–3654* ⊕ *www.princecharlescinema.com* Ⓤ *Leicester Sq., Piccadilly Circus.*

THEATRE

Soho Theatre. This sleek theater in the heart of Soho is devoted to fostering new writing and is a prolific presenter of work by emerging writers and comedy performance. ⊠ *21 Dean St., Soho* ☏ *0207/478–0100* ⊕ *www.sohotheatre.com* Ⓤ *Tottenham Court Rd.*

Shopping

WORD OF MOUTH

"We arrived home a couple days ago from our long awaited trip to London, the Cotswolds, and Bath. All I will say is that the success of this trip was largely due to the wonderful advice and helpful hints that I received from my friends on Fodor's. This is now the third trip that I've planned with help from Fodor's, and they've all been winners."

—freberta

SHOPPING PLANNER

Top Shops

Dover Street Market. Run by Comme des Garçons designer Rei Kawakubo, this concept store is a combination art gallery and department store, and also hosts design retrospectives.

Hamleys. With floor after floor of treasures for every child on your list, this is *the* London toy shop.

Liberty. In a Tudor-style building, Liberty has an outstanding collection of clothing crafted from its famous prints and furniture, as well as cutting-edge fashion.

Mint. Fans of contemporary furniture and housewares should head to Mint, which showcases the work of both leading and up-and-coming designers.

Portobello Road Market. Whether you are a serious antiques buyer or just want to browse the stalls and people-watch, Portobello Road is London's most dynamic market.

Rellik. Celebs like Sienna Miller love Rellik for its superb collection of vintage clothing, ranging from classic Dior to Ossie Clark and Vivienne Westwood.

Opening Hours

Most shops are open from about 9:30 or 10 am to 6 or 6:30 pm. Some may open at 11 and stay open until 7. Because shop hours, particularly for the smaller shops, are varied, it's a good idea to phone ahead. Stores that have late shopping—and not all do—are usually open until 7 or 8 pm on Wednesday or Thursday only. Most department stores stay open late during the week. On Sunday, many shops open between 11 am and noon and close at 5 or 6 pm. Most stores are open on Sunday in December for the Christmas season.

A Word About Service

American standards of customer service are rare in London—salespeople can seem abrupt or rude, but don't take it personally.

Watch Your Language

Locals like to say that Brits and Americans are separated by a common language. Here are a few confusing terms to watch for when out and about in the shops:

Pants means underwear. Every other type of long-legged bottoms (except jeans) are called **trousers.**

Knickers are ladies' underwear. If you want pantyhose, ask for **tights.**

Jumper means sweater—unless it's a cardigan, in which case it's often shortened to **cardie.** If you ask for a **sweater,** you may be offered a sweatshirt.

Men use **braces** to hold up their trousers; in England **suspenders** is another word for garters.

If you want some Adidas- or Nike-type athletic shoes, ask for **trainers,** not sneakers.

Don't ask for a **pocketbook** or a **purse** if you mean a handbag—the former will be incomprehensible, and the latter will produce a coin purse.

Nightgowns are usually abbreviated to **nighties** and bathrobes are always **dressing gowns.**

CAMDEN TOWN
cheap
second-hand
and club gear

CLERKENWELL
a historical
hotspot for
crafts and design

MARYLEBONE
small shops
in village-like
setting

BLOOMSBURY

**HOXTON &
SHOREDITCH**
edgy young
designers

NOTTING HILL
antiques, vintage
clothing, and
boho boutiques

**OXFORD
CIRCUS**
global flagships,
department stores,
and street style
on Carnaby

SOHO
books abound
on Charing
Cross Road

**COVENT
GARDEN**
an urban-wear
mecca around
Seven Dials

BAYSWATER

MAYFAIR
catwalk names
on Bond St.,
trad tailors on
Savile Row

ST JAMES'S
old-fashioned
specialists, from
hatters to
shirtmakers

HYDE PARK

KNIGHTSBRIDGE
luxe labels
and, of course,
Harrods

BELGRAVIA

WESTMINSTER

LAMBETH

CHELSEA
the King's Rd.
spans fashion
to furniture

VICTORIA

REGENT'S
PARK

Green
Park

St. James's
Park

River
Thames

0 — 1/2 mile
0 — 1/2 km

KNIGHTSBRIDGE, CHELSEA, AND SOUTH KENSINGTON

All the big British brands like Burberry and Pringle are here, as well as the big department stores like Harvey Nichols and Harrods. If you're a design buff or love antiques, then make a beeline to Chelsea.

These are some of most exclusive shopping areas in London, so expect to find yummy mummies with money to burn, Russian heiresses, and celebrities—along with plenty of chauffeur-driven Bentleys idling outside stores. Start at the top of Sloane Street, which has all the big designer names, and as you head into South Kensington, you'll find more independent boutiques and plenty of cafés and restaurants that are perfect for a shopping break. Even if your bank account has fewer zeros than you'd like, wander down the King's Road to check out the home design and antiques shops. You never know, you might just score a bargain, or at the very least, you'll come away feeling design-inspired. The King's Road also has plenty of High-street chains, such as Oasis, Whistles, and Warehouse, which are gentler on the wallet.

BEST TIME TO GO

Weekends are crowded, so try to hit the shops midweek for a calmer experience. On the other hand, people-watching is part of the true Kensington and Chelsea experience, so take your time and soak it all up. The bi-annual sales, in January and July, make shops busy no matter what the day.

BEST FIND FOR YOUR BEST FRIEND

For something affordable in these neighborhoods, pick up a beautifully packaged bottle of Grapefruit or Vintage Gardenia perfume at **Jo Malone**. A box of luxury correspondence cards from **Smythson** is another classic gift.

REFUELING

Chic ladies sip lattes and nibble on goat-cheese tarts or a salad Niçoise at **Aubaine**, a simple yet elegant French café and boulangerie. For something more substantial, tuck into a hearty meal at **Admiral Codrington**, a gastropub known as "The Cod" to the locals. You can't go wrong with an order of crispy fish-and-chips served with chive butter, or salmon and crab cakes, all washed down with a pint of beer or a glass of wine.

WHAT YOU'LL WANT

BEST OF THE BRITISH

Harvey Nichols. The capital's best department store is a must.

Jimmy Choo. Every woman needs a pair of sexy, sky-high Jimmy Choos.

Pringle of Scotland. There's nothing dowdy here. The traditional plaids still crop up, but the latest designs are edgy and cool.

Vivienne Westwood. Her World's End boutique, with the crazy clock outside, is where it all started.

TRENDSETTERS

All Saints. Limited stock and fresh-from-the-catwalk designs here mean original looks—you won't be walking around looking like everyone else.

Austique. For the über-feminine London shopper, look no further than this two-floor boutique on the King's Road, which offers chic dresses and accessories.

Bruce Oldfield. Come for an Oscar-worthy couture gown or a glam wedding dress.

Marie-Chantal. For exclusive baby and children's clothing fit for a prince or a princess.

18

ST. JAMES'S AND MAYFAIR

CLOTH SOLD BY THE METRE

If you love old-fashioned tailoring and shops that seem unchanged since Victorian times, then hit one of the many traditional shops in St. James's and Mayfair.

Mayfair is one of the most elegant places to shop in London—not only because of the big-name designers who have their flagships here, but because the cobblestone streets and hushed atmosphere add to the exclusivity. Serious fashionistas can make their way through Nicole Farhi, Armani, Versace, and Ralph Lauren on Bond Street and New Bond Street before heading to tiny South Molton Street, which is home to Browns and plenty of great shoe stores. But for shoppers who aren't as big on the latest catwalk fashions, spend an afternoon on St. James's Jermyn Street, which has a lost-in-time quality and carries on the tradition of producing high-quality handmade shirts, hats, and suits. The area is also home to Savile Row—synonymous with handmade suits—and also the place where Prince Charles and rocker David Bowie have had their clothing made. If your budget won't stretch for a suit or a pair of shoes, head to the food section of Fortnum & Mason to stock up on beautifully packaged teas or jams.

BEST TIME TO GO

Because this area covers some of the most exclusive shopping streets in the capital, don't expect huge crowds. South Molton Street can get a bit busy, whereas the area surrounding Jermyn Street is relatively quiet. Many of the independent stores are closed on Sunday.

BEST FIND FOR YOUR DAD

Long-established shirt maker **Hilditch & Key** makes bespoke and ready-to-wear dress shirts. Alternatively, for something a bit less expensive, pick up a formal shirt from **Thomas Pink** or **Charles Tyrhwhitt**.

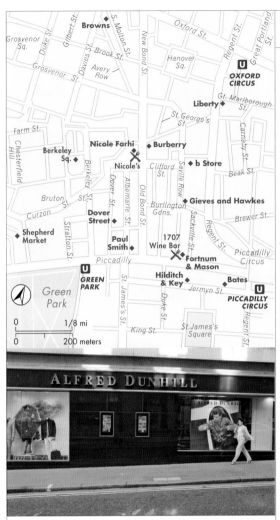

REFUELING

Nicole's restaurant in the basement of the Nicole Farhi shop is ideal for a quick lunch between purchases. The two-story restaurant was designed by Ms. Farhi, as was the menu, which features modern British cuisine with a California twist. For the quickest service, head to the upper level; reservations are recommended for the more formal dining room. Or pop in for a glass of wine at the 1707 Wine Bar inside Fortnum & Mason. The elegant lower level is part of the recent 300th-birthday expansion and is one of four restaurants in the Queen's grocery store.

WHAT YOU'LL WANT

DESIGNER CHIC

b store. Models flock here for the ever-changing stock of clothing and accessories by emerging talent.

Browns. This mini-department store stocks big names as well as plenty of up-and-coming designers.

Dover Street Market. Alongside Alber Elbaz and Alaïa fashion, expect to see art exhibits and one-off events at this concept store.

Paul Smith. Known for his classics-with-a-twist, his furniture and curio shop has the same quirky design ethos.

OLD MADE NEW

Burberry. Once dowdy, this landmark label is now super-chic thanks to Christopher Bailey, the designer who's made this into the British Gucci.

Liberty. All the great Art Nouveau and Aesthetic Movement textiles and accessories are still lovingly crafted here for today's Mrs. Dalloways.

Gieves and Hawkes. Grand bespoke suits of yore and custom-tailored uniforms (for Prince William) keep young the grand old craft of British menswear.

18

SOHO AND COVENT GARDEN

Soho and Covent Garden house a plethora of independent boutiques and some of the best High-street chain stores including Zara, H&M, and Oasis. A three-floor Banana Republic, a favorite American outpost, is now along Long Acre.

Although some never make it past the covered market area of Covent Garden (which is fine for a browse through the stalls), it's best to venture off onto one of the smaller streets in the area. Neal's Yard is an idyllic alcove for all things vegetarian and bohemian while Seven Dials, known as Covent Garden's "Hidden Village" for shopping, is bound to provide ample opportunities for worthwhile purchases. Monmouth Street, part of Seven Dials, is easily one of the best areas for fashionable boutiques. Some of the bigger names in fashion, such as Ted Baker, Radley, and Agnes B, have set up shop on the pretty, cobblestone Floral Street, and Earlham Street is a happy mishmash of stalls and shops, which includes the trendy but affordable Urban Outfitters. Brighten your day with some fresh flowers at the low-key Wild Bunch.

BEST TIME TO GO

It's almost always crowded, so go with the flow—or get there early in the morning.

BEST FIND FOR YOUR ANGLOPHILE FRIEND

Couldn't make it to Scotland this trip? Leave room in your luggage for a bottle or two of single-malt whisky from **Milroy's of Soho**, on Greek Street, which stocks whiskies from every distillery in Scotland. Or stop by the **Tea House** on Neal Street, which sells more than 100 varieties of tea along with pots and mugs to make the perfect brew and the perfect gift.

REFUELING

Wahaca serves up delicious yet inexpensive dishes inspired by Mexican street food. The wait for a seat is worth it, and you'll have money left over to continue shopping your way through Covent Garden. If you're looking for a caffeine jolt, head to **Monmouth Coffee**, which roasts all its own beans and boasts some of the best coffee around, or pick up some delectable cheese to nibble on from the nearby **Neal's Yard Dairy**.

WHAT YOU'LL WANT

TOYS R THEM

Benjamin Pollock's Toyshop. Billionaires buy the antique toy theaters on sale in this legendary and historic emporium, while the rest of us adore the new paper reproductions, complete with dollhouse sets for *The Mikado*.

Hamleys. Santa Claus's London pied-à-terre, this is the city's biggest toy store, and heaven to most children.

QUIRKY COOL

Paul Smith. Taking the classics and giving them a Smith twist, with rainbow stripes, Mona Lisa eyes, and flamboyant linings, is one sure way to give any fashionplate their creds.

Topshop. A fashion mecca for all that is young, stylish, and fun, this is half runway, half department store, and not surprisingly was founded by superstar Kate Moss.

BOOKS AND PRINTS

Stanfords. With the British long known as fabled explorers, it is little wonder London boasts one of the greatest travel book shops anywhere.

Foyles. Five floors of every title imaginable, this bibliophile's wonderland has everything from art history to opera scores.

18

Updated by
Erin Huebscher

As befits one of the great trading capitals of the world, London's shops have been known to boast, "You name it, we sell it." Finding and buying "it" can be a delight (the private fitting rooms at couturier Vivienne Westwood) or a trial (mobbed Oxford Street on a Saturday morning). No matter where you head in this city, you'll find you can melt as much plastic as your wallet can stand. You can shop like royalty at Her Majesty's glove maker, run down a leather-bound copy of Wuthering Heights at a Charing Cross bookseller, or find flea-market goodies on Portobello Road. Whether out for fun—there's nothing like those amazing street markets to stimulate the acquisitive juices—or for fashion, London can be the most rewarding of hunting grounds.

Although it's impossible to pin down one particular look that defines the city, homegrown designers like Vivienne Westwood, Matthew Williamson, Paul Smith, and Alice Temperley stand out for their quirky, eccentric designs. London is, after all, the city that introduced punk, miniskirts, and Mod fashion to the world. If you're after a more traditional look, however, head to Jermyn Street and Savile Row, which still retain their old-world look and feel—and there's no better place in the city to buy custom-made shirts and suits. If your budget can't stretch to Savile Row, no problem. The city's High-street chain stores like Topshop, Oasis, Reiss, and French Connection are excellent places to pick up designs straight from the catwalk, at a fraction of the price. And don't forget London's markets, known for their size, variety, and sheer street theater.

Know Your Shopping Personality

"Where is the best place to shop in London?" is an age-old question, akin to "How long is a piece of string?" There are thousands of shops in the city, and dozens of neighborhoods worth shopping in. Start by identifying your shopping personality to narrow your choices for a successful outing.

Whirlwind. If you're after a one-stop shopping experience, head to one of London's biggest department stores. Selfridges and Liberty are near the Bond Street and Oxford Circus Tube stations, while Harvey Nichols and Harrods share Knightsbridge Tube.

Fashionista. When only the top designers will do, start at Harvey Nichols, in Knightsbridge, then take in the designer boutiques along Sloane Street before hopping on the Tube for Green Park. From there, peruse New and Old Bond streets, and finish at Fenwick. If you still have time and energy, aim for South Molton Street or St. Christopher's Place, opposite Bond Street Tube, for more independent boutiques.

Eclectic. If you don't want to be pinned down and prefer beautiful workmanship and originality, start at Liberty on Regent Street, then head to either the Holland Park/Notting Hill or Marylebone neighborhoods. Both provide enough idiosyncratic lifestyle shops for hours of browsing.

Funky and Avant-Garde. For cutting-edge fashion and housewares, head east to the city's coolest neighborhoods, chiefly Hoxton and Shoreditch. Start at Columbia Road, and then have a wander around Spitalfields and Brick Lane, which boast excellent markets. Then work your way north to Hoxton and Shoreditch, which are chock-full of less mainstream stores.

Easygoing. If you want to pop in and out of a variety of shops, as well as avoid the crowds around Oxford Street, head to the King's Road in Chelsea. You'll find department store Peter Jones, Marks & Spencer, and plenty of High-street chains, as well as trendy boutiques. Another safe bet is High Street Kensington for the big chains like Topshop, Oasis, and Zara.

18

Apart from bankrupting yourself, the only problem you may encounter is exhaustion. London's shopping districts are spread out all over the city, so do like the locals do. Plan your excursion with military precision, taking in only one or two areas in a day, and stop for a hearty English lunch with a glass of wine or a pint at a pub.

SPECIALTY STORES

ANTIQUES

Investment-quality items or lovable junk—London has loads. For the best range of merchandise, and plenty of character, try the markets first. Some argue that Portobello Road in Notting Hill has become a bit of a tourist trap, but if you acknowledge that it's a circus and get into the spirit, it's a lot of fun, if expensive. Kensington Church Street and the shops along the King's Road have some of the best antiques in the city, but the prices are high, unless you're willing to wake up early and try your luck at the Lots Road Auction, near the swanky Chelsea Design Centre. Also stop by Alfie's Antique Market in Marylebone; the small shops lining Church Street sell everything from large-scale 19th-century English and European furniture to Art Deco ceramics and vintage shop fittings.

Listed below is a selection of stores in which to whet your appetite. ■ TIP→ Opening times vary: many places that are open on the weekend are closed Monday or Tuesday.

APPLIED ARTS AND HANDICRAFTS

London, with its prestigious design colleges, multiple design fairs, and myriad galleries, is a magnet for artisans and craftspeople in glass, textiles, jewelry making, ceramics, metal, leather, and woodwork. Open-studio weekends (usually late May/early June and late November/early December) allow you to buy direct from makers. Two of the most convenient are Craft Central (⊕ *www.craftcentral.org.uk*), formerly the Clerkenwell Green Association, and Cockpit Arts (⊕ *www.cockpitarts.com*).

BEAUTY

Skin-care junkies and perfume fans will be hard-pressed to walk away empty-handed from some of London's best beauty emporiums. Visitors should try to visit at least one of London's most venerable perfumeries—the old-school favorites Floris or Penhaligon, as well as relative newcomers like Miller Harris or Jo Malone. London's organic pioneer, Neal's Yard Remedies, is still going strong but has plenty of competition from brands like Cowshed or Space NK.

BOOKS AND PRINTS

Charing Cross Road has long been a center of London bookselling, but books are big business in London and the trade spreads into many corners of the city. Every decent London High street has its Waterstone's, Borders, or local independent, some complete with coffee shops and, in some cases, even cocktail bars. Bloomsbury, around London University and the British Museum, is good territory for used books and eccentric specialists.

London, of course, has a vast array of specialist book shops, from art to travel. The English gentleman's library, with its glass-front cabinets full of rare leather-bound books, may be a film and literary cliché, but there's no denying that London is also one of the world's great centers for rare-book collectors. There's still quite a concentration of used bookstores on Charing Cross Road, with additional book and print specialists tucked away in Cecil Court, a pedestrian alley linking it with St. Martin's Lane. (See ⊕ *www.cecilcourt.co.uk* for a full list of the shops in this unique enclave.) Other well-respected specialists reside in Mayfair.

CLOTHING

London has joined Paris and New York as one of the world's fashion capitals, and every designer you've ever heard of is available. But it's the city's eccentric street style that gives fashion here its special edge. London women may not look as chic as French or Italian women, but many are daring and colorful fashion risk-takers. This is where the trends that show up on the European catwalks

WORD OF MOUTH

"Our favorite day was walking thru Marylebone High Street. Great shops, nice shopkeepers. We loved Daunt, the bookstore there. The folks there were great and the selection was wonderful. The store has very quaint architecture, too."
—paris1953

really begin. What makes London clothes shopping so much fun—for both men and women—is that you can buy high-quality traditional British clothing, bespoke tailoring, today's best fashion labels, delicious vintage clothing, and outrageous directional street style without traveling farther than a couple of Tube stops.

As one of the world's great fashion capitals, London has shops to dress women in style—whether their taste is trendy or traditional, and their budget rummage or royal. High-street chains like Miss Selfridge, Topshop, New Look, and Warehouse take aim at the young, adventurous, and slim; Hobbs, Whistles, and Jaeger provide updated classics for the more sophisticated; and fashion-oriented department stores—Harvey Nichols, Harrods, Selfridges, Liberty, Fenwick—cater to women of all ages and tastes. The hottest names on the London catwalks have their headquarters here—Alexander McQueen's flagship store is at 4–5 Old Bond Street, Mayfair, and, nearby, Stella McCartney's collections are showcased in a town house at 30 Bruton Street.

18

When it comes to stylish accessories, whether men or women are looking for a sturdy umbrella, a traditional hat, or a bag that will last a lifetime, London's specialists are known for their high level of craftsmanship—and today's designers draw on centuries of expertise.

Several of the lower-price adult chains, including H&M, Next, Monsoon, and Zara, have cheap and cheerful children's lines. In select Jigsaw branches, Jigsaw Junior has classics with a twist for girls. London parents swear by no-nonsense department store John Lewis, on Oxford Street, for fair prices and high-quality goods. But if you're looking for something more than run of the mill, expect to pay for it.

Finally, when it comes to menswear, London is even more celebrated for its trendsetters than for its womenswear. The department stores listed here have good menswear departments, but Selfridges and Liberty deserve special mentions for interesting designer offerings. London's Savile Row tailors are still the spot where a man orders a bespoke suit once he has really "arrived," but British style has loosened up considerably in recent years. Ozwald Boateng, with his sharp designs, and colorful suits and linings, is typical of the new wave of bespoke tailors. Not bespoke but still sublimely stylish is the famed Paul Smith emporium. Those with more flash than cash should seek out the trendsetting fashion chains: Topman, Reiss, and Zara.

LONDON SHOPPING STEALS AND DEALS

Although London has never been known as a budget-shopping destination, when the pound is strong, prices can seem stratospheric. No matter what currency you are using, there are still bargains to be had, as long as you know where, and when, to look. To get the maximum mileage out of your cash, visit during the widespread biannual sales, which kick off in late June and just after Christmas, and last about a month. For the best choices and biggest discounts, head to a department store such as Selfridges.

Fashion insiders attend the many sales held throughout the year, from big warehouse clearances, such as the Designer Warehouse Sales (⊕ www.designerwarehousesales. com) and Designer Sales UK (⊕ www. designersales.co.uk), to individual designers' sample sales—check out ⊕ www.fashionconfidential.co.uk or ⊕ www.dailycandy.com/london for information, and to register for updates. London outlets, such as Browns Labels for Less, Paul Smith Sale Shop, and the Joseph Sale Shop on the King's Road, offer year-round designer bargains. If time permits, travel outside London to Bicester Village (⊕ www.bicestervillage.com),

a luxury outlet mall in Oxfordshire. It's completely worth the nearly one-hour train journey, if only for the opportunity to score an item from such highly coveted British brands as Alexander McQueen, Temperley, Mulberry, and Thomas Pink.

If you're not fussy about labels, there are even more choices. **Primark** (✉ 499 Oxford St., Soho ☎ 020/7495–0420 Ⓤ Marble Arch) is fantastic for low-cost, high-fashion clothing. The huge, two-story Oxford Street flagship is the best place to shop, although keep in mind you get what you pay for; some of the fabrics and finishes betray their low prices. You may think having a suit custom-made in the city famous for its tailoring traditions is beyond your means, but there are less costly options away from hallowed Savile Row. Contemporary tailors **Pokit** (✉ 132 Wardour Street., Soho ☎ 020/7434–2875 ⊕ www.pokit. co.uk ⊙ Closed Sun. Ⓤ Tottenham Court Road) offer sharp but comfortable made-to-measure suits for men and women from just £500. And if your budget is tighter, you can score a secondhand Savile Row suit at Old Hat (⇨ see Vintage London).

DEPARTMENT STORES

FOOD AND DRINK

London excels at posh nosh, and the selection has gotten even bigger with European integration—but be prepared to pay quite a lot for it. The Food Halls at Harrods are internationally famous, almost as much for the beautiful displays and ceramic-tile ceilings as for the packaged teas, chocolates, biscuits, fresh produce, fish, and game. Selfridges is less daunting but more international in its selection, and the grande dame of London food halls is Fortnum & Mason. Marks & Spencer, almost as well known for its high-quality ready-made meals as its underwear, has M&S Simply Food stores around town.

HOME DECOR

London's main department stores have just about everything you might need; John Lewis, on Oxford Street is especially good for practical items, such as kitchen equipment. Terence Conran no longer owns Habitat, but his good-design-on-a-budget philosophy is still apparent. For something more unusual, head to Cheshire Street in the East End. Independent home-design shops have sprouted up here over the past

> **BESPOKE LONDON**
>
> Having anything made to order used to be an upper-class distinction in London. One had one's tailor, one's milliner, one's dressmaker, and so forth. Things are more democratic these days, but whether you want a custom-made Savile Row suit or handmade leather shoes, the price is steep.

few years, including the wonderfully British Labour & Wait, which sells stylish yet practical goods. Most are open only on weekends, when the Brick Lane and Spitalfields markets bring customers to the area.

English bone china is legendary, and the famous brands—Royal Doulton, Royal Worcester, Spode, Wedgwood, Minton, and the like—are still made in England, most in the Staffordshire towns around Stoke-on-Trent known as "The Potteries." The top brands are all over London, and Harrods and Selfridges both have excellent selections.

JEWELRY

If you are suddenly overcome with the need to invest in serious rocks, London won't let you down. All the major international players are here: Cartier, Tiffany, Bulgari, Fred, Boucheron, De Beers, Van Cleef and Arpels, Graff, David Morris, and Britain's own Mappin & Webb among them. Bond Street, in particular, is good hunting grounds for megawatt stocking fillers. ■TIP➔ Bargain hunters who know their gems head for Hatton Garden, London's traditional diamond center. It's lined with small, independent dealers. For a selection of unusual designer jewelry under one roof, try Liberty, Selfridges, or Fenwick. Widespread chain Links of London is a good bet for classic sterling silver and gold pieces, especially charm bracelets and cufflinks, and Melissa McArthur Jewellry is a fantastic little shop in Chelsea for purchasing beautifully handmade earrings or a necklace—all for prices that won't leave you gasping.

MUSIC

Although their supremacy is increasingly challenged by Internet downloads, global megastores such as HMV and Zavvi (formerly Virgin Megastore) are still busy. There are also specialty stores galore for cutting-edge music mixed by club DJs, and for stocking up your own collection of good old-fashioned vinyl. ■TIP➔ Consider that CDs cost anywhere from 10% to as much as 50% more in the United Kingdom than they do in North America. So look for the kind of music you really can't find at home. Long-standing independent record-shop enclave Berwick Street, in Soho has seen some recent closures, but several shops remain, including the wide-ranging Sister Ray (Nos. 34–35), and Vinyl Junkies

VINTAGE LONDON

The trend for vintage clothing on both sides of the Atlantic shows no sign of letting up, and the British, with their love of theatrical style, have embraced it with particular gusto. Many boutiques have integrated vintage items into their stock. Liberty, Selfridges, and Topshop all have vintage sections. You can find retro from the recent past at Camden Market or on the fringes of Portobello Road and Brick Lane/Spitalfields. Listed below are some of the best specialty shops:

Absolute Vintage is a warehouse of handpicked items from the 1930s through the 1980s, but the specialty here is shoes. The shop has the largest collection of vintage shoes in the United Kingdom (more than 1,000 pairs). Best of all, prices are reasonable. ⊠ *15 Hanbury St., Spitalfields/East End* ☎ *020/7247–3883* ⊕ *www.absolutevintage.co.uk* Ⓤ *Aldgate East, Liverpool St.*

Beyond Retro stocks more than 10,000 vintage items for men and women. From cowboy boots to bowling shirts to prom dresses, they've got the largest collection of American retro in the United Kingdom. ⊠ *110–112 Cheshire St., Spitalfields/East End* ☎ *020/7729–9001* ⊕ *www.beyondretro.com* Ⓤ *Whitechapel, Bethnal Green Rail.*

Orsini is a tiny but choice boutique. Eveningwear with Hollywood-style glamour is the trademark here, with clothes from the 1920s to the 1970s. Victoria Beckham is a fan. ⊠ *76 Earl's Court Rd., Kensington* ☎ *020/7937–2903* Ⓤ *Earl's Court.*

Every piece of clothing at **Palette London** is in immaculate condition, which can save a lot of digging.

Owner Mark Ellis sells Ossie Clark, Missoni, Pucci, as well as Chanel from the 1940s up to the '90s. ⊠ *21 Canonbury La., Islington* ☎ *020/7288–7428* Ⓤ Highbury & Islington.

★ **Fodor'sChoice Rellik** is favored by the likes of Kate Moss and originally began as a street stall on Portobello Road. Today vintage hunters looking to splurge can find a selection of YSL, Chanel, and Dior, as well as items from lesser-known designers. Prices range from £30 to £1,000. ⊠ *8 Golborne Rd., Notting Hill* ☎ *020/8962–0089* ⊕ *www.relliklondon.co.uk* Ⓤ *Westbourne Park.*

Rokit consists of two shops along Brick Lane that stock everything from handbags and ball gowns to jeans, military, and Western wear, and the ever-changing collection spans from the 1920s to the 1990s. Magazine and rock stylists love it. There are also branches in Camden and Covent Garden. ⊠ *101 and 107 Brick La., Spitalfields/East End* ☎ *020/7375–3864* ⊕ *www.rokit.co.uk* Ⓤ *Shoreditch High St.*

Virginia, Virginia Baker's collection of vintage clothing, may be the best in London. Dresses, hats, and accessories from early Victorian (circa 1850) to the early 1930s are available. These are wearable collectors' items and priced accordingly. ⊠ *98 Portland Rd., Holland Park* ☎ *020/7727–9908* ⊗ *Closed Sun.; open Sat. by appointment only* Ⓤ *Holland Park, Ladbroke Grove.*

(No. 94), and there are more dotted in surrounding streets. Camden Market is also good for a browse through secondhand and independent music stores.

SHOES

It's no accident that Manolo Blahnik, the luxury shoe designer, made his name in London and still lives here. Audrey Hepburn, Kate Moss, and even the *Sex and the City* girls have all worn Manolos. Blahnik still trades from his original shop in Chelsea, just off the King's Road, hidden away on Old Church Street. Jimmy Choo is another "native son" who began his career quietly in London's East End before Tamara Mellon turned his name into a global luxury brand. The British capital is still a hotbed of shoemaking talent: Georgina Goodman, Beatrix Ong, and Rupert Sanderson are some of the most exciting names of the moment. Stop in at one of the King's Road branches of Office, Kurt Geiger, or Dune for British-designed shoes at slightly more affordable prices.

> ### ROYAL WARRANT
>
> Many stores carry items with the Royal Warrant seal (even some sugar brands). Though not personally endorsed by the royals, it does mean that the palace has used the item for five consecutive years—and it could enliven a gift for royal-watchers.

STATIONERY AND GRAPHIC ARTS

Whether you're looking for monogrammed calling cards or a pretty box of note cards to bring back as a gift, you're in luck. At the top of the range is Smythson, where many a socialite and celebrity have their personal stationery made, while shops like Paperchase are crammed with brightly colored notebooks and writing accessories.

TOYS AND MODELS

If you're traveling with kids in tow, there are plenty of shops that cater to children. Forget about taking them to check out the latest game system; London is the place to shop for traditional toys like soldiers, puppets, teddy bears, and those divinely wonderful toy theaters from Pollock's that have been delighting children ever since the days of Queen Victoria.

BLOOMSBURY, HOLBORN, AND ISLINGTON

BLOOMSBURY

ACCESSORIES

James Smith & Sons Ltd. This has to be the world's ultimate umbrella shop, and a must for anyone interested in real Victorian London. The family-owned shop has been in business since 1857 in the same New Oxford Street corner, and sells every kind of umbrella, cane, and walking stick imaginable. The decor is unchanged since the 19th century; you will feel as if you have stepped back into time. If the umbrellas are out of

BRING A BIT OF ENGLAND HOME

To avoid panic-buying a bulk pack of Cadbury chocolate or a "My sister went to London" T-shirt at Heathrow, it's wise to plan your gift purchasing with care.

For everything under one roof, unique department store Liberty is hard to beat—here, you'll find everything from exquisite Miller Harris fragrances by British perfumer Lyn Harris to small leather goods embossed with the famous Liberty prints.

Fortnum & Mason is also a good bet for traditional offerings, such as leather-covered hip flasks and its beautifully packaged biscuits, teas, and unusual condiments.

For the men back home, consider some traditional shaving cream from Geo. F. Trumper.

The museum shops are also bursting with original gift ideas, from Brit Art books and posters at Tate Modern to double-decker bus models and Tubemap mouse mats at the recently refurbished London Transport Museum in Covent Garden.

For truly unique items, check out the craft showrooms listed under Applied Arts and Handicrafts. The shops below will further inspire—and are all close to each other for easy browsing.

A. Gold. All the foodstuffs sold in this Dickensian-looking shop, occupying an old milliner's premises near Spitalfields Market, are sourced from or grown in the United Kingdom. A bottle of mead, a jar of English wildflower honey, or Somerset brandy are all great Brit gifts. Stylish gift baskets and old-fashioned picnic hampers are available. ✉ 42 Brushfield St., East End ☎ 020/7247–2487 Ⓤ Liverpool St.

Geo. F. Trumper. If you don't have time for their old-fashioned hot towel shave, pick up some accessories to take home for yourself or as a gift. The Extract of West Indian Lime is a popular, zingy aftershave, or pick up a Coconut Oil Hard Shaving Soap, which comes in a hand-turned wooden bowl. There is also a store at 9 Curzon Street in Mayfair. ✉ 1 Duke of York St., St. James's ☎ 020/7734–1370 ⊕ www.trumpers.com ⊗ Closed Sun. Ⓤ Piccadilly Circus.

Labour & Wait. Although household items like colanders and clothespins may not sound like ideal souvenirs, this shop may make you reconsider. The owners are on a mission to revive functional, old-fashioned British goods, such as enamel kitchenware, "Brown Betty" glazed teapots, Guernsey sweaters, and vintage Welsh blankets. ✉ 85 Redchurch St., East End ☎ 020/7729–6253 ⊗ Closed Sun. Ⓤ Shoreditch High St.

Shelf. Near Labour & Wait, this gift shop, run by an artist and designer, sells stationery, books, small household items, and original artworks and oddities made in London and Europe. ✉ 40 Cheshire St., East End ☎ 020/7739–9444 ⊗ By appointment only Mon.–Thurs. Ⓤ Aldgate East, Liverpool St.

your price range, James Smith also sells smaller accessories and hand-made wooden bowls. ⊠ *Hazelwood House, 53 New Oxford St., Blooms-bury* ☎ *020/7836–4731* ⊕ *www. james-smith.co.uk* ⊗ *Closed Sun.* ⓤ *Tottenham Court Rd., Holborn.*

BOOKS

Gay's the Word. Open since 1979, this is London's leading gay and lesbian bookshop. Thousands of titles, from literature, thoughtful nonfiction to erotica, and even detective novels, fill the shelves. The shop is a well-loved fixture on the scene, and often hosts discus-sion groups, readings, and other events. ⊠ *66 Marchmont St., Blooms-bury* ☎ *020/7278–7654* ⊕ *www.gaystheword.co.uk* ⊗ *Closed Sun. morning* ⓤ *Russell Sq.*

Persephone Books. A must for all lovers of feminist fiction and non-fiction, Persephone is on Lamb's Conduit Street in the heart of Blooms-bury. A gem of a bookshop specializes in reprinting mostly neglected 20th-century stories from predominately female writers. The exqui-sitely decorated covers make for perfect gifts for your bibliophile friends. ⊠ *59 Lamb's Conduit St., Bloomsbury* ☎ *020/7242–9292* ⊕ *www.persephonebooks.co.uk* ⊗ *Closed Sun.* ⓤ *Russell Sq.*

STATIONERY

Paperchase. The stationery superstore of London, Paperchase sells writ-ing paper in every conceivable shade and in a dozen mediums. There are lovely cards, artists' materials, notebooks, and loose stationery. The three-floor store has a café. Other branches in London include the King's Road in Chelsea, and The Piazza in Covent Garden. ⊠ *213–215 Tottenham Court Rd., Bloomsbury* ☎ *020/7467–6200* ⊕ *www. paperchase.co.uk* ⓤ *Goode St.*

HOLBORN

ANTIQUES

★ **London Silver Vaults.** Housed in a basement vault, this extraordinary space holds stalls from more than 30 silver dealers. Products range from the spectacular to the over-the-top, but you can also pick up smaller items, from a set of Victorian cake forks to a teaspoon or candlesticks. ■TIP➜ Most of the silver merchants actually trade out of room-size, underground vaults, which were originally rented out to London's upper crust to store their valuables. ⊠ *53–64 Chancery La., Holborn* ☎ *020/7242–3844* ⊕ *www.thesilvervaults.com* ⊗ *Closed Sat. after 1, and Sun.* ⓤ *Chancery La.*

18

ISLINGTON

HOUSEHOLD

TwentyTwentyOne. Open since 1996, TwentyTwentyOne showcases the best in both modern and vintage furniture. There are design classics like a chaise longue from Le Corbusier, as well curvy daybeds from designer Jacob Pringiers. The kids' range is particularly cool, such as the plastic elephants designed by the Eames brothers, and small accessories like tote bags and cushion covers will easily fit into your luggage. ⊠ *274 Upper St., Islington* ☎ *020/7288–1996* ⊕ *www.twentytwentyone.com* Ⓤ *Highbury & Islington.*

THE CITY AND SOUTH BANK

THE CITY

ART GALLERY

★ **Lesley Craze Gallery.** This serene gallery displays jewelry by some 100 young designers from around the world, with a strong British bias, featuring both precious and semiprecious stones. There's also a textiles room showcasing unusual and colorful handmade scarves, bags, and cushions. Prices are reasonable. ⊠ *33–35A Clerkenwell Green, Clerkenwell* ☎ *020/7608–0393* ⊕ *www.lesleycrazegallery.co.uk* ⊗ *Closed Sun.; open Mon. in Nov. and Dec. only* Ⓤ *Farringdon.*

THE SOUTH BANK

ART

Bargehouse. Many varied artisans have to pass rigorous selection procedures to set up in the prime riverside workshops where they make, display, and sell their work. The workshops are glass walled, and you're welcome to explore, even if you're just browsing. There are around 30 studios, spread over two floors. The Oxo Tower Restaurant & Brasserie on the top floor is expensive, but with its fantastic view of London, it's worth popping up for a drink. There's also a public terrace where you can take in the view. ⊠ *Oxo Tower Wharf, Bargehouse St., South Bank* ☎ *020/7401–4255* ⊗ *Closed Mon.* Ⓤ *Southwark, Waterloo.*

MUSIC

MDC Music & Movies. Perfectly placed for music lovers attending concerts at the Royal Festival Hall, classical specialist MDC also stocks jazz and world music. Staff here, and at sister shop MDC Opera next to the ENO Coliseum, are knowledgeable and helpful. ⊠ *Festival Riverside, Royal Festival Hall, South Bank* ☎ *020/7620–0198* Ⓤ *Waterloo.*

Continued on page 399

TO MARKET, TO MARKET

Londoners love a good market. With their cluttered stalls and crowds of people, they are a visible reminder that, in this world of global chain stores and supermarkets, London is still, in many respects, an Old World European city.

Every neighborhood has its cluster of fruit, vegetable, and flower stalls, or its weekend car-boot sales—gigantic garage sales where ordinary people pay a fiver for the privilege of selling their castoffs. Some, like Broadway Market in London Fields, run for miles. Others, like Brixton Market, Europe's biggest Caribbean-food market, featuring more than 300 stalls, specialize in ethnic ingredients and products. Still others crop up in the most unexpected places: on Berwick Street in the heart of Soho, for example, media moguls, designers, ad execs, actors,

dancers, and ladies of the night mingle over the punnets of strawberries, wedges of cheddar, and slabs of wet fish.

The big specialty markets, traditionally open on weekends, are not only great for the occasional bargain but also for people-watching, photo ops, and all around great days out. And though the markets are popular with visitors, they aren't tourist traps. In fact, browsing the London markets is one of the few activities in London where natives and tourists mix and enjoy themselves as equals.

PORTOBELLO ROAD MARKET

🕐 Sat. 8 am–6 pm

✉ Portobello Rd., Notting Hill

Ⓤ Ladbroke Grove
(Hammersmith & City
Line), Notting Hill (District,
Circle, or Central Line)

☞ Antiques, fruits and
vegetables, vintage
clothing, household goods

★ Fodor'sChoice **London's most famous market** still wins the prize for the all-around best. It sits in a lively multicultural part of town; the 1,500-odd antiques dealers don't rip you off (although you should haggle where you can); and it stretches over a mile, changing character completely as it goes.

The southern end is lined with antiques shops and arcades; the middle, above Elgin Crescent, is where locals buy fruits and vegetables. This middle area was the setting for the lovely sequence in the movie *Notting Hill* where Hugh Grant walks along the market and through the changing seasons. The section near the elevated highway (called the Westway) has the best flea market in town, with vintage-clothing stores along the edges. Here, young designers sell their wares in and around the Portobello Green arcade. After that, the market trails off into a giant rummage sale of the kinds of cheap household goods the British call tat.

Some say Portobello Road has become a bit of a tourist trap, but if you acknowledge that it's a circus and get into the spirit, it's a lot of fun. Perhaps you won't find many bargains, but this is such a cool part of town that just hanging out is a good enough excuse to come. There are some food and flower stalls throughout the week, but to see the market in full swing, Saturday is the only day to come.

A PORTOBELLO DAY

In good weather the market gets very crowded by midday. For a Londoner's day at Portobello, come as early as you can (7 am) and enjoy the market when the traders have time for a chat and you can actually get near the stalls. By 10:30 you'll have seen plenty of the market and can stop for a late breakfast or brunch at the **Electric Brasserie** (✉ 191 Portobello Rd. ☎ 020/7908–9696), next to the area's famous Electric Cinema. If you still have the will to shop, move on to the less crowded boutiques along Westbourne Grove, Blenheim Crescent, or Ledbury Road.

BOROUGH MARKET

🕐 **Thurs. 11–5, Fri. noon–6, Sat. 8–5**

✉ Borough High St., South Bank

Ⓤ London Bridge (Jubilee or Northern Line),

🛒 Cheese, olives, coffee, baked goods, meats, fish, fruits, vegetables

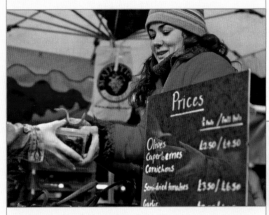

★ **There's been a market** in Borough since Roman times. This one, spread under the arches and railway tracks leading to London Bridge Station, is the successor to a medieval market once held on London Bridge. Post-millennium, it has been transformed from a noisy collection of local stalls to a trendy foodie center. Named the best market in London by a local magazine and the best market in Britain by a national newspaper, the Farmers Market held on Thursdays (some stalls), Fridays and Saturdays has attracted some of London's best merchants of comestibles. Fresh coffees, gorgeous cheeses, olives, and baked goods complement the organically farmed meats, fresh fish, fruit, and veggies.

Don't make any other lunch plans for the day; celebrity chef Jamie Oliver's scallop man cooks them up fresh from the Dorset coast at Shell Seekers; wild boar sausages sizzle on a grill, and there is much more that's tempting to gobble on the spot. There are chocolates, preserves, and Mrs. Bassa's handmade Indian condiments to take home, but the best souvenirs are the memories. If you'd rather eat sitting down, pop into the sleek reaturant Roast, which specializes in local seasonal food—much of it purchased at the market.

A BARGAIN DAY ON THE SOUTH BANK

Combine a visit to the Tate Modern (free) and a walk across the Millennium Bridge from the Tate to St. Paul's with a Thames-side picnic of goodies foraged at Borough Market. There are gourmet breads and farmhouse cheeses from France and Italy.

Or how about a wedge of Stinking Bishop cheese (Wallace and Gromit's favorite) from Neal's Yard Dairy? Fishmonger Applebee's serves up freshly sautéed garlic prawns in a wrap with chili and crème fraîche.

A PUB RIGHT OUT OF DICKENS

On the way back to Borough Tube station, stop for a pint at the **George Inn** (✉ 77 Borough High St., Southwark SE1 ☎ 020/7407-2056 Ⓤ London Bridge), mentioned by Dickens in *Little Dorrit*. This 17th-century coaching inn was a famous terminus in its day, and is the last galleried inn in London. Now owned by the National Trust, it is leased to a private company and still operates as a pub.

THE EAST END MARKETS

Brick Lane. The noisy center of the Bengali community is a hubbub of buying and selling. Sunday stalls have food, hardware, household goods, electrical goods, books, bikes, shoes, clothes, spices, and saris. The CDs and DVDs are as likely as not to be counterfeit, and the bargain iron may not have a plug—so be careful. But people come more to enjoy the ethnic buzz, eat curries and Bengali sweets, or indulge in salt beef on a bagel at Beigel Bake, London's 24-hour bagel bakery, a survivor of the neighborhood's Jewish past. Brick Lane's activity spills over into nearby Petticoat Lane Market with similar goods but less atmosphere.

From Brick Lane it's a stone's throw to the **Columbia Road Flower Market**. It's only 52 stalls, but markets don't get much more photogenic than this. Flowers, shrubs, bulbs, trees, garden tools, and accessories are sold wholesale. The local cafés are superb.

Stop to smell the roses and have Sunday brunch on Columbia Road before plunging into **Spitalfields**. The covered market (once London's wholesale meat market) is at the center of this area's boho revival. The original building has been restored to its Victorian splendor, and a modern shopping complex that respects its character has been developed around it, with a covered area housing additional stalls. Wares include crafts, retro clothing, handmade rugs, soap, and cakes. And, from Spanish tapas to Thai satays, it's possible to eat your way around the world.

BRICK LANE

⊙ **Sun. 8 am–2 pm**

✉ Brick La., East End

Ⓤ Aldgate East (Hammersmith & City or District Line), Liverpool Street (Hammersmith & City, District, or Circle Line)

☞ Food, hardware, household goods, electric goods, books, bikes, shoes, clothes, spices, saris

COLUMBIA ROAD FLOWER MARKET

⊙ **Sun. 8–4**

✉ Columbia Rd., East End

Ⓤ Old Street (Northern Line)

☞ Flowers, shrubs, bulbs, trees, garden tools, accessories

SPITALFIELDS

⊙ **Stalls Thurs., Fri. 10–4, Sun. 9–5. Restaurants weekdays 11 AM–11 pm, Sun. 9–5. Retail shops daily 11 am–7 pm.**

✉ Brushfield St., East End

Ⓤ Liverpool St. (Hammersmith & City, Circle, or Bakerloo Line), Aldgate East (Hammersmith & City or District Line)

☞ Crafts, foods, vintage clothing, rugs, soap, cakes

BERMONDSEY ANTIQUES MARKET

🕐 Fri. 4 am–about 1 pm

✉ Long La. and Bermondsey Sq., South Bank

Ⓤ London Bridge (Jubilee or Northern Line), Borough (Nothern Line)

☞ Antiques (silverware, paintings, furniture)

Come before dawn and bring a flashlight to bag a bargain antique at this famous market. Dealers arrive as early as 4 AM to snap up the best bric-a-brac and silverware, paintings, objets d'art, fine arts, and furniture. The early start grew out of a wrinkle in the law under which thieves could sell stolen goods with impunity in the hours of darkness when provenance could not be ascertained. That law was changed, and the market has been shrinking ever since.

What should be one of London's most important antiques markets is in decline and in desperate need of a significant rebrand to survive. The recent establishment of the Saturday morning Bermondsey Farmer's Market, as well as the 2009 redevelopment of Bermondsey Square (⊕ www.bermondseysquare. co.uk) should attract more customers to the Antiques Market. The square now includes a hotel, an arthouse cinema, shops, and restaurants.

THE CAMDEN MARKETS

CAMDEN MARKET
🕐 **Daily 9:30 am–6 pm**

CAMDEN LOCK MARKET, STABLES MARKET, AND CANAL MARKET
🕐 **Daily 10–6**

ELECTRIC MARKET
🕐 **Sun. 10–5**

✉ Camden Town

Ⓤ Camden Town, Chalk Farm (Northern Line)

☞ Vintage clothing, antiques, jewelry, candlesticks, ceramics, mirrors, toys

This area's actually several markets gathered around a pair of locks in the Regent's Canal. Camden Lock Market proper began in 1973 on the site of a former timber yard. The lock studios attracted artists with reasonable rents and gave customers the chance to see goods being made. Today, the market includes some of London's most creative types, with products designed on site and market stalls offering a spectacular array of merchandise: vintage and new clothes, antiques and junk, jewelry and scarves, candlesticks, ceramics, mirrors, and toys.

The markets on Camden High Street (both outdoors and within the Electric Ballroom) mainly sell cheap T-shirts, secondhand clothes, and tacky pop-culture paraphernalia; it's best to head to Camden Lock and Stable Markets. Though much of the merchandise is youth oriented, the markets have a lively appeal to aging hippies, fashion designers, and anyone with a taste for the bohemian who doesn't mind crowds and a bit of a madhouse scene. Don't miss the Horse Hospital (weekends only) for quirky antiques dealers.

THE GREENWICH MARKET

On weekends, the focus is on crafts, while on Wednesdays it's on fresh produce and housewares, on Thursdays and Fridays it's on antiques: china, old books, cameras, vintage clothing, marine memorabilia, and other curiosities. On weekends, the Village Market down the road offers yet more flea-market miscellany and cheap goods. Less crowded than Camden, less touristy than Covent Garden, this part-indoor, part-outdoor market is surrounded by interesting shops and close to historic sites. If you make a day of it, you can see the Greenwich Observatory and stand on Longitude 0 (marked in brass and stone in front of the observatory). But, sadly, due to setbacks in the Cutty Sark's restoration after fire damage in Spring 2007, the famous tea clipper will be closed until Spring 2011.

🕐 Wed. 11 am–6 pm
Thurs.–Sun. 10–5:30 pm

✉ Greenwich High Rd., Greenwich

Ⓤ DLR: Cutty Sark for Maritime Greenwich

☞ Antiques, arts, crafts, books, toys, paraphernalia

Know-How

■ **TWO MARKET TIPS TO REMEMBER →** In the end, if you like something and you can afford it, it's worth buying; you're the best judge of that. But it's annoying to buy an "English antique" only to find the Made in China label when you get home. To avoid disappointment:

Look for hallmarks. A lot of what passes for English silver is plate or outright fake. English gold and silver must, by law, be marked with hallmarks that indicate their material and the year in which they were made. Books of hallmarks are inexpensive to buy in London bookshops.

Buy crafts items directly from the makers. Ceramicists, jewelers, needleworkers and other artisans often sell their own work at markets. Besides buying the item, you may have a conversation worth remembering.

■ **MARKET ETIQUETTE →** You've probably heard that you're expected to bargain with the market traders to get the best price. That's true to a degree, but London markets are not Middle Eastern souks, and most bargaining is modest. Unless you are an expert in the item you want to buy and really know how low you can go, don't offer a ridiculously low price. Instead ask the dealer, "Is that the best you can do?" If the dealer is willing to bargain, he or she will suggest a slightly lower price, maybe 10% less. You might try to get another 10% off and end up meeting in the middle.

THE EAST END

SPITALFIELDS

ACCESSORIES: HATS

★ **Bernstock Speirs.** Paul Bernstock and Thelma Speirs turn traditional hats on their head with street-smart trilbies and knitted hats that feature unusual colors and quirky details. It's no wonder that this store has caught the eye of Liam Gallagher and Kylie Minogue. ⊠ *234 Brick La., Spitalfields* ☎ *020/7739–7385* ⊕ *www.bernstockspiers.com* Ⓤ *Liverpool St., Bethnal Green.*

CLOTHING

★ **Junky Styling.** This brand was launched by designers Annika Sanders and Kerry Seager, who used to "deconstruct" old clothing when they wanted something unique to wear clubbing. They recycled traditional suits and shirts into wild outfits, and the business grew from there. The highly original (and eco-friendly) garments, for both men and women, are funky but retain the sophistication of their tailored origins. ⊠ *12 Dray Walk, The Old Truman Brewery, 91 Brick La., Spitalfields* ☎ *020/7247–1883* ⊕ *www.junkystyling.co.uk* Ⓤ *Liverpool St., Aldgate East.*

★ **The Laden Showroom.** Sienna Miller, Victoria Beckham, and Noel Gallagher are among the celebs who regularly check out emerging talent at this East End showroom for young designers. The store retails the work of more than 70 new designers, some selling one-off items—so the look you find is likely to be original. ⊠ *103 Brick La., Spitalfields* ☎ *020/7247–2431* ⊕ *www.laden.co.uk* Ⓤ *Shoreditch High St.*

MUSIC

★ **Rough Trade East.** Whereas some London record stores are struggling, this veteran indie-music specialist seems to have gotten the formula right. In 2007 it opened this spacious new East End branch that's as much a hangout as a shop, complete with a stage for live gigs, a café, and even Internet access. ⊠ *Dray Walk, Old Truman Brewery, 91 Brick La., Spitalfields* ☎ *020/7392–7788* Ⓤ *Liverpool St.*

18

KENSINGTON, CHELSEA, KNIGHTSBRIDGE, AND BELGRAVIA

BELGRAVIA

ACCESSORIES

★ **Lulu Guinness.** Famous for her flamboyantly themed bags (think the satin "bucket" topped with roses or the elaborately beaded red snakeskin "lips" clutch). Guinness also showcases vintage-inspired vanity cases, shoes, beauty products, and bed linens in this frilly little shop, which is just as whimsical as her designs. ⊠ *3 Ellis St., Belgravia* ☎ *020/7823–4828* ⊕ *www.luluguinness.com* ⊘ *Closed Sun.* Ⓤ *Sloane Sq.*

Philip Treacy. Treacy's magnificent hats are annual showstoppers on Ladies Day at the Royal Ascot races and regularly grace the glossy magazines' society pages. Part Mad Hatter, part Cecil Beaton, Treacy's creations always guarantee a grand entrance (remember Sarah Jessica Parker at the London premiere of the *Sex and the City* movie?). In addition to the extravagant, haute couture hats handmade in the atelier, ready-to-wear hats and bags are also for sale. ⊠ *69 Elizabeth St., Belgravia* ☎ *020/7730–3992* ⊕ *www.philiptreacy.co.uk* ☉ *Closed Sun.* Ⓤ *Sloane Sq.*

CHELSEA

ACCESSORIES
The Shop at Bluebird. The "concept store" has officially arrived in London. The brainchild of the couple behind popular womenswear brand Jigsaw, this 10,000-square-foot space in the old Bluebird garage brings together fashion, furniture, books, and music—all chosen for style and originality. It's worth visiting for the displays alone, which change regularly, although the funky ceiling-light installation of more than 1,000 bulbs seems to be a constant feature. After browsing, unwind with a treatment at the on-site spa or join the ladies who lunch at Terence Conran's restaurant in the same complex. ■TIP→ It's a good 20-minute walk from the nearest Tube station at Sloane Square, so catch a No. 11 or No. 22 bus along the King's Road. ⊠ *350 King's Rd., Chelsea* ☎ *020/7351–3873* ⊕ *www.theshopatbluebird.com* Ⓤ *Sloane Sq.*

BOOKS
Green & Stone. This fabulous cave of artists' materials, papers, art books, easels, and mannequins is one of the longest-running shops on the King's Road, with a distinguished arts pedigree. It began life in 1927 as part of the Chenil Gallery, under the directorship of Augustus John and George Bernard Shaw. At the current location since 1934, it also has a framing service, antique paint boxes, and artists' tools. ⊠ *259 King's Rd., Chelsea* ☎ *020/7352–0837* ⊕ *www.greenandstone.com* Ⓤ *Sloane Sq.*

CLOTHING
Austique. For fans of such feminine brands as Shoshanna, Alice + Olivia, or Mara Hoffman, look no further than Austique. Situated along the trendy King's Road, this sophisticated boutique, which debuted in 2004 by sisters Linda Lopes and Katie Canvin, is home to a gorgeous array of dresses, lingerie, jewelry, and accessories for the ultimate fashionista. It's almost impossible to leave empty-handed. ⊠ *330 King's Rd., Chelsea* ☎ *020/7376–4555* ⊕ *www.austique.co.uk* Ⓤ *Sloane Sq.*

☉ **Brora.** The knitwear is cozy, but the taste temperature is cool in this contemporary Scottish cashmere emporium for men, women, and kids. There are dressed-up camisoles, sweaters and cardigans, adorable baby ensembles, plus noncashmere items such as picnic blankets and scarves. There are branches in Notting Hill, Marylebone, Islington, as well as Wimbledon. ⊠ *344 King's Rd., Chelsea* ☎ *020/7352–3697* ⊕ *www.brora.co.uk* Ⓤ *Sloane Sq.*

CLOTHING: MENSWEAR

Bamford & Sons. The men's and boys' wear at Bamford & Sons combines the British heritage of tailoring and fabrics with a suave modernity. Dashing city wear, romantically nonchalant country clothes, plus fine leather and cashmere accessories are all available. There is also a small but exquisite women's collection ⊠ *31 Sloane Sq., Chelsea* ☎ *020/7881–8010* Ⓤ *Sloane Sq.*

CLOTHING: WOMEN'S

Rigby & Peller. Those who love luxury lingerie shop here for brands like Prima Donna and Aubade, as well as R&P's own line. If the right fit eludes you, and you fancy being fitted by the Queen's corsetiere, have a bra made to measure (starting around £300). Most of the young royal and affluent women buy here, not only because the store holds the royal appointment, but also because the quality is excellent and the service much friendlier than you might expect. There are a number of stores across town, all of which are open on Sunday except the Conduit Street location. ⊠ *13 Kings Rd., Chelsea* ☎ *0845/076–5545* ⊕ *www. rigbyandpeller.com* Ⓤ *Sloane Sq.*

FOOD

L'Artisan du Chocolat. Praised by top chefs Gordon Ramsay and Heston Blumenthal, L'Artisan raises chocolate to an art form. Its abstract "Couture" chocolates are infused with fruits, nuts, and spices (including such exotic flavorings as Szechuan pepper and tobacco). It is also one of the few chocolate shops in the world that makes liquid salted caramels. Leave the kiddies at home, though; this shop is total wish fulfillment for grown-up chocolate lovers. ⊠ *89 Lower Sloane St., Chelsea* ☎ *020/7824–8365* Ⓤ *Sloane Sq.*

HOUSEHOLD

The Conran Shop. This is the domain of Sir Terence Conran, who has been informing British taste since he opened Habitat in the 1960s. Although no longer associated with Habitat, the stores are still a bastion of clean, unfussy modernist design. Home enhancers from furniture to stemware—both handmade and mass produced, by famous names and young designers—are displayed in a suitably gorgeous building that is a modernist design landmark in its own right. Both the flagship store and the branch on Marylebone High Street are bursting with great gift ideas. ⊠ *Michelin House, 81 Fulham Rd., South Kensington* ☎ *020/7589–7401* ⊕ *www.conranshop.co.uk* Ⓤ *South Kensington.*

Designers Guild. Tricia Guild's exuberantly colored modern fabrics, wallpapers, paints, furniture, and bed linens have inspired several decades' worth of home owners and apartment dwellers, and her soft-furnishings book has taught many a budget-conscious do-it-yourselfer how to reupholster a sofa or make lined draperies. The shop also stocks contemporary furniture, wallpapers, and home accessories by other designers. ⊠ *267 King's Rd., Chelsea* ☎ *020/893–7620* ⊕ *www.designersguild. com* ☾ *Closed Sun.* Ⓤ *Sloane Sq.*

18

JEWELRY

★ **Butler & Wilson.** Long before anybody ever heard the word bling, this shop was marketing the look—in diamanté, colored rhinestones, and crystal—to movie stars and secretaries alike. Specialists in bold costume jewelry, they've added semiprecious stones to the collections and the look is anything but subtle, so it may not suit all tastes unless you're in the market for a rhinestone Union Jack pin. Even if you're not a fan, the shop is worth a visit for its vintage (and vintage-influenced) clothes, once used only to display the jewelry. There's also another shop at 20 South Molton Street. ✉ *189 Fulham Rd., South Kensington* ☎ *020/7352–3045* ⊕ *www.butlerandwilson.co.uk* Ⓤ *South Kensington.*

Melissa McArthur Jewellry. Tucked between Vivienne Westwood's shop and the Bluebird in Chelsea, this small but mighty jewelry store is a must-see on the King's Road. With everything handmade in-house using precious and semiprecious gems (don't forget the pearls), stocking up on gifts for female loved ones is easy here. The price points are also very reasonable for such eternally wearable and gorgeous items. ✉ *378 King's Rd., Chelsea* ☎ *020/7351–1551* ⊕ *www.mmjlondon.com* Ⓤ *Sloane Sq.*

SHOES

★ **Manolo Blahnik.** Blink and you'll miss the discreet sign of this little shoe shop. Here, in the heart of Chelsea, the man who single-handedly managed to revive the sexy stiletto and make it classier than ever has been trading since 1973. It's a must for shoe lovers with a generous budget. If you're wearing your Manolos, hop on the No. 11 or No. 22 bus or into a cab—the nearest Tube is about a 20-minute walk away. ✉ *49–51 Old Church St., Chelsea* ☎ *020/7352–3863* ⊕ *www.manoloblahnik. com* ☾ *Closed Sun.* Ⓤ *Sloane Sq.*

KENSINGTON

CLOTHING: CHILDREN

☺ **Marie-Chantal.** If you love beautiful, tasteful clothing for babies and children, head to this boutique that is the brainchild of Princess Marie-Chantal of Greece. As you'd imagine, the look is regal and the price is high. Materials used include silk, linen, and Liberty prints. ✉ *148 Walton St., South Kensington* ☎ *020/7838–1111* ⊕ *www.mariechantal. com* Ⓤ *South Kensington.*

HOUSEHOLD

Fodor's Choice **Mint.** Owner Lina Kanafani has scoured the globe to stock an eclectic
★ mix of furniture, art, ceramics, and home accessories. Mint also showcases works by up-and-coming designers and sells plenty of limited edition and one-off pieces. If you don't want to ship a couch home, consider a miniature flower vase or a handmade ceramic pitcher. ✉ *2 North Terr., South Kensington* ☎ *020/7225–2228* ⊕ *www.mintshop. co.uk* Ⓤ *South Kensington.*

WOMEN'S WEAR

★ **Jigsaw.** Popular with women in their twenties through forties, Jigsaw toes the line between trendy and classic (similar to Banana Republic). Prices are reasonable for feminine dresses, practical T-shirts, and knitwear in high-quality fabrics and distinctive yet subtle colors. There are several other branches are around town. Girls get in on the act, too, with their own line, Jigsaw Junior. ⊠ *The Chapel, Duke of York Sq., King's Rd., Chelsea* ☎ *020/730–4404* ⊕ *www.jigsawonline.com* Ⓤ *Sloane Sq.*

KNIGHTSBRIDGE

ACCESSORIES

★ **Anya Hindmarch.** Exquisite leather bags and personalized, printed canvas totes are what made Hindmarch famous, along with her hit 2007 "I'm Not A Plastic Bag" eco-creation. Her designs are sold at Harrods and Harvey Nichols, but in her stores you can see her complete collection of bags and shoes, and have your own photograph immortalized on a bag from a choice of sizes and styles. There are also branches around the corner on Bond Street in Mayfair and Ledbury Road in Notting Hill. ⊠ *157–158 Sloane St., Belgravia* ☎ *020/7730–0961* ⊕ *www.anyahindmarch.com* Ⓤ *Sloane Sq., Knightsbridge.*

CLOTHING

Egg. Tucked away in a residential mews a short walk from Harvey Nichols, this shop is the brainchild of Maureen Doherty, once Issey Miyake's right-hand person. Minimalist, unstructured styles for men and women in natural fabrics, such as silk, cashmere, and antique cotton, have an artisanal quality. The shop is a former Victorian dairy, and garments are casually hung on hooks or folded on wooden tables in the simple, white space. The price tags, however, are anything but humble. Unusual ceramics and jewelry are also on display. ⊠ *36 Kinnerton St., Knightsbridge* ☎ *020/7235–9315* ☉ *Closed Sun. and Mon.* Ⓤ *Knightsbridge.*

CLOTHING: CHILDREN

☺ **Rachel Riley.** Looking for traditional English style for the younger ones? Riley's expensive, vintage-inspired collection includes classics like duffle coats, cashmere booties, and floral dresses for girls and teens. Mothers who love the Riley look can pick even up coordinating outfits for themselves at the Knightsbridge or Marylebone High Street locations. ⊠ *14 Pont St., Knightsbridge* ☎ *020/7259–5969* ⊕ *www.rachelriley.com* Ⓤ *Knightsbridge.*

CLOTHING: MENSWEAR

Hackett. If J. Crew isn't preppy enough for you, try Hackett. What once started as a posh thrift shop, Hackett once recycled cricket flannels, hunting pinks, Oxford brogues, and similar British wear. Now it makes its own attire, and it has become a genuine—and very good—gentlemen's outfitter. The look is traditional and classic, and some of the best buys include polo shirts, corduroys, and striped scarves. ⊠ *Main store: 137/138 Sloane St., Knightsbridge* ☎ *020/7730–3331* ⊕ *www.hackett.com* Ⓤ *Sloane Sq.*

CLOTHING: WOMEN'S WEAR

★ **Agent Provocateur.** Created by Vivienne Westwood's son, these shops purvey sexy, naughty-but-nice lingerie in gorgeous fabrics and lace. The original shop is in the almost-red-light area of Soho, but there are now branches across the city—and across the Atlantic. Selections are

18

also available in Harrods, Harvey Nichols, and Selfridges. ⊠ *16 Pont St., Knightsbridge* ☎ *020/7235–0229* ⊕ *www.agentprovocateur.com* ⊘ *Closed Sun.* Ⓤ *Knightsbridge, Sloane Sq.*

DEPARTMENT STORES

Fodor's Choice
★ **Harrods.** A fabled encyclopedia of luxury brands, this Knightsbridge institution has more than 300 departments and 20 restaurants, all spread over 1 million square feet. If you approach Harrods as a tourist attraction rather than a fashion store, you won't be disappointed. Focus on the spectacular food halls, the huge ground-floor perfumery, the marble-clad accessory rooms, and the theme park–like Egyptian Room—at the bottom of the nearby Egyptian escalator there's a commemorative memorial to Diana and Dodi (whose father owns Harrods). ■TIP➔ Be prepared to brave the crowds (avoid visiting on a Saturday if you can), and be prepared to pay if you want to use the bathroom on some floors(!). ⊠ *87–135 Brompton Rd., Knightsbridge* ☎ *020/7730–1234* ⊕ *www.harrods.com* Ⓤ *Knightsbridge.*

★ **Harvey Nichols.** While visiting tourists flock to Harrods, true London fashionistas shop at Harvey Nichols, aka "Harvey Nicks" as it's called. The fashion and accessories departments are outstanding, carrying designs from Prada to 3.1 Phillip Lim. The furniture and housewares are equally gorgeous (and pricey), but bargains abound during the twice-annual sales in January and July. The Fifth Floor restaurant is a place to see and be seen, but if you're after a quick bite, pick up a sandwich and some chocolates from the Foodmarket or Daylesford Organic. ⊠ *109–125 Knightsbridge, Knightsbridge* ☎ *020/7235–5000* ⊕ *www.harveynichols.com* Ⓤ *Knightsbridge.*

SHOES

Jimmy Choo. It's the name on every supermodel's and fashion editor's feet, even though it is Tamara Mellon who launched and now owns the company. The brand's exquisite and elegant designs combine luxurious materials and details with shapes (pointy toes and slim high heels are signatures) that are classic enough to have fashion staying power—essential given the prices. The handbags are also a hit with fans. ⊠ *32 Sloane St., Knightsbridge* ☎ *020/7823–1051* ⊕ *www.jimmychoo.com* Ⓤ *Knightsbridge.*

NOTTING HILL

BOOKS

Books for Cooks. It may seem odd to describe a bookshop as delicious-smelling, but between the products of its test kitchen and its regularly scheduled cooking workshops, Books for Cooks is hard to resist. Just about every world cuisine is represented on its shelves, along with the complete lineup of celebrity-chef editions. You can sample lunch dishes, cakes, and coffee at one of a handful of tables in the back. ■TIP➔ Before you come to London, visit the shop's Web site, www.booksforcooks. com, to sign up for a cooking class. ⊠ *4 Blenheim Crescent, Notting Hill* ☎ *020/7221–1992* ⊘ *Closed Sun. and Mon.* Ⓤ *Notting Hill Gate, Ladbroke Grove.*

CLOTHING

Aimé. French-Cambodian sisters Val and Vanda Heng-Vong launched this shop to showcase the best of French clothing and designer housewares. Expect to find fashion by Isabel Marant, Antik Batik, and A.P.C. You can also pick up scents by Esteban and a well-edited collection of ceramics. Just next door at 34 Ledbury Road, Petit Aimé sells children's clothing. ✉ *32 Ledbury Rd., Notting Hill* ☎ *020/7221–7070* ⊕ *www.aimelondon.com* Ⓤ *Notting Hill Gate.*

MUSIC

Music & Video Exchange. This store—actually a conglomeration of several shops on Notting Hill Gate—is a convenient destination for seekers of unusual and mainstream chart music as well as classical and pop. Rare records and CDs are upstairs, the soul and dance branch is at No. 42, and the classical branch is at No. 36. There are also branches in Soho, Greenwich, and Camden. ✉ *38 Notting Hill Gate, Notting Hill* ☎ *020/7243–8574* ⊕ *www.mveshops.co.uk* Ⓤ *Notting Hill Gate.*

SHOES

Emma Hope. The signature look at Emma Hope is vintage inspired. Mules and kitten-heeled shoes have exquisite embroidery and beading. Her ballet flats will appeal to those who favor comfort, but the filigree stilettos and bejeweled court shoes are the real showstoppers. Her stores also stock shoes and accessories for men. ✉ *207 Westbourne Grove, Notting Hill* ☎ *020/7313–7490* ⊕ *www.emmahope.com* Ⓤ *Notting Hill Gate.*

ST. JAMES'S, MAYFAIR, AND MARYLEBONE · 18

MARYLEBONE

ANTIQUES

★ **Alfie's Antique Market.** A large and exciting labyrinth on four floors, it has dealers specializing in anything and everything, but particularly in vintage clothing, decorative accessories, and furniture. Highlights include the fabulous collection of cocktail dresses and kitsch bar accessories at the Girl Can't Help It, and Vincenzo Caffarrella's spectacular Italian lighting. There's also a rooftop restaurant if you need a coffee break. In addition to the market, this end of Church Street is lined with excellent antiques shops. ✉ *13–25 Church St., Marylebone* ☎ *020/7723–6066* ⊙ *Closed Sun. and Mon.* Ⓤ *Edgware Rd.*

BEAUTY

Space NK. A cult favorite among beauty product fiends, this upscale chain boasts more than 20 locations throughout London. The minute you step inside, you're surrounded by very luxurious and sought-after brands like Kate Somerville, Chantecaille, and Rodial. Whether you're shopping for someone else or for just for yourself, you'll no doubt be the envy of every beauty lover when they see you toting a Space NK bag around town. ✉ *83a Marylebone High St., Marylebone* ☎ *020/7486–8791* ⊕ *www.spacenk.co.uk* Ⓤ *Baker St.*

BOOKS

Daunt Books. The most striking Daunt branch is the Edwardian store in Marylebone. The travel section is housed in a dramatic oak room, illuminated by a lofty conservatory roof and stained-glass windows. Guidebooks, poetry, and other literature are organized by country. There's also an excellent children's section and, at the entrance, biographies and fiction are piled on tables for eclectic browsing. There are also branches in Belsize Park, Chelsea, Hampstead, and Holland Park. ⊠ 83 Marylebone High St., Marylebone ☎ 020/7224–2295 ⊕ www. dauntbooks.co.uk Ⓤ Baker St.

CERAMICS

Emma Bridgewater. Peruse this shop for fun and funky casual plates, mugs, jugs, and breakfast tableware embellished with polka dots, hens, hearts and flowers, amusing mottoes, or matter-of-fact labels (sugar or coffee). Other locations include Fulham and Chiswick. ⊠ 81a Marylebone High St., Marylebone ☎ 020/7486–6897 Ⓤ Baker St.

CLOTHING

Margaret Howell. These quintessentially English clothes are understated yet manage to look utterly contemporary. Howell mixes impeccable British tailoring and traditional fabrics (linen, cashmere, tweed) with relaxed modern cuts. A fan of 20th-century household design, the designer also showcases vintage Ercol furniture at her boutique. ⊠ 34 Wigmore St., Marylebone ☎ 020/7009–9006 ⊕ www.margarethowell. co.uk ♥ Closed Sun. Ⓤ Bond St.

DEPARTMENT STORES

Marks & Spencer. You'd be hard-pressed to find a Brit who doesn't have something in their closet from Marks & Spencer (or "M&S" as it's affectionately known). This major chain whips up classic, dependable clothing for men, women, and children. It occasionally scores a fashion hit with its Per Una and Autograph lines, but the best buys here are the classics, such as cashmere and wool sweaters, socks and underwear, and believe it or not, machine-washable suits. The food department at M&S is consistently superb, and a great place to pick up a sandwich or premade salad on the go. (Look for their M&S Simply Food stores all over town.) The Marble Arch branch is the flagship, and has a fast stock turnover, but the 173 Oxford Street location also has an extensive fashion department. ⊠ 458 Oxford St., Marylebone ☎ 020/7935–7954 ⊕ www.marksandspencer.com Ⓤ Marble Arch.

Fodor's Choice ★ **Selfridges.** This giant, bustling store gives Harvey Nichols a run for its money as London's leading fashion department store. It's packed to the rafters with clothes for everyone in the family, from midprice lines to the latest catwalk names. The store continues to break ground with its striking modern design—especially the men's and women's high-fashion Superbrands sections, and the ground-floor Wonder Room, which showcases extravagant jewelry and luxury gifts. The frenetic cosmetics department is, according to the store, the largest in Europe. There are so many zones with pulsating music that merge into one another—from fashion to sports gear to audio equipment—that you practically need a map. ■ TIP→ Take a break with a glass of wine from the Wonder Bar, or pick up some rare tea in the Food Hall as a gift. ⊠ *400 Oxford St., Marylebone* ☎ *0800/123–400* ⊕ *www.selfridges.com* Ⓤ *Bond St.*

JEWELRY

★ **Kabiri.** A dazzling array of exciting contemporary jewelry by emerging and established designers from around the world is packed into this small shop. There is something to suit most budgets and tastes, from flamboyant statement pieces to subtle, delicate adornment. Look out for British talent Johanne Mills, Scott Stephen, and Tatty Devine, among many others. ⊠ *37 Marylebone High St., Marylebone* ☎ *020/7224–1808* ⊕ *www.kabiri.co.uk* Ⓤ *Baker St.*

MAYFAIR

ACCESSORIES

Connolly. Connolly used to produce the leather for Rolls-Royces and Aston Martins, and that heritage lives on in its deluxe motoring accessories, from sleek luggage to an espresso machine designed for your car. Today the brand is owned by fashion designer Joseph Ettedgui, and the Andree Putman–designed shop sells a broad range of luxurious clothing and accessories for men and women, including butter-soft leather and suede jackets, wallets, and driving gloves. ⊠ *41 Conduit St., Mayfair* ☎ *020/7439–2510* ⊕ *www.connollylondon.com* ⊘ *Open Sun. in Dec. only* Ⓤ *Oxford Circus, Bond St.*

Mulberry. This luxury goods company has produced many a season's It bag, including the Roxanne and the Bayswater. In addition to the leather handbags, Mulberry also produces gorgeous leather accessories, from wallets to luggage. In 2008 the company unveiled its first line of shoes. Aside from the New Bond Street flagship, there are branches in Knightsbridge, Covent Garden, and Notting Hill. The boutique-size store at St. Christopher's Place stocks accessories only. ⊠ *41–42 New Bond St., Mayfair* ☎ *020/7491–3900* Ⓤ *Bond St.*

ANTIQUES

Grays Antique Market. Open every Saturday from 11 to 5, Grays boasts more than 100 dealers under one roof, specializing in everything from Sheffield plate to Asian antiquities (although the majority of stalls focus on jewelry). Bargains are not impossible, and proper pedigrees are guaranteed. Also try Grays in the Mews around the corner—it has less-expensive merchandise, including the large Biblion bookshop and excellent vintage clothing at Vintage Modes. ⊠ *58 Davies St., Mayfair* ☎ *020/7629–7034* ⊕ *www.graysantiques.com* ⊘ *Closed Sun.* Ⓤ *Bond St.*

BOOKS AND STATIONERY

Maggs Brothers Ltd. How could any book lover resist a shop with such a deliciously Dickensian name? In a Georgian townhouse in one of Mayfair's elegant squares, Maggs was established in 1853, and is one of the world's oldest and largest rare-book dealers. Shop staff act as advisers to important collectors, but they are, nonetheless, friendly and helpful to all interested visitors. ⊠ *50 Berkeley Sq., Mayfair* ☎ *020/7493–7160* ⊕ *www.maggs.com* ⊘ *Closed weekends* Ⓤ *Green Park.*

18

Simon Finch Rare Books Ltd. This unpretentious dealer spans all periods, from Babylonian tablets to modern first editions. English history and literature, medical texts, and photography are among the eclectic specialties. ✉ *Floors 1–4, 26 Brook St., Mayfair* ☎ *020/7499–0974* ⊕ *www.simonfinch.com* ⊗ *Closed weekends* Ⓤ *Bond St.*

★   **Smythson of Bond Street.** Hands down, this is the most elegant stationer in Britain. No hostess of any standing would consider having a leather-bound guest book made by anyone else, and the shop's distinctive pale-blue–page diaries and social stationery are thoroughly British. Bespoke stationery sets come with a form and a sample so that recipients can personalize their gift. Smythson also produces a small range of leather handbags and purses. There are branches on Sloane Street within Harvey Nichols, Harrods, and even at Selfridges. ✉ *40 New Bond St., Mayfair* ☎ *020/7629–8558* Ⓤ *Bond St., Green Park.*

Waterstone's. For book buying as a hedonistic leisure activity, the monster-size store near Piccadilly Circus caters to all tastes. Sip a gin-and-tonic or get a bite while browsing through a book and admiring the view from the top floor until 9 pm at the 5th View Bar & Food. Waterstone's is the country's leading book chain, and they've pulled out all the stops to make their flagship as comfortable and relaxed as a bookstore can be. ✉ *203–206 Piccadilly, Mayfair* ☎ *020/7851–2400* ⊕ *www.waterstones.com* Ⓤ *Piccadilly Circus.*

CLOTHING

Burberry. A few years ago, Burberry was the victim of its own success, with the company's ubiquitous plaid appearing on everything from baseball hats to baby strollers and bikinis. These days, the brand has cultivated a more rock-and-roll image, thanks to its poster boy and creative director, Christopher Bailey, whose designs now include fetish-y boots and sexy leather jackets perfect for any catwalk. The raincoats are still a classic buy, along with the plaid scarves in every color imaginable. If you're up for a trek, there's a huge factory outlet in Hackney on Chatham Place with clothing for men, women, and children, as well as accessories, at half price and less. There are also branches at Brompton Road in Knightsbridge and Regent Street in Soho. ✉ *21–23 New Bond St., Mayfair* ☎ *020/3367–3000* ⊕ *www.burberry.com* Ⓤ *Piccadilly Circus.*

Fodor'sChoice   **Dover Street Market.** Visiting this six-floor emporium isn't just about
★   buying; with its arty displays and eccentric mix of merchandise, it is as fascinating as any gallery. The creation of Comme des Garçons' Rei Kawakubo, it showcases all of the label's collections for men and women alongside other designers such as Lanvin, Alaïa, and exclusive Japanese lines, plus curiosities including antique medical specimens, avant-garde art books, and vintage couture. You never know what you will find, which is half the fun. ■TIP➔ **An outpost of the Rose Bakery on the top floor makes for a yummy break.** ✉ *17–18 Dover St., Mayfair* ☎ *020/7518–0680* ⊕ *www.doverstreetmarket.com* ⊗ *Closed Sun.* Ⓤ *Green Park.*

CLOTHING: MENSWEAR

Gieves and Hawkes. One of the grandest of grand old names for London bespoke tailoring; this company made its name outfitting Britain's Royal Military officers and still supplies bespoke military uniforms. Prices for a bespoke suit start around £3,600, or choose an off-the-peg design starting at around £600. ⊠ *1 Savile Row, Mayfair* ☎ *020/7434–2001* ⊕ *www.gievesandhawkes.com* Ⓤ *Piccadilly Circus.*

★ **Ozwald Boateng.** Ozwald Boateng's (pronounced Bwa-teng) is one of the funkiest tailors working on Savile Row these days. His made-to-measure suits in eye-popping colors (even the more conservative suits sport bright silk linings), luxurious fabrics, and leading-edge styling have been worn by rock and club-land luminaries including Jamie Foxx, Mick Jagger, and Laurence Fishburne. ⊠ *30 Savile Row, Mayfair* ☎ *020/7440–5231* ⊕ *www.ozwaldboateng.co.uk* ⊗ *Closed Sun.* Ⓤ *Piccadilly Circus.*

CLOTHING: WOMEN'S WEAR

★ **Browns.** This shop—actually a series of small shops on South Molton Street—was a pioneer designer boutique in the 1970s and continues to talent-spot the newest and best around. You may find the windows showcasing the work of top graduates from this year's student shows or displaying well-established designers such as Marni, Chloé, Alexander McQueen, YSL, Dries Van Noten, or Temperley. The men's store at No. 23 has a similar selection, whereas Browns Focus, across the street at Nos. 38–39, showcases young, hip designs, and denim. Browns also has its own label, a bargain outlet at No. 50, and a designer bridal boutique at 11–12 Hinde Street. There is also a smaller boutique at 6C Sloane Street, and another at 59 Book Street, off New Bond Street, which solely sells shoes. ⊠ *24–27 South Molton St., Mayfair* ☎ *020/7514–0000* ⊕ *www.brownsfashion.com* ⊗ *Closed Sun.* Ⓤ *Bond St.*

b Store. Some people regard b Store as the best little clothing boutique in London. At the end of Savile Row, b Store couldn't be farther away in terms of style from the traditional tailors down the street. Head here for cutting-edge pieces from avant-garde designers such as Diana Brinks and Ute Ploeir, plus the store's quirky own-label shoes. ⊠ *24A Savile Row, Mayfair* ☎ *020/7734–6846* ⊕ *www.bstorelondon.com* ⊗ *Closed Sun.* Ⓤ *Piccadilly Circus, Oxford Circus.*

Fenwick. A haven of realistically priced fashion, Fenwick is found in a shopping area where most things cost the earth. Five floors of chic clothes and accessories for men and women, lingerie, and home furnishings highlight lesser known and emerging designers from all over Europe. ⊠ *163 New Bond St., Mayfair* ☎ *020/7629–9161* ⊕ *www.fenwick.co.uk* Ⓤ *Bond St.*

Nicole Farhi. Busy women willing to invest in quality greatly value Nicole Farhi's softly tailored yet functional dresses and separates. The style manages to be contemporary yet timeless, making these standbys in many a working woman's wardrobe. Of the numerous locations, the New Bond Street store sells clothes for both men and women, but the full men's collection is available at the Floral Street branch. ⊠ *158 New Bond St., Mayfair* ☎ *020/7499–8368* ⊕ *www.nicolefarhi.com* Ⓤ *Bond St.*

18

Vivienne Westwood. This is where it all started: the pompadour-punk ball gowns, Lady Hamilton vest coats, and foppish landmark getups are the core of Westwood's first boutique in Chelsea, where you can still buy ready-to-wear (mainly the more casual Anglomania diffusion line and exclusive Worlds End label based on the archives) under the spinning clock. The designer still represents the apex of high-style British couture. Head for the Conduit Street flagship for all the collections. The small Davies Street boutique sells only the Gold Label and made-to-measure couture. ⊠ *44 Conduit St., Mayfair* ☎ *020/7439–1109* Ⓤ *Oxford Circus* ⊠ *Original boutique, 430 King's Rd., Chelsea* ☎ *020/7352–6551* ☉ *Closed Sun.* Ⓤ *Sloane Sq.*

DEPARTMENT STORES

★ **Browns.** Launched in the 1970s, mini-department store Browns caters to the very label-conscious customer. You will find men's and women's fashion from Alexander McQueen and Marni and Chloe, as well as lesser-known designers like Nicholas Kirkwood and jewelry by Muriel Grateau. The beauty department is also worth a look, especially for hard-to-find brands like London cult favorite Vaishaly, a facialist to celebs like British chef Nigella Lawson. ⊠ *24–27 South Molton St., Mayfair* ☎ *020/7514–0000* ⊕ *www.brownsfashion.com* Ⓤ *Bond St.*

Fodor's Choice **Liberty.** With a wonderful black-and-white mock-Tudor facade, Liberty
★ is a peacock among the chain-store pigeons on Regent Street. In the 19th century, Liberty's designers, leaders in the art nouveau and aesthetic movements, created classic fabric and home-furnishing designs. Those Liberty prints are still world famous today, and grace fashionable goods, from silk kimonos to embossed leather bags, wallets, and photo albums. Inside, the store is a labyrinth of nooks and crannies stuffed with goodies. The carpet and furniture departments are worth a look even if you're not buying. The jewelry and accessories departments contrast the unusual and bohemian with deluxe international labels. Fashion, for men and women, focuses on high quality and beautiful fabric. ⊠ *Regent St., Mayfair* ☎ *020/7734–1234* ⊕ *www.liberty.co.uk* Ⓤ *Oxford Circus.*

Thomas Goode. This spacious luxury homeware shop has been at the same smart Mayfair address since 1827. The china, silver, crystal, and linens are either of the store's own design and manufacture or are simply the best that money can buy. Originally, customers here were mainly international royals and heads of state. The store still holds three royal warrants, but anyone who can afford it can have their own bespoke set of china. ■TIP➜ If such luxury is beyond you, visit anyway for the shop's archive of antique plates and those designed for royalty, including a pattern for Charles and Diana's wedding. ⊠ *19 S. Audley St., Mayfair* ☎ *020/7499–2823* ⊕ *www.thomasgoode.co.uk* Ⓤ *Green Park.*

FOOD

Charbonnel et Walker. Britain's master chocolatier since 1875, this Mayfair shop specializes in traditional sweets (violet and rose-petal creams, for example) and has been serving up beautifully packaged, high-quality chocolates long before most of the fashionable new brands appeared. ■TIP➜ Some of their "drawing room" boxes are real works of art, and their drinking chocolate—coarsely grated fine chocolate in a tin—is worth carrying home in a suitcase. ⊠ *One the Royal Arcade, 28 Old Bond St., Mayfair* ☎ *020/7491–0939* ⊕ *www.charbonnel.co.uk* ⊗ *Closed Sun.* Ⓤ *Green Park.*

JEWELRY

★ **Asprey.** Exquisite jewelry and gifts are displayed in a discreet and very British environment at the "global flagship" store, designed by Lord Foster and British interior designer David Mlinaric. The setting oozes money, good taste, and comfort. If you're in the market for an immaculate 1930s cigarette case, a crystal vase, a lizard-bound diary, or a pair of pavé diamond and sapphire earrings, you won't be disappointed. Bespoke jewelry is available as well. ⊠ *167 New Bond St., Mayfair* ☎ *020/7493–6767* ⊕ *www.asprey.com* Ⓤ *Green Park.*

Garrard. Formally known as "Garrard, the Crown Jeweler," this is the company that, since Queen Victoria's day, has set the Kohinoor diamond into more than one royal crown. Many of the company's jewels can be found in the Tower of London. Today, the focus is on diamonds and precious gems in simple, classic settings, and the store also sells silver accessories. Although some collections such as Knightrider and the Wings line (featuring winged hoop earrings and pendants) are definitely bling, tradition rules, and you can still drop in to pick up a jeweled tiara. ⊠ *24 Albemarle St., Mayfair* ☎ *0870/871–8888* ⊕ *www.garrard. com* Ⓤ *Green Park.*

SHOES

★ **Beatrix Ong.** This young designer trained under Jimmy Choo, and her collection is just as sexy and bold. Her Burlington Arcade shops sells a ready-to-wear collection of strappy sandals and stilettos, and brides-to-be are also well catered to. ⊠ *200/206 Regent St., Mayfair* ☎ *020/979–1100* ⊕ *www.beatrixong.com* Ⓤ *Oxford Circus.*

Georgina Goodman. Former fashion stylist Georgina Goodman's original, colorful designs for women have been praised by the great Manolo Blahnik himself. Featuring such signature flourishes as hand-painted leather and unusual heel shapes, her footwear is influenced by, but not enslaved to, current fashion. The pretty flat "slippers" in seasonally changing materials are affordable best sellers. ⊠ *44 Old Bond St., Mayfair* ☎ *020/7493–7673* ⊕ *www.georginagoodman.com* ⊗ *Closed Sun.* Ⓤ *Green Park.*

★ **Rupert Sanderson.** Designed in London and made in Italy, Sanderson's elegant shoes have been a huge hit in fashion circles. Ladylike styles, bright colors, smart details, and a penchant for peep toes are signature elements. Prices reflect the impeccable craftsmanship. There's now a tiny outpost next to Harrods at 2A Hans Road. ⊠ *33 Bruton Pl., Mayfair* ☎ *0207/491–2220* ⊕ *www.rupertsanderson.com* ⊗ *Closed Sun.* Ⓤ *Bond St., Green Park.*

18

ST. JAMES'S

ACCESSORIES: HATS

James Lock & Co. Ltd. Need a silk opera hat, a flat-weave Panama, or a traditional tweed flat cap? James Lock of St. James's has been making hats from its cozy little shop since 1676, and has dressed the heads of Admiral Lord Nelson, Jackie Onassis, Frank Sinatra, and, recently, hip young musicians and models. ⊠ *6 St. James's St., St. James's* ☏ *020/7930–8884* ⊕ *www.lockhatters.co.uk* ⊘ *Closed Sun.* Ⓤ *Green Park, Piccadilly Circus.*

★ **Swaine Adeney Brigg.** This shop has been selling practical supplies for country pursuits since 1750. Not just for the horsey set, the store has golf umbrellas, walking sticks, and hip flasks—all beautifully crafted and ingenious. Or pick up your own Poet Hat, the iconic hat worn by Harrison Ford in every Indiana Jones film, and which the company has been making since the 1890s. On a frosty morning, you shouldn't be without the umbrella with a slim tipple-holder flask secreted inside the stick. Traditional menswear (tweeds, cashmere sweaters, and Herbert Johnson hats) can be found downstairs. ⊠ *54 St. James's St., St. James's* ☏ *020/7409–7277* ⊕ *www.swaineadeney.co.uk* ⊘ *Closed Sun.* Ⓤ *Green Park.*

BEAUTY

Fodor'sChoice
★ **Floris.** One of the most beautiful shops in London, Floris boasts gleaming glass-and-Spanish-mahogany showcases from the Great Exhibition of 1851. As well as beautifully packaged soaps, bath essences, perfumes, and its famous rose-scented mouthwash, gift possibilities include goosedown powder puffs and cut-glass atomizers. Queen Victoria used to dab her favorite Floris fragrance on her lace handkerchief. True to its origins as a barbershop, Floris makes shaving products as well as scents for both men and women. ⊠ *89 Jermyn St., St. James's* ☏ *0845/702–3239* ⊕ *www.florislondon.com* ⊘ *Closed Sun.* Ⓤ *Piccadilly Circus.*

BOOKS

Fodor'sChoice
★ **Hatchards.** This is London's oldest bookshop, open since 1797 and beloved by writers themselves (customers have included Oscar Wilde, Rudyard Kipling, and Lord Byron) thanks to its cozy, independent character. Independence, however, is a matter of appearance only—Hatchards is owned by the same corporate giant as the omnipresent Waterstone's chain. Nevertheless, you can revel in its old-fashioned charm while perusing the well-stocked shelves lining the winding stairs. The staff has retained old-fashioned helpfulness, too. ⊠ *187 Piccadilly, St. James's* ☏ *020/7439–9921* ⊕ *www.hatchards.co.uk* Ⓤ *Piccadilly Circus.*

CLOTHING: MEN

Thomas Pink. The chain still makes some of the most colorful and most stylish dress shirts around for both men and women in fine fabrics such as Sea Island and Egyptian cotton. Bespoke shirts for men are available at the Jermyn Street branch. ⊠ *85 Jermyn St., St. James's* ☏ *020/7930–6364* Ⓤ *Green Park, Piccadilly Circus.*

★ **Turnbull & Asser.** This is *the* custom shirtmaker, dripping exclusivity from every fiber—after all, Prince Charles is a client and James Bond wore the shirts on film. At least 28 separate measurements are taken, and the cloth, woven to their specifications, comes in 1,000 different patterns—the cottons feel as good as silk. The first order must be for a minimum of six shirts, starting from £180 each. There are less expensive, though still exquisite, ready-to-wear shirts available as well as jackets, cashmeres, suits, ties, and accessories like pajamas perfect for the billionaire who has everything. ✉ *71–72 Jermyn St., St. James's* ☎ *020/7808–3000* ⊕ *www.turnbullandasser.com* ⊗ *Closed Sun.* Ⓤ *Green Park.*

FOOD

Berry Bros. & Rudd. Although wine is sold in British supermarkets and there are decent High-street chains for wine (like Oddbins and Nicolas), try Berry Bros. & Rudd for special bottles and a unique shopping experience. A family-run wine business since 1698, "BBR" stores its vintage bottles and casks in vaulted cellars that are more than 300 years old. The shop is quirky yet charming and the staff is extremely knowledgeable—and not snooty if your budget isn't huge. ✉ *3 St. James's St., St. James's* ☎ *020/7396–9600* ⊕ *www.bbr.com* ⊗ *Closed Sun.* Ⓤ *Green Park.*

Fodor's Choice ★ **Fortnum & Mason.** Although it's the Queen's grocer, this store is, paradoxically, the most egalitarian of gift shops. It has plenty of irresistibly packaged luxury foods, stamped with the gold "By Appointment" crest, for less than £5, which make ideal gifts. Try the teas, preserves (unusual products include rose-petal jelly), condiments, chocolate, tins of pâté, Gentleman's Relish (anchovy paste), or a box of Duchy Originals oatcakes—like Paul Newman, the Prince of Wales has gone into the retail food business. Fortnum's celebrated its tercentenary in 2007 with a major refurbishment—although the impeccably mannered staff still sport traditional tailcoats. The gleaming food hall spans two floors, and there's also a sleek wine bar designed by David Collins. The rest of the store is devoted to upscale gifts, toiletries, and house wares, and there are four more restaurants to choose from, including an indulgent ice-cream parlor. Afternoon tea is also offered at each one of the restaurants. ✉ *181 Piccadilly, St. James's* ☎ *020/7734–8040* ⊕ *www.fortnumandmason.com* Ⓤ *Green Park.*

TOYS

The Armoury of St. James's. The fine toy soldiers and military models in stock here are collectors' items. Painted and mounted knights only 6 inches high can cost more than £1,200 (though figures start at a mere £7.50 for a Beefeater). Besides lead and tin soldiers, the shop has regimental brooches, porcelain figures, military memorabilia, and military antiques. ✉ *17 Piccadilly Arcade, St. James's* ☎ *020/7493–5082* ⊕ *www.armoury.co.uk* ⊗ *Closed Sun.* Ⓤ *Piccadilly Circus, Green Park.*

18

SOHO AND COVENT GARDEN

COVENT GARDEN

HOUSEHOLD

Cath Kidston. If you love chintz and bright patterns, then stop by Cath Kidston. Her signature look is bright, girly prints—ginghams, polka dots, and miles and miles of roses—pasted over everything in sight, from ceramics and bed linens to fine china, stationery, and doggie beds. There are several clothing and nightwear lines for women and children, along with handbags, totes, and cosmetic bags. Everything in this shop is basically a canvas for Kidston's sugary prints. ✉ *28–32 Shelton St., Covent Garden* ☏ *020/7836–4803* ⊕ *www.cathkidston.co.uk* Ⓤ *Covent Garden.*

BOOKS AND PRINTS

★ **Grosvenor Prints.** London's largest collection of 17th- to early-20th-century prints includes a good selection of rare, early Americana. The main emphasis is on London views and architecture as well as sporting and decorative prints. It's an eccentric collection, with prices ranging from £5 into the thousands. ✉ *19 Shelton St., Covent Garden* ☏ *020/7836–1979* ⊕ *www.grosvenorprints.com* ⊘ *Closed Sun.* Ⓤ *Covent Garden.*

Stanfords. When it comes to encyclopedic coverage, there is simply no better travel-book and map shop on the planet. Stanfords is packed with a comprehensive selection of map and travel-book series. Whether you're planning a day trip to Surrey or an adventure to the South Pole, this should be your first stop. ✉ *12–14 Long Acre, Covent Garden* ☏ *020/7836–1321* ⊕ *www.stanfords.co.uk* Ⓤ *Covent Garden.*

CLOTHING

★ **Paul Smith.** British classics with colorful and irreverent twists define Paul Smith's collections for both women and men. Beautifully tailored men's suits in exceptional fabrics might sport flamboyant linings or unusual detailing. Women's lines tend to take familiar and traditional British ideas and turn them on their heads with humor and color. Accessories, including wallets, scarves, diaries—and even a soccer ball—in his signature rainbow stripes make great gifts. There are several branches, including a Notting Hill mansion at 120–122 Kensington Park Road; a small, funky outpost at 13 Park Street near Borough Market; a vintage furniture shop at 9 Albemarle Street in Mayfair; and, not far away, a sale shop at 23 Avery Row. There is also a shoes and accessories shop on Marylebone High Street. ✉ *40–44 Floral St., Covent Garden* ☏ *020/7379–7133* ⊕ *www.paulsmith.co.uk* Ⓤ *Covent Garden.*

CLOTHING: WOMEN'S WEAR

★ **Koh Samui.** Named for a Thai island resort, this shop stocks designer clothes for the kind of hip young woman who thinks nothing of flying there for a week's detox at the drop of a hat. On the rails are the likes of Marc Jacobs, Matthew Williamson, and Balenciaga, plus hot young design talent and select vintage pieces. ✉ *65–67 Monmouth St., Covent Garden* ☏ *020/7240–4280* Ⓤ *Covent Garden.*

Office. Inexpensive but imaginative takes on catwalk looks are the stock in trade at this popular chain. Styles for men and women feature trend-conscious shapes and funky patterns and finishes. Upscale sibling stores Poste (⊠ *10 South Molton St.*) and Poste Mistress (⊠ *61–63 Monmouth St.*) stock cutting-edge designer shoes for men and women, respectively. ⊠ *57 Neal St., Covent Garden* ☎ *020/7379–1896* ⊕ *www.office.co.uk* Ⓤ *Covent Garden.*

Orla Kiely. This Irish designer is probably best known for her bags and wallets with the signature leaf print, but her appealingly simple retro-tinged prints (cars, mugs, leaves, abstracts) grace everything from dresses to lamp shades—all showcased in this airy flagship store. If you want something a little less busy, her line of clothing is a safer bet. ⊠ *31 Monmouth St., Covent Garden* ☎ *020/7240–4022* ⊕ *www. orlakiely.com* Ⓤ *Covent Garden.*

TOYS

Ⓒ Fodor's Choice ★ **Benjamin Pollock's Toyshop.** This independently owned Covent Garden Piazza shop carries on in the tradition of its founder and namesake, who sold "theatrical sheets" for toy theaters from the mid-19th century to his death in 1937. Robert Louis Stevenson was a fan who wrote, "If you love art, folly, or the bright eyes of children, speed to Pollock's." Magical toy theaters (most of the antique theaters or toy scenery now costs a fortune, if even available, but there are some nice "new" reproductions that are reasonable in cost) are the main stock in trade, but nostalgic puppets, mechanical toys, and paper dolls are also available. ⊠ *44 The Market, Covent Garden* ☎ *020/7379–7866* Ⓤ *Covent Garden.*

SOHO

18

BOOKS

Fodor's Choice ★ **Foyles.** A quirky, labyrinthine, family-run business, this store was founded in 1903 by the Foyle brothers, after they failed the civil service exam. Today Foyles' five floors carry almost every title imaginable. One of London's best sources for textbooks, the store stocks everything from popular fiction to military history, sheet music, medical tomes, opera scores, and fine arts. Store-within-a-store Ray's Jazz has a cool café, and there's even a piranha tank on the children's floor. In 2005, a branch opened in the South Bank, followed by a concession within Selfridges department store and an outpost in St. Pancras International, home of Eurostar. ⊠ *113–119 Charing Cross Rd., Soho* ☎ *020/7437–5660* Ⓤ *Tottenham Court Rd.* ⊠ *Royal Festival Hall, South Bank* ☎ *020/7437–5660* Ⓤ *Waterloo.*

CLOTHING

Aquascutum. Known for its trench coats (worn by Churchill, no less), Aquascutum also offers clothing for men and women in classic British style. The men's suits and sweaters are timeless, and the women's collection has become surprisingly funky, offering fresh takes on overcoats and items like tunics and jersey dresses. The brand is also available at Harrods, Selfridges, and other big department stores around town. ⊠ *100 Regent St., Soho* ☎ *020/7675–8200* ⊕ *www.aquascutum.co.uk* Ⓤ *Piccadilly Circus.*

CLOTHING: WOMEN'S WEAR

Fodor's Choice
★

Topshop. Plenty of foreign fashion editors make Topshop their first port of call when visiting London for this standby has successfully made the transition from "cheap and cheerful" to genuine fashion hot spot (with mostly affordable prices). Clothing and accessories are geared to the younger, trendier end of the market (although women who are young at heart find plenty of wearable items here such as the Kate Moss for Topshop collection). Although the store also has its own catwalk line, Topshop Unique, the aim is to copy runway trends as fast as possible. Every season, an ever-changing array of designers create small collections for the in-store boutique, as well as other lines from affordable independent designers. Innovations, such as personal style advisers and an on-site "Blow Dry Bar," are constantly being introduced. Topman brings the same fashion approach to clothing for men. ■TIP➔ If the crowds become too much, head to one of the smaller Topshops in town, such as the Kensington High Street branch. ⊠ *214 Oxford St., Soho* ☎ *020/927–7634* ⊕ *www.topshop.com* Ⓤ *Oxford Circus* ⊠ *42–44 Kensington High St., Kensington* ☎ *020/7938–1242* Ⓤ *High Street Kensington.*

FOOD

The Vintage House. If whisky is more to your taste than wine, you may want to visit the Vintage House, which has the country's largest selection of single malts (more than 1,400), many notable for their age. The shop is open late—to 11 pm most nights. ⊠ *42 Old Compton St., Soho* ☎ *020/7437–2592* Ⓤ *Piccadilly Circus, Leicester Sq.*

MUSIC

BM Soho. House, drum 'n' bass, electro, dubstep—this shop (formerly Blackmarket Records) stocks the hottest club music around. They carry some CDs, but this is really a shop for vinyl lovers. ⊠ *25 D'Arblay St., Soho* ☎ *020/7437–0478* ⊕ *www.bm-soho.com* Ⓤ *Oxford Circus, Tottenham Court Rd.*

TOYS

☺
Fodor's Choice
★

Hamleys. Every London child puts a trip to Hamleys at the top of his or her wish list. A Regent Street institution, the shop has demonstrations, a play area, a café, and every cool toy on the planet—as soon as it's launched. The huge stock, including six floors of toys and games for children and adults, ranges from traditional teddy bears to all the latest technological gimmickry. It's a mad rush at Christmastime, but Santa's grotto is one of the best in town. ⊠ *188–196 Regent St., Soho* ☎ *0871/704–1977* ⊕ *www.hamleys.com* Ⓤ *Oxford Circus, Piccadilly Circus.*

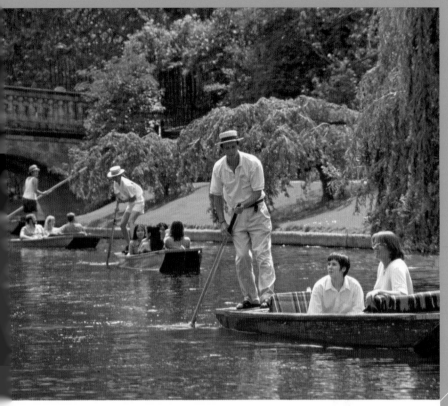

Side Trips from London

WORD OF MOUTH

"THE major 'new' museum in the region is Oxford's Ashmolean. Though it's Britain's oldest, the 2009 extension has created what really is a totally new institution, with far, far more of the 4 million items in its archive on display—infinitely more attractively than before. A very pleasant half day (book your train ticket sufficiently in advance, and the travel cost is peanuts)."

—flanneruk

SIDE TRIPS PLANNER

Getting Around

Normally the towns covered in this chapter are best reached by train. Bus travel costs less, but can take twice as long. Wherever you're going, plan ahead: check the latest timetables before you set off, and try to get an early start. ⇨ *Also see the Travel Smart chapter.*

Station Tips

You can reach any of London's main-line train stations by Tube. London's bus stations can be confusing for the uninitiated. Here's a quick breakdown:

Green Line Coach Station is on Bulleid Way (in front of the Colonnades Shopping Centre on Buckingham Palace Road) and is the departure point for most Green Line and Megabus services.

Victoria Coach Station is on Buckingham Palace Road: it's a five-minute walk from Victoria Tube station. This is where to go for coach departures; arrivals are at a different location, a short walk from here.

Victoria Bus Station is where many of the local London bus services arrive and depart, and is directly outside the main exits of the train and Tube stations.

What it Costs in Pounds

	£	££	£££	££££	£££££
Restaurants	under £10	£10–£14	£15–£19	£20–£25	over £25

Price per person for an average main course or equivalent combination of smaller dishes at dinner.

To Get To . . .

	TAKE THE TRAIN FROM . . .	TAKE THE BUS FROM . . .
Cambridge	King's Cross (48–73 minutes; every 10 or 20 minutes)	Victoria Coach (about 2 hours; hourly)
Canterbury	Victoria (85–100 minutes; every 20 minutes)	Victoria Coach (1 hour, 50 minutes; hourly)
Oxford	Paddington (55–100 minutes; every 20 minutes)	Victoria Coach (1 hour, 40 minutes; every 15–20 minutes)
Stratford-upon-Avon	Paddington (2 hours, 20 minutes to 3 hours, 30 minutes); Marylebone (2 hours, 10 minutes to 3 hours, 23 minutes); or Euston (2 hours, 40 minutes); Trains leave every 20 or 40 minutes or hourly	Victoria Coach (3 hours; about 3 times daily)
Windsor	Paddington (40 minutes; every 20 minutes, every half hour, or hourly) or Waterloo (1 hour; every 12 minutes or every 20 minutes)	Green Line Coach Station (1 hour; hourly)

Updated by
Ellin Stein

Londoners are undeniably lucky. Few urban populations enjoy such glorious—and easily accessible—options for day-tripping. Even if vacationers or travelers have only one day to spare, head out of the city. A train ride past hills dotted with sheep, a stroll through a medieval town, or a visit to one of England's great castles could make you feel as though you've added another week to your vacation.

Not only is England extremely compact, the train and bus networks, although somewhat inefficient and expensive compared with their European counterparts, are extensive and user-friendly, making "a brilliant country holiday" an easy thing to accomplish.

Although you could tackle any one of the towns in this chapter on a frenzied day trip—heavy summer crowds make it difficult to cover the sights in a relaxed manner—consider staying for a day or two. You'd then have time to explore a very different England—one blessed with quiet country pubs, tree-lined lanes, and neatly trimmed farms. No matter where you go, lodging reservations are a good idea from June through September, when foreign visitors saturate the English countryside.

19

CAMBRIDGE

60 mi (97 km) north of London.

With the spires of its university buildings framed by towering trees and expansive meadows, its medieval streets and passages enhanced by gardens and riverbanks, the city of Cambridge is among the loveliest in England. The city predates the Roman occupation of Britain, but the university was not founded until the 13th century. There's disagreement about the birth of the university: one story attributes its founding to impoverished students from Oxford, who came in search of eels—a cheap source of nourishment. Today a healthy rivalry persists between the two schools.

London Side Trips

KEY

Ferry Lines

North Sea

English Channel

FRANCE

TO CALAIS

Channel Tunnel

TO JERSEY & GUERNSEY

20 miles

20 kilometers

This university town may be beautiful, but it's no museum. Even when the students are on vacation, there's a cultural and intellectual buzz here. It's a preserved medieval city of some 109,000 souls and growing, dominated culturally and architecturally by its famous university (whose students make up around one-fifth of the inhabitants), and beautified by parks, gardens, and the quietly flowing River Cam. A quintessential Cambridge pursuit is punting on the Cam (one occupant propels the narrow, square-end, flat-bottom boat with a long pole), followed by a stroll along the Backs, the left bank of the river fringed by St. John's, Trinity, Clare, King's, and Queens' colleges, and by Trinity Hall.

VISITING THE COLLEGES

College visits are certainly a highlight of a Cambridge tour, but remember that the colleges are private residences and workplaces, even when school isn't in session. Each is an independent entity within the university; some are closed to the public, but at others you can see the chapels, dining rooms (called halls), and sometimes the libraries, too. Some colleges charge a small fee for the privilege of nosing around. All are closed during exams, usually from mid-April to late June, and the opening hours often vary. Additionally, all are subject to closures at short notice, especially King's; check the Web sites in advance. For details about visiting specific colleges not listed here, contact **Cambridge University** (☎ *01223/337733* ⊕ *www.cam.ac.uk*).

By far the best way to gain access without annoying anyone is to join a walking tour led by an official Blue Badge guide—in fact, many areas are off-limits unless you do. The one or two-hour tours (£11–£12.50) leave from the **Tourist Information Centre.** Hours vary according to the tour, with the earliest leaving at 11 and the latest at 2. (⊠ *Peas Hill* ☎ *0871/226–8006, 1223/464732 from abroad* ⊕ *www.visitcambridge. org* ⊙ *Apr.–Sept., weekdays 10–5, Sat. 10–5, Sun. 11–3; Oct.–Mar., weekdays 10–5, Sat. 10–5.*

ESSENTIALS

Visitor Information **Cambridge** (☎ *0871/226–8006, 1223/464732 from outside U.K.* ⊕ *www.visitcambridge.org*).

EXPLORING

Emmanuel College (1584) is the alma mater of one John Harvard, who gave his books and his name to the American university. A number of the Pilgrims were Emmanuel alumni; they named Cambridge, Massachusetts, after their onetime home. ⊠ *St. Andrew's St.* ☎ *01223/334200* ⊕ *www.emma.cam.ac.uk* 🎟 *Free* ⊙ *Daily 9–6.*

Fodor'sChoice ★ One of England's finest art galleries, the **Fitzwilliam Museum** houses an outstanding collection of art, as well as striking antiquities from ancient Egypt, Greece, and Rome. Highlights include two large Titians, an extensive collection of French impressionist paintings, and many paintings by Matisse and Picasso. The gallery holds occasional free classical music concerts. ⊠ *Trumpington St.* ☎ *01223/332900* ⊕ *www. fitzmuseum.cam.ac.uk* 🎟 *Free* ⊙ *Tues.–Sat. 10–5, Sun. noon–5.*

19

Fodor's Choice **King's College** (1441) is notable as the site of the world-famous Gothic-style
★ **King's College Chapel** (built 1446–1547). Some deem its great fan-vaulted
roof, supported by a delicate tracery of columns, the most glorious example of Perpendicular Gothic in Britain. It's the home of the famous cho-
risters, and, to cap it all, Rubens's *Adoration of the Magi* is tucked away
behind the altar. The college's Back Lawn leads down to the river, from
which the panorama of college and chapel is one of the university's most
photographed views. ⊠ *King's Parade* ☎ *01223/331212* ⊕ *www.kings.*
cam.ac.uk ⊡ *£5* ☉ *Term time, weekdays 9:30–3:30, Sat. 9:30–3:15, Sun.*
1:15–2:15; out of term, Mon.–Sat. 9:30–4:30, Sun. 10–5. Hrs may vary,
grounds closed during exams; call in advance or see Web site.

Pembroke College (1347) has delightful gardens and bowling greens. Its
chapel, completed in 1665, was the architect Christopher Wren's first
commission. ⊠ *Trumpington St.* ☎ *01223/338100* ⊕ *www.pem.cam.*
ac.uk ⊡ *Free* ☉ *Daily 9–4.*

In 1284 the Bishop of Ely founded **Peterhouse College,** Cambridge's smallest
and oldest college. Take a tranquil walk through its former deer park, by
the river side of its ivy-clad buildings. ⊠ *Trumpington St.* ☎ *01223/338200*
⊕ *www.pet.cam.ac.uk* ⊡ *Free* ☉ *Daily 9–5 (groups 1–5).*

★ **Queens' College.** Originally established in 1447 as the College of St. Bernard's, one of Cambridge's most eye-catching colleges was re-founded a
year later by Margaret of Anjou, queen of Henry VI, and then re-founded
again in 1475 by Elizabeth, queen of Edward IV—hence the new name.

Cross over the Cam via the **Wooden Bridge,** also known as the Mathematical Bridge. A popular myth tells of how it was built by Isaac
Newton without any binding save gravity, then dismantled by curious
scholars eager to learn Sir Isaac's secret. However, the bridge wasn't
actually put together until 1749, 22 years after Newton's death.
⊠ *Queens' La.* ☎ *01223/335511* ⊕ *www.queens.cam.ac.uk* ⊡ *£2.50,*
free Nov.–mid-Mar., Oct. weekdays, closed mid-May–mid-June (call
for info) ☉ *Mid-Mar.–mid-May, daily 10–4:30; mid-June–Sept., daily*
10–4:30; Oct., weekdays 2–4, weekend 10–4:30.

The only Cambridge College founded by townspeople (in 1352) is **Corpus**
Christi College, whose beautiful, serene, 14th-century Old Court is the oldest
college quadrangle in Cambridge. The college's Parker Library contains one
of the world's finest collections of medieval manuscripts. ⊠ *Trumpington*
St. ☎ *01223/338000* ⊕ *www.corpus.cam.ac.uk* ⊡ *Free* ☉ *Daily 2–4.*

St. John's College (1511), the university's second largest, has noted alumni
(Wordsworth studied here), a series of beautiful courtyards, and two of
the finest sights in town: the **School of Pythagoras,** the oldest house in
Cambridge; and the 1831 **Bridge of Sighs,** a replica of its Venetian coun-
terpart. The windowed, covered stone bridge reaches across the Cam to
the mock-Gothic New Court (1825–31). The New Court cupola's white
crenellations have earned it the nickname "the wedding cake." ⊠ *St.*
John's St. ☎ *01223/338600* ⊕ *www.joh.cam.ac.uk* ⊡ *£3.20* ☉ *Mar.–*
Oct., daily 10–5:30; Nov.–Feb., daily 10–3:30.

Fodor's Choice **Trinity College** was founded by Henry VIII in 1546, and has the largest
★ student population of all the colleges. It's also famous for having been
attended by Byron, Thackeray, Tennyson, Bertrand Russell, Nabokov,

Nehru, and 31 Nobel Prize winners. Many of Trinity's features reflect its status as one of Cambridge's largest colleges, not least its 17th-century "great court," scene of the university race in *Chariots of Fire*. Don't miss the wonderful library by Christopher Wren, where you can see a letter written by alumnus Isaac Newton with early notes on gravity, and A. A. Milne's handwritten manuscript of *The House at Pooh Corner*. ⊠ *Trinity St.* ☎ *01223/338400* ⊕ *www.trin.cam.ac.uk* ⊡ *£3 mid-Mar.–Oct.* ☉ *College daily 10–5; library weekdays noon–2, Sat. in term time 10–noon; hall and chapel open to visitors, but hrs vary.*

WHERE TO EAT

£   ✕ **Fitzbillies.** Usually filled with students' visiting parents, this traditional
CAFÉ café is famous for its exceptionally sticky Chelsea buns (if you don't want to sit down, the bakery next door has the same pastries to take away). It also serves filling and tasty lunches, afternoon teas, and dinners (Friday and Saturday) with such dishes as risotto, confit of duck salad, and goat cheese and sweet shallot tart. ⊠ *52 Trumpington St.* ☎ *01223/352500* ⊕ *www.fitzbillies.co.uk* ▭ *AE, MC, V.*

£££££   ✕ **Midsummer House.** In fine weather the gray-brick Midsummer House's
ECLECTIC conservatory, beside the River Cam, makes for a memorable lunchtime
★ jaunt. Choose from a selection of innovative French and Mediterranean dishes. You might get braised turbot, pumpkin and cep cannelloni, or slow-cooked duck with beetroot puree. ⊠ *Midsummer Common* ☎ *01223/369299* ⊕ *www.midsummerhouse.co.uk* ⌲ *Reservations essential* ▭ *AE, MC, V* ☉ *Closed Sun. and Mon. No lunch Tues.*

CANTERBURY

60 mi (97 km) southeast of London.

A bustling medieval cathedral town, charming Canterbury has good shopping, plenty of history, and just enough to see in a day—making it an ideal day trip from London.

As you might remember from high-school English classes spent studying Chaucer's *Canterbury Tales,* the height of Canterbury's popularity came in the 12th century, when thousands of pilgrims flocked here to see the shrine of Archbishop (and later Saint) Thomas à Becket, murdered when four knights misunderstood King Henry II's complaints about the "troublesome priest." The humble ancient buildings that served as pilgrims' inns still dominate the streets of Canterbury's pedestrian center.

Dig a little deeper and there's evidence of prosperous society in the Canterbury area as early as the Bronze Age (around 1000 BC). Canterbury was an important Roman city, as well as an Anglo-Saxon center in the Kingdom of Kent; it's currently headquarters of the Anglican Church. The town remains a lively place, a fact that has impressed visitors since 1388, when Chaucer wrote his stories.

ESSENTIALS

Visitor Information Canterbury (☎ *01227/378100* ⊕ *www.canterbury.co.uk*).

19

EXPLORING

You can easily cover Canterbury in a day. The 90-minute journey south-east from London's Victoria Station leaves plenty of time for a tour of the cathedral, a museum visit or two, and (if the weather's right) a walk around the perimeter of the old walled town. Canterbury is bisected by a road running northwest, along which the major tourist sites are clustered. This road begins as St. George's Street, then becomes the High Street, and finally turns into St. Peter's Street.

If you're seeing several sights while in town, consider purchasing an Attractions Passport from the visitor center. It costs £20 and gives you admission to the Canterbury Cathedral, the Canterbury Tales, St. Augustine's Abbey, and another museum of your choice.

On St. George's Street a lone church tower marks the site of **St. George's Church**—the rest of the building was destroyed in World War II—where playwright Christopher Marlowe was baptized in 1564.

★ The **Canterbury Roman Museum** is below ground level, in the ruins of the original Roman town. There's a colorful restored Roman mosaic pavement and a hypocaust (the Roman version of central heating), as well as a display of excavated objects. Get a feel for what it once looked like via the computer-generated reconstructions of Roman buildings. ✉ *Butchery La.* ☎ *01227/452747* ⊕ *www.canterbury-museums.co.uk* ✎ *£3.10* ⏱ *June–Sept., Mon.–Sat. 10–4:30, Sun. 1:30–4:40; Oct.–June, Mon.–Sat. 10–4.*

Mercery Lane, with its medieval-style cottages and massive, overhanging timber roofs, runs right off Canterbury High Street and ends in the tiny **Buttermarket,** a square that was known in the 15th century as the Bullstake: animals were tied here for baiting before slaughter at market. Today it's a town square surrounded by small bars and restaurants, and is often crowded with people visiting the cathedral.

The immense **Christchurch Gate,** built in 1517, leads into the cathedral close. As you pass through, look up at the sculpted heads of two young figures: Prince Arthur, elder brother of Henry VIII, and the young Catherine of Aragon, to whom he was betrothed. After Arthur's death, Catherine married Henry. Her inability to produce a male heir after 25 years of marriage led to Henry's decision to divorce her, creating an irrevocable breach with the Roman Catholic Church and altering the course of English history.

Fodor's Choice The massive heart of the town, towering **Canterbury Cathedral** was the
★ first of England's great Norman cathedrals. The mother church of worldwide Anglicanism and the seat of its head, the Archbishop of Canterbury, the Cathedral Church of Christ Canterbury (its formal name) is a living textbook of medieval architecture.

The cathedral was only a century old, and still relatively small in size, when Thomas à Becket, the Archbishop of Canterbury, was murdered here in 1170. An uncompromising defender of ecclesiastical interests, Becket had angered his friend Henry II, who supposedly exclaimed, "Who will rid me of this troublesome priest?" Thinking they were carrying out the king's wishes, four knights burst in on Becket in one of

Canterbury Cathedral, the destination of Chaucer's pilgrims in *The Canterbury Tales*.

the church's side chapels, chased him through the halls, and stabbed him to death. Two years later Becket was canonized, and Henry II's subsequent penitence helped establish the cathedral as the undisputed center of English Christianity.

Becket's tomb, destroyed by Henry VIII in 1538 as part of his campaign to reduce the power of the Church and confiscate its treasures, was one of the most extravagant shrines in Christendom. In **Trinity Chapel,** which held the shrine, you can still see a series of 13th-century stained-glass windows illustrating Becket's miracles. The actual site of Becket's murder is down a flight of steps just to the left of the nave, and marked with a simple sign that says only "Becket." If time permits, be sure to explore the **Cloisters, the Romanesque Crypt,** and the small monastic buildings north of the cathedral. ⊠ *Cathedral Precincts* ☎ *01227/762862* ⊕ *www.canterbury-cathedral.org* ✉ *£8; free for services* ⊙ *Easter–Oct., Mon.–Sat. 9–5:30, Sun. 12:30–2:30; Nov.–Easter, Mon.–Sat. 9–5, Sun. 12:30–2:30. Last entry 30 min before closing. Restricted access during services.*

To learn more about Chaucer's legendary pilgrims on their way to Canterbury, visit the **Canterbury Tales,** an audiovisual (and occasionally olfactory) dramatization of 14th-century English life. You'll "meet" Chaucer's pilgrims at the Tabard Inn near London and view tableaux illustrating five tales. In summer, actors in period costumes play out scenes from the town's history. ⊠ *St. Margaret's St.* ☎ *01227/479227* ⊕ *www.canterburytales.org.uk* ✉ *£7.75* ⊙ *Nov.–Dec., daily 10–4:30; Mar.–June, Sept., and Oct., daily 10–5; July and Aug., daily 9:30–5.*

★ The medieval Poor Priests' Hospital is now the site of the **Museum of Canterbury** (previously the Canterbury Heritage Museum). Its exhibits provide an excellent overview of the city's history and architecture from Roman times to World War II, although the displays are a strange mix of the serious (the Blitz) and the silly (cartoon characters Bagpuss and Rupert Bear). It also touches on the mysterious death of the 16th-century poet and playwright Christopher Marlowe. It's definitely child-friendly—kids can even look at "medieval poo" under a microscope. Visit early in the day to avoid the crowds. ⊠ *20 Stour St.* ☎ *01227/452747* ⊕ *www.canterbury-museums.co.uk* ✆ *£3.60* ⊘ *Jan.–May and Oct.–Dec., Mon.–Sat. 11–4:30; June–Sept., Mon.–Sat. 11–4:30, Sun. 1:30–4:30; last admission at 4.*

☾ Only one of the city's seven medieval gatehouses survives, complete with twin castellated towers; it now contains the **West Gate Towers Museum.** Inside are medieval bric-a-brac and armaments used by the city guard, as well as more contemporary weaponry. Built in the 14th century, the building became a jail in the 15th century, and you can view the prison cells. Climb to the roof for a panoramic view of the city spires. Because it's accessed by spiral stone stairs, this museum is only for those without mobility problems. ⊠ *St. Peter's St.* ☎ *01227/452747* ⊕ *www. canterbury-museums.co.uk* ✆ *£1.30* ⊘ *Sat. 11–12:30 and 1:30–3:30; last admission 15 min before closing. Closed Christmas wk.*

Perhaps the best view of Canterbury's medieval past comes from following its 13th- and 14th-century **medieval city walls,** which were themselves built on the line of the original Roman walls. Those to the east have survived intact, towering some 20 feet high and offering a sweeping view of the town. You can access these from a number of places, including Castle and Broad streets.

Augustine, England's first Christian missionary, was buried in 597 at **St. Augustine's Abbey,** one of the oldest monastic sites in the country. When Henry VIII seized the abbey in the 16th century, he destroyed some of the buildings and converted others into a royal manor for his fourth wife, Anne of Cleves. A free interactive audio tour vividly puts events into context. The abbey is the base for Canterbury's biennial Sculpture Festival (held in odd-number years). Contemporary sculpture is placed on the grounds, and in other locations in the city, May through August. ⊠ *Longport* ☎ *01227/767345* ⊕ *www.english-heritage.org.uk* ✆ *£4.50* ⊘ *Apr.–June, Wed.–Sun. 10–5; July and Aug., daily 10–6; Sept. and Oct., weekends 10–5; Nov.–Mar., weekends 11–4.*

☾ Dane John Gardens (the name is a corruption of *donjon,* French for a castle keep) offers a children's maze and a historic monument, **Dane John Mound,** the remains of a Norman fortress that formed part of the city defenses and today offers excellent cathedral views. ⊠ *Watling St.* ☎ *01227/452747* ⊕ *www.canterbury-museums.co.uk.*

WHERE TO EAT

£ ✕ **City Fish Bar.** Long lines and lots of satisfied finger-licking attest to the
BRITISH deserved popularity of this excellent fish-and-chips outlet in the center of town. Everything is freshly fried, the batter is crisp, and the fish is

tasty; the fried mushrooms are also surprisingly good. It closes at 7. ✉ *30 St. Margaret's St.* ☎ *01227/760873* ▭ *No credit cards.*

£–££
BRITISH

✕ **Duck Inn.** About 5 mi outside of Canterbury, this lovely, low-roof traditional pub is a great favorite among regular visitors to the city. Its pleasant rural location yields a bit of country charm, and dishes such as game pies are delightfully traditional. The name is said to come from the fact that the beams above the entrance are so low that you must duck as you enter or risk bashing your head. ✉ *Pett Bottom, near bridge* ☎ *01227/830354* ▭ *AE, MC, V.*

£–££
BRITISH
★

✕ **Weavers.** In one of the Weavers' Houses (the Weavers were Huguenots and Walloons who fled persecution in continental Europe in the 16th and 17th centuries) on the River Stour, this popular restaurant in the center of town is an ideal place to revel in the Tudor surroundings and feast on generous portions of British comfort food. Traditional pies and grills, seafood, and pasta dishes are served along with a good selection of wines. Ask for a table in the more sedate ground-floor dining area. ✉ *1 St. Peter's St.* ☎ *01227/464660* ▭ *AE, MC, V.*

OXFORD

62 mi (100 km) northwest of London.

The university that educated former Prime Minister Tony Blair, former President Bill Clinton, and writers J. R. R. Tolkien, Percy Bysshe Shelley, Oscar Wilde, W. H. Auden, and C. S. Lewis is the heart and soul of the town. Its fabled "dreaming spires" can be seen for miles around, and it's not at all unusual to see robed students rushing to class or harried dons clutching mortarboards as they race to exams on bicycles. Dating from the 12th century, Oxford University is older than Cambridge, and the city is bigger and more cosmopolitan than its competitor to the east. It's satisfyingly filled with hushed quadrangles, chapels, canals, rivers, and vivid gardens. Bikes are inevitably propped against picturesque wrought-iron railings, and students propel flat-bottom boats down the little River Cherwell with long poles. (It's harder than it looks, but you can rent a punt yourself at the foot of Magdalen Bridge.)

In the end, though, central Oxford is also a bit of an illusion. Outside of the eminently photographable university area, it's a major industrial center, with sprawling modern suburbs and large car and steel plants around its fringes.

19

VISITING THE COLLEGES

The same concerns for people's work and privacy hold here as in Cambridge. Note that many of the colleges and university buildings are closed around Christmas (sometimes Easter, too) and on certain days from April to June for exams and degree ceremonies.

If you have limited time, get a detailed map from the tourist office and focus on selected sights. The Oxford University Web site (⊕ *www.ox.ac. uk*) is a great source of information if you're planning to go it alone.

TOURS

Guided city walking tours (both themed and general) leave the **Oxford Tourist Information Centre** at different times throughout the day. ✉ *15–16 Broad St.* ☎ *01865/252200* ⊕ *www. visitoxford.org* ✉ *Tours from £7* ⊙ *Mon.–Sat. 9:30–5, Sun. 10–4.*

Oxford also features the hop-on, hop-off guided bus tours that have been such a hit in major destinations around the world. While they have stops throughout the city, the main terminus location is at

ESSENTIALS

Visitor Information Oxford (☎ *01865/252–2000* ⊕ *www.visitoxford.org*).

EXPLORING

Any Oxford visit should begin at its very center—a pleasant walk of 10 minutes or so east from the train station—with the splendid **University Church of St. Mary the Virgin** (1280). Climb 127 steps to the top of its 14th-century tower for a panoramic view of the city. ✉ *High St.* ☎ *01865/279111* ⊕ *www.university-church.ox.ac.uk* ✉ *Church free, tower £3* ⊙ *Church admission Sept.–June, Mon.–Sat. 9–5, Sun. noon–5; July and Aug., Mon.–Sat. 9–6, Sun. noon–6.*

Fodor'sChoice Among Oxford's most famous sights, the gorgeous, round **Radcliffe**
★   **Camera** (1737–49) is the most beautiful of the buildings housing the extensive contents of the august **Bodleian Library.** The baroque domed rotunda with an octagonal base sits in a lovely square where your photographic instincts can run riot. Not many of the 6-million-plus volumes are on view to those who aren't dons, but you can see part of the collection if you call ahead to book a regular or self-guided audio tour. Note that children under 11 are not admitted. ✉ *Broad St.* ☎ *01865/277224* ⊕ *www.bodleian.ox.ac.uk* ✉ *Bodleian self-guided audio tour £2.50; 30-min guided tour £4.50, 1-hr guided tour £6.50, extended guided tour £13* ⊙ *Weekdays 9–5, Sat. 9–4:30, Sun. 11–5; Divinity School weekdays 9–5, Sat. 9–4:30, Sun. 11–5 (admission £1). Closed for University functions and events (check Web site).*

★   The **Sheldonian Theatre,** built between 1664 and 1668, was Sir Christopher Wren's first major work (the chapel at Pembroke College was his first commission). The theater, which he modeled on a Roman amphitheater, made his reputation. It was built as a venue for the university's public ceremonies, and graduations are still held here—entirely in Latin, as befits the building's spirit. Outside is one of Oxford's most striking sights—a metal fence topped with stone busts of 18 Roman emperors (modern reproductions of the originals, which were eaten away by pollution). ✉ *Broad St.* ☎ *01865/277299* ⊕ *www.sheldon.ox.ac.uk* ✉ *£3* ⊙ *Mar.–Oct., Mon.–Sat. 10–12:30 and 2–4:30; Nov.–Feb., Mon.–Sat. 10–12:30 and 2–3:30. Closed for 10 days at Christmas and Easter and for degree ceremonies and events.*

Radcliffe Camera, an unmissable circular library at Oxford University.

Outside the "new" (they're actually Victorian) college gates of prestigious **Balliol College** (1263), a cobblestone cross in the sidewalk marks the spot where Archbishop Cranmer and bishops Latimer and Ridley were burned in 1555 for their Protestant beliefs. The original college gates (rumored to have existed at the time of the scorching) hang in the library passage, between the inner and outer quadrangles. ⊠ *Broad St.* ☎ *01865/277777* ⊕ *www.balliol.ox.ac.uk* ⊠ *£1* ☉ *Daily 10–5, or dusk if earlier.*

★ The **chapel of Trinity College** (1555) is an architectural gem—a tiny place with a delicately painted ceiling, gorgeously tiled floor, and elaborate wood carvings on the pews, pulpit, and walls. Some of the superb carvings were done by Grinling Gibbons, a 17th-century master carver whose work can also be seen in Hampton Court Palace and St. Paul's Cathedral, and who inspired the 18th-century cabinetmaker Thomas Chippendale. ⊠ *Broad St.* ☎ *01865/279900* ⊕ *www.trinity.ox.ac.uk* ⊠ *£2* ☉ *Weekdays 10–noon and 2–4, or dusk if earlier. Weekends noon–4:30 during term, 10–4:30 outside term.*

Fodor's Choice ★ The **Ashmolean Museum,** founded in 1683, is one of Britain's oldest public museums. Some of the world's most precious art objects are stashed here—drawings by Michelangelo and Raphael, European silverware and ceramics, a world-class numismatic collection, and Egyptian, Greek, and Roman artifacts. A renovation by noted architect Rick Mather, creating 39 additional galleries and a rooftop restaurant, opened in November 2009. ⊠ *Beaumont St.* ☎ *01865/278000* ⊕ *www. ashmolean.org* ⊠ *Free* ☉ *Tues.–Sun. 10–6.*

St. John's College (1555), former Prime Minister Tony Blair's alma mater, is worth a stop for its historic courtyards, world-renowned symmetrical gardens, and its library, where you can view some of Jane Austen's letters and an illustrated 1483 edition of *The Canterbury Tales* by the English printer William Caxton. ⊠ *St. Giles* ☎ *01865/277300* ⊕ *www. sjc.ox.ac.uk* 🖾 *Free* ☉ *Daily 1–5, 1–dusk in winter.*

College members, but not visitors, can enter the university's largest college via **Tom Gate.** This massive gatehouse is surmounted by Christopher Wren's **Tom Tower,** which contains Great Tom, a giant clock that strikes each hour with high and low notes.

☾ **Christ Church College.** Traditionally called "the House" by its students,
★ Christ Church has the largest quadrangle in town. This is where Charles Dodgson, better known as Lewis Carroll, was a math don; a shop across from the parkland (known as "the meadows") on St. Aldate's was the inspiration for the shop in *Through the Looking Glass.* More recently, various college locations appeared in the Harry Potter films. Don't miss the 800-year-old chapel, or the Tudor dining hall, with its portraits of former students—John Wesley, William Penn, and six of the 13 prime ministers who attended the college. ⊠ *St. Aldate's* ☎ *01865/276492* ⊕ *www.chch. ox.ac.uk* 🖾 *£6, with additional £2 for"Behind the Scenes" tour* ☉ *Weekdays 9–5, Sun. 2–5. Dining hall weekdays 2:30–5 during school year.*

WHERE TO EAT

££–£££ ✕ **Brasserie Blanc.** Raymond Blanc's Conran-designed brasserie is sophis-
CONTINENTAL ticated even by London standards. The top British chef populates his
★ menu with modern European and regional French dishes: you might see steamed Loch Fyne mussels in a white wine–and-cream sauce, or a Barbary duck breast in a blackberry sauce. At £12.50 for two courses or £14.95 for three, the prix-fixe lunch is an incredible value, and well worth the short walk north of the town center. ⊠ *71–72 Walton St.* ☎ *01865/510999* ⊕ *www.brasserieblanc.com* 🍴 *Reservations essential* 🖃 *AE, MC, V.*

£ ✕ **Grand Café.** In a lovely 1920s building, this inexpensive café looks as
CAFÉ if it should cost the world. Golden tiles, carved columns, and antique marble floor fill the place with charm, and the menu of tasty sandwiches, salads, and tarts, as well as afternoon tea, perfect coffee drinks and desserts, make it a great place for lunch or an afternoon break. At night it puts away its menus and transforms itself into a popular cocktail bar. ⊠ *84 High St.* ☎ *01865/204463* ⊕ *www.thegrandcafe.co.uk* 🖃 *AE, DC, MC, V.*

£ ✕ **Pizza Express.** Many people are surprised to discover that this uniquely
ITALIAN situated restaurant in the former sitting room of the 15th-century Golden Cross—Shakespeare's stopover lodging on his frequent trips from Stratford to London—is part of a nationwide chain. Creativity is encouraged here, so vegetarians, vegans, and meat eaters alike can enjoy inventing their own dream pizzas. A terrace is open in summer, but be sure to check out the medieval paintings and friezes inside the restaurant before heading out. ⊠ *8 The Golden Cross, Cornmarket St.* ☎ *01865/790442* ⊕ *www.pizzaexpress.com* 🖃 *AE, MC, V.*

STRATFORD-UPON-AVON

104 mi (167 km) north of London.

Stratford-upon-Avon has become adept at accommodating the hordes of people who stream in for a glimpse of William Shakespeare's world. Filled with all the distinctive, Tudor half-timber buildings your heart could desire, this is certainly a handsome town. But it can feel, at times, like a literary amusement park, so if you're not a fan of the Bard, you'd probably do better to explore a historic English market town.

TOURS AND TICKETS

It's difficult to avoid feeling like a herd animal as you board the Shakespeare bus, but tours like City Sightseeing's **Stratford and the Shakespeare Story** (✉ *Pen and Parchment pub, Bridgefort* ☎ *01789/412680* ⊕ *www.city-sightseeing.com* ✉ *£11.50*), with a hop-on, hop-off route around the five Shakespeare Birthplace Trust properties (two of which are out of town), can make a visit infinitely easier if you don't have a car.

It's worth purchasing a combined ticket to the **Shakespeare's Birthplace Trust properties,** which include Shakespeare's Birthplace Museum, Nash's House, Hall's Croft, Anne Hathaway's Cottage, and the Shakespeare Countryside Museum. The ticket, which is valid for one year and is available at any of the properties, costs £19 for all the sites, or £12.50 for the three in-town properties (not including Anne Hathaway's Cottage and Mary Arden's House). Note that you cannot buy a ticket for just one of the in-town sites. ☎ *01789/204016* ⊕ *www.shakespeare.org.uk.*

ESSENTIALS

Visitor Information Stratford-upon-Avon (☎ *01789/264–293* ⊕ *www.shakespeare-country.co.uk*).

> ## WORD OF MOUTH
>
> "Most visitors have only enough time in a hectic schedule to walk from the coach park or train station through the center to the Birthplace. If they stayed for longer and visited Anne Hathaway's Cottage by *walking* from the center (15 minutes) across the fields where undoubtedly Shakespeare walked, or visited Charlecote Park, a beautiful Elizabethan house by the Avon, they might return home with happier memories of Stratford-upon-Avon!"
> —bellini

19

EXPLORING

Most visitors to Stratford start at **Shakespeare's Birthplace.** The half-timber building in which Shakespeare was born in 1564 is a national treasure. It was owned by his descendants until the 19th century, and it became a national memorial in 1847. It's been furnished and decorated with simple whitewashed walls and brightly colored fabrics that were popular in Shakespeare's time. All the textiles have been hand-dyed using period methods. The revamped visitor center tells the story of Shakespeare's life in great detail, which makes a good starting point for any tour of Stratford. ✉ *Henley St.* ☎ *01789/204016* ⊕ *www.shakespeare.org.uk* ✉ *£12, includes admission to Nash's House and Hall's Croft* ☉ *Apr.–Oct., daily 9–5; Nov.–Mar., daily 10–4, July and Aug. 10–6.*

Nash's House contains an exhibit charting the history of Stratford, against a backdrop of period furniture and tapestries. The main attraction is really the extravagant gardens around the adjacent remains of **New Place,** the home where Shakespeare spent his last years, and where he died in 1616. A gorgeous Elizabethan knot garden, based on drawings of gardens from Shakespeare's time, grows around the remaining foundation of the house, which was destroyed in 1759 by its last owner, the Reverend Francis Gastrell, in an attempt to stop the tide of visitors. ⊠ *Chapel St.* ☎ *01789/204016* ⊕ *www.shakespeare.org.uk* ✇ *£12.50, includes admission to Shakespeare's Birthplace and Hall's Croft* ۞ *Nov.–Mar., daily 11–4; Apr.–Oct., daily 10–5, July and Aug. 10–6.*

★ **Hall's Croft** is Stratford's most beautiful Tudor town house. This was—almost definitely—the home of Shakespeare's daughter Susanna and her husband, Dr. John Hall. It's outfitted with furniture of the period and the doctor's dispensary. The walled garden is delightful. ⊠ *Old Town St.* ☎ *01789/204016* ⊕ *www.shakespeare.org.uk* ✇ *£12.50, includes admission to Shakespeare's Birthplace and Nash's House* ۞ *Nov.–Mar., daily 11–4; Apr.–Oct., daily 10–5.*

"Shakespeare's church," the 13th-century **Holy Trinity,** is fronted by a beautiful avenue of lime trees. Shakespeare is buried here, in the chancel. The bust of the Bard is thought to be an authentic likeness, executed a few years after his death. ⊠ *Trinity St.* ☎ *01789/266316* ✇ *Church free, chancel £1.50* ۞ *Mar., Mon.–Sat. 9–5, Sun. noon–5; Apr.–Sept., Mon.–Sat. 8:30–6, Sun. noon–5; Oct., Mon.–Sat. 9–5, Sun. noon–5; Nov.–Feb., Mon.–Sat. 9–4, Sun. 12:30–5.*

Fodor'sChoice   At long last, the **Royal Shakespeare Theatre,** famously set on the bank
★   of the Avon and landmark home of the Royal Shakespeare Company in Stratford has reopened after massive renovations began in 2007. Now classic productions of the Bard can be seen in the newly refurbished **Main Theatre,** along with the smaller **Swan Theatre** in the same building is now reopened. Check the Web site to see what's going to be on during your visit. It's always best to book in advance, especially now that the renovated theater has garnered its fair share of world headlines; day-of-performance tickets are sometimes available. ⊠ *Waterside* ☎ *0844/800–1110 ticket hotline and general information* ⊕ *www.rsc.org.uk.*

STRATFORD ENVIRONS

The two remaining stops on the Shakespeare trail are just outside Stratford.

★ **Anne Hathaway's Cottage,** the early home of the playwright's wife, is perhaps the most picturesque thatched cottage in the world. It has been gorgeously restored to reflect the comfortable middle-class Hathaway life. You can walk here from town—it's just over a mile from central Stratford. ⊠ *Cottage La., Shottery* ☎ *01789/204016* ⊕ *www.shakespeare.org.uk* ✇ *£7.50* ۞ *Apr.–Oct., daily 9–5; Nov.–Mar., daily 10–4.*

☺ **Mary Arden's Farm** uses 16th-century methods to grow food on its working farm. This stop is great for kids, who can see the lambs and calves, listen as the farmers explain their work in the fields, and watch the cooks prepare food in the Tudor farmhouse kitchen. This site was formerly referred to as Mary Arden's House, and believed to be where Shakespeare's mother grew up. In late 2000, research findings based on newly discovered real-estate records revealed that the

real **Mary Arden's Farm,** hitherto known as Glebe Farm, was actually nearby and (thankfully) already owned by the Shakespeare Birthplace Trust. ⊠ *Wilmcote* ☎ *01789/204016, 01789/293455 for information on special events* ⊕ *www.shakespeare.org.uk* ✎ *£9.50; children £5.50* ⊙ *Nov.–Mar. closed; Apr.–Oct., daily 10–5.*

⊙ Some 8 mi north of Stratford in the medieval town of Warwick, **War-★ wick Castle** fulfills the most clichéd Camelot daydreams. This medieval, fortified, much-restored, castellated, moated, landscaped (by Capability Brown) castle, now managed by the experts at Madame Tussauds, is a true period museum—complete with dungeons and a torture chamber, state rooms, and the occasional battle reenactment or joust. Note: It gets very crowded in summer, when lines for tickets, as well as food and drink, can be long, so it's not for those looking for a quiet, historic retreat to explore. Tickets are cheaper if purchased in advance on the Web site, and you'll also avoid some lines. ⊠ *Castle La. off Mill St., Warwick* ☎ *01926/495421, 0871/265–2000 24-hr information line* ⊕ *www.warwick-castle.co.uk* ✎ *£19.95–£25.45 on the day, £14.36–£20.36 online* ⊙ *Apr.–Sept., daily 10–6; Oct.–Mar., daily 10–5; last admission 30 min before closing.*

WHERE TO EAT

19

£–££ ✕ **The Black Swan/The Dirty Duck.** The only pub in Britain to be licensed
BRITISH under two names (the more informal one came courtesy of American GIs who were stationed here during WWII), this is one of Stratford's most celebrated pubs—it has attracted actors since the 18th-century thespian David Garrick's days. A little veranda overlooks the theaters and the river here. Along with a pint of bitter, it's a fine place to enjoy English grill specialties, as well as braised oxtail and honey-roasted duck. You can also choose from an assortment of bar meals. ⊠ *Waterside* ☎ *01789/297312* ▭ *AE, MC, V.*

££ ✕ **Lambs of Sheep Street.** Sit downstairs to appreciate the hardwood
BRITISH floors and oak beams of this local epicurean favorite; upstairs, the look is more contemporary. The updates of tried-and-true dishes include rib-eye steak with vine tomatoes, and slow-roasted lamb shank. Daily fish specials keep the menu seasonal, and the desserts are fantastic. A £11.50 fixed-price lunch is a good deal for two courses. ⊠ *12 Sheep St.* ☎ *01789/292554* ⊕ *www.lambsrestaurant.co.uk* ✑ *Reservations essential* ▭ *MC, V.*

Stratford-upon-Avon honors Shakespeare's Birthday with an annual procession.

££–£££ ✕ **The Opposition.** Hearty, warming meals are offered at this informal,
BRITISH   family-friendly restaurant, more commonly known as the "Oppo," in
           a 16th-century building on the main dining street near the theaters.
           The American and modern European dishes on the menu win praise
           from the locals. Try the roast chicken. ✉ *13 Sheep St.* ☎ *01789/269980*
           ⊕ *www.theoppo.co.uk* ⊟ *MC, V.*

WINDSOR CASTLE

24 mi (39 km) west of London.

The tall turrets of Windsor Castle, believed to be the world's largest
inhabited castle, can be seen for miles around. The grand stone building
is the star attraction in this quiet medieval town—though Eton College, England's most famous public school, is also just a lovely walk
away across the Thames. The castle is the only royal residence to have
been in continuous royal use since the days of William the Conqueror,
who chose this site to build a timber stockade soon after his conquest
of Britain in 1066. It was Edward III in the 1300s who really founded
the castle: he built the Norman gateway, the great Round Tower, and
the State Apartments. Charles II restored the State Apartments during the 1600s, and, during the 1820s George IV—with his mania for
building—converted what was still essentially a medieval castle into
the palace you see today.

ESSENTIALS

Visitor Information Windsor (☎ *01753/743900* ⊕ *www.windsor.gov.uk*).

EXPLORING

The massive citadel of **Windsor Castle** occupies 13 acres, but the first part you notice on entering is the **Round Tower,** on top of which the Standard is flown and at the base of which is the 11th-century Moat Garden. Passing under the portcullis at the Norman Gate, you reach the **Upper Ward,** the quadrangle containing the State Apartments—which you may tour—and the sovereign's Private Apartments.

Processions for foreign heads of state and other ceremonies take place here, as does the Changing of the Guard when the Queen is in residence. A short walk takes you to the Lower Ward, where the high point is the magnificent **St. George's Chapel,** home of the Order of the Garter, the highest chivalric order in the land, founded in 1348 by Edward III. Ten sovereigns are buried in the chapel—a fantastic Perpendicular Gothic vision 230 feet long, complete with gargoyles, buttresses, banners, swords, and choir stalls. This is also where royal weddings take place.

The **State Apartments** are as grand as Buckingham Palace's and have the added attraction of a few gems from the Queen's vast art collection: choice canvases by Rubens, Rembrandt, Van Dyck, Gainsborough, Canaletto, and Holbein; da Vinci drawings; Gobelin tapestries; and lime-wood carvings by Grinling Gibbons. The entrance is through a grand hall holding cases crammed with precious china—some still used for royal banquets. Don't miss the outsize suit of armor, made for Henry VIII, in the armory. Make sure you take in the magnificent views across to Windsor Great Park, which are the remains of a former royal hunting forest.

One unmissable treat is **Queen Mary's Dolls' House,** a 12:1 scale, seven-story palace with electricity, running water, and working elevators, designed in 1924 by Sir Edwin Lutyens. The detail is incredible—even the diminutive wine bottles hold the real thing. ✉ *Windsor Castle* ☎ *020/7766–7304 tickets, 01753/831118 opening hours* ⊕ *www.royalcollection.org.uk* 🎫 *£16 (£42 family ticket) for Precincts, State Apartments, Gallery, St. George's Chapel, Albert Memorial Chapel, and Queen Mary's Dolls' House; £8.50 when State Apartments are closed* ⊙ *Mar.–Oct., daily 9:45–5:15, last admission at 4; Nov.–Feb., daily 9:45–4:15, last admission at 3; St. George's Chapel closed Sun. except to worshippers. Hrs vary; check Web site.*

★ The splendid redbrick Tudor-style buildings of **Eton College,** founded in 1440 by King Henry VI, border the north end of High Street. During the college semesters, schoolboys dress in their distinctive striped trousers, swallow-tailed coats, and stiff collars to walk to class—it's all terrifically photogenic. The Gothic **Chapel** rivals St. George's at Windsor in size and magnificence, and is both austere and intimate. The

19

Museum of Eton Life has displays on the school's history. Admission to the school is with a prebooked guided tour only. ✉ *Main entrance off Eton High St.* ☎ *01753/671177* ⊕ *www.etoncollege.com* 🎟 *£6.20 short tour, £8.50 extended tour* ⊙ *Tours mid-Mar.–Oct., daily at 2 and 3:15. Closed Mon. and Tues. and Thurs. during term time, also closed weekends Nov.–Feb. Check Web site for details.*

WHERE TO EAT

£   ✕ **Two Brewers.** Two small, low-ceiling rooms make up this 17th-cen-
BRITISH   tury pub where locals congregate and palace staff unwind after work. Children are not welcome, but adults will find a suitable collection of wine, espresso, and local beer, plus an excellent little menu. Reservations are essential on Sunday, when the pub serves a traditional roast. ✉ *34 Park St.* ☎ *01753/855426* ⊟ *AE, MC, V* ⊙ *No full dinner Fri. and Sat.*

UNDERSTANDING LONDON

LONDON AT-A-GLANCE

ENGLISH VOCABULARY

BOOKS AND MOVIES

LONDON AT-A-GLANCE

FAST FACTS

Type of government: Representative democracy. In 1999 the Greater London Authority Act reestablished a single local governing body for the Greater London area, consisting of an elected mayor and the 25-member London Assembly. Elections, first held in 2000, take place every four years.

Population: Inner city 3 million, Greater London 7.7 million

Population density: 12,331 people per square mi

Median age: 38.4

Infant mortality rate: 5 per 1,000 births

Language: English. More than 300 languages are spoken in London. All city government documents are translated into Arabic, Bengali, Chinese, Greek, Gujurati, Hindi, Punjabi, Turkish, Urdu, and Vietnamese.

Ethnic and racial groups: White British 70%, White Irish 3%, Other White 9%, Indian 6%, Bangladeshi 2%, Pakistani 2%, other Asian 2%, Black African 6%, Black Caribbean 5%, Chinese 1%, Other 3%.

Religion: Christian 58%, nonaffiliated 15%, Muslim 8%, Hindu 4%, Jewish 2%, Sikh 1%, other religion 1%, Buddhist 0.8%

When a man is tired of London, he is tired of life; for there is in London all that life can afford.

—Samuel Johnson

GEOGRAPHY AND ENVIRONMENT

Latitude: 51° N (same as Calgary, Canada; Kiev, Ukraine; Prague, Czech Republic)

Longitude: 0° (same as Accra, Ghana). A brass line in the ground in Greenwich marks the prime meridian (0° longitude).

Elevation: 49 feet

Land area: City, 67 square mi; metro area, 625 square mi

Terrain: River plain, rolling hills, and parkland

Natural hazards: Drought in warmer summers, minor localized flooding of the Thames caused by surge tides from the North Atlantic

Environmental issues: The city has been improving its air quality, but up to 1,600 people die each year from health problems related to London's polluted air. Only half of London's rivers and canals received passing grades for water quality from 1999 through 2001. More than £12 million ($22 million) is spent annually to ensure the city's food safety.

I'm leaving because the weather is too good. I hate London when it's not raining.

—Groucho Marx

ECONOMY

Workforce: 3.8 million; financial/real estate 28%, health care 10%, manufacturing 4%, education 7%, construction 5%, public administration 5%

Unemployment: 7.2%

Major industries: The arts, banking, government, insurance, tourism

London: a nation, not a city.

—Benjamin Disraeli, Lothair

ENGLISH VOCABULARY

You and a Londoner may speak the same language, but some phrases definitely get lost in translation once they cross the Atlantic.

British English	American English

BASIC TERMS AND EVERYDAY ITEMS

British English	American English
bill	check
flat	apartment
lift	elevator
nappy	diaper
holiday	vacation
note	bill (currency)
plaster	Band-Aid
queue	line
row	argument
rubbish	trash
tin	can
toilet/loo/WC	bathroom

CLOTHING

British English	American English
braces	suspenders
bum bag	fanny pack
dressing gown	robe
jumper	sweater
pants/knickers	underpants/briefs
rucksack	backpack
suspender	garter
tights	pantyhose
trainers	sneakers
trousers	pants
vest	undershirt
waistcoat	vest

TRANSPORTATION

British English	American English
bonnet	hood
boot	trunk

coach	long-distance bus
pavement	sidewalk
petrol	gas
pram	baby carriage
puncture	flat
windscreen	windshield

FOOD

aubergine	eggplant
banger	sausage
biscuit	cookie
chips	fries
courgette	zucchini
crisps	potato chips
jam	jelly
main course (or main)	entrée
pudding	dessert
rocket	arugula
starter	appetizer
sweet	candy
tea	early dinner

SLANG

all right	hi there
cheers	thank you
chuffed	pleased
fit	attractive
geezer	dude
guv'nor, gaffer	boss
hard	tough
mate	buddy
sound	good
ta	thank you

BOOKS AND MOVIES

London has been the focus of countless books and essays. For sonorous eloquence, you still must reach back more than half a century to Henry James's *English Hours* and Virginia Woolf's *The London Scene*. Today most suggested reading lists begin with V. S. Pritchett's *London Perceived* and H. V. Morton's *In Search of London*, both decades old. Four more-up-to-date books with a general compass are Peter Ackroyd's *Thames* and anecdotal *London: The Biography*, which traces the city's growth from the Druids to the 21st century; John Russell's *London*, a sumptuously illustrated art book; and Christopher Hibbert's *In London: The Biography of a City*. Stephen Inwood's *A History of London* explores the city from its Roman roots to its swinging '60s heyday. Piet Schreuders's *The Beatles' London* follows the footsteps of the Fab Four.

That noted, there are books galore on the various facets of the city. *The Art and Architecture of London* by Ann Saunders is fairly comprehensive. *Inside London: Discovering the Classic Interiors of London*, by Joe Friedman and Peter Aprahamian, has magnificent color photographs of hidden and overlooked shops, clubs, and town houses. For a wonderful take on the golden age of the city's regal mansions, see Christopher Simon Sykes's *Private Palaces: Life in the Great London Houses*. For various other aspects of the city, consult Mervyn Blatch's helpful *A Guide to London's Churches*, Andrew Crowe's *The Parks and Woodlands of London*, Sheila Fairfield's *The Streets of London*, Ann Saunders's *Regent's Park*, Ian Norrie's *Hampstead, Highgate Village, and Kenwood*, and Suzanne Ebel's *A Guide to London's Riverside: Hampton Court to Greenwich*. For keen walkers, there are two books by Andrew Duncan: *Secret London* and *Walking Village London*. *City Secrets: London*, edited by Robert Kahn, is a handsome book of anecdotes from London writers, artists, and historians about their favorite places in the city. For the last word on just about every subject, see *The London Encyclopaedia*, edited by Ben Weinreb and Christopher Hibbert. HarperCollins's *London Photographic Atlas* has a plethora of bird's-eye images of the capital. For an alternative view of the city, it would be hard to better Iain Sinclair's witty and intelligent *London Orbital: A Walk Around the M25* in which he scrutinizes the history, mythology, and politics of London from the viewpoint of its ugly ring road. Sinclair is also the editor of *London: City of Disappearances*, an anthology exploring what has vanished.

Of course, the history and spirit of the city are also to be found in celebrations of great authors, British heroes, and architects. Peter Ackroyd's massive *Dickens* elucidates how the great author shaped today's view of the city; Martin Gilbert's magisterial, multivolume *Churchill* traces the city through some of its greatest trials; J. Mansbridge's *John Nash* details the London buildings of this great architect. Liza Picard evokes mid-18th-century London in *Dr. Johnson's London*. For musical theater buffs, Mike Leigh's *Gilbert and Sullivan's London* takes a romantic look at the two artists' lives and times in the capital's grand theaters and wild nightspots. *Rodinsky's Room* by Rachel Lichtenstein and Iain Sinclair is a fascinating exploration of East End Jewish London and the mysterious disappearance of one of its occupants.

Maureen Waller's *1700: Scenes from London Life* is a fascinating look at the daily life of Londoners in the 18th century. Nineteenth-century London—the city of Queen Victoria, Tennyson, and Dickens—comes alive through *Mayhew's London*, a massive study of the London poor by Henry Mayhew, and Gustave Doré's *London*, an unforgettable series of engravings of the city (often reprinted in modern editions) that detail its horrifying slums and grand avenues. When it comes to fiction, of course, Dickens's immortal works top the list. Stay-at-home detectives have long walked the streets of London, thanks to great mysteries by Dorothy L. Sayers, Agatha Christie, Ngaio Marsh, and Antonia Fraser. Cops and bad guys wind their way around 1960s London in Jake Arnott's pulp fiction books, *The Long Firm* and *He Kills Coppers*. Martin Amis's *London Fields* tracks a murder mystery through West London. For so-called "tart noir," pick up any Stella Duffy book. Marie Belloc-Lowndes's *The Lodger* is a fictional account of London's most deadly villain, Jack the Ripper. Victorian London was never so salacious as in Sarah Waters's story of a young girl who travels the theaters as a singer, the Soho squares as a male prostitute, and the East End as a communist in *Tipping the Velvet*. Late-20th-century London, with its diverse ethnic makeup, is the star of Zadie Smith's famed novel *White Teeth*. The vibrancy and cultural diversity of London's East End come to life in Monica Ali's *Brick Lane*.

Many films—from *Waterloo Bridge* and *Georgy Girl* to *Secrets and Lies* and *Notting Hill*—have used London as their setting. The great musicals Walt Disney's *Mary Poppins*, George Cukor's *My Fair Lady*, and Sir Carol Reed's *Oliver!* evoke the Hollywood soundstage version of London.

Children of all ages enjoy Stephen Herek's *101 Dalmatians*, with Glenn Close as fashion-savvy Cruella de Vil. King's Cross Station in London was shot to cinematic fame by the movie version of J.K. Rowling's *Harry Potter and the Philosopher's Stone*. Look for cameos by the city in all other *Harry Potter* films.

The swinging '60s are loosely portrayed in M. Jay Roach's *Austin Powers: International Man of Mystery*, full of references to British slang and some great opening scenes in London. For a truer picture of the '60s in London, Michelangelo Antonioni weaves a mystery plot around the world of a London fashion photographer in *Blow-Up*. British

gangster films came into their own with Guy Ritchie's amusing tales of London thieves in *Lock, Stock, and Two Smoking Barrels*, filmed almost entirely in London, and the follow-up *Snatch*. More sobering portraits of London criminal life include Neil Jordan's *Mona Lisa*, Paul McGuigan's *Gangster No. 1*, and John Mackenzie's *The Long Good Friday*. Of course, the original tough guy is 007, and his best exploits in London are featured in the introductory chase scene in *The World Is Not Enough*.

Sir Arthur Conan Doyle knew the potential of London as a chilling setting, and John Landis's *An American Werewolf in London* and Hitchcock's *39 Steps* and *The Man Who Knew Too Much* exploit the Gothic and sinister qualities of the city. For a fascinating look at Renaissance London, watch John Madden's *Shakespeare in Love*. Dickens's London is indelibly depicted in David Lean's *Oliver Twist*.

Some modern-day romantic comedies that use London as a backdrop are Peter Howitt's *Sliding Doors* with Gwyneth Paltrow and the screen adaptations of Helen Fielding's *Bridget Jones's Diary* (and its sequel), starring Renée Zellweger, Hugh Grant, and Colin Firth. Glossy London is depicted in Woody Allen's *Match Point*, bohemian London in David Kane's *This Year's Love*, gritty London in Shane Meadow's *Somers Town*, and post-zombie London in Danny Boyle's *28 Days Later*, while Patrick Kellior's *London* offers a uniquely informed, idiosyncratic view of the city.

Travel Smart London

GETTING HERE AND AROUND

Central London and its surrounding districts are divided into 32 boroughs—33, counting the City of London. More useful for finding your way around, however, are the subdivisions of London into postal districts. Throughout the guide we've given the full postal code for some listings. The first one or two letters give the location: N means north, NW means northwest, and so on. Don't expect the numbering to be logical, however. You won't, for example, find W2 next to W3. The general rule is that the lower numbers, such as W1 or SW1, are closest to Buckingham Palace, but it is not consistent—SE17 is closer to the city center than E4, for example.

▌ AIR TRAVEL

Flying time to London is about 6½ hours from New York, 7½ hours from Chicago, 11 hours from San Francisco, and 21½ hours from Sydney.

For flights out of London, the general rule is that you arrive one hour before your scheduled departure time for domestic flights and two hours before international flights for off-peak travel.

Airline Security Issues Transportation Security Administration (⊕ www.tsa.gov).

AIRPORTS

International flights to London arrive at either Heathrow Airport (LHR), 15 mi west of London, or at Gatwick Airport (LGW), 27 mi south of the capital. Most flights from the United States go to Heathrow, which is the busiest and is divided into five terminals, with Terminals 3, 4, and 5 handling transatlantic flights. Gatwick is London's second gateway. It has grown from a European airport into an airport that also serves dozens of U.S. destinations. A smaller third airport, Stansted (STN), is 35 mi northeast of the city. It handles mainly European and domestic traffic, although there's also scheduled

service from New York. Two smaller airports, Luton (LTN), 30 mi north of town, and business-oriented London City (in East London E16) mainly handle flights to Europe.

Airport Information Gatwick Airport (☎ 0844/335–1802 ⊕ www.gatwickairport. com). **Heathrow Airport** (☎ 0844/335–1801 ⊕ www.heathrowairport.com). **London City Airport** (☎ 020/7646–0088 ⊕ www.londoncityairport.com). **Luton Airport** (☎ 01582/405–100 ⊕ www.london-luton.co.uk). **Stansted Airport** (☎ 0844/355–1803 ⊕ www.stanstedairport.com).

GROUND TRANSPORTATION

London has excellent if pricey bus and train connections between its airports and Central London. If you're arriving at Heathrow, you can pick up a map and fare schedule at the Transport for London (TfL) Information Centre located in the underground station serving Terminals 1, 2, and 3. Train service can be quick, but the downside (for trains from all airports) is that you must get yourself and your luggage to the train via a series of escalators and connecting trams. Airport link buses (generally National Express Airport buses) may ease the luggage factor and drop you closer to central hotels, but they're subject to London traffic, which can be horrendous and make the trip drag on for hours. Taxis can be more convenient than buses, but beware that prices can go through the roof. Airport Travel Line has additional transfer information and takes advance booking for transfers between airports and into London. The BAA (British Airport Authority) Web site is a useful resource, giving all transport options from Gatwick, Heathrow, and Stansted.

FROM HEATHROW TO CENTRAL LONDON		
Travel Mode	Time	Cost
Taxi	1 hour+	£50+
Heathrow Express Train	15 min	£16.50 (£32 round-trip) and £26 for first class
Underground	50 min	£4.50 one-way (less with Oyster card)
National Express Bus	1 hour	£4 one-way
Hotel by Bus	1 hour+	£22 one-way

Heathrow by Bus: National Express buses take one hour to reach the city center (Victoria) and costs £5 one-way and £10 round-trip. A rival service, easyBus, offers buses from as little as £2. The National Express Hotel Hoppa service runs from all airports to around 20 hotels located near the airport (£4). Alternatively, nearly every hotel in London itself is served by the Hotel By Bus service. Fares to Central London average around £22. SkyShuttle also offers a shared minibus service between Heathrow and any London hotel. The N9 night bus runs every half hour from midnight to 5 am to Trafalgar Square; it takes an hour and costs £4.

Heathrow by Train: The cheap, direct route into London is via the Piccadilly line of the Underground (London's extensive subway system, or "Tube"). Trains normally run every four to eight minutes from all terminals from early morning until just before midnight. The 50-minute trip into central London costs £4.50 one-way and connects with other central Tube lines. The Heathrow Express train is comfortable and convenient, if costly, speeding into London's Paddington Station in 15 minutes. Standard one-way tickets cost £16.50 (£32 round-trip) and £26 for first class. Book ahead (online is the cheapest option, at a counter/kiosk less so), as tickets are more expensive to buy on board. There's daily

NAVIGATING LONDON

London is a confusing city to navigate, even for people who've visited it a few times. Its streets are arranged in medieval patterns that no longer make much sense, meaning that you can't always use logic to find your way around. A good map is essential, and public transportation can be a lifesaver: buses will take you magically from point A to point B, and the Tube is often the quickest way to reach your destination. Here are some basic tips to help you find your way around:

■ Although free tourist maps can be handy, they're usually quite basic and include only major streets. If you're going to be doing lots of wandering around, buy the pocket-size map book *London A–Z* sold in bookstores and Tube and train stations throughout the city. Its detailed maps are lifesavers.

■ To find your way, look for tall landmarks near where you are headed: the London Eye, for example, or the cross atop St. Paul's Cathedral—or the most obvious of all, Big Ben.

■ If you get properly lost, the best people to ask are the Londoners hustling by you, who know the area like nobody else. The worst people to ask are the people working in souvenir kiosks, and street vendors handing out the local *Evening Standard* newspaper; they're famously rude and unhelpful to lost tourists.

■ The tourist hubs of Soho, Covent Garden, Leicester Square, and Trafalgar Square are separated from one another by only a few blocks. Taking the Tube from one to another actually takes longer than walking.

■ On the other hand, when you're lost, the Tube is often the shortest distance between two points. Don't hesitate to use it.

London
Postal Districts

service from 5:10 am (5:50 am on Sunday) to 11:25 pm (10:50 pm on Sunday), with departures every 15 minutes. The Heathrow Connect service leaves from Paddington station and makes five local stops before arriving at Terminals 1, 3, and 5. At 25 minutes, journey time is only slightly slower than the Express and one-way tickets are £7.90.

Gatwick by Bus: Hourly bus service runs from Gatwick's north and south terminals to Victoria Station with stops at Hooley, Coulsdon, Mitcham, Streatham, Stockwell, and Pimlico. The journey takes up to 90 minutes and costs from £4.50 one-way. The easyBus service runs a service to west London (Fulham) from as little as £2; the later the ticket is booked online, the higher the price (up to £10 on board).

Gatwick by Train: The fast, nonstop Gatwick Express leaves for Victoria Station every 15 minutes 5:15 am–midnight. The 30-minute trip costs £16.90 one-way, £23. round-trip. Book in advance, as tickets cost more on board. The First Capital Connect rail company's non-express services are cheaper; Capital Connect train runs regularly throughout the day until midnight to St. Pancras International, London Bridge, and Blackfriars stations; departures are every 15 to 30 minutes, and the journey takes almost one hour. Tickets are from £8 one-way. FlyBy service to Victoria (£10 single) is not express, but the fare applies only on trains operated by Southern Trains.

Stansted by Bus: Hourly service on National Express Airport bus A6 (24 hours a day) to Victoria Coach Station costs from £10 one-way, £17 round-trip, and takes about 1 hour and 40 minutes. Stops include Golders Green, Finchley Road, St. John's Wood, Baker Street, Marble Arch, and Hyde Park Corner. The easyBus service to Victoria via Baker Street costs from £2.

Stansted by Train: The Stansted Express to Liverpool Street Station (with a stop at Tottenham Hale) runs every 15 minutes 4:10 am–11:25 pm daily. The 45-minute

trip costs £18.80 one-way, £26.70 round-trip if booked online. Tickets cost more when purchased on board.

Luton by Bus and Train: A free airport shuttle runs from Luton Airport to the nearby Luton Airport Parkway Station, from which you can take a train or bus into London. From there, the First Capital Connect train service runs to St. Pancras, Farringdon, Blackfriars, and London Bridge. The journey takes about 25 minutes. Trains leave every 10 minutes or so from 5 am until midnight. Single tickets cost £13.50. The Green Line 757 bus service from Luton to Victoria Station runs three times an hour, takes about 90 minutes, and costs from £14 (£15 return).

Heathrow, Gatwick, Stansted, and Luton by Taxi: This is an expensive and time-consuming option. The city's congestion charge (£8) may be added to the bill if your hotel is in the charging zone, you run the risk of getting stuck in traffic, and if you take a taxi from the stand, the price will be even more expensive (whereas a minicab booked ahead is a set price). The trip from Heathrow, for example, can take more than an hour and cost more than £50.

TRANSFERS BETWEEN AIRPORTS

Allow at least two to three hours for an inter-airport transfer. The cheapest option—but most complicated—is public transport: from Gatwick to Stansted, for instance, you can catch the non-express commuter train from Gatwick to Victoria Station, take the Tube to Liverpool Street Station, then catch the train to Stansted from there. To get from Heathrow to Gatwick by public transport, take the Tube to King's Cross, then change to the Victoria Line, get to Victoria Station, and then take the commuter train to Gatwick.

The National Express Airport bus is the most direct option between Gatwick and Heathrow. Buses pick up passengers every 15 minutes from 5:20 am to 11 pm from both airports. The trip takes around 70 minutes, and the fare is £19.50 one-way. It's advisable to book tickets in advance.

National Express buses between Stansted and Gatwick depart every 30 to 45 minutes and take around 3 hours and 45 minutes. The adult single fare is £30.20. Some airlines may offer shuttle services as well—check with your travel agent in advance of your journey.

Contacts BAA (⊕ www.baa.com). easyBus (⊕ www.easybus.co.uk). First Capital Connect (⊕ www.firstcapitalconnect.co.uk). Gatwick Express (☎ 0845/850–1530 ⊕ www.gatwickexpress.com). Heathrow Express (☎ 0845600–1515 ⊕ www.heathrowexpress.com). National Express (☎ 0870/580–8080 ⊕ www.nationalexpress.com). SkyShuttle (☎ 0845/481–0960 ⊕ www.skyshuttle.co.uk. com). Stansted Express (☎ 0845/850–0150 ⊕ www.stanstedexpress.com).

Transfer Information Airport Travel Line (☎ 0871/200–2323).

FLIGHTS

British Airways is the national flagship carrier and offers mostly nonstop flights from 16 U.S. cities to Heathrow and Gatwick airports, along with flights to Manchester, Birmingham, and Glasgow. It also offers flights to New York from London City Airport near Docklands.

Airline Contacts American Airlines (☎ 800/433–7300, 0207/365–0777 in London ⊕ www.aa.com). British Airways (☎ 800/247–9297, 0844/493–0787 in U.K. ⊕ www.ba.com) to Heathrow, Gatwick. Delta Airlines (☎ 800/221–1212 for U.S. reservations, 800/241–4141 for international reservations, 0845/600-0950 in U.K. ⊕ www.delta. com). United Airlines (☎ 800/864–8331 for U.S. reservations, 800/538–2929 for international reservations, 0845/844–4777 in U.K., 800/231–0856 for international reservations for Continental Airlines, now merged with United ⊕ www.united.com). US Airways (☎ 800/428–4322 for U.S. and Canada reservations, 800/622–1015 for international reservations, 0845/600–3300 in U.K ⊕ www. usairways.com). Virgin Atlantic (☎ 800/ 821–5438, 0844/209–7777 in U.K. ⊕ www. virgin-atlantic.com).

▌ BUS TRAVEL

ARRIVING AND DEPARTING

National Express is the biggest British coach operator and the nearest equivalent to Greyhound. It's not as fast as traveling by train, but it's comfortable (with washroom facilities on board). Services depart mainly from Victoria Coach Station, a well-signposted short walk behind the Victoria mainline rail station. The departures point is on the corner of Buckingham Palace Road; this is also the main information point. The arrivals point is opposite at Elizabeth Bridge. National Express buses travel to all large and midsize cities in southern England and the midlands. Scotland and the north are not as well served. The station is extremely busy around holidays and weekends. Arrive at least 30 minutes before departure so you can find the correct exit gate. Smoking is not permitted on board.

Another bus company, Megabus, has been packing in the budget travelers in recent years, since it offers cross-country fares for as little as £1 per person. The company's single- and double-decker buses serve an extensive array of cities across Great Britain with a cheerful budget attitude. In London, buses for all destinations depart from the Green Line bus stand at Victoria Station. Megabus does not accommodate wheelchairs, and the company strictly limits luggage to one piece per person checked, and one piece of hand luggage.

Greyhound itself recently launched a low-cost bus service connecting London Victoria with several destinations on England's south coast, as well as Cardiff and Swansea in Wales.

Green Line serves the counties surrounding London, as well as airports. Bus stops (there's no central bus station) are on Buckingham Palace Road, between the Victoria mainline station and Victoria Coach Station.

Tickets on some long-distance routes are cheaper if purchased in advance, and traveling midweek is cheaper than over weekends and at holiday periods.

GETTING AROUND LONDON

Private, as opposed to municipal, buses are known as coaches. Although London is famous for its double-decker buses, long articulated buses (locally known as "bendy buses") replaced the oldest buses—the beloved rattletrap Routemasters, which had the jump-on/off back platforms, under the previous mayor. However, these proved both unpopular and money-losing and are being phased out, to be replaced by a redesigned Routemaster in the near future. Two Routemaster "heritage" routes keep the old familiar double-decker buses working, however: the No. 9 travels through Piccadilly, Trafalgar Square, and Knightsbridge, and the No. 15 travels from Trafalgar Square down Fleet Street and on to St. Paul's Cathedral.

Bus stops are clearly indicated; signs at bus stops feature a red TfL symbol on a plain white background. You must flag the bus down at some stops. Each numbered route is listed on the main stop, and buses have a large number on the front with their end destination. Not all buses run the full route at all times; check with the driver to be sure. You can pick up a free bus guide at a TfL Travel Information Centre (at Euston, Liverpool Street, Piccadilly Circus, King's Cross, and Victoria Tube stations; and at Heathrow Airport).

Buses are a good way of seeing the town, particularly if you plan to hop on and off to cover many sights, but don't take a bus if you're in a hurry, as traffic can really slow them down. To get off, press the red "Stop" buttons mounted on poles near the doors. You will usually see a "Bus Stopping" sign light up. Expect to get very squashed during rush hour, from 8 am to 9:30 am and 4:30 pm to 6:30 pm.

Night buses, denoted by an "N" before their route numbers, run from midnight to 5 am on a more restricted route than day buses. However, some night bus routes should be approached with caution and the top deck avoided. All night buses run by request stop, so flag them down if you're waiting or push the button if you want to alight.

All journeys cost £2, and there are no transfers. If you plan to make a number of journeys in one day, consider buying a Travelcard (⇨ *Underground Tube Travel*), good for both Tube and bus travel. Also consider getting a prepaid Oyster card, as single journeys are just over a pound using a prepaid card. Travelcards are also available in one-, three-, or seven-day combinations. Visitor Oyster cards cost £2 and can be topped up. They are available from ticket desks at Gatwick and Stansted airports or at any Tube station and are transferable if you have money left over. Traveling without a valid ticket makes you liable for a fine (£20). Buses are supposed to swing by most stops every five or six minutes, but in reality, you can often expect to wait a bit longer, although those in the center of town are quite reliable.

In central London, if you don't have a prepaid Travel- or Oyster card, you must pay before you board the bus. Automated ticket machines are set up at these bus stops, which are clearly marked with a yellow sign "Buy Tickets Before Boarding". Otherwise, you can buy tickets at most central London Tube stations as well as at newsagents and shops that display the sign "Buy Your TravelCards & Bus Passes Here". Outside the central zone, payment may be made to the driver as you board (exact change is best so as to avoid incurring the driver's wrath).

Bus Information EasyBus (⊕ www.easybus.com). **Green Line** (☏ 0870/608–7261 ⊕ www.greenline.co.uk). **Greyhound UK** (☏ 0900/096–0000 ⊕ www.greyhounduk.com). **Megabus** (☏ 0871/266–3333 ⊕ www.megabus.com). **National Express** (☏ 0871/781–8181 ⊕ www.nationalexpress.com). **Transport for London** (☏ 0207/222–1234 ⊕ www.tfl.gov.uk). **Victoria Coach Station** (☏ 0207/730–3499).

▌ CAR TRAVEL

The best advice on driving in London is this: don't. London's streets are a winding mass of chaos, made worse by one-way roads. Parking is also restrictive and expensive, and traffic is tediously slow at most times of the day; during rush hours—from 8 am to 9:30 am and 4:30 pm to 6:30 pm—it often grinds to a standstill, particularly on Friday, when everyone wants to leave town. Avoid city-center shopping areas, including the roads feeding Oxford Street, Kensington, and Knightsbridge. Other main roads into the city center are also busy, such as King's Cross and Euston in the north. Watch out also for cyclists and motorcycle couriers, who weave between cars and pedestrians and seem to come out of nowhere, and you may be fined heavily for straying into a bus lane during its operating hours—check the signs.

If you are staying just in London on this trip, there's virtually no reason to rent a car since the city and its suburbs are widely covered by public transportation. However, you might want a car for day trips to castles or stately homes out in the countryside. Consider renting your car in a medium-size town in the area where you'll be traveling, and then journeying there by train and picking up the car once you arrive. Rental rates are generally reasonable, and insurance costs are lower than in comparable U.S. cities. Rates generally begin at £42 a day for a small economy car (such as a subcompact General Motors Vauxhall, Corsa, or Renault Clio), usually with manual transmission. Air-conditioning and unlimited mileage generally come with the larger-size automatic cars.

In London your U.S. driver's license is acceptable (as long as you are over 23 years old, with no endorsements or driving convictions). If you have a driver's license from a country other than the United States, it may not be recognized in the United Kingdom. An International Driver's Permit is a good idea no matter what; it's available from the American (AAA) or Canadian Automobile Association and, in the United Kingdom, from the Automobile Association (AA) or Royal Automobile Club (RAC). International permits are universally recognized, and having one may save you a problem with the local authorities.

Remember that Britain drives on the left, and the rest of Europe on the right. Therefore, you may want to leave your rented car in Britain and pick up a left-side drive if you cross the Channel (⇨ *The Channel Tunnel*).

CONGESTION CHARGE

Designed to reduce traffic through central London, a congestion charge has been instituted. Vehicles (with some exemptions) entering central London on weekdays from 7 am to 6 pm (excluding public holidays) have to pay an £8 daily fee; it can be paid up to 90 days in advance, on the day of travel, or on the following charging day, when the fee goes up to £10. Day-, month-, and year-long passes are available on the Congestion Charging page of the Transport for London Web site, at gas stations, parking lots (car parks), by mail, by phone, and by SMS text message. One day's payment is good for all access into the charging zone on that day. Traffic signs designate the entrance to congestion areas, and cameras read car license plates and send the information to a database. Drivers who don't pay the congestion charge by midnight of the next charging day following the day of driving are penalized £120, which is reduced to £60 if paid within 14 days.

Information Congestion Charge Customer Service (✉ *Freepost NAT 6416, Box 2985, Coventry CV7 8BR* ☎ *0845/900–1234* ⊕ *www.cclondon.com*). **Transport for London** (⊕ *www.tfl.gov.uk*).

GASOLINE

Gasoline (petrol) is sold in liters and is expensive (at press time in spring 2011 about £1.20 per liter—around $7 per gallon—at this writing). Unleaded petrol, denoted by green pump lines, is predominant. Premium and Super Premium are the two varieties, and most cars run on regular Premium. Supermarket pumps usually offer the best value. You won't find many service stations in the center of town; these are generally on main, multilane trunk roads out of the center. Service is self-serve, except in small villages, where gas stations are likely to be closed on Sunday and late evening. Most stations accept major credit cards.

PARKING

During the day—and probably at all times—it's safest to believe that you can park nowhere except at a meter, in a pay-and-display bay, in a garage, otherwise, you run the risk of an expensive ticket, plus possibly even more expensive clamping and towing fees (some boroughs are clamp-free). Restrictions are indicated by the "No Waiting" parking signpost on the sidewalk (these restrictions vary from street to street), and restricted areas include single yellow lines or double yellow lines, and Residents' Parking bays. Parking at a bus stop or in a bus lane is also restricted. On Red Routes, indicated by red lines, you are not allowed to park or even stop. It's illegal to park on the sidewalk, across entrances, or on white zigzag lines approaching a pedestrian crossing.

Meters have an insatiable hunger in the inner city—a 20p piece may buy just three minutes—and some will permit only a two-hour stay. Meters take 20p and £1 coins, pay-and-display machines 10p, 20p, 50p, £1, and £2 coins. Some take payment by credit card. In some parts of central London, meters have been almost entirely replaced by pay-and-display machines that require payment by cell phone. You will need to set up an account to do this (⊕ *www.westminster. gov.uk*). Meters are free after 6:30 or 8:30 in the evening, on Sunday, and on holidays. Always check the sign. In the evening, after restrictions end, meter bays are free. After meters are free, you can also park on single yellow lines—but not double yellow lines. In the daytime, take

advantage of the many NCP parking lots in the center of town (about £4 per hour, up to eight hours).

Information NCP (☎ 0845/050-7080 ⊕ www.ncp.co.uk).

ROADSIDE EMERGENCIES

If your car is stolen, you're in a car accident, or your car breaks down and there's nobody around to help you, contact the police by dialing ☎ 999.

The general procedure for a breakdown is the following: position the red hazard triangle (which should be in the trunk of the car) a few paces away from the rear of the car. Leave the hazard warning lights on. Along highways (motorways), emergency roadside telephone booths are positioned at intervals within walking distance. Contact the car-rental company or an auto club. The main auto clubs in the United Kingdom are the Automobile Association (AA) and the RAC. If you're a member of the American Automobile Association (AAA), check your membership details before you depart for Britain, as, under a reciprocal agreement, roadside assistance in the United Kingdom should cost you nothing. You can join and receive roadside assistance from the AA on the spot, but the charge is higher—around £75—than a simple membership fee.

Emergency Services American Automobile Association (☎ 800/564-6222). **Automobile Association** (☎ 0870/085-2721, 44-161-333-0004 from outside U.K., 0800/887-766 for emergency roadside assistance from mobile phones, 08457/887766). **RAC** (☎ 01922/437-000, 0800/828-282 for emergency roadside assistance).

RULES OF THE ROAD

London is a mass of narrow, one-way roads, and narrow, two-way streets that are no bigger than the one-way roads. If you must risk life and limb and drive in London, note that the speed limit is either 20 or 30 mph—unless you see the large 40 mph signs found only in the suburbs. Speed bumps are sprinkled about with abandon in case you forget. Speed is strictly controlled by cameras mounted on occasional lamposts, which photograph speeders for ticketing.

Medium-size circular intersections are often designed as "roundabouts" (marked by signs in which three arrows curve into a circle). On these, cars travel left in a circle and incoming cars must yield to those already on their way around from the right. Signal when about to leave the roundabout.

Jaywalking is not illegal in London and everybody does it, despite the fact that striped crossings with blinking yellow lights mounted on poles at either end—called "zebra crossings"—give pedestrians the right of way to cross. Cars should treat zebra crossings like stop signs if a pedestrian is waiting to cross or already starting to cross. It's illegal to pass another vehicle at a zebra crossing. At other crossings (including intersections) pedestrians must yield to traffic, but they do have the right-of-way over traffic turning left at controlled crossings—if they have the nerve.

Traffic lights sometimes have arrows directing left or right turns; try to catch a glimpse of the road markings in time, and don't get into the turn lane if you mean to go straight ahead. A right turn is not permitted on a red light. Signs at the beginning and end of designated bus lanes give the time restrictions for use (usually during peak hours); if you're caught driving on bus lanes during restricted hours, you will be fined. By law, seat belts must be worn in the front and back seats. Drunk-driving laws are strictly enforced, and it's safest to avoid alcohol altogether if you'll be driving. The legal limit is 80 milligrams of alcohol per 100 milliliters of blood, which roughly translated means two units of alcohol—two small glasses of wine, one pint of beer, or one glass of whiskey.

▌ UNDERGROUND TRAVEL

London's extensive Underground train (Tube) system has color-coded routes, clear signage, and many connections. Trains run out into the suburbs, and all stations are marked with the London Underground circular symbol. (Do not be confused by similar-looking signs reading "subway"—in Britain, the word subway means "pedestrian underpass.") Trains are all one class; smoking is *not* allowed on board or in the stations. There is also an Overground network serving the further reaches of Inner London. These now accept Oyster cards.

Some lines have multiple branches (Central, District, Northern, Metropolitan, and Piccadilly), so be sure to note which branch is needed for your particular destination. Do this by noting the end destination on the lighted sign on the platform, which also tells you how long you'll have to wait until the train arrives. Compare that with the end destination of the branch you want. When the two match, that's your train. ▌TIP➜ Service on many Tube lines will be disrupted, especially on weekends, as a widespread improvements program continues before the 2012 Olympics. Check the TfL Web site for up-to-date information.

London is divided into six concentric zones (ask at Underground ticket booths for a map and booklet, which give details of the ticket options), so be sure to buy a ticket for the correct zone or you may be liable for an on-the-spot fine of £20. Don't panic if you do forget to buy a ticket for the right zone: just tell a station attendant that you need to buy an "extension" to your ticket. Although you're meant to do that in advance, generally if you're an out-of-towner, they don't give you a hard time.

For single fares paid in cash, a flat £4 price per journey now applies across all six zones, whether you're traveling one stop or 12 stops. If you're planning several trips in one day, it's much cheaper to buy a tourist Oystercard or Travelcard, which is good for unrestricted travel on the Tube, buses, and some overground railways for the day. The off-peak Oystercard fare for Zones 1–2, for example, is £1.80. Bear in mind that Travelcards cost much more if purchased before the 9:30 am rush-hour threshold. A one-day Travelcard for Zones 1–2 costs £7.20 if purchased before 9:30 am, and £5.60 if bought after 9:30 am. The more zones included in your travel, the more the Travelcard will cost. For example, Kew is Zone 4, and Heathrow is Zone 6. If you're going to be in town for several days, buy a seven-day Travelcard (£25.80 for Zones 1–2, £47.60 for Zones 1–6). Children 11–15 can travel at discounted rates on the Tube and free on buses and trams with an Oyster photocard (order at least four weeks before date of travel), while children under 11 travel free on the Tube if accompanied by an adult or with an Oyster photocard and on buses at all times. Young people 16–18 and students over 18 get discounted Tube fares with an Oyster photocard.

Oyster cards are "smart cards" that can be charged with a cash value and then used for discounted travel throughout the city. Each time you take the Tube or bus, you swipe the blue card across the yellow readers at the entrance and the amount of your fare is deducted. The London mayor is so eager to promote the cards that he set up a system in which those using Oyster cards pay lower rates. Oystercard Tube fares start at £1.30 and go up depending on the number of zones you're covering, time of day, and whether you're traveling into Zone 1. You can open an Oyster account online or pick up an Oyster card at any London Underground station, and then prepay any amount you wish for your expected travel while in the city. Using an Oyster card, bus fares are £1.20p instead of £2. If you make numerous journeys in a single day, your Oyster card deductions will always be capped at the standard price of a one-day Travelcard.

Trains begin running just after 5 am Monday–Saturday; the last services leave central London between midnight and 12:30 am. On Sunday, trains start two hours later and finish about an hour earlier. The frequency of trains depends on the route and the time of day, but normally you should not have to wait more than 10 minutes in central areas.

There are TfL Travel Information Centres at the following Tube stations: Euston, Liverpool Street, Piccadilly Circus, King's Cross, and Victoria, open 7:15 am–9:15 pm; and at Heathrow Airport (in Terminals 1, 2, and 3), open 6:30 am–10 pm.

Information **Transport for London** (☏ *0207/222-1234* ⊕ *www.tfl.gov.uk*).

▌TAXI

Universally known as "black cabs" (even though many of them now come in other colors), the traditional big black London taxicabs are as much a part of the city's streetscape as red double-decker buses, and for good reason: the unique, spacious taxis easily hold five people, plus luggage. To earn a taxi license, drivers must undergo intensive training on the history and geography of London. The course, and all that the drivers have learned in it, is known simply as "the Knowledge." There's almost nothing your taxi driver won't know about the city.

Hotels and main tourist areas have cabstands (just take the first in line), but you can also flag one down from the roadside. If the yellow "For Hire" sign on the top is lighted, the taxi is available. Cabdrivers often cruise at night with their signs unlighted so that they can choose their passengers and avoid those they think might cause trouble. If you see an unlighted, passengerless cab, hail it: you might be lucky.

Fares start at £2.20 and charge by the minute—a journey of a mile (which might take between 5 and 12 minutes) will cost anything from £4.60 to £8.60 (the fare goes up between 10 pm and 6 am—a system designed to persuade more taxi drivers to work at night). A surcharge of £2 is applied to a telephone booking. At Christmas and New Year, there is an additional surcharge of £4. You can, but do not have to, tip taxi drivers 10% of the tab. Usually passengers round up to the nearest pound.

Minicabs, which operate out of small, curbside offices throughout the city, are generally cheaper than black cabs, but are less reliable and trusted. These are usually unmarked passenger cars, and their drivers are often not native Londoners, and do not have to take or pass "the Knowledge" test. Still, Londoners use them in droves because they are plentiful and cheap. If you choose to use them, do not ever take an unlicensed cab: anyone who curb-crawls looking for customers is likely to be unlicensed. Unlicensed cabs have been associated with many crimes and can be dangerous. All cab companies with proper dispatch offices are likely to be licensed. Look for a small purple version of the Underground logo on the front or rear windscreen with "private hire" written across it.

There are plenty of trustworthy and licensed minicab firms. For London-wide service try Lady Mini Cabs, which employs only women drivers, or Addison Lee, which uses comfortable minivans but requires that you know the full postal code for both your pickup location and your destination. When using a minicab, always ask the price in advance when you phone for the car, then verify with the driver before the journey begins.

Black Cabs Dial-a-Cab (☎ 0207/253–5000). Radio Taxis (☎ 0207/272–0272).

Minicabs Addison Lee (☎ 0844/800–6677). Lady MiniCabs (☎ 0207/272–3300).

▌DLR: DOCKLANDS LIGHT RAILWAY

For destinations in East London, the quiet, driverless Docklands Light Railway (DLR) is a good alternative, offering interesting views of the area.

The DLR connects with the Tube network at Bank and Tower Hill stations as well as at Canary Wharf. It goes to London City Airport, the Docklands financial district, and Greenwich, running 5:30 am–12:30 am Monday–Saturday, 7 am–11:30 pm Sunday. The DLR takes Oyster cards and Travelcards, and fares are the same as those on the Tube. A £14.50 River Rover ticket combines one-day DLR travel with hop-on, hop-off travel on City Cruises riverboats between Westminster, Waterloo, Tower and Greenwich piers.

Information Transport for London (☎ 0207/222–1234 ⊕ www.tfl.gov.uk).

▌RIVER BUS

In the run-up to the 2012 Olympics, a new push is being made to develop river travel as part of London's overall public transport system. The service stops at 10 piers between the London Eye/Waterloo and Greenwich, with peak-time extensions to Putney in the west and Woolwich Arsenal in the east. The Waterloo-Woolwich commuter service runs every 20 minutes from 6 am to 1 am on weekdays, 8:30 am–midnight on weekends. Tickets are £5.30, with a one-third discount for Oyster card and Travelcard holders (full integration into the Oyster card system is expected in 2011). When there are events at the O2 (North Greenwich Arena), a half-hourly express service runs to and from Waterloo starting three hours before the event. There is also a special Tate-to-Tate express, a 20-minute trip between Tate Modern and Tate Britain that costs £5. Boats run every 40 minutes from 10 to 5. A £12 River Roamer ticket offers unlimited river travel 10–10 weekdays and 8 am–10 pm on weekends.

Contacts **Thames Clippers** (☎ 0870/781–5049 ⊕ www.thamesclippers.com).

▌TRAIN TRAVEL

The National Rail Enquiries Web site is the clearinghouse for information on train times and fares as well as to book rail journeys around Britain—and the earlier the better. Tickets bought two to three weeks in advance can cost a quarter of the price of tickets bought on the day of travel. However, journeys within commuting distance of city centers are sold at unvarying set prices, and those can be purchased on the day you expect to make your journey without any financial penalty. You may also be able to purchase a PlusBus ticket, which adds unlimited bus travel at your destination. Note that, in busy city centers such as London, all travel costs more during morning rush hour. You can purchase tickets online, by phone, or at any rail station in the United Kingdom. Check the Web site or call the National Rail Enquiries line to get details of the train company responsible for your journey and have them give you a breakdown of available ticket prices. Regardless of which train company is involved, many discount passes are available, such as the 16–25 Railcard (for which you must be under 26 and provide a passport-size photo), the Senior Railcard, and the Family & Friends Travelcard, which can be bought from most mainline stations. But if you intend to make several long-distance rail journeys, it can be a good idea to invest in a BritRail Pass (which you must buy in the United States).

You can get a BritRail pass valid for London and the surrounding counties, for England, for Scotland, or for all of Britain. Discounts (usually 20%–25%) are offered if you're between 16 and 25, over 60, traveling as a family or a group, or accompanied by a British citizen. The pass includes discounts on the Heathrow Express and Eurostar. BritRail passes come in two basic varieties. The Classic pass allows travel on consecutive days, and the FlexiPass allows a number of travel days within a set period of time. The cost (in U.S. dollars) of a BritRail Consecutive Pass adult ticket for eight days is $359 standard and $509 first-class; for 15 days, $535 and $759; and for a month, $759 and $1,139. The cost of a BritRail FlexiPass adult ticket for four days' travel in two months is $315 standard and $445 first-class; for eight days' travel in two months, $459 and $649; and for 15 days' travel in two months, $689 and $975. Prices drop by about 25% for off-peak travel passes between November and February.

Most long-distance trains have refreshment carriages, called buffet cars. Most trains these days also have "quiet cars" where use of cell phones and music devices is banned, but these rules are not enforced with any enthusiasm. Smoking is forbidden in all rail carriages.

Generally speaking, rail travel in the United Kingdom is expensive: for instance, a round-trip ticket to Bath from London can cost around £143 per person at peak times. The fee drops to around £27 at other times, so it's best to travel before or after the frantic business commuter rush (after 9:30 am and before 4:30 pm). Credit cards are accepted for train fares paid both in person and by phone.

Delays are not uncommon, but they're rarely long. You almost always have to go to the station to find out if there's going to be one (because delays tend to happen at the last minute). Luckily, most stations have coffee shops, restaurants, and pubs where you can cool your heels while you wait for the train to get rolling. National Rail Enquiries provides an up-to-date state-of-the-railways schedule.

Most of the time, first-class train travel in England isn't particularly first-class. Some train companies don't offer at-seat service, so you still have to get up and go to the buffet car for food or drinks. First class is generally booked by business travelers on expense accounts because crying babies and noisy families are quite rare in first class, and quite common in standard class.

Short of flying, taking the Eurostar train through the channel tunnel is the fastest way to reach the continent: 2 hours and 15 minutes from London's St. Pancras International Station to Paris's Gare du Nord. The high-speed Eurostar trains use the same tunnels to connect St. Pancras International directly with Midi Station in Brussels in around two hours. If purchased in advance, round-trip tickets from London to Belgium or France cost from around £125, cheaper in the very early or very late hours of the day. If you want to bring your car over to France, you can use the Eurotunnel Shuttle, which takes 35 minutes from Folkestone to Calais, plus at least 30 minutes to check in. The Belgian border is just a short drive northeast of Calais.

Information BritRail Travel (☎ 866/938–7245 in U.S. ⊕ www.britrail.com). **Eurostar** (☎ 08432/186–186 in U.K., 44–123–367–7575 outside U.K. ⊕ www.eurostar.com). **National Rail Enquiries** (☎ 0845/748–4950, 207/278–5240 outside U.K. ⊕ www.nationalrail.co.uk).

Channel Tunnel Car Transport Eurotunnel (☎ 0844/35–3535 in U.K., 070/22–32–10 in Belgium, 0810–63–03–04 in France, 33–321–002–061 from outside Europe ⊕ www.eurotunnel.com).

ESSENTIALS

■ BUSINESS SERVICES AND FACILITIES

There are several FedEx Kinko's and Mail Boxes Etc. locations in London to handle your photocopying, next-day mail, and packaging needs. Check their Web sites for more locations.

Contacts FedEx Kinko's (✉ *1 Curzon St., Mayfair, London* ☎ *0207/717–4900* ⊕ *www.kinkos.co.uk*). **Mail Boxes Etc.** (✉ *19–21 Crawford St., Marylebone, London* ☎ *0207/224–2666* ⊕ *www.mailboxes-etc.co.uk*).

■ COMMUNICATIONS

INTERNET

If you're traveling with a laptop, carry a spare battery and adapter: new batteries and replacement adapters are expensive; if you do need to replace them, head to Tottenham Court Road (W1), which is lined with computer specialists. For Macintosh computers, Micro Anvika is a good chain for parts and batteries, and the Apple Stores on Regent Street off Oxford Street and in the Covent Garden Piazza do repairs. John Lewis department store and Selfridges, on Oxford Street (W1), also carry a limited range of computer supplies.

The United Kingdom is finally catching up to the United States in terms of the spread of broadband and Wi-Fi. In London, free Wi-Fi is increasingly available in hotels, pubs, coffee shops—even certain branches of McDonald's—and broadband coverage is widespread; generally speaking, the pricier the hotel, the more likely you are to find Wi-Fi there. To find your nearest free hot spot, see the Wi-Fi FreeSpot Web site.

Contacts Cybercafes (⊕ *www.cybercafes.com*) lists more than 4,000 Internet cafés worldwide. **My Hot Spot** (⊕ *www.myhotspost.co.uk*).

PHONES

The good news is that you can now make a direct-dial telephone call from virtually any point on earth. The bad news? You can't always do so cheaply. Calling from a hotel is almost always the most expensive option; hotels usually add huge surcharges to all calls, particularly international ones. Calling cards usually keep costs to a minimum, but only if you purchase them locally. And then there are mobile phones, which are sometimes more prevalent—particularly in the developing world—than landlines; as expensive as mobile phone calls can be, they are still usually a much cheaper option than calling from your hotel.

The minimum charge from a public phone is 60p for a 110-second call. To make cheap calls it's a good idea to pick up an international phone card, available from newsstands, which can be used from residential, hotel, and public pay phones. With these, you can call the United States for as little as 5p per minute.

To dial from the United States or Canada, first dial 011, then Great Britain's country code, 44. Continue with the local area code, dropping the initial "0." The code for London is 020 (so from abroad you'd dial 20), followed by a 7 for numbers in central London, or an 8 for numbers in the Greater London area. Freephone (toll-free) numbers start with 0800, 0500 or 0808; low-cost national information numbers start with 0845 or 0844.

A word of warning: 0870 numbers are *not* toll-free numbers; in fact, numbers beginning with this, 0871, or the 0900 prefix are "premium rate" numbers, and it costs extra to call them. The amount varies and is usually relatively small when dialed from within the country but can be excessive when dialed from outside the United Kingdom.

CALLING WITHIN BRITAIN

There are three types of phones: those that accept (1) only coins, (2) only British Telecom (BT) phone cards, or (3) BT phone cards and credit cards, although with the advent of cells, it's increasingly difficult to find any type of public phone, especially in London.

The coin-operated phones are of the push-button variety; the workings of coin-operated telephones vary, but there are usually instructions on each unit. Most take 10p, 20p, 50p, and £1 coins. Insert the coins *before* dialing (the minimum charge is 10p). If you hear a repeated single tone after dialing, the line is busy; a continual tone means the number is unobtainable (or that you have dialed the wrong—or no—prefix). The indicator panel shows you how much money is left; add more whenever you like. If there is no answer, replace the receiver and your money will be returned.

There are several different directory-assistance providers. For information anywhere in Britain, try dialing 118–888 (49p per call, then 9p per minute) or 118–118 (49p per call, then 14p per minute); you'll need to know the town and the street (or at least the neighborhood) of the person or organization for which you're requesting information. For the operator, dial 100.

You don't have to dial London's central area code (020) if you are calling inside London itself—just the eight-digit telephone number. However, you do need to use it if you're dialing an 0207 (Inner London) number from an 0208 (Outer London) number, and vice versa.

For long-distance calls within Britain, dial the area code (which begins with 01), followed by the number. The area-code prefix is used only when you are dialing from outside the destination. In provincial areas, the dialing codes for nearby towns are often posted in the booth.

CALLING OUTSIDE BRITAIN

For assistance with international calls, dial 155.

To make an international call from London, dial 00, followed by the country code and the local number.

When calling from overseas to access a London telephone number, drop the first 0 from the prefix and dial only 20 (or any other British area code) and then the eight-digit phone number.

The United States country code is 1.

Access Codes **AT&T Direct** (☎ *0800/013–0011*). **MCI** (☎ *0800/89–0222 in U.K., 800/888–8000 for U.S. and other areas*). **Sprint International Access** (☎ *0800/890–877*).

CALLING CARDS

Public card phones operate either with cash or with special cards that you can buy from post offices or newsstands. Ideal for longer calls, they are composed of units of 10p, and come in values of £3, £5, £10, and more. To use a card phone, lift the receiver, insert your card, and dial the number. An indicator panel shows the number of units used. At the end of your call, the card will be returned. Where credit cards are taken, slide the card through, as indicated.

MOBILE PHONES

If you have a multiband phone (Britain uses different frequencies from those used in the United States) and your service provider uses the world-standard GSM network (as do T-Mobile, AT&T, and Verizon), you can probably use your phone abroad. Roaming fees can be steep, however: 99¢ a minute is considered reasonable. And overseas you normally pay the toll charges for incoming calls. It's almost always cheaper to send a text message than to make a call, since text messages have a very low set fee (often less than 5¢).

If you just want to make local calls, consider buying a new SIM card (note that your provider may have to unlock your phone for you to use a different SIM card) and a prepaid service plan in London. You'll then have a local number and can make local calls at local rates. If your trip is extensive, you could also simply buy a new cell phone in your destination, as the initial cost will be offset over time.

■TIP→ If you travel internationally frequently, save one of your old mobile phones or buy a cheap one on the Internet; ask your cell phone company to unlock it for you, and take it with you as a travel phone, buying a new SIM card with pay-as-you-go service in each destination.

Any cell phone can be used in Britain if it's tri-band/GSM. Travelers should ask their cell phone company if their phone is tri-band and what network it uses, and make sure it is activated for international calling before leaving their home country.

You can rent a cell phone from most car-rental agencies in London. Some upscale hotels now provide loaner cell phones to their guests. Beware, however, of the per-minute rates charged, as these can be shockingly high.

Contacts Cellular Abroad (☎ 800/287–5072 ⊕ www.cellularabroad.com) rents and sells GMS phones and sells SIM cards that work in many countries. **Mobal** (☎ 888/888–9162 ⊕ www.mobal.com) rents mobiles and sells GSM phones (starting at $49) that will operate in 150 countries. Per-call rates vary throughout the world. **Planet Fone** (☎ 888/988–4777 ⊕ www.planetfone.com) rents cell phones, but the per-minute rates are expensive. **Rent a Mobile Phone** (☎ 0207/353–7705 ⊕ www.rent-mobile-phone.com) has phones with short contract.

▊ CUSTOMS AND DUTIES

You're always allowed to bring goods of a certain value back home without having to pay any duty or import tax. But there's a limit on the amount of tobacco and liquor you can bring back duty-free, and some countries have separate limits for perfumes; for exact figures, check with your customs department. The values of

so-called "duty-free" goods are included in these amounts. When you shop abroad, save all your receipts, as customs inspectors may ask to see them as well as the items you purchased. If the total value of your goods is more than the duty-free limit, you'll have to pay a tax (most often a flat percentage) on the value of everything beyond that limit.

There are two levels of duty-free allowance for entering Britain: one for goods bought outside the European Union (EU) and the other for goods bought within the EU.

Of goods bought outside the EU you may import the following duty-free: 200 cigarettes or 100 cigarillos or 50 cigars or 250 grams of tobacco; 4 liters of still wine and 16 liters of beer and, in addition, either 1 liter of alcohol over 22% by volume (most spirits), or 2 liters of alcohol under 22% by volume (fortified or sparkling wine or liqueurs).

Of goods bought within the EU, you should not exceed the following (unless you can prove they are for personal use): 3,200 cigarettes, 400 cigarillos, 200 cigars, or 3 kilograms of tobacco, plus 10 liters of spirits, 20 liters of fortified wine such as port or sherry, 90 liters of wine, or 110 liters of beer.

Pets (dogs and cats) can be brought into the United Kingdom from the United States without six months' quarantine, provided that the animal meets all the PETS (Pet Travel Scheme) requirements, including microchipping and vaccination. Other pets have to undergo a lengthy quarantine, and penalties for breaking this law are severe and strictly enforced.

Fresh meats, vegetables, plants, and dairy products may be imported from within the EU. Controlled drugs, flick knives, obscene material, counterfeit or pirated goods, and self-defense sprays may not be brought into the United Kingdom, although firearms (both real and imitation) and ammunition, as well as souvenirs made from endangered plants or animals, are barred except with relevant permits.

Information HM Revenue and Customs (*Crownhill Court, Tailyour Rd., Plymouth* ☎ *0845/010–9000* ⊕ *www.hmrc.gov.uk*). **U.S. Customs and Border Protection** (⊕ *www.cbp.gov*).

■ ELECTRICITY

The electrical current in London is 220–240 volts (coming into line with the rest of Europe at 230 volts), 50 cycles alternating current (AC); wall outlets take three-pin plugs, and shaver sockets take two round, oversize prongs. For converters, adapters, and advice, stop in one of the many STA Travel shops around London or at Nomad Travel.

Consider making a small investment in a universal adapter, which has several types of plugs in one lightweight, compact unit. Most laptops and mobile phone chargers are dual voltage (i.e., they operate equally well on 110 and 220 volts), and thus require only an adapter. These days the same is true of small appliances such as hair dryers. Always check labels and manufacturer instructions to be sure. Don't use 110-volt outlets marked "For Shavers Only" for high-wattage appliances such as hair dryers.

Contacts Nomad Travel (✉ *43 Bernard St., Bloomsbury* ☎ *0207/833–4114* ✉ *52 Grosvenor Gardens, Victoria* ☎ *0207/823–5823* ⊕ *www.nomadtravel.co.uk*). **STA Travel** (⊕ *www.statravel.co.uk*). **Steve Kropla's Help for World Travelers** (⊕ *www.kropla.com*) has information on electrical and telephone plugs around the world. **Walkabout Travel Gear** (⊕ *www.walkabouttravelgear.com*) offers some helpful advice on electricity under "Adapters."

■ EMERGENCIES

London is a relatively safe city, though crime does happen (even more so than in New York City), especially in areas of built-up social housing or tourist meccas.

If you need to report a theft or an attack, head to the nearest police station (listed in the Yellow Pages or the local directory) or dial 999 for police, fire, or ambulance (be prepared to give the telephone number you're calling from). National Health Service hospitals, several of which are listed below, give free round-the-clock treatment in Accident and Emergency sections, where waits can be an hour or more. As a non-EU foreign visitor, you will be expected to pay for any treatment you receive before you leave the country. Prescriptions are valid only if made out by doctors registered in the United Kingdom. All branches of Boots are dispensing pharmacies, and the one listed is open until midnight.

Doctors and Dentists Dental Emergency Care Service (☎ *0207/748–9365* ⊕ *www.24hour-emergencydentist.co.uk*). **Medical Express Clinic** (✉ *117A Harley St.* ☎ *0207/499–1991* ⊕ *www.medicalexpressclinic.com*). **UCL Eastman Dental Hospital** (✉ *256 Gray's Inn Rd.* ☎ *0207/915–1000* ⊕ *www.uclh.nhs.co.uk*).

Foreign Embassies U.S. Embassy (✉ *24 Grosvenor Sq., Mayfair* ☎ *0207/499–9000* ✉ *londonpassport@state.gov* ⊕ *www.usembassy.org.uk*).

General Emergency Contacts Ambulance, fire, police (☎ *999*).

Hospitals and Clinics Charing Cross Hospital (✉ *Fulham Palace Rd., Fulham* ☎ *0203/311–1234* ⊕ *www.imperial.nhs.uk/charingcross/index/htm*). **Royal Free Hospital** (✉ *Pond St., Hampstead* ☎ *02077794–0500* ⊕ *www.royalfree.nhs.uk*). **St. Thomas's Hospital** (✉ *Westminster Bridge Rd., Lambeth* ☎ *0207/188–7188* ⊕ *www.guysandstthomas.nhs.uk*). **University College Hospital** (✉ *235 Euston Rd., Bloomsbury* ☎ *0845/155–5000* ⊕ *www.uclh.co.uk*).

Hotlines Samaritans (☎ *0845/790–9090*) for counseling.

Pharmacies Boots (✉ *44–46 Regent St., Piccadilly Circus* ☎ *0207/734–6126* ⊕ *www.boots.com*).

HOLIDAYS

Standard holidays are New Year's Day, Good Friday, Easter Monday, May Day (first Monday in May), spring and summer bank holidays (last Monday in May and August, respectively), Christmas, and Boxing Day (December 26). On Christmas Eve and New Year's Eve, some shops, restaurants, and businesses close early. Some museums and tourist attractions may close for at least a week around Christmas, or operate on restricted hours—call to verify.

MAIL

Stamps can be bought from post offices (generally open weekdays 9–5:30, Saturday 9–noon), from stamp machines outside post offices, and from some newsagents and newsstands. Mailboxes are known as post or letter boxes and are painted bright red; large tubular ones are set on the edge of sidewalks, whereas smaller boxes are set into post-office walls. Allow seven days for a letter to reach the United States. Check the Yellow Pages for a complete list of branches, though you cannot reach individual offices by phone.

Airmail letters up to 10 grams (0.35 ounce) to North America, Australia, and New Zealand cost 67p. Letters under 9.4 inches x 6.4 inches within Britain are from 41p for first class, 32p for second class. Large letters (over 9.4 inches x 6.4 inches, under 13.8 inches x 9.8 inches) cost from 66p first-class, 51p second-class within the U.K., depending on weight. Airmail is assessed by weight alone.

If you're uncertain where you'll be staying, you can have mail sent to you at the London Main Post Office, c/o poste restante. The post office will hold international mail for one month.

Contact **Post Office** (☎ 0845/774–0740 ⊕ www.postoffice.co.uk).

Main Branches **London Main Post Office** (✉ 24–28 William IV St., Trafalgar Sq. ⊕ www.postoffice.co.uk ✉ 43–44 Albemarle St., Mayfair ✉ 111 Baker St., Marylebone ✉ 54–56 Great Portland St., Fitzrovia ✉ 181 High Holborn, Holborn).

SHIPPING PACKAGES

Most department stores and retail outlets can ship your goods home. You should check your insurance for coverage of possible damage. Private delivery companies such as DHL, FedEx, and Parcelforce offer two-day delivery service to the United States, but you'll pay a considerable amount for the privilege.

Express Services **DHL** (☎ 0844/248–0844 ⊕ www.dhl.com). **FedEx** (☎ 0845/607–0809 ⊕ www.fedex.com). **Parcelforce** (☎ 0844/800–4466 ⊕ www.parcelforce.com).

MONEY

No doubt about it, London is one of the most expensive cities in the world: getting around is expensive, eating can be expensive, travel is pricey, and hotels aren't cheap. However, for every yin there's a yang, and travelers do get a break in other places: most museums are free, for example, and Oyster cards help cut the price of travel.

ATMS AND BANKS

Your own bank will probably charge a fee for using ATMs abroad; the foreign bank you use may also charge a fee. Nevertheless, you'll usually get a better rate of exchange at an ATM than you will at a currency-exchange office or even when changing money in a bank. And extracting funds as you need them is a safer option than carrying around a large amount of cash.

■TIP➡ PIN numbers with more than four digits are not recognized at ATMs in many countries. If yours has five or more, remember to change it before you leave.

Credit cards or debit cards (also known as check cards) will get you cash advances at ATMs, which are widely available in London. To make sure that your Cirrus or Plus card (to cite just two of the leading names) works in European ATMs, have your bank reset it to use a four-digit PIN number before your departure.

CREDIT CARDS

Throughout this guide, the following abbreviations are used: AE, American Express; DC, Diners Club; MC, Master-Card; and V, Visa.

■TIP→ Remember to inform your credit-card company before you travel, especially if you're going abroad and don't travel internationally very often. Otherwise, the credit-card company might put a hold on your card owing to unusual activity—not a good thing halfway through your trip. Record all your credit-card numbers— as well as the phone numbers to call if your cards are lost or stolen—in a safe place, so you're prepared should something go wrong. Both MasterCard and Visa have general numbers you can call (collect if you're abroad) if your card is lost, but you're better off calling the number of your issuing bank, since Master-Card and Visa usually just transfer you to your bank; your bank's number is usually printed on your card.

If you plan to use your credit card for cash advances, you'll need to apply for a PIN at least two weeks before your trip. Although it's usually cheaper (and safer) to use a credit card abroad for large purchases (so you can cancel payments or be reimbursed if there's a problem), note that some credit-card companies *and* the banks that issue them add substantial percentages to all foreign transactions, whether they're in a foreign currency or not. Check on these fees before leaving home, so there won't be any surprises when you get the bill.

■TIP→ Before you charge something, ask the merchant whether he or she plans to do a dynamic currency conversion (DCC). In such a transaction the credit-card *processor* (shop, restaurant, or hotel, not Visa or Mas-terCard) converts the currency and charges you in dollars. In most cases you'll pay the merchant a 3% fee for this service in addition to any credit-card company and issuing-bank foreign-transaction surcharges.

Dynamic currency conversion programs are becoming increasingly widespread. Merchants who participate in them are supposed to ask whether you want to be charged in dollars or the local currency, but they don't always do so. And even if they do offer you a choice, they may well avoid mentioning the additional surcharges. The good news is that you *do* have a choice. And if this practice really gets your goat, you can avoid it entirely thanks to American Express; with its cards, DCC simply isn't an option.

Credit cards are accepted virtually everywhere in London.

Reporting Lost Cards **American Express** (☎ 800/528–4800 in U.S., 01273/696–933 in U.K. ⊕ www.americanexpress.com). **Diners Club** (☎ 800/234–6377 in U.S., 702/797–5532 collect from abroad. ⊕ www.dinersclub. com). **MasterCard** (☎ 800/627–8372 in U.S., 0800/964–767 in U.K. ⊕ www.mastercard.com). **Visa** (☎ 800/847–2911 in U.S., 0800/891–725 in U.K. ⊕ www.visa.com).

CURRENCY AND EXCHANGE

The units of currency in Great Britain are the pound sterling (£) and pence (p): £50, £20, £10, and £5 bills (called notes); £2, £1 (100p), 50p, 20p, 10p, 5p, 2p, and 1p coins. At this writing, the exchange rate was about Australian $1.65, Canadian $1.64, New Zealand $2.16, U.S. $1.58, and €1.78 to the pound (also known as quid).

Even if a currency-exchange booth has a sign promising no commission, rest assured that there's some kind of huge, hidden fee. (Oh . . . that's right. The sign didn't say no *fee.*) And as for rates, you're almost always better off getting foreign currency at an ATM or exchanging money at a bank or post office.

■TIP→ Banks never have every foreign currency on hand, and it may take as long as a week to order. If you're planning to exchange funds before leaving home, don't wait until the last minute.

Currency Conversion **Google** (⊕ *www.google. com*) does currency conversion. Just type in the amount you want to convert and an explanation of how you want it converted (e.g., "14 Swiss francs in dollars"), and then voilà. **Oanda.com** (⊕ *www.oanda.com*) also allows you to print out a handy table with the current day's conversion rates. **XE.com** (⊕ *www.xe.com*) is another good currency conversion Web site.

▌PACKING

London's weather is unpredictable. It can be cool, damp, and overcast, even in summer, but the odd summer day can be uncomfortable, as not very many public venues, theaters, or the Tube are air-conditioned. In general, you'll need a heavy coat for winter and light clothes for summer, along with a lightweight coat or jacket. Always pack a small umbrella that you can easily carry around with you. Pack as you would for any American city: jackets and ties for expensive restaurants and nightspots, casual clothes elsewhere. Jeans are popular in London and are perfectly acceptable for sightseeing and informal dining. Sports jackets are popular with men. In five-star hotels men can expect to be asked to wear a jacket and tie in the restaurant and bar, and women might feel out of place unless they're in smart clothes. Otherwise, for women, ordinary dress is acceptable just about everywhere.

▌PASSPORTS AND VISAS

U.S. citizens need only a valid passport to enter Great Britain for stays of up to six months. If you're within six months of your passport's expiration date, renew it before you leave—nearly extinct passports are not strictly banned, but they make immigration officials anxious, and may cause you problems.

PASSPORTS

We're always surprised at how few Americans have passports—only 25% at this writing. This number is expected to grow now that it is impossible to reenter the United States from trips to neighboring Canada or Mexico without one.

Remember this: A passport verifies both your identity and nationality—a great reason to have one.

U.S. passports are valid for 10 years. You must apply in person if you're getting a passport for the first time; if your previous passport was lost, stolen, or damaged; or if your previous passport has expired and was issued more than 15 years ago or when you were under 16. All children under 18 must appear in person to apply for or renew a passport. Both parents must accompany any child under 14 (or send a notarized statement with their permission) and provide proof of their relationship to the child.

There are 24 regional passport offices, as well as 7,000 passport acceptance facilities in post offices, public libraries, and other governmental offices. If you're renewing a passport, you can do so by mail. Forms are available at passport acceptance facilities and online.

The cost to apply for a new passport is $110 for adults, $80 for children under 16; renewals are $110. There is an additional "execution fee" of $25. Allow six weeks for processing, both for first-time passports and renewals. For an expediting fee of $60 you can reduce this time to about two weeks. If your trip is less than two weeks away, you can get a passport even more rapidly by going to a passport office with the necessary documentation. Private expediters can get things done in as little as 48 hours, but charge hefty fees for their services.

▌**TIP→** Before your trip, make two copies of your passport's data page (one for someone at home and another for you to carry separately). Or scan the page and e-mail it to someone at home and/or yourself.

VISAS

A visa is essentially formal permission to enter a country. Visas allow countries to keep track of you and other visitors—and generate revenue (from application fees). You *always* need a visa to enter a foreign country; however, many countries routinely issue tourist visas on arrival, particularly to U.S. citizens. When your passport is stamped or scanned in the immigration line, you're actually being issued a visa. Sometimes you have to stand in a separate line and pay a small fee to get your stamp before going through immigration, but you can still do this at the airport on arrival. Getting a visa isn't always that easy. Some countries require that you arrange for one in advance of your trip. There's usually—but not always—a fee involved, and said fee may be nominal ($10 or less) or substantial ($100 or more).

If you must apply for a visa in advance, you can usually do it in person or by mail. When you apply by mail, you send your passport to a designated consulate, where your passport will be examined and the visa issued. Expediters—usually the same ones who handle expedited passport applications—can do all the work of obtaining your visa for you; however, there's always an additional cost (often more than $50 per visa).

Most visas limit you to a single trip—basically during the actual dates of your planned vacation. Other visas allow you to visit as many times as you wish for a specific period of time. Remember that requirements change, sometimes at the drop of a hat, and the burden is on you to make sure that you have the appropriate visas. Otherwise, you'll be turned away at the airport or, worse, deported after you arrive in the country. No company or travel insurer gives refunds if your travel plans are disrupted because you didn't have the correct visa.

U.S. Passport Information U.S. Department of State (☎ 877/487–2778 ⊕ *travel.state. gov/passport*).

U.S. Passport and Visa Expediters
A. Briggs Passport & Visa Expeditors (☎ 800/806–0581 or 202/388–0111 ⊕ *www.abriggs.com*). **American Passport Express** (☎ 800/455–5166 or 603/559–9888 ⊕ *www.americanpassport.com*). **Passport**

Express (☎ *800/362–8196* ⊕ *www.passportexpress.com*). **Travel Document Systems** (☎ *800/874–5100 or 202/638–3800* ⊕ *www.traveldocs.com*). **Travel the World Visas** (☎ *866/886–8472 or* ⊕ *www.world-visa.com*).

▌ SAFETY

The rules for safety in London are the same as in New York or any big city. If you're carrying a considerable amount of cash and do not have a safe in your hotel room, it's a good idea to keep it in something like a money belt, but don't get cash out of it in public. Keep a small amount of cash for immediate purchases in your pocket or handbag.

Beyond that, use common sense. In central London, nobody will raise an eyebrow at tourists studying maps on street corners, and don't hesitate to ask for directions. However, outside of the center, exercise general caution about the neighborhoods you walk in: if they don't look safe, take a cab. After midnight, outside of the center, take cabs rather than waiting for a night bus. Although London has plenty of so-called "minicabs"—normal cars driven by self-employed drivers in a cab service—don't ever get into an unmarked car that pulls up offering you "cab service." Take a licensed minicab only from a cab office, or, preferably, a normal London "black cab," which you flag down on the street. Unlicensed minicab drivers have been associated with a slate of violent crimes in recent years.

If you carry a purse, keep a firm grip on it (or even disguise it in a local shopping bag). Store only enough money in the purse to cover casual spending. Distribute the rest of your cash and any valuables among deep front pockets, inside jacket or vest pockets, and a concealed money pouch. Some pubs and bars have "Chelsea clips" under the tables where you can hang your handbag at your knee. Never leave your bag beside your chair or hanging from the back of your chair. Be careful with backpacks, as pickpockets can unzip them on the Tube, or even as you're traveling up an escalator.

■**TIP➜ Distribute your cash, credit cards, IDs, and other valuables between a deep front pocket, an inside jacket or vest pocket, and a hidden money pouch. Don't reach for the money pouch once you're in public.**

Advisories U.S. Department of State (⊕ *travel.state.gov*).

▌TAXES

Departure taxes are divided into four bands, depending on destination. The Band A tax on a per-person Economy fare is £12, Band B is £60, Band C is £75, and Band D is £85. The fee is subject to government tax increases.

The British sales tax (V.A.T., value-added tax) is 20%. The tax is almost always included in quoted prices in shops, hotels, and restaurants.

Most travelers can get a V.A.T. refund by either the Retail Export or the more cumbersome Direct Export method. Many, but not all, large stores provide these services, but only if you request them; they will handle the paperwork. For the Retail Export method, you must ask the store for Form VAT 407 when making a purchase (you must have identification—passports are best). Some retailers will refund the amount on the spot, but others will use a refund company or the refund booth at the point when you leave the country. For the latter, have the form stamped like any customs form by U.K. customs officials when you leave the country, or, if you're visiting several European Union countries, when you leave the EU. After you're through passport control, take the form to a refund-service counter for an on-the-spot refund (which is usually the quickest and easiest option), or mail it to the address on the form (or the envelope with it) after you arrive home. You receive the total refund stated on the form (the retailer or refund company may deduct a handling fee), but the processing time can be long, especially if you request a credit-card adjustment. This may be preferable to a check, however, as U.S. banks will charge a fee for depositing a check in a foreign currency.

With the Direct Export method, the goods are shipped directly to your home. You must have a Form VAT 407 certified by customs, the police, or a notary public when you get home and then send it back to the store, which will refund your money. For inquiries, contact Her Majesty's Customs & Excise office.

Global Refund is a worldwide service with 240,000 affiliated stores and more than 200 Refund Offices. Its refund form, called a Tax Free Check, is the most common across the European continent. The service issues refunds in the form of cash, check, or credit-card adjustment. Again, the cost of cashing a foreign currency check may exceed the amount of the refund.

V.A.T. Refunds Global Refund (☎ *866/706–6090 in U.S., 800/321–1111 in U.K.* ⊕ *www.globalrefund.com*). **Her Majesty's Revenue & Customs** (☎ *0845/010–9000 within U.K., 292/050–1261 from outside U.K.* ⊕ *www.hmrc.gov.uk/vat*).

▌TIME

London is five hours ahead of New York City. In other words, when it's 3 pm in New York (or noon in Los Angeles), it's 8 pm in London. Note that Great Britain and most European countries also move their clocks ahead for the one-hour differential when daylight saving time goes into effect (although they make the changeover several weeks after the United States).

Time Zones Timeanddate.com (⊕ *www.timeanddate.com/worldclock*) can help you figure out the correct time anywhere in the world.

▌ TIPPING

Tipping is done in Britain just as in the United States, but at a lower level. So, although it might make you uncomfortable, tipping less than you would back home in restaurants—and not tipping at all in pubs—is not only accepted, but standard. Tipping more can look like you're showing off. Do not tip movie or theater ushers, elevator operators, or bar staff in pubs—although you can always offer to buy them a drink.

TIPPING GUIDELINES FOR LONDON	
Bartender	In cocktail bars, on the other hand, if you see a tip plate, it's fine to leave £1 or £2. For table service, tip 10% of the cost of the bill. However, the gratuity is often included in the check at more expensive bars.
Bellhop	£1 per bag, depending on the level of the hotel.
Hotel Concierge	£5 or more, if a service is performed for you.
Hotel Doorman	£1 for hailing taxis or for carrying bags to check-in desk.
Hotel Maid	It's extremely rare for hotel maids to be tipped; £1 or £2 would be generous.
Porter at Airport or Train Station	£1 per bag
Skycap at Airport	£1–£3 per bag
Taxi Driver	Optional 10%–12%, perhaps a little more for a short ride.
Tour Guide	Tipping optional; £1 or £2 would be generous.
Waiter	10%–15%, with 15% being the norm at high-end restaurants; nothing additional if a service charge is added to the bill.
Other	Restroom attendants in expensive restaurants expect some small change (50p or so). Tip coat-check personnel £1 unless there is a fee (then nothing). Hairdresser and barbers get 10%–15%.

▌ TOURS

BIKE TOURS

London's mayor, Boris Johnson, is a real cycling enthusiast and keen to make the capital more bike-friendly. A 24-hour cycle-for-hire scheme, the Barclays Cycle Hire, was introduced in 2010 to enable Londoners to pick up a bicycle at one of more than 400 docking stations and return it at another. You can find a map of docking stations at the Web site below. The first 30 minutes are free. After that, charges rise incrementally from £1 for one hour up to £50 for the entire 24 hours. There is also a £1 per-day access charge. Fees are payable online, by phone or at docking stations, by credit or debit cards only—cash is not accepted. To sign up, a user goes to the TfL (Transport for London) Web site and then receives a bike key in the mail, so this scheme is really meant for locals, not tourists. But whether you join the Barclays Cycle Hire scheme or just, per usual, hire a bike for rent from a rental shop, remember that London is still a busy metropolis: unless you're familiar with riding in London traffic, the best way to see it on two wheels is probably to contact one of the excellent cycle tour companies that aim to take you around town, avoiding all the busy routes and traveling along cycle lanes and river paths, down quiet backstreets and through parks.

Tour Operators Barclays Cycle Hire (☏ 0845/026–3630 within U.K., 208/216–6666 from outside U.K. ⊕ www.tfl.gov.uk/roadusers/ cycling/14808.aspx). **Cycle Tours of London** (☏ 0207/737–4802 ⊕ www.biketoursoflondon. com). **Fat Tire Bike Tours** (☏ 0788/238–779 within U.K., 0788/238–8779 from outside U.K. ⊕ www.fattirebiketours.com). **London Bicycle Tour Company** (☏ 0207/928–6838 ⊕ www.londonbicycle.com).

BOAT TOURS

Year-round, but more frequently from April to October, boats cruise the Thames, offering a different view of the London skyline. Most leave from Westminster Pier,

Charing Cross Pier, and Tower Pier. Downstream routes go to the Tower of London, Greenwich, and the Thames Barrier via Canary Wharf. Upstream destinations include Kew, Richmond, and Hampton Court (mainly in summer). Most of the launches seat between 100 and 250 passengers, have a public-address system, and provide a running commentary on passing points of interest. Some include musical entertainment. Depending upon the destination, river trips may last from one to four hours.

Details on all other operators are available as a PDF from Transport for London's River Services page

River Cruise Operators Bateaux London (☎ *0207/695–1800* ⊕ *www.bateauxlondon. com*). **London Duck Tours** (☎ *0207/928–3132* ⊕ *www.londonducktours.co.uk*). **Thames Cruises** (☎ *0207/928–9009* ⊕ *www.thamescruises.com*). **Thames River Boats** (☎ *0207/930–2062* ⊕ *www.wpsa.co.uk*). **Thames River Services** (☎ *020/930–4097* ⊕ *www.thamesriverservices.co.uk*).

BUS, COACH, AND TAXI TOURS

Guided sightseeing tours from the top of double-decker buses, which are open-top in summer, are a good introduction to the city, as they cover all the main central sights. Numerous companies run daily bus tours that depart (usually between 8:30 and 9 am) from central points. In hop-on, hop-off fashion, you may board or alight at any of the numerous stops to view the sights, and reboard on the next bus. Most companies offer this hop-on, hop-off feature but others, such as Best Value, remain guided tours in traditional coach buses. Tickets can be bought from the driver and are good all day. Prices vary according to the type of tour, although £20 is the benchmark. For that more personal touch, try out a tour in a guided taxi. Other guided bus tours, like those offered by Golden, are not open-top or hop-on, hop-off, but enclosed (and more expensive) coach bus versions.

Bus Tour Operators Best Value Tours (⊕ *www.bestvaluetours.co.uk*). **Big Bus Tours** (☎ *0207233–9533* ⊕ *www.bigbustours. com*). **Black Taxi Tour of London** (☎ *0207/935–9363* ⊕ *www.blacktaxitours. co.uk*). **Golden Tours** (☎ *0207/233–7030 in U.K., 800/548–7083 in U.S.* ⊕ *www.goldentours. co.uk*). **Original London Sightseeing Tour** (☎ *02088877–1722* ⊕ *www.theoriginaltour. com*). **Premium Tours** (☎ *0207/713–1311* ⊕ *www.premiumtours.co.uk*).

CANAL TOURS

The tranquil side of London can be found on narrow boats that cruise the city's two canals, the Grand Union and Regent's Canal; most vessels operate on the latter, which runs between Little Venice in the west (nearest Tube: Warwick Avenue on the Bakerloo Line) and Camden Lock (about 200 yards north of Camden Town Tube station). Fares start at about £8.50 for 1½-hour round-trip cruises.

Canal Tour Operators Canal Cruises (☎ *0208/440–8962* ⊕ *www.londoncanalcruises. com*). **Jason's Trip** (☎ *020/7286–3428* ⊕ *www.jasons.co.uk*). **London Waterbus Company** (☎ *020/7482–2550* ⊕ *www.londonwaterbus.co.uk*).

EXCURSIONS

Evan Evans, Green Line, and National Express all offer day excursions by bus to places within easy reach of London, such as Hampton Court, Oxford, Stratford, and Bath.

Tour Operators Evan Evans (☎ *020/7950– 1777, 800/422–9022 in U.S.* ⊕ *www.evanevanstours.co.uk*). **Green Line** (☎ *0844/801–7261* ⊕ *www.greenline.co.uk*). **National Express** (☎ *0871/781–8181* ⊕ *www.nationalexpress.com*).

WALKING TOURS

One of the best ways to get to know London is on foot, and there are many guided and themed walking tours from which to choose. Richard Jones's London Walking Tours includes the Jack the Ripper Walk following in the footsteps of the titular killer, as does the Blood and Tears

Walk. Other tours include Secret London, The West End with Dickens, and Hampstead—A Country Village. Context London's expert docents lead small groups on walks with art, architecture, and similar themes. The London Walks Company hosts more than 100 walks every week on a variety of themes, including a Thames pub walk, Literary Bloomsbury, and Spies and Spycatchers. For more options, pick up a copy of *Time Out* magazine and check the weekly listings for upcoming one-off tours.

Walking Tour Operators **Blood and Tears Walk** (✆ 07905/746–733 ⊕ www.shockinglondon.com). **Blue Badge** (✆ 020/7403–1115 ⊕ www.blue-badge-guides. com). **Context London** (✆ 0207/193–9158, 800/691–6036 in U.S. ⊕ www.contexttravel. com/london). **London Walks** (✆ 020/7624–3978 ⊕ www.walks.com). **Richard Jones's London Walking Tours** (✆ 0208/530–8443 ⊕ www.walksoflondon.co.uk). **Shakespeare City Walk** (✆ 07905/746–733 ⊕ www.shakespeareguide.com).

▌VISITOR INFORMATION

When you arrive in London, you can get good information at the Travel Information Centre near the Eurostar arrivals area at St. Pancras International train station and at Victoria and Liverpool Street Stations. These are helpful if you're looking for brochures for London sights, or if something's gone horribly wrong with your hotel reservation—if, for example, you don't have one—as they have a useful reservations service. The Victoria Station center, opposite Platform 8, is open Monday–Saturday 7:15 am–9:15 pm, Sunday 8:15 am–8:15 pm, as are the St. Pancras and Liverpool Street centers. A Travel Information Centre at Euston station has the same hours but closes Saturday at 6:15 pm, while one at the Piccadilly Circus Tube station is open daily 9:15 am–7 pm. The Travel Information Centre at Heathrow is open daily 7:15 am–9 pm, while the Britain and London Visitor Centre on Lower Regent Street is a worthwhile stop for travel, hotel, and entertainment information; it's open Monday 9:30–6 during October–March and 9:30–6:30 during April–September, Tuesday–Saturday 9–6 during October–March and 9–6:30 during April–September, and weekends and public holidays 10–4. There are also London Tourist Information Centres in Greenwich and some other Outer London locations.

Official Web Sites ⊕ www.visitbritain.com, ⊕ www.visitlondon.com.

Other Web sites ⊕ www.londontown.com, the *Evening Standard*'s online ⊕ www.thisislondon. com, No. 10 Downing Street (⊕ www.number-10.gov.uk), and the BBC (⊕ www.bbc.co.uk).

Entertainment Information ⊕ www.timeout. com/london, ⊕ www.officiallondontheatre. co.uk, and ⊕ www.kidslovelondon.com.

INDEX

PHOTO CREDITS

1, Sylvain Grandadam / age fotostock. 2-3, Heeb Christian/age fotostock. 5, Rich B-S/Flickr. Chapter 1: Experience: 8-9, William Helsel/age fotostock. 10, Angelina Dimitrova/Shutterstock. 11 (left), British Tourist Authority. 11 (right), PCL/Alamy. 12, gary718/Shutterstock. 13 (left), Pres Panayotov/Shutterstock. 13 (right), Kathy deWitt/Alamy. 14, Jan Kranendonk/Shutterstock. 15 (left), Dominic Burke/Alamy. 15 (right), Doug Scott/age fotostock. 17, Marc Pinter/Shutterstock. 18 (left), Sean Nel/Shutterstock. 18 (top center), Vinicius Tupinamba/Shutterstock. 18 (bottom center), WH Chow/Shutterstock. 18 (top right), Jan Kranendonk/iStockphoto. 18 (bottom right), Thomas Sztanek/Shutterstock. 19 (top left), Bob Masters/Alamy. 19 (bottom left), Andrew Ward/Life File/Photodisc. 19 (top center), Jack Sullivan/Alamy. 19 (bottom center), Dominic Burke/Alamy. 19 (right), Walter Bibikow/viestiphoto.com. 20 (left), wikipedia.org. 20 (top center), The Print Collector/Alamy. 20 (bottom center and top right), wikipedia.org. 20 (bottom right), www.wga.hu. 21 (top left, bottom left, and right), wikipedia.org. 21 (top center), newsphoto / Alamy. 23 (left), London 2012. 23 (right). Christopher Steer/iStockphoto. 25 (left and right), British Tourist Authority. 27 (left), Lebrecht Music and Arts Photo Library/Alamy. 27 (right), and 28, Visit London. 29 (left), Danilo Donadoni/Marka/age fotostock. 29 (right), British Tourist Authority. 32, Sylvain Grandadam/age fotostock. 33 and 34, British Tourist Authority. 35, David Peta/Shutterstock. 36 (top left), UK21/Alamy. 36 (bottom left), wikipedia.org. 36 (right), Kobby Dagan/Shutterstock. 37 (left), Mike Booth/Alamy. 37 (top right), wikipedia.org. 37 (bottom right), INTER-FOTO Pressebildagentur/Alamy. 38 (top left), Robert Stainforth/Alamy. 38 (bottom left), Jeffrey Blackler/Alamy. 38 (right), Andrew Dunn/wikipedia.org. 39 (left), Eric Nathan/Alamy. 39 (right), Chris Batson/Alamy. 40 (left), Directphoto.org/Alamy. 40 (top right), Zaha Hadid/wikipedia.org. 40 (bottom right), Nigel Young/British Museum. Chapter 2: Westminster & Royal London: 41, British Tourist Authority. 43, Eric Nathan/ britainonview.com. 44, Peter Adams/age fotostock. 47, ktylerconk/Flickr. 48, Mark William Richardson/Shutterstock. 51, Pres Panayotov/Shutterstock. 54-55, Doug Pearson/age fotostock. 56, British Tourist Authority. 58, John Sturrock/Alamy. 61, Sean Nel/Shutterstock. 65 (left), F. Monheim/R. von Göt/Bildarchiv Monheim/age fotostock. 65 (top right), Dean and Chapter of Westminster. 65 (center right), Mark Thomas/Alamy. 65 (bottom right) and 67, Dean and Chapter of Westminster. 69, British Tourist Authority.Chapter 3: St. James's & Mayfair: 71, Roberto Herrett / age fotostock. 73, British Tourist Authority. 74, David Noton Photography/Alamy. 76, Tibor Bognar / age fotostock. 77, Jess Moss. 79, Pawel Libera/Alamy. 80, Derek Croucher/Alamy. 83, Matthew Mawson/Alamy. Chapter 4: Soho & Covent Garden: 85, 87 and 88, British Tourist Authority. 89, Julian Love/John Warburton-Lee Photography/photolibrary.com. 90, Jon Arnold/age fotostock. 92, Ann Steer/iStockphoto. 95, British Tourist Authority. Chapter 5: Bloomsbury & Legal London: 97, Michael Jenner/Alamy. 99 and 100, British Tourist Authority. 102, Jarno Gonzalez Zarraonandia/Shutterstock. 103 and 104 (top), British Museum. 104 (bottom), Grant Rooney/Alamy. 106, British Museum. 107, James McCormick/britainonview.com. 108, Eric Nathan/Alamy. Chapter 6: The City: 113, PSL Images/Alamy. 115, Ryan Fox/age fotostock. 116-17, Jason Hawkes. 118, Jerry Millevoi/age fotostock. 121 (left), F. Monheim/R. von Göt/Bildarchiv Monheim/age fotostock. 121 (top right), Jeff Gynane/Shutterstock. 121 (center right), Ken Ross/viestiphoto.com. 121 (bottom right), Marcin Stalmach/iStockphoto. 123, Rene Ramos/Shutterstock. 125, Russ Merne/Alamy. 127, Imagestate/age fotostock.com. 129, iStockphoto. 131 (left), Walter Bibikow/viestiphoto.com. 131 (right), Tom Hanley/Alamy. 132 (top), Natasha Marie Brown/HRP/newsteam.co.uk. 133, Peter Phipp/Peter Phipp/age fotostock. 134 (left), Mary Evans Picture Library/Alamy. 134 (center), Reflex Picture Library/Alamy. 134 (right), Classic Image/Alamy. 135, Jan Kranendonk/iStockphoto. Chapter 7: The East End: 137, Janine Wiedel Photolibrary/Alamy. 139, Neil Setchfield/Alamy. 140, foybles/Alamy. 143, Jon Arnold/age fotostock. 146, Elly Godfroy/Alamy. Chapter 8: The South Bank: 149, Mike Peel/wikipedia/org. 151, Eric Nathan/britainonview.com. 152, PCL/Alamy. 155 (top), Shutterstock. 155 (bottom), Duncan Soar/Alamy. 156, Vehbi Koca/Alamy. 157 (top), Lebrecht Music and Arts Photo Library/Alamy. 157 (bottom), Eric Nathan/britainonview.com. 159, AA World Travel Library/Alamy. 161, Terry Walsh/Shutterstock. Chapter 9: Kensington, Chelsea & Knightsbridge: 165, Cahir Davitt/age fotostock. 167, British Tourist Authority. 168, Robert Harding Picture Library Ltd/Alamy. 171, John Warburton-Lee Photography/Alamy. 172, Londonstills.com/Alamy. 173, British Tourist Authority. 176, Ant Clausen/Shutterstock. 177, PCL/Alamy. Chapter 10: Notting Hill & Bayswater: 179, Roger Cracknell 01/classic / Alamy. 181, Doug Scott/age fotostock. 182, David H. Wells/age fotostock. 184, Peter Cook/age fotostock. 185, Corbis. 187, Joe Viesti/viestiphoto.com. 188, TNT MAGAZINE/Alamy. 189 (left), Andrew Holt/Alamy. 189 (top right), Dominic Burke/Alamy. 189 (bottom right), David Berry/Shutterstock. Chapter 11: Regent's Park & Hampstead: 191, Earl Patrick Lichfield/britainonview.com. 193, British Tourist Authority. 194, Bildarchiv Monheim GmbH/Alamy. 198, ARCO/R. Kiedrowski/age fotostock. 200, PCL/Alamy. 203, Pictorial Press Ltd/Alamy. 205, PCL/Alamy. Chapter 12: Greenwich: 207, Michael Booth/Alamy. 209,

NOTES

ABOUT OUR WRITERS

Astrid deRidder grew up in the Rocky Mountains of Colorado but came to love the urban bustle of New York City. A passionate Anglophile, she packed up her cats and books (and husband) in 2009 and moved across the ocean. She now calls England home and works as an editor near London Bridge, not too far from the two neighborhood chapters she updated for this edition: Soho and Bloomsbury.

Londoner and freelance writer Damian Harper was born and raised in Kensington and has been authoring guidebooks for more than a decade. He currently lives in Honor Oak Park in southeast London and updated the Experience London, Westminster, and St. James's chapters for this book.

Julius Honnor has lived in, and written about, London for 12 years. Though he is often disappearing off to write and take photographs for guidebooks to places such as Morocco, Italy, and Bolivia, he always hurries home to a fine pint of ale in one of his favorite pubs. Not surprisingly, for this edition, he updated our Pubs and Nightlife chapter along with our Arts and Entertainment chapter.

Erin Huebscher's love affair with London officially began during her undergrad years at the University of Iowa when she studied abroad for a semester and became enthralled with English culture and fashion. She recently obtained her Master's in Creative Writing from London Metropolitan University (with one eye on her career as a "chick lit" novelist) but, when not writing, she thoroughly enjoys perusing London's dazzling boutiques and markets (Borough Market is her personal favorite), updating our Shopping chapter as she goes.

A Londoner since public transport was cheap, Jack Jewers has reviewed pubs for Time Out and directed films for the BBC in addition to writing for several Fodor's titles. For this edition, he updated our Where to Stay chapter, along with our neighborhood chapters on Notting Hill, Regent's Park, Greenwich, and the Thames Upstream. An ancestor of his was a notorious pirate who was hanged at Tyburn (now part of Oxford Street). As London-related jobs go, Jack's may be somewhat less glamorous, but at least his career trajectory is better.

Hertfordshire lass Michelle Rosenberg is a freelance writers, published author, and mother of two gorgeous gals. She has written for London's *Big Issue* magazine and her first book, *Inspiring Women*, focuses on women entrepreneurs. A baby-naming book and coffee shop business guide were published recently. She loves being a tourist in her own city and spends most of her time (and money) at legendary Charing Cross bookstore Foyles. For this edition, she updated our City, East End, and South Bank chapters.

Ellin Stein has written for publications on both sides of the Atlantic, including the *New York Times*, the *Times of London*, the *Guardian*, the *Telegraph*, the *Independent*, the *Village Voice*, *People* magazine, and *InStyle*, for whom she was European correspondent. Originally from Manhattan, she has lived in London for 16 years and is married to a native. For this edition, she updated our Kensington, Side Trips, and Travel Smart chapters.

By day, Londoner Alex Wijeratna works as a global hunger activist for Action-Aid: at all other times, he hunts down the best food in town. With his mixed roots, Alex is well aware that London's restaurant boom is built in ethnic diversity. He's written for the *Times*, *Guardian*, *Independent* and the *Daily Mail*, and for this edition, Alex updated the Where to Eat chapter.